T[MIKE SAYER

HUGH DELLAR   ANDREW WALKLEY

ADVANCED
OUTCOMES

Australia · Brazil · Mexico · Singapore · United Kingdom · United States

ngl.cengage.com/outcomes

PASSWORD outcomes!C4#

NATIONAL GEOGRAPHIC
L E A R N I N G

Outcomes *Advanced Teacher's Book*
Mike Sayer

Publisher: Gavin McLean
Publishing Consultant: Karen Spiller
Development Editor: Sue Jones
Editorial Manager: Scott Newport
Head of Strategic Marketing, ELT: Charlotte Ellis
Senior Content Project Manager: Nick Ventullo
Manufacturing Manager: Eyvett Davis
Cover Design: eMC Design
Text Design: Studio April
Compositor: Q2A Media Services Pvt. Ltd.
Illustrations: Q2A Media Services Pvt. Ltd.
National Geographic Liaison: Leila Hishmeh

For product information and technology assistance, contact us at
Cengage Learning Customer & Sales Support, cengage.com/contact

For permission to use material from this text or product,
submit all requests online at **cengage.com/permissions**
Further permissions questions can be emailed to
permissionrequest@cengage.com

ISBN: 978-1-305-26819-7

National Geographic Learning
Cheriton House, North Way, Andover, Hampshire, SP10 5BE
United Kingdom

National Geographic Learning, a Cengage Learning Company, has a mission to bring the world to the classroom and the classroom to life. With our English language programs, students learn about their world by experiencing it. Through our partnerships with National Geographic and TED Talks, they develop the language and skills they need to be successful global citizens and leaders.

Locate your local office at **international.cengage.com/region**

Visit National Geographic Learning online at **NGL.Cengage.com/ELT**
Visit our corporate website at **www.cengage.com**

Printed in China by RR Donnelley
Print Number: 03   Print Year: 2019

CONTENTS

INTRODUCTION TO *OUTCOMES* ADVANCED

In this introduction we try to answer these questions:
- What are the goals of language students?
- How did we choose language for students at this level?
- What makes *Outcomes* better for teachers?
- How can we help students learn?

GOALS AND OUTCOMES

The Common European Framework of Reference for Languages (CEFR) states that language learning and teaching overall goals should be:
1.1 to deal with the business of everyday life in another country, and to help foreigners staying in their own country to do so;
1.2 to exchange information and ideas with young people and adults who speak a different language and to communicate their thoughts and feelings to them;
1.3 to achieve a wider and deeper understanding of the way of life and forms of thought of other peoples and of their cultural heritage.
(Council of Europe, 2001, *Common European Framework of Reference for Languages*, p3)

These ideas underpin everything we do in the *Outcomes* series. At Advanced, we look at some can-do statements at C1 as a guide to what students might want to achieve. On the **opening double-page** of each unit you will see a list of outcomes. The vocabulary, grammar and skills practice that is provided in each unit aim to help students to do these things better.

Business of everyday life
Outcomes has a strong practical thread. For example, students at Advanced learn the grammar and vocabulary to:
- handle arguments in a constructive manner, pages 52–53
- give better presentations, pages 108–109
- take part in meetings and take minutes, pages 128–129.

For many students passing **exams** is also the business of everyday life, which is why *Outcomes* has a **Grammar reference** with exercises on all the grammar you'd expect. The **Review pages** after every two units also make use of exercise types found in common exams such as **Cambridge First**, including cloze tests, wordbuilding and transformation exercises. **Writing** sections deal with both practical types of writing task (covering letters, pages 158–159) and exam-type writing (a review, pages 154–155; an article, pages 160–161).

Communicating thoughts and feelings
Practicalities are important, but just as important, and perhaps more motivating, is the ability to communicate in a way which reflects your personality, feelings and opinions. That's why most of the **Developing conversations** and **Conversation practice** sections work towards practising typical conversations we have to establish and maintain friendships. For example:
- talk about other people, page 17
- talk about sports you watch or do, page 99
- comment on news stories, page 117

This is also why we constantly give students the chance to exchange their ideas, through **Speaking**, practice activities in **Vocabulary** and **Grammar**, the lead-ins to **Reading** and **Listening** and discussions about the texts.

Understanding other cultures
Students will best understand other cultures by talking with other students and by having the language to express themselves, which the language input and **Speaking** activities in *Outcomes* always encourage. However, many classrooms may not have people from a large mix of backgrounds, which is why we use texts and **National Geographic videos** with international contexts to reflect cultures throughout the world, both English-speaking and non-English speaking. Students may well realise they share many of the same desires and concerns as others from very different cultures. You'll watch videos about:
- constructing skyscrapers in New York, page 22
- Aboriginal songlines and culture (Australia), page 40
- providing astronomy books for blind children, page 58
- maths and the basic instincts of babies, page 76
- the drama of an animal operation, page 94
- investigations into the myth of King Arthur, page 112
- how we can combat counterfeiters, page 130
- the long-necked women of Myanmar, page 148.

Choosing specific outcomes
We want to work towards specific conversations and outcomes. We consulted documents such as the ALTE can-do statements which identify situations and levels for the purposes of writing exams. For example, they provide the following specific suggestions for what students should be able to achieve at C1 level:
- Can show visitors around and give a detailed description of a place.
- Can enquire effectively about health services provided, entitlements and procedures involved.
- Can participate in casual conversation with appropriacy and good understanding of humour, irony and implicit cultural references.

We also make judgements based on the kinds of things we ourselves talk about (as people rather than authors!) and the kinds of conversations we've had with students over the the years.

LANGUAGE AND *OUTCOMES* ADVANCED

In *Outcomes* it is generally the topic and conversation that comes first. We sometimes write dialogues or texts and work backwards to consider what vocabulary and grammar will help students have those conversations, talk about those topics, or read / listen to those texts. We grade the texts and choose language input in the following ways:

- to reflect CEFR level descriptors
- to meet expectations of grammar input at this level
- to include frequent words students are likely to use and see / hear outside the classroom

CEFR level

Advanced students are aiming to achieve a C1 level, where students are, for example, expected to 'understand a wide range of demanding, longer texts, and recognise implicit meaning ... express him / herself fluently and spontaneously without much obvious searching for expressions ... use language flexibly and effectively for social, academic and professional purposes ... produce clear, well-structured, detailed text on complex subjects, showing controlled use of organisational patterns, connectors and cohesive devices'.
(*Common European Framework of Reference for Languages*, page 24)

Grammar

You will see the same grammar syllabus as you would expect in other books at this level. We know because we've checked! In fact there are not only the 32 **Grammar** sections, but a different kind of grammar is often seen in **Developing conversations**. The grammar presentation may differ slightly from other books in that texts may only have one or two examples of the key grammar, and the text may not always have an example of all forms (e.g. question, statement, negative). That's because we write the texts for the outcome and to sound natural, and often negatives or questions are much less common. We want to show the grammar as it is really used. However, the Grammar reference and other exercises will normally give examples of how these other forms are used. We sometimes suggest that your students translate the target grammar pattern into their own language in order to identify where the differences and similarities lie; this is an optional activity presented in the Teacher's Book and can be very effective with classes who all have the same L1.

Frequent words

We refer to frequency guides in the British National Corpus (phrasesinenglish.org) and published dictionaries such as Cobuild and Macmillan which provide information on frequency. We try to choose those words with a higher frequency (top 5,000 most common words). This is especially true when we focus on words with **reading** and **listening** texts. In some cases, the word you really need is not frequent within the whole of the language but might be within a topic (e.g. *asthma*). In this case, we may teach it. All these important words are found in the **Vocabulary Builder**, with phonetics,

definitions, collocations (often very frequent words) and examples where relevant.

Other words will appear that are part of a story but aren't otherwise worth teaching and remembering. These words are glossed or ignored and don't appear in the Vocabulary Builder.

BETTER FOR TEACHERS

Most teachers need or want material that:
- is quick and easy to prepare
- motivates students.

Quick and easy to prepare

A Student's Book is easy to use when the relation between input and outcomes is clear, and we hope you already see that this is the case with *Outcomes*. However, other aspects of the Student's Book and components should help you just pick up the book and teach:

- **Grammar** and **Vocabulary** have clear links to texts and / or topics.
- **Clear, structured grammar presentations** which get students to do the work:
  - short explanation boxes allow you to introduce grammar points
  - examples from the texts with questions or tasks get students to think about the rules
  - grammar reference provides short clear explanations for students to check their ideas
  - simple to more difficult tasks allow students to check and practise their understanding
- **Fully integrated pronunciation**. Pronunciation work is integrated as part of language input and listening tasks. The video pages include Understanding fast speech activities, which show how words in spoken English are grouped in chunks, and help students to understand and imitate fast speech.
- **Simple instructions** in the Student's Book fully explain tasks.
- **Straightforward numbering** of exercises and audio on each page helps teachers orient students and manage the class.
- **New design** makes navigation around the pages easy.
- **Regular unit structure** allows you to teach as discrete lessons.
- Every spread has its own identity and **lesson title**, which is usually a fixed expression or collocation, using every opportunity to teach students real English.
- **There is thorough recycling and revision of language** throughout the course.
- **The Teacher's Book** provides background information, additional activities and language support. Audio scripts and full answer keys with additional explanations accompany the activity notes.
- **Tests** in the Teacher's Book allow you to assess students' progress after every unit, and to review and assess what they have learnt so far on the course at regular intervals through the year.
- **Quickly-prepared photocopiables** provide additional practice. They involve limited cutting, are quick to set up and provide full practice and revision of language in the Student's Book.

- The **Vocabulary Builder** follows the spreads of the book so you and your students can easily look up words in class. All of the target vocabulary is contained in a database on the website (ngl.cengage.com/outcomes). Students can search for specific words, create their own word lists, add translations and examples, as well as print out pdfs organised by spread.
- **ExamView tests** allow you to make your own revision tests in a matter of minutes.
- **Course website** gives access to all of the additional materials, videos and audio.
- **MyOutcomes online resource.** Teachers can use the online resources practising grammar and vocabulary if they apply for an access code. Go to myelt.heinle.com and request a MyELT instructor's account. This will allow you to set specific work for all your students and then receive their results. You can then store these results through the Grade book, so both you and your student have a record of their marks and progress.
  1 Go to MyELT.heinle.com.
  2 Click Create an Account!
  3 Click Instructor and then click Next.
  4 Complete the online form and click Submit Request. New accounts will be processed within 72 business hours. You will receive a verification email after submitting your account request. A second email will include instructions for logging in to MyELT once your account has been approved. Please print and / or save these emails for your records.

Motivating students

As a teacher, motivating students will be a major part of your job. However, we know a Student's Book can often work against student motivation by having irrelevant or boring content, unclear, unrealistic or unfulfilled outcomes or simply by a dull design. *Outcomes* helps you motivate students by having:
- **outcomes** that reflect many students' wants and needs
- **vocabulary** and **grammar** input and tasks that really help to fulfil those outcomes
- a beautiful design which makes the material clear and easy to navigate
- **National Geographic photos** that inspire, including a full double-page spread photo as the starting point for each unit, intended to raise questions and provoke debate
- **National Geographic videos** that bring in real world content and speech
- fun and funny **Conversation practice videos** on the DVD-ROM, which incorporate role plays into the lesson, and include a Karaoke feature!
- **reading** and **listening** texts based on authentic sources that we think you'll find by turns informative, funny, even moving
- a range of **speaking** tasks that allow for play, humour and gossip, as well as serious discussion.

KEY TO LEARNING

There are many ways to learn but it seems there are a few essentials:
- Students need to notice.
- Students need to understand.
- Students need to remember language.
- Students need to practise – spoken, written, receptive.
- Students need to make mistakes.
- Students need to repeat these steps a lot.

Noticing and understanding

Obviously, **Grammar** and **Vocabulary** encourage students to notice and understand language. Grammar has simple explanation boxes, lots of examples and questions and tasks that guide students to notice form and understand meaning. Words in bold help students to notice key words. Explanations in the **Vocabulary Builder** and many additional collocates and examples allow students to see and understand useful vocabulary. Finally, **reading** and **listening** tasks often ask students to notice words and how they are used.

Remember

Students do have to remember the language they have studied if they are going to use it. That's why you will see exercises in the Student's Book which encourage students to study, cover and remember language. Students often will avoid this work! In class they may say things like 'it's impossible'! Don't give in. Give students time to study in class, and encourage them. They won't remember everything – which is why you need to repeat over time (see below) – but they will remember more than they (and perhaps you) think! Regular **Review** units get students to recall language, and additional tests in the Teacher's Book review and assess what students have learnt so far on the course at regular intervals throughout the year. Additionally, **ExamView** allows you to create your own tests. Further practice that helps students remember the language they have studied includes photocopiable **communicative activities** in the Teacher's Book, and some of the **reading** and **listening** tasks that provide key words and encourage students to try to remember how they were used.

Practice

There are controlled, written practice tasks for all the **Vocabulary** and **Grammar** sections, **in the Grammar reference**, **Workbook** and **Vocabulary Builder**. However, students also need to try and make language their own and there is always an opportunity to experiment with the language that's presented and practise real communication. You might model some of these activities to show students how they can make use of the language taught. Encourage students to incorporate some of the new language – but don't expect them to use it all or get it right (see Making mistakes below). **Photocopiable activities** in this Teacher's Book also provide more of this kind of practice.

Making mistakes

Students will make mistakes with new language as part of the process of learning how to use it. See this as a positive thing and use these moments to extend their knowledge. Not all teaching and input can or should be provided by the Student's Book. We all know from experience and research that people learn new language when they are struggling to express something and the 'correct' or better word is given. This is also why we have lots of **Speaking** activities and speaking after **Listening** and **Reading** texts. They are not just opportunities for students to practise what they know; they are chances for them to try to say something new, stretch themselves and make mistakes, which you can then correct.

Repetition

Seeing a word once is not enough! Some say you need to see and understand vocabulary ten times before you have learnt to use it! Maybe grammar takes even longer. Recycling and revision is therefore a key part of the design of *Outcomes*. We try to repeatedly re-use language from **Vocabulary** in **Listening** and **Reading**; in **Grammar** and **Grammar reference**; in **Developing conversations**; in Workbook texts; in exercises and texts in other units of the Student's Book and even in other levels of the series. We also re-use grammar structures in vocabulary exercises. And as we have seen, the **Speaking** and **Conversation practice** exercises also allow students to re-use language they've learnt, because we work backwards from the outcome to the language.
You as a teacher can help recycle vocabulary and grammar by correcting students after they speak and asking questions about language as you go through exercises. The **Teacher's Book** gives tips and advice on this.

Grammar and vocabulary is also specifically revised and tested in the **Workbook**, **MyOutcomes** online resource, **Reviews** after every two units, **Grammar reference**, and grammar-focused exercises in the **Vocabulary Builder**. You can help students by using these elements over time rather than in one go. For example, you could:

- tell students to study the relevant Vocabulary Builder pages before you teach pages in the Student's Book
- set grammar homework from the reference or MyOutcomes the night after they do it in the Student's Book
- ask students to use the Vocabulary Builder material to create their own word lists, adding their own translations and examples
- ask students to start working through the Workbook exercises after they finish the whole unit
- get students to prepare for the review unit by doing the Vocabulary Builder exercises
- do the review unit in class
- set an ExamView test every four or five units.

1 CITIES

SPEAKING

Aim
to set the scene and introduce the theme with a photo; to get students describing cities and city life; to revise adjectives used to describe places

1   Start by telling the class that in this unit they're going to be learning how to describe cities, discussing city life and urban problems, and telling stories and urban myths.
• Ask students to look at the photo on pages 6–7. Ask: *What can you see?* Elicit a brief description.
• Organise the class into groups of three or four. You could elicit one advantage and one drawback to get them started. Go round the room and check students are doing the task and help with ideas and vocabulary if necessary. Listen for errors, new or difficult language that students try to use, or any interesting ideas that you could use in feedback.
• Ask different groups to present their advantages and drawbacks.
• In feedback, look at good language that students used, and language students didn't quite use correctly. Show students better ways of saying what they were trying to say. You could write some useful new phrases on the board with gaps and ask the whole class to complete the sentences.

> **Possible answers**
> Advantages: very green, close to the water and so good if a person is into water sports, etc., small enough to have a close-knit community, safe
> Drawbacks: potentially very dull, no nightlife or cultural amenities, too homogenous

Culture notes

The photo shows a housing development in West Palm Beach in the US state of Florida. West Palm Beach is one of South Florida's three main cities, and has a population of about 100,000. It is not far from Miami. Strung out along the shoreline, the city has an imposing skyline of skyscrapers as well as historic districts dating from the early twentieth century.

2   Elicit from the class to what degree they would apply *dull* to the place in the photo to get students started. Then ask students to work with a partner to discuss the meaning of the words in the box as they apply them to the place. Monitor and help with ideas and vocabulary.
• In feedback, ask pairs to share their ideas and get them to justify their reasons. Look at good language that students used, and language students didn't quite use correctly.

Optional extra activity   Pre-teach the vocabulary. In pairs, ask students to organise the words in the box into positive and negative words, or ask them to say which words match to simpler synonyms that you could read out. (See Background language notes below.)

Background language notes for teachers

run-down = in bad repair
affluent = rich
congested = crowded
sprawling = stretched out
vibrant = lively
spotless = clean
Note the stress: congested, polluted.
Note the pronunciation: sprawling /ˈsprɔːlɪŋ/.

3   Personalise the topic by asking students to discuss whether they would like to live in West Palm Beach or not as an open-class activity. Again, encourage students to justify reasons.

Teacher development: using *Outcomes* photos

Outcomes aims to start each unit with a large, interesting photo to stimulate interest in the topic and to get students 'on board' with the theme and topics. You can often use the photo to do the following:
1 to get students talking and to personalise the topic
2 to get students interacting and sharing ideas and opinions
3 to introduce key or useful vocabulary
4 to preview language that will come up in the unit (here, descriptive adjectives), and to find out what they already know

A REAL BUZZ ABOUT THE PLACE
Student's Book pages 8–9

Communicative outcomes
In this two-page spread, students will practise asking about and describing cities using present forms.

VOCABULARY City life

Aim
to introduce and practise words used to describe cities and city life

1 Ask students to describe the photo on the page in their own words in open class. Write up any interesting words or phrases used on the board.

• Tell students to check the words in bold and put the words in the box in the sentences. Encourage students to use the context to try to work out any words they are not sure of. Let students compare their answers in pairs before discussing as a class.

• In feedback, check any words that are causing problems. Elicit student definitions or provide your own definitions, synonyms or examples.

Answers
2 There are a lot of **muggings** and shootings.
3 ... and it all runs very **smoothly**.
4 you have to wear a mask or you'd **choke** on the fumes.
5 The cars just **crawl** along most of the time ...
6 ... with people **showing off** their wealth.
7 Apparently, you can get fined heavily for **dropping** it.
8 A lot of buildings should just be **condemned** and rebuilt.

Teacher development: using context to work out meaning

Encourage students to work out meaning from context instead of relying on dictionaries. One way of developing this skill is to ask questions about the words in bold. For example, point out the word 'buzz' in the first sentence and ask: *Is it a noun or a verb? Is it positive or negative? Does it describe the atmosphere of a place?* Then tell students to apply the same technique of asking questions for each of the other words in bold.

• You could further develop the skill of using context to guess meaning by asking pairs to prepare and write questions to ask about each of the words in bold, which they could then share with other pairs.

Background language notes for teachers

buzz = a positive, exciting feel
conspicuous consumption = a term used to refer to consumers who buy expensive items to display wealth and income rather than to cover their real needs (the term was introduced by the Norwegian-American economist and sociologist Thorstein Veblen in his book *The Theory of the Leisure Class*, published in 1899)

crawl = go slowly
might as well = a phrase indicating that it is probably better to do something than not to do it
muggings = a type of street robbery in which valuables are taken using violence
slum = a building or area of a city which is poor and in bad condition
smog = thick fog in cities caused by smoke and pollution
spring up = appear suddenly
trace = a small or barely visible amount

Culture notes

The photo on the page shows a view of Vienna, the capital of Austria, from the bar of the Hotel Sofitel Stephansdom in Vienna.

2 Organise the class into pairs and ask them to discuss the questions. Monitor and help with ideas and vocabulary. In feedback, round up by asking pairs to share their ideas, and getting them to justify their reasons.

Possible answers
1 Adjectives to describe the places mentioned in Exercise 1:
   (1) vibrant (2) chaotic (3) well-run (4) polluted
   (5) congested (6) affluent (7) spotless (8) run-down

Possible ideas for opposites:
1 dull / hit hard by the recession / poor / badly affected / run-down
2 well-run / safe and secure
3 chaotic / poorly connected / badly designed / badly run
4 very clean and fresh / unpolluted
5 it's a great city to drive in / there's hardly any traffic
6 run-down / poor / impoverished
7 filthy / there's litter everywhere
8 very affluent area / it's buzzing / newly built / gentrified

2 great clubs / bars / nightlife, a local successful sports team, lots of new galleries, boutiques, cafés, etc. springing up
3 food / a bone
4 people driving big expensive cars / people wearing designer brands, Rolex watches, gold, etc.

Optional extra activity Ask students to brainstorm (or find in dictionaries) other collocations with words from Exercise 1 (e.g. *a / no trace of evidence, footprints; thick, impenetrable smog; run-down slum*).

LISTENING

Aim
to practise listening for general understanding, and to hear key phrases in a spoken context

3 🔊 1 Ask students to read the situation and the task. Play the recording. Students listen and note answers.

4 Let students compare their answers in pairs before discussing as a class. In feedback, ask students to speculate about the cities, express personal opinions, and work together as a class to put together what they have collectively understood from the listening.

Answers

Conversation 1

Good: it's a wild place, the nightlife is crazy, the whole city is still buzzing at 4 in the morning; the downtown is very vibrant – with all the skyscrapers and neon lights, etc.

Bad: the traffic is terrible, it's incredibly congested, the traffic just crawls along and it's quicker to walk; it's very humid and hard to walk around there; it's very polluted; the smog is terrible. You almost choke on the fumes when you're outside.

Conversation 2

Good: affluent (though this also contributes to it being boring!) and spotless; good place to bring up kids; spotlessly clean; everything runs very smoothly.

Bad: very conservative and monied / affluent; very dull; not much going on, no music scene or anything.

🔊 1

Conversation 1

A: How was your trip?

B: Great. Really amazing. Have you ever been there?

A: No. What's it like?

B: It's really wild. It took me by surprise, actually.

A: Yeah?

B: Yeah. I don't know what I expected, really. I just thought it'd be quieter, but the nightlife is totally insane.

A: Really?

B: Honestly. We went out with these people and ended up in a place at about four in the morning and it was absolutely packed.

A: Yeah?

B: Seriously. You literally couldn't move. In fact, the whole city was still buzzing. You can still get stuck in traffic at that time of night.

A: Wow!

B: Actually, that was a bit of a pain, the congestion.

A: Really? Is it bad?

B: Unbelievable! You just spend hours and hours in the taxi crawling along, with everyone sounding their horns. You'd be quicker walking, really.

A: So did you?

B: No, it's unbearably humid, so at least the car has air con. Honestly, you walk out of your hotel and it's like hitting this thick wall of heat. You just die walking in that heat for any length of time.

A: There must be a fair amount of pollution, then.

B: That as well. The smog is incredible. I mean our hotel was supposed to have this amazing view – and I guess it would be on a clear day, but half the time you can hardly see a thing. And you nearly choke on the fumes when you're outside.

A: Sounds pretty awful. Are you sure it's so great?

B: Well, you know, it does have its drawbacks but, as I say, it just has a real buzz – especially downtown with the skyscrapers and the neon lights flashing and the people and the noise. It's just a really, really vibrant place.

Conversation 2

C: What's your home town like? It's supposed to be nice, isn't it?

D: It is, if you like that sort of place.

C: What do you mean?

D: It's just very conservative. You know, it's very affluent – you see loads and loads of people in fur coats and posh cars, and the streets are spotless, but it's also just incredibly dull. There's not much going on.

C: Right.

D: I know it's a bit more run-down here, but at least it's more lively. There's more of a music scene, you know.

C: Yeah, I know what you mean. So you wouldn't consider going back to live there?

D: Maybe. I mean, don't get me wrong, it is a good place to live if you're bringing up kids – everything works very smoothly and, as I say, there's not a trace of litter on the streets. So if I were to settle down, I might move back. It's just not what I want right now.

C: Fair enough.

5 🔊 1 Ask students to read through the ten sentences carefully first, and to guess or recall which words are missing. Play the recording again. Students listen and complete the sentences. Let them compare their answers in pairs.

• If students find it hard to complete the gaps, play the recording a second time, and pause after each set of missing words.

Answers

1 took me by surprise
2 ended up in a place
3 a bit of a pain
4 it's like hitting
5 have its drawbacks
6 that sort of place
7 more of a music scene
8 consider going back
9 get me wrong
10 were to settle down

Background language notes for teachers

That was a bit of a pain = used to describe a situation that was annoying

Don't get me wrong = used to explain or rephrase when you think someone might not understand what you say, or be upset by it

6 Organise students into groups of four or five to discuss the questions. Ask them to take turns to ask and answer questions. Monitor closely and note interesting and useful language, as well as errors. Use the feedback to point out good examples, correct errors, and to provide examples of how students can express their ideas better.

Optional extra activity Organise Exercise 6 as a mingle. Ask students to walk round the class and interview three or four other students.

UNDERSTANDING VOCABULARY
Emphasising and exaggerating

Aim
to introduce and practise ways of emphasising and exaggerating

7　Read through the information in the box with the class. Ask students to give you other examples of repetition, intensifying adverbs, extreme verbs and expressions with *like* from their language learning experience.

• Organise the class into pairs to do the task. Encourage students to use their own ideas. However, if they have access to dictionaries or digital media, you could ask them to find other examples. In feedback, elicit answers, and check any words or uses that are causing problems.

> **Possible answers**
> There are lots of possible answers, so respond to what your students come up with. Here are some possibilities:
> 1 intensifying adverbs: remarkably, preposterously, greatly, hugely, absolutely, terribly, deeply, etc.
> 2 extreme adjectives: filthy, vast, brilliant, dreadful, awful, incredible, tiny, enormous, fascinating, etc. extreme verbs: devastate, bombard, smash, crush, soar, rocket, plummet, etc.
> 3
> *It was like being at a rock concert.*
> – being at the theatre for a modern play, where the audience stands up and applauds a lot
> – being at a conference where a famous speaker gives a plenary
> – being at a wildly popular classical music concert
>
> *It was like living in a war zone.*
> – living with very noisy argumentative housemates
> – living in an area where there's lots of crime and maybe gang activity
>
> *It's like Buckingham Palace.*
> – a lovely big house that someone has bought
> – a new office that's very big and well decorated
>
> *It was like the Arctic in there.*
> – a cold store room in a big store
> – a room that has the air conditioning turned up very high
>
> *It's like talking to a brick wall.*
> – trying to talk to someone who just won't listen to you
> – trying to explain to a bad worker what they've done wrong and getting nowhere with the conversation

Background language notes for teachers

Here, *like* is a preposition and is followed by a noun or gerund. It means 'similar to'.

8　Start students off by eliciting and writing up on the board one or two further ways of rewriting the first sentence.

• Organise the class into pairs to do the task. Monitor and prompt, and encourage students to use all four of the different ways of emphasising and exaggerating. In feedback, write up any particularly interesting or informative sentences students come up with and analyse them for the class. You could also write up incorrect sentences and get the class to correct them.

> **Possible answers**
> 2 They're doing *loads and loads of* / *an incredible amount of* building work.
> They're doing so much building work the whole city is *absolutely covered* in clouds of dust!
> 3 The city's *really, really* run-down. / The city is so run-down that half the buildings there are *totally* crumbling and falling to pieces.
> 4 It's *really, really* cheap there.
> It's so cheap there it's *like* you hardly even notice you're spending money!
> 5 Some areas are *incredibly* rough / *really, really* dangerous.
> It's *extremely* dangerous. It's *like* the whole area is controlled by organised criminals and there are *loads and loads* of shootings and muggings every day!
> 6 It's *absolutely* fascinating.

Teacher development: feedback on error

Being corrected is a key part of learning, so use the feedback stage to deal with any errors students have made with the sentences they have prepared. In Exercise 8, students have time to think up and prepare their own sentences, so keep an eye on the sentences they produce at the preparation stage. Go round and see what they are writing, and either prompt students to correct errors as you go round, or note any errors a number of students are making which you can focus on in more detail in the feedback stage. In feedback, it is better to write up incorrect sentences and get students to correct them than it is to just correct orally – by getting students to think, and self-correct or peer correct, they are more likely to process what they are learning.

DEVELOPING CONVERSATIONS
Reinforcing and exemplifying a point

Aim
to introduce and practise ways of reinforcing and exemplifying a point

9　Read through the information in the box as a class.
• Ask students to read and match the sentences to the examples. Let students compare answers in pairs. In

feedback, check that students know all the words (*posh* = expensive and desirable; *conspicuous* = noticeable and different – here the speaker is saying they stand out and feel uncomfortable because they are so different).

Answers

1 e	2 b	3 a	4 c	5 d

10 Ask students to work in pairs. Tell them to prepare first by looking at the sentences and examples, and thinking of how they could add adverbs to make the conversations more interesting. Give students plenty of time to practise their conversations from the prompts. Go round, and correct and praise, paying attention to the stress and intonation. Students should be attempting exaggerated intonation on words like *Really?* and *Honestly.*

CONVERSATION PRACTICE

Aim
to practise language from the lesson in a free, communicative, personalised speaking activity

11 Ask students to make notes about cities and at least one thing that happened to them in a city. Go round and help with ideas.

12 Organise the class into pairs and ask them to have conversations about their cities. Encourage pairs to have a go three or four times – practice makes perfect.
• Organise the class into new pairs. Alternatively, you could extend this with a mingle. Ask students to stand up and find new partners to talk to. As students speak, note errors, new language or interesting conversations to use in feedback.
• In feedback, look at good language that students used, and language students didn't quite use correctly. Show students better ways of saying what they were trying to say. You could write some useful new phrases on the board with gaps and ask the whole class to complete the sentences.

▶ 1 Refer students to the video and activities on the DVD-ROM.

Teacher development: using the video

The video and activities on the DVD-ROM can be used in various ways:
1 as an alternative to the conversation practice
2 instead of the listening activity in some units, particularly with weaker groups. Students can first practise reading out the dialogues and work on some of the key phrases / structures in a controlled way before having a go themselves.
3 at the end of the unit as a revision exercise

Communicative outcomes
In this two-page spread, students will read about and compare three cities; they will present proposals for the change and recovery of a city.

READING

Aim
to practise reading for specific information using a jigsaw reading activity

1 Start by checking the meaning of any unknown words in the box.
• Organise the class into groups of three or four to discuss the questions. (Ideally, you want an equal number of groups with an equal number of students in each because this will help the management of the jigsaw reading that follows). Monitor closely and note ideas and interesting and useful language, as well as errors.
• In feedback, ask different groups to tell the class what they discussed. On the board build up a list of useful phrases and language that comes up, and correct any errors or rephrase what students are trying to say.
• Also look at good language that students used, and language students didn't quite use correctly.

Possible answers
an economic downturn: businesses go bankrupt, people get made redundant, poverty increases, homelessness goes up, crime may well go up
a hurricane: destroys buildings, devastates areas
an armed conflict: may result in men getting drafted and civilian deaths, affects the economy, leads to problems reintegrating soldiers after the war, spikes in domestic violence, etc.
an earthquake: buildings collapse, people are crushed to death, can be hard to get relief and aid into the areas if they're remote; can lead to frustration with the government
flooding: people drown, houses get flooded, areas have to be evacuated, costs a fortune to repair damage, frustration with government can develop if relief efforts are slow
a high crime rate: middle class people leave the area, it goes downhill, gangs take over whole areas, areas become no-go zones for the police
severe pollution: people go out less, health is affected terribly, middle classes move out
terrorism: destroys infrastructure, kills innocent people, leads to fear and possible demonising of and revenge attacks on groups seen as being responsible, costs a lot to rebuild, affects tourism
a huge fire: destroys buildings, maybe kills people, causes traffic chaos

Background language notes for teachers

an economic downturn = a period when the economy has negative growth – rising prices, fewer jobs, etc.
an armed conflict = a fight between two countries, or between government or rebels – not quite serious enough to describe as a war

Teacher development: monitoring

At the Advanced level, students are usually confident about using English and comfortable with expressing opinions or sharing ideas in pairwork or groupwork activities. However, this does not mean they are always accurate with their use and pronunciation. By listening proactively whenever students are doing speaking tasks, you are in a position not only to gauge interest and prompt for ideas, but also to notice ingrained errors, communication breakdown, and gaps in students' lexis and grammar. It is a good idea to get into the habit of listening carefully and noting what students say, either mentally or with a notebook. Signal that you are listening in, and monitor equally, paying attention to each conversation going on in the class. The information you gather when monitoring will allow you to feedback on errors, introduce better ways of saying things, and highlight good examples of language use.

2 Organise the class into A, B and C groups. Make sure that, as far as possible, there are an equal number of groups with an equal number of students in each. Ask students to find and read their texts. Set a five-minute time limit for reading.

3 In the same A, B and C groups, students carry out the tasks. Monitor, prompt and help. One way of doing this, with groups of four, is to ask students to work in pairs then have a quick check at the end with the whole of their group. There are no fixed answers here, but you need to be available to help students with vocabulary they're not sure of, and answer any questions about the texts.

Background language notes for teachers

Bogotá:
large-scale reforms = major changes
clear a large slum = knock down and take away the buildings in a slum (an area of poverty)
created a barrier = here, separated the two communities
expropriated the land = took the land away from its previous owners
tackle congestion = deal with problems of too much traffic
protests = demonstrations to demand a different situation
imposed restrictions = introduced measures to stop or cut back on something – in this case car use
poured money into = a way of saying invested large amounts of money
increase in enrolment = increase in the number of people going to school
escape criticism = avoid being criticised
Manchester:
devastated the city centre = ruined or destroyed the centre

evacuated the area = moved all the people out of the area
undergone some changes = some changes happened
host the Commonwealth Games = if a city 'hosts' an event, it means the event takes place in the city
badly neglected = not looked after well
launched an international competition = started or set up a competition for different countries
diverting main roads = making the roads / traffic go in different directions
to boost tourism = to increase tourism
key in attracting = important in bringing in (investors)
inequality has also increased = here, inequality refers to the gap between rich and poor people
lost some of its soul = here, lost the feeling that made the city real and individual
Bilbao:
the gallery symbolises = what it represents or means to the city
unemployment soar = *soar* means 'go up to very high levels'
discouraged inward investment = caused investors to feel negative about bringing their money into the city
abandoned the city = left the city (*abandoned* suggests giving up on the place)
ongoing heavy investment = *ongoing* means 'continuing'
voices of opposition = people who oppose or disagree and express that view
survive the major recession = a recession is a period when the economy is negative – fewer jobs, higher prices, etc.

4 Organise the class into new A, B and C groups, each with three students who have read a different text. Students tell each other about the city they read about and decide on three similarities. Set a short time limit.

> **Possible answers**
> All three cities have managed to overcome huge obstacles.
> They all used to be more run-down / divided / poor than they are now.
> They all reinvented space in the city.
> They've placed an emphasis on bringing the city centres back to life.
> They've all been the victims of violence / terrorism.
> There's been some criticism of each project, claiming it's benefitted some more than others, affecting working class people, etc.

5 In the same groups, students find the answers in the texts. In feedback, ask different groups to justify answers by saying where they found the information in the texts.

> **Answers**
> 1 Bilbao:
>   Other cities trying to replicate the so-called "Guggenheim effect" may have failed because they didn't take up the other strands of Bilbao's regeneration project.
> 2 Bogotá:
>   Peñalosa's administration then expropriated the land of a private country club in the north side of the city. Its golf course and polo fields were converted into a free park with sports facilities for all.

3 Manchester:
Making more of the city's historical sites and creating the Urbis building, which now houses The National Museum of Football. In turn, these changes have been key in attracting new investors such as the Qatari royal family, who own Manchester City Football Club.
4 Bogotá:
They also imposed restrictions on car use and increased taxes on petrol, the proceeds from which went back into the new transport system.
5 Bilbao:
Up until the early 80s, Bilbao had been dominated by steel plants and shipbuilding. To halt the decline, the city embarked on a strategy to reinvent itself as a centre for culture, tourism and new technologies. It also modernised what remained of its more traditional industries and attracted new companies to the technology park on the outskirts of the city.
6 Bogotá:
The ex-mayor of Bogotá, Enrique Peñalosa, has argued that if we ever achieve a successful city for children, we will have built the perfect city for all citizens.
7 Bilbao:
Nevertheless, it's difficult to deny it's been a success which has seen the city return to its previous population levels and survive the major recession that began in 2008.
8 Manchester:
So, dreadful though the bombing was, it actually provided an opportunity to start again that might not have happened otherwise.

Culture notes

Bogotá: Enrique Peñalosa Londoño was born in 1954 in Washington, D.C. He was mayor of Bogotá from 1998 until 2001, and was re-elected in 2015 for the 2016–2019 term.
Manchester: After over 25 years of bombings and other terrorist activities, the IRA disarmed in 2005 following the success of the Good Friday Agreement which brought peace to the region.
The Commonwealth Games takes place every four years. Like the Olympics, it has a different venue each time, has an opening and closing ceremony, and hosts a range of sports. The countries that take part are all members of the Commonwealth, a loose grouping of countries which were once part of the British Empire.
Bilbao: After years of terrorist activity, ETA announced a ceasefire in 2010. On 24 November 2012, it was reported that the group was ready to negotiate an end to its operations and disband completely. The Basque people of southwestern France and northern Spain are linguistically and culturally different to the people of France and Spain. Designed by Canadian-American architect Frank Gehry, the Guggenheim Museum Bilbao houses modern and contemporary art exhibitions. The building is designed to look like a ship.

6 Ask students to discuss the questions. In feedback, encourage ideas from different groups, and open out any interesting points for class discussion.

Optional extra activity 1 If you have a multinational class, ask students to compare their home cities in groups and find five similarities.

Optional extra activity 2 Write five of the phrases in bold in the texts on the board at random. Ask students in groups to discuss their home city or a city they know well using the phrases in bold as prompts.

VOCABULARY Recovery and change

Aim
to introduce and practise verbs used to describe recovery and change

7 Ask students to match and replace the verbs. Elicit the answer to the first one to get students started. Let students compare their answers in pairs before going through the answers.
• In feedback, point out which words are more academic.

Answers
1 undergone (*undergone* is more academic than *gone through*)
2 poured (*invested* is more academic than *poured*)
3 demolished (*demolished* is more academic than *knocked down*)
4 initiated (*initiated* is more academic than *set out*)
5 been neglected (*been neglected* is more academic than *become run-down*)
6 flourishing (*flourishing* is more academic than *doing very well*)
7 soared (*soared* is more academic than *gone up a lot*)
8 imposed (*imposed* is more academic than *brought in*)

Optional extra activity Show the following sentences on the board and ask students to write them in their language:
The city has gone through huge changes in recent years – not entirely for the better.

I'm not happy about it, but I guess it's probably for the best.

I think it was a change for the worse.

He's in hospital. He took a turn for the worse last night.

Remove the English sentences from the board, and ask students to translate their sentences back into English. Then show the originals again for them to compare.

8 Ask students to think of examples in pairs. In feedback, open up a brief discussion about places or people students know about and can describe using the new vocabulary.

GRAMMAR Perfect forms

Aim
to check students' understanding of how to use perfect forms to emphasise that something happened or started before another event or point in time

9 Read through the information in the box as a class.
• Organise students into pairs to complete the sentences. Do the first as an example in open class. Monitor and notice how well students understand the uses.
• In feedback, elicit the students' answers. They can check their answers using the Grammar reference on page 166.

> **Answers**
> 1 has become
>   = happened before now
> 2 have been
>   = before now
> 3 had ... created
>   = before it was condemned and knocked down
> 4 had been dominated
>   = before the economic downturn of the late 1980s
> 5 hadn't secured
>   = before Peñalosa initiated his large-scale reforms
> 6 will have built
>   = before achieving a perfect city in the future
> 7 may have failed
>   = before now
> 8 Having cleared
>   = before Peñalosa's administration expropriated the land of a private country club

 Students complete Exercise 1 in the Grammar reference on page 166.

> **Answers to Exercise 1, Grammar reference**
> 1 a haven't called
>   b don't call
> 2 a was done up
>   b has been done up
> 3 a had been struck
>   b was struck
> 4 a will have changed
>   b will change
> 5 a consult
>   b have consulted
> 6 a was / were here (*was* is more common)
>   b had been
> 7 a Having spent
>   b Spending
> 8 a underwent
>   b had undergone

Background language notes for teachers: perfect forms

• The present perfect is used to talk about 'before now' and to show the result of actions that began or were in the past: *I've been here for a week* (= I arrived a week ago and I'm still here now); *I've lost my wallet* (= I lost it in the past and haven't got it now); *I've sailed round the world* (= I did this in the past, but it has relevance now – it's an experience I have). Advanced students need to recognise that the present perfect is used when that link between the past and the present result is important.

• The past perfect is used to talk about 'before another past event': *I left for work. I had already had breakfast* (= I had breakfast then I left for work).
• The future perfect is used to talk about 'before a future time': *I will have written the essay before Friday* (= after now, but before Friday).

10 Elicit from the class two or three ways their city has changed to get students started. Then ask students to work with a partner to discuss the questions. Monitor and note errors, as well as interesting uses of language, particularly in the use of perfect forms.
• In feedback, look at good language that students used, and language students didn't quite use correctly. Show students better ways of saying what they were trying to say. You could write some useful new phrases on the board with gaps and ask the whole class to complete the sentences.

 For further practice, see Exercise 2 in the Grammar reference on page 166.

> **Answers to Exercise 2, Grammar reference**
> 1 will have left by
> 2 had never seen anything
> 3 having been there recently
> 4 had been initiated
> 5 people had not been evacuated
> 6 to have improved

SPEAKING

Aim
to make a presentation to the class

11 Organise the class into groups of four. In a medium to large size class, it is a good idea for students to work with new partners at this stage. Ask students to read the information first, and to briefly discuss any words or phrases they aren't sure about in their group. When they're ready, ask students to discuss and agree on an order of priority. Monitor and help students at this stage, encouraging them to make decisions about spending and time scale.
• Once students have made their decisions, in feedback, ask each group what their main priorities are.

12 Ask each group to prepare a presentation. Encourage everybody in the group to contribute to the preparation. When ready, one person from each group should read out their presentation.
• Use the feedback to point out good examples, correct errors, and to provide examples of how students can express their ideas better.

Web research activity
• Ask students to find out about how the following once run-down American cities are being regenerated: Detroit, Cleveland, Baltimore.
• In the next lesson, ask students to present what they have found out about one of the cities.

URBAN TALES
Student's Book pages 12–13

Communicative outcomes
In this two-page spread, students will read about and listen to urban tales or myths.

SPEAKING

Aim
to introduce the theme of the lesson and reading text

1 Organise the class into groups. Ask students to read the comments and discuss the questions. In feedback, you could ask students to share any urban myths they have heard.

READING

Aim
to give students practice in reading for specific information; to focus on useful chunks of language used in the text

2 Ask students to read the questions.
• Students read the article and find the answers. Let students discuss their answers in pairs before discussing the answers as a class.

> **Answers**
> 1 The story was that an organised gang was planning to drug visitors to the New Orleans Mardi Gras and take their kidneys out, to sell them on the black market. It sparked panic – lots of people called the police.
> 2 It's an old story, and dates back over 30 years. In the 1980s Guatemala was gripped by stories of Americans kidnapping local children and harvesting their organs; by the early 1990s, there were stories in the States about Latino women tempting American men to a similar fate and before long the idea appeared in TV dramas and movies – variations started to appear all over the world.
> 3 They're all examples of urban myths – stories that just emerge from the popular subconscious and take on lives of their own!

3 Organise students into pairs to find the words in bold and use them to complete the phrases. Encourage them to make guesses by looking at the context and the phrases before checking the meaning of any unknown words as a class.

> **Answers**
> 1 raises
> 2 compelled
> 3 drug
> 4 emerge / emerged
> 5 calm
> 6 sparking
> 7 unites
> 8 gripped

Background language notes for teachers

compelled = forced, obliged
emerge = come out of / from
spark = start or cause
a wave of protests = a number of protests happening one after the other
gripped = held firmly in a way that suggests you have the complete attention of someone or you are completely taken over by something

4 Ask students to work in groups of three to five to think of ideas. Organise the class into new groups to discuss their reasons. Monitor closely and note interesting and useful language.
• In feedback, ask any individual students with interesting comments to share them with the class. Look at good language that students used, and language students didn't quite use correctly. Show students better ways of saying what they were trying to say. You could write some useful new phrases on the board with gaps and ask the whole class to complete the sentences.

> **Possible answers**
> Reasons: just for fun, or to be funny, to offer a moral lesson, as part of a conspiracy theory showing distrust in the government, a malicious attempt to scare people, embarrass them, or get them to do things

Optional extra activity Write on the board: 'Urban myths are an important part of popular culture, experts say, offering insight into our fears and the state of society.' Ask students to discuss what urban myths in their country show about their culture and society.

LISTENING

Aim
to practise listening for general understanding, and to hear key phrases in a spoken context

5 ♫2 Ask students to read the situation and the task. Play the recording. Students listen and answer the questions.

> **Answers**
> **Speaker 1**
> 1 a woman the speaker used to work with
> 2 where she lived
> 3 the police, who she called ... whoever stole the car ... her friend, who she invited to the concert
> 4 she came home and found her car had been stolen ... the next day, it suddenly reappeared
> **Speaker 2**
> 1 a guy from Tokyo
> 2 on a golfing holiday he went on
> 3 hospital staff ... detective
> 4 he ended up in hospital, having been poisoned
> **Speaker 3**
> 1 a guy that a friend of the speaker's brother knows
> 2 in a supermarket
> 3 an old lady – a supermarket cashier

4 the fact (the old lady said) he looked just like her dead son and wanted him to pretend that's who he was

💿2
1
A really terrible thing happened to a woman I used to work with. One day, she woke up and found her car had been stolen from outside her house, so she called the police and reported it, but when she got back home from the office that night, the car had been returned. It was in the driveway. It'd been completely cleaned and there was a note on the driver's seat apologising for taking it. Whoever had written the note said that his mum had been taken ill and he'd had to drive her to hospital. Next to the note there were a couple of tickets for a concert the following day. The woman was really thrilled, you know, so happy – her car back, two free tickets, fantastic. So she called a friend and they both went to the concert and had a really fantastic time. Once she got home though, …
2
Someone told me a story about a guy from Tokyo who'd gone on a golfing holiday. On the third or fourth day, he suddenly collapsed and had to be rushed to hospital for treatment. Eventually, they diagnosed him as having been poisoned and they reported the incident to the police. The detective in charge of the case questioned the man, but he couldn't think of any reason why anybody would want to poison him. It was something really silly in the end. They worked out …
3
This mad thing happened to a guy that a friend of my brother knows. Apparently, one day, he went to a supermarket to buy a few bits and pieces and as he was walking up and down the aisles, looking for the bread, he noticed this elderly woman just staring at him with these desperately sad eyes. He turned away, grabbed a loaf and went off in search of some milk. Once he'd found the milk, he turned round only to see the same woman there again – still just staring like mad at him. Anyway, he was getting a bit freaked out by this – as you would – so he rushed off to pay, but then he remembered that he'd run out of toilet paper and so he went back to get some. When he got back to the cashier, there was the old woman again – in front of him in the queue and her trolley was almost full to the brim. This time she turns to him and she says, 'I'm really sorry for staring, but the thing is, you're the spitting image of my son who died last year.' She's wiping her eyes, getting all tearful, and she says, 'You've got the same eyes, the same hair. It's incredible.' As she was packing all her stuff away, she whispered to the guy and said, 'Could you do me a tiny little favour? Could you just say 'Goodbye, Mum' when I leave? It'd mean the world to me.' Well, what was he going to do? This little old lady and her tragic story, trying to hold back the tears. So as she's leaving the store, struggling with all her shopping, he shouts out, 'Goodbye Mum.' He felt like he'd done his good deed for the day, but then …

6 💿2 Pre-teach *freaked out* (= lost control because of being shocked or scared) and *spitting image* (= exactly the same appearance as someone). Ask students to work in pairs to retell the stories. Monitor, prompt and encourage. When students are ready, play the recording. In feedback, ask how their retelling of the stories differed from the recording.

> **Answers**
> Ideally, students will retell more or less the whole stories, using much of the language from the listening. Use the summaries below, shown in words that aren't exact, to rephrase and support what students tell you:
> 1 one day, she woke up and found her car had been stolen from outside her house
> she called the police and reported it,
> when she got back home the car was in the driveway
> there was a note on the driver's seat
> the note said that the thief's mum had been taken ill and he'd had to drive her to hospital
> next to the note there were a couple of tickets for a concert the following day
> she went with a friend and they both had a fantastic time
> 2 he suddenly collapsed and had to be rushed to hospital
> they diagnosed him as having been poisoned
> they reported the incident to the police
> the detective in charge of the case questioned the man, but he couldn't think of any reason why anybody would want to poison him
> 3 he noticed this elderly woman just staring at him with these desperately sad eyes
> he turned away, grabbed a loaf
> he was getting a bit freaked out by the old woman staring
> he remembered that he'd run out of toilet paper and so he went back to get some
> when he got back to the cashier, there was the old woman again
> her trolley was almost full to the brim
> she said he was the spitting image of her dead son
> she asked if he could do her a favour and say *goodbye mum* as she left
> so he did, feeling like he'd done his good deed for the day

7 💿3 Ask students to discuss the endings in pairs. Play the recording. In feedback, find out how accurately students guessed the endings.

💿3
1
Once she got home though, she discovered she'd been burgled and all her valuables had been stolen. Then to top that, about a week later, the police called her and told her that her car had been used as the vehicle to get away from a major bank robbery on the day that it had gone missing. That is so unlucky, no?

2
It was something really silly in the end. They worked out that the man had actually poisoned himself by accident. Apparently, when he was playing golf he used to hold the tee – that plastic thing you put the golf ball on – between his teeth as he was walking round between the holes, but the golf course had been sprayed with pesticide, so he was basically just sucking in toxic pesticide.

3
He felt like he'd done his good deed for the day, but then the cashier told him his bill was like £300. He said there must've been a mistake as he'd only bought a few things, but then the cashier explained. She said, 'Yes, I know, but your mother said you'd pay for all of her shopping as well!'

8   Organise students into groups of four or five to discuss the questions. Encourage everybody in the group to contribute.
• Use the feedback to point out good examples, correct errors, and to provide examples of how students can express their ideas better.

UNDERSTANDING VOCABULARY
Binomials

Aim
to introduce and practise binomials (pairs of words usually linked together by *and*)

9   Read the information in the box with the class. Ask students if they can provide any examples of binomials from their own language learning experience.
• Ask students to complete the sentences individually. Elicit the first as an example. Let students compare their answers in pairs.

Answers
1 off
2 miss
3 then
4 quiet
5 hard
6 there
7 tired
8 order
9 regulations
10 foremost

Teacher development: noticing pronunciation and stress and using prompt drills

When introducing or revising vocabulary or structure, it is important to listen to how accurately your students pronounce the words, and to help them notice and have a go at key features. In Exercise 9 above, for example,

a feature of these binomial expressions is the weak stress and pronunciation of the word 'and' which is reduced to /n/. You could deal with this in a number of ways:
1 By explicitly pointing out the weak stress when feeding back on answers.
2 By briefly drilling the students, asking them to repeat the binomials (or some of them) after your model.
3 By doing a prompt drill: for example, you say *sick*, students say *sick and tired*.

10   Ask students to work in groups of four to discuss the questions.

Possible answers
1 a park, a zoo, a coffee shop, a library, a museum
2 getting married, which college to go to, which course to study, which house or flat to buy or rent
3 traffic, travelling to work, noise, crowds, pollution, litter
4 civil war, riots, recession
5 students' opinions

Optional extra activity Write one word from each of the binomials taught on the board (e.g. *now, long, there, foremost*, etc.) at random. Then give students in pairs a topic to discuss (e.g. holidays) and tell them to chat about holidays for one minute while trying to include as many binomials in the conversation as they can. The words are on the board as prompts to help them remember which binomials to include. After one minute, change the topic, and ask students to have a second conversation.

SPEAKING

Aim
to make a presentation to the class

11   Organise the class into new pairs. Give students time to find the texts. Ask students to read and prepare their stories. When they are ready, ask them to tell the stories without looking at the originals.
• If you have access to the Internet in class, get students to find and prepare an urban myth they find online. You will have to go round and support students by explaining any difficult words in the texts they find.
• Monitor closely and note interesting and useful language, as well as errors. Use the feedback to point out good examples, correct errors, and to provide examples of how students can express their ideas better.

Web research activity
• If you didn't ask students to research an urban myth on the Internet in the lesson, ask them to do so for homework.
• In a future lesson, ask students to retell the story.

2 RELATIONSHIPS

SPEAKING

Aim
to set the scene and introduce the theme with a photo; to get students talking about friendships and people they know

1 Start by telling the class that in this unit they're going to be describing people they know, and talking about marriage and science, and different relationships.
- Ask students to look at the photo on pages 14–15. Ask: *What can you see?* Elicit a brief description, and establish what happens at a school reunion.
- Organise the class into groups of four or five to discuss the questions. Go round the room and check students are doing the task and help with ideas and vocabulary if necessary.
- In feedback, ask different groups to tell the class what they discussed.
- Once you have fed back on content, look at good language that students used, and language students didn't quite use correctly during the activity.

> **Possible answers**
> Thomas Edison, Benjamin Franklin, Bill Gates and Albert Einstein all dropped out of school or college early before becoming successful.

Optional extra activity Write the names of three of your former schoolmates (that you are still in touch with) on the board. Ask students in pairs to think of questions to ask about them then and now. Listen to and answer your students' questions in a Q and A session.

Teacher development: live listening

Outcomes aims to provide plenty of personalised spoken practice between students. However, nothing beats listening to and interacting with a native or near-native speaker. Here are some ways of incorporating 'live listening' into your lessons:
1 Model personalised activities in which students have to interview each other by getting the class, or individuals in the class, to interview you first.
2 Extend listening tasks in which people describe personal experiences by describing personal experiences of your own.
3 Take opportunities during the course to tell stories, describe experiences, or answer questions from your class at length.

Communicative outcomes
In this two-page spread, students will practise describing people.

VOCABULARY Describing people

Aim
to introduce and practise ways of describing people

1 Ask students to look at the photo collage and describe the people they can see. Write up on the board any interesting words or phrases students come up with.
- Ask students to choose the correct options. Start them off by eliciting the first answer, pointing out that *snobbish* is an adjective, and *snob* a noun. Let students compare their answers in pairs before discussing as a class.

> **Answers**
>
> | | |
> |---|---|
> | 1 snob | 7 arrogance |
> | 2 cynical | 8 incompetent |
> | 3 principles | 9 stubborn |
> | 4 charming | 10 intense |
> | 5 really | 11 willing |
> | 6 a pain | 12 slacker |

Teacher development: checking words

When you feedback on a vocabulary task, don't assume that students know all the words simply from doing the task. Check the part of speech, and use or ask for examples, or synonyms and antonyms, to check the words.
Here are some suggestions for checking the words in Exercise 1:
1 Which word in item 2 is an adjective? (*cynical*) How do you know? (the suffix -al)
2 Which word is the opposite of *easy-going*? (*stubborn*)
3 Is *slacker* a positive or negative word? (negative) What adjectives can you use to describe a slacker? (*lazy, idle*)

Optional extra activity Focus on the stress in these words if you think your students have problems in this area. Briefly drill the following: *cynical, principled, arrogant, incompetent, stubborn, intense*.

2 Organise the class into pairs to think of ideas. Monitor and help students with ideas and how to express them. In feedback, elicit ideas and get the rest of the class to comment on them. If students find it difficult to think of things that show the meaning of the words well, share the examples provided below.

Possible answers

cynic: They don't really want to help people – they're just doing it for the money.

principled: It's just wrong! / I wouldn't do it no matter what you paid me.

charming: But you can't have children that age – you look far too young!

bitchy: He thinks he's clever, but he's such an idiot!

a pain: I can't do it now – you'll have to come back later.

arrogant: Listen, you know I'm right because i'm always right.

incompetent: I didn't plug it in! Oh, silly me.

stubborn: I don't care what you say – I'm not doing it.

intense: Yes, but what does it all mean? What's the meaning of life?

willing: If you ever want to talk it over, please just ask.

laid-back: I'll do it later – it'll be fine. Don't worry.

---

3 Ask students to work individually to complete the sentences. The aim of this exercise is to get students to put together, learn and use chunks of useful language. Focus on the example before students start so that they can see that 'mind' is a noun which collocates with 'make up' and that 'back down' is a phrasal verb, and its meaning is shown by the sentence: 'won't' and 'even if he's in the wrong'. Students will need to think about the part of speech and context to do the activity.

• Let students compare their answers in pairs before discussing as a class. In feedback, elicit answers and check any idiomatic uses students may be unsure of.

Answers

2 She's constantly <u>going behind my back</u> and saying things to <u>undermine me</u>.

3 He never <u>seems that bothered by criticism</u> or bitchy comments. He just <u>takes no notice of</u> it all.

4 She <u>stands up for what she believes in</u> and she <u>sticks to her principles</u>. She's not easily bullied.

5 <u>He's one of those people who</u> never panics. He just <u>takes everything in his stride</u>

6 She's <u>not exactly shy and retiring</u>. She loves to be <u>the centre of attention</u>.

7 He's <u>not the easiest person to talk to</u>. I wish he'd <u>lighten up a little</u>.

8 You'll need to <u>remind her about</u> it. She <u>is prone to forgetting</u> things like that.

9 He's <u>a bit prone to exaggerating</u>, so I would<u>n't take what he said too seriously</u>.

10 <u>She's the kind of person who</u>'s constantly <u>sucking up to the boss</u> in order to get ahead.

Background language notes for teachers

bothered = concerned, upset

stick to your principles = stand up for what you believe in even when under pressure to change your view

take (things) in your stride = deal with a problem or difficulty calmly and not to allow it to influence what you are

lighten up = relax, stop being too serious

prone to = likely to, tend to

suck up to (someone) = try to make someone in authority approve of you by doing and saying things that will please them (a negative word)

Optional extra activity Show the following sentences on the board and ask students to write them in their language:

He's one of those people who'll just never accept they've made the wrong decision.

She's one of those people who never worry about anything.

He's one of those people who are always willing to try new things.

Remove the English sentences from the board, and ask students to translate their sentences back into English. Then show the originals again for them to compare.

4 Organise the class into new pairs to think of adjectives or nouns to match to the sentences.

Possible answers

1 stubborn

2 bitchy

3 (self-) confident / thick-skinned / laid-back

4 principled

5 laid-back / (self-) confident / easy-going

6 out-going / extrovert / loud / arrogant (last two examples are more negative)

7 intense / serious

8 forgetful / absent-minded / incompetent (last example is very negative)

9 unreliable / liar (second example is very strong)

10 (overly) ambitious / a creep

---

5 Ask students to prepare and practise two-line exchanges in pairs. Monitor and notice how well students use and pronounce the new words. Provide feedback on any errors or examples of good language use.

Optional extra activity Ask students in groups to describe friends, family members and / or celebrities using some of the words and phrases from the lesson.

DEVELOPING CONVERSATIONS

Giving your impression

Aim

to introduce and practise ways of giving your impression about people

6 Read through the information in the box as a class.

• Ask students to work in pairs to prepare their ideas. You could start students off by eliciting names of celebrities they might want to talk about first, and eliciting a couple of ways they might describe them.

Background language notes for teachers

strikes (someone) as = used to describe the impression created by someone on an onlooker
comes across as = used to describe the particular opinion of someone formed by their appearance or actions
Note the use of *as* here. It is used to say how somebody or something is considered or described. It can be used in many other phrases: *It / He is seen / regarded / described as ...*

7 Ask students to share impressions in pairs using the prompts. Monitor and note down errors of form, use and pronunciation. Use the feedback to point out good examples, correct errors, and to provide examples of how students can express their ideas better.

Optional extra activity Ask students to write three sentences to describe how they think they come across to other people in public. Collect the sentences, mix them up, and hand them to groups in the class. Ask students to read the sentences and say who they think is being described.

LISTENING

Aim
to practise listening for general understanding and to hear chunks of language in a listening text

8 🌑 **4** Ask students to read the situation and the task. Play the recording. Students listen and note answers.
• After playing the recording, ask students to compare answers in pairs. In feedback, elicit answers. Note that the descriptions in question 2 will vary. You may wish to make a judgement on how many of the descriptions you expect students to give and which language to accept.

Answers
Conversation 1
1 manager (dragging the whole team down / go over his head / blame everyone else especially below him)
2 incompetent / arrogant / sucks up to boss / maybe bitchy (blames everyone else)
Conversation 2
1 rock / pop star
2 decent / principled (other speaker disagrees – fake / cynical – wants to sell more records)
Conversation 3
1 flatmate (in a student residence / dorm / house) (corridor / lectures / medicine / shared bathroom)
2 friendly, bright and chatty / a good laugh / annoying (taking over bathroom)

🌑 **4**
Conversation 1
A: So, how's it all going? Any better?
B: I'd say things are worse if anything, to be honest. He doesn't seem to have a clue how the department should work or what's expected of him – and he's dragging the whole team down with him. I've tried to talk to him about it,

but he always just gets really defensive and puts up this great big barrier and basically just tells me to get on with my work. What really drives me mad, though, is the man's arrogance. He's so full of himself! He's one of those people who'll just never accept they've made the wrong decision. He just blames it all on everyone else – mainly those below him!
A: Sounds like an idiot to me! Maybe you need to go over his head and talk to his line manager about it.
B: Oh, it's not worth it. He isn't exactly the most approachable person and from what I've heard he wouldn't take any notice anyway. They seem oblivious to criticism, these people. All they're interested in is sucking up to whoever is above them in order to get ahead.
Conversation 2
C: I can't stand him.
D: Really? I've always thought he comes across as a really decent guy.
C: You're joking, aren't you? He's so fake!
D: Do you think so? In what way?
C: All that rubbish about saving the world and helping the starving millions that he's always going on about.
D: What's wrong with that? I quite admire the fact he's prepared to stand up for what he believes in. There are plenty of people in the public eye who just aren't bothered about those things. It'd be easier for him to just keep his mouth shut.
C: I wouldn't say that. I'd say it's all just self-promotion. It's just to sell more of his music. If he was really bothered, he'd give his millions away and really help people. He just likes to be seen to be doing good.
D: I just think you've got him wrong. He's done a lot to raise awareness of various different causes and he works really hard to make a difference. You're just a cynic.
C: And you're just naive!
Conversation 3
E: So what're the people on your corridor like? Are you getting on OK with them all?
F: Yeah, more or less. I haven't really seen much of the guy next door. I think he studies Medicine so he's either at lectures or studying – he certainly keeps himself to himself, anyway.
E: OK.
F: But the girl opposite is great. She's really nice and very bright and chatty. We hit it off straightaway.
E: That's good, then.
F: Yeah, she's from the States and came over to do a Master's in International Law.
E: Really? So she's a bit older than you, then.
F: Yeah, but she certainly doesn't make a thing of it. She's a great laugh. The only problem is she kind of takes over the bathroom every morning. She's in there for hours doing her hair and her make-up. It's really annoying because we've only got the one bathroom.
E: Oh no! Really? That'd drive me mad, that would!

> F: And the guy on the other side of me seems
>   pleasant enough, but he strikes me as a bit of
>   a slacker. I mean, I see him throwing a Frisbee
>   around with people outside the hall or sitting
>   around smoking, but I've never seen him go to any
>   lectures or anything and he just seems ... well ...
>   extremely laid-back about it.
> E: To the point of horizontal, then, eh?

9 ♨ 4 Ask students to work in pairs to write the
missing words. Play the recording for students to check
their answers. If students have problems hearing the
missing words, play it again and pause the recording
after each phrase.

Answers
1 a dragging the whole team down
  b puts up this great
  c go over his head
2 a comes across as
  b done a lot to raise awareness
3 a hit it off straightaway
  b takes over the bathroom
  c strikes me as

Background language notes for teachers

drag (someone) down = make (someone) feel worse or
less hopeful or perform worse
hit it off = have a good relationship immediately

10 Organise the class into groups of four or five to
discuss the questions. In feedback, encourage students to
share any interesting experiences.

CONVERSATION PRACTICE

Aim
to practise language from the lesson in a free,
communicative, personalised speaking activity

11 Give students a short amount of time to think
of what to say, and go round to help with ideas
and vocabulary.

12 Organise students into pairs to ask and answer
about the people on their lists.
• In feedback, look at good language that students used,
and language students didn't quite use correctly. Show
students better ways of saying what they were trying
to say. You could write some useful new phrases on the
board with gaps and ask the whole class to complete
the sentences.

▶◀ **2 Refer students to the video and activities on the DVD-ROM.**

Teacher development: using the video

The video and activities on the DVD-ROM can be used in
various ways:
1 as an alternative to the conversation practice
2 instead of the listening activity in some units,
   particularly with weaker groups. Students can first
   practise reading out the dialogues and work on some
   of the key phrases / structures in a controlled way
   before having a go themselves.
3 at the end of the unit as a revision exercise

Web research activity
• Ask students to type the name of three or four well-
known international celebrities followed by the words
'descriptive adjectives' into a search engine. Tell them
to note down five adjectives they find connected with
that celebrity.
• In a future lesson, ask students to share their findings
in groups.
• A search of 'George Clooney descriptive adjectives'
came up with *charming, funny, arrogant, toffee-nosed* and
gravelly-voiced.

GETTING TOGETHER
Student's Book pages 18–19

Communicative outcomes
In this two-page spread, students read and discuss an article about love and relationships, and will practise using phrasal verbs.

SPEAKING

Aim
to discuss different ways of meeting a partner; to lead in to the topic of the lesson

1 Organise the class into groups of four or five to discuss the questions. Go round the room and check students are doing the task and help with ideas and vocabulary if necessary.
• In feedback, ask different pairs to tell the class what they discussed. Once you have fed back on content, look at good language that students used, and language students didn't quite use correctly during the activity.

Possible answers
Arranged marriage:
Pros: likely to marry someone suitable that your family will approve of; correct way to act in some cultures; takes away the stress of having to find a partner of your own; both people in partnership have family support and a degree of security
Cons: no individual choice; you may not like your partner or find them attractive or have much in common; feel pressured by culture or community to accept your partner; no romantic love before the marriage
Going on a blind date:
Pros: difficult to find people to go out with in everyday life; can be fun and exciting
Cons: may have some difficult or embarrassing evenings out; may be meeting someone you can't trust; some feel that it isn't as romantic as meeting someone in real life
Meeting through work or university:
Pros: have a lot in common; chance to get to know someone slowly and as friends first; know you can trust them
Cons: can be problematic if you split up; too similar – same friends and activities
Meeting via an Internet dating site:
Pros: difficult to find people to go out with in everyday life; can be fun and exciting; can meet lots of different people
Cons: may have some difficult or embarrassing evenings out; may be meeting someone you can't trust; some feel that it isn't as romantic as meeting someone in real life
Students may suggest that these are advertisements asking for a partner. Work with however students interpret this photograph (see Culture notes).

Other ways of meeting people: dating agency, at a disco or nightclub, through friends or relatives, Facebook friends, through hobbies, sports or other club activities, on holiday, on a language learning course.
Pros and cons: students' answers

Culture notes

The photo shows personal ads hanging in People's Park, Shanghai, China. Parents with unmarried children are browsing the ads, seeking suitable matches.

READING

Aim
to give students practice in reading for specific information; to find and learn chunks of language in the reading context

2 Ask students to read the headline and the questions and to predict what the text might be about. Then ask students to read and find answers to the questions. Let students compare their answers in pairs before discussing as a class.

Answers
1 Social science
Basic answer: Social scientists have been doing research into why couples stay together – and what their secrets are.
Extra information students may come up with, or you may want to add: couples stay together longer if share housework, talk rather than text when they have problems, get enough sleep and don't have kids
Neuroscience
Basic answer: Neuroscientists have found which parts of the brain light up when you're in love, so they can 'see' attraction and affection.
Extra information students may come up with, or you may want to add: brain scans of new couples may be sufficiently revealing to see if the feelings are strong and mutual
Computer science
Basic answer: Mathematical formula can help to narrow down partners you might like and help you find most compatible dates.
Extra information students may come up with, or you may want to add: collaborative filtering process helps this by dividing people up into similar groups
2 Not very. The writer sounds sceptical and says: 'The degree to which this will ensure marital success remains highly contested. Perhaps in the end we may have to accept that chemistry will never be completely understood by scientists!'

3 Organise students into pairs. Ask them to discuss the reason why the phrases were mentioned. Monitor and help students find answers, or share them with you to see if they are right. In feedback, briefly go through the reasons.

Answers
1 doing your own thing – helps couples keep things fresh
2 changing partners – doesn't work / no happier afterwards
3 patience and perseverance – central to long lasting marriage
4 artists, poets and playwrights – love was previously their domain (as opposed to science)
5 kids – marriages tend to last longer without them
6 thousands upon thousands of online profiles – this was what early online dating sites offered
7 collaborative filtering – technique for narrowing down choices to people with similar outlooks
8 arranged marriage – the old way of getting married was through arranged marriage, nowadays we've just replaced the matchmaker with a computer

4 Ask students to complete the phrases individually. Elicit the first one to get them started. Let students compare their answers in pairs before discussing as a class.

Answers
1 keep things fresh
2 pride ourselves on
3 drawing lessons from
4 a wealth of studies
5 be sufficient to determine whether
6 researchers working in the field of
7 may well prove to be
8 lived to tell the tale

5 Organise the class into groups of four to choose and prepare topics. You could ask students to work individually or let them prepare ideas in pairs first. Give them about five minutes preparation time. Monitor and help students with ideas and vocabulary if necessary.
• As students share their ideas, monitor closely and note interesting and useful language, as well as errors. Use the feedback to point out good examples, correct errors, and to provide examples of how students can express their ideas better. You could write some useful new phrases on the board with gaps and ask the whole class to complete the sentences.

Optional extra activity Have a class debate on one of these topics – the pros and cons of having children, having an arranged marriage, or meeting a partner online.

UNDERSTANDING VOCABULARY

Phrasal verbs

Aim
to introduce and practise phrasal verbs

6 Read through the information in the box with the class. Ask students to provide examples from their own learning of three-part phrasal verbs (*get on with*), verbs that are usually used in the passive (*the brochure was beautifully laid out*) or require objects (*hit it off*; *turn it on*).

• Ask students to complete each set of phrases with phrasal verbs from the article. Elicit the first answer to get them started. Let students compare answers in pairs before discussing as a class.

Answers
1 sort out
2 be subjected to
3 move into
4 sound out
5 narrow down
6 end up

7 Ask students to work in pairs to discuss the phrasal verbs. Start them off by eliciting and explaining how *bring in* takes an object, and is usually separable. With a pronoun, it has to split: *Legislators brought them in*. With nouns, they can be split or not: *They brought rules in*; *They brought in rules*.

8 ✦ 5 Play the recording so students can check their answers. Explain that students should listen to hear whether the object is before or after the particle. In feedback, summarise the rules for students by listing them on the board or providing a handout.

Answers
Pronoun comes between verb and particle:
1 brought them in
2 dragging us down
4 gave it all away
6 knock them down
7 set it out
8 set it up
10 takes it over
Pronoun comes after the particle:
3 embark on it
5 gone through them all
9 stick to them

✦ 5
1 The new restrictions? Oh, they brought them in last year.
2 He's not just messing up his own career. He's dragging us down as well.
3 We realised as soon as we embarked on it that it was a good strategy.
4 He made millions, but then gave it all away.
5 Life brings many changes – and I've gone through them all!
6 The buildings aren't fit to live in anymore so they've decided to knock them down.
7 It's quite an ambitious plan so make sure you set it out clearly.
8 There's a big recycling centre there. They set it up a few years ago.
9 If those are your principles, you've got to stick to them.
10 I can never get in the bathroom in the morning. She totally takes it over.

9 Organise the class into new groups of four or five to discuss the questions. Give them two or three minutes to prepare their ideas first, and monitor briefly and help if necessary. As they speak, encourage students to particularly focus on using the phrasal verbs from the lesson.
• In feedback, ask different groups to tell the class what they discussed. Look at good language that students used, and language students didn't quite use correctly.

Optional extra activity Write the following on the board and tell students they are the last lines of short stories:
We ended up hitchhiking all the way back from the northernmost town in Scotland.
Unsurprisingly, once they narrowed down the candidates on the list, I was no longer included.
I can honestly say that I will never go through such an ordeal again.
Ask students to choose one closing line and imagine what happened in the story that went before it. Elicit some ideas in feedback.

MIXED MESSAGES
Student's Book pages 20–21

Communicative outcomes
In this two-page spread, students will practise language used to talk about relationships, and will practise sharing and talking through problems.

SPEAKING

Aim
to get students talking about relationships; to lead in to the topic of the lesson

1 Start by pre-teaching any key words: *siblings* (= brothers and sisters); *life partner* (= a modern way to describe a long-term relationship which covers unmarried and same sex relationships as well as that between husband and wife); *colleague* (= somebody you work with).
• Tell students to work individually first to order their relationships. Organise the class into groups of four or five to compare and explain their choices. Go round the room and check students are doing the task and help with ideas and vocabulary if necessary.
• In feedback, ask different groups to tell the class what they discussed. Once you have fed back on content, look at good language that students used, and language students didn't quite use correctly during the activity.

Optional extra activity This is an opportunity for a live listening. As a model before the activity, or an extension after it, describe an important relationship in your life and encourage students to ask you questions about it.

LISTENING

Aim
to listen for general and specific understanding

2 ♦6 Give students time to read the situation and the task. Play the recording and ask students to note answers. Let students compare their answers in pairs before discussing as a class. In feedback, ask students to justify answers by saying what they heard.

> **Answer**
> Speaker 1
> grandmother of Toby (my son and his mother / unsteady on her feet)
> Speaker 2
> a class teacher of Toby (bright boy / change desks / call the Head)
> Speaker 3
> Toby's coach (turn professional / dispute on the pitch / part of the game / training / matches)
> Speaker 4
> doctor (operation went well / complete recovery / discharge him) of the victim Toby helped / hurt
> Speaker 5
> ex-girlfriend / classmate of Toby (went out / committed / awkward in class)

☘6

1

When he was a toddler, I'd do the childcare most days and he was always a bit of a handful. I did try and instil a bit of discipline into him, but I'm not sure it really happened at home. My son would shout and tell him off, but then he'd burst into tears and his mother would comfort him – so totally mixed messages. I knew it would come to no good, but you can't really interfere, can you? Not that he's all bad. He's helped me out sometimes since I've been unsteady on my feet. But really, if it's true, I hope they treat him severely. It's what he needs to get back on the straight and narrow.

2

The frustrating thing is he's a bright lad, but I would say he has a stubborn streak and he's been prone to outbursts and answering back. I remember once I asked him to change desks to sit next to this girl and he just wouldn't – just refused point blank – and then we got into this ridiculous confrontation with neither of us willing to back down. I had to call the Head in the end. So yeah, I guess it doesn't entirely surprise me he's ended up in this kind of trouble. What should happen now? Well, he should obviously be punished, but after that I'd still give him another chance rather than exclude him permanently. I'm sure he'll learn.

3

Oh yeah. Hugely talented and I would've thought he could go all the way and turn professional, so this has come as a big shock. Maybe there's more to it than appears to be the case. He certainly conducted himself well here. You know, I push them hard, but he's just taken that in his stride and done everything I've asked of him. He's had the odd dispute on the pitch, but I always took that to be part of the game rather than something particular to him. He confided that his parents were going through a rough patch and I was aware that he had a few issues at school, but I think training and matches were always an escape from that and I made sure he was always focused. Hopefully this is just a setback rather than the end of his career prospects.

4

I've been treating him since he came in here. He suffered some quite severe blows, but the operation went very well. It helped he was in remarkably good health for someone of his age and although he's a little frail now, I'd expect him to make a complete recovery. We're going to monitor him for a few more days, but we'll probably discharge him next week. From what I understand, he's still a bit confused about what happened, but he seems to think the young man who was arrested had actually come to his aid.

5

He's in my class and we kind of went out for a while. He can turn on the charm and that, but he was just too unreliable. When it came down to it, the only thing he was committed to was his football. We'd arrange something, but then it'd be like, 'Oh, the coach wants to put us through our paces', or 'Coach says we're getting complacent. Gotta stay on', 'Early night. Coach says I've gotta conserve my energy for the game.' Tttch! I said you might as well go out with coach cos you've let me down too often. I would've probably stayed with him if he'd apologised, but he's too proud, inne. Just walked away. It was cold. It's been awkward in class. I actually saw him the night it happened at this friend's party. I don't know what was up with him. He was acting strangely – staring at the people I was with – and there was like a bit of a scene, but I still doubt he'd do something like that.

3 ☘6 Organise the class into pairs to discuss the phrases. Check the meaning briefly in feedback and elicit students' answers to the questions before playing the recording again. In feedback, make sure you both provide answers and ask students to justify them.

Answers
1 mixed messages: dad (and grandmother) strict / mother soft when he was punished
2 get back on the straight and narrow: proper punishment (treat him severely)
3 ridiculous confrontation: he wouldn't change desks
4 unwilling to back down: he didn't want to sit next to a particular girl / used to getting his own way / didn't like the teacher / unhappy at home
5 come as a shock: he has conducted himself well / he has taken things in his stride
6 confide to his coach: his parents were unhappy (going through a rough patch) and issues at school
7 remarkably good health: because of his age and because he suffered severe blows
8 who came to his aid: a young man / Toby
9 when it came down to it, why did they split up: Toby wasn't committed enough to her and he was totally committed to football
10 where was there a scene and what do you think caused it: a friend's party – Toby was unhappy to see his ex- girlfriend, and was perhaps jealous of the people she was with

Background language notes for teachers

mixed messages = when you are told something which can be interpreted in two ways, or when one thing you are told contradicts another
get back on the straight and narrow = return to acting in a good way (e.g. a criminal stopping committing crimes or a drug addict giving up drugs)
unwilling to back down = not prepared to allow somebody else to win an argument or fight
confide to (someone) = tell a secret to someone
when it came down to it = in the end
a scene = a situation in which there is an argument or a display of anger

Teacher development: justifying answers

In the feedback to a reading or listening text, encourage students to justify their answers by summarising what they have heard or read in their own words, or, in the case of a reading text, by asking them to find and read out supporting sections. Encourage students to do this in pairs when checking answers before feedback, and in the feedback session itself. This creates spoken interaction, demands that students are proactive and autonomous, and gets students to read and listen more intensively.

GRAMMAR *Would*

Aim
to introduce and practise different uses of *would*

4   Read through the information in the box as a class.
• Organise students into pairs to match the sentences and discuss the rules. Monitor and notice how well students understand the rules.
• In feedback, elicit the students' answers. They can check their answers using the Grammar reference on page 167.

Answer					
1 d	2 e	3 c	4 b	5 a	6 f

Students complete Exercise 1 in the Grammar reference on page 167.

Answers to Exercise 1, Grammar reference
1 would completely agree with you
2 would not say he was / would say he was not
3 would not accept any of
4 would not get involved
5 he would not bitch about people
6 I would kick him out
7 would not imagine I would get / buy // would imagine I will not buy / get
8 I would expect it to

Background language notes for teachers: *would*

Would is a modal verb which is often shortened to *'d*. It is followed by an infinitive of the verb without *to*.
It is used in the following situations:
1 expressing unlikely or unreal hypothesis: *We wouldn't be here if we had taken the train.*
2 expressing a past hypothesis or regret: *I wouldn't have failed if I'd worked harder.*
3 expressing habitual past with active verbs: *As a child, I'd walk to school every day.*
4 expressing the future in the past: *She met the man she would one day marry.*
5 expressing a refusal: *The car wouldn't start.*
6 giving advice: *If I were you, I'd stop smoking now.*
7 introducing cautious opinions: *I'd say ... I'd imagine ...*
8 making polite requests, and expressing wants and preferences: *Would you mind opening the window? I'd like to leave now. I'd prefer to go by train.*

9 past of *will* (often in reported speech): *She said she would come.*

5   Ask students to work individually to write sentences. Monitor, prompt and help with ideas and vocabulary.

6   Organise students into pairs or small groups to compare and agree on ideas. In feedback, elicit some ideas from students. Write up and point out good examples that you hear, and correct any *would* errors. Use the suggested ideas below to provide good examples for students if they find the activity demanding.

Possible answers
what his childhood was like and his relationship with his parents:
– I'd say he had a difficult childhood. Because his parents would argue a lot and they wouldn't spend a lot of time with him.
why the different people have the opinions they do:
– I'd say the grandmother doesn't like her daughter-in-law and blames her.
– I would've thought Toby still liked his ex-girlfriend.
– I don't suppose the coach would think that way if he was rubbish at football.
why you think he was arrested and if it could have been avoided:
– He might have just been in the wrong place at the wrong time.
– It wouldn't have happened if he'd stayed at home.
– They wouldn't have arrested him if the victim had spoken to the police sooner.
what you think / hope / imagine would happen to Toby now:
– I'd imagine he'd get off.
– I wouldn't expect him to be found guilty.
– I'd hope the victim would explain what happened.
what you would advise him and the people he knows:
– I'd tell him to get some counselling.
– I'd advise his parents to be clearer about the rules and punishments they set.
– If I was the teacher, I'd recommend that he be excluded from school.

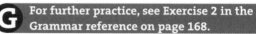
For further practice, see Exercise 2 in the Grammar reference on page 168.

Answers to Exercise 2, Grammar reference
1 correct
2 I often got into trouble at school just because I ~~would have~~ **had** really long hair.
3 correct
4 My parents wish we ~~would live~~ **lived** a bit closer to them.
5 I wouldn't be here if I ~~wouldn't have~~ **hadn't** had the surgery.
6 correct
7 Seriously, I wish my brother **would** shut up sometimes.
8 correct
9 It doesn't surprise me. I knew ~~he'll~~ **he'd** say that! He's so predictable!
10 correct

VOCABULARY Relationships

Aim
to introduce and practise chunks of language used to describe relationships

7 Organise the class into pairs to discuss the phrases. In feedback, use check questions, synonyms and examples to check the meaning of the phrases.

Possible answers
1 a life partners
  b bad – going through rough patch
2 a neighbours
  b good – keeping an eye / caring
3 a pupil – teacher (teenager / interest in science)
  b good – sparked my interest
4 a colleagues – collaborated / projects
  b good – taught me a lot
5 a colleagues – in meetings
  b bad – not on speaking terms / awkward
6 a doctor – patient (go and see him / professional not usually on first name terms)
  b good (first name terms)
7 a colleagues – professional
  b bad – don't see eye to eye / disagree (but good in that it stays professional)
8 a parent – child (competing for my attention)
  b bad – get on each other's nerves
9 a doctor – patient (reassures them of the whole process)
  b good – puts them at their ease
10 a parent – child, teacher – student, coach – athlete
   b depends on your point of view (bad – causes stress / good – stretches and improves)
11 a neighbours – don't know them (possibly colleagues)
   b not that good, but not bad (keep ourselves to ourselves)
12 a colleagues / siblings / flatmates
   b bad – doesn't pull her weight / friction

Background language notes for teachers

a rough patch = a difficult period of time in a relationship
keep an eye on someone = observe someone because you are concerned about their health or behaviour
spark (interest) = do something to start or create (interest)
collaborate with = work with (in partnership)
not on speaking terms with = not speaking because you have fallen out or had a disagreement with someone
on first-name terms = this suggests you are friendly and familiar with someone
don't see eye to eye = don't agree
get on (someone's) nerves = annoy or irritate someone
put (someone) at their ease = make someone feel relaxed and less nervous
push (a child) = make demands, e.g. force them to do lots of homework to get into a good college
keep ourselves to ourselves = don't get involved with other people, probably in order to avoid problems or difficult situations

he doesn't pull his weight = he doesn't work hard enough or as hard as other people
friction = bad feeling, disagreements

Optional extra activity Ask students to think of someone in their family and somebody in their public life (e.g. a work colleague). Tell them to prepare and deliver a description of the two people using words and phrases from the lesson.

SPEAKING

Aim
to practise language from the lesson in a free, communicative, personalised speaking activity

8 Organise the class into groups of three. Tell students in each group to decide who is A, who is B, and who is C. Tell students to find and read their files in the back of the Student's Book, and plan how to describe the problem they choose. Monitor and help with ideas at this stage, and suggest language students might use to talk about their problem.

9 When students are ready, ask them to roleplay a conversation. Monitor closely and note interesting and useful language, as well as errors. In feedback, point out good examples, correct errors, and provide examples of how students can express their ideas better. You could write some useful new phrases on the board with gaps and ask the whole class to complete the sentences.

10 Extend the activity by asking students to prepare and roleplay other problems in the files or by preparing their own scenarios.

Optional extra activity Ask confident groups to roleplay their conversation for the class.

VIDEO 1: BIG CITY CONSTRUCTION
Student's Book page 22

Aim
to provide insight into the challenge of constructing skyscrapers in New York; to improve students' ability to follow and understand fast speech in a video extract; to practise fast speech and to improve pronunciation, stress and intonation

1   Lead in to the topic by asking students to look at the photo and say what they can see. Pre-teach the phrases provided (*blast a hole* = use explosives to make a hole; *adjacent* = next to or nearby). Organise the class into pairs to discuss the questions. In a brief feedback session, elicit students' ideas and write up interesting ideas or pieces of language on the board.

Culture notes

The photo shows a building site in a densely-built-up area of a major city. It is an aerial view of a construction site in London. Cranes and foundations are visible.
The video is about The Bank of America Tower at One Bryant Park in the Midtown area of Manhattan in New York City. It is located on Sixth Avenue, between 42nd and 43rd Streets, opposite Bryant Park. It is the fourth tallest building in New York, and the sixth tallest building in the United States. Construction was completed in 2009.

2   Organise the class into groups to rank the topics. In feedback, ask different groups to suggest the three most difficult aspects, and discuss to agree on a class top three.

3   ⬛◀3 Give students time to read through the task first. As students watch the video, they should note the answers. Let them compare their notes in pairs before discussing as a class.

Answer
1 making a hole for the enormous foundations without disturbing subway lines (resolved by digging rather than blasting foundations)
2 bringing materials into a major city centre (resolved by lifting materials into the building right away by crane; resolved by bringing large pieces into the city early in the morning)
3 the size of materials, particularly the spire (resolved by bringing in pieces by escort and assembling them above ground)

---

4   ⬛◀3 Organise the class into pairs. Let students read through the sentences first to see what numbers they remember based on their first viewing. As students watch the video again, they should add to and correct their answers. Let them compare answers in pairs. In feedback, write up the missing numbers on the board.

Answer
1 6,000	4 200	7 260,000
2 198,000	5 23	8 70 / 275
3 42,000 / 30	6 3	9 365

---

5   This exercise offers students the chance to relate the topic of the video to their own experiences, ideas and opinions.
• Give students time to prepare their ideas then put them in groups to discuss the questions.
• Monitor and listen to each group. Help with pronunciation and ideas if necessary.
• When most students have finished, stop the class and give some feedback, either by rephrasing some of the things students tried to say for the whole class, or by asking students to correct or fill in gaps in sentences you've written on the board, based on what you heard students saying.

Understanding fast speech

6   ⬛◀4 Play the recording. Students listen and write what they hear. Let them compare answers in pairs.

7   ⬛◀5 Students listen again to a slower version to check and improve what they have written. Let them compare answers in pairs.

8   Students check what they wrote in File 10 on page 189. Encourage them to practise saying the extract several times.

Video script ⬛◀3
Narrator: New York City is home to almost 6,000 high-rise buildings. It's an impressive sight. But have you ever wondered what it's like to erect a building in one of the most crowded places in the world? Let's find out from the people working on One Bryant Park. As you will learn, it's quite a challenge. Especially on the corner of 42nd Street and 6th Avenue, one of the busiest spots in the whole city. The first hurdle was digging the enormous foundation.
Man 1: Typically blasting is the most efficient quickest way to get through all that rock, but we have subway tunnels on 42nd Street, and another subway line coming up and down 6th Avenue, which are right there and right there. And we can't really blast adjacent to that.
Narrator: Dynamite is not an option. It took a full year for workers to remove 198,000 cubic metres of earth. But once the foundation was complete, the building materials could start coming in. Thousands of kilograms arrive at the site each day. And in the heart of mid-town Manhattan, there's very little room. So everything has to be lifted or picked into the building right away.
Joseph Haggerty: To give you an idea of how much tonnage comes in on one truck – it's about 42,000 pounds. We'll make about 30 picks today.
Narrator: About 200 metres above ground, the crews work furiously. The crane operator is so high up he can't see the load that's down below. He has to rely on the directions of his crew.
Crane assistant: Basically, I've gotta tell him what's going on here – give him a countdown of where his line is for his boom. And erm, just ... and I got another signal guy up top and we just communicate to the operator, to let him know what's going on.

Narrator: The biggest job is lifting the enormous steel beams that form the structure of the tower. But first the beams have to make it there. They arrive on large flatbed trucks.

Thomas Kenney: This is just an average load. It's about 23 ton – in that range – give or take a couple hundred pounds.

Narrator: Getting a truck this size through city traffic can be a nightmare.

Thomas Kenney: We come in, like, five in the morning – for traffic reasons. Mike'll call us and say, 'Alright, come on up' and so then we start coming up. But that's the biggest nightmare, is getting here.

Narrator: As the day moves on, the traffic only gets worse.

Thomas Kenney: I need a long distance to make a turn now, like I can't, there's no way I could make one of these turns down these streets. I'm going to have to go down and cut over three lanes to make a left-hand turn down there. There's no room to park on these streets, so that's the issue.

Narrator: Once the steel arrives, the men work quickly. With a building this size everything is big, and that always presents a challenge. This is one of five water tanks that will hold a total of 260,000 litres of water. Its size makes it difficult to place. But if you think this looks hard, the greatest challenge is yet to come! The spire. It's so large, it comes in 70 pieces.

Michael Keen: Going into New York City, you basically lose two days. And it is true what they say: this is a city that never sleeps and there is always traffic out there to deal with. It gets a little hairy at times, you know, but you have an escort behind you and he kind of blocks it off a little bit. Even though New York is a really big city, the streets aren't the biggest.

Narrator: Each piece must be lifted and assembled 275 metres above ground. At this height, the smallest mistake can be fatal. With its spire, One Bryant Park stands 365 metres high, making it one of New York's tallest buildings. So the next time you stop to admire the city's skyline, it's sure to look even more remarkable.

REVIEW 1
Student's Book page 23

Aim
to consolidate vocabulary and grammar from Units 1 and 2

Answers
1
1 would
2 had / needed
3 like (virtually / nearly / almost)
4 having
5 fewer
6 would
7 order
8 foremost
9 sick
10 in
11 have
12 to
2
1 and large, we would play
2 have said he pushes
3 has gone / been through
4 not / never have been subjected to
5 to have narrowed down the
6 had not knocked / pulled down
3
1 have heard
2 set it up
3 having been elected
4 had done
5 would fail, embarked on it
4

| 1 b | 3 a | 5 d | 7 e |
| 2 f | 4 h | 6 g | 8 c |

5
areas and buildings: condemned, vibrant, sprawling, congested, affluent
people: stubborn, prone, principled, laid-back, willing
6

1 in	5 of
2 to	6 about
3 behind	7 at
4 on	8 on

7

1 snobbish	5 incompetence
2 arrogance	6 muggings
3 charming	7 confrontations
4 cynical	8 remarkably

8

1 now	5 laid-back
2 end up	6 weight
3 friction	7 lighten up
4 trace	8 spotless

3 CULTURE AND IDENTITY

SPEAKING

Aim
to set the scene and introduce the theme with a photo; to get students talking about culture and society; to introduce key words

1   Start by telling the class that in this unit they're going to be discussing culture and society, and personal and national identities, while improving their ability to express feelings and opinions and to agree and disagree politely.
• Ask students to look at the photo on pages 24–25. Ask: *What can you see?* Elicit a brief description.
• Organise the class into pairs to discuss the questions. Go round the room and check students are doing the task and help with ideas and vocabulary if necessary.
• In feedback, ask different pairs to tell the class what they discussed.
• Once you have fed back on content, look at good language that students used, and language students didn't quite use correctly. Show students better ways of saying what they were trying to say. You could write some useful new phrases on the board with gaps and ask the whole class to complete the sentences.

> **Possible answers**
> The people might be in traditional costume, or preparing for a festival or celebration. From the dress and reaction of the man, perhaps this is something to do with a marriage ceremony (he is seeing his bride dressed up and looks shocked). The country could be in Southern or Eastern Europe, or North Africa or the Near East.
> Somebody is filming the event.
> This is a country which is maintaining old traditions even though most people usually wear modern dress. Perhaps only women continue to wear traditional clothes.

Culture notes

The photo shows a bride named Fatme Inus, her face painted white and decorated with sequins, smiling after her groom Mustafa Sirakov has carried her into his bedroom at his home towards the end of the couple's two-day wedding in 2014 in Ribnovo, in Bulgaria. The practice of painting the bride's face white and decorating it with sequins and coloured paint is called 'gelena' in Bulgarian, and is unique to Ribnovo. It is a tradition going back centuries. Ribnovo weddings only take place in the winter and the entire village participates with group dances on the main square.

2   Ask students to check the words. Go round the room and help with ideas and vocabulary if necessary.
• Once you have fed back on content, look at good language that students used, and language students didn't quite use correctly during the activity.

Background language notes for teachers

hospitality = welcoming and being kind to guests, strangers and foreigners (this can be interpreted in different ways – some cultures have a tradition of being extravagant when welcoming guests, serving them with the best food and drink, for example, while others may interpret hospitality as welcoming refugees or immigrants into their country)
male-dominated = a society in which men have more power and are in positions of power
conform = behave in a way that accepts the rules and expectations of your society
You could bring out words that are opposite to those provided: *inhospitable, insular, intolerant, equality, rebel, rebellious.*

Optional extra activity   Ask students to individually write down three words that best describe their culture and society. Then, if your students are from the same country, organise them into groups to discuss the three words each student wrote, and to work together to come up with a set of three words that they agree on as a group. Alternatively, if your students are from different countries, ask them to share their three words in groups and to comment on whether they see the speaker's country in that way or not.

Teacher development: feedback on language and errors

After any speaking stage, it is good practice to highlight or teach new language based on what students have tried to say. This is especially important at the start of a new level. As a teacher, you want students to feel that they aren't just chatting away, but that you have listened to them and understood them and given them some new language or useful feedback.
Here are three feedback ideas:
1 Write up new or difficult words or phrases students said (or tried to say).
2 Write up sentences they said (correctly or incorrectly) with two or three words missing. Students must fill in the words.
3 Write up incorrect sentences and ask students to correct them in pairs.

THINGS ARE DIFFERENT THERE
Student's Book pages 26–27

Communicative outcomes
In this two-page spread, students will practise challenging what people say, using cleft sentences, and agreeing or disagreeing with things that people like or dislike about a place.

DEVELOPING CONVERSATIONS
Challenging overgeneralisations

Aim
to introduce and practise ways of challenging overgeneralisations

1 Start by asking students to look at the photo on page 26. Ask: *What does the photo show? What stereotypical views might people in the photo have of the culture of the other people in the photo?* Elicit ideas and check that students understand *stereotype* and *stereotypical* (they describe a firm, simple view of what a nationality or class of person are like).
• Read through the information in the box with the class. Model the phrases in bold by reading them out, and ask the class to rephrase some of the phrases with their own ideas, e.g. *It's like saying all Italians eat ice cream.* or *There must be millions of Americans who never go to McDonalds.*
• Organise the class into pairs to prepare and practise ways of responding to the overgeneralisations. You may need to pre-teach *hypocrite* (= somebody who is insincere in their actions or beliefs). Go round the room and check students are doing the task accurately, and help with ideas and vocabulary if necessary.
• In feedback, ask different pairs to share some phrases they used. Correct any errors or rephrase what students are trying to say.

Possible answers
1
What? All men?
Come on! It's not as though all men are like that.
That can't be true! It's like saying women talk too much!
Just because you're a man, doesn't mean you can't be good at listening.
I wouldn't go that far. There are / must be loads of men who are good listeners.

Culture notes

The photo shows National Geographic Explorer Conrad Anker in the Himalayan Region during an expedition to climb Mount Everest.
Conrad Anker is an American mountaineer and author, and a National Geographic Explorer. He is most famous for his ascents in the high Himalayas and in the Antarctic. In 1999, he located the body of celebrated 1920s climber George Mallory on Everest.

2 Organise the class into groups of four or five to discuss the questions. As students speak in pairs, go round and monitor, and note any interesting comments students make which you could bring up in feedback.
• In feedback, comment on any errors students made, or point out any really good sentences students used.

Culture notes

National and regional stereotypes can be a sensitive area, so, in a multicultural class, it is best to stick to students commenting on their own culture and its stereotypes rather than that of other students. Avoid expressing any stereotypical views of your own – let students share their views.

Optional extra activity In a class in which your students are of the same background, write the following adjectives on the board and ask them to say which nationalities they would most associate the words with and why: *trustworthy, hard-working, outgoing, easy-going, romantic, hospitable, funny, serious, trendy.*
Ask students to discuss whether there is any truth in such generalisations or not.

LISTENING

Aim
to practise listening for general and specific understanding, and to introduce cleft sentences in context

3 ✿7 Ask students to read the situation and the task.
• Play the recording. Students listen and note answers. Let students compare answers in pairs before discussing as a class. You could follow up by asking students if they can remember any specific phrases or chunks of language they heard and remembered which justify their answers.

Answers
Conversation 1
1 People and how they interact (hypocrisy / take the mickey / polite / superficial)
2 No, the speakers are talking about their culture compared to Mehdi's.
3 Negative (Mehdi doesn't like it / can't fit in)
Conversation 2
1 Bureaucracy and people's attitudes to it
2 No, the speakers are talking about where they currently live (the bureaucracy here).
3 Negative (drives me insane / frustrates me)
Conversation 3
1 People (hospitality / traditions / women's roles)
2 No, the speakers are talking about the culture of a place both speakers have visited (the people there / they).
3 Positive feelings from the first speaker (amazing hospitality / loved ... the fact that they've managed to maintain their culture and traditions)
More negative feelings from the second speaker – it must be difficult if you don't conform / women are still looked down on and have fewer rights

♪7
Conversation 1
C = Chrissy, Z = Zoe
C: Zoe! I'm over here.
Z: Chrissy. How are you? You're looking great!
C: Thanks – so are you. I like that top.
Z: Yeah, it's nice, isn't it? Mehdi got it for me.
C: Very good taste. How is he?
Z: Oh, … he's OK. A bit down.
C: Really? Fed up with the miserable winter.
Z: No, no, not really. <u>It's the people that he seems to be struggling with</u>.
C: Oh?
Z: Yeah, apparently he's sick of our British hypocrisy!
C: Oof, that's a bit harsh, isn't it? It's not as though everyone's like that.
Z: I have pointed that out …
C: Oh, so what's brought that on? Doesn't sound like him.
Z: It's not – and I try not to take it personally. It's really more about his work.
C: Oh? Not paying him enough?
Z: Well, that too probably. No, <u>what he hates is all the bitchy comments and gossip</u>.
C: Really? He's not just misinterpreting it? You know, people sometimes just take the mickey and don't mean things to be taken seriously.
Z: Yeah, I know it can be like that sometimes here … and they are more formal where he's from – at least in the work setting.
C: Mmm.
Z: Then again, it might not be the usual jokes.
C: Right.
Z: And I guess the bottom line is that he's just not like that and it makes it difficult to fit in.
C: Tttch – that's not good.
Z: No. I mean, people are polite to him, but he just feels it's a bit superficial and that he's always going to be an outsider.
C: Aww, that's such a shame – he's such a lovely bloke.

Conversation 2
A: How did it go?
B: Oh man, the bureaucracy here! It just drives me insane. We're in the 21st century! You should be able to do everything online rather than doing it in person.
A: I know. Mind you, <u>the thing that really frustrates me is the fact that they only ever seem to have one person serving you</u>.
B: Yeah, yeah. When I went this morning … it wasn't that they were short-staffed. There were plenty of others in the rest of the office, but <u>all they did was stare at their computer screens or file papers</u>.
A: I know! And when I went to get a parking permit, there was a queue of about 100 people even before the place opened, but they only had two people actually dealing with them all.
B: Oh! Tell me about it!
A: Still, people were very funny about it, in that dry, understated way they have here, you know, which I guess is the best outlook to have.
B: Yeah, but then again how will anything ever change?

Conversation 3
C: So how did you find it?
D: Really, really amazing.
C: Yeah, the people there are so welcoming – and the hospitality!
D: I know. I was invited into people's homes or offered tea or dinner so many times.
C: Absolutely. And the other thing I loved about it was the fact that they've managed to maintain their culture and traditions.
D: I guess.
C: You don't think?
D: Yeah … but the flip side is it must be difficult if you don't conform.
C: Mmm, I suppose so.
D: And women are still looked down on and have fewer rights.
C: I'm not sure about that. Just because most take on that traditional home-building role, it doesn't mean they're looked down on, does it?
D: No, of course not, but what I heard from people there is that, with the economy developing, more women are starting to study and even work now and it's the women who are pushing the government to do more to break down barriers so, you know, there's still a fair way to go.
C: Oh right. OK. I hadn't grasped all that.

4 ♪7 Let students read through the sentences first, and decide whether they are true, false or not mentioned based on their first listening.
• Play the recording again. Let students compare their answers in pairs before discussing as a class. In feedback, ask students to justify their answers by telling you what they heard on the recording.

Answers
1a T (he's sick of our British hypocrisy / they are more formal where he's from / he's always going to be an outsider)
1b N (his colleagues do make comments / take the mickey, but we don't know if it's about him or not)
1c N (he's a bit down – doesn't say he wants to change jobs)
2a F (it wasn't that they were short-staffed – but all they did was stare …)
2b F (people were very funny about it, in that dry, understated way they have here – suggests they are used to it, and deal with it through dry humour – suggests they're not happy!)
3a N (invited into people's homes – doesn't say where they actually stayed)
3b T (most take on the traditional home-building role / more women are starting to study and even work now … there's still a fair way to go)
3c F (it's the women pushing the government)

Background language notes for teachers

a bit down (= feeling negative or depressed)
fed up with, sick of (= bored or frustrated with)
bitchy (= always making negative or rude comments)
take the mickey (= make personal jokes)
not fit in (= not belong to a cultural group)
an outsider (= different from others)
the flip side (= the other side of an argument or point of view)
break down barriers (= do things to help make people understand each other better)
I hadn't grasped that (= I hadn't realised / understood that)

5   Organise the class into groups of four to discuss the questions. Ask them to take turns to ask and answer questions. Monitor and note errors and interesting uses of language.
• Once you have fed back on content, look at good language that students used, and language students didn't quite use correctly. Show students better ways of saying what they were trying to say. You could write some useful new phrases on the board with gaps and ask the whole class to complete the sentences.

Teacher development: getting the most out of listening texts

Rather than 'testing' students on what they don't hear, the approach to listening texts should be to find out what students do hear, and to give them a platform to say what they hear, discuss what they heard with others, and to listen as many times as they wish to get a good understanding.
Here are some suggestions:
1 Use the first listening as a 'what did you catch' exercise. The first task in *Outcomes* is generally designed to be broad enough to allow students to just comment on anything they catch. By allowing students to discuss what they heard in pairs and in open class, students build up a good mosaic of what they collectively heard.
2 The second listening expects students to show they have understood specific information, or interpreted what was said correctly. However, by allowing a full discussion, and getting different students to justify their answers the process can be positive and collaborative.
3 Play the recording a third time, or play extracts from the recording to help students confirm things they aren't sure about. Use the audio script as a reference at the end to allow students to read the parts they found tricky.

GRAMMAR Cleft sentences

Aim
to check students' understanding of how to use cleft sentences

6   Read through the information in the box as a class.
• Organise students into pairs to find the cleft sentences which relate to the sentences in the box. They are underlined in audio script 7 on page 199 to help students

find them. Ask students to discuss the questions. Monitor and notice how well students understand the uses.
• In feedback, elicit the students' answers. They can check their answers using the Grammar reference on page 168.

> **Answers**
> 1 We change the order of the sentence, fronting nouns or phrases we wish to emphasise or focus on:
> *It* + conjugated form of *to be* + X + subordinate clause
> *What* + subordinate clause + conjugated form of *to be* + X
> *All* + subordinate clause + conjugated form + X
> 2 It's ... / what ... / all they did ... / the thing that ...
> 3 is / was (verb *to be*) (that) / (all they) did / is the fact that
> 4 In order to focus on how we feel / the cause / the action, etc. ...

 G   **Students complete Exercise 1 in the Grammar reference on page 168.**

> **Answers to Exercise 1, Grammar reference**
> 1 it, that
> 2 was, way, that / which
> 3 did, suggest, what, is
> 4 thing, me, that
> 5 reason, he, happened, was

Background language notes for teachers: cleft sentences

Cleft sentences add emphasis by fronting nouns or phrases that we want to focus on. So *I blame the government* can be changed to *It's the government I blame* in order to emphasise 'government' – the target of the speaker's frustration. As detailed in the Grammar reference, we can also use set phrases to emphasise feelings, reasons, places, etc.
Form and pronunciation are the two most challenging aspects of cleft sentences for students. In practice, you will need to give students plenty of time to have a go at forming sentences using prompts, and before and during speaking practice make sure students emphasise the stress on the key parts of the phrases.

7   Start by eliciting the first cleft sentence in the dialogue to get students started. Ask students to read the dialogue carefully and form the other cleft sentences from the prompts. You could choose to let students work individually before checking with a partner, or you could make it a collaborative exercise by asking students to work in pairs. As students work, go round and monitor, and prompt students to correct any errors they are making.
• In feedback, elicit answers and do some revision work on the board by writing up any problem sentences and eliciting why they are wrong and how they can be corrected.

Answers
1 The thing I like about our way of life is the fact that you can be yourself.
2 Yeah, but what concerns me is that people are losing touch with their roots.
3 In fact, one thing that frustrates me is the lack of social mobility.
4 It's not the government that should be doing / should do something; it's people's attitudes that need to change.
5 (The) One thing that gives me hope is the fact that young people don't seem all that interested in people's backgrounds.
6 All they want to do is go shopping.

8   Organise the class into pairs to practise the dialogue. Go round and monitor, and prompt students to correct any errors they are making. Make sure they are putting a strong stress on any words that are fronted in the sentences.

9   Elicit two or three ideas from students to get them started. Ask students to work individually to complete the sentences.

10   Organise the class into pairs to compare their answers, and discuss why they feel as they do. Monitor, and note down any interesting language you hear.
• In feedback, look at good language that students used, and language students didn't quite use correctly. Show students better ways of saying what they were trying to say. You could write some useful new phrases on the board with gaps and ask the whole class to complete the sentences.

Possible answers
1 The thing I find most *annoying* about my *brother* is *the fact that he's so bad at keeping in touch.*
2 The main thing I *love* about *my mum* is *her ability to make everyone around her feel better.*
3 All I tend to do most *weekends* is *sleep* and *eat!*
4 The place I'd most like to visit is *Ethiopia.*
5 One *thing* I have absolutely no interest in *trying* is *skydiving.* / One *place* I have absolutely no interest in *visiting* is New Zealand.
6 The main reason that I *go running* is *it stops me getting even more out of shape than I already am.* / The main reason that I *love travelling* is *that I love meeting people.*

Optional extra activity   Write more sentence starters on the board to practise other types of cleft sentences: *What I love about ... is ...; It's ... that I hate about ...; All that happens when I ... is ...*

 For further practice, see Exercises 2 and 3 in the Grammar reference on page 169.

Answers to Exercise 2, Grammar reference
1 frustrates + lack	5 concerns + number
2 upset + seeing	6 worrying + level
3 disturbs + stance	7 angered + the fact
4 drives + way	8 amazes + amount

Answers to Exercise 3, Grammar reference
1 surprised me was how cosmopolitan the city is
2 disturbs me is how nationalistic he can be
3 concerns me is the growing wealth gap
4 I find scary / scares me is the alarming rate that the whole society is ageing (or how fast society is ageing)
5 makes me angry / angers me is the way people assume I must love football just because I'm Brazilian

CONVERSATION PRACTICE

Aim
to practise language from the lesson in a free, communicative, personalised speaking activity

11   Organise the class into small groups. Ask students to prepare their lists individually. You could help by eliciting two or three ideas from the class to get them started. Go round and help with ideas and vocabulary as necessary.

12   When students are ready, ask them to share their ideas in groups and to discuss them. Listen for errors, new language or interesting conversations to use in feedback.
• In feedback, look at good language that students used, and language students didn't quite use correctly. Show students better ways of saying what they were trying to say. You could write some useful new phrases on the board with gaps and ask the whole class to complete the sentences.

 6 Refer students to the video and activities on the DVD-ROM.

Teacher development: using the video

The video and activities on the DVD-ROM can be used in various ways:
1 as an alternative to the conversation practice
2 instead of the listening activity in some units, particularly with weaker groups. Students can first practise reading out the dialogues and work on some of the key phrases / structures in a controlled way before having a go themselves.
3 at the end of the unit as a revision exercise

Communicative outcomes
In this two-page spread, students read and discuss an article about differences people notice when living in another country; they talk about household objects.

SPEAKING

Aim
to discuss household objects and how they reflect nationality or identity; to lead in to the topic of the lesson

1 Organise the class into groups of four or five to discuss the questions. Monitor and help with ideas and vocabulary if necessary.
• In feedback, ask different pairs to tell the class what they discussed. Once you have fed back on content, look at good language that students used, and language students didn't quite use correctly.

VOCABULARY Household objects

Aim
to introduce and practise phrases connected with household objects

2 Ask students to match verbs and objects. Do the first as an example to get them started. Let students compare answers in pairs before discussing as a class. Students may come up with things not specified but which seem plausible. If so, let them explain and accept if it sounds fine to you.

> **Answers**
> climb: ladder
> cover: pan
> cut: string
> fill: bucket, dishwasher, pan, sink
> flush: toilet
> heat: oven, pan
> lay: carpet
> load: dishwasher
> run: tap, dishwasher
> spread: glue
> stick in: a pin, needle
> thread: needle
> unblock: sink, toilet, dishwasher
> wring out: cloth

Background language notes for teachers

flush = pull the lever or press the button to get rid of the waste in a toilet
lay the carpet = put down and fix to the floor
thread = put the small piece of thread through the 'eye' at the top of the needle
wring out = hold the cloth tightly in your hands and twist so that the water comes out

3 Organise the class into pairs. Elicit the first answer to get students started. In feedback, elicit answers, and sort out any confusion by drawing pictures on the board or miming the actions of the objects.

> **Answers**
> rope and string – rope is a lot thicker and stronger (and usually longer)
> a mop and a brush – a mop is used to clean up liquids; a brush is used to clean up dust, broken glass, etc.
> wire and cable – wire is usually thinner; cable may have several wires in it
> a nail and a screw – you use a hammer to hit a nail, you use a screwdriver to turn a screw (may need to draw / act this)
> a cloth and a sponge – a sponge is thicker and takes up more water; a cloth is used for cleaning; a sponge is used for washing a body or cars
> a ladder and stairs – a ladder can be moved around / has rungs, is straight; stairs are fixed / angled / between floors
> a bucket and a bowl – a bucket has a handle / is deeper and narrower than a bowl
> a knee pad and a bandage – a knee pad is thicker (sponge) to protect your knees so that you don't get injured; a bandage is usually cloth and is put on after you've been injured
> a drill and a hammer – you use a drill to make holes; you use a hammer to hit nails, etc.
> soap and washing-up liquid – soap is usually used to wash hands / bodies; washing-up liquid used to wash dishes

4 In the same pairs, students discuss problems and solutions. Elicit the first answer to get them started.

> **Answers**
> Problems
> spill some water – need a mop and bucket
> flood the kitchen – need a mop and bucket / plunger or plumber!
> rip your trousers – need needle and thread / sewing machine
> stain your top – need stain remover
> drop a glass – need a dustpan and brush (and maybe mop and bucket)
>
> Solutions
> sweep the floor – it's dirty / dusty
> soak your jeans – they're dirty / stained
> rinse a glass – it's soapy / dirty
> mend your shirt – it's ripped / torn
> wipe the table – it's dirty / has crumbs on it

5 Ask students in the same pairs to take turns drawing or miming actions involving the objects in Exercises 2, 3 and 4. Their partner must guess which verb and object they are miming.

READING

Aim
to read for general and specific understanding; to summarise an introduction

6 Ask students to read the introduction to the article and to decide on the best summary. Elicit ideas from the class.

> **Answers**
> Definitions of normality vary across time and across different countries.

7 Organise the class into pairs to discuss the questions. Pre-teach *take for granted* (= fail to fully appreciate something or assume that something is normal or typical). Monitor and help with ideas and vocabulary if necessary.
• In feedback, ask different pairs to tell the class what they discussed. At this stage, elicit as many ideas as you can from the class but don't confirm or deny any stories. The 'correct' answer isn't important. Pick up on and check any interesting phrases students use in their stories.

8 Ask students to read the rest of the article and to discuss the questions with a partner. It is a good idea to change partners at this stage to provide a variety of interaction and focus. Elicit ideas from the class.

Teacher development: varying focus and interaction when reading

At the Advanced level, students are expected to read lengthy and complex texts, and do a number of tasks when reading. Here, for example, there are four tasks that involve in-depth reading. To avoid students feeling isolated and reading at different speeds, and to make sure students are on task and collaborating, think carefully about how to manage the interaction. Here are some suggestions:
1 Instruct students to work with a partner when reading. Tell them to read in order to share their answers or check their answers with their partner.
2 Mix pairs halfway through so students do one task with one partner, and the second task with another.
3 Ask pairs to check their answers with another pair so that they try out their answers before whole class feedback.

9 Ask students to read the article carefully and find which of the four people match each statement. This requires a more intensive read. Encourage students to work with a partner, sharing information and pointing out where they have found the correct references. In feedback, ask students to point out extracts from the text to justify their answers.

> **Answers**
> 1 Jim (basement flat – people here find really weird)
> 2 Ed (reduced the scope of my cooking)
> 3 Kasia (bath)
> 4 In-ha (old and draughty houses)
> 5 Jim (Best of all, though, is the *brasero* ... It's lovely and cosy when everyone's sitting round the table.)
> 6 Ed (apartments that don't have fridges)
> 7 Kasia (the deep sink for washing delicate clothes)
> 8 In-ha (what drives you really mad / useless!)

Background language notes for teachers

draughty houses = houses with poor insulation so the wind gets in
clamp = implement for holding two things together firmly
soak in a bath / soak clothes = if you soak in a bath, you stay in it for a long time; if you soak clothes, you leave them in the water for a long time
staple = something that is fundamental, and always there
Note the use of many words for *strange*: *odd, bizarre, weird, extraordinary, ridiculous*.

Culture notes

Belfast is the capital of Northern Ireland, which is a part of the United Kingdom.
Lublin is the ninth largest city in Poland, approximately 170 kilometres (106 miles) southeast of the capital, Warsaw.
Belo Horizonte (meaning Beautiful Horizon) is the sixth largest city in Brazil.
Qingdao is a major seaport on China's east coast.

10 Ask students to work individually to think about their answers.
• Organise the class into groups of four or five to discuss their ideas. In feedback, encourage ideas from different pairs, and open out any interesting points for class discussion.

Optional extra activity Ask students to research the text for as many household objects as they can find. Tell them to brainstorm other objects to add to the list.

Web research activity
• Ask students to choose two different places in the world (e.g. France and Australia) and to go to estate agent sites in those countries and find images and descriptions of typical houses.
• Ask students to find as many differences as they can between houses, rooms and objects.

Communicative outcomes
In this two-page spread, students will talk about nationality and identity in the UK and in their own countries.

Preparation: You will need to bring in a set of class dictionaries or direct students to online dictionaries in order to do Exercise 8.

SPEAKING

Aim
to discuss what they know about culture in the UK; to lead in to the topic of the lesson

1 Organise the class into groups of four or five to discuss the questions. Go round the room and check students are doing the task and help with ideas and vocabulary if necessary.
• In feedback, ask different pairs to tell the class what they discussed. Once you have fed back on content, look at good language that students used, and language students didn't quite use correctly during the activity.

Possible answers
The photos show (clockwise from top left):
(top left) A photo from Northern Ireland. Many Protestants there are also unionists, and committed to the union with the rest of Great Britain and with the British crown. The street art on the end of the terraced building is celebrating the Union Flag and Her Majesty (H.M.) Queen Elizabeth II. Her Golden Jubilee (50 years on the throne) was celebrated in 2002. The flag on the wall to the left shows the Ulster Banner, the flag of Northern Ireland that Protestants recognise.
(top middle) A photo from Wales. It shows an eisteddfod, a traditional arts festival, many of which are still held annually in Wales.
(bottom middle) A photo from Scotland. The crowd are holding Scottish flags of St Andrew and YES banners. They are campaigning for a Yes vote in the Scottish Independence referendum of 2015 – a vote for independence. In the event, the Scottish people voted to remain part of the UK.
(bottom left) A photo from England. It shows a cricket match taking place in a typical English village.

Culture notes

Bonfire Night = On November 5th each year, bonfires are lit, fireworks are set off, and people gather at fireworks parties to eat toffee apples and baked potatoes. It traditionally celebrates the foiling of the Gunpowder Plot on November 5th 1605 when a Catholic radical called Guy Fawkes was caught red-handed in the cellars of the Houses of Parliament with barrels of gunpowder. He was part of a Catholic plot to blow up Parliament and kill King James I. Along with his co-conspirators, Fawkes was executed. Nowadays, the anti-Catholic nature of the original celebration is downplayed (effigies of the Pope as well as Guy Fawkes used to be burnt on Bonfire Night). However, the event is still widely celebrated.
car boot sales = People gather in open fields, often on the edge of towns, park their cars in a row, and sell things from the boot of their cars. It is a way of getting rid of unwanted items when clearing out the house or loft, and car boot sales are very popular on weekend mornings.
Carnival = Although Carnival is seen by the rest of the world to be an event synonymous with Latin countries like Brazil and Spain, one of the world's biggest Carnivals actually takes place in London each year. It is the Notting Hill Carnival, which is led by members of London's West Indian community, and takes place over two days in August.
curry = Although curry dishes originally come from India and south-east Asia, curry houses are an important aspect of British life. Because of the colonial connection with the Indian sub-continent, many British people living there in the eighteenth and nineteenth centuries developed a taste for Indian curry dishes. The first curry house opened in London in 1810. Today, largely because of the significant numbers of people of Bengali, Punjabi and Indian descent, there is at least one curry restaurant in every town in the country. Many curry sauces such as Balti and Tikka Masala were actually invented in the UK by chefs of Bengali or Indian descent. The curry Chicken Tikka Masala is commonly considered the most popular dish in the UK.
fish and chips = Battered fish (usually cod or haddock dipped in a mixture of flour, baking soda and water and then deep fried) and chips is considered traditionally British. The first takeaway fish and chip shop opened in the northern town of Oldham in the mid-nineteenth century and the first shop in London opened in 1860. It became a stock meal among the working classes, and is still popular today, especially in seaside towns.
football = The modern game of football (or soccer) began in English public schools in the early nineteenth century. In 1863 the Football Association was formed in London and the rules of the game we now know were codified. England hosted and won the World Cup in 1966. Today, the English Premier league is one of the richest and most popular leagues in the world, and Manchester United, Arsenal, Manchester City and Chelsea are major teams. Bobby Charlton, George Best, Gary Lineker, David Beckham, Wayne Rooney and Gareth Bale are well-known British players.
Glastonbury = The Glastonbury Festival takes place annually in fields near the small village of Glastonbury in the south-west of England. It is the largest greenfield festival in the world, and is now attended by around 175,000 people every year. It features the biggest names in the music industry.
God Save the Queen = This is the national anthem of the UK, a patriotic song first sung in the 1740s. The current British queen is Elizabeth II. When her son or grandson ascends the throne, the song will change to God Save the King. The punk rock band Sex Pistols famously produced an anarchist version of the song, which begins, 'God Save the Queen,/ And the Fascist regime ...'

Islam = Islam is the second largest religion in the UK according to the 2011 census. The UK Muslim population in 2011 was 2.7 million, 4.5% of the total population.
the NHS = The National Health Service was founded in 1948. It provides free healthcare at the point of need for British citizens, and is funded by the taxpayer. Although many are concerned about standards and bureaucracy in the NHS, and the burden on the taxpayer, the NHS remains a very popular institution according to surveys.
the public school system = Public schools are actually private, independent, fee-paying schools, and the most illustrious and exclusive (notably Eton College, Harrow School, Charterhouse, Rugby School, Shrewsbury, Westminster and Winchester College) are frequented by the children of the rich and privileged. Princes William and Harry went to Eton College, which was founded in 1440, as did nineteen British Prime Ministers, including David Cameron. Many consider the system to be systematic of Britain's class-conscious society. At the time of writing, the Prime Minister, Mayor of London, and Archbishop of Canterbury are all Old Etonians.
regional autonomy = The United Kingdom of Great Britain and Northern Ireland is made up of England, Scotland, Wales and Northern Ireland. Scotland has a separate parliament, First Minister, law system and education system, and a lot of autonomy from the UK government in London. There is a strong movement campaigning for an independent Scotland. Wales and Northern Ireland have their own assemblies but fewer powers than Scotland.
St George's Day = St George is the patron saint of England. The saint's day is on April 23rd. Some celebrate the day by flying the English flag (the cross of Saint George) patriotically. Pubs are keen to do this. However, it is not an event that is widely celebrated.
the trade union movement = Legalised in 1871, the Trade Union Movement was instrumental in founding the Labour Party in the UK. The movement is still influential in the politics of the Labour Party. With the decline of industry in the UK, the power of the unions has declined.

Optional extra activity Ask students in pairs to research one of the things in the box on the Internet and present their findings to the class or to other students in groups.

LISTENING

Aim
to practise listening for general and detailed understanding, and to introduce phrases with *thing*

2 🔊8 Ask students to read the situation and the task.
• Play the recording. Students listen and note answers. Let students compare their answers in pairs. In feedback, elicit answers from the class.

Answers
Speaker 1
Carnival – went to Notting Hill Carnival every year; uses it as an example of how multi-racial and multicultural Britain is
curry – grew up eating it; again, it's an example of multiculturalism

---

car boot sales – lives in the country and likes them – often finds mad stuff at them
Speaker 2
the public school system – people who went to public school dominate the government and so not so left wing
regional autonomy – sees Scotland as a separate country and wants more control
God Save the Queen – is a republican and only sings a punk version
Speaker 3
fish and chips – owns a fish and chip shop
Islam – he's Muslim
football – explains his support of the Pakistan cricket team

🔊8
1 Savannah
I grew up in London, which is incredibly multicultural, so my feelings about British culture have obviously been influenced by that. Half my friends were mixed race like me and we all grew up going to the Notting Hill Carnival, eating curry and kebabs, listening to Jamaican music, American music, you know. A real mixed bag of stuff. Now, though, I live in Lincolnshire, which is much more what you might call traditionally English. It's much whiter, for a start! I'm enjoying it, though, I have to say, I love the countryside up here and the big, empty skies, and I love all the local car boot sales as well. I've picked up some mad stuff there. I've started gardening too, and getting into baking, which is a whole new thing for me. My London friends would die laughing if they could see me now!

2 Callum
One thing that bugs me is people talking about 'British' culture when what they really mean, whether they're aware of it or not, is English! Scotland's a separate country with its own distinct cultural heritage. Politically, we're more left wing, but that's not reflected in the British government, which is still dominated by these southern English public school boys.
We're more in control of what goes on up here than we used to be, but personally I'd like even more autonomy – and maybe one day independence! Also, I don't understand why we still cling on to the Royal family. The only 'God Save the Queen' I'll sing along to is an old anti-royalist punk song! In some ways, I'd like to be seen as a republican and a citizen of the world first, then European and Scottish, or even British – but never English!

3 Amir
Some people might not expect someone like me to be running a fish and chip shop, but for most of my customers it's just not an issue. I was born here as were my parents and I'm as British as anyone else. I just happen to be Muslim as well, that's all. It's no big thing. I mean, it's not exactly unusual nowadays, is it? I do get the occasional comment about it, but I don't let it bother me.

> The only time I ever feel vaguely conflicted about my identity is when England play Pakistan at cricket. I can't help it, but I always want Pakistan to do well. There's generally a bit of friendly joking about that with the local lads, but, as I always say, I'm sure most English blokes who end up moving to Spain still want their kids to support the English football team. It's human nature, isn't it?

3 🔊 8 Let students read through the sentences first, and decide whether they are true or false based on their first listening.

• Play the recording again. Let students compare their answers in pairs before discussing as a class. In feedback, ask students to justify their answers by telling you what they heard on the recording.

Answers
1
a T (*half my friends are mixed race like me*)
b F (*it's much whiter*)
c F (*My London friends would die laughing if they could see me now!*)
2
a T (*one thing that annoys me is …*)
b F (*We're more in control of what goes on up here than we used to be …*)
c F (*citizen of the world first*)
3
a T (*some might not expect …*)
b F (*I don't let it bother me*)
c T (*The only time I ever feel vaguely conflicted about my identity is when England play Pakistan at cricket. I can't help it, but I always want Pakistan to do well.*)

4 Organise the class into pairs to discuss the questions.
• Once you have fed back on content, look at good language that students used, and language students didn't quite use correctly during the activity. Show students better ways of saying what they were trying to say. You could write some useful new phrases on the board with gaps and ask the whole class to complete the sentences.

Teacher development: personal response

The aim of Exercise 4 is to give students the opportunity to engage in the topic by expressing personal experiences and views. It is important at this level to give adults the opportunity to say what they think, relate what they are reading to their own experience, and be heard. Here are four things to do after every listening or reading:
1 Ask what they notice or respond to.
2 Ask what they think about views expressed.
3 Ask what their experiences are.
4 Ask what it is like in their country.

UNDERSTANDING VOCABULARY
Words and phrases

Aim
to introduce and practise fixed phrases using the word *thing*

5 Read through the information in the box with the class.
• Ask students to complete the phrases. Elicit the first answer from students to get them started. Let students compare answers in pairs before discussing as a class. In feedback, ask for definitions or synonyms, and ask students to think of situations where they might use the phrases.

Answers
1 Don't make such a fuss. It really is no big thing.
2 It's rude. It is just not the done thing in our society.
3 I'd love to do it, but chance would be a fine thing!
4 It is the furthest thing from my mind at the moment.
5 I always do it first thing in the morning.
6 It's the sort of thing that makes you glad to be alive.
7 It's difficult, what with one thing and another.
8 I didn't plan it. Just one thing led to another. / One thing just led to another.

Background language notes for teachers

no big thing = not important
not the done thing = not acceptable
chance would be a fine thing = it is very unlikely that he / she will have an opportunity to do it
furthest thing from my mind = not thinking about it all (because there are many other more important things to think about)
first thing = very early; before doing anything else
what with one thing and another = this is vague language – people say it because they don't want to be precise about what things they are doing
one thing led to another = used an excuse or an explanation to say why something happened after a series of events

6 Organise the class into pairs.
• Ask students to discuss what *it* refers to in the sentences in Exercise 5. In feedback, elicit answers and explanations.

Possible answers
1 winning an award / diploma, etc.; winning a sporting competition; performing a heroic act like saving someone from a river
2 smoking indoors / belching at the end of a meal / chewing loudly (in the UK)
3 going to a posh restaurant / travelling round the world (something expensive and / or difficult)
4 having a holiday / getting married (something pleasurable you might do usually which you can't afford to do time-wise or for other reasons)
5 exercises / have a shower / go for a run / meditate
6 sitting on a beach / a bracing walk in the country
7 life / marriage / helping people out
8 an affair / a baby / getting into debt

7 🎧 **9** Play the recording. Ask students to listen and notice the stress. Ask them to either put a dot over the stressed syllables, or underline them. Let students discuss answers with a partner, and play the recording a second time if necessary to ensure they have heard and marked the stress correctly.
- Play the recording again. Students listen and repeat.

🎧 **9 and answers (stress shown underlined)**
1 It's <u>really</u> no <u>big</u> thing.
2 It's just <u>not</u> the <u>done</u> <u>thing</u>.
3 <u>chance</u> would be a <u>fine</u> thing
4 It's the <u>furthest</u> <u>thing</u> from my <u>mind</u>.
5 <u>first</u> <u>thing</u> in the <u>morning</u>
6 It's the <u>sort</u> of <u>thing</u> that makes you <u>glad</u> to be a<u>live</u>.
7 what with <u>one</u> thing and a<u>nother</u>
8 <u>one</u> thing just <u>led</u> to a<u>nother</u>

8 Organise the class into small groups to brainstorm as many phrases as they can. It is best to make this a dictionary task. In feedback, ask different groups to present a couple of phrases they found, complete with their example sentences.

Possible answers
die happy / rich / young; die of thirst / boredom; die a death (e.g. **The show died a death** = it failed); **I nearly died** (= I was very embarrassed); **I'd rather die first than talk to him** (= I refuse to do something); **Never say die** (= never stop trying)
burst out laughing; don't make me laugh; laugh all the way to the bank; **it's no laughing matter** (= it's serious); it's good for a laugh; **we did it for a laugh** (= just for fun); laugh at somebody

Teacher development: dictionaries in class

The use of class dictionaries depends, naturally, on your school policy and school resources. At this level, many vocabulary research tasks are dependent on students checking meaning and use, and finding further examples, in dictionaries. Here are three things to do to make sure students are using helpful dictionaries rather than dictionary resources that merely translate or provide inadequate information:

1 Bring in class dictionaries for students to use, or, if there is Internet access in class, or students have their own devices, direct them to the same, high-quality online dictionary.
2 Spend time in class doing a comparison of paper or online dictionaries. Ask students to look up words or phrases from a lesson in a variety of dictionaries. Ask them to decide on the dictionary that is easiest to navigate around, provides the best examples, provides the clearest pronunciation check, and gives the best extra information (e.g. collocations, connotations, or whether a word is common or particular to certain user groups).
3 Once students have selected (or you have provided) a particular paper or online dictionary to use, set research tasks for homework to help them get familiar with how to use it.

LISTENING

Aim
to practise listening to a lecture and summarising the main message; listening for general and detailed understanding

9 🎧 **10** Ask students to read the situation and the task.
- Play the recording. Students listen and note ideas for the summary. Let students compare notes and think of how to express the main message. In feedback, elicit suggestions, and agree on a main message.

Possible answers
Culture and identity is to do with your individual experiences and roles, and national cultures, as far as they exist, are simply an invention of those in power.

🎧 **10**
As you're no doubt all aware, we live in troubled times, and one reaction to global uncertainty has always been to cling onto this idea of a unified national culture, a culture that everyone living in a particular land shares and participates in. It's an idea that many find very comforting. Sadly, though, I'm afraid it's also something of a myth.
The reality is that identity is a very personal thing, and the individual cultural identities of people living in pretty much any society that you care to name vary so much that it's basically impossible to define common features. And, of course, our identities aren't fixed or static. They change over time as a result of our interactions. And in an increasingly globalised world, a world that's driven by commerce, our interactions are becoming more and more complex and multi-layered.
We can easily find ourselves eating a breakfast that's been manufactured by a Swiss company while watching a French TV show we recorded last night on our Korean-made TV. We might then put on a Chinese-produced T-shirt, some American-made jeans and some Italian shoes before getting into a German-made car to drive to work.
I should know. That's exactly what I did this morning!

If our habits as consumers complicate our ideas about what it means to belong to a national culture, then so too do our relationships with others. As we get older, we often grow into the many distinct roles we play in life. These different roles often exist independently of each other; and when playing a particular role, we sometimes end up only interacting with those directly affected by whatever the role is. This is why it's quite possible for one person to be, for instance, a mother, a wife, a ballet lover, Welsh, British, Jamaican, black, and a marketing manager – without any contradiction.

At the same time, though, we also need to realise that for some people, these different roles can cause terrible tensions and can result in individuals abandoning certain roles as they feel they're no longer compatible with the main ways in which they have come to see themselves. I'm sure you can all think of examples of this kind of thing from your own experience of the world.

So where does all of this leave national identity? The historian Eric Hobsbawm has argued that many of the ideas about national cultures that are spread through the education system, through the media, and through public ceremonies and monuments are basically a form of myth-making – and it's the ruling elite who encourage these stories and, of course, who benefit.

10 Ask students to work in pairs to compare their ideas, and to say how far they agree with the message.

11 🔊 10 Let students read through the six topics first, and decide why they were mentioned based on their first listening.

• Play the recording again. Let students compare their answers in pairs before discussing as a class. In feedback, ask students to justify their answers by telling you what they heard on the recording.

Answers
1 We react to global uncertainty by clinging on to the idea of a national unified culture.
2 Identities change as a result of interaction and increasingly our interactions are driven by commerce.
3 They are examples of the lecturer's multilayered cultural interactions.
4 They are examples of two roles / identities that one person may take on.
5 Sometimes different roles cause tensions and are incompatible.
6 The ruling elite encourage the idea of national identity.

12 Organise the class into new pairs to discuss the sentences. Ask them to justify their suggestions from what they hard on the recording. In feedback, use the notes below to help students if they find it hard to summarise their ideas.

Possible answers
1 Yes – resort to the idea of a national unified culture
2 No – seems to think globalised commerce is fine. The economy is not mentioned.
3 Yes – the reality is that identity is a very personal thing – and the individual cultural identities of people living in pretty much any society that you care to name vary
4 No – it's mainly the ruling elite
5 No – education tends to be used to reinforce culture not criticise it as a concept
6 Yes – in an increasingly globalised world, a world that's driven by commerce, our interactions are becoming more and more complex and multi-layered

SPEAKING

Aim
to present and discuss lists of important people

13 Organise the class into groups of four to decide on a task. Once they have decided, ask students to prepare lists individually. Elicit one or two ideas to get students started. Go round the room and help with ideas.

14 Ask students in their groups to take turns to present their lists. Monitor and note errors and interesting uses of language.

• Once you have fed back on content, look at good language that students used, and language students didn't quite use correctly. Show students better ways of saying what they were trying to say. You could write some useful new phrases on the board with gaps and ask the whole class to complete the sentences.

Optional extra activity Write three things that are important to you culturally on the board. Tell the class to ask you questions to find out about the people and things and to hear why they are so important to you.

Web research activity
• Ask students to research an aspect of culture in the UK. It could be something from this lesson (the Queen, curry, football) or something not mentioned (e.g. Winston Churchill, pasties, rugby).
• Ask students to write about their findings and report them to the class.

4 POLITICS

SPEAKING

Aim
to set the scene and introduce the theme with a photo; to get students talking about politics and politicians; to revise nouns used to describe personal qualities

1 Start by telling the class that in this unit they're going to be learning how to describe politicians and their qualities, give opinions about politics, tell jokes, and discuss voting and elections.
- Ask students to look at the photo on pages 32–33. Ask: *What can you see?* Elicit a brief description.
- Organise the class into pairs to discuss the questions. Go round the room and check students are doing the task and help with ideas and vocabulary if necessary.
- In feedback, ask different groups to present ideas and share experiences.
- Once you have fed back on content, look at good language that students used, and language students didn't quite use correctly. Show students better ways of saying what they were trying to say. You could write some useful new phrases on the board with gaps and ask the whole class to complete the sentences.

> **Possible answers**
> No fixed answers here, but students may point out that the appearance of the building suggests a warm country, a significant country (or one that thinks it is significant), and a country that wants to portray itself as very modern and cutting edge.

Culture notes

The photo shows Brazil's National Congress building in the modern, purpose-built capital Brasilia.

2 Mix the pairs so that students are working with someone new. Start them off by eliciting whether they would choose 'honesty' as a quality needed by politicians. Ask students to discuss the meaning of the words with partners as they apply them to politicians. Go round the room and check students are doing the task and help with ideas and vocabulary if necessary.
- In feedback, round up by asking pairs to share their ideas, and getting them to justify their reasons. Once you have fed back on content, look at good language that students used, and language students didn't quite use correctly.

Optional extra activity You may wish to pre-teach the vocabulary before students start. Ask them in pairs to provide an example of a situation in which a politician has shown any of the qualities.

Background language notes for teachers

ruthlessness = the quality of someone who will do anything to achieve what they want
charisma = attractiveness or charm which makes people like him or her, and makes them want to follow them
the ability to compromise = the ability to find agreement between two different points of view by agreeing to change his or her demands

Teacher development: providing a task and a goal

Outcomes aims to encourage a lot of personalised speaking, in which students find out about each other, their interests and their opinions. The pairwork activity on this spread is an example of this. However, you may wish to vary this task type to make it more fun or more goal-orientated:
Ask students to do a class survey or questionnaire. Ask them first to work in pairs to adapt the questions and tasks in Exercise 1 to prepare a survey. They then each interview four students from the rest of the class, collate their answers, and present what they found out to the class.

I DON'T KNOW WHERE I STAND
Student's Book pages 34–35

Communicative outcomes
In this two-page spread, students will practise giving opinions.

DEVELOPING CONVERSATIONS
Giving opinions

Aim
to introduce and practise phrases used to give opinions

1 Ask students to pair the sentences. Elicit the answers to the first pair to get students started. Let students compare answers in pairs before discussing in feedback.

> **Answers**
> 1 I'm a huge fan of the idea.
> 12 I'm totally in favour of it.
>
> 2 I don't really know where I stand.
> 5 I can't pass judgement. I don't know enough about it.
>
> 3 I'm totally against it.
> 10 I'm completely opposed to it.
>
> 4 I think the negatives far outweigh the positives.
> 8 I have some major doubts about it.
>
> 6 It's a good idea in theory, just not in practice.
> 9 It's OK in principle. I just think it's unworkable.
>
> 7 I am in favour. I just have some slight reservations.
> 11 It's not without problems, but on the whole I like it.

Background language notes for teachers

Point out some of the interesting collocations here (e.g. *a huge fan, pass judgement, major doubts, slight reservations*). Point out that the intensifiers *totally* and *completely* both collocate with *against* and *opposed*, so you can say *completely against* and *totally opposed*.

in favour = in support
unworkable = not practical
on the whole = in general

Teacher development: noticing collocation

Outcomes aims to encourage students to learn language in useable chunks, which is why vocabulary is taught in context and as part of a useable phrase which students can use in specific situations. It is essential that students learn language, not as isolated words (e.g. *huge* = very big), but as part of a phrase that can be learnt and used as a whole (e.g. *I'm a huge fan of* ...). Take every opportunity to get students to notice which words collocate, what words they are dependent on, and which chunks of language they can most usefully adopt into their own usage.

2 Organise the class into groups of four to six. Ask them to take turns to give opinions. Go round the room and check students are doing the task and notice errors and examples of good language use.
• Once you have fed back on content, look at good language that students used, and language students didn't quite use correctly during the activity.

Optional extra activity Ask students to choose three of the phrases from the lesson that they would particularly like to memorise and use. Tell them to write three personalised phrases using them.

LISTENING

Aim
to practise listening for a general understanding; to listen intensively for specific words

3 🔊 **11** Ask students to read the situation and the task. Explain that *Where do you stand?* = What is your point of view?
• Play the recording. Students listen and note the answers. In feedback, ask why, and find out what students heard, but don't worry if they didn't catch everything at this stage.

> **Answers**
> Conversation 1
> Limiting size of salaries / maximum wage
> Woman A is in favour – benefits far outweigh the difficulties
> Woman B – likes it in principle but thinks it's unworkable
>
> Conversation 2
> Holding the Olympics
> Man – totally opposed to it
> Woman – not sure where she stands

> 🔊 **11**
> **Conversation 1**
> A: I don't know about you, but personally I'm in favour of limiting the salaries of people like bankers and executives.
> B: Yeah? Really? How would you do that, though?
> A: I don't know. I'm sure it's not without problems, but something's got to be done. Honestly, I just think some of these salaries are obscene – especially when there are people in the same company who you know are earning peanuts.
> B: Hmm, yeah. I do know what you mean.
> A: And it just distorts everything else because if they're earning that much, it encourages other people to ask for more, and it all just pushes up prices.
> B: Mmm, restricting salaries may be OK in principle, but in practice? I mean, even if they do manage to introduce this new law, it's basically going to be unworkable, isn't it?

A: I don't see why. We have a minimum wage, so why not a maximum one? The bottom line is that as long as there's the official desire to make it work, then it'll work.

B: Maybe, I guess. So how would this maximum amount be decided? And what would you include in pay? Supposing they were given a boat, or whatever, instead of money?

A: Well, they'd just declare it as part of their income in the normal way, no? And it could be, say, ten times the lowest wage.

B: Only ten? I'm sure they'd be able to find ways round it. And you don't think it'd discourage people from doing those jobs?

A: Some, maybe, but I don't see that as a bad thing. I mean, maybe they'd think about doing other jobs that are more useful. Anyway, I thought you said it was a good idea in theory.

B: I did. I'm just playing devil's advocate. But, as I said, I do have major doubts about how it'd work.

A: Well, personally I think the benefits far outweigh the difficulties.

Conversation 2

C: Did you hear about this proposal to bid to hold the Olympics here?

D: Yeah. You don't sound that happy about it.

C: No, absolutely not! I'm totally opposed to it. It's a complete waste of money. Aren't you against it?

D: I'm not really sure where I stand on it, to be honest. Won't the Games make a lot of money if we get them?

C: No! They always talk about them leaving a good legacy and boosting the economy, but it's all rubbish.

D: Really? I can't pass judgement. I don't know enough about it.

C: Doh! Have a look on the Internet. I mean, take Montreal, for example. The Olympics were held there way back in 1976 and the city then took another 30 years to clear off the debt the whole thing created!

D: Seriously?

C: I'm telling you! It's lucky we don't have a hope in hell, so they'll only waste the money on the bid. Imagine if we actually won it, though! It'd be a recipe for disaster. It'd probably bankrupt us.

4 🔊11 Organise students into pairs. Let students read through the sentences first, and decide which are incorrect based on their first listening and correct the incorrect ones (note that we mean incorrect in this particular context – all the words can be correct in another context).

• Play the recording again for students to correct. In feedback, write the corrected words up on the board.

Answers
1 Some of these salaries are obscene.　CORRECT
2 It all just ~~puts~~ **pushes** up prices.
3 They'd just ~~detail~~ **declare** it as part of their income.
4 They'd be able to find ways ~~through~~ **round** it.

5 I'm just playing devil's advocate.　CORRECT
6 Did you hear about this proposal to bid to hold the Olympics here?　CORRECT
7 Won't the games ~~earn~~ **make** a lot of money?
8 They always talk about them leaving a good ~~facility~~ **legacy**.
9 We don't have a hope in hell.　CORRECT
10 It'd be a ~~receipt~~ **recipe** for disaster.

Background language notes for teachers

Note that people *put up prices* and *earn money*; events *push up prices* (i.e. cause them to rise) and *make money* (i.e. make a profit).
• Latin speakers tend to confuse *receipt* and *recipe*.

5 Let students work in the same pairs to discuss the questions. Monitor closely and note interesting and useful language, as well as errors. Use the feedback to point out good examples, correct errors, and to provide examples of how students can express their ideas better.

Possible answers
playing devil's advocate
Advantages: allows you to see both sides of debate; encourages other speaker to come up with good arguments for his or her point of view; challenges established opinions; (point out that interviewers on news or political shows often play devil's advocate in order to force politicians to explain and defend their views fully)
Downsides: may make people accept a view you don't believe in; may confuse the issue; may upset people

Cities might run up debts by spending too much on infrastructure, housing, crime, etc.; they may choose to spend more than they have for political reasons – trying to force central government to give more; natural disasters or crime may cause problems; corruption

Optional extra activity Play *Devil's Advocate*. Explain that the phrase means 'arguing in favour of something even if you don't actually hold that view'. Then write some controversial phrases on the board:
Everybody should be able to smoke anywhere they like.
War is a useful tool of international diplomacy.
Education is a privilege and should only be available to those who pay for it.
Ask groups to choose a statement they totally oppose, then think of and present arguments in favour of it.

GRAMMAR Conditionals 1

Aim
to check students' understanding of how to form and use conditional forms to talk about general truths as well as probable or imagined events now or in the future

6 Read through the information in the box as a class.
• Organise the class into pairs to match the sentence halves. Monitor and notice how well students understand the rules.
• In feedback, elicit the students' answers.

Answers
1 c	4 a
2 e	5 d
3 b	

7 Once you have confirmed answers to Exercise 6, ask students to work in the same pairs to discuss the questions in Exercise 7.
• In feedback, elicit the students' answers. They can check their answers using the Grammar reference on page 169.

Answers
1 4a
2 2e and 5d
3 3b and 1c
4 present / past
5 past / going to / would / present / will
6 imagine if / supposing / even if / as long as

Students complete Exercise 1 in the Grammar reference on page 170.

Answers to Exercise 1, Grammar reference
1 don't
2 bound / sure / likely / going
3 would
4 should (or could)
5 never (or not), would
6 puts
7 knew, don't
8 be, was / were
9 'd, didn't (or 'll, don't)
10 couldn't / wouldn't, had (or don't, 's)
11 does, will (or did, would)
12 would, did

Background language notes for teachers: conditionals

At this level, students should be familiar with forming conditionals. Concentrate on meaning:
• compare *things that are generally or always true* (If I don't like them, I don't vote for them) to *a likely / possible event in the future* (If you vote for them, they'll probably win)
• compare *a likely / possible event in the future* (If you vote for them, they'll probably win) to *an imagined / hypothetical event* (Even if I were old enough to vote, I still wouldn't bother).

8 Elicit two or three possible responses to the first one to get students started. Then ask them to produce their own in pairs. Go round the class and help with ideas and vocabulary. Ask pairs to compare with another pair before open-class feedback.

Possible answers
Answers will vary. An example is given for number 1.
1 What if everyone did that? What would happen then?
If you don't vote, you're letting other people decide for you.
If you voted for X, they would make a difference.

 For further practice, see Exercise 2 in the Grammar reference on page 170.

Answers to Exercise 2, Grammar reference
1 Unless they win / have / get popular support
2 provided they do not spend / provided it does not cost
3 whether you like it or
4 Supposing an accident happens / happened (or *Supposing there was / were an accident*)
5 as / so long as the economy
6 or things / the situation will get
7 Assuming (the) opinion polls are

Optional extra activity Write the following on the board:
Supposing you won a million dollars …
Imagine if you were the American president …
Supposing you could go anywhere …
Ask students in groups to share their thoughts on each of these subjects.

VOCABULARY Consequences

Aim
to introduce and practise ways of expressing consequences

9 Read through the words in the box as a class.
• Ask students to complete the sentences individually then check with a partner. In feedback, ask students how they worked out the answer (meaning, collocation with nouns or dependent prepositions, context, etc.).

Answers
1 discourage (<u>from</u> working)
2 benefit (someone / an organisation – the opposite of *harm*)
3 boost (make better – the word 'economy' collocates with *boost*)
4 devastate (destroy – it collocates with *area*)
5 bankrupt (the phrase 'strain on finances' suggests this is the correct verb)
6 compound (make worse – it collocates with 'the (existing) problem' – note that *exacerbate* also collocates here)
7 trigger (cause to start / happen – it collocates with *an election*)
8 undermine (make worse – it collocates with *relations*)
9 reduce (could also be *discourage*)
10 lead (<u>to</u> tension)

10 Start by eliciting two or three further examples of events for the first sentence to get students started. Then organise the class into pairs to think of other ideas. Go round and help with ideas and vocabulary. In feedback, ask a few pairs to share their best ideas with the class.

Possible answers
1 if they reduce pay / if they extend working hours
2 if they cut taxes / if they remove unemployment benefits
3 if they cut business tax / if they increased public spending on infrastructure
4 if the car plant closes down
5 if we held the Olympics here
6 if they abolished unemployment benefit
7 if they lose the parliamentary vote
8 if they expel their diplomats for spying / if they increase arms spending
9 if they legalised cannabis / increased penalties for drug trafficking
10 if they allow a vote on independence

11 Start by eliciting which verbs in Exercise 9 are opposites of the verbs in the box (*damage / benefit, encourage / discourage, resolve / compound, strengthen / undermine*). Then ask students to prepare sentences. Let students compare answers in pairs before feedback.

Answers
It'll damage the economy and result in the loss of jobs.
It might encourage people to work more.
It's a good idea. If anything, it'll help resolve the existing social problems.
It'll strengthen relations between the two countries.

Optional extra activity Ask students in pairs to think of three or four policies of the current government in their countries, and to write them down. When students are ready, ask pairs to announce their policies. Ask the rest of the class to praise or criticise by saying what they think the consequences of such policies would be if introduced in their countries.

CONVERSATION PRACTICE

Aim
to practise language from the lesson in a free, communicative, personalised speaking activity

12 Ask students to work in pairs and think of two proposals. Give them about five minutes to prepare ideas and consider the possible consequences. Encourage students to make brief notes which will help them with their new partner in Exercise 13.

13 Organise the class into new pairs. Tell them to start conversations with the phrases given. Allow pairs to have a go three or four times – practice makes perfect. As you monitor, listen for errors, new language or interesting conversations to use in feedback.

• In feedback, look at good language that students used, and language students didn't quite use correctly during the activity. Show students better ways of saying what they were trying to say. You could write some useful new phrases on the board with gaps and ask the whole class to complete the sentences.

7 Refer students to the video and activities on the DVD-ROM.

Teacher development: using the video

The video and activities on the DVD-ROM can be used in various ways:
1 as an alternative to the conversation practice
2 instead of the listening activity in some units, particularly with weaker groups. Students can first practise reading out the dialogues and work on some of the key phrases / structures in a controlled way before having a go themselves.
3 at the end of the unit as a revision exercise

NO LAUGHING MATTER
Student's Book pages 36–37

Communicative outcomes
In this two-page spread, students read and discuss an article about Prime Minister's Questions in the UK Parliament; they listen to and practise telling jokes.

READING

Aim
to practise reading for general and specific information; to discover language in the context of an article

1 Organise the class into groups of four or five to discuss the questions. Ask one person from each group to briefly share two or three things from their discussion with the rest of the class in feedback.

> **Answers**
> Work with what your students know. However, the information in the culture notes below may be useful.

Culture notes

The photo shows Prime Minister David Cameron at Prime Minister's Questions (PMQs). Francis Maude, a member of the Government is behind him and they are both clearly laughing at and mocking the Opposition leader and party.
The House of Commons is the lower house of the Parliament of the United Kingdom. It meets in a chamber of the Palace of Westminster. On the front benches on one side of the Commons sit government ministers, with their supporting members of Parliament sitting behind them. On the front benches on the other side of the Commons sit leading members of the opposition parties, with their supporting members of Parliament sitting behind them. As a result, the situation is face-to-face and very adversarial. In the middle sits the Speaker, shouting 'Order! Order!' It is his or her job to announce speakers, and to stop speakers who are being too aggressive or long-winded.
PMQs takes place at noon on Wednesdays and lasts 30 minutes. The leader of the second largest party (the leader of Her Majesty's Opposition) can ask the PM six questions. The leader of the third largest can ask two. Other questions then come from backbench MPs (i.e. not ministers) who have to submit their questions in advance and have them selected. Naturally, the PM is well-briefed each morning before facing such a barrage of questions. Although generally criticised in the UK because they are so theatrical, PMQs are also popular. The exchange is widely reported and highlights are shown on the evening news.
The BBC Parliament Channel broadcasts all UK parliamentary debates, and PMQs are broadcast on mainstream TV and radio every week.

2 Ask students to read the article and answer the questions. Set a five-minute time limit to ensure students don't take too long reading. Let them compare and discuss their answers in pairs before discussing as a class.

> **Answers**
> 1 The leader of the opposition asks a question, and the Prime Minister answers it. But this is just an excuse for the leader of the opposition to make a joke, and for the Prime Minister to poke fun in return.
> 2 The author is critical, saying it symbolises much that is wrong with politics, MPs laughing like hyenas, politics as mere entertainment, just a game, mock abuse, and discouraging engagement with politics.
> 3 and 4 Students' own ideas

3 Let students read through the sentences, and decide whether they are true, false or not mentioned based on their first reading.
• Students read the article again. Let them compare their answers in pairs before discussing as a class. In feedback, ask students to justify their answers.

> **Answers**
> 1 N (only says they have to come on Wednesday – nothing else)
> 2 T (laughing like hyenas as they compete to demonstrate loyalty)
> 3 N (The text says satirical comments in the British parliament date back to the 18th century but there's no other mention of the birth of satire or of whether satire was in existence earlier elsewhere.)
> 4 T (As 'opposing' parties have more or less adopted the same economic outlook.)
> 5 F (They aim to take the mickey equally out of all politicians based on character more than policy. As a result, all politicians are seen as bad and political engagement is discouraged.)
> 6 T
> 7 F (They issue shocking, ridiculous press releases that exaggerate official positions in order to force back into the news stories that corporations would rather bury.)
> 8 N (It doesn't say explicitly this is what he wants, despite the implications. It could be the case the writer just wants PMQs reformed.)

Teacher development: exploiting a reading text

At this level, the approach to reading a text in class needs to differ from lower levels. Students are generally quite comfortable with the general comprehension of a text, so there is no need to spend too long checking they understand. Adult advanced students are also sometimes reluctant to spend a lot of class time merely reading, so it is important to set tasks that include a lot of collaborative speaking and discussion, and personal reflection on what they have read. Here are some suggestions:

1 Set a first task which is broad, asking students to report on what they find out or find interesting, rather than on checking they understand. Make sure there is plenty of pairwork discussion around this task.

2 Set a second task which gets students to research the text closely. On this spread, students must infer from the text to answer questions. Again, this results in lots of collaborative speaking.

3 Use the text as a way of finding useful words and phrases students can learn actively or passively.

4 Ask students to look through the the article again and write the missing words. Let them compare answers in pairs before discussing as a class.

Answers	
1 representation	5 loyal
2 emerged	6 identity / identification
3 engaged	7 satire
4 merely	8 opposed

5 Organise the class into groups of three or four to discuss the questions. Go round the room and check students are doing the task and help with ideas and vocabulary if necessary.

• In feedback, ask different groups to summarise their discussion. Correct any errors or show students better ways of saying what they were trying to say.

Optional extra activity Write up the following verbs from the article on the board: *insult, mock, ridicule, poke fun at, satirise, abuse.* Ask students to look up the words in dictionaries, and to say which are the strongest, and in what different contexts the words can be used.

LISTENING

Aim
to practise listening to a joke

6 🔊 **12** Start by asking students if they know any jokes about politicians.

• Play the recording. Students listen and decide on answers. Let students compare answers in pairs.

Answers
1 Students' own answers
2 Lies told by politicians at elections
3 Students' own answers

🔊 **12**

A politician has died and has arrived at the gates of heaven **clutching** his bags. The gatekeeper stops him and says, 'Don't make up your mind just yet. Try out hell and heaven first and see what you think.' The politician **hops** in the lift down to hell and when he gets out he finds he's in an incredible seven-star hotel.

Many of his old friends are lounging round the huge pool, sipping expensive drinks and **chattering** to each other. When they see him, they all **cheer**, 'Hello' and welcome him over. Later in the day, he **strolls** round the fantastic golf course with his best friend and scores his lowest score ever. Later in the evening there's a huge party and he dances the night away. The following day, he goes back to heaven with the music and laughter ringing in his ears. He **steps** into heaven and into a lovely restaurant overlooking a beautiful beach. There is soft classical music and the murmur of gentle conversation. After his meal he **strolls** along the beach and **gazes** at the beautiful sunset. He returns to his hotel and settles into his super-comfy bed and falls fast asleep.

In the morning he goes to the gatekeeper who asks him, 'So what do you think? Have you decided?' And the politician says, 'You know, don't get me wrong, heaven was great – all very relaxing and lovely – but, I have to say, I would never have imagined that hell could be so much fun.' So he waves goodbye and happily **skips** into the lift to take him down to hell. When the doors open, though, he is faced with a scene of devastation. It's like there's been an earthquake or something. He **peers** into the distance and **spots** some people on the horizon. As he walks towards them he sees that they are his friends **trudging** along under the weight of heavy rocks while the devil **yells**, 'Work harder.' Some are **crawling** on the floor in exhaustion and hunger. The politician goes up to the devil and **gasps**, 'But what are you doing? What's happened? Where's the hotel? The golf? The party?'

The devil chuckles and shakes his head. 'Oh dear, you should know – that was the election campaign and now you've voted.'

UNDERSTANDING VOCABULARY

'Ways of' verb groups

Aim
to practise using descriptive verbs with distinctive patterns

7 Read through the information in the box as a class.
• Ask students to work in pairs to find and categorise the words in bold in audio script 12 on page 201. Encourage them to try to guess meaning from context, explain the words to each other, and only use dictionaries to check once they have had a guess at the words.

Answers				
Groups				
go / move	**look**	**say**	**hold**	**laugh**
hop	gaze	yell	clutch	chuckle
stroll	peer	cheer		
step	spot	gasp		
skip		chatter		
trudge				
crawl				

8 Ask students to work in pairs to categorise the words in the box.

Answers				
Groups				
go / move	**look**	**say**	**hold**	**laugh**
race	glare	mutter	grab	giggle
creep	stare	mumble		
stagger		scream		

Background language notes for teachers

stroll = walk slowly in a relaxed way (stroll in the park)
trudge = walk heavily, when tired or on difficult ground (they trudged uphill in the mud)
gaze = look into the distance for a long time or at a view
yell = shout loudly to get attention
clutch = hold tight
chuckle = laugh quietly and happily
creep = walk carefully so that nobody hears you
stagger = walk in an unbalanced way, perhaps because you are concussed, injured or drunk
glare = stare angrily
mutter = speak under your breath (often when complaining)

Optional extra activity Mime some of the words from Exercises 7 and 8 and ask students to say which words you are miming. Then ask students to practise miming and guessing words in pairs or small groups.

9 Organise the class into new pairs to prepare and practise telling jokes. Ask students to decide who is A and B, read their jokes, and prepare how to tell the jokes. Monitor and help as they prepare. As students tell their jokes, monitor and notice how well students use the language.
• In feedback, look at good language that students used, and language students didn't quite use correctly during the activity. Show students better ways of saying what they were trying to say. You could write some useful new phrases on the board with gaps and ask the whole class to complete the sentences.

Optional extra activity Tell a joke of your own.

Web research activity
• Ask students to find a funny story on the Internet in English, and to prepare to tell it in their own words.
• Ask students to share their story in the next class.

CAST YOUR VOTE
Student's Book pages 38–39

Communicative outcomes
In this two-page spread, students will read about and discuss Switzerland and the Swiss electoral system; they will discuss voting and elections.

READING

Aim
to read for general and detailed understanding and respond personally to the text; to learn words and phrases in context

1 Organise the class into groups of four or five to discuss the questions. In feedback, ask one person from each group to report back to the class.

Answers
Work with what your students know. However, the information in the culture notes below may be useful.

Culture notes

Switzerland is a federal republic, a landlocked country in south central Europe with Germany to the north and Italy to the south. The capital is Bern. German, French, Italian and Romansch are its four official languages. It is famous for its lakes (Lake Geneva, Lake Lucerne), its mountains (the Alps, the Eiger, the Matterhorn), its cows and cheese (gruyere, emmenthal), its banks, its neutrality, its flag (a white cross on a red background – the symbol of the Red Cross which was founded in Switzerland), the Swiss Army pen knife, and its chocolate (Suchard, Lindt, Tobler). Historically, the country was founded in the late thirteenth century as a confederacy of cantons. Napoleon conquered the region. However, since 1815, it has been independent and neutral.
Famous people: Albert Einstein (physicist), Le Corbusier (architect), Roger Federer, Martina Hingis (tennis players), Peter Sauber (F1 boss), Johanna Spyri (wrote *Heidi* – the Swiss children's classic novel), William Tell (a fictional character)

2 Ask students to read the article and find the information. Let students compare their answers in pairs before discussing as a class.

Answers
1 MPs have modest salaries; they only sit for 12 weeks a year; they have second jobs
2 they can challenge parliamentary decisions; they can petition for / propose new laws; they can vote in referenda
3 Senate: two elected reps per canton; National Council: by a form of proportional representation based on lists of candidates
4 there's not much change in the makeup of government, which rules by consensus

3   Ask students to read the article again. Emphasise that there are no right or wrong answers here – it depends on their point of view.

4   Organise the class into pairs. Let students compare their answers and discuss differences with their country before discussing as a class.

5   Ask students to find the words in bold with their partner. You could start students off by eliciting the meaning of the first one. You could make this a dictionary task – asking students to check their guesses in dictionaries – or you could elicit and check the meanings in the feedback session.

Answers

allocates: gives or shares
counterparts: people with the same position in another institution
federal: federal laws apply to the whole country rather than regional / state law
petition: a list of signatures supporting or criticising a policy (and wanting a change)
referendum: a vote on a single subject – it's a yes / no choice (plural is *referenda*)
proportional representation: electoral system where the number of MPs a party gets is in proportion to the number of votes it gets. If you get 10% of the votes, you get 10% of MPs.
ballot papers: the papers where you mark the party / candidate or choice you want when you vote
the party line: the policy / opinion that the whole party has decided to support
lobby: talk to groups to persuade them to support your cause
consensus: when everyone agrees on the policy / course of action (reach a consensus)

Optional extra activity   Ask students to find and underline three other words they aren't sure of in the article. Tell them to ask another student to try to explain the word.

VOCABULARY Elections and politics

Aim
to learn and use vocabulary connected with elections and politics

6   Ask students to complete the phrases. Do the first as an example to get students started. Let them compare their answers in pairs before discussing as a class.

Answers

1 figure	5 scandal
2 election	6 MP
3 poll	7 vote
4 consensus	8 victory
not needed – party, strike	

---

7   Check that students understand all the phrases by asking them to underline any new ones and to write personalised example sentences (e.g. *In my country, so-and-so is a hate figure because ...*).

Background language notes for teachers

a prominent figure = an important, well-known person
rig an election = unlawfully predetermine the result of an election (also, *vote-rigging*)
the run-up to ... = the period just before
a broad consensus = an agreement among a wide number of people
a landslide victory = a victory by a large margin
a hollow victory = a victory that feels disappointing or meaningless

8   Organise the class into pairs. Ask students to compare their sentences and match the nouns to other words. Again, this could be a dictionary task. In feedback, elicit a few interesting ideas.

Possible answers

1 a leading figure, a historical figure
2 General Election, local election, presidential election, hold an election
3 standing in the polls, opinion poll
4 a general consensus, result in a consensus, made by consensus
5 a scandal breaks, expose a scandal, a financial scandal
6 a left-wing / independent / socialist MP, a sitting MP, elect an MP
7 win / lose votes, have a vote, put to the vote, split the vote
8 achieve victory, cruise to victory, a complete victory, an unexpected victory

---

LISTENING

Aim
to practise listening for general and specific information

9   Organise students into groups of four or five to discuss the questions. In feedback, elicit answers and ideas.

Answers

1 You vote for a person or party: an election for a student council, a general election, a local election, a talent show vote; you vote for a law or action: a referendum, a strike ballot, a vote in parliament
2 In top to bottom order: Column 1: students, the general public, the public in a particular region or city, selected members of the public; Column 2: the general public, workers, MPs
3 Students' own ideas
4 an opinion poll – although you don't elect a person, or decide on a law or action, it allows people to see what people think; in elections, opinion polls are used by pollsters to find out how the public might vote, so, in that respect it is connected to voting in elections
5 Possible answers: you might vote for a mayor, a police chief, sports personality of the year
6 Students' own ideas

---

10 ☕13 Ask students to read the situation and the task. Play the recording. Students listen and match speakers to events. Let students compare answers in pairs.
• In feedback, elicit answers from the class.

Answers
Speaker 1
a talent show vote
Speaker 2
a strike ballot
Speaker 3
a referendum
Speaker 4
an opinion poll
Speaker 5
an election for student council

☕13
1
I used to like watching Star Quality, but since this scandal has erupted I've lost interest in it. This story leaked out that they were encouraging people to phone in even though they'd already decided the result. They were manipulating things so that one guy didn't get voted off because it helped the programme's ratings if they had a kind of hate figure. I might not have minded so much if the calls were free, but they're making a fortune on them.

2
We only called a vote because negotiations were going absolutely nowhere and, despite the massive support we've received from our members, the management is persisting with a ridiculous offer that will basically result in a drop in the value of wages next year. If they hadn't been so reluctant to negotiate, we would not be taking this action now. We understand the public's anger and frustration – we share it – but the blame for this dispute lies firmly with the train company, not with us.

3
I'm totally in favour of a vote on the issue. The way the current system works, some parties get a seat with only 100,000 votes, while others who poll more than twice that don't get any. In the run-up to the election, the New Party had promised to hold one if they got into power, but in the event all that talk has faded away. I guess if they hadn't won a landslide victory, they'd be keener to bring about electoral reform, but I truly believe the vast majority of the electorate still wants to see a change and would vote yes, whatever their reservations.

4
To be honest, I suspect that if they'd called on another day, I wouldn't have taken part, but I was at a bit of a loose end when the researcher called and so had some time to spare. It took about half an hour and I have to admit I quite enjoyed it – moaning

about the government. Mind you, when the results were published in the paper, I was a bit taken aback. It seems I'm in a small minority. People must be mad!

5
It's easy to be cynical and to say that it changes nothing – that it's all just done to create the illusion of fairness and inclusivity – but I can assure you that simply isn't the case here. Given that relatively few people vote these days, we feel it's essential for young people to learn that democracy can contribute to positive change. Apart from deciding things like the end-of-term trips, pupil reps can also decide on policy. It's unlikely we would've abolished uniforms if we didn't have a body like this. It isn't compulsory to vote, but nearly everyone does.

11 ☕13 Play the recording again. Students listen for the answers. Let students compare answers in pairs.
• In feedback, elicit answers from the class.

Answers
a Speaker 3
b Speaker 1
c Speaker 5
d –
e Speaker 4
f Speaker 2

GRAMMAR Conditionals 2

Aim
**to check students' understanding of how to form
and use conditional forms to talk about general past
truths, imagined events in the past and imagined
events in the past and present**

12 Read through the information in the box as a class.
• Students work individually to match the sentences to the functions. Let them compare their answers with a partner.
• In feedback, elicit the students' answers. They can check their answers using the Grammar reference on page 170.

Answers
a = 1
b = 3
c = 3
d = 2
e = 3

 Students complete Exercise 1 in the Grammar reference on page 170.

Answers to Exercise 1, Grammar reference
1 could've / would've won, had changed
2 would've voted, didn't like
3 might / would be, hadn't been mixed up
4 wouldn't be, hadn't made
5 hadn't given, might not / wouldn't be
6 needed, would be / was, had, would go

Background language notes for teachers

Note the form of the three different uses:
• General past truths
If they had a hate figure, it boosted ratings. (*If* + past, past)
or *If there was an election, all the posters would go up.*
(*If* + past, *would* + infinitive)
Compare this use to the section in Conditionals 1.
Effectively, the tenses are going one back, from present to past, from *will* to *would*, when talking about past truths rather than general truths.
• Imagined events in the past
If they'd called on another day, I wouldn't have taken part.
(*If* + *had* + past participle, *would* + *have* + past participle)
The situation is hypothetical because they did call and on that day, not another day.
• Imagined events in the past and present
Often called a mixed conditional, here one clause uses *had* + participle or *would* + *have* + past participle, while the other clause uses the past or *would* + infinitive.

13   Ask students to discuss the options in pairs. Monitor and support students, prompting them to explore differences in meaning.

> **Answers**
> 1 If the parliamentary vote goes against the government next week, it could trigger / it'll trigger / ~~it triggered~~ an election.
>   *could* is less certain than *will*
> 2 The government should've done more for the middle classes if they want / wanted / ~~would've wanted~~ to win the election.
>   *want* suggests a current situation (what they put in the manifesto for the next election) as opposed to a finished situation
> 3 If they complain, tell / I wouldn't tell / ~~I told~~ the boss.
>   *tell* is more certain – imperative, the other is advice
> 4 If I'd heard something, ~~I'd told /~~ I would tell / I would've told you.
>   *would tell you now* and *would've told you before now*
> 5 If it hadn't been for him, I *wouldn't be working* / ~~wouldn't have been working~~ / *would never have got a job* here.

14   Elicit one or two possible sentences from students to get them started. Give them a few minutes to think of their own ideas. Let students compare their answers in pairs before discussing as a class.

> **Answers**
> 1 The Liberals would have won if they had a more charismatic leader. / If more younger people had voted, the result might have been very different.
> 2 We would have lost the war if he hadn't been our leader.
> 3 If I hadn't gone to university, I wouldn't have got my current job.

Optional extra activity   Tell the class about famous figures in your country and important moments in your life, using conditional forms.

 For further practice, see Exercise 2 in the Grammar reference on page 171.

> **Answers to Exercise 2, Grammar reference**
> 1 a, b, d
> 2 a, d, e
> 3 a, c, e
> 4 a, c, e

SPEAKING

Aim
to provide speaking practice on the topic of the lesson

15   Ask students to work in groups of four or five. Tell them to read through the questions individually first and decide which ones they have most to say about. Ask one student in each group to lead the discussion and make sure everybody else gets a chance to contribute.
• In feedback, ask one person from each group to tell the class what they discussed.
• Once you have fed back on content, look at good language that students used, and language students didn't quite use correctly during the activity. Show students better ways of saying what they were trying to say. You could write some useful new phrases on the board with gaps and ask the whole class to complete the sentences.

VIDEO 2: SONGLINES OF THE ABORIGINES
Student's Book page 40

Aim
to find out about the Songlines (ancient historical and cultural songs) and culture of the aboriginal people of Australia; to improve students' ability to follow and understand fast speech in a video extract; to practise fast speech and to improve pronunciation, stress and intonation

1 Lead in to the topic by asking students to look at the photo and say what they can see. Organise the class into small groups to discuss the questions. In feedback, elicit students' ideas and write up interesting ideas or pieces of language on the board.

Culture notes

The photo shows the Aboriginal artist, Turkey Tolson Tjupurrula (1938–2001) who was an important figure in Contemporary Indigenous Australian art. He painted for over 30 years. Several of his paintings are in major Australian public galleries.
The *outback* is the name given to the dry, flat land of central Australia away from the towns.

2 ⬛8 Give students time to read through the task and the sentences first, and to predict what they might see and hear. Students watch and note their answers. Let them compare in pairs before discussing as a class.

Answers
1 N
2 T (their millennia-old culture survives today)
3 N
4 F (nearly 90% of the population had perished)
5 T (once people settled into places ... people were separated from the very thing upon which the culture depended)
6 T (practical purpose – they chart territory, maps for finding food, mark borders; symbolic purpose – represent a spiritual journey, as they walk they sing songs about the moment the world was born)
7 N
8 F (the Dreaming are mythical stories)

3 ⬛8 Organise the class into pairs. Let students try to complete the sentences first to see what they can remember based on their first viewing. As students watch the video again, they should add to and correct their answers. Let them compare answers in pairs. In feedback, write up the missing words on the board.

Answers
1 pockets
2 cradle
3 attempts / results
4 links
5 respect / connection
6 footsteps
7 borders / clans
8 journey

4 This exercise gives students the chance to relate the topic of the video to their own experiences, ideas and opinions. Organise the class into pairs to discuss the questions.
• When most students have finished, stop the class and give some feedback, either by rephrasing some of the things students tried to say for the whole class or by asking students to correct or fill in gaps in sentences you've written on the board, based on what you heard students saying.

Understanding fast speech

5 ⬛9 Play the recording. Students listen and write what they hear. Let them compare in pairs.

6 ⬛10 Students listen again to a slower version to check and improve what they have written. Let them compare answers in pairs.

7 Students check what they wrote in File 10 on page 189. Encourage them to practise saying the extract.

Video script ⬛8
Narrator: Around 55,000 years ago, the Aborigines first arrived in Australia. Their millennia-old culture survives today in remote pockets of the outback. And that's where we're headed.
We're heading east now into Arnhem Land in the Northern Territory of Australia. In a sense, this is the cradle of what became one of the greatest civilizations in the history of humanity.
Sadly, when the Europeans arrived, that's not what they saw. Adam Macfie, an Australian anthropologist, explains.
Adam Macfie: When Europeans first came to Australia, what they saw – in their eyes – were just these savages, living on the land and not doing anything with it. And in fact, they missed out on one of the greatest subtle philosophies of any culture on the planet.
European attempts to 'civilise' the Aborigines had tragic results. By the mid-20th century, nearly 90% of the population had perished.
We just pulled into Ramingining, which is a community that probably was established, I don't know, in the early 70s or so, when people started moving off the land. You know, once people settled into places like Ramingining, suddenly people were separated from the very thing upon which the culture depended: the incredible link, spiritually, metaphysically, to landscape.
The Aborigines' beliefs are founded on a deep respect for and connection to the land.
So it's no wonder that their ancient rituals involve long walks, tracing the footsteps of their ancestors, following the ancient pathways of the Songlines. Thousands of Songlines interlace across the Australian continent. Some are as short as a mile or two; others span hundreds of miles.

Narrator: Songlines have a practical purpose. They are vital for survival: they chart the territory, indicating waterways, mountains, depressions; they are maps for finding food, and they even mark borders between clans.

But Songlines also represent a spiritual journey. On their walks, the Aborigines sing songs about the mythical stories of the Dreaming, a time when the world as we know it was born. When they sing the songs and follow the Songlines, Aborigines return to that moment of creation. And each time they sing, the world is created all over again.

REVIEW 2
Student's Book page 41

Aim
to consolidate vocabulary and grammar from Units 3 and 4

Answers

1

1 would (should)	6 no
2 first	7 reason
3 with	8 was
4 that	9 didn't
5 is	10 though (or *if*)

2
1 thing / sight / place worth seeing there is
2 isn't the done thing
3 hadn't led to another
4 he does is stare at
5 stop giggling if it had
6 is the way / fact he mumbles

3

1 fine	4 asked
2 staggered	5 scamper
3 muttered	6 amount

4
society: welcoming, family-centred, diverse, male-dominated
politicians: outspoken, ruthless
both: hypocritical, secular, right-wing (more commonly used for politicians), conservative, liberal, powerful (though it's more usually used to talk about societies and organisations and clubs and the like, rather than society as a general whole)

5

1 d	3 a	5 c	7 e	9 f
2 j	4 b	6 g	8 i	10 h

6

1 bureaucratic	5 emergence
2 unworkable	6 judgement
3 mobility	7 influential
4 outlook	8 strengthen

7
1 triggered
2 exposed
3 mixed up
4 cover (it) up
5 landslide
6 polls
7 prominent
8 charisma (charm)
9 favour
10 boosting (though *bolstering* also possible)
11 benefitted
12 stand

5 GOING OUT, STAYING IN

SPEAKING

Aim
to set the scene and introduce the theme with a photo; to get students talking about nights out

1   Start by telling the class that in this unit they're going to be talking about nights out, tourism and tourists sites; students will practise commenting on what people say, changing the subject, and describing and reviewing books.
• Ask students to look at the photo on pages 42–43. Ask: *What can you see?* Elicit a brief description of the photo, and introduce any key words students might need.
• Let students work individually to choose which sentence best describes their feelings about the night out. Organise the class into pairs to compare and discuss their answers.

2   Ask students to work in the same pairs to discuss the questions. Go round the room and check students are doing the task and help with ideas and vocabulary if necessary.
• In feedback, ask different pairs to tell the class what they discussed. Look at good language that students used, and language students didn't quite use correctly during the activity. Show students better ways of saying what they were trying to say. You could write some useful new phrases on the board with gaps and ask the whole class to complete the sentences.

> **Possible answers**
> The photo was probably taken at a nightclub in the early hours of the morning.
> Best: fun, funny, good to be with friends, great music, getting dressed up to go, taking funny photos, meeting new people
> Worst: embarrassing, lots of drunk or annoying people, tiring, headache
> Other occasions: carnival, festivals, fancy dress parties, Halloween, Day of the Dead, Christmas or New Year Parties

Culture notes

The photo actually shows a foam party in the Amnesia Club on Ibiza (Eivissa), one of the Balearic Islands, in Spain. The party has an Elvis Presley fancy dress theme!

Background language notes for teachers

induce = persuade / give cause to
give it a go = try it out
tailor-made for = perfectly designed for / exactly right for

Optional extra activity Ask students to tell the class what other types of event would be a brilliant night out for them, tailor-made for them, or their idea of hell.

Teacher development: handling feedback

After a speaking activity, feed back on both content and language use.
• It is important that you give the class an opportunity to say what they found out about each other, to share interesting ideas or queries, and to show that they completed the task. Do this first before commenting on the students' language use.
• It is also important to comment on how well students did the task, so write up any interesting chunks of language students used when speaking in pairs or groups, and check the meaning and pronunciation. You could also write up phrases they didn't use, but might have used, or phrases they used incorrectly, which you could correct and improve. Responding to what students say, and confirming, correcting or improving their utterances is a way of giving your class immediate and specific input. It means you are helping them say what they want to say.

I BET THAT WAS FUN
Student's Book pages 44–45

Communicative outcomes
In this two-page spread, students will practise talking about nights out; they will practise commenting on what is said.

VOCABULARY Nights out

Aim
to introduce and practise phrases used to talk about nights out

1 Start by asking the class to look at the pairs of words in the box. Ask students to work individually to complete the sentences. Do the first as an example to get them started. Let students compare answers in pairs before discussing as a class. In feedback, use examples, mime or drawings on the board to check the meaning of any words students are not sure of.

> **Answers**
> 1 yawning, bored
> 2 exhausted, crawl
> 3 overwhelmed, tears
> 4 courses, burst
> 5 stitches, hilarious
> 6 mortified, swallow
> 7 disappointment, hype
> 8 rough, do
> 9 bits, floods
> 10 scene, awkward

Background language notes for teachers

Note the collocations and idiomatic language in these expressions. Some involve exaggeration for effect (bored out of your mind, burst into tears, floods of tears), whereas one uses understatement (a bit of a scene). Students need to learn them as whole chunks.
bored out of your mind = completely bored
burst into tears = suddenly start crying
on the floor in stitches = laughing so much as though you're in physical pain
absolutely mortified = extremely embarrassed or ashamed – often used for dramatic or comic effect
live up to the hype = be as good as people or advertising said it would be
go to a do = go to a party or event (*do* is used informally to describe any organised event: a family do, a works do, a big do)
in floods of tears = crying uncontrollably
a bit of a scene = an embarrassing situation, e.g. an argument in a restaurant

2 The aim here is to get students to take responsibility for their learning by thinking about which phrases are most useful for them. Ask them to think about the phrases individually.

> **Answers**
> There are no fixed answers here, but students may choose phrases because they include new words they want to learn (*I couldn't stop yawning; It was hilarious*), or because they are phrases relevant to their lives (a twenty year old may think *I didn't crawl into bed until …* and *I feel a bit rough* are useful phrases), or because they just like the sound of the expression (*We were all on the floor in stitches*). You could point out that some expressions (*It was such a disappointment; It caused a bit of a scene; It was quite awkward*) might suit more mature speakers.

3 Organise the class into pairs to compare their chosen words and phrases.

4 Let students work in the same pairs to think of situations. You could start them off by providing one or two examples. Monitor and notice how well students use the new vocabulary. In feedback, point out any errors students make with use and pronunciation.

> **Possible answers**
> 1 an afternoon at your grandparents / a rainy day on holiday / a long bus journey / a dull lecture
> 2 winning a race or competition that you have worked hard for / passing an important exam / kind words from someone
> 3 a funny comedy on TV / a live stand-up comedian telling a good joke / a YouTube clip / something funny your friend does or says
> 4 any really embarrassing situation – going to a wedding in the same dress as the bride's mother / being rude about your teacher or boss just as she or he enters the room
> 5 a film, play or show that everybody has said was great but left you feeling bored
> 6 any party – a family do, a do at work, a small do with friends, or a big do with lots of people there
> 7 a funeral / a sad film / a book with a sad ending
> 8 an argument between boyfriend and girlfriend in a restaurant or other public place / a colleague losing his temper at work / a teacher shouting at a student

Optional extra activity Ask students to work in pairs to prepare a dialogue in which they each use two of the phrases from the lesson. When students are ready, ask a few to act out their conversations. Tell them to cover what they prepared, and to improvise the conversations.

LISTENING

Aim
to listen for a general understanding; to listen for specific phrases in a conversation

5 🔊**14** Give students a moment to read through the questions.
• Play the recording. Students listen and note answers. Let students compare answers before discussing in feedback.

Answers

Conversation 1
1 a surprise party
2 dancing

Conversation 2
1 a meal out
2 arranging a big meeting

🎧 14
Conversation 1

A: Hey, Maddy. You're in late today. Are you OK? You look tired.
B: I am. I'm exhausted. I didn't crawl home till almost three.
A: Yeah? How come?
B: Oh, this friend of mine ... it was her 25th and we'd organised a surprise party.
A: Oh, that's nice. I bet she was pleased.
B: Yeah, she was, although she actually burst into tears when she first came in.
A: Oh no!
B: Yeah. She's been through a lot recently, which is partly why we'd planned the do.
A: Cheer her up?
B: Yeah, exactly. Anyway, she was clearly a bit overwhelmed by it all at first, but she soon got over it.
A: Oh, well. That's good. Where was it?
B: In this bar in town. We hired a room and managed to book this band who were friends of hers.
A: Oh really? Were they any good?
B: Yeah, brilliant. They do this kind of old school rock and roll stuff, and they went down really, really well. Honestly, everyone was up dancing.
A: Was Marco there?
B: But of course! Giving it his all on the dance floor as usual.
A: Oh, he's so full of himself, that guy. He thinks he's God's gift to women!
B: Oh, that's a bit harsh. He seems pretty harmless to me. He just loves a good dance.
A: Yeah? Well, it could just be me, I suppose. Glad he behaved himself, anyway.
B: Yeah. Hey, talking of dancing, are you still going to those tango classes?
A: Yeah, on and off.
B: You must be getting quite good, then.
A: I wouldn't go that far. I'm still a bit prone to treading on toes.

Conversation 2

C: Oh Almir. Hi. I'm glad I caught you. I just wanted to check whether you've managed to sort everything out for the big meeting yet.
D: Yup. It's all in hand – and I've also booked a table at St John's for the evening.
C: That sounds perfect. I didn't mean to hassle you. I'm just stressing about it.
D: That's all right. I'm sure it'll all be fine.
C: Yeah, of course it will. It's just that I could do without it at the moment. I've got far too much on.

D: I can imagine. Anyway, as I said, it's all under control.
C: That's great. Thanks for being so on top of things.
D: No problem at all.
C: Oh, by the way, how was your meal the other night?
D: It was great, thanks. We went to this new place, Porchetta?
C: Oh yeah. How was the food?
D: Amazing, but there was so much of it. They do something like six or seven courses. I lost count after a while.
C: That must've been quite filling!
D: It was. I was ready to burst by the end of it all. It was a bit too much, to be honest.
C: Hmmm.
D Actually, I almost forgot ... there was a bit of a scene while we were there.
C: Oh?
D: Yeah. This guy at a table in the corner just suddenly burst out screaming at one of the waiters.
C: Really? How come?
D: I'm not sure, actually. I didn't catch it all, but it was about something daft, like a dirty fork or something.
C: Strange!
D: I know. There was a kind of awkward silence in the room while it was all going on.
C: I bet. That can't have been much fun.
D: Mmm.
C: So what happened in the end, then?
D: Oh, they managed to get him to leave. But otherwise, yeah, it was good.

6 🎧 **14** Play the recording again. Students listen and note the phrases used. Let students compare answers before discussing in feedback.

Answers
Conversation 1
exhausted
crawl
burst into tears
overwhelmed (by it all)

Conversation 2
(ready to) burst
a bit of a scene
awkward (silence)

7 Ask students to complete the sentences based on the listening. Let them compare answers in pairs. Ask students to look at audio script 14 on page 201 and check their answers. Alternatively, you could play the recording at this stage again as an intensive listening to confirm the answers.

Answers

Conversation 1	Conversation 2
1 through	7 in
2 over	8 without
3 down	9 on
4 of	10 on
5 of	11 by
6 to	12 out

Teacher development: listening intensively for chunks of language

In Exercise 6, students are asked to listen intensively for particular words. In Exercise 7, students are asked to remember the missing prepositions or adverbs, and, if you play the recording, to listen to a text very intensively to hear the words. This develops intensive listening as it tests students' abilities to hear particular chunks of sound. It also introduces students to a set of useful and common chunks of language, which they can learn and use.

In order to develop your students' ability to listen for chunks, do the following:

1 Give them time to predict what words might be missing, or what parts of speech the words might be before they listen.

2 Allow them to listen two or three times to extracts from the listening so that they can really work at hearing chunks of language.

3 Introduce your students to the way words link together when spoken naturally, the way pronouns and auxiliary verbs contract, and the way words such as *of* and *to* are reduced to weak forms.

8 Organise the class into groups of four or five to discuss the questions. Monitor closely and note interesting and useful language, as well as errors. Use the feedback to point out good examples, correct errors, and to provide examples of how students can express their ideas better.

Optional extra activity Ask students to ask you the questions, and to note any interesting answers you provide. It is a good idea to provide a 'live listening' in class, especially if you are a native or near native speaker.

DEVELOPING CONVERSATIONS
Commenting on what is said

Aim
to introduce and practise short phrases used to comment on what people say

9 Read through the information in the box as a class.
• Check the meaning and form of the phrases used. Point out that *I bet* is used to mean *I suspect* or *It is my belief that*. Point out the form after *must* and *can't*.
• Ask students to rewrite the comments. Let them compare their answers in pairs.

10 🔊 15 Play the recording. Students listen and check. In feedback, ask students to say which comments were accurate and why.

Suggested answers
1 That must've been pretty dull.
2 You can't be feeling your best at the moment.
3 He can't have been very pleased when he found out.
4 You must be glad you didn't go now.
5 That can't have been cheap.

---

6 She must've been feeling quite unwell.
7 Judging from his accent, he can't be from here.
8 You must be joking!

1, 3, 4, 6, and 7 were accurate.

🔊 15
1 A: That must've been pretty dull.
　B: Awful! I couldn't stop yawning.
2 A: You can't be feeling your best at the moment.
　B: Actually, I feel surprisingly fresh.
3 A: He can't have been very pleased when he found out.
　B: You can say that again! He went totally mental!
4 A: You must be glad you didn't go now.
　B: Absolutely! It obviously didn't live up to the hype.
5 A: That can't have been cheap.
　B: You'd be surprised, actually. It wasn't as pricey as you'd think.
6 A: She must've been feeling quite unwell.
　B: Yeah, I guess so. I mean, she's usually the last person to leave, isn't she?
7 A: Judging from his accent, he can't be from here.
　B: No, I know. He sounds Australian or something, I thought.
8 A: You must be joking!
　B: No, honestly! I'm deadly serious.

Background language notes for teachers

totally mental = crazy, completely out of control, extremely angry

11 Organise the class into new pairs. Give students time to prepare their dialogues around the comments. Monitor and help with ideas and vocabulary. In feedback, pick out two or three interesting examples you spotted and comment on the language use.

Optional extra activity Ask students to practise the conversations in their pairs.

CONVERSATION PRACTICE

Aim
to practise language from the lesson in a free, communicative, personalised speaking activity

12 Ask students to choose a task and prepare ideas individually. Monitor and help with ideas and vocabulary.

13 Once students have prepared their ideas, ask them to practise in pairs. Encourage them to have three or four attempts – practice makes perfect. Tell them to take turns to play each role. Monitor closely and note interesting and useful language, as well as errors. Use the feedback to point out good examples, correct errors, and to provide examples of how students can express their ideas better.

Teacher development: using the video

The video and activities on the DVD-ROM can be used in various ways:
1 as an alternative to the conversation practice
2 instead of the listening activity in some units, particularly with weaker groups. Students can first practise reading out the dialogues and work on some of the key phrases / structures in a controlled way before having a go themselves.
3 at the end of the unit as a revision exercise

▶ 11 Refer students to the video and activities on the DVD-ROM.

Communicative outcomes
In this two-page spread, students talk about tourism, and use noun phrases to write about places.

READING

Aim
to introduce and practise ways of talking about tourism and tourist sites

1 Organise the class into pairs to list sites and things to do. Set a three-minute time limit to make students think quickly, then elicit ideas. Ask students which ideas sound best.

Culture notes

This activity depends, naturally, on how well your students are likely to know London. If your students know very little, you could share some of the information below. Otherwise, just work with their knowledge.
Top ten attractions in London: Tower of London, London Eye, British Museum, Palace of Westminster (Houses of Parliament and Big Ben), Westminster Abbey, St Paul's Cathedral, Buckingham Palace, Madame Tussaud's Waxworks Museum, National Gallery, Science Museum

2 Focus students on the task then ask them to read the article and find answers. Set a five-minute time limit to encourage students not to read too intensively.

Possible answers
1 People who follow the crowd are sometimes called 'sheep'. So, all the tourists go to the same places. The article is encouraging people to go to different places 'off the beaten track'.
2 They're not seeing the real London. They aren't going anywhere apart from the centre and the classic sites, and so they're only getting a superficial view of London.

3 Ask students to read the rest of the article and match the headings. Let them compare answers in pairs before discussing as a class.

Answers
1 b Free view (The Shard is the tallest building in London and it costs a lot to go up it. The alternative is the view from Hampstead Heath which is free.)
2 e True insights (British Museum not very British so if you really want to see how we've lived ...)
3 f East End Playhouse (Hackney Empire Theatre / contrast with West End theatres)
4 g Not just chippies (you can get a variety of food – 'chippie' is a traditional fish and chip shop)
5 c Far out night out (takes a while to get there – 'far out' used to be a trendy way to say cool or great)
6 h Quiet Night Out (silent disco at London Zoo)

4 Explain that the phrases in italics have the same meaning as differently-expressed phrases in the text. Ask students to discuss the phrases and check in the article together. In feedback, answer any queries about the meaning of words.

> **Answers**
> 1 ventured beyond
> 2 some go for a dip all year round
> 3 feeling peckish
> 4 houses
> 5 a theatre that once hosted Charlie Chaplin
> 6 a peculiarly British show
> 7 embraced a huge array
> 8 a toss-up
> 9 synonymous with social deprivation
> 10 are tucked up in

Culture notes

a waxwork of Cristiano Ronaldo = Cristiano Ronaldo is a world-famous Portuguese footballer who, at the time of writing, plays for Real Madrid. The point being made here is that seeing a waxwork of a foreign footballer has nothing to do with experiencing London

ventured beyond Zone 1 = The London Underground is organised into zones. Zone 1 contains all the central London districts, most of the major tourist attractions, the major rail terminals, the City of London, and the West End. It is about 6 miles (9.7 km) from west to east and 4 miles (6.4 km) from north to south. There are five further zones. The cost of a ticket goes up the further you travel across zones.

The Shard = It is a 95-storey skyscraper in Southwark, which opened in 2012. At over 300 metres high, it is the fourth tallest building in Europe. A ticket for the viewing gallery costs £25.95.

Charlie Chaplin = Although he became famous in Hollywood movies, Chaplin was a Londoner who started out as a child performer on the London stage.

Pantomimes = Pantomime (or panto) is a type of musical comedy stage production, designed for family entertainment. It was developed in England and is still performed there, generally during the Christmas and New Year season and, to a lesser extent, in other English-speaking countries. Modern pantomime includes songs, slapstick comedy and dancing, and has a story loosely based on a well-known fairy tale.

London is made up of lots of small towns, which were swallowed up as the city grew during the nineteenth and twentieth centuries. So, places like Hampstead Heath, Hackney, Harringay, Southall and Muswell Hill are more than just suburbs. They all have their own centres, often containing old and historical buildings. People from different ethnic groups have settled in different suburbs, hence Turkish food in Harringay, and Indian food in Southall.

5 Students work in the same pairs to discuss the questions. Go round the room and check students are doing the task and help with ideas and vocabulary if necessary.

• In feedback, ask different pairs to tell the class what they discussed.
• Once you have fed back on content, look at good language that students used, and language students didn't quite use correctly. Show students better ways of saying what they were trying to say. You could write some useful new phrases on the board with gaps and ask the whole class to complete the sentences.

Optional extra activity Ask students in pairs to discuss and suggest two or three 'off the beaten track' places to go to in their town.

UNDERSTANDING VOCABULARY
Noun + *of*

Aim
to practise using nouns with *of*

6 Read through the information in the box as a class. Then ask students to match nouns to endings. Organise the class into pairs to compare answers. In feedback, elicit answers from the class.

> **Answers**
> 1 e   5 c
> 2 f   6 b
> 3 h   7 a
> 4 g   8 d

7 Organise the class into pairs to produce their own personalised sentences.

> **Possible answers**
> Students' own ideas, but you could provide one or two example sentences to help: I always give my grandmother a bunch of flowers on her birthday. / The answer's on the tip of my tongue – I just can't remember it.

Optional extra activity Ask students to listen to you saying some of the phrases and repeating them, paying attention to the weak stress of the word *of*, and the linking between words.

Teacher development: drilling for pronunciation

Notice when a vocabulary set requires a focus on pronunciation, and incorporate a repetition drill to give students practice. Select four or five short phrases (e.g. *a bunch of flowers, a swarm of bees*), say the phrase clearly and ask students to repeat chorally and individually. Here, *of* needs to be weakly stressed /əv/, and there is a clear linking between consonant and vowel sounds: *bunch of* (bʌntʃ_əv).

GRAMMAR Noun phrases

Aim
to check students' understanding of how to form and use noun phrases

8 Read through the information in the box as a class. Then organise the class into pairs to do the matching task. Monitor and notice how well students understand the rules of form.

• In feedback, elicit the students' answers. They can check their answers using the Grammar reference on page 171.

> **Answers**
> a adding a name of something to the kind of thing it is (or vice versa)
> 2 – the 18th-century stately home, Kenwood House
> b adding a noun before the main noun to describe it
> 3 – cream teas
> c adding several adjectives
> 6 – our best multicultural cheap eats
> d using a compound adjective with a number and noun
> 7 – a six-hour course
> e adding a prepositional phrase to show a feature
> 1 – round Hampstead Heath with its natural ponds
> f a relative clause
> 4 – Geffrye Museum, which contains 11 living rooms from different periods of history
> g a reduced relative clause using an *-ing* participle
> 5 – four period gardens showing changing trends
> h a reduced relative clause using a past participle
> 8 – 'chippie' run by second-generation Greek immigrants
> i a reduced relative clause using an adjectival phrase
> 9 – places in town, full of trendy bars and restaurants

 Students complete Exercises 1 and 2 in the Grammar reference on page 171.

> **Answers to Exercise 1, Grammar reference**
> 1 Joel Riley gives a talk. 2 Solitary retreat is explored in this book. 3 The parents are seeking damages.
>
> **Suggested answer to Exercise 2, Grammar reference**
> John Moffit, the 37-year-old award-winning character actor from Canada, playing in his first leading role, stars in the three-hour action-packed road movie *The Dying* based on the book by Tom Daley.

Background language notes for teachers: noun phrases

There are numerous ways of building noun phrases. Watch out for some of the following problems students may have:
Pluralising the first noun – *cream teas* not *creams teas*
Hyphenating numbers and nouns – *a five-mile journey*
Deciding between present and past participles in reduced relative clauses – we use present when an active

verb is involved (*a cinema which shows classic films … a cinema showing classic films*) and past when a passive verb is involved (*a film which was shown round the world … a film shown round the world …*)

9 Elicit three or four ideas from the class for the first sentence to get students started. Then ask students to work in pairs to prepare their sentences. In feedback, find out which pair has the longest accurate sentence.

> **Possible answers**
> 1 The 19th-century National Museum houses a remarkable collection of ceramic vases.
> 2 A tall, handsome, well-built man seeks a French woman with a wide range of interests.
> 3 A well-known German man has won a prestigious prize for his scientific research.

10 Ask pairs to work together to think of places to describe, and to prepare sentences. Monitor and help with ideas and vocabulary. Prompt students to correct as you go round. Note errors and interesting uses of language.

• Once students have completed their paragraphs, you could pass them round the class and ask other students to correct and comment on them, or you could put them on classroom walls so students can walk round and read each other's work.

• In feedback, look at good language that students used, and language students didn't quite use correctly.

 For further practice, see Exercises 3 and 4 in the Grammar reference on page 172.

> **Answers to Exercise 3, Grammar reference**
> 1 Visit the awe-inspiring cathedral designed by the architect Antonio Gaudi.
> 2 I read a fascinating article in the paper by the novelist Anne Tyler.
> 3 The exhibitions held in the centre are accompanied by workshops suitable for all ages.
> 4 There is a wealth of exhibits on show, dating back thousands of years.
>
> **Answers to Exercise 4, Grammar reference**
> 1 The six-week course provides guidelines for quick and effective weight loss.
> 2 The supply of arms to other countries is a controversial matter / a matter of controversy.
> 3 There's a lot of opposition to the creation of a new car tax.
> 4 The building / erection / construction of the monument celebrated the centenary / 100th / 100-year anniversary of Jonson's birth / of the birth of Jonson.

Web research activity Ask students to find out more about places in London that are off the beaten track. Here are some places they could search for: Sir John Soane's Museum, The Thames Path, Wilton's Music Hall, Wallace Collection, Fulham Palace.

• Ask students to share what they found out in the next class.

IT CAME HIGHLY RECOMMENDED
Student's Book pages 48–49

Communicative outcomes
In this two-page spread, students will listen to and discuss a radio feature about book clubs, and will describe and recommend books.

SPEAKING

Aim
to introduce the theme of the lesson and listening text; to get students talking in a personalised speaking activity

1   Organise the class into groups of four or five. Ask them to discuss the questions. Go round the room and check students are doing the task and help with ideas and vocabulary if necessary.
• In feedback, ask different pairs to tell the class what they discussed. Once you have fed back on content, look at good language that students used, and language students didn't quite use correctly. Show students better ways of saying what they were trying to say. You could write some useful new phrases on the board with gaps and ask the whole class to complete the sentences.

Culture notes

A book club is a group of people who meet to discuss a book or books that they have read and express their opinions, likes and dislikes. It can also be called a book discussion club, reading group, book group, and book discussion group. Book clubs may meet in private homes, libraries, bookstores, online forums, pubs, and in cafés or restaurants.
People may join because they love reading or literature, but, more often, they join to make friends, or to enjoy intelligent conversation.

LISTENING

Aim
to practise listening for key information; to introduce words in a text

2   ◍ **16**   Give students a moment to read through the sentences. Ask them what they can predict about the text from the information (explain that Mark Zuckerberg is well-known as an American computer programmer and Internet entrepreneur, and best known as a co-founder of the social networking website Facebook).
• Play the recording. Students listen and make notes. Let students compare their answers in pairs before discussing as a class.

Answers
Work with students' ideas. The information below, however, is what you may try to elicit from the group. Don't worry about not getting all of it.
1 Every year Zuckerberg makes his New Year's Resolutions public and they have included: only eating meat that he'd killed himself, learning Mandarin Chinese, and trying to meet a different new person who wasn't an employee every single day.
2 It makes a huge difference to sales. (For example, *Purchases of The End Of Power by Venezuelan journalist Moisés Naím rocketed after it was chosen as the first title for consideration, with the book jumping to the top of Amazon's economics chart overnight!*)
3 Social media has influenced reading habits quite a lot. (For example, people use hashtags like amreading / fridayreads to share what they're reading on Twitter.)
   Also, mobile phones have created a mobile reading revolution across the developing world (according to one study, 62% now read more as books are easier to access online / there are things like the Africa-wide cell phone book clubs).
4 If you'd googled 'book club' back in 2003, it would've returned around 400,000 hits; try it today and you're guaranteed more than 30 million! (In Britain alone, there are now an estimated 40,000 reading groups – including lots of specialist groups such as the vegan book club and socialist feminist groups.)
5 If, for instance, each of the 40,000 reading groups in the UK has around ten members and picks perhaps six books a year, then that's 60 books per club – and almost two and a half million sales – per year. Before you even factor in the power of Facebook.
6 Not everyone sees them in a positive light. Critic Brian Sewer sees them as gossiping circles or dating clubs in disguise. (He also thinks the discussions are trivial and shallow and that there's too much reading of cheap sentimental autobiographies.)
7 One book club favourite, *Reading Lolita in Tehran*, by Azar Nafisi, details the transformational experience of reading and discussing frequently banned Western books in the Iranian capital in the 1990s.

◍ **16**

P = presenter, BS = Brian Sewer
P: For several years now, Mark Zuckerberg, the billionaire co-founder of Facebook, has been making very public – and often quite eccentric – New Year's resolutions. There was the year he promised to only eat meat that he'd killed himself and the time he vowed to learn Mandarin Chinese; then there was the year when he tried to meet a different new person who wasn't an employee every single day. And then in 2015, he announced he'd be switching his media diet towards reading

more books. He planned to get through one every fortnight. To aid him in this pursuit, he set up a page called A Year of Books on his own social networking site, where recommendations could be dissected and discussed. Its impact was both dramatic and immediate.

With its focus on learning about different cultures, beliefs, histories and technologies, the page soon had half a million followers and was making a huge difference to sales of selected titles. Purchases of *The End Of Power* by Venezuelan journalist Moisés Naím rocketed after it was chosen as the first title for consideration, with the book jumping to the top of Amazon's economics chart overnight!

The degree to which Zuckerberg will continue to influence popular purchases remains to be seen, but the venture is very much in keeping with broader cultural trends. Social media has had a marked influence on reading choices over recent years, with, for instance, tens of thousands sharing current enthusiasms on Twitter, using hashtags like 'amreading' or 'fridayreads'. We are also seeing what UNESCO has dubbed 'a mobile reading revolution' across the developing world, where in the past paper-based products were hard to come by. Now, though, according to one recent survey, 62% read more as they can freely access books on their phones. This has resulted in initiatives such as the Africa-wide cell phone book club, started by a Zimbabwean librarian.

Of course, all this online activity is an extension of the face-to-face reading groups which have thrived since the start of the century. If you'd googled the phrase 'book club' back in 2003, it would've returned around 400,000 hits; try it today and you're guaranteed more than 30 million! In Britain alone, there are now an estimated 40,000 reading groups, with people meeting to discuss their latest literary loves in private homes or cafés, in libraries and in bookstores. This phenomenon has resulted in specialist gatherings such as a Vegan Book Club and a Socialist Feminist group, as well as meetings specifically targeted at lovers of crime novels and even comics! Now, let's say each club has around ten members and picks perhaps six books a year, then that's 60 books per club – and almost two and a half million sales – per year. And that's before you even factor in the power of Facebook! Not everyone, though, sees these trends in such a positive light. Here's literary critic Brian Sewer.

BS: Let's face it, most reading groups are little more than gossiping circles, or else simply a literary guise for dating clubs! I know from my own observations that when members do finally get round to discussing books, the discourse is generally basic and displays limited insight or intelligence. I also suspect that these groups consume far too much sentimental autobiographical writing. One can only assume it must be easier for a mass audience to digest.

P: Such opinions, though, seem to have had little impact and certainly haven't halted the spread of communal reading. Indeed, one book club favourite, *Reading Lolita in Tehran*, by Azar Nafisi, details the impact that the experience of reading and discussing frequently banned Western books in the Iranian capital in the 1990s had on the lives of eight young women. The appeal, it would seem, is universal.

3 Ask students to match verbs to the words they were used with. Elicit the first answer to get students started. Let students compare their answers in pairs before discussing as a class. In feedback, write answers up on the board.

Answers			
1 e		5 g	
2 d		6 c	
3 h		7 b	
4 a		8 f	

4 Organise students into groups of four or five to discuss the questions.
• As students speak, go round and monitor, and note down any interesting pieces of language you hear.
• In feedback, look at good language that students used, and / or language students didn't quite use correctly. Show students better ways of saying what they were trying to say. You could write some useful new phrases on the board with gaps and ask the whole class to complete the sentences.

VOCABULARY Describing books

Aim
to introduce and practise words and phrases useful in a book review

5 Start by asking students to look at the photo on the page, and the titles of the books, and names of authors. Ask: *What sort of text are you about to read? What type of books will be described? What sort of words or phrases do you expect to see in the texts?* Elicit ideas to establish and predict as much as you can about the text type and likely content. You could ask students to skim the text before doing the first task, just to confirm their predictions.
• Ask students to read the reviews and choose the correct options. Let them compare their answers in pairs before discussing as a class.

Answers
The Son
1 centres (centres *on* / revolves *around*)
2 plot (argument in a theory / academic paper - false friend with some languages)
3 protagonist (star in a film / play only)
4 dialogue (write / give a speech)

Lies My Mother Never Told Me
1 memoir (a memoir is full of memories)
2 struggle
3 deals with (*treat* is a false friend with some languages)
4 recommend

The Hunger Games
1 Tackling
2 revolving (revolving *around* / basing *on*)
3 traces
4 exploring

Katherine
1 based (based on a true story / rooted in real life)
2 bring (... to life)
3 set
4 tale (it's fiction – characters / stories; histories are non-fiction)

Things My Girlfriend and I Have Argued About
1 (told in the) first person (from the viewpoint of the main character)
2 narrator (commentator on a match / political situation)
3 turns (*by* turns / *in* episodes)
4 insight

Culture notes

Jo Nesbø (born 1960) is a Norwegian writer and musician and former economist. He is primarily known for his crime novels about Inspector Harry Hole.
Kaylie Jones (born 1960) is an American memoirist and novelist. *Lies My Mother Never Told Me* (2009) describes her life as the child of a celebrated author and a beautiful, competitive and witty mother.
Suzanne Collins (born 1962) is an American television writer and novelist. *The Hunger Games* is a 2008 science fiction novel set in a dystopian, post-apocalyptic North America, and written from the perspective of a sixteen-year-old girl.
Anya Seaton (1904–1990) was an American author of historical romances. *Katherine* tells the story of Katherine Swynford, the wife of John of Gaunt. She was a direct ancestor of the modern British royal family.
Robert 'Mil' Millington is a British author of humorous books. *Things My Girlfriend and I Have Argued About* began as a website hosted on Wolverhampton University's web servers.

6 This is an opportunity for students to discuss and find out about words they don't know in the text. Let students work in pairs while monitoring to help. In feedback, you could choose four or five words to focus on with the class.

Background language notes for teachers

protagonist = the central character in a novel or film
flaws = weaknesses (in someone's character)
crisp dialogue = short, sharp exchanges when people speak to each other
heart-wrenching = really sad and moving
transcendence = managing to get over or beyond a difficult period
gripping = very exciting
vivid portrayal = a very clear, colourful, detailed description

7 Ask students in pairs or small groups to discuss the questions. This activity allows students to respond personally and naturally to the material in the reviews. In feedback, comment on any errors or good uses of language.

Optional extra activity Ask students in pairs to write three sentences using the phrases in the reviews to describe a classic work of fiction. Emphasise that it should be a very well-known piece of fiction. Ask pairs to read out their sentences. The rest of the class must guess which book is being described.

SPEAKING

Aim
to provide extended speaking practice, and to practise using phrases to describe books

8 Ask which students have belonged to a book club, what books they have read or recommended, and what books work best in a book club. Tell students to work individually to think of the book they would like to recommend, and why. Go round and help with ideas and vocabulary.

9 Organise the class into groups of four to six. Try to mix students so they are with people they work with less regularly. When students are ready, ask them to sit in a circle with their groups and present the book they think the group should read. You could set a one-minute time limit for each presentation. Students listen to each suggested book then vote on which to choose.
• In feedback, ask groups to give reasons why they have chosen each book. Use the feedback to point out good examples, correct errors, and to provide examples of how students can express their ideas better.

Optional extra activity Bring in a set of books or readers that you would like your students to read. Ask students in groups to choose one individually to present to their groups. Ask each group to choose a book to read together which they can talk about at a later date either in or out of class.

6 CONFLICT AND RESOLUTION

SPEAKING

Aim
to set the scene and introduce the theme with a photo; to get students talking about arguments

1 Start by telling the class that in this unit they're going to be learning how to handle arguments in a constructive manner, defend and excuse positions and behaviour and discuss conflict and resolution; students will talk about how they would like things to be different and will use extended metaphors.
• Ask students to look at the photo on pages 50–51. Ask: *What can you see?* Elicit a brief description of the photo, and introduce any key words students might need.
• Organise the class into pairs to discuss the questions. Monitor and help with ideas and vocabulary if necessary. In feedback, discuss students' ideas as a class.

> **Possible answers**
> The relationship might be husband and wife. They seem to be about the same age. He seems very angry and appears to be telling her to leave.

Background language notes for teachers

let off steam = express feelings of anger or frustration (without hurting anyone)
lose your temper = lose control of feelings of anger and shout
a good row = a row /raʊ/ is a noisy argument in which people lose their temper and shout – it is often used to talk about domestic situations rather than serious debates – *a good row* is one in which there is a positive outcome because it 'clears the air' – people know exactly how others feel and there is no longer any tension

2 Organise the class into new pairs to discuss their ideas. Tell them to choose which topics to discuss – they needn't discuss all of them. Monitor and note errors, as well as interesting uses of language.

> **Possible answers**
> Careers: husband and wife might argue about whose career should take priority (*You're so selfish; It's not fair – your job always comes first*); parents might argue with child about choice of career (*I can do what I like*; *You have to think about the future*)
> Politics: difference of opinion between friends – somebody being opinionated in their views (*You don't know what you are talking about*; *The country would be in a mess if we did that*)

> Silly annoyances: husband and wife, flatmates, siblings, etc. arguing about people not taking the rubbish out, not clearing up, not switching something off, etc. (*I have to do everything round here*; *Stop being such a pain*)
> Exes: ex-husbands, ex-wives, ex-partners might argue about custody of children, visiting rights, splitting their property, who should pay who and how much (*I'm not giving you a penny more*; *It's your turn to have the kids*)
> Religion: difference of opinion between friends – somebody being opinionated in their views (*You should respect my views*; *I beg to differ*)
> Household chores: see silly annoyances
> Homework: parents and child (*If you don't do your homework, you won't get any dinner*; *It's not fair*)
> Sport: disagreement between players or between players or coaches and referees (*Come on, ref*; *You need glasses*; *That's a blatant foul*)
> Stress and tiredness: new parents with a crying baby or colleagues at work (*It's your turn to get up*; *You are constantly undermining me*)
> In-laws: couple might argue about interfering in-laws or about having to visit them or invite them over (*I'm not going over to your mother's again*)
> Kids: not tidying rooms, staying out late, making a noise (*Keep the noise down*; *Have you done your homework?*; *Where do you think you're going?*)
> Time spent together: a couple or parents and kids (*I never see you*; *You're always so busy at work*; *Why don't you stay in once in a while?*)
> Money: a couple worried about bills, or flatmates arguing about who should pay bills (*It's your turn to pay*; *You can't buy that – it's too expensive*)
> Work: colleagues being competitive (*Stop undermining me*; *Get on with your own work*)

3 Ask pairs to decide on the three things that cause the worst arguments. In feedback, ask different pairs to briefly summarise their ideas.
• Once you have fed back on content, look at good language that students used, and language students didn't quite use correctly during the activity.

Optional extra activity Ask students to think of the last time they had an argument. Who was it with, what was it about, how was it resolved? Tell them to tell their partner about it.

Teacher development: organising pairs

Outcomes aims to encourage lots of spoken interaction between students by means of pairwork and groupwork. However, this can become frustrating for students if they always end up with the same partner. That's why the Student's Book regularly mixes pairs during the unit opener.

Here are some tips for varying pairwork:

1 Encourage adult students to speak to different people in the class, and get to know them, by mixing pairs during the initial warmer or lead-in parts of the lesson. Use instructions like *find a partner you didn't speak to in the last lesson* or *find a partner who has been to the same famous place as you* to empower students to seek out new speaking partners. This builds relationships and class dynamics.

2 On the other hand, don't mix pairs for the sake of it. Adult students often want to sit with a partner they are comfortable with when talking about grammar rules, doing vocabulary exercises, or checking answers to a reading text, for example. However, aim to change pairs when the task is creative or productive. So, students should have a new partner when they do a speaking or writing task.

3 When preparing to do a speaking or writing activity, ask students to prepare with one partner. Then do the activity with another partner.

Communicative outcomes

In this two-page spread, students practise arguing and discussing and talk about how they'd like things to be different.

VOCABULARY

Arguments and discussions

Aim

to introduce and practise chunks of language used in arguments

1 Ask students to work individually to make phrases. Do the first as an example in open class to get students started. Let them compare their answers in pairs. In feedback, model the pronunciation of phrases that are difficult to say.

Answers
1 I hear what you're saying, but try to see it from my point of view.
2 That's not what I meant at all. You're twisting my words.
3 I think we've got our wires crossed. That wasn't my intention at all.
4 Hey, chill! There's no need to raise your voice. I can hear you perfectly well.
5 I've obviously done something to upset you, so I think we should clear the air.
6 OK. You've made your point and I heard you. Now can we just move on? / Can we just move on now?
7 Sorry, that came out all wrong. Just pretend I didn't say that.
8 Alright! Calm down! It's not the end of the world!
9 It's done. Just forget about it. There's no point crying over spilt milk.
10 We're getting nowhere here. We're just going round in circles. Can we just agree to disagree?

Background language notes

twisting my words = deliberately misunderstanding what I'm saying
got our wires crossed = we have misunderstood each other
that came out all wrong … pretend I didn't say that = used to apologise for saying something rude or inappropriate
It's not the end of the world = whatever it is that has upset you is not as important as you think
no point crying over spilt milk = no reason to worry about things that have happened which can't be changed
We're getting nowhere here. We're just going round in circles = we're repeating the same arguments and achieving nothing

2 Ask students to work in pairs to do the task. In feedback, elicit answers.

Answers
1 Answers depend on students' first language. The discussion will take place in English.
2 Answers may vary if students can make an argument for their point of view, but suggested answers are:
   1 calm the argument – asking for balance
   2 make things worse (suggesting the other person is manipulating words)
   3 calm the argument – recognition of a misunderstanding
   4 make things worse (I'm not raising my voice!)
   5 calm the argument – being reasonable and understanding
   6 could be both depending on how it's said and if the other person wants to move on
   7 calm the argument – apologising
   8 could be both depending on how it's said and what the situation is
   9 could be both depending on how it's said and what the situation is; it can sound a bit dismissive
   10 calm the argument – being reasonable and understanding

3 Ask students to work individually to decide what the word is. Let them compare their answer in pairs. In feedback, ask students to think of translations of *point* in their own L1 and to compare in pairs whether they have one word like *point* that's used in each translation or whether they have different words.

Answers
point

Background language notes

Here, *point* means 'idea, opinion or reason'.

4 Organise the class into pairs. Students close their books and see how many phrases they can remember from Exercises 1 and 3. Alternatively, you could give students two minutes to look at and memorise the phrases before closing their books. In feedback, find out which pairs remembered the most phrases.

5 Organise the class into groups. Ask students to discuss the phrases and say when they may have used them.

Possible answers
1 speaking to a friend who has failed an exam or lost a match
2 explaining to a colleague or client when there has been a misunderstanding, e.g. thinking a delivery has been made when it hasn't
4 feeling frustrated when talking about or arguing about a subject, and never agreeing
5 acknowledging the argument a friend or colleague is making

Optional extra activity Ask students to look up *point* in their dictionaries, and find as many different meanings for the word as they can.

LISTENING

Aim
to practise listening for general and specific understanding; to contextualise language used when defending and excusing in an argument

6 🔊 **17** Ask students to read the situation and the task.
• Play the recording. Students listen and note answers. Let them compare answers in pairs. In feedback, elicit answers from the class.

Answers
Conversation 1
untidiness / leaving things lying around
Conversation 2
poor communication

🔊 **17**
Conversation 1
A: Aargh!!
B: What've you broken? Oh my word! What a mess!
A: Don't!
B: OK! Calm down! It's not the end of the world!
A: Don't tell me to calm down. If only you'd put things away properly!
B: I'm sorry?
A: That is your bag, isn't it?
B: Oh ... yeah, I was going to take it to my room ...
A: Well, I wish you had. I almost broke my neck!
B: OK. Sorry. It's not as though I did it deliberately.
A: That's not the point. You're constantly leaving your stuff lying around. You know, I'm not your mother to clear up after you.
B: Right, of course – Mr Perfect!
A: Come on! That's not what I'm saying!
B: Well, that's what it sounds like. It's not as if you're the only one who does stuff round the house.
A: Yeah. OK. Whatever. Listen, forget it. I wish I hadn't said anything.
B: No, if that's how you really feel ...
A: No, it came out wrong. I'm sorry. It's just that it's been a long day and this was the last straw.
B: OK. Well, I am sorry. I will make an effort, although in this particular case I went to answer a phone call and then I forgot about it.
A: Whatever. It's done. Can we just move on?
B: OK. Can I give you a hand?
A: Yeah. Can you grab the dustpan and brush?

Conversation 2
C: Miriam, Could I have a word?
D: Erm. Could we not talk later? I'm actually in a bit of a hurry, as it happens.
C: I'd rather not leave it.
D: Oh, OK. What's wrong?
C: Listen. I just had a phone call from that group who were coming in July and they're cancelling.
D: What? You're joking?
C: I wish I was. Apparently, they were unhappy with the service they were getting.

D: What? They haven't even been in touch recently. I assumed everything was fine.

C: They said they'd asked about discounts, but you hadn't got back to them.

D: Er ... yes, but I passed that on to you.

C: When?

D: A couple of weeks ago! I assumed you'd dealt with it.

C: Why? Didn't you even reply to them?

D: No.

C: Or think to bring it to my attention?

D: Well, you were the one who said you wanted to take control of everything.

C: What? When?

D: Last month – in the departmental meeting.

C: What? That's not what I said at all.

D: You said, 'We've got a to get a grip of costs' and that everything had to go through you.

C: That was different.

D: Really? You kind of left us feeling as if we were doing it all wrong and it was as though we'd been wasting money left, right and centre.

C: Really? That certainly wasn't my intention. I wish you'd said something sooner.

D: I would have, but you hardly come out of that office.

C: Well, it's just that I have tremendous amount on.

D: We actually understand that, but try to see it from our point of view. We want to help, but how can we if you don't communicate more with us.

C: I send out a weekly update.

D: OK ... no offence, but that's not exactly the most human thing. I'm not saying it's not helpful – it's just that we'd all appreciate a bit more face-to-face contact.

C: OK, I hear you. And I can see we've got our wires crossed.

D: That's OK, I should've followed up the email. I was probably being a bit petulant, for which I apologise.

C: OK. Well, it's done now. I'm glad we've cleared the air.

D: Is it worth getting back to them?

C: No, I've spoken to them already. Let's just move on. There's no point crying over spilt milk.

7 🌑 **17** Give students time to decide which conversation the situations refer to.

• Play the recording again. Students listen and check their answers. Let them compare their answers with a partner before discussing as a class. In feedback, ask students to justify their answers.

Answers

a Conversation 1 (I almost broke my neck)
b Conversation 2 (they're cancelling)
c Conversation 2 (it's just that I have a tremendous amount on)
d Conversation 1 (Right – of course, Mr Perfect!')
e Neither
f Conversation 1 (if that's how you really feel)
g Neither
h Neither

---

i Conversation 1 (it's been a long day and this was the last straw)
j Conversation 2 (you were the one who said you wanted to take control of everything / Last month – in the departmental meeting

8 Ask students to discuss the questions in pairs. In feedback, ask different pairs to briefly summarise their ideas.

• Once you have fed back on content, look at good language that students used, and language students didn't quite use correctly during the activity.

Answers
Argument 1 is resolved with an apology (*I'm sorry. It's just that it's been a long day and this was the last straw*), a suggestion that they stop arguing, (*Can we just move on?*), and an offer of help (*Can I give you a hand? / Yeah. Can you grab the dustpan and brush?*). Argument 2 is resolved with a recognition of misunderstanding (*I can see we've got our wires crossed*), an apology (*I should've followed up the email. I was probably being a bit petulant, for which I apologise*), and an agreement to move on (*Let's move on. There's no point crying over spilt milk*).

DEVELOPING CONVERSATIONS
Defending and excusing

Aim
to introduce and practise ways of defending and excusing ourselves in an argument

9 Read through the information in the box as a class. Point out that we use *It's not as though* ... to defend our position, and *It's just that* ... to introduce an excuse.

• Organise the students into pairs to complete the exchanges. You could elicit one or two suggested ideas to get students started. Monitor and help with ideas and vocabulary.

Possible answers
1 ... it's difficult to make myself heard / ... I'm tired
2 B: ... it's your money / ... it was expensive
   A: ... you've got one already / ... you don't even know how to ski!
3 A: ... I have nothing to do / ... everyone else is rushed off their feet
   B: ... you do it so well / ... the client specifically asked for you
4 B: ... I bite / ... I haven't offered before
   A: you're always so busy / ... you looked a bit stressed
5 ... it hurt anyone / ... I do it all the time, is it?

---

10 Organise the class into new pairs. Ask students to act out and improvise dialogues. Encourage them to try out the same dialogue two or three times. Practice makes perfect.

• Monitor closely and note interesting and useful language, as well as errors. Use the feedback to point out good examples, correct errors, and to provide examples of how students can express their ideas better.

Teacher development: practice makes perfect

Outcomes aims to encourage lots of practice using new phrases or chunks of language. The only way students will get familiar with new chunks, and learn to use them confidently and accurately, is to practise. Encourage students to see pairwork practice activities as an opportunity to have a go at using new language over and over again. By repeating and repairing exchanges students fine-tune their ability to use language for real.

Optional extra activity Write the following on the board and ask students to defend or excuse their actions:
Why did you …
… arrive late for the lesson?
… put your headphones on during the lesson?
… make a phone call during the film?
Why didn't you …
… remember my birthday?
… do the washing up?
… go to the interview?

GRAMMAR *Wish* and *if only*

Aim
to check students' understanding of how to use *wish* and *if only* to talk about things we want to be different

11   Read through the information in the box as a class.
• Organise students into pairs to complete the sentences and explain the functions. Monitor and notice how well students understand the rules.
• In feedback, elicit the students' answers. They can check their answers using the Grammar reference on page 172.

Answers
1 'd (would) – a habit (explaining how you want someone to behave differently)
2 had – a regret about the past (*I wish you had taken it to your room …*) (explaining how you'd like the past to be different)
3 was – (impossible situation now) (referring to things in the present that we want to be different)
4 'd – (criticism / regret about past) (explaining how you'd like the past to be different)
5 would – (hypothetical result about something before now – *I would have said it if you came out of your office more often*) (replying to a wish / if only comment)

 Students complete Exercise 1 in the Grammar reference on page 172.

Answers to Exercise 1, Grammar reference
1 had, didn't, would've / might've
2 was / could, could, 'll
3 had, would've, wasn't / weren't, would
4 weren't, 'll, could've
5 hadn't, wouldn't, wouldn't

Background language notes for teachers: *wish* and *if only*

The key thing for students to grasp in terms of form is that English has no conditional form in effect, and goes one tense back when expressing hypothesis, so *I didn't say that* becomes *I wish I hadn't said that* or *If only I'd said that* (*didn't say* goes one tense back to *had / hadn't said*).
• Note that we use the past form to say we want the present to be different (*I wish I was / were richer now*) and the past perfect form to express a regret about the past or to say we wish the past was different (*I wish I had worked harder*).
• To criticise the actions of others, and, therefore, to say that we want them to behave differently, we use *would* + infinitive (*I wish you would be quiet*).
• Note that we can't use this form to talk about ourselves or the past: (*I wish I would be taller; I wish I would have worked harder*).

12   Read through the example as a class. Ask students to work in pairs to make their own exchanges. Once students have created some exchanges, encourage them to practise with their partner. Encourage students to practise two or three times, and think about mixing pairs or asking pairs to perform dialogues for the class in order to maximise practice.
• Monitor closely and note interesting and useful language, as well as errors. Use the feedback to point out good examples, correct errors, and to provide examples of how students can express their ideas better.

Possible answers
2 So you didn't pull out of the course in the end? / I wish I had. The whole thing's a nightmare. / Well, you could still pull out now.
3 Joe tells me you're going to Munich for the weekend. / To be perfectly honest, I wish I didn't have to. / Why's that? Are you busy?
4 I've got three tickets for the concert. / If only you'd mentioned that an hour ago. / Why? You haven't bought tickets, have you?
5 Would you like to go away for the weekend? / I wish I could. / Oh dear, you're not still studying, are you?
6 So you've volunteered to help clean the park? / Yeah. We wouldn't have if you hadn't been so keen. / Well, don't worry. It'll be fun.

---

13   Organise the class into groups of four. Give students time individually to prepare things to say. Go round and help with ideas as they prepare. When students are ready, ask them to discuss in groups. Elicit two or three ideas for each item.
• Monitor for errors or good language use and feedback on what you heard at the end.

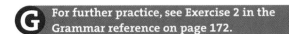 For further practice, see Exercise 2 in the Grammar reference on page 172.

Answers to Exercise 2, Grammar reference
1 only I had not / hadn't spoken
2 wish I could have gone
3 wish you were not so
4 would not fight so / as
5 we did not have to
6 If only you had / 'd told me

Optional extra activity Ask students to turn the prompts in Exercise 13 into questions. Then ask the class to interview you. Speak at length, as a live listening.

CONVERSATION PRACTICE

Aim
to practise language from the lesson in a free, communicative, personalised speaking activity

14 Organise the class into pairs. Ask each pair to decide who is A and who is B. Tell them to find their information pages (pages 187 and 188), then give them time to read their files and to think of what to say.

15 When students are ready, ask them to roleplay the conversations. Early finishers can swap roles and act out the conversations again.
• Monitor the students and note errors and good uses of language.
• In feedback, look at good language that students used, and language students didn't quite use correctly during the activity. Show students better ways of saying what they were trying to say. You could write some useful new phrases on the board with gaps and ask the whole class to complete the sentences.

 12 Refer students to the video and activities on the DVD-ROM.

Teacher development: using the video

The video and activities on the DVD-ROM can be used in various ways:
1 as an alternative to the conversation practice
2 instead of the listening activity in some units, particularly with weaker groups. Students can first practise reading out the dialogues and work on some of the key phrases / structures in a controlled way before having a go themselves.
3 at the end of the unit as a revision exercise

Communicative outcomes
In this two-page spread, students read and discuss a text about Peace Studies, and talk about conflict and resolution.

READING

Aim
to read for specific understanding; to find nouns that collocate with given adjectives in the text

1 Ask students to look at the photo on page 55. Organise the class into small groups to discuss the questions. Go round the room and check students are doing the task and help with ideas and vocabulary if necessary.
• In feedback, ask different pairs to tell the class what they discussed. Once you have fed back on content, look at good language that students used, and language students didn't quite use correctly during the activity.

Possible answers
They could be holding candles at a peace rally.
Peace Studies involves looking at the causes of conflict (terrorism, poverty, social inequality) and peace building (integrating ex-soldiers, improving communication).
Graduates may perhaps end up working for the United Nations or other international peace bodies, charities, or in government.

2 Ask students to read the questions carefully and predict what they can from the questions.
• Students read the article and note their answers. Let them compare their answers in pairs before discussing as a class.
• In feedback, elicit answers and ask students what they read which helped them with their answers.

Answers
1 It's a football competition between the Department of War Studies at King's College, London and Bradford University's Department of Peace Studies. It's named after Tolstoy's novel, *War and Peace*.
2 growth of nation states and legal systems
increasingly globalised trade
increased respect for women
globalised mass media and greater freedom of movement
increased importance of reason
3 It's become more mainstream and accepted. (It was a fringe area but since the 1970s and 1980s it's spread throughout the world.) People want to find new ways of solving conflicts. (*the increasing desire to solve conflict by means other than war*)
4 politics and economics (terrorism, poverty, social inequality, hunger), psychology (group dynamics and aggression), geography (climate change, resource shortages, etc.)

> 5 surrender of weapons and reintegration of soldiers, and developing social and political institutions, encourage community relations and economic development

3 Ask students in pairs to discuss the questions. Let them read the text to check and confirm what they remembered from their first reading.

Possible answers
1 it's an upcoming event and so is newsworthy; it's unusual; it grabs the reader's attention by being novel and unusual
2 because in all but one match, the Peace Studies students have beaten the War Studies students, and this could be seen as ironic, as many people feel war is triumphing over peace in the wider world
3 to show us / as evidence of the fact that – contrary to popular belief – violence is in decline
4 to provide a link to the football match and to show the football match can be seen as an example of war by other means. This then leads nicely into the part about solving conflict by means other than war. The Orwell quote is a bridge / link here.
5 When Bradford University first started offering Peace Studies courses in the 1970s, students were stereotypically seen as little more than hippies who sat around all day listening to John Lennon. Nuclear weapons are mentioned because of their proliferation in the 1970s and 1980s and this led to Peace Studies being taken more seriously
6 to show the incredibly broad range of subjects that Peace Studies courses actually cover now – and peacebuilding is mentioned as it's the heart of the subject
7 it ties the article up nicely – and the writer makes the point that the Peace Studies players give their all on the pitch – and hopes they'll do the same when they graduate and give their all for peace in the world

Culture notes

The Tolstoy Cup is named after Russian author Count Leo Tolstoy (1828–1910) who wrote *War and Peace* (which follows events surrounding the French invasion of Russia, and the impact of the Napoleonic era on Tsarist society) and *Anna Karenina*.
The Oxford-Cambridge Boat Race takes place on the Thames in London every spring. It is a boat race between Oxford and Cambridge University.
Martin Luther King (1929–1968) was an American civil rights leader, and Mahatma Gandhi (1869–1948) was the pre-eminent leader of the Indian movement for independence. George Orwell (1903–1950) was a British journalist and writer famous for writing *Animal Farm* and *1984*.
Steven Pinker (1954–) is a Canadian-born American cognitive scientist, psychologist, linguist, and popular science author.

4 Ask students to match the adjectives from the box to nouns or noun phrases in the article. Elicit the word that goes with *annual* to get students started.
• Let students compare answers in pairs before discussing as a class. Once you have checked answers, ask students to suggest examples from real life or from recent news stories to illustrate the collocations.

Answers
annual event	diverse range of topics
notable peace campaigners	aggressive tendencies
historical forces	former soldiers
dramatic reduction	legitimate state institutions
associated threat	lasting peace

Possible examples
Christmas is an annual event. / There has been lasting peace in much of Europe since the end of WWII. / Former soldiers often suffer from mental health problems. / A diverse range of topics was covered at the conference. / There's been a dramatic reduction in the size of the army over the last year.

5 Organise students into new pairs to discuss the questions. Give students two or three minutes to prepare their ideas first.
• Monitor carefully and note interesting comments and examples of good language to focus on in feedback.

Optional extra activity Ask students to work in pairs to prepare a list of what they would cover if they were to design a course in Peace Studies.

VOCABULARY Conflict and resolution

Aim
to introduce and practise phrases connected with conflict and resolution

6 Ask students to order the groups of words. Start them off by eliciting the first set. Let students compare answers in pairs before discussing as a class.

Answers
1 be invaded
defend yourself / lose ground / join forces / gain ground / defeat the enemy
2 tension rises
fighting breaks out / the conflict escalates / war rages / negotiate a ceasefire
3 be surrounded
be under siege for weeks / run out of food / surrender / become a prisoner of war
4 plant a bomb
cause casualties and fatalities / claim responsibility / track down / arrest / put on trial
5 plot to overthrow the president
stage a coup / seize control of the country / suffer sanctions / undermine economic stability / return to democracy

6 receive reports of human rights violations
  seek a UN resolution / send in international troops /
  re-establish security / withdraw troops
7 declare a ceasefire
  begin negotiations / talks break down /
  restart negotiations / achieve a resolution /
  sign a peace agreement

7 Organise the class into groups of four or five to prepare ideas. Pre-teach *a coup* /kuː/ or *coup d'etat* (a sudden appropriation of leadership or power, often by the military using force).
• Monitor carefully and note interesting comments and examples of good language to focus on in feedback.
• In feedback, look at good language that students used, and language students didn't quite use correctly during the activity. Show students better ways of saying what they were trying to say. You could write some useful new phrases on the board with gaps and ask the whole class to complete the sentences.

Optional extra activity Write the following famous names on the board and ask students to say which phrases from Exercise 6 could be connected with their life and times: *John F Kennedy, Lenin, Mao Tse Tung, Nelson Mandela.*

Communicative outcomes
In this two-page spread, students will practise using extended metaphors, and will hold a debate on current and universal issues.

UNDERSTANDING VOCABULARY
Extended metaphors

Aim
to introduce and practise extended metaphors

1 Ask students whether they know what an extended metaphor is. Elicit ideas. Read through the information in the box as a class.
• Organise the class into pairs to read and discuss the article. In feedback, elicit answers.

Answers
1 sport, health and medicine, business, law and politics
2 Students' own answers
3 Students' own answers

2 Ask students to work individually to complete the sentences. The first answer has been done to get them started.

Answers
2 The party has recruited a huge **army** of volunteers for the campaign.
3 They are desperately trying to attract female voters and have been **bombarding** them with messages seeking support.
4 They're gaining ground in the polls and hope to **capture** 20 new seats.
5 They have a huge sales force compared to ours so we have to really **target** our efforts.
6 She has won her fight to stop the photos being published, which she said was an **invasion** of privacy.
7 All the big **guns** are through to the semi-finals of the competition so it's going to be a tight battle to get through.
8 The fifth set became a **battle** of wills as both players tired and it was Murray who finally surrendered.
9 They've had to join forces to fight off new businesses that are **challenging** their position in the market.
10 Tiredness can often reduce our **defences** against viruses that attack our bodies.

3 Organise the class into pairs and ask them to compare their answers and decide which area of life is being discussed before discussing as a class.

Answers
1 business
2 politics
3 politics
4 politics
5 business
6 law
7 sport
8 sport
9 business
10 medicine

4 Ask students to underline the words that are part of the same metaphor before discussing as a class.

Answers
2 The party has <u>recruited a huge army</u> of volunteers for <u>the campaign.</u>
3 They are <u>aggressively pursuing</u> the middle-class vote and have been <u>bombarding them with messages</u> seeking support.
4 They're <u>gaining ground</u> in the polls and hope to <u>capture</u> 20 new <u>seats</u>.
5 They have a <u>huge sales force</u> compared to ours so we have to really <u>target our efforts</u>.
6 She has <u>won her fight</u> to stop the photos being published, which she said was <u>an invasion of privacy</u>.
7 All the <u>big guns</u> are through to the semi-finals of the competition so it's going to be a <u>tight battle</u> to get through.
8 The fifth set became <u>a battle of wills</u> as both players tired, and it was Murray who <u>finally surrendered</u>.
9 They've had to <u>join forces</u> to <u>fight off new start-ups</u> that are <u>challenging their position</u> in the market.
10 Tiredness can often <u>reduce our defences</u> against viruses that <u>attack our bodies</u>.

5 Organise the class into new pairs to discuss the questions. Give students a minute to prepare ideas first.
• Monitor the students and note errors and good uses of language.
• In feedback, ask different pairs to tell the class what they discussed. Look at good language that students used, and language students didn't quite use correctly during the activity.

Possible answers
1 poor diet, stress and working too much can reduce defences against a virus
2 poverty can be combatted by providing welfare relief, providing jobs and opportunities, providing education; disease can be combatted by providing medicines and drugs, and making sure people eat and exercise well; addiction can be combatted with advice and education, personal support, and other drugs
3, 4, 5 Students' own ideas and experiences

Optional extra activity Ask pairs to look up key words in a dictionary to find further useful metaphors. Key words

to write on the board: battle (*do battle, battle against illness, battle of wits*), fight (*pick a fight, put up a good fight, fight for survival*), war (*wage war against poverty, a war of words*), gun (*gunning for somebody, go great guns, under the gun, with all guns blazing, put a gun to his head*).

LISTENING

Aim
to practise listening for general and specific understanding; to contextualise noun phrases in news stories

6 Organise the class into groups of four to predict the content of the news stories from the headlines. Monitor and help with ideas and vocabulary. In feedback, you could write up any useful language students came up with when predicting.

Teacher development: predicting the content of listening texts

Predicting content creates an interesting and motivating pre-listening task which prepares students for what they are about to listen to, creates a motivating first task (listening to confirm predictions), and gives you an opportunity to elicit or pre-teach any key words students may need which will come up in the listening. Here are some suggested tasks:
1 Ask students to predict the content from any clues on the page – photos, headlines or titles, the questions in the first listening task, the topic of the unit / lesson.
2 Ask students to predict words or phrases they expect to hear in the text.
3 Write key words or phrases on the board before listening, check their meaning, and ask students to say what they reveal about the likely content of the listening.
4 Make sure students are clear about the text type, the task, and the number of speakers and their relationship before they listen. Ask them what they can predict about the text from this knowledge.

7 🔊 18 Ask students to read the situation and the task.
• Play the recording. Students listen and note answers. Let students compare answers in pairs. In feedback, elicit answers. At this stage, ask students whether the actual stories differed from their predictions, and, if so, to what extent.

Answers
1 A high-level manager at Jazz Drinks is said to have sold crucial strategic information to Pit-Pots for over two million dollars.
2 TV presenter Jonas Bakeman is fighting to save his career after stories appeared of his affair with a researcher on his programme, 'Justice Fight'.
3 Campaigners have claimed victory in their battle against full body scanners in airports, saying it is a gross invasion of privacy as the scanners can see through clothing.

4 Farmer Tim Langford has agreed to the pink statue of his prize-winning pig being relocated to a nearby sculpture gallery after many complained about it.

Let students decide on least serious to most serious. Story 4 is, perhaps, the least serious, 1 is very serious because it involves a criminal act, but students may argue that 2 (a person's reputation) and 3 (a fight for a cause) may claim to be more serious.

🎧 18
1
A manager of the soft drinks company Jazz Drinks is standing trial today accused of spying for its biggest rival, Pit-Pots. Dan Craddock, a high-level manager at Jazz, is said to have sold crucial strategic information to Pit-Pots for over two million dollars. Over recent years, the two companies have been engaged in a fierce battle to capture market share, pouring money into ever more extravagant advertising campaigns. Last year was Jazz Drinks' best ever, and, as Pit-Pots was losing ground, it is claimed they secretly recruited Mr Craddock, a sales director at Jazz, to pass on information on marketing and pricing strategy for the coming year. Mr Craddock denies the charges. The case continues.

2
The TV presenter Jonas Bakeman is fighting to save his career after stories appeared of his affair with a researcher on his programme, 'Justice Fight'. As reporters laid siege outside his home, he released a statement expressing regret over the affair, but defended himself against allegations that he'd initiated it after aggressively pursuing the woman, Petra Campbell. He claimed the affair had been brief and he had simply surrendered to a foolish moment of weakness at a production party. However, Ms Campbell has made available evidence that she had been bombarded with emails and text messages of a personal nature and that the affair had been far from 'brief'. Bosses of the TV company are to meet tomorrow to consider Mr Bakeman's future.

3
Campaigners have claimed victory in their battle against full body scanners in airports following a court decision supporting a woman who refused to accept a scan. A number of civil liberties groups had joined forces to back the woman in an attempt to defeat the government's proposals that everyone travelling by plane should have to pass through the machines. The campaigners say it is a gross invasion of privacy as the scanners can see through clothing. The government has said that it will not retreat in its policy and believes the scanners play a crucial role in protecting the public from terrorism. It plans to appeal against the decision.

4
And finally, peace has now broken out in the village of Paulston. A dispute had been raging over a statue of St John of Bidshire, the multi-prize-winning pig of local farmer Tim Langford. The three-metre pink sculpture, which had been standing at the entrance of the village for over a year, had split the village, with half saying it was hideous, while supporters of Mr Langford said it stood as a proud symbol of the local produce for which Paulston is famous. Protesters had marched onto Mr Langford's land and sprayed the statue with paint. There were then revenge attacks against the vandals. Now the local council has stepped in as peacemaker to solve the dispute. Mr Langford has agreed to the statue being relocated to a nearby sculpture gallery, but it will be moved back to the village during the three-day summer festival.

8 🎧 18 Play the recording again. Students listen and note which answers are true. Let them compare answers in pairs. In feedback, elicit answers.

Answers
1a Dan Craddock has been found guilty of spying.
NOT TRUE – he has been accused
1b Mr Craddock was a manager for Pit-Pots.
NOT TRUE – he was a manager for Jazz Drinks
1c Jazz Drinks has a bigger market share now.
TRUE – Pit-Pots was losing ground
2a Jonas Bakeman is in danger of losing his job.
TRUE – he's fighting to save his career
2b Bakeman spoke to the press and fully apologised.
NOT TRUE – he expressed regret, which isn't the same as fully apologising, and then went on to defend himself, saying he didn't aggressively pursue the woman in question
2c Ms Campbell claims she didn't initiate the affair.
NOT STATED – Ms Campbell has made evidence available to show Mr Bakeman pursued her and that the affair was not brief, but she doesn't say that she didn't initiate it (There WERE allegations, but we can't 100% say that she made them.)
3a A court decided people didn't have to submit to body scans at airports.
TRUE – court decision supported woman who refused to accept a scan
3b One lobby group funded the woman's defence.
NOT TRUE – a number of civil liberties groups joined forces
3c The government has accepted the ruling.
NOT TRUE – it will not retreat and it plans to appeal
4a Pig farming is an important industry in Paulston.
TRUE – local produce for which it's famous
4b Both sides in the dispute inflicted some kind of damage.
TRUE – protestors sprayed the statue ... then there were revenge attacks against the vandals
4c The sides agreed a settlement between themselves.
NOT TRUE – local council stepped in as peacemaker

9 🔊 **19** Ask students to work in pairs to complete the sentences based on the listening.
• Play the recording. Students listen and check their answers. Let them compare answers in pairs. In feedback, elicit answers.

Answers
1 fierce / to capture market share
2 on marketing / pricing strategy / the coming
3 expressing regret over the affair
4 text / of a personal nature
5 against full body scanners / airports
6 crucial / in protecting / public from
7 multi-prize-winning pig of
8 proud / local produce for which

🔊 **19**
1 The two companies have been engaged in a fierce battle to capture market share.
2 ... to pass on information on marketing and pricing strategy for the coming year.
3 He released a statement expressing regret over the affair.
4 She had been bombarded with emails and text messages of a personal nature.
5 Campaigners have claimed victory in their battle against full body scanners in airports.
6 The scanners play a crucial role in protecting the public from terrorism.
7 ... a statue of St John of Bidshire, the multi-prize-winning pig of local farmer Tim Langford.
8 It stood as a proud symbol of the local produce for which Paulston is famous.

Optional extra activity Show the following sentences on the board and ask students to write them in their language:
They've been pouring money into ever more extravagant advertising campaigns.
Last year was Jazz Drinks' best ever.
It comes against a backdrop of ever-increasing tension.
There are more weapons than ever on our streets.
As ever, she managed to calm things down.
The government is, as ever, committed to peace.
Remove the English sentences from the board, and ask students to translate their sentences back into English. Then show the originals again for them to compare.

10 Organise the class into small groups to discuss stories. Give students a short time to prepare their ideas first.
• Monitor closely and note interesting and useful language, as well as errors. Use the feedback to point out good examples, correct errors, and provide examples of how students can express their ideas better.

Optional extra activity Bring in today's newspapers, or ask students to find English language newspapers online (for example, theguardian.com, telegraph.co.uk). Give groups one minute to skim the headlines and find a story worth telling. Ask them to read the story they choose then report it to the class in their own words.

SPEAKING

Aim
to practise language from the lesson in a debate

11 This is an opportunity for students to practise their debating skills. Decide which subjects to debate as a class. You could do this by getting students to vote on which statements are the most interesting, or by finding out which topics divide opinion most clearly in the class.
• Organise the class into two groups. In a small class, ask students to decide which group to be in.

Teacher development: preparation time with large classes

Preparing for open-class activities, like a debate, when your class is large can be demanding. Asking ten students, say, to form a group and discuss ideas is not practical. So, if you have a large class, organise the class into four groups instead of two. Two groups are in agreement with the statements. Two groups are opposed. Let students prepare in small groups then share ideas with the groups who prepared for the same argument before beginning the debate. You could have four speakers in the debate presenting ideas, two on one side, two on the other.

12 Give groups five to ten minutes to prepare their ideas. Each group should also choose a spokesperson (or perhaps two spokespeople, who deliver half the argument each). Monitor and help with ideas and vocabulary.

13 Ask the debating group to come out to the front of the class to debate the first statement. The rest of the class must listen and decide on the winner at the end. Encourage the watching students to ask follow-up questions to challenge information used by speakers in the debate.

14 When students have finished, ask them to debate the second statement in the same way.
• Once you have fed back on content, look at good language that students used, and language students didn't quite use correctly. Show students better ways of saying what they were trying to say. You could write some useful new phrases on the board with gaps and ask the whole class to complete the sentences.

Web research activity
• Ask students to type some of the extended war metaphors from the lesson into a search engine. They should find and note which news stories are revealed. For example, typing 'a battle of wills' revealed a news story about how the government and doctors in the UK are in a struggle about work and conditions.
• In a future lesson, ask students to briefly tell groups about their news story and how it relates to the metaphor.

VIDEO 3 THE BRAILLE HUBBLE
Student's Book page 58

Aim
to find out about astronomy books for blind children; to improve students' ability to follow and understand fast speech in a video extract; to practise fast speech and to improve pronunciation, stress and intonation

1 Lead in to the topic by asking students to look at the photo and say what they can see. Organise the class into pairs to discuss the questions. In feedback, elicit students' ideas and write up interesting ideas or pieces of language on the board.

Culture notes

The photo is called The Pillars of Creation. It shows the Eagle Nebula, a young open cluster of stars in the constellation Serpens. The photo was taken by NASA.

2 ▢◀13 Give students time to read through the task first. Students watch and note their answers. Let them compare in pairs before discussing as a class.

Answers
1 It is aimed at children who are blind or have sight problems.
2 Each photo comes with a transparent plastic sheet overlay covered with raised dots and ridges, giving visually impaired readers a feel for the limitless reaches of space.
3 Their opinions and feedback shaped the way the book was presented to people who are blind around the world.

3 ▢◀13 Organise the class into pairs to discuss the questions. As students watch the video, they should add to and correct their notes. Let them compare answers in pairs once more.

Answers
1 No
2 The student says: '... it says red for sulphur, green for hydrogen and blue for oxygen, but the problem with that is, I can't tell the different coloured gases, these lines are all the same.'
3 Noreen says: 'We can bring images that people might have only imagined, and we can bring it close to them so people can understand what these objects are in the universe and I think better understand their place within the universe.'
4 The students were happy just to be involved at first, then they realised their opinions would shape the way the book was presented to people who are blind around the world.
5 Part of the problem with the early versions of the plastic overlays is that they had touch points for everything in the photograph. Fingers got lost in the galaxy of dots and ridges. Later versions of the book provided more room to manoeuvre.

4 Ask students to work individually to complete the sentences. Elicit the first answer to get them started. Let students compare their answers in pairs before discussing as a class.

Answers
1 way
2 sheet
3 ridges
4 feel
5 place
6 prototype
7 room
8 window

Background language notes for teachers

prototype = the first form of something new, made before it is produced in large quantities
ridges = raised line along the surface of something

5 This exercise offers students the chance to relate the topic of the video to their own experiences, ideas and opinions. Organise the class into small groups of four or five to discuss the questions.
• Monitor closely and note interesting and useful language, as well as errors. Use the feedback to point out good examples, correct errors, and to provide examples of how students can express their ideas better. You could ask students to correct or fill in gaps in sentences you've written on the board, based on what you heard students saying.

Understanding fast speech

6 ▢◀14 Play the recording. Students listen and write what they hear. Let them compare in pairs.

7 ▢◀15 Students listen again to a slower version to check and improve what they have written. Let them compare answers in pairs.

8 Students check what they wrote in File 10 on page 189. Encourage them to practise saying the extract.

Video script ▢◀13
Narrator: From the endless reaches of space images that delight the eye are admired in a most unlikely place: a Colorado school for the deaf and blind.
Student 1: Are these stars?
Narrator: Where students have the universe at their fingertips.
Nimer Jaber: I got Jupiter.
Student 2: That ones, of these shows the arms of the galaxies.
Student 3: Let's see, I see those moons and, um, I see like those, the stars.
Narrator: Images taken by the Hubble Space Telescope have found their way into a classroom for students with different levels of vision loss. These are the critics who were chosen to review a new book that displays some of the most spectacular space images ever produced.

Student 2: Now it says red for sulphur, green for hydrogen and blue for oxygen, but the problem with that is, I can't tell the different coloured gases, these lines are all the same.

Narrator: The book is called *Touch the Universe: A NASA Braille Book of Astronomy*. Each photo comes with a transparent plastic sheet overlay covered with raised dots and ridges, giving visually impaired readers a feel for the limitless reaches of space.

Nimer Jaber: I always wondered about space, you know, what it feels like, what it, you know what ... how big it really was.

Noreen Grice: I mean you can't just reach out and touch the stars, nobody can, but we can bring it to people's fingertips. We can bring images that people might have only imagined, and we can bring it close to them so people can understand what these objects are in the universe and I think better understand their place within the universe.

Narrator: When asked to feel test prototypes of the book, the students were happy just to be involved, then they realised their opinions would shape the way the book was presented to people who are blind around the world.

Ben Wentworth: Then they started ... tearing the images up.

Narrator: Part of the problem with early versions of the plastic overlays is that they had touch points for everything in the photograph. Fingers got lost in the galaxy of dots and ridges. Later versions of the book provided more room to manoeuvre.

Nimer Jaber: It has great pictures, I can, you know ... you could feel them better, you could, you know, you know what their shapes are.

Narrator: Revisions were duly noted.

Noreen Grice: Alright, I can, I can make that change in the plate.

Student 2: Yeah, and that's all I really ... the suggestions I have.

Noreen Grice: OK.

Narrator: Exactly what these students see in their mind's eye remains a mystery for sighted people.

Student 1: This one reminds me of ... onion rings.

Narrator: Still it's clear that with each raised ridge and dot, an image of space that makes sense reveals itself.

Student 4: That's pretty cool.

Ben Wentworth: To get the kids to say, 'Oh, that's what you're seeing.' And I ... that's what's so unique about the Hubble book.

Narrator: The images provided by the Hubble Space Telescope continue to astonish and amaze and provide a window on the wonders of space, no matter how you see them.

REVIEW 3
Student's Book page 59

Aim
to consolidate vocabulary and grammar from Units 5 and 6

Answers
1
1 could	6 come
2 did	7 competition
3 about	8 war
4 who	9 big
5 battle	10 only

2
1 had floods of emails complaining
2 after / following the creation of the
3 the tip of the iceberg
4 wouldn't bombard me with
5 had joined forces
6 two-week course taught by (run by)

3
1 hadn't	4 dating
2 ground	5 from the hotel
3 army	

4
Possible answers:
The notorious American politician **Joel Riley**, who was the subject of a shocking documentary about corruption and the cigarette industry a few years ago, **gives a talk** at New Haven College tonight, promoting his new book and explaining why he's really not as bad as people think he is.
The Nobel-Prize-winning scientist **Joel Riley**, who is perhaps best known for his ground-breaking work on the ways in which cells repair damaged DNA, **gives a talk** tonight as part of our free webinar series, available to all subscribers of the Science Today channel.

5
Possible answers:
1 **Books**: (have a serious / a fatal / a major) flaw, plot (develops) / follow the plot, (a likeable / the main) protagonist, (display real / limited / be full of) insight, (a moving) memoir
2 **War**: (be under / lay) siege, talks (break down), (negotiate / declare a) ceasefire, (suffer / impose) sanctions, (cause) casualties

6
1 d	3 i	5 j	7 h	9 c
2 a	4 b	6 g	8 e	10 f

7
1 out of	3 over	5 around
2 from	4 in	6 into

8
1 annoyances	4 lasting
2 resolution	5 overwhelming
3 responsibility	6 notable

9
1 traces	7 stage
2 overthrow	8 seize
3 signed / signs	9 track down
4 rages	10 defeat
5 surrendering	11 gripping
6 undermining	12 yawning

7 SCIENCE AND RESEARCH

SPEAKING

Aim
to set the scene and introduce the theme with a photo; to get students talking about science and scientists

1 Start by telling the class that in this unit they're going to be talking about areas of work in the field of science, news stories about science, science fiction films, and the uses and abuses of statistics; students will also study how to express surprise and disbelief, and form nouns and adjectives.
• Ask students to look at the photo on pages 60–61. Ask: *What can you see?* Elicit a brief description of the photo, and introduce any key words students might need.
• Organise the class into pairs to discuss the questions. Go round the room and check students are doing the task and help with ideas and vocabulary if necessary.
• In feedback, ask different pairs to tell the class what they discussed.
• Once you have fed back on content, look at good language that students used, and language students didn't quite use correctly.

> **Possible answers**
> Other major projects worldwide:
> The Relativistic Heavy Ion Collider on Long Island, New York where scientists are trying to re-create the conditions that existed during the first millionth of a second after the big bang.
> The Very Large Array (VLA) in New Mexico is one of the largest telescopes in the world.
> Juno is an orbiter in Space on a mission to Jupiter.
> the International Space Station

Culture notes

The Large Hadron Collider (LHC) was built by the European Organisation for Nuclear Research (CERN) between 1998 and 2008. It is the largest single machine in the world, and the world's largest and most powerful particle collider. Built in collaboration with over 10,000 scientists and engineers from over 100 countries, it lies in a tunnel 27 kilometres in circumference, 175 metres beneath the Swiss-French border near Geneva.
The LHC was built to test different theories of particle physics and high-energy physics, including the nature of dark matter and the existence of the Higgs Boson. It fires protons at extraordinary speeds around a tunnel circuit, and analyses the data that is produced when the protons collide with each other.

2 Mix the pairs so that students are working with someone new. Ask students to discuss the questions. Go round the room and check students are doing the task and help with ideas and vocabulary if necessary.

• Once you have fed back on content, look at good language that students used, and language students didn't quite use correctly during the activity.

> **Possible answers**
> Some famous scientists: Albert Einstein (physicist); Marie Curie (chemist); Charles Darwin (biologist); Stephen Hawking (mathematician and physicist); Louis Pasteur (chemist); Jacques Cousteau (marine biologist); Isaac Newton; Galileo Galilei; Archimedes
> Kinds of scientists (the stress is underlined):
> agricultural scientist: someone who studies commercial plants, animals and cultivation techniques to improve the productivity and sustainability of farms and agricultural industries
> anthropologist: someone who studies human societies, customs and beliefs
> astronomer: someone who studies the stars and planets using scientific equipment, including telescopes
> neurologist: a doctor who's an expert in the study of the nervous system and the diseases that affect it
> geologist: a scientist who studies the structure of the earth, how it was formed and how it's changed over time
> hydrologist: a scientist who studies the properties, distribution, and effects of water on the earth's surface, in the soil and underlying rocks, and in the atmosphere
> immunologist: someone who studies how diseases can be prevented and how the immune system works
> marine biologist: someone who studies life in the oceans and seas
> military scientist: someone who studies military processes, institutions and behaviour, along with the study of warfare, and the theory and application of organised coercive force
> educational psychologist: someone who is concerned with helping children or young people who are experiencing problems within an educational setting with the aim of enhancing their learning. Challenges may include social or emotional problems or learning difficulties.

Optional extra activity 1 Ask students in pairs or groups to think of as many words as they can that they associate with the scientists (e.g. geologist: *rocks, excavate, fossils*).

Optional extra activity 2 You could extend Exercise 2 into a mingle. Students go round and ask each other about the different kinds of scientist, and find people who can both define them and give famous examples of the types of scientist.

Teacher development: mingles

It is a good idea to encourage students to get out of their chairs, walk round, and speak to a number of students in mingles or milling activities when they're practising new language. It creates a more realistic task than just talking in pairs or open class. It also encourages interaction between students who don't often speak to each other. It creates variety and a change of focus in class. Here are some management tips:

1 Provide lots of preparation time so students are clear about their role and what they need to say.
2 Participate in the mingle to provide a good model of what you want students to say.
3 Set clear time limits and goals. So, tell students how long they have, how many people they must speak to, and what they must find out, before they do the mingle.
4 Ensure there is a good space for students to use. This could involve moving desks, or moving students to a clear space in the room. Make sure you plan this before doing the mingle.
5 At the end, ask students to sit down, and feed back on both content and errors.

Communicative outcomes

In this two-page spread, students will practise talking about science; they will practise telling science news stories, and expressing surprise and disbelief.

VOCABULARY Talking about science

Aim

to introduce and practise words and phrases to talk about science

1 Start by writing some of the words in the box on the board (e.g. *adverse, carry out, root*) and asking students if they can give you a synonym or antonym for the words.
• Ask students to replace the words in italics in the sentences with the synonyms. You could elicit the answer to the first to get them started.
• In feedback, ask them to justify their decisions, and check any unknown words by providing definitions or examples. Model and drill any words that are difficult to pronounce or stress correctly.

Answers	
1 step forward	7 lead to
2 root	8 reproduce
3 remove	9 due
4 inserted	10 adverse
5 a slippery slope	11 disorder
6 carried out	12 devised

Background language notes for teachers

A slippery slope and *the thin end of the wedge* are two synonymous idioms. They describe an action or procedure of little importance in itself, but one likely to lead to more serious developments. They are often used when criticising an action, e.g. *It might seem OK to make students carry ID cards. But it's a slippery slope / the thin end of the wedge in my view – soon everybody will be forced to carry one.*

2 Ask students to work in pairs to test each other on how well they can remember the words.

Optional extra activity Write down three famous scientific breakthroughs on the board:
Gutenberg's invention of the printing press
Newton's discovery of the law of gravity
Einstein's theory of relativity
Ask students to describe them using phrases from Exercise 1.

LISTENING

Aim
to practise listening to confirm predictions and take notes

3 Start by giving students a minute to read the headlines on their own. Check that they understand them, and deal with any words or phrases they're not sure of.
• Organise the class into pairs to discuss the headlines. In feedback, elicit ideas from the whole class, and accept any plausible ideas.

4 🔊 20 Play the recording. Students listen and note answers.

5 Organise the class into pairs to compare notes. Ask students to reconstruct and retell as much of the stories they heard about as they can. Monitor and notice how well students can do this task.
• In feedback, round up ideas from the whole class. Accept whatever comes back, so long as it's accurate. Try wherever possible to rephrase student ideas using actual language from the listening itself.

> **Answers**
> Work with the notes students take – there are no specific answers here.
> Conversation 1 (Scientists successfully transplant mosquito nose)
> Conversation 2 (Backing for space sun shield)

🔊 20
Conversation 1
A: Did you read that thing about transplanting the noses of mosquitoes?
B: What? Are you serious? I didn't think mosquitoes even had noses!
A: Yeah, well, it's obviously not a nose in the sense of our noses, but apparently it's like the smelling receptors on the antennae on their heads ... and what they do is they somehow get these receptors to grow inside frog's eggs so that they can do tests on them.
B: How on earth do they do that?
A: To be perfectly honest, I'm not really sure. They extract the DNA from the receptors or something and then insert it into the eggs. It's a bit beyond me, really. I just thought it was amazing.
B: It sounds a bit peculiar, if you ask me. I mean, what's the point?
A: Well, apparently, they use them to see what smells trigger the receptors.
B: And?
A: Well, it's to stop the spread of malaria. Obviously, mosquitoes are strongly attracted to the smell of human sweat, but if they can find smells which create a bigger stimulus or which produce no trigger, then they could use those smells to manufacture traps to tempt the mosquitoes away from humans or spray-on repellents that mask human smells.

B: OK. I suppose that makes sense. I have to say, though, I still find all that gene manipulation a bit worrying.
A: What do you mean?
B: Well, it's a slippery slope, isn't it? One moment it's mosquito noses, the next they'll be engineering babies.
A: Come off it! It's hardly the same thing!

Conversation 2
C: Did you read that thing about building a sun shield in space to prevent global warming?
D: No. It sounds a bit unlikely, though. I mean, how big would it have to be?
C: Well, apparently, about 60,000 miles long!
D: 60,000! That's ridiculous! I mean, how on earth are they going to build something that big, let alone get it up there? They struggle to build a stadium here on time and on budget.
C: Well, that's it – the idea with this is it's not like one big structure; it's millions of little reflectors which form a massive 'cloud'.
D: But how many would you need?
C: Trillions. They reckon if they launched a pile of these things every five minutes or so, it'd take ten years to make.
D: Hardly an instant solution, then!
C: No.
D: And what about the cost?
C: I've no idea, to be honest, but they claim it's all quite possible. Anyway, this guy got a grant to look into it further.
D: You're joking! What a waste of money! Are you sure it isn't just a scam or some made-up story?
C: It was on a fairly reliable website. They wouldn't have just made it up.
D: Pah! Mind you, I sometimes wonder whether the whole climate change thing isn't all just a scam. I mean, there are a lot of rich and powerful people out there who stand to benefit from us being scared into believing it's all true.
C: You're not serious, are you?
D: Yeah, why not?
C: Because the evidence is pretty conclusive.
D: Says who?

6 🔊 20 Ask students to complete the sentences based on the listening. Let them compare answers with a partner.
• Play the recording again. Students listen and check answers. Let students compare answers in pairs again. You could play and pause if you think students will have problems noticing the phrases.

> **Answers**
> Conversation 1
> 1 How on earth
> 2 a bit beyond me
> 3 if you ask me
> 4 that makes sense
> 5 Come off it

Conversation 2
6 let alone
7 Hardly an instant solution
8 You're joking
9 Mind you, I sometimes wonder
10 Says who

7   Ask students to discuss the questions in pairs. Go round the room and check students are doing the task and help with ideas and vocabulary if necessary.
• Once you have fed back on content, look at good language that students used, and / or language students didn't quite use correctly during the activity.

Optional extra activity   Show the following sentences on the board and ask students to write them in their language:
It's hardly the same thing!
Hardly an instant solution, then!
It's hardly surprising people are concerned about it.
Hardly a day goes by without hearing one of these stories.
I hardly know anyone who agrees with it.
There's hardly any funding available for research into it.
Remove the English sentences from the board, and ask students to translate their sentences back into English. Then show the originals again for them to compare.

DEVELOPING CONVERSATIONS
Expressing surprise and disbelief

Aim
to introduce and practise ways of expressing surprise and disbelief

8   ✎ 21 Read through the information in the box as a class.
• Play the recording. Students listen and repeat. It is a good idea to play the first two or three questions and ask students what they notice (see notes below). Then play all the sentences, pausing so that students can repeat after each one.

✎ 21
1 What on earth for?
2 Why on earth would they want to do that?
3 What on earth's that?
4 Who on earth would buy something like that?
5 Where on earth are they going to get the money for that?
6 What on earth is he going on about?

Background language notes for teachers

In these questions, *on earth* goes between the question word and the auxiliary verb. There is linking between *on* and *earth*, and the word *earth* is very strongly stressed. Encourage students to make sure their intonation rises over the strongly stressed word.
to go on about something = to talk at length and without coming to the point
Less common alternatives to ... *on earth* include *Why in the world ...? Who in creation ...?*

9   Start by eliciting a possible question for the first comment from the class. Then ask students to work in pairs to prepare possible questions. Elicit good examples from students, and correct or rephrase any errors.

Possible answers
1 What on earth is a Nanobridge? / What on earth is one of those? What on earth is that?
2 What on earth for? / Why on earth do they want to do that? / How on earth did they do that?
3 Where on earth is that? / Why on earth have they based themselves there?
4 What on earth for? / Why on earth do / would they want to do that?
5 What on earth for? / Why on earth would you do something like that? / What on earth will that involve, then?
6 What on earth for? / Why on earth would anyone want to buy them? / How on earth did they create them?

10   Model the activity first with a reliable student. Ask them to read out the first comment, respond with a question using *on earth*, then try to continue the conversation with the student for as long as possible.
• Organise the class into pairs to try out conversations using the other comments and their prepared questions. You could mix pairs to encourage a degree of improvisation. Tell students to try out conversations two or three times. Practice makes perfect. Monitor and correct any errors with form or pronunciation.
• Note that it doesn't really matter if the students don't know what these things are, e.g. a nanobridge or where Flitwick is. The point is to try and keep a dialogue going, even if they're inventing rather crazy things on the spot.

Possible answers
Work with your students' ideas. Encourage them to be creative and humorous if they wish. Here is an example dialogue for the first situation (which also explains what a Nanobridge is):
1
We're developing a Nanobridge.
  What on earth is a Nanobridge?
It's a way of supporting wireless connections.
  You mean wifi?
That's right. It's very technological.
  OK. Too complicated for me then, I guess.

Teacher development: modelling activities

A useful way of introducing pairwork speaking activities is to model the activity first. If students have seen a clear model of what they are trying to achieve when they speak, they are likely to speak longer and more accurately, and to feel inspired to try to achieve a good result. It also has the advantage of being clearer than long-winded spoken instructions. Here are some suggestions:
1 Model by yourself. In other words, say the first line of a given or improvised dialogue as Speaker A, then turn and respond as Speaker B.

2 Model with a reliable student. Nominate a student you can trust to act out the model dialogue with you.

3 Model with three or four students. Act out the required example exchange with three or four class members so that everybody feels involved.

4 Use a student-to-student model. Ask one pair to show the rest of the class what is expected in the dialogue.

CONVERSATION PRACTICE

Aim
to practise language from the lesson in a free, communicative, personalised speaking activity

11 Organise the class into groups of three. Ask each group to decide who is A, who B, and who C. Tell them to find their information pages (pages 187, 190 and 195), then give them time to read their files and prepare what to say. Monitor and help with vocabulary and understanding.

12 When students are ready, they take turns to introduce the topics of their texts and to respond to their partners' queries. Encourage students to express surprise and disbelief.
• In feedback, look at good language that students used, and language students didn't quite use correctly during the activity. Show students better ways of saying what they were trying to say. You could write some useful new phrases on the board with gaps and ask the whole class to complete the sentences.

Optional extra activity This works well as a mingle. Ask students to stand up, walk round, and talk to as many students as they can in five minutes.

Web research task
• Ask students to research a surprising true science news story on the Internet.
• Ask students to present it in the next class. The class must think of ways of responding to the story.

▶ 16 Refer students to the video and activities on the DVD-ROM.

Teacher development: using the video

The video and activities on the DVD-ROM can be used in various ways:
1 as an alternative to the conversation practice
2 instead of the listening activity in some units, particularly with weaker groups. Students can first practise reading out the dialogues and work on some of the key phrases / structures in a controlled way before having a go themselves.
3 at the end of the unit as a revision exercise

THE TEST OF TIME
Student's Book pages 64–65

Communicative outcomes
In this two-page spread, students read about and discuss science fiction films.

SPEAKING

Aim
to introduce the theme of the reading text; to get students motivated and interested in the topic

1 Ask students to discuss the questions in groups of three to five. Go round the room and check students are doing the task and help with ideas and vocabulary if necessary.
• In feedback, ask different groups to tell the class what they discussed.
• Once you have fed back on content, look at good language that students used, and language students didn't quite use correctly during the activity.

Culture notes

The Time Machine = Originally, this was a novella by British author HG Wells, published in 1895. Hollywood film versions were made in 1960 and 2002. In the original story a time traveller uses the machine to go forward into the future where he meets a race of beautiful, incurious people called the Eloi who are routinely captured by a race of underground people called the Morlocks. Wells uses the story to reflect his own socialist political views, his view on life and abundance, and the contemporary angst about industrial relations.
Avatar = A 2009 film directed by James Cameron, notable for its huge budget and amazing special effects. Humans are colonising Pandora, a distant moon, in order to mine a super-conductor, and their actions threaten the existence of the Na'vi, a humanoid species. As the review the students will read says, Cameron explores issues such as colonisation, exploitation of resources, and control of the Web.
Star Wars = An epic film series comprising seven films with two more planned. The first film released, directed by George Lucas in 1977, is a battle between good and evil – the Empire against the Rebel Alliance.
Godzilla = Called *Gojira* in Japanese, Godzilla is a monster or *daikaiju* originating from a series of *tokusatsu* films of the same name from Japan. It looks a bit like a large carnivorous dinosaur and first appeared in Ishirō Honda's 1954 film *Godzilla*. Today it is a worldwide pop culture icon, appearing in video games, novels, comic books and TV shows. There have been 28 Japanese *Gojira* movies, and two Hollywood films.
The Stepford Wives = Originally a 1975 film based on a novel by Ira Levin, it tells the story a young housewife who moves to a suburban estate and is surprised by how perfect and submissive all the other wives are. She realises they have been turned into robots by their husbands, a fate that catches up with her at the end of the film. It is a powerful feminist statement about the

role of women and the way they were thwarted by their husbands at the time. There was a 2004 remake starring Nicole Kidman.
Interstellar = Directed by Christopher Nolan in 2014, the film is about a crew of astronauts who travel through a wormhole to find a new home for humanity.

Optional extra activity Ask students to research the films in Exercise 1 online and to say what inspired the films and what message they have.

READING

Aim
to give students practice in reading for specific information; to find and use words in the reading text

2 Ask students to read the task and to say what sort of text they expect to read (a review) and what they expect it to be about. Ask them what the subtitle 'all roar and no bite' suggests. Let students compare answers in pairs after they have read the text. In feedback, elicit answers from the class, and encourage them to justify their ideas.

> **Possible answers**
> New *Godzilla* – good special effects but poor story – message doesn't carry weight – misses the point
> *Gojira* – very meaningful for the time – though laughably unrealistic
> *Stepford Wives* (mid 1970s) – very good – a chilling thriller
> New *Stepford Wives* – poor – a lame comedy
> *Avatar* – standing the test of time – incredible 3D – resonates – like all the best sci fi ...

3 Ask students to read the eight statements and decide whether they are true, false or not mentioned. Let students compare with their partner. Tell students to read the text again to check and confirm answers.
• Monitor and be available to prompt and help at this stage. In feedback, elicit answers from the class, and ask them to justify their answers by reference to the text.

> **Answers**
> 1 F (*the original "Godzilla"'s box office success* – this is the film *Gojira*)
> 2 T (*make it more real, more impressive. Of course, in terms of special effects they have ...*)
> 3 T (*at the time of an accelerating arms race*)
> 4 T (*few would place nuclear war high on their list of priorities*)
> 5 T (*submit to their husbands' wills*)
> 6 N
> 7 T (*companies exploiting private data and governments spying*)
> 8 N

4 Organise the class into pairs to discuss the questions. Encourage students to explain their reasons.
• Monitor closely and note interesting and useful language, as well as errors. Use the feedback to point out good examples, correct errors, and to provide examples of how students can express their ideas better.

5 Ask students to complete the sentences. Let them compare their answers with their partner. In feedback, elicit answers from the class.

> **Answers**
> 1 prompts   6 stood
> 2 reflected   7 resonated
> 3 addresses   8 parallels
> 4 unfolds   9 metaphor
> 5 came out   10 hanging

6 Organise the class into small groups to discuss the questions. Mix students so that they are with people they haven't worked with earlier in the lesson.
• In feedback, look at good language that students used, and language students didn't quite use correctly during the activity. Show students better ways of saying what they were trying to say.

> **Possible answers**
> 1 Frankenstein
> 2 Mad Men
> 3 Amour
> 4 2001: A Space Odyssey
> 5 A Clockwork Orange
> 6 Jaws
> 7 Wild Tales
> 8 a Shakespeare play
> 9 Rise of the Planet of the Apes
> 10 Lord of the Rings: The Fellowship of the Ring

UNDERSTANDING VOCABULARY
Forming nouns and adjectives

Aim
to introduce and practise ways of forming nouns or adjectives by adding suffixes

7 Read through the information in the box with the class.
• Ask students to complete the rules individually. Elicit the first answer to get them started. Let students compare their answers in pairs.
• As you go through the answers, you might ask students to give you examples (see Answers below).

> **Answers**
> 1 adjectives based on nouns
> 2 adjectives based on verbs
> 3 nouns based on adjectives
> 4 nouns based on verbs
>
> Here are some common examples students will already know: *comical, commercial, industrial, musical, practical, funny, messy, colourless, wonderful, useful, creative, active, bored, interested, interesting, laughable, irritant, density, tolerance, movement, sensation, variance.*

Background language notes for teachers: pronunciation

As well as rules of form, there are also rules of pronunciation and stress involved in adding suffixes. You may wish to point out the following:
When adding the suffixes below, a word is stressed one syllable before the suffix:
-ic, -tion / -sion, -ish
For example: re*la*tion
When adding the suffixes below, a word is stressed two syllables before the suffix:
-cy, -ty, -gy, -phy, -fy, -ian, -ate
For example: ge*o*graphy

8 Ask students to correct the sentences individually. Elicit the first answer to get them started. Tell students that some sentences have more than one. Let students compare answers in pairs.

> **Answers**
> 1 I don't get the point of films about time travel when it's a complete **impossibility**.
> 2 I hate the utter **stupidity** of action films. They're just meaningless.
> 3 The **technological** advances over the last 50 years are incredibly **impressive**.
> 4 The level of **ignorance** of science among the public is a big concern.
> 5 **Investment** in space **exploration** is a total waste of money!
> 6 There's great **reluctance** to take **preventative** measures against global warming.
> 7 Scientists are not sufficiently **reflective** about the **implications** of their research.
> 8 I'm a bit **cynical** about drug companies' **involvement** in medical research.

9 Organise the class into small groups to discuss the questions. Encourage students to explain their reasons.
• In feedback, look at good language that students used, and language students didn't quite use correctly during the activity. Show students better ways of saying what they were trying to say.

Optional extra activity Ask students in pairs to look at the first paragraph of the text on page 65 and find as many words as they can that could be changed by adding a suffix. Here are some answers: speculate (-*tion*), doubt (-*ful, -less*), ambitious (-*tion*), original (-*ity*), success (-*ful*), thought (-*less*), impressive (-*ion*), effects (effective), point (-*less*). You could ask students to make a sentence with the new words they create to ensure they can use them in context.

Communicative outcomes
In this two-page spread, students will discuss statistics and practise using passive forms.

SPEAKING

Aim
to introduce the theme; to get students motivated and interested in the topic

1 Organise the class into small groups to discuss the questions. Go round the room and check students are doing the task and help with ideas and vocabulary if necessary.
• In feedback, ask different groups to tell the class what they discussed.
• Once you have fed back on content, look at good language that students used, and language students didn't quite use correctly during the activity.

> **Possible answers**
> Important uses of data and statistics include samples, surveys and polls in the advertising industry, polling in politics and elections, using statistical data to test cars and other machines, using statistics in a census of the population.

VOCABULARY Statistics

Aim
to introduce and practise phrases used when talking about statistics

2 Ask students to complete the sentences individually. Elicit the first answer to get them started. Let students compare answers in pairs. Tell students that they can use a dictionary or ask the teacher for help if they need to check the meaning of any words.
• As you go through the answers, point out common collocations (*popular belief, a vested interest*, for example).

> **Answers**
> | | |
> |---|---|
> | 1 belief | 6 ends |
> | 2 research | 7 interest |
> | 3 link | 8 scrutiny |
> | 4 evidence | 9 anomaly |
> | 5 correlation | |

3 Organise the class into pairs to discuss the questions. Encourage the use of phrases from Exercise 2, and as you monitor pick up any useful and accurate phrases students use which you could highlight in feedback. Note that the topic of the answers below comes up in the listening so you might give limited feedback to focus on correct use of language rather than the factual truth and details of students answers.

Possible answers

1 The commissioning person may have a vested interest in a result. The company might twist the figures to suit its own ends.
2 If the data isn't collected at random, the results might not stand up to scrutiny. You get more chance of exaggerated results if the people are self-selected. Self-selection might confirm popular beliefs held by the group.
3 Usually the bigger the sample, the more accurate the results because anomalies become less important.
4 You get experts to check figures to see if they stand up to scrutiny. They spot flaws in the research. They may be less likely to have vested interests, or to have to declare them.
5 There may be some variables that weren't covered. Perhaps the results were caused by those variables rather than the ones which were included in the study. Without full context one may draw the wrong conclusions or twist them to suit. They may hide conflicting evidence.
6 People may just make the wrong connections – correlations don't necessarily prove cause. Researcher may have ignored conflicting evidence. May not be able to explain the conclusions – there is no overall theory.

LISTENING

Aim
to listen for general and detailed understanding

4 ✿22 Give students time to read the task and the question.
• Play the recording. Students listen and note answers. Let them compare their answers in pairs before discussing as a class.

Possible answers

1 The research can be used to manipulate and sell stuff (agrees with presenter + food company example). If funded for a purpose, researchers may be pressurised to get 'correct' results. They may get sacked or lose funding.
2 Self-selected groups through social media tend to attract people with similar views.
3 If the sample is too small, it exaggerates 'grouping effects' of self-selection.
4 Peer reviews filter out poor research more than anonymous publications.
5 may not have both absolute and relative figures when comparing
   may not have a full series of figures (just one or two years) or information that shows if it is a trend or an anomaly
6 Wrong conclusions can be drawn from data – may highlight an absolute or relative figure to present a 'good' result / conclusion. Correlations do not prove causal links.

✿22

P = presenter, T = Tom Hunter

P: So next, statistics – often thought to be the worst kind of lying there is! A recent survey found that 60% of Britons believed the probability of tossing a coin twice and getting two heads is 50%, rather than the correct answer of 25%. Our guest today, Tom Hunter, thinks this is a worry and says we need to get to grips with stats. Tom, welcome.

T: Hi.

P: So, what's the problem? We don't really make use of stats and probabilities in our daily lives, do we?

T: Oh my! Well, that's a common belief, but gosh! I mean, we're surrounded by statistics: opinion polls, crime figures, product claims in advertising …

P: Exactly! I mean, it's just used to sell stuff – and so we ignore it!

T: Well, of course, statistics can be used to manipulate, but they also inform policy development, scientific progress and many individual decisions. The heart of the matter is that there are good statistics and bad ones. And knowing the difference is empowering.

P: OK. So how can we tell the good from the bad?

T: Well, we need to recognise that different approaches to data collection have different degrees of validity. And we need to look for underlying problems with any research we encounter.

P: For example?

T: Well, say a food company is having some research done to see if its product has health benefits, right? It has a vested interest in the process, so researchers may get pressured into finding positive results. They may worry about not being employed again, which may affect their conclusions. Similarly, asking 50 people on social media will be less valid than a survey of 5,000 people chosen at random. That's not just because the sample size is too small, but also because social media will tend to attract people of similar views, so this grouping effect may exaggerate the results further.

P: Shouldn't publishers filter out this poor research?

T: Mmm, you'd hope so. Obviously, research in a respected journal, reviewed by other experts, will be better than something published anonymously online, but even peer reviews can underestimate aspects like sample size. And interpretations can also be wrong. So we always need to be on our guard.

P: Yeah, you mean the wrong conclusions may be drawn, whatever the data?

T: Absolutely. Take the issue of relative and absolute figures.

P: Relative and absolute?

T: Yeah. Say Company A produced 10,000 units last year and increased it to 12,000 this year. That'd be a 20% rise relative to its previous performance and an absolute increase of 2,000 units. Company B, on the other hand, produced 1,000 units last year and 1,400 this year – a rise of 40%. So by comparing the relative changes, Company B could say it performed twice as well as its rival, but in absolute terms its rival produced an extra 1,600 units compared to Company B.

P: I see.
T: But what's more, Company B may have employed more people to get its increase, while Company A may have achieved theirs whilst cutting staff. So, far from doing 100% better than a rival, Company B's actually being hugely outperformed. And, of course, one year doesn't make a trend. It could just be an anomaly.
P: Maybe they had one client who ordered a huge amount and won't repeat it.
T: Exactly. So you can see it's the focus on either a relative or absolute figure and choosing the start and end point for the figures that can be used to twist data to suit your own ends.
P: Sure. So, what about the probabilities we started with?
T: Well, the initial problem is basic maths. However, people also misunderstand how probability works as a prediction tool. They don't understand variables and the degree to which they're dependent.
P: OK ...
T: If you had just thrown a head, or indeed six heads or ten, the probability of the next throw being a head is still 50% not 25% or smaller. That's because these are random events out of your control. However, the probability of having a heart attack, say, is dependent on whether you've had one before. If you have, the risk of another is greatly increased.
P: Time to cut down on salt!
T: Well, maybe, but claims about direct correlations also need to be treated sceptically. As an extreme comparison, the fact that TV sales may increase in line with crime does not prove that one affects the other!
P: Well, you're beginning to convince me, but can you give some other examples ...

5 🎧22 Ask students to discuss what they think the numbers refer to with a partner based on the listening.
• Play the recording again. Students listen and note answers. Let them compare their answers in pairs before discussing as a class. You will need to decide whether you require students to give only the general connection or whether you want them to explain specifics in detail. Both are given in the answers below.

Answers
1 Talking about people's understanding of probability
60% of people say that if you throw a coin twice the probability of getting two heads is 50% when in fact it's 25%.
2 Talking about sample size
50 people interviewed through social media is not as good as 5,000 people chosen at random.
3 This shows how the relative figures are calculated for Company A
Initially produces 10,000 a year and this rises to 12,000 – an increase of 20%.
4 This shows how the relative figures are calculated for Company B

Initially produces 1,000 a year and the next year 1,400 – a 40% increase.
5 Comparing the relative increases, Company B can claim to be performing twice as well as its rival but in absolute terms it produces 1,600 fewer extra units over the last year than Company A.
6 50% – probability each time you throw a head

6 Organise the class into new pairs to discuss the questions. As students speak, go round and monitor, and note down any interesting pieces of language you hear. In feedback, encourage students to explain their choices.
• In feedback, look at good language that students used, and language students didn't quite use correctly during the activity. Show students better ways of saying what they were trying to say. You could write some useful new phrases on the board with gaps and ask the whole class to complete the sentences.

Possible answers
Two other variables that may affect studies into the relationship between gaming and bad behaviour:
– level of education, class or income / amount of hours played
Two examples of causal links that have been conclusively proved:
– smoking and cancer / poverty and (ill)health / education and economic performance
Two things that have not yet been proved because of conflicting evidence:
– fat and heart disease / prison sentences and crime

GRAMMAR Passives

Aim
to check students' understanding of how to form and use passives to focus on who or what an action affects

7 Read through the information in the box as a class.
• Organise the class into pairs to do the task. Monitor and notice how well students understand the rules.
• In feedback, elicit the students' answers. They can check their answers using the Grammar reference on page 173.

Answers
a Far from doing 100% better than a rival, Company B's actually being hugely outperformed. (Company A is the doer)
Company A is hugely outperforming Company B.
b Statistics can be used to manipulate, but they also inform policy development. (the doer is a person or people in general – perhaps the people, agencies or companies that commission the research)
People manipulate statistics, but they also use them (statistics) to inform policy development ...
c Researchers may get pressured into finding positive results. (the doer is a person or people in general – perhaps the people, agencies or companies that commission the research)

They (The government) may put pressure on researchers to encourage them to find positive results.

d A food company <u>is having some research done</u> to see if its product has health benefits. (the researchers are the doers)
Researchers are doing some research for a food company to see if ...

e So next statistics – <u>often thought to be</u> the worst kind of lying there is! (the doer is a person or people in general)
People often think statistics are the worst kind of lying there is.

f They may worry about not <u>being employed</u> again, which may affect their conclusions. (the doer is the person or people who do the employing – the employer)
They may be worried about losing their jobs. / They may be worried employers won't employ them.

g Obviously, research in a respected journal, <u>reviewed by other experts</u>, will be better than something <u>published</u> anonymously online. (the doers are experts and people who publish online)
Obviously, research in a respected journal, that experts have reviewed, will be better than something that people have published online.

 G **Students complete Exercise 1 in the Grammar reference on page 173.**

Answers to Exercise 1, Grammar reference
1 has been achieved
2 was given an injection
3 is believed to be
4 had one of my wisdom teeth taken
5 be supported by
6 being / getting employed by
7 is thought to be caused by a mineral
8 to be funded by

Background language notes for teachers: passives

Passive forms can sometimes look complex to students, but actually they are just *be* (or *get*) + past participle. To form different passives, you merely change or add to the auxiliary verb *be* or *get*.

In a monolingual class, it is worth looking at how the passive sentences in Exercise 7 might be translated. Other languages may avoid the passive, using reflexive forms, for example, instead. By doing a grammar comparison, students may better see how English uses the passive when the subject is unknown or not important.

Teacher development: approaches to checking grammar understanding

At this level, students are often confident about rules of grammar. Errors tend to be individual (based on ingrained problems, L1 interference, or misunderstandings) rather than collective errors that all the class share. This is particularly the case if you have a multilingual class. In such a class, the same area of grammar might seem too easy to one student but confusing to another. With this in mind it is important to bear the following in mind when checking grammar:

1 Avoid spending time 'presenting' grammar (i.e. explaining rules of form and use in an initial presentation). Instead, encourage students to show what they know, and share what they know with other students, first. This could involve matching rules to examples or analysing examples.

2 Be ready to answer queries from students. However, don't feel that you should be on the spot, and that it is your job to explain everything. Let students explain rules or misunderstandings to each other. Encourage students to research answers in the Grammar reference. Make learning about grammar a collective effort.

3 Be aware that practice, and feeding back on errors made, is more useful at this level than explaining rules. In this lesson, for example, spend more time on Exercise 8 than Exercise 7. It is more important that students have opportunities to use grammar in accuracy speaking or writing activities. Errors made here can then be explained, and learning is directed towards problems students actually have.

4 While some students may feel grammar is important, and may judge lessons on how well it is covered, others prefer to learn by using language. Encourage students to see 'grammar' as being accurate and meaningful with the language patterns they use. Let them see that using language accurately is more important than knowing the rules. Students learn more by using language patterns correctly, and being corrected when they make errors, than they do by studying rules.

8 Ask students to complete the stories individually. Elicit the first answer to get them started. Let students compare their answers in pairs before discussing as a class.

Answers
1 fell
2 had been reported
3 lead / be led
4 was dumped
5 (which was) published
6 found
7 were kept / had been kept
8 was defined
9 were forced
10 (which were) treated
11 revealed
12 (which are) conducted
13 to be tightened
14 was reduced

9 Organise the class into groups of four to discuss the problems. Refer them to the questions in Exercise 3 to guide their discussion.

10 **23** Play the recording so students can check whether they were right about the problems. In feedback, look at good language that students used, and language students didn't quite use correctly.

23

Story 1
The main issue here is that it's difficult to interpret this story without knowing the number of accidents per journey or mile travelled. If there were twice as many journeys in fair weather, then the snowstorm has indeed led to an increase in the accident rate. Really, you'd need more evidence over a period of time to fully establish a correlation between accidents and weather. It could be that bad weather really does reduce incidents due to people driving more carefully.

Story 2
The statistics themselves in this study were accurately collected and described. However, the lobby group who commissioned the study were so-called 'stay-at-home mums', and in the interpretation and the narrow time frame of the study, there was a strong element of twisting the data to fit a conclusion they'd set out to find.
The truth, which was ignored in the analysis, is that aggression is a normal developmental stage in which children test boundaries. Not only is aggression normal, it doesn't usually last. The study failed to measure the stay-at-home toddlers' behaviour when they were mixed in groups, where the same levels of aggression can be observed. Indeed, a follow-up study by different researchers discovered that those kids who had been kept at home exhibited more aggression later at school than those who'd been in nursery, i.e. it simply appeared at a later stage.

Story 3
This statistic seems counterintuitive, but only if you ignore other evidence. The study fails to mention that the number of fatalities dropped dramatically. As more people survive accidents, more are treated for injury. Of course, the statistic as it stands also tells us nothing about the severity of the injuries.

Story 4
The group was self-selecting, so we might imagine those strongly against animal testing would be more likely to take part, and there's already probably a bias in terms of the readership of the magazine. Furthermore, the poll was actually conducted following a news report on cruelty and mistreatment in one laboratory.

Story 5
The base numbers are all true. However, the starting point that was chosen was the year when there had been a terrorist bombing in the city, which obviously inflated the figures. In previous years, the figures had actually been 94 and 98. Of course, whether any fall in murders can be attributed to government policy is another thing. There could be a number of underlying causes.

G For further practice, see Exercise 2 in the Grammar reference on page 173.

Answers to Exercise 2, Grammar reference
1 is being carried out
2 affected, have been vaccinated
3 undertaking, be produced
4 have been caused, being exposed
5 being extracted / having been extracted, was tested
6 set back, is hoped, prevent

SPEAKING

Aim
to practise language from the lesson in a free, communicative, personalised speaking activity

12 Organise the class into groups of four or five to discuss the quotations.
• As students speak, go round and monitor, and note down any interesting language you hear.
• In feedback, look at good language that students used, and language students didn't quite use correctly. Show students better ways of saying what they were trying to say. You could write some useful new phrases on the board with gaps and ask the whole class to complete the sentences.

Optional extra activity Here are two other quotes for fast finishers to discuss:
There are two kinds of statistics, the kind you look up and the kind you make up.
Statistics are used much like a drunk uses a lamppost: for support, not illumination.

8 NATURE AND NURTURE

SPEAKING

Aim
to set the scene and introduce the theme with a
photo; to get students sharing experiences of seeing
animals in the wild

1 Start by telling the class that in this unit they're going to be describing scenery and natural landscapes, discussing stereotypes, and describing animals, their habitats and habits; students will tell the stories behind photos and talk about communication; they will learn how to emphasise opinions.
• Ask students to look at the photo on pages 68–69. Ask: *What can you see?* Elicit a brief description of the photo, and introduce any key words students might need.
• Organise the class into pairs to roleplay the interview.

2 When they have done the interview once, students change roles. Go round the room and check students are doing the task and help with ideas and vocabulary if necessary.
• In feedback, ask different pairs to tell the class what their stories were.
• Once you have fed back on content, look at good language that students used, and language students didn't quite use correctly during the activity.

> **Possible answers**
> The photo shows a man giving a young gorilla
> a piggyback. Possible stories could be that the
> photographer came across a researcher rescuing
> gorillas from a sanctuary that has been flooded
> or otherwise damaged, or that the researcher is
> returning the gorilla to the wild.

3 Organise the class into groups. Give students time to prepare their own stories. You may need to go round and prompt students, or help them with names of animals. Tell students that this could be a fox in the street – it doesn't have to be a lion or tiger! Ask students to share stories.
• Once you have fed back on content, point out good examples, correct errors, and provide examples of how students can express their ideas better.

Optional extra activity Extend Exercise 3 into a mingle. Students go round and share stories.

Teacher development: sharing personal experiences

A key part of being able to use a foreign language is to be able to relate personal experiences and stories to other people. Take the opportunity in class to get students to prepare and share stories from their own experiences in pairs, groups or mingles, at both the lead-in and follow-up stages of lessons. This builds rapport in the class, since students get to know about each other. It is also motivating because students feel empowered to use language for real – adult learners are most motivated when they can see that the language they are learning is instantly useable. It also creates interest and personal involvement in the theme of the lesson and its texts.

Here are three suggestions:
1 Provide some preparation time with support so students can get ready to tell stories as accurately as they can.
2 Vary interaction in the class so students share stories with different students, and get to know everybody in class.
3 Provide some feedback on the content of their story-telling – finding out about the best or most interesting stories, for example, or asking individuals to share a 'highlight' from their story with the class.

Communicative outcomes
In this two-page spread, students will practise describing scenery and landscapes, and describing photos.

VOCABULARY   Describing scenery

Aim
to introduce and practise words used to describe scenery

1   Ask students to look at the picture and say what they can see. Elicit as many words as you can. Ask students to look at the words in the box and to use them to label the picture. Let them compare their answers in pairs. In feedback, check answers and drill pronunciation when necessary.

Answers		
1 range	7 dunes	
2 peak	8 plains	
3 crater	9 river mouth	
4 ridge	10 glacier	
5 waterfall	11 cove	
6 gorge	12 cliff	

Background language notes for teachers

range /reɪndʒ/ (*of mountains*) = a group of mountains
dunes /djuːnz/ = hills of sand on a beach or in a desert
cove /kəʊv/ = a small area of sea partly surrounded by land
peak /piːk/ = pointed top of a mountain
ridge /rɪdʒ/ = the long narrow upper edge of a mountain; a chain of mountains
gorge /ɡɔːdʒ/ = a deep valley with high sides where a river cuts through rock

2   Ask students to work in pairs to decide on the correct words. In feedback, check answers and drill pronunciation when necessary.

Answers
1 It's very popular with birdwatchers because it's at the mouth of a river / ~~some dunes~~ and there's a lot of wetland / ~~craters~~ that attract birds.
2 There's a very narrow / steep ridge leading up to the main peak and the views are breathtaking / stunning – if you're not too scared to look down!
3 We sometimes gather mushrooms in the woodland near us, but you have to be careful not to stray from / ~~stick to~~ the paths as it's so thick / dense you can easily get lost.
4 It's miles from civilisation, really. You just drive along these dirt roads / tracks across these huge flat / rolling plains. And it's all pretty ~~lush~~ / barren – just brown grassland.

5 It's a mecca for climbers because there are these amazing sheer / jagged cliffs on either side of the valley / gorge. I saw quite a few people climbing without ropes. They must be nuts.
6 The road winds along the coastal cliffs and there are these little coves where you can scramble down to sandy / rocky beaches and have a dip. The water's amazing – crystal clear / ~~very murky~~.

3   Organise the class into pairs to discuss the questions. Monitor closely and note interesting and useful language, as well as errors. Use the feedback to point out good examples, correct errors, and to provide examples of how students can express their ideas better.

Optional extra activity   Ask students to match words from Exercise 1 to the world-famous places below: the Himalayas, Niagara, the Arctic, Sahara, the Nile, the Alps, Serengeti. Alternatively, ask students to come up with their own examples.

LISTENING

Aim
to practise listening for general and specific information

4   🔊 24   Ask students to read the situation and the task.
• Play the recording. Students listen and note answers. Let students compare their answers in pairs.
• In feedback, elicit answers from the class.

Answers
Conversation 1
1 Dolomites, Italy
2 climbing
3 mountainous / breathtaking views / rocky ridges / peaks and deep gorges / sheer cliffs
Conversation 2
1 Mauritius, Indian Ocean
2 on holiday – visiting family
3 tropical island / thick jungle / waterfall / volcanic crater / sandy beaches / crystal clear water / palm trees

🔊 24
Conversation 1
A: Is that you there?
B: Yeah.
A: Where is that? It looks pretty high up.
B: It was in the Dolomites. It's a range in northern Italy. That peak was about 3,000 metres, I think.
A: Wow! The view from up there must've been pretty breathtaking!
B: Yeah, it was stunning, it really was.
A: So was there a cable car or something?
B: Cable car! What? You don't think I'm fit enough to climb up?
A: No, no. It's not that. It's just that it looks pretty terrifying. I mean, that's a proper rocky ridge.

B: Yeah, it looks a bit worse than it actually was, to be honest, and there are these fixed metal ropes that you can clip yourself onto. I mean, it's a bit of a scramble, but you don't need any great technical expertise. You can more or less just pull yourself up the worst bits.

A: Really? I'm not sure I'd trust some rusty old cables.

B: No, they're fairly secure. I mean, you need a head for heights, but it's fine. It's not like these guys we saw base jumping.

A: What?

B: You know what it is, yeah? Where they just throw themselves off a cliff and parachute down?

A: Yeah, yeah. It's nuts.

B: I know! We saw people doing it. I mean, all round that area there are these peaks and deep gorges with these incredible sheer cliffs and we watched some guys jump off one in these kind of flying suits.

A: They must have a death wish, those people, they really must.

B: There are videos of them all on YouTube – just search Dolomites and base jumping.

A: Wugh! It gives me the fear just thinking about it.

Conversation 2

C: Who's that, then?

D: Oh, that's my uncle and cousins ... and that's me.

C: Uh? Oh yeah! How old are you there?

D: I must've been seven or eight, I guess.

C: So where is that?

D: Mauritius. My dad's from there originally and there was a family reunion.

C: Really? So where is Mauritius?

D: It's basically a tropical island in the Indian Ocean.

C: Wow! I was going to say – you look like you're in a jungle.

D: Yeah, I think it's a national park. There are some more photos if you flick through.

C: Wow! Look at that! Is that a waterfall there?

D: Yeah. That's where we went. I think it might be an old volcanic crater. I'm not sure, I might be making that up.

C: What? And you walked through that?

D: Yeah. They've already hacked trails through it so it's not that hard. I mean, anywhere else and it's really thick dense jungle. You really have to stick to the tracks.

C: Aww. Look at him there in this one, looking all upset.

D: Alright, alright. There's no need to take the mickey. You would've been a bit freaked-out if you'd just been attacked by some creepy-crawly.

C: Aww! Shame. Your poor thing.

D: Yeah, yeah. Actually, my mum said I moaned pretty much incessantly on that trip.

C: Oh gosh! Yeah! You look miserable there too, you really do. How can you not be happy there? Look at that. White sand, crystal clear water, palm trees. What's wrong with you? It's like paradise. It's amazing.

D: I was a little English boy, wasn't I? It was too hot. And there's scorpions and snakes and jellyfish and stuff. I was missing home!

C: Man, I'd love to go there, I really would.

D: Yeah, well, I'd probably appreciate it more now.

C: You haven't been there since?

D: Nah, can't afford it. Dad said he spent years in debt from that trip! Hopefully, one day though.

5 🔊 24 Organise the class into pairs to discuss what they remember from the listening.
• Play the recording again so that students can check their answers.
• In feedback, elicit answers from the class. Students don't need to produce the exact words.

Answers

Conversation 1
1 asked if she'd taken a cable car to the peak
2 it was a bit of a scramble to the top
3 listener wouldn't trust rusty cables to hold him / be safe
4 you need a head for heights to climb up
5 base jumpers must have a death wish

Conversation 2
6 a family reunion was the reason the speaker went to Mauritius
7 he'd just been attacked by some creepy-crawly before the photo was taken
8 listener thinks the place looks like paradise
9 speaker doesn't like jellyfish and other dangerous animals
10 the holiday left them in debt which was the reason why they didn't go again

---

Optional extra activity Show the following sentences on the board and ask students to write them in their language:
There are these little coves where you can scramble down to sandy beaches.
It's a mecca for climbers because there are these amazing sheer cliffs on either side of the valley.
Did you hear about this proposal to bid to hold the Olympics here?
This guy at a table in the corner just suddenly burst out screaming.
We hired a room and managed to book this band who were friends of hers.
He always just gets really defensive and puts up this great big barrier.
We stayed in that hotel you recommended.
I haven't felt this fit in years.
It wasn't that bad.
Remove the English sentences from the board, and ask students to translate their sentences back into English. Then show the originals again for them to compare.

6 Organise the class into pairs to discuss the questions. In feedback, elicit some of the more interesting ideas students made, and comment on good examples of language use.

Optional extra activity Show photos from your own holidays. If possible, use your classroom technology to show them on a big screen. Answer questions about them from your class.

DEVELOPING CONVERSATIONS
Emphatic tags

Aim
to introduce and practise tags to emphasise opinions

7 Read through the information in the box as a class.
• Ask students to work individually to add emphatic tags. It is a good idea to elicit the first answer from the class, and to get students to explain how they formed the tag. Let students compare answers in pairs.

8 ♻ 25 Play the recording. Students listen and compare answers. In feedback, provide answers, and comment on errors students have made. Follow up by asking students to practise saying the sentences in pairs.

> ♻ **25 and answers**
> 1 I wouldn't drive it if I were you, I really wouldn't.
> 2 The views were just stunning, they really were.
> 3 The scenery takes your breath away, it really does.
> 4 I just love it there, I really do.
> 5 It made no difference whatsoever, it really didn't.
> 6 He'll never change, he really won't.
> 7 I've never been anywhere like it, I really haven't.
> 8 That sounds amazing, it really does.

9 Ask students to work in pairs to form replies with emphatic tags. Work through the examples to show students what is required. Elicit ideas from different pairs in feedback.

> **Possible answers**
> 2 So was it worth climbing to the top?
>   Yeah, it was breathtaking, it really was.
>   Yeah, but it was exhausting, it really was.
> 3 What was your tour guide like?
>   Oh, he was great, he really was.
>   He knew his stuff, but he wouldn't shut up, he really wouldn't.
> 4 You cycled there, didn't you?
>   Yeah, but I wouldn't do it again, I really wouldn't.
>   Yeah, it was a real adventure, it really was.
> 5 It must've been nice being away from civilisation for a few days.
>   Oh yeah, we had a great time, we really did.
>   It was OK, but the kids didn't stop complaining, they really didn't.
> 6 What did you think of the place?
>   Oh, it's a dump, it really is.
>   It was OK, but it poured with rain the whole time, it really did.

Optional extra activity Ask students to practise the questions and replies in dialogues. Tell them to pay attention to the stress on *really*, and expand and improvise dialogues.

CONVERSATION PRACTICE

Aim
to practise language from the lesson in a free, communicative, personalised speaking activity

10 Give students a short amount of preparation time to choose a task and prepare what to say.

11 Organise the class into pairs to practise. Set a short time limit. Monitor closely as students speak to notice how well they use the new language. After a few minutes, ask one student in each pair to move on in a clockwise direction to start a new conversation with a new partner. Alternatively, do this activity as a mingle.
• In feedback, look at good language that students used, and language students didn't quite use correctly during the activity. Show students better ways of saying what they were trying to say. You could write some useful new phrases on the board with gaps and ask the whole class to complete the sentences.

▶ 17 Refer students to the video and activities on the DVD-ROM.

Teacher development: using the video

The video and activities on the DVD-ROM can be used in various ways:
1 as an alternative to the conversation practice
2 instead of the listening activity in some units, particularly with weaker groups. Students can first practise reading out the dialogues and work on some of the key phrases / structures in a controlled way before having a go themselves.
3 at the end of the unit as a revision exercise

Communicative outcomes

In this two-page spread, students talk about gender differences and gender stereotypes; they talk about how they take notes and how they communicate.

SPEAKING

Aim

to get students talking about gender differences; to lead in to the topic of the lesson

1 Organise the class into groups of four or five to read the introduction and discuss the questions. You could break up the task by setting a gist task for the reading (*What are the two books mentioned and what are they about?*) and feeding back on that before asking students to discuss the questions.

• In feedback, ask different pairs to tell the class what they discussed. Once you have fed back on content, look at good language that students used, and language students didn't quite use correctly during the activity.

Possible answers

Reasons for popularity: people need books that try to explain aspects of their own lives and relationships; people who have problems seek answers; self-help books are optimistically promoted as having answers

Teacher development: using the section heading

A feature of *Outcomes* is unit and section headings. Why not start your lesson by asking students to predict what the unit or section will be about in terms of topic from the heading, and tell you which words and phrases they expect to come across during the unit / section. In this section, it is a way of making sure students understand nature (hard-wired through evolution) and nurture (learnt behaviour as a result of culture or upbringing).

LISTENING

Aim

to give students practice in listening and taking detailed notes

2 🔊 26 Ask students to read the situation and the task. You could ask students to predict what they expect the lecturer to say (for example, women talk more than men, men use different words to women, women / men are more polite / uncertain / aggressive with language, etc.).

• Play the recording. Students listen and take notes.

3 Let students compare their answers in pairs. At this stage, monitor discreetly to see how well students have understood the text, but do not provide any feedback yet.

4 🔊 26 Ask students to answer as many of the questions as they can with their partner using their notes.

• Play the recording again. Let students compare their answers again. In feedback, elicit answers from the class, and ask students to say what they heard to justify their answers.

Answers

Answers will vary. Suggested ideas are listed below:

1 How are the figures 20,000, 7,000, 16,000 and 45,000 connected?
   Number of words spoken per day by women and men. Previously claimed to be 20,000 by women and 7,000 by men. 16,000 is in fact the average for both men and women with a maximum of 45,000 words per day.

2 Which figures are more reliable? Why?
   16,000 & 45,000 are more reliable – they come from *Science*, a research journal. Brizendine couldn't cite a source for the other figures.

3 What are the findings of studies by Hyde and Chambers?
   Hyde – men and women interrupt equally unless there's a power dynamic (more powerful person interrupts more)
   Chambers – no real difference in the way sexes communicate

4 Why does the speaker cite the study in Gapun?
   It shows how different cultures may have different stereotypes of gender and communication. Evidence that language difference between men and women is not down to nature.

5 What do Deborah Cameron and Simon Baron-Cohen disagree about?
   Whether the jobs men and women do is based on the structure of the brain (nature) or on social power and cultural factors (nurture)

6 What's the lecturer's conclusion?
   Nurture is a stronger influence and stereotypes based on the 'nature' of gender are politically motivated / suppress women.

🔊 26

It's common knowledge that men and women do things differently, isn't it? The male of the species, we're told, goes quiet and retreats into a cave to brood at the slightest sign of stress, whilst the female reaches out and shares her feelings. After all, women are better communicators, aren't they? That's certainly what writers like John Gray would have us believe, but on what basis do they make this argument? And does it matter?

It's easy to assume these books must be based on valid scientific research, but in reality very few are. Indeed, even a cursory inspection of the literature of linguistics and gender reveals that men and women communicate in remarkably similar ways. Take the notion that women talk more. A book in 2007 reported that women used 20,000 words a day and men just 7,000, but when the claim was challenged, the author, Louann Brizendine, couldn't provide a source and promised to withdraw it from later editions. In fact, <u>research</u> in the journal *Science* has shown both sexes talk equally as much - and in doing so use on average 16,000 words per day. There's obviously huge variety – from 500 to 45,000 words a day – but, significantly, the three chattiest people in the <u>study</u> were all men!

Then there's the belief that men interrupt more because they are biologically more aggressive and programmed to use language more competitively. <u>Evidence</u> from Janet Hyde actually suggests that in neutral situations where people speak on equal terms, women and men interrupt equally. The neutrality of the situation is important. *Some* men do speak over others more, but this is not to do with gender but rather the power relationship between the speakers. When talking to a boss *we* won't butt in, but *they* will. In fact, when Chambers reviewed a number of linguistic <u>studies</u> investigating gender difference in this and other areas such as empathising, aggression and wordplay, he found an overlap of 99.75% in the way the sexes communicate. In short, no difference whatsoever!

Finally, if these supposed language differences were biological we would expect them to be universal to all cultures. However, to take just one example, a study in the village of Gapun, Papua New Guinea, found the men pride themselves on their ability to speak indirectly and never say what they mean, while the women frequently give voice to their anger by launching into lengthy swearing sessions – behaviour which is a reversal of the Mars and Venus <u>stereotypes</u> of aggression and indirectness.

So, why do these <u>myths</u> of biological difference and communication persist? Well, sweeping generalisations such as, 'Women are more in touch with their feelings' appeal because they match long-standing <u>stereotypes</u>. We look for and cite <u>evidence</u> to back up a traditional view, but ignore or fail to search for contradictory <u>evidence</u>! Take the psychologist Simon Baron-Cohen, who argues in his book *The Essential Difference* that male brains are analytical and goal-orientated, which makes them wonderful scientists and lawyers; while the female's empathetic brain is best for jobs like teaching and counselling.

However, as Deborah Cameron notes, a career in education or as a therapist just requires a mix of verbal, people and analytical skills, and Baron-Cohen's choice is simply based on the fact jobs in such fields have traditionally been occupied by women. And why have they? Because they're less well paid, less varied, and have less power in a society that has been dominated by men for centuries. Furthermore, all of this is often reinforced by our biased use of language, where we'll still often specify a *male* nurse or a *female* doctor.

Ultimately then, when and how people communicate has far more to do with social status and power than it does with genetic make-up and 'nature'. It's vital to challenge these <u>myths</u>, because, in many cases, <u>stereotypes</u> around gender and communication serve to hide the structural problems in societies that maintain male power and hold back women.

5 Organise the class into small groups to discuss the questions about taking notes. As students speak, go round and monitor, and note down any interesting comments about note-taking systems or ways of improving note-taking.

• In feedback, elicit good ideas from the students. You could build up a list of tips for note-taking on the board.

Possible answers
The following pointers for taking notes in lectures or lessons may help you add to what your students say:
1 Use a binder instead of a spiral or bound book. Pages can be easily removed for reviewing and handouts can be inserted into your notes.
2 Bring highlighters to class. Highlighting notes will help remind you later that this is definitely something you need to know.
3 Start each new lecture on a new page, and date and number each page. The sequence of material is important.
4 Write on one side of the paper only.
5 Leave blank spaces. This allows you to add comments or note questions later.
6 Make your notes as brief as possible. Use short notes and write key words.
7 Develop a system of abbreviations and symbols you can use wherever possible.
8 Review and edit notes shortly after the lecture or lesson.

6 Ask students to work in pairs to go through the text. You may want to set a time limit for the task or make it a competition between pairs: *Who can find the most in five minutes? Who can be the first to find twenty?*

Answers
be based on research
valid scientific research
research ... has shown

evidence suggests
look for evidence
cite evidence
evidence backs up a view
ignore evidence
(fail to) search for evidence
contradictory evidence

review a study
linguistic studies
studies investigate
a study found

myths persist
challenge a myth

match stereotypes
long-standing stereotypes
stereotypes serve (to hide problems / maintain male power / hold back)

a claim was challenged
withdraw a claim

7 Organise the class into groups of four or five to discuss the questions.
• Monitor the students and note errors and good uses of language.
• In feedback, look at good language that students used, and language students didn't quite use correctly during the activity. Show students better ways of saying what they were trying to say. You could write some useful new phrases on the board with gaps and ask the whole class to complete the sentences.

GRAMMAR Auxiliaries

Aim
to check students' understanding of how to use auxiliary verbs

8 Read through the information in the box as a class.
• Ask students to complete the sentences. Monitor and note how well students understand the rules. Let students compare answers in pairs.
• In feedback, elicit the students' answers. They can check their answers using the Grammar reference on page 174.

> **Answers**
> 1 aren't (used as a tag to check understanding / elicit agreement)
> 2 have (used as a short rhetorical question to avoid repetition of the whole verb phrase: *Why have they been traditionally occupied by these sexes?*)
> 3 will (to avoid repetition of the whole verb phrase: *but they will butt in*)
> 4 doing (to avoid repetition of the verb phrase: *and in talking equally as much, use … .*)
> 5 do (to add emphasis – often as part of making a contrast)

 Students complete Exercise 1 in the Grammar reference on page 174.

> **Answers to Exercise 1, Grammar reference**
> 1 am, are
> 2 won't (*wouldn't* also possible)
> 3 does, does, doesn't
> 4 wouldn't
> 5 won't
> 6 did, Wouldn't
> 7 wasn't / weren't, can't
> 8 haven't, will
> 9 did, am

9 Ask students to work individually to write responses. Elicit the first answer to get them started. Let them compare answers with a partner before checking in feedback. It is a good idea to hear or have a look at students' ideas before moving on to the practice stage in Exercise 10.

> **Possible answers**
> 2 I don't think you can just totally dismiss stereotypes.
> You don't get stereotypes without any truth to them, do you?
> Don't you? I'd say it's all nonsense.
> 3 I'd love to live on a tropical island.
> So would I! It'd be great.
> Yeah, me too, but my husband wouldn't – he hates the heat.
> 4 I wasn't allowed to play with dolls when I was a kid.
> Weren't you? Aww, poor you.
> I was, but I really didn't like it much.
> 5 I don't have much of a head for heights.
> Don't you?
> That's a shame. I was going to take you up the Shard, but I won't now.
> 6 I find baking quite fascinating, as weird as that may sound.
> You're right, it does sound weird.
> Actually, so do I. You see, we're made for each other!

10 Start by modelling the activity with a reliable student. Read out the first statement, elicit a response, then keep the conversation going. Once students have the idea, put them in pairs to practise. Monitor and prompt students, and help them produce sentences. Make sure you correct errors at this stage.

11 Organise the class into new pairs to find things in common. Give them a minute to prepare questions to ask individually before they start. As students speak, encourage them to use auxiliaries appropriately.
• In feedback, look at good language that students used, and language students didn't quite use correctly. Show students better ways of saying what they were trying to say. You could write some useful new phrases on the board with gaps and ask the whole class to complete the sentences.

 For further practice, see Exercises 2 and 3 in the Grammar reference on page 174.

> **Answers to Exercise 2, Grammar reference**
> 1 He **does** live up to
> 2 I **did** like the country
> 3 My son **does** really enjoy
> 4 species **does** participate
> 5 Tigers **did** use to be
> 6 He **does** talk over you
>
> **Answers to Exercise 3, Grammar reference**
> 1 I did
> 2 It doesn't
> 3 We will
> 4 It does
> 5 It is

VOCABULARY Communicating

Aim
to introduce and practise phrases used to talk about communicating

12   Ask students to work individually to complete the sentences. Elicit the first answer to get them started. Let them compare their answers in pairs before discussing as a class. In feedback, check any new words.

> **Answers**
> 1 gossip, rumours
> 2 mince, blunt
> 3 shuts up, word
> 4 twisting, words
> 5 manners, butting into
> 6 listener, shoulder
> 7 articulate, struggle
> 8 bush, point

Background language notes for teachers

she doesn't mince her words = she says things very directly
you can't get a word in edgeways = you get no chance to speak because (the person) just talks non-stop
put words into (someone's) mouth = to say that someone means one thing when the person really meant something else
beat about the bush = not say something clearly or directly

13   Organise the class into groups of four or five to discuss the questions.
• Monitor closely and note interesting and useful language, as well as errors. Use the feedback to point out good examples, correct errors, and to provide examples of how students can express their ideas better.

SPEAKING

Aim
to provide speaking practice on the topic of the lesson

14   Ask students to work in groups of four or five. Tell them to read through the questions individually first and decide which ones they have most to say about. Ask one student in each group to lead the discussion and make sure everybody else gets a chance to contribute.
• In feedback, ask one person from each group to tell the class what they discussed.
• Once you have fed back on content, look at good language that students used, and language students didn't quite use correctly. Show students better ways of saying what they were trying to say. You could write some useful new phrases on the board with gaps and ask the whole class to complete the sentences.

Communicative outcomes
In this two-page spread, students will read and talk about animals.

VOCABULARY Animals

Aim
to introduce and practise phrases used to talk about animals

1   Ask students to work in pairs to share what they know about each animal. In feedback, check the name of each animal and elicit students' knowledge.

Background language notes for teachers

an Alpine ibex: a species of wild goat that lives in the mountains of the European Alps
an aye-aye (pronounced /ai-ai/): a nocturnal lemur native to Madagascar that has rodent-like teeth and a really long, thin middle finger that it uses to find grubs and insects
a Bactrian camel: a large camel native to the steppes of Central Asia – it is much rarer than the single-humped dromedary
a Eurasian sparrow hawk: a small bird of prey that hunts woodland birds – it is now very common in Europe
a dog snapper: a fish which lives in the Atlantic Ocean
a star-nosed mole: a small mole found in wet parts of eastern Canada and the north-eastern United States, which has 22 pink fleshy appendages ringing its snout
a lilac-breasted roller: the national bird of Kenya, it lives in sub-Saharan Africa
a chameleon: a lizard that lives in deserts or rainforests and eats insects – species come in a range of colours, and many species have the ability to change colours

2   Ask students to work in pairs to label the animals with the words in the box. In feedback, point out any difficult pronunciation.

> **Answers**
> Ibex: hoof, teeth, nostrils, horn, fur
> Aye-aye: fur, tail, nostrils, teeth
> Camel: hump, fur, nostrils, teeth
> Hawk: claw, tail, beak, wings, breast
> Fish: scales, teeth
> Mole: nostrils, fur, claw, feelers
> Bird: legs, tail, beak, wing, breast
> Chameleon: nostrils, toe, scales, tail
> All except the fish have legs.

Background language notes for teachers

Point out the different ways of saying hand or foot with animals: *hooves* (singular, *hoof*) = cows, horses, antelopes, camels; *claws* = hunting birds; *paws* = cats, dogs.

3 Ask students to match the sentence halves. Elicit the first answer to get students started. Let students compare their answers in pairs before discussing as a class in feedback.

Answers

1	It builds	e	a nest.
2	It can sense	g	the slightest movement.
3	It tunnels	j	down into the earth.
4	It can blend	f	into the background.
5	It can withstand	i	freezing temperatures.
6	It gnaws	a	through tree bark.
7	It puffs up	d	its chest.
8	It leaps out	h	and snatches its prey.
9	It stores	c	reserves of fat.
10	It lets out	b	a high-pitched squeal.

Background language notes for teachers

gnaw = bite at something persistently
a squeal = a high scream, often produced in fear or pain

4 Organise the class into pairs to think of examples. Go round the room and check students are doing the task and help with ideas and vocabulary if necessary.
• In feedback, ask different pairs to tell the class what examples they thought of. Once you have fed back on content, look at good language that students used, and language students didn't quite use correctly during the activity.

Possible answers
1 birds build nests – to make a secure, warm place to lay eggs and raise young
2 a spider can sense the slightest movement – to capture prey
3 a mole tunnels down into the earth – home, find food, escape predators
4 a stick insect can blend into the background – escape predators, hide to leap out and catch prey
5 a polar bear can withstand freezing temperatures – to survive in cold northern climate
6 a beaver gnaws through tree bark – to eat, find prey, sharpen teeth, get logs to build dams
7 a gorilla / ape puffs up its chest – to attract a mate, as a warning signal
8 a shark or killer whale might leap out of the water and snatch its prey – to eat
9 seals / bears store reserves of fat – when they hibernate, to withstand freezing temperatures
10 pigs let out a high-pitched squeal – being killed, a warning, a mating call

Optional extra activity You could ask students to do a web search to find animals that can be described with the sentences.

5 ✇ 27 Play the recording. Students listen and note answers. Let students compare their answers in pairs before discussing as a class.

Possible answers
1 mole, sparrow hawk
2
mole
claws – digging
fur – remain underwater
tail – store fat
feelers – sense movement
nose – blow bubbles to smell underwater

sparrow hawk
wings and tail – manoeuvre quickly through trees
markings on breast – blend into the background / leap out and snatch prey
legs, toe and claw – grasp and kill prey in mid-flight
hooked beak – plucking and tearing flesh

✇ 27
1
Unusually for this species, it can swim underwater as well as tunnel underground, which is handy as it inhabits low wetland areas. Its long claws are adapted for tunnelling through the earth and its water-resistant fur allows it to remain underwater. The long thick tail is thought to store extra fat to draw upon during the mating season. The mole is functionally blind, which is why it has developed the distinctive star-shaped set of feelers that give it its name. These feelers allow it to sense nearby movement.
Uniquely, the mole can also smell underwater. It does this by blowing out tiny bubbles through its nose in order to capture scents that are sucked back in. These adaptations are highly efficient and the star-nosed mole is apparently the fastest eater in the animal kingdom, being able to identify, snatch and consume its prey all in a matter of milliseconds.

2
While the sparrow hawk is more commonly found in woodland, its short, broad wings and long tail allow it to manoeuvre quickly through the trees, while the light striped markings on its breast and its darker upper parts help it to blend into the background, as it tends to lie in wait for its prey before shooting out. It has relatively long legs that enable it to kill in mid-flight. The long slender central toe is adapted to grasp, while a small projection on the underside of the claw enables it to grip and hold on to its prey whilst flying. Its small hooked beak is used for plucking and tearing flesh rather than killing. It also sometimes hunts on foot through vegetation. In recent years, it has appeared more and more in cities, where it has no predators and where it is often seen as a pest, damaging garden bird populations.

Understanding vocabulary
Compound adjectives

Aim
to introduce and practise compound adjectives

6   Read through the information in the box as a class.
• Ask students to work in pairs to think of nouns to match to the compound adjectives in the box. In feedback, check students are clear about the meanings of the words.

Possible answers
water-resistant coat / material / watch
star-shaped object / light
award-winning film / actor / play
long-term project / plan / memory
child-friendly restaurant / hotel
self-help group / book
high-powered job / sports car / senior executives
six-lane highway / bridge
life-threatening disease / injuries / illness
tailor-made suit / course

7   Ask students to work in pairs to think of compound adjectives. Make this a competition – after five minutes, stop the activity, and check their answers. Don't forget to check the answers of the pair who claim to have won.

Possible answers
water-friendly farming, star-crossed lovers, long-standing problems, long-sighted, long-suffering parents, long-winded explanation, life-saving operation, sweat-resistant vest, drug-resistant bacteria, wrinkle-resistant suit, egg-shaped, oval-shaped, U-shaped objects, prize-winning, medal-winning athlete, match-winning performance, short-term view, mid-term elections, user-friendly gadget, well-made, badly-made toys
Note that students may also give you examples in which the two parts of the compound are not normally hyphenated: childproof lid, childlike behaviour, childbearing age, lifelong friends, homemade cakes, waterproof jackets.
There are no real rules as to why a compound is hyphenated or not. It's a matter of usage.

Reading

Aim
to read for specific detail and to share information from a jigsaw reading activity

8   Organise the class into groups of four. Ask each group to decide who are As and who are Bs. Tell Bs to find their text on page 190. Students read their texts and find the answers. Tell them they can take brief notes, but that they should try to remember the information as much as possible.

9   Ask students to work with their A or B partners to compare understanding, and do the tasks. Encourage students to refer to the text to explain answers.

Answers
Camel
the animal's habitat – Gobi desert – extremes of temperature and arid
its habits – eats snow / drink salt water, hardly sweats or urinates, resistant to disease, eats sharp thorns, travels vast distances
threats it's facing – hunted, poisoned from illegal mining, breeding with domestic Bactrians and losing ability to drink salt water
Aye-aye
the animal's habitat – Madagascan rain forest
its habits – nests in a tree, taps, gnaws and pokes to find food, travels a distance for food, solitary apart from mating
threats it's facing – habitat being destroyed, hunted

Background language notes for teachers

form a protective barrier = make a barrier or 'wall' which stops things getting into the eye (such as sand)
draws upon these fat reserves = uses the extra fat stored in its body (when there is no food or water)
the sharp thorns of desert shrubs = plants (shrubs are small plants) in the desert which have pointed pieces sticking out from them which stop animals eating them
roam widely in small herds = animals that 'roam' walk very long distances in search of food – 'herds' are large groups of animals such as cows, buffalo, antelope, camels
threatened from a number of angles = in danger from many directions
illegal mining activities = taking coal, gold, minerals, etc. without legal permission
crack down = stop or prevent
captive breeding programme = a programme or plan to breed animals in zoos, away from the wild

10   Within their groups of four, students change partners so that they are with someone who read a different text. Students share information using the phrases in bold in the text. Monitor and prompt at this stage. In feedback, briefly elicit what conclusions students came to, and what phrases they found most useful.

11   Students work in the same pairs to discuss the sentences. Tell them to check answers with reference to the text.

Answers
1 Aye-aye (habitat is being destroyed)
2 Both (camels travel vast distances, aye-aye may cover over four kilometres a night)
3 Camel (drought and famine)
4 Aye-aye (believed to be evil)
5 Camel (they are heavily hunted ... where there is competition for water from domestic herds)
6 Camel (still unknown how it processes salt water)

7 Aye-aye (only one other animal uses the same technique)
8 Both (captive breeding programmes)
9 Camel (lives in a herd)
10 Camel (interbreeding with domestic Bactrians leads them to lose the capability to drink salt water)

SPEAKING

Aim
to practise language from the lesson in a free, communicative, personalised speaking activity

12 Give students a short amount of preparation time to choose two topics, and prepare what to say individually.
• Organise the class into groups of four or five and let students share their ideas.
• Monitor closely and note interesting and useful language, as well as errors.
• In feedback, look at good language that students used, and language students didn't quite use correctly during the activity. Show students better ways of saying what they were trying to say. You could write some useful new phrases on the board with gaps and ask the whole class to complete the sentences.

Web research activity
• Make the Speaking task in Exercise 12 a web research activity.
• Ask students to research one of the topics in class or for homework online. Tell them to find pictures or data to support a talk on one of the topics in Exercise 12.
• In the next class, ask students to present findings to the class or their group.

VIDEO 4: BABY MATH
Student's Book page 76

Aim
to find out about the basic instincts of babies; to improve students' ability to follow and understand fast speech in a video extract; to practise fast speech and to improve pronunciation, stress and intonation

1 Lead in to the topic by asking students to look at the photo and say what they can see. Organise the class into pairs to discuss the questions. In feedback, elicit students' ideas and write up interesting ideas or pieces of language on the board.

Culture notes

The photo is illustrative. It shows how instinctive it is for very young babies to swim underwater without drowning.

2 ▶ 18 Give students time to read through the task and to look at the words, and check their meaning. Students watch and note their answers. Let them compare in pairs before discussing as a class.

> **Answers**
> 1 If you **submerge** a baby under water, it'll intuitively hold its breath. Other mammals, birds and reptiles share the same instinct.
> 2 A touch on the cheek makes a baby turn its head and **suck**.
> 3 A touch on the palm of the hand makes a baby **grasp** your finger – perhaps the trace of an ancestral instinct inherited from monkeys, where the young grasp their mothers' backs.
> 4 A **startle** causes the baby to throw out its arms and legs – as if to grasp onto a tree branch while falling, like monkeys do.
> 5 Babies are pre-programmed to walk. One hour after birth, if a baby's feet touch the ground, they'll start to take **steps**.

Background language notes for teachers

submerge = go under water
suck = pull liquid into your mouth using the muscles of the cheek and tongue (babies suck milk from a bottle)
grasp = hold tightly
startle = surprise or shock
steps = here, small individual leg movements when walking

3 Ask students to discuss the questions in pairs. Encourage them to share their ideas in feedback but don't confirm or deny at this stage.

4 ▶ 18 Ask students to watch the video, and answer the questions in Exercise 3. Let them compare their notes in pairs before discussing as a class. Find out how many answers students predicted.

Answers
1 By measuring how long babies look at certain things that show arithmetical situations.
2 Hard to know what babies are thinking; they can't verbalise things yet.
3 Babies notice when numbers don't add up; babies as young as four months seem to know how to add up or subtract.

5   After students have checked the meaning of the vocabulary in bold with their partner, ask them to discuss what the pronouns refer to.

Answers
1 It = a baby (*reflexes* = very quick ways of reacting that you do without thinking about it)
2 It = a submerged baby (*intuitively* = naturally, without learning to, using feelings to guide you)
3 This = the fact that babies will grasp your finger if you touch it on the palm (*trace* = a small sign of something that has been present or has happened, *ancestral* = connected to your ancestors, those related to you who lived long long ago)
4 it = a baby (*blank slate* = something in its original state / condition and not yet changed by experience)
5 It = a baby (*barrage* = an overwhelming quantity of – in a negative way, like you're being attacked by these things)
6 it = baby doing the experiment with puppets, this outcome = the one they find surprising or unexpected (*outcome* = final result of the process)
7 They = the results of the research (*pretty consistent* = very similar time and time again, not changing in any major way)
8 They = pigeons, this = the number of crumbs on a street corner (*glance* = a very quick look)

6   This exercise offers students the chance to relate the topic of the video to their own experiences, ideas and opinions.
• Give students time to read the questions then put them into groups and give them seven or eight minutes to discuss them.
• Monitor and listen to each group. Help with pronunciation and ideas if necessary.
• Use the feedback to point out good examples, correct errors, and to provide examples of how students can express their ideas better. You could ask students to correct or fill in gaps in sentences you've written on the board, based on what you heard students saying.

Understanding fast speech

7   ▢◀19 Play the recording. Students listen and write what they hear. Let them compare in pairs.

8   ▢◀20 Students listen again to a slower version to check and improve what they have written. Let them compare answers in pairs.

9   Students check what they wrote in File 10 on page 189 of the Student's Book. Encourage them to practise saying the extract.

Video script ▢◀18
Narrator: When a baby comes into the world, it arrives with a set of reflexes to help it survive. If you submerge a baby under water, for example, it will intuitively hold its breath, an instinct we share with other mammals, birds and reptiles. A touch on the cheek makes a baby turn its head and suck. A touch on the palm makes a baby grasp your finger, perhaps the trace of an ancestral instinct for holding onto a mother's back. And a startle causes the baby to throw out his arms and legs, as if to grasp onto a tree branch while falling. Babies are even pre-programmed to walk. Just one hour after birth, if a baby's feet touch the floor, they will begin to take steps. And it turns out that our instincts are not just physical. Yale psychologist Karen Wynn believes that human babies are much smarter than we think.
Karen Wynn: One popular notion is that the baby starts out in the world with a completely blank slate mind, no expectations and finds the world this incredibly confusing, chaotic, barrage of impressions and sensations. In fact, this is very, very far from, from the truth.
Where is he going?
Narrator: She's convinced that babies can even do math.
Karen Wynn: Watch the screen.
Narrator: Using toys, she shows babies simple math problems. But it's not easy to know what a baby is thinking, so she relies on what is called the looking-time method.
Karen Wynn: What a good looker you are.
It's well known that babies tend to look longer at things that they find surprising or unexpected. So, we can show them little arithmetical situations, if you will, little magic shows in which babies see some number of objects being added to some other number. And by sneakiness on the part of the experimenter, we can either make the outcome be the correct outcome or an incorrect outcome.
Narrator: Two minus one equals one. This ten month old is bored and looks away after just a few seconds. But when things don't add up ... one ... plus one ... equals one ... the baby seems surprised and stares at the outcome much longer.
Karen Wynn: Good job, Bella! Good job!
Narrator: The results are pretty consistent. And they suggest that babies as young as six or even four months know how to add and subtract. For most of us, these results are surprising, but for Wynn they make evolutionary sense.
Karen Wynn: I would've been surprised not to get that finding because it's actually very consistent with what we know from findings in a lot of non-human species.

Narrator: Bees know where to find pollen by counting landmarks, and pigeons can judge which street corner has more crumbs with a simple glance. The reflexes we are wired with help us survive after birth and allow us to begin a lifelong journey of discovery.

Aim
to consolidate vocabulary and grammar from Units 7 and 8

Answers
1

1 being	8 been
2 is	9 got
3 given / offered	10 life
4 winning	11 did
5 are / were	12 doing
6 was	13 be
7 being	14 am

2
1 the sheer stupidity of
2 is being carried out
3 reluctance to help is understandable
4 child-friendly site has been awarded
5 is known to be helpful

3
1 interactivity
2 fullness
3 star-shaped
4 disappearance
5 hopelessness
6 captivity, extinction
7 breathable, waterproof

4
Parts of animals: claw, beak, hoof, scales, horn, fur, hump
Landscape: cliff, cove, range, crater jungle, peak, ridge, gorge

5

1 c	3 d	5 h	7 f	9 i
2 e	4 a	6 b	8 j	10 g

6
1 to
2 at
3 by / in
4 in
5 to
6 in
7 on
8 about / around, to
9 into

7
1 upwards
2 contradictory / conflicting
3 prevalent
4 findings
5 field
6 flawed
7 correlation / connection
8 stand up
9 down
10 variables
11 linked
12 paving

9 WORK

SPEAKING

Aim
to set the scene and introduce the theme with a photo; to get students talking about working in an office

1 Start by telling the class that in this unit they're going to be describing what people do at work, discussing experiences of work, talking about conditions of employment, and discussing issues related to dismissal and tribunals.
• Ask students to look at the photo on pages 78–79. Ask: *What can you see?* Elicit a brief description of the photo, and introduce any key words students might need.
• Ask students to discuss the questions in pairs. Monitor and help with ideas and vocabulary if necessary. In feedback, ask different pairs to briefly tell the class how they interpreted the photo.
• Once you have fed back on content, look at good language that students used, and language students didn't quite use correctly during the activity.

> **Possible answers**
> The photo shows the modern, open-plan lobby of a company.
> The man in the foreground is taking a nap in the nap pod at Google headquarters in California.
> The office may be set up to give a sense of openness and light.
> Advantages of working in an office: with colleagues, technology at your fingertips, modern offices provide a stimulating work environment, own desk
> Disadvantages: have to travel to work, distractions from other colleagues

2 With the same partner, ask students to discuss the work-related abbreviations and acronyms. Go round the room and check students are doing the task.
• Once you have fed back on the answers, ask students if they know any other work-related abbreviations or acronyms.

> **Possible answers**
> *a rep* = a representative. Usually, this means a sales representative, a person who presents products to clients, but it could also be a holiday rep or a travel rep, who deals with issues between the travel agency and the local hotel.
> *in IT* = in information technology. The IT department installs computers, software and networks, troubleshoots problems, mans a help desk, and maintains and orders other technological tools.
> *a CEO* = a Chief Executive Officer. This is the boss of the company (depending on the size of the company). This person sets the agenda and strategy, makes final decisions and is a figurehead of a company. The CEO represents a company publicly, and lobbies government and the like.

> *in R&D* = in research and development. This part of a company researches and develops new ideas. It depends on the kind of company, but it may include doing experiments or surveys and building prototypes and testing products. It may liaise closely with marketing.
> *a PA* = a personal assistant. Some top managers might have a personal assistant to organise their diary, set up meetings, make travel arrangements, take minutes at meetings, answer emails on their behalf, etc.
> *in admin* = people who do administrative tasks such as inputting data, booking rooms and travel, processing orders or expenses, filing and maintaining databases, etc.
> *in HR* = in human resources. This department of a company deals with contractual issues, manages recruitment and redundancy or sacking, and advises managers on dealing with disciplinary issues.

3 Organise the class into small groups to discuss the questions.
• Once you have fed back on content, look at good language that students used, and language students didn't quite use correctly during the activity.
Optional extra activity If some or all of your students have worked in an office, ask them to describe positive and negative experiences of being in an office environment.

Teacher development: personalisation

Outcomes aims to use personalisation to get students interested in a topic, and to make communication meaningful. Using a new language to talk about your own experiences and opinions brings it alive. Think of other ways you can personalise a topic for students. Here are some examples of ways of personalising topics further:
1 Ask students to bring in photos or objects connected with the topic which others can ask about. And bring in your own photos or objects.
2 Ask students to prepare and tell stories from their own experience connected with the topic.
3 Ask students to prepare questionnaires, quizzes and interviews in order to question their classmates about interests, experiences and opinions.

SHOW YOU THE ROPES
Student's Book pages 80–81

Communicative outcomes
In this two-page spread, students will practise describing roles and tasks at work.

VOCABULARY Roles and tasks

Aim
to introduce and practise words to describe roles and tasks at work

1 Start by asking students what the section head 'Show you the ropes' means (see Culture notes below). Ask students to complete the sentences. Elicit the first answer to get them started. Let students compare their answers in pairs before discussing as a class. In feedback, model the pronunciation of words that are difficult to say, pointing out strong stress and difficult vowel sounds.

Answers	
1 input	6 come up with
2 troubleshoot	7 liaise
3 network	8 place
4 process	9 schedule
5 oversee	10 draw up

Background language notes for teachers

troubleshoot problems = deal with and solve problems
network (verb) = if you network, you contact people both socially and professionally, and keep in touch with people; networking is a way of influencing people, so it is important to people in sales and marketing, for example
liaise /lɪˈeɪz/ *with designers* = contact and talk to designers in order to share ideas and concerns
draw up a contract = make a contract

Culture notes

I'll show you the ropes means 'I'll show you round and help you to understand what you have to do' – it is said by someone experienced to someone on their first day at work. It comes from a nautical term – an experienced sailor showing a new sailor how to find their way around and operate the complicated ropes on a ship.

2 Ask students to discuss the questions in pairs. Go round the room and check students are doing the task and help if necessary.
• In feedback, ask students to share their experiences with the class.

Optional extra activity Ask students to describe the roles and tasks of people they can see in the photo on the page.

LISTENING

Aim
to practise listening for general understanding; to listen and take notes and hear new and interesting words

3 🔊 28 Ask students to read the situation and the task.
• Play the recording. Students listen and note answers.

4 Let students compare answers in pairs. Monitor closely and notice how well students have made notes. Play the recording a second time if necessary. In feedback, elicit the students' answers.

Possible answers
Tasneem – person showing Harry (the new person) the ropes / going to work together / liaises with external service providers
Harry – new person / just moved to Redditch
Bianca – main admin person / sorts out travel and bookings (students may also comment on her character – jokey / funny)
the photocopier – temperamental / jams easily (doesn't work very well)
Mary – managing director / down-to-earth (students may comment she doesn't talk to staff or at least Tasneem much)
the company – expanding (taking on new staff) / everyone very busy / open plan office

🔊 28
H = Harry, T = Tasneem, B = Bianca
H: Hi, I'm looking for Tasneem.
T: That's me. You must be Harry.
H: That's right.
T: Nice to meet you. Did you find us OK?
H: Yeah, yeah. Well, I came here before for my interview.
T: Right. So, where do you live? Does it take you long to get here?
H: I've just moved to Redditch, but it was quicker than I expected. I've actually been hanging around in the coffee bar over the road for the last hour.
T: Really? You were eager to get here, then.
H: Well, I didn't want to be late and, you know, first-day nerves and all that.
T: Sure. Anyway, I'm sure you'll settle in quickly. We're a pretty good bunch. Nobody bites. Well, almost nobody!
H: Right.
T: So, raring to go, then?
H: Absolutely.
T: OK, well, just dump your stuff down here for the moment and I'll show you the ropes.
H: OK.
T: I should've said, we'll be working alongside each other on this new project. I liaise with our external service providers. I was just emailing one of them to schedule a time for us all to meet when you arrived. Anyway, as you can see, the office is mainly open-plan. We'll sort you out with a spot later.

H: Right.

T: It's a bit chaotic at the moment with all the changes. We've been rushed off our feet so it'll be good to have more people.

H: I'm not the only one who's being taken on now, then.

T: No. Three or four more are joining in the next couple of weeks.

H: That's good. There'll be some others in the same boat.

T: Yeah. This is Bianca. She's our main admin assistant. She'll sort out any travel or bookings and other stuff. Bianca, this is Harry.

B: Hiya. Nice to meet you. Hope Taz is treating you well. She's a real slave driver, you know.

H: Really?

B: Oh yeah, she's probably being all kind and helpful now but wait till you get started.

H: That sounds ominous.

T: Take no notice. She's just pulling your leg. You need to watch her!

B: I don't know what you mean! Actually, Harry, can I just take a quick photo while you're here? I'm just sorting out your entry card and setting up your email.

H: Sure.

B: OK. Say cheese ... lovely, very handsome. That's it. Anything you need or you're not sure about, don't hesitate to ask.

H: Thanks. I'll get the card later, then, yeah?

B: If that's OK.

T: OK, let's move on. That lot over the far side are the sales team. We won't disturb them now. I can introduce you later. To be honest, you won't be having that much to do with them in your day-to-day dealings.

H: OK. What about these rooms? Are they offices?

T: Um, the last two are the boardrooms for meetings. The near one is Mary's office. She's the managing director.

H: OK. What's she like?

T: She's OK. She comes across as being quite down-to-earth ... the few times we've talked.

H: She's not in the office that much, then.

T: No, she's here most days, but as I said, I guess we've all been so busy that everybody just sticks to their own tasks. Anyway, just going back to the rooms ... that one with the door open is the photocopier room. I'd better show you how it works. It's a bit temperamental. It has a tendency to jam if you don't treat it with tender loving care.

H: OK.

T: So how come you moved to Redditch? It's not that close to here.

H: No, but I'd been thinking about moving out there for a while and I happened to get the house just before I got this job.

5 🔊 **28** Ask students to work in pairs to recall any words or phrases they can first. You could elicit some examples.

• Play the recording and ask students to write down four new words or phrases they hear. Students compare in

pairs again before looking at audio script 28 on page 205. In feedback, elicit a few phrases students heard or found, and explain them to the class.

> **Answers**
> You may need to explain some of the words or phrases below. However, don't feel you need to explain all of these. Be guided by what your students ask about.
> *You were eager to get here*
> *first-day nerves*
> *I'm sure you'll settle in quickly*
> *dump your stuff*
> *external service providers*
> *the office is mainly open-plan*
> *We'll sort you out with a spot later*
> *rushed off our feet*
> *slave driver*
> *That sounds ominous*
> *day-to-day dealings*
> *She comes across as being quite down-to-earth*
> *temperamental*
> *It has a tendency to jam*
> *treat it with tender loving care*

Background language notes for teachers

eager = keen, enthusiastic
dump your stuff = put your belongings down – it doesn't matter where
rushed off your feet = very busy
slave driver = a jokey way to describe a boss who wants you to work hard
ominous = makes you think something bad will happen (it is often said humorously to say 'I'm worried by that' or 'Should I be worried by that?')
tendency to jam = paper is likely to get stuck in the machine
treat it with tender loving care = a jokey way to say 'be gentle and careful when using it'

Optional extra activity Ask students to personalise and practise the phrases by saying which ones could be used to describe their experiences of work or school.

6 Ask students to discuss the questions in pairs. Go round the room and check students are doing the task and help if necessary.

• In feedback, ask students to share experiences with the class.

DEVELOPING CONVERSATIONS

Making deductions

Aim
to introduce and practise ways of making deductions

7 🔊 **29** Read through the information in the box as a class.

• Play the recording so that students can notice the rising intonation.

• Ask students to do the task. Let them compare answers in pairs. In feedback, elicit answers from the class.

Answers
You were eager to get here, then.
1 I've actually been hanging around in the coffee bar over the road for the last hour.
2 Well, I didn't want to be late and, you know, first-day nerves and all that.

I'm not the only one who's being taken on now, then.
1 We've been rushed off our feet so it'll be good to have more people.
2 No. Three or four more are joining in the next couple of weeks.

She's not in the office that much, then.
1 She comes across as being quite down-to-earth ... the few times we've talked.
2 No, she's here most days, but as I said, I guess we've all been so busy that everybody just sticks to their own tasks.

🔊 29
You were eager to get here, then.
I'm not the only one who's being taken on now, then
She's not in the office that much, then

8 Read through the example with the class. Then ask students to work in pairs to come up with deductions, or ask them to work individually before comparing ideas with a partner.

Possible answers
2 You were up late last night, then.
3 He's not very nice, then.
4 He's called in sick again, then.
5 You've been to Russia, then.
6 You're working really hard, then.

9 Organise the class into pairs to practise the exchanges. Monitor and prompt, and notice how well students use the new language and the correct intonation. Use the feedback to comment on good uses of language, and to correct any errors students make.

Optional extra activity Ask students in pairs to choose one of the situations and pairs of phrases in Exercise 8, and to build a more extended dialogue around the situation. Ask some pairs to perform their dialogue for the class.

GRAMMAR Continuous forms

Aim
to check students' understanding of how to use continuous forms

10 Read through the information in the box as a class. Then ask students to complete the sentences individually. Organise the class into pairs to check and discuss answers. Monitor and notice how well students understand the rules.
• In feedback, elicit the students' answers.

Answers
1 've actually been hanging around
2 'll be working
3 was just emailing
4 's being taken on
5 are joining
6 's probably being
7 won't be having
8 'd been thinking

Teacher development: deductive and inductive grammar learning

These are the two approaches generally applied to grammar teaching and learning:
1 Using the deductive approach involves learners being given a general rule, which they then apply to specific language examples before doing practice exercises.
2 Using the inductive approach involves learners noticing patterns and working out rules for themselves before doing practice exercises.
• At the Advanced level, students should be capable of both applying learnt knowledge and noticing patterns in language. Encourage students to work out meaning from what they know and notice, using the knowledge of other class members to confirm or shape their ideas.

11 Ask students to discuss why the different forms are used in pairs. Monitor and notice how well students understand the rules.
• In feedback, elicit the students' answers. They can check their answers using the Grammar reference on page 175.

Answers
1 focus on the activity happening over a period of time – as opposed to the result
2 talk about arrangements and activities based on a previous decision
3 show an action or event is / was unfinished at a particular point in time or at the time of another action.
4 talk about arrangements and activities based on a previous decision
5 talk about arrangements and activities based on a previous decision
6 emphasise that we see an action or situation as temporary – rather than permanent
7 talk about arrangements and activities based on a previous decision
8 focus on the activity happening over a period of time – as opposed to the result

Answers to Exercise 1, Grammar reference
1 have drawn up, have been drawing up / am drawing up
2 were losing / had been losing, lost
3 will be dealing with / is dealing with, will deal with
4 were having / had been having, had had
5 are processed, is being processed
6 wouldn't be sitting, wouldn't sit
7 was being interviewed, was interviewed
8 show, be showing

Background language notes for teachers: continuous forms

Continuous aspect is used with active verbs. They describe temporary rather than permanent activities, (compare *I'm living in Paris right now; I live in Paris =* the city of my birth). They describe activities that are unfinished and in progress rather than finished (compare *We've been working on a major project; We've worked on three or four major projects – all of which went well*). They focus on duration and activity (compare *I've been painting the ceiling all morning; I've painted the ceiling*).

12 Ask students to discuss the sentences in pairs. You could ask students to refer to the Grammar reference on page 175 to check their understanding. In feedback, elicit and discuss ideas.

Answers
1a The company went bankrupt last year. **finished**
1b The company was going bankrupt last year. **unfinished** – the company's fortunes may possibly now have been turned around. We might also say *it was on the verge of bankruptcy*.
2a She's a pain. **always** – that's her character.
2b She's being a pain. **at the moment** – this is temporary. Examples include a child nagging or someone refusing to do something.
3a You must have been struggling. **in the past**
3b You must be struggling. **now**
4a They should sort it out. **in the future** – you want them to do it at some time in the future or you believe they will. The focus is on the solution / result.
4b They should be sorting it out. **now** – you believe that they are doing it now. The focus is on the activity.
5a Things are improving a lot. **now** – in effect 5a and 5b have a similar meaning. Improvement is happening now. It depends on time phrase (at the moment / nowadays).
5b Things have been improving a lot. **up to now** – focus here is before and including now. It depends on different time phrases (over the past / last few years, etc.).

13 Start by eliciting a possible dialogue from the class with reference to 1b in Exercise 12. Once students have the idea, organise them into pairs to prepare other dialogues. Monitor and help students with ideas and vocabulary, and prompt them to correct any errors. In feedback, you could elicit good examples from the class or ask a few pairs to act out situations for the class.

Possible answers
A: I would recommend investing in Fiji Electronics.
B: But I thought they were making big losses.
A: Well, the company was going bankrupt last year, but their finances have improved a lot.
B: So, it's safe to buy shares in the company, then.
A: Absolutely. They're doing well now.

 For further practice, see Exercise 2 in the Grammar reference on page 176.

Answers to Exercise 2, Grammar reference
1 correct
2 He must've been doing at least 80km/h when he crashed.
3 The company took over a chain of shops last year so they own over 1,000 stores now.
4 We can't meet in the office at the moment because it's being done up.
5 We're actually supposed to be taking on some new people soon, but I don't know when.
6 Apparently, he's been seeing the boss's daughter for the last year, but the boss still doesn't know.
7 correct
8 correct
9 I'll be sorting out those files later, so if you finish early, come and give me a hand.
10 I don't know why he's being such a pain, he's not normally like that.

CONVERSATION PRACTICE

Aim
to practise language from the lesson in a free, communicative, personalised speaking activity

14 Give students four or five minutes to draw a plan and to prepare what to say. Go round and help with ideas and vocabulary at this stage. When students are ready, organise them into pairs to show each other their plan and describe their places of work or study.
• In feedback, look at good language that students used, and language students didn't quite use correctly. Show students better ways of saying what they were trying to say. You could write some useful new phrases on the board with gaps and ask the whole class to complete the sentences.

Optional extra activity Write the following phrases on the board before students do the conversation practice: *Things are going well, then. You've been working there for quite a while, then. She's extremely friendly, then.* Ask students to try to say each phrase at some stage in their conversations, in response to aspects of their partner's descriptions.

 21 Refer students to the video and activities on the DVD-ROM.

Teacher development: using the video

The video and activities on the DVD-ROM can be used in various ways:
1 as an alternative to the conversation practice
2 instead of the listening activity in some units, particularly with weaker groups. Students can first practise reading out the dialogues and work on some of the key phrases / structures in a controlled way before having a go themselves.
3 at the end of the unit as a revision exercise

OUT OF THE OFFICE
Student's Book pages 82–83

Communicative outcomes

In this two-page spread, students read about and talk about different experiences of work.

READING

Aim

to read for general and specific understanding; to work out the meaning of words in context

1 Organise the class into pairs and ask students to look at the title of the book (*The Living Dead*) and the photo from the book cover on page 83, and predict what it might be about. In feedback, elicit ideas from the class. Answers will vary. Don't force a 'correct' answer on students but ask them to explain their ideas. Use the feedback to point out good examples, correct errors, and to provide examples of how students can express their ideas better.

Culture notes

The Living Dead was published in 2015. British management writer David Bolchover coined the phrase to describe demotivated, disengaged employees. In his writings, he argues that placing so-called 'talented' employees in high-earning positions is a bad idea as it means they play safe instead of being innovative.

2 Ask students to look at the questions first (explain *in his shoes* = in his position). Then tell them to read the article. Let them compare their answers in pairs before discussing as a class. In feedback, you could ask students whether they correctly predicted the theme of the book.

Possible answers
1 He's been off work – at home, travelling, etc., but still getting full pay – because the company has 'forgotten about him'.
2 He's jealous.
3 and 4   Answers will vary – don't force a 'correct' answer on students but ask them to explain ideas and correct language, if necessary.

3 Ask students to work individually then check with a partner before discussing in feedback.

Answers
1 Bolchover did an MBA but his company then couldn't find him a suitable job. His boss didn't care because he was retiring and he was passed around various other people who didn't really want to sort it out.
2 He was made redundant eventually after ten months of no work.
3 The office workers like him who don't have enough work to do.

4 Elicit the first answer to get students started. Let them work in pairs to compare answers and to look at the text if necessary to check their answers.

Answers
1 i   my vitality drained away
2 a   acquire new skills
3 g   sponsor me
4 e   sparked my interest
5 d   get the most out of its investment
6 f   his mind was drifting off
7 j   set the wheels in motion
8 c   passed this on to someone else
9 b   which begs the question
10 h   get a redundancy payment

Background language notes for teachers

spark my interest = made me suddenly very interested
My mind was drifting off = I wasn't concentrating because I was tired or bored
set the wheels in motion = start a series of actions
begs the question = invites the question

5 Organise the class into pairs to retell the story. Monitor and notice how well students can tell the story. Prompt them to use the new phrases. In feedback, briefly focus on any phrases students weren't sure how to use, and feedback on any errors you heard.

6 In the same pairs, students discuss the questions.
• In feedback, ask different pairs to tell the class what they discussed. Ask them which of their ideas have the most potential to help. Once you have fed back on content, look at good language that students used, and language students didn't quite use correctly. Show students better ways of saying what they were trying to say.

Optional extra activity Write the following phrases from the text on the board: *on the payroll, sitting on your backside, screwed the system, my shoulders slumped, make some small talk*. Ask students to say what they mean and to say how they relate to the narrative in the text.

LISTENING

Aim

to listen for general and detailed understanding

7 🔊 30 Give students a moment to read the instruction and the task and make sure they are clear about what to listen for from Exercise 6.
• Play the recording. Students listen and note answers. Let students compare answers in pairs.

Possible answers
1 Maybe – although being able to stay at home doing nothing and getting paid is unusual, Bolchover argues that being at work and doing nothing isn't.
2 Bolchover blames the disconnection workers feel when they are employed by big companies. They don't see how their small contributions fit the whole picture.
3 Bolchover's lesson is that we should break up large companies and make people feel their role at work is more important.

♻30

Is David Bolchover's experience a freak occurrence? Well maybe, but only in the sense that he was allowed to stay at home to not work. Bolchover argues that much of the workforce in many big companies is badly under-employed at work and backs up his arguments with a barrage of statistics. One in three of all mid-week visitors to a UK theme park had phoned in sick. In one year, there were nine million questionable requests for sick notes from the doctor. That's about a third of the working population! Two-thirds of young professionals have called in sick because of a hangover, and on it goes.

Once at work, things don't improve. On average, employees spend 8.3 hours a week accessing non-work-related websites and 14.6% of all so-called 'working' Americans say they surf the net constantly at work. 18.7% send up to 20 personal emails a day and 24% said they had fallen asleep at their desk, in a toilet or at a meeting.

Bolchover argues that there's a conspiracy of silence over this workplace slacking. Workers have no vested interest in saying they do nothing, while businesses want to maintain their image of being highly efficient. Under-employment happens, he suggests, because workers feel a disconnection with big companies. Unlike with small companies, employees don't see how their small contributions fit into the whole picture. Furthermore, managers typically fail to develop or motivate workers because, he claims, in large corporations people progress not by looking down but by looking up. Instead of managing effectively and getting the most out of those under you, the way to get ahead is by advertising yourself and networking with those above you. People below you don't give promotions.

With smaller companies, slacking happens less because workers see how failure to pull your weight can directly impact on colleagues and the company. Bolchover suggests the solution, therefore, is to break up large companies into smaller competitive units. From a worker's view, doing nothing might seem fun at first, but in the end it's soul-destroying and a waste of talent.

8 **♻30** Give students two minutes to read the questions.
• Play the recording again. Students listen and note answers. Let students compare answers in pairs.

Answers
1 one in three mid-week visitors to a UK theme park had phoned in sick, employees spend 8.3 hours a week accessing non-work-related websites, 24% (of working Americans) said they had fallen asleep at their desk, in a toilet or at a meeting. Bolchover's point is that we slack (are lazy) in the workplace and nobody wants to do anything about it.
2 the conspiracy is that it suits both sides to keep quiet – workers have no vested interest in saying they do nothing, and businesses don't want to say they're inefficient – they want to maintain their image of being highly efficient.

3 Because workers feel a disconnection with big companies. Unlike with small companies, employees don't see how their small contributions fit into the whole picture
4 Bolchover suggests breaking up large companies into smaller competitive units so that workers can see how failure to pull their weight can directly impact on colleagues and the company.

9 Organise the class into small groups to discuss the questions.
• Once you have fed back on content, look at good language that students used, and language students didn't quite use correctly during the activity.

UNDERSTANDING VOCABULARY
Adverb-adjective collocations

Aim
to introduce and practise adverb-adjective collocations

10 Read through the information box with the class. Ask students to complete the sentences individually. Point out that there are no correct answers – only personal ones. Elicit an answer to the first one to get students started.

11 Let students compare and discuss their answers in pairs.

Background language notes for teachers

mind-numbingly boring = a fixed collocation which suggests that something is so boring that your mind goes 'numb' (no feeling)
inherently interesting = interesting for its own sake
blissfully happy = an extreme state of happiness

12 Ask students to make their own sentences individually. Monitor and help with ideas as they prepare. Organise students into pairs to compare and discuss their ideas. In feedback, point out examples of good language use and correct errors.

Optional extra activity Ask students to describe the following sports using phrases from Exercise 10: football, golf, swimming, table tennis, paragliding.

Web research activity
• Ask students to research David Bolchover and find out more about his ideas and his books.
• Ask students to share what they found out in the next class.

Communicative outcomes
In this two-page spread, students will talk about conditions at work; they will discuss issues related to dismissal and tribunals.

SPEAKING

Aim
to introduce the topic; to get students talking about work conditions around the world

1 Start by writing *Working Conditions* on the board, and asking students what might be covered by this title (Answer: rates of pay, hours of work, holiday entitlement, breaks, maternity and paternity leave, sick pay, etc.). Ask students to read the fact file and discuss the questions with a partner. In feedback, ask different pairs to briefly tell the class about their countries.
• Once you have fed back on content, look at good language that students used, and language students didn't quite use correctly during the activity.

Culture notes

IMF = International Monetary Fund
GDP = gross domestic product (the monetary value of all the finished goods and services produced within a country's borders in a specific time period)

VOCABULARY The world of work

Aim
to introduce and practise phrases used when describing work and working conditions

2 Ask students to look at the words in the box and say how many words they are not sure of (*crèche*, *perk* and *absenteeism* may be new). Ask students to complete the sentences individually. Elicit the answer to the first one as a class to get them started. Let students compare answers in pairs before discussing as a class.

> **Answers**
> 1 quit, notice
> 2 subsidised, perk
> 3 compassionate leave, grateful
> 4 crèche, childcare
> 5 early retirement, pension
> 6 absenteeism, crackdown
> 7 tribunal, dismissal
> 8 raise, opposition
> 9 cuts, voluntary redundancy
> 10 unions, casualisation

Background language notes for teachers

subsidised travel = here, the company is paying for reduced prices on bus or train travel to and from work

perk = something extra at work
crèche /krɛʃ/ = a day nursery for very young children
absenteeism = used to describe persistent failure to appear for work
voluntary redundancy = when you choose to give up your job, usually in return for payment (redundancy pay)
casualisation of the workforce = a term used to describe the situation when workers lose rights and become 'casual workers' – they no longer have contractual working conditions such as sick pay, the right to a period of notice before being made redundant, holiday leave, etc.

3 Organise the class into pairs. Start by eliciting the answer to the first one to get students started. Then ask pairs to take turns remembering the verbs and their collocations Encourage students to work hard at this, trying to remember and fix in their minds the collocations taught.

4 Once students have finished, tell them to check their answers by looking at Exercise 2, and encourage students to note new phrases in a way that is useful for them.

> **Answers**
> give a week's notice
> granted compassionate leave
> take early retirement
> live on the state pension
> launch a crackdown
> take someone to a tribunal
> awarded compensation
> raise the minimum wage
> face a lot of opposition
> take voluntary redundancy

Optional extra activity Ask students to choose three new phrases to memorise and learn, and remember to check which phrases they have learnt at the start of the next lesson.

5 Organise students into groups of four or five to discuss the questions. As students speak, go round and monitor, and note down any interesting pieces of language you hear.
• In feedback, look at good language that students used, and language students didn't quite use correctly.

Optional extra activity Ask students to research the following words online or in a dictionary and to say how they differ in meaning: *holiday, vacation, leave, break, recess, time off, sabbatical, leave of absence, long weekend.*

LISTENING

Aim
to listen for general and detailed understanding

6 ◗31 Give students a moment to read the instructions and the task and make sure they are clear about what to listen for.
• Play the recording. Students listen and match the stories to the sentences. Let students compare answers in pairs.

Answers

Conversation 1

b The employee did something illegal. He stole some biscuits – was taken to court and fined.

Conversation 2

d The union are accusing the employer of breaking an agreement. The employers want employment laws changed to delay retirement. The firefighter's union has concerns about the ability of staff to fulfil all their duties beyond 55 and claims the government has gone back on promises to guarantee the pensions of firefighters who fail a compulsory medical.

Conversation 3

a The employer did something illegal. The tribunal concluded that sacking him was a step too far as his previous leave had been legitimate and managers had failed to inform Mr Portman that he could have applied for compassionate leave.

Conversation 4

f The union want employment laws changed. The ECA is a pilots' union. The ECA is concerned about the implications of casualisation on training and safety and is calling for new rules to crack down on the practice.

Conversation 5

c The employer proved to be right in a dispute. A woman has failed in her case of constructive dismissal because the company which employed her refused to pay her wages in full when she went on maternity leave. The employer was relieved at the verdict, saying he'd fulfilled the statutory requirements.

🎧 31

1

A 27-year-old call centre worker has been fined and has lost his job after eating a colleague's biscuits. While working a night shift, Michael Campbell decided to dip into what remained of a biscuit tin that had been left in the office. The following day, however, a co-worker returned to find her £7 gift selection gone – and decided to search CCTV footage so as to find the culprit. Campbell was charged with stealing and brought before a magistrate, who ordered him to repay the cost of the biscuits as well as a £150 fine. He was also dismissed from his job as a result of the incident and is currently retraining as a bar manager.

2

Firefighters are holding a one-day strike today as part of a long-running dispute over pensions. With swingeing cuts taking place throughout the public sector, the government wants to raise the retirement age for firefighters from 55 to 60 and say it'll mean they can avoid making redundancies in the service. The firefighter's union, however, has concerns about the ability of staff to fulfil all their duties beyond 55 given the nature of the work. It claims the government had previously promised to guarantee the pensions of firefighters who fail the compulsory medical at 55, but now it was going back on that promise.

The government denies this and condemned the strike, and is assuring the public that emergency calls will be dealt with. The action has also prompted some MPs to call for legislation preventing employees in essential services from striking.

3

A postman who was sacked after taking a week off work to mourn the death of a pet has been awarded £10,000 compensation. The employment tribunal was told David Portman had a history of sick leave due to a number of accidents and injuries, and had been absent for a total of 137 days in just five years. In his defence, Mr Portman claimed the majority of his injuries were incurred during the course of his duties at work. However, when he took further leave following the death of his dog, he was sacked. The tribunal concluded this was a step too far as his previous leave had been legitimate and managers had failed to inform Mr Portman that he could have applied for compassionate leave.

4

A report commissioned by the ECA, which represents European pilots, has raised concerns about aviation safety. The report found 17% of pilots were on insecure contracts and not employed directly by the airline, with young pilots being particularly badly affected. Many of them have no guarantees of work and not only have to pay for initial training, uniforms and overnight stays, but in some cases even subsidise the airline through pay-to-fly schemes, whereby young pilots can gain flying experience. The ECA is concerned about this casualisation of contracts because the report found pilots in this group were more reluctant to disobey the airline's instructions even if they had safety or health concerns. It also claims the pilots may miss out on important training. The pilot union is therefore calling for new rules to crack down on these atypical contracts.

5

A woman has failed in her discrimination claim against the company which employed her, which refused to pay her wages in full when she went on maternity leave. What makes the case unusual is that the company, Kapp's Kitchen Tiles, is a family business run by her own father. Mandy Platt claimed the decision was the final straw in a series of incidents, where her father had expressed displeasure at the pregnancy. Her father, Andy Kapp, was relieved at the verdict saying he'd fulfilled the statutory requirements with regards to his daughter, and was simply ensuring his business remained secure to pass on to all his children.

7 Organise the class into pairs to tell the stories. Monitor and prompt, and help with ideas and vocabulary. It is a good idea to walk round the class with the audio script handy, to help you prompt.

8 🎧 31 Play the recording again. Students listen and check ideas. Let students compare answers in pairs. In feedback, find out which stories students think are true, and elicit reasons why.

Answers
The last story is NOT true – the others are. There was a similar case though between a mother and daughter who owned an estate agency. The daughter left and set up her own estate agency and they sued each other – one for stealing clients and one for harassment.

9   Ask students to work in groups of four or five to discuss the questions. Monitor closely and note interesting and useful language, as well as errors.
• Once you have fed back on content, look at good language that students used, and language students didn't quite use correctly. Show students better ways of saying what they were trying to say. You could write some useful new phrases on the board with gaps and ask the whole class to complete the sentences.

SPEAKING

Aim
to practise language from the lesson in a personalised, communicative speaking activity

10   Start by organising the class into groups of three. Mix students so that they are with new partners. Tell students to find file 20 on page 191, and to read the cases. Ask students to decide on what they think should be done, and to make brief notes if necessary. Monitor and help with ideas and vocabulary.

11   When students are ready, ask them to discuss what they think should be done. At the end, ask each group to present their decision briefly. Feedback on good examples of language use and errors you heard.

12   Ask students to discuss the questions in the same groups. Monitor and note errors or examples of good language use.

10 HEALTH AND ILLNESS

SPEAKING

Aim
to set the scene and introduce the theme with a photo; to get students talking about visiting the doctor

1 Start by telling the class that in this unit they're going to be describing medical procedures, approaches to medicine, and discussing issues doctors face; students will practise using vague language and describing what the mind and body do.
• Ask students to look at the photo on pages 86–87. Ask: *What can you see?* Elicit a brief description of the photo, and introduce any key words students might need.
• Ask students to discuss the questions in groups of four or five. Monitor and help with ideas and vocabulary if necessary. In feedback, ask different groups to briefly tell the class what they discussed.
• Once you have fed back on content, look at good language that students used, and language students didn't quite use correctly during the activity.

Possible answers
Problems the place has:
nothing is digitalised, so record-keeping is hard;
lack of access to medicine / specialised care, which is all too expensive
long waiting times in cramped spaces
brain drain of skilled local staff to other, better-paid contexts
In the UK, the most common reasons for visiting doctors include: skin problems, joint disorders, back problems, cholesterol problems, colds and flu, mental illness, high blood pressure, headaches and migraines, etc.
Most common operations include: cataract surgery, prostate surgery, caesarean sections, abortions, hernia operations, hip replacement, blood transfusion, etc.

Culture notes

The photo shows the administrative office of the Tekle Haimanot Higher Clinic in Addis Ababa, the capital of Ethiopia in Africa.

Optional extra activity Brainstorm *illnesses* and *operations* and write them on the board. Find out how many words and phrases under the two headings students already know.

Teacher development: brainstorming and using the board

Outcomes aims to encourage students to show what they already know, and to recall and recycle language they have. Brainstorming during a lead-in is a positive way of getting students to recall language.
• Write up headings in web diagrams, so, here, write *illnesses* and *operations* on the board, put a circle round each word, and draw short lines from each circle. Then ask students to give you ideas. Encourage lots of different ideas from around the class. Don't write up everything. Write up anything relevant or interesting, and repair or rephrase inaccurate uses. At the end, check any difficult words and point out any vocabulary or structures of interest that students thought of.

UNDER THE KNIFE
Student's Book pages 88–89

Communicative outcomes
In this two-page spread, students will talk about medical procedures and discuss medical experiences; they will use vague language to describe medical procedures they are unfamiliar with.

VOCABULARY Operations

Aim
to introduce and practise chunks of language used to describe operations

1 Ask students to order the groups of words in pairs. Start them off by eliciting the first answer. In feedback, model the pronunciation of words that are difficult to say.

Answers
1 damaged her knee quite badly: the knee joint swelled up – had to have a scan – had it operated on – underwent extensive physiotherapy
2 broke his leg in three places: had to fast for twelve hours – was given an anaesthetic – had an operation to insert metal rods – eventually had them removed
3 the pain became excruciating: had a filling – it somehow got infected – had to have the whole tooth out – had to have a few stitches
4 was diagnosed with kidney disease: was put on a waiting list – finally found a donor – had a transplant – took part in a rehabilitation programme
5 suffered severe burns: was rushed to hospital – was put on a drip – had a skin graft – had to wait for the scarring to heal
6 found a lump: it was diagnosed as cancer – underwent chemotherapy – it went into remission – suffered a relapse – had an operation to have it removed

2 Elicit one or two examples for the first one to get students started. Ask them to work in pairs to discuss and answer the questions. It may well be the case that students know and produce ideas not mentioned in the answers below, due to experience or specialised knowledge, so be prepared to explore their answers, and ask questions about them to find out what they know.

Possible answers
1 when you're pregnant, when you have knee or back problems, when you have a head injury, when you have cancer
2 putting increasing amounts of weight on a joint, extending flexibility, lots of stretching and moving, doing fixed exercises again and again every day

3 for religious reasons like during Ramadan for many Muslims, for health reasons or because they're dieting using something like the 5:2 method (five days eating and two days with no food)
4 heart transplant, liver transplant, kidney and lung transplants, bone marrow transplant and recently they've done the first face transplant
5 when you're recovering from drug addiction or alcoholism, when you're recovering from any kind of serious illness or operation
6 to ensure fluids and / or medicine goes directly into their blood
7 causes fatigue and tiredness, loss of appetite, hair loss, feelings of nausea, feelings of numbness in hands and feet, etc.
8 start drinking or taking drugs again when trying to get over addiction, athletes suffer relapses when trying to recover from serious illnesses or injuries and when pushing themselves hard

Teacher development: organising vocabulary

Organising new words and vocabulary into categories using tables, diagrams and spidergrams is a good way of helping students note, learn and remember words. Here, for example, ask students to think of ways of recording and organising the chunks:
1 students could copy out their ordered lists in a flow diagram
2 students could write headings / a circle in the middle of a spidergram and write the chunks around the circle. Headings might be: A lump, Toothache, A swollen knee, etc.
3 students could draw circles and write five or six key words from each list in the circle: at a future date, these key words can act as prompts to make students remember all the chunks they have learnt. For example, key words for number 1 in Exercise 1 could be: *damaged, operated, extensive, joint, swelled, scan.*

Optional extra activity Write key words on the board (e.g. *damaged, operated, extensive, joint, swelled, scan*) and ask students in pairs to try to recall and use as many of the chunks from number 1 in Exercise 1 as they can. Repeat the activity with other sets of key words for 2 to 6.

LISTENING

Aim
to practise listening for general understanding and for detail

3 🔊 32 Ask students to read the situation and the task.
• Play the recording. Students listen and note answers. Let students compare answers in pairs before discussing as a class.

Answers

Conversation 1

1 having your eyes done / having laser treatment on your eyes / having your eyes fixed by laser
2 they numb your eyes with eye drops and give a couple of Xanax to keep you calm, and kind of clamp the eyes open ... then they slice a tiny flap in the front of the eye, and you stare at a laser for a few seconds and that reshapes the inside of your eye
3 he doesn't need further treatment, but he has to go back for aftercare ... basically, however, the next day it was fine

Conversation 2

1 a root canal at the dentist's
2 they drill a hole in the back of the tooth, clean everything up, then stick some kind of temporary filling in there to prevent bacteria getting in
3 yes, has to go back and have the temporary filling taken out, then they'll put a more permanent thing in

🎵 32

Conversation 1

A: You look really different without your glasses on. I almost didn't recognise you there.
B: Hey, the glasses have gone! They're a thing of the past.
A: Yeah?
B: Yeah. After months and months of toying with the idea, I finally got round to having my eyes done the other day.
A: Cor! Really? Did you get them lasered?
B: Yeah.
A: Woah! That's brave of you. Didn't it hurt? I've always imagined it must be really painful.
B: No, not really. It's actually pretty quick and easy these days. Well, at least if you're shortsighted, like I am ... was!
A: OK.
B: It is a bit scary, though, because what they do is they numb your eyes and then they sort of clamp them open so they can slice this tiny little flap in the front of the eye – and you kind of have to watch as the whole thing happens.
A: Oh! It sounds horrendous, it really does! How did they give you the anaesthetic? Was it an injection or something?
B: No, they just poured in a load of these eye drops and they did the job. Oh, and they dosed me up with a couple of Xanax as well, just to calm me down.
A: So how long does the whole thing take?
B: It's over in a matter of minutes. After they cut the eye open, you have to stare at this laser for a few seconds and that reshapes the inside of your eye – and then you're done.
A: And how long does it take to recover from?

B: To be honest, the next day I woke up and I pretty much had perfect vision. They're still a bit sore and I have to go back a few times for the aftercare and everything, but it's all very quick. I should've got it done years ago, honestly!
A: Right. Wow! I still think I'll stick with contact lenses for the time being, though, personally.

Conversation 2

C: So, where did you rush off to the other day, then?
D: Oh, sorry. Didn't I tell you? I had to get to the dentist's.
C: Oh no! How come?
D: Well, about a week ago or so, I got this excruciating pain in my upper jaw so I went along to get it looked at and he told me that one of my teeth had died somehow and that I'd need a root canal.
C: Died? How did that happen?
D: Don't really know, to be honest. He said I must've taken some kind of knock. I'm not sure, but I think it might've been my daughter, actually, thrashing her arms and legs around while I was changing her nappy one day, you know.
C: Kids, eh! All that work and that's the kind of thanks you get.
D: Tell me about it! And then today I went in and he drilled a hole in the back, cleaned everything up and then he stuck some kind of temporary filling in to prevent bacteria or anything getting in.
C: That can't have been much fun! Did it hurt at all?
D: No, not really. I mean, I was conscious of what he was doing, but I couldn't feel anything.
C: Do you have to go back again sometime?
D: Yeah, next week. They'll remove the temporary filling and put a more permanent thing in, but then I'm done.
C: How much is all that going to set you back, then? It must be quite expensive.
D: It's not that bad, but it's not cheap either. I mean, I won't see much change from £500.

Culture notes

Xanax = Xanax is the brand name of a drug with the generic name alprazolam. It is a benzodiazepine used to treat anxiety disorders, panic disorders, and anxiety caused by depression.

a root canal = a treatment used to repair and save a tooth that is badly decayed or becomes infected. During a root canal procedure, the nerve and pulp are removed and the inside of the tooth is cleaned and sealed.

4 🎵 32 Let students read through the sentences first, and decide whether they are true or false based on their first listening.
• Play the recording again. Students listen and choose true or false. Let students compare answers in pairs before discussing as a class. In feedback, ask students to justify their answers by telling you what they heard on the recording.

Answers
Conversation 1
1 T (*slice this tiny little flap in the front of the eye ...*)
2 F (*How did they give you the anaesthetic? Was it an injection or something? // No, they just poured in a load of these eye drops and they did the job.*)
3 F (*they dosed me up with a couple of Xanax as well, just to calm me down.*)
4 F (*They're still a bit sore ...*)
5 T (*I still think I'll stick with contact lenses for the time being, though, personally.*)

Conversation 2
6 T (*about a week or so ago, I got this excruciating pain in my upper jaw ...*)
7 F (*How did that happen? // Don't really know, to be honest. He said I must've taken some kind of knock. I'm not sure, but I think it might've been my daughter ...*)
8 T (*then stuck some kind of temporary filling in, to prevent any bacteria or anything getting in.*)
9 F (*I was conscious of what he was doing, but I couldn't feel anything.*)
10 F (*I won't see much change from £500.*)

5 Organise students into groups of four or five to discuss the questions. Give them two minutes to read the questions first, and to decide which ones they have most to talk about. When students are ready, ask them to discuss.
• In feedback at the end, look at good language that students used, and language students didn't quite use correctly during the activity.

DEVELOPING CONVERSATIONS
Vague language

Aim
to introduce and practise vague language to show we can't find the right word or wish to avoid a complicated word

6 Ask students to work in pairs to complete the sentences. Ask students to look at audio script 32 on page 207 and check their answers. Alternatively, you could play the recording at this stage again as an intensive listening to confirm the answers.

Answers
1 sort of
2 or something
3 a load of
4 and everything
5 or so
6 somehow
7 some kind of
8 some kind of, or anything

7 Ask students to discuss the sentences in pairs. Find out whether they can work out use from their previous knowledge and from context. You could elicit and discuss ideas as a class in feedback or ask students to use the information in the box to check their ideas.

Answers
1 We use *sort of* before verbs to show we can't find the exact word.
2 We add *or something* to suggest a non-specific alternative to the thing mentioned.
3 We use *a load of* to refer to a large, unspecified amount.
4 We add *and everything* to refer vaguely to other associated things.
5 We use *or so* with periods of time to show we are not being exact.
6 We use *somehow* with verbs to show we do not know exactly how.
7 We use *some kind of* before nouns to show we do not know what kind exactly.
8 We use *some kind of* before nouns to show we do not know what kind exactly, and we use *or anything* to suggest an absence of things.

8 Elicit one or two examples to get students started. Let students work individually before comparing in pairs. In feedback, you could write up some of the best examples on the board.

Possible answers
1 I asked for a second opinion, but they just **sort of / kind of** ignored me.
2 He used **some kind of / some sort of** (or **a load of**) bleach solution on my teeth.
OR He used bleach solution **and everything** on my teeth.
OR He used bleach solution on my teeth **and everything**.
3 If you want a check-up **and everything**, it should cost about €100.
4 They told me that a build-up was damaging blood vessels in my brain **or something**.
OR They told me that **some kind of / some sort of** build-up was damaging blood vessels in my brain.
OR They told me that a build-up was damaging **a load of** blood vessels in my brain.
5 They use this tiny little knife **or something** to make the incision.
OR They used **some kind of / some sort of** tiny little knife to make the incision.
6 It was quite a traumatic birth, but they **somehow** managed to deliver her after about an hour **or so**.
7 They just **sort of / kind of** glued the skin back together again using some **sort of / kind of** clear plastic tape **or something**.
8 Mercifully, there were no needles **or anything** involved – just massage and **some kind of** traditional medicine.
OR Mercifully, there were no needles **or anything** involved – just massage and traditional medicine **and everything**.

9 Organise the class into pairs to practise using vague language. Point out that you don't expect them to know exactly how to do these procedures. You want them to have a go at describing them in 'vague' terms. Give students two minutes' thinking time before they speak to prepare some ideas or notes about what to say. Monitor and correct any errors.

Answers
There are no fixed answers. Work with whatever
students come up with. Below are descriptions of
the procedures:

BACK PAIN: There's usually some kind of scan to
establish what's wrong; they make a small incision
and maybe remove disc material that's pressing on
nerves and causing pain; they use a microscope of
some kind to view area being operated on.

HIP REPLACEMENT: You're given anaesthetic; a cut
is made along the top of the hip; move the muscles
connected to the thighbone to allow a better view.
Next, the ball portion of the joint is removed by
cutting the thighbone with some kind of saw. Then
an artificial joint is attached to the thighbone using
either cement or a special material that allows the
remaining bone to somehow attach to the new joint.
The doctor then sort of prepares the surface of
the hipbone – removing any damaged cartilage –
and attaches the replacement socket part to the
hipbone. The new ball part of the thighbone is then
inserted into the socket part of the hip. A drain may
be put in to help drain any fluid. The doctor then
reattaches the muscles and closes the incision.

LIPOSUCTION:
The surgeon will mark out lines on the patient's body,
indicating where treatment will take place. Photos of
the target area, and sometimes the patient's whole
body may be taken; they will be compared to pictures
of the same areas taken afterwards. The patient is
given anaesthetic; several litres of a saline solution
with a local anaesthetic is pumped below the skin in
the area that is to be suctioned. The fat is sucked out
through small suction tubes.

TOOTH WHITENING:
There are a few ways to have your teeth
professionally whitened at a dentist's.
The "laser light" method involves sitting for about
one or two hours. A gel is painted on your teeth and
the light beam is positioned to be directly over the
gel. It is safe and produces instant results and is more
costly than other methods. During the process, if your
teeth start to become sensitive, the gel is removed.
Another professional method is the professional
trays made by the dental team. An impression is
taken so as to custom fit a soft plastic retainer on
top of your teeth. You will be given instructions to
place a gel within the tray and place on top of your
teeth for a certain time period. This could be from
30 minutes to overnight depending on your choice
and the dentist's recommendation. You take the
trays out, rinse and spit.
Another option is the same professional trays with
a 'boost', which means the trays are used at the
dentist's with a 45% concentration of bleach. Your
gums are protected, the trays with the gel are placed
on your teeth, and you wait about 30 minutes, rinse
and spit. The bleach is specially formulated to avoid
sensitivity.

Optional extra activity If you want to give students extra
practice, write the following questions on the board and
ask students to answer them:
How do they get parachutes in the small parachute bag?
How do helicopters take off?
How do fish 'breathe'?

CONVERSATION PRACTICE

Aim
to practise language from the lesson in a free,
communicative, personalised speaking activity

10   Organise the class into threes and ask them to
decide which task to choose. Give students four or five
minutes to read role cards (pages 191, 186 and 197) or
prepare things to say. When students are ready, ask them
to do the task.
• In feedback, look at good language that students used,
and language students didn't quite use correctly during
the activity. Show students better ways of saying what
they were trying to say. You could write some useful new
phrases on the board with gaps and ask the whole class
to complete the sentences.

 22 Refer students to the video and activities on the DVD-ROM.

Teacher development: using the video

The video and activities on the DVD-ROM can be used in
various ways:
1 as an alternative to the conversation practice
2 instead of the listening activity in some units,
    particularly with weaker groups. Students can first
    practise reading out the dialogues and work on some
    of the key phrases / structures in a controlled way
    before having a go themselves.
3 at the end of the unit as a revision exercise

Web research activity
• Revise vocabulary from the lesson by brainstorming
a list of ten ailments from the class. For example: a
sprained wrist, a sore throat, a migraine, an insect bite,
etc. Ask students in pairs to choose three ailments and to
decide how they would treat the problem.
• Ask them to research online and find out whether
the way they would treat each ailment is backed up by
Internet advice.

Communicative outcomes
In this two-page spread, students read about and talk about mindfulness, meditation and depression; they talk about things you do with the mind and body.

SPEAKING

Aim
to lead in to the topic of the lesson; to do a questionnaire to find out about negative feelings

1 Organise the class into pairs to take turns to ask the questions. Go round the room and check students are doing the task and help with ideas and vocabulary if necessary.
• In feedback, ask different pairs to tell the class what they discussed. Once you have fed back on content, look at good language that students used, and language students didn't quite use correctly during the activity.

READING

Aim
to read and take notes; to use phrases and sentence starters to retell parts of the text

2 Ask students to look at the photo on page 91, and say what it shows (people doing yoga or meditation). Ask them what they expect the text to be about. Give students a moment to read the list of topics and think about what they know about them. Then ask them to work in pairs to discuss the topics. In feedback, elicit interesting ideas students may wish to share with the class. If your students know little or nothing, accept whatever ideas they come up with, and reassure them that they'll learn more shortly.

3 Ask students to read through the phrases first. Check any unknown words. Then ask them to work with the same partner to say how the phrases are connected to the topics. You could feedback briefly to find out what students think before they read, and get students to explain their choices and decisions. What's important here is that they understand the language used in the phrases, so be prepared to check meaning.

4 Ask students to read the text and take notes. Let them compare notes in pairs. Elicit answers briefly.

Answers
Try to elicit or cover at least some of the following:
Mindfulness and meditation
mindfulness originates in ancient Buddhist practices
used to be fairly unknown in the west, but has become more popular
widely used now by among others the US military!
it's basically a kind of meditation therapy designed to train people to focus on inner processes happening now

Depression and anxiety
evidence suggests mindfulness can help to break cycles of depression and anxiety
people suffering depression find moods often accompanied by negative thoughts and these thoughts usually disappear after meds prescribed or episode passes
but this has created pattern in the brain and so a mood swing caused by something small like bad weather can trigger off negative thoughts, and start another bout of depression
the more this happens, the more it recurs, making it harder to treat with drugs
mindfulness encourages people to be more aware of their patterns of thought
helps to break the cycle by resetting neural pathways

Life expectancy and well-being in the developed world
Western medicine has been good at extending life expectancy
in many countries, life expectancy doubled in the 20th century
many infectious diseases were eradicated
but we live longer in sickness, not health
Western medicine less good at encouraging well-being
unless you're in severe pain, Western doctors have little to offer

Patients that doctors refer to as 'the worried well'
often patients suffering low-level complaints or long-term illnesses are dismissed by doctors as the worried well
Western doctors often not good at treating such patients at all

Traditional Chinese Medicine
more focused on maintaining good health and well-being than most Western models
better at relieving minor conditions like eczema, back pain and migraine
TCM includes acupuncture, herbal remedies, massage

5 Ask students to use the phrases to retell parts of the article. Monitor and help with ideas and vocabulary at this stage, and prompt students to produce accurate sentences. Elicit answers briefly.

Possible answers
Work with your students' ideas. It doesn't matter if they don't summarise the whole text. Here are a few possible examples of what they might cover:
Mindfulness therapy can help people suffering from depression. It can break the downward spiral of depressed moods accompanied by negative thoughts. The negative thoughts that come with the bad moods spark neural connections and thus future mood swings can trigger symptoms of depression. Mindfulness can stop this by helping sufferers become more aware of patterns of thought.

Western medicine has been good at <u>eradicating infectious diseases</u>, which has increased life expectancy a lot and has <u>improved mortality</u>. Western medicine is only really any good at dealing with people in <u>excruciating pain</u> or with something life-threatening. It's not so good at dealing with those who have <u>low-level complaints</u>. Traditional Chinese Medicine (TCM) helps them more. TCM is also better at <u>relieving minor conditions</u>.

6   The aim here is for students to respond personally to the information in the text. Give students two or three minutes to prepare things to say before discussing with a partner. There are no fixed answers here, so work with the personal reactions students come up with.

Optional extra activity   Show the following sentences on the board and ask students to write them in their language:
The more this happens, the more likely it is to recur.
The longer you leave it, the more difficult it'll be.
The richer the country, the healthier the people tend to be.
The older people get, the more prone they are to high blood pressure.
Remove the English sentences from the board, and ask students to translate their sentences back into English. Then show the originals again for them to compare.

VOCABULARY Mind and body

Aim
to introduce and practise phrases used to describe actions involving the mind and body

7   Ask students to work in pairs to discuss the actions. Start them off by eliciting the first answer. Monitor and notice how well students understand the phrases. In feedback, check meanings and model the pronunciation of words that are difficult to say.

Possible answers
1 you're bored, you're stuck in class / at work, you suddenly start reflecting on the past, you're tired
2 you're trying to think of who did something, you're worried about someone or something, you're suddenly having amazing ideas about future possibilities, you're having some kind of panic attack
3 you're excited, you're scared, you're exercising – or have just been running
4 you're breathing deeply, you're sleeping, you're very relaxed and doing mindfulness therapy
5 you may shudder with unease, discomfort, fear, disgust or pleasure
6 you're sweating
7 you're surprised, you're expressing irony
8 to answer a question in class, to ask a question at the end of a presentation, to vote
9 you're in pain / having a heart attack, to express deep joy or relief
10 in time with music, when you're dancing, to get someone's attention

11 you're losing in a game, you feel defeated, you're depressed, you're giving up
12 to show you don't know something, or don't care
13 you're angry, to show defiance, to demonstrate and protest; if you raise a clenched fist it's a gesture of solidarity and support – especially for oppressed peoples
14 it hurts / aches, you're recovering from back surgery, you've been hunched over your computer for a long time
15 to get some fresh air, to exercise, after a long flight or meeting or lesson, because you're bored and fancy a walk
16 to flirt with someone you find attractive

8   Give students two minutes to think of ideas individually. Monitor and prompt as students do this exercise. Let students compare answers in pairs before discussing as a class.

Answers
you sniff using your nose
you use your hands – and particularly your fingernails – to scratch other parts of your body
you glare angrily at someone using your eyes
you stroke pets or hair or skin using your hand, especially the cupped palm of your hand
you blink with both eyes
you frown by moving your eyebrows down and closer together – the frown can also be seen on your forehead
if you crouch down, you move your body close to the ground by bending your knees and leaning forward slightly
you hug with both arms and the front part of your body touches the front part of the person you hug
if you grin, you smile, usually showing your teeth, so you use your mouth
you pat people on the back or head using the palm of your hand
if you spit, you use your mouth to release saliva
if you punch, you use your fist (your closed hand) to hit someone or something

9   Organise the class into new pairs to test each other. Monitor and note and correct errors.

Optional extra activity   Play 'Simon Says' (a popular children's game). Ask five students to stand in a row at the front of the class. The class must give them instructions. For example, they say, *Simon says shrug your shoulders*. The students at the front must obey and perform the action. The class then say, *Stretch your legs*, without saying *Simon says*. If any student moves, even flinches, they are out and must sit down. Students continue. If they say *Simon says*, the students must obey. If they don't say *Simon says*, they mustn't move. Continue until only one student remains standing – the winner!

BEDSIDE MANNER
Student's Book pages 92–93

Communicative outcomes
In this two-page spread, students will talk about health issues, and roleplay medical situations.

SPEAKING

Aim
to lead in to the topic of the lesson; to talk about being a doctor

1 Organise the class into groups of four or five to discuss the questions. Go round the room and check students are doing the task and help with ideas and vocabulary if necessary.
• In feedback, ask different groups to tell the class what they discussed. Once you have fed back on content, look at good language that students used, and language students didn't quite use correctly during the activity.

Optional extra activity Ask students in their groups to produce a list of five nouns to describe the qualities a doctor should have. An example list: *patience, expertise, consideration, knowledge, tiredness.*

LISTENING

Aim
to read for general understanding and for phrases in context in a text

2 ✪ 33 Ask students to read the situation and the task.
• Play the recording. Students listen and note answers.

3 ✪ 33 Students compare their answers in pairs.
• Play the recording again. Students listen and add to their notes.

4 Students compare their answers in pairs once more. Then elicit answers from the class. Ask students to justify their answers in feedback.

Possible answers
Speaker 1 – the only one who is training doctors, whilst the others are either doctors or studying to become doctors
Speaker 2 – the only one who criticises patients and admits to getting rid of them quickly, whilst the others all seem very caring
Speaker 4 – the only one studying rather than working at present
Speaker 5 – the only one who has done medical research

✪ 33

1
Medical dramas on TV here have changed a fair bit over the years. Before, the doctor was just a saint that could do no wrong, but nowadays they'll have more flawed characters and the hospitals are more like my own. My favourite remains *House*, even though it finished a while back. It's basically about this highly unconventional doctor and the team he leads. He's a brilliant clinician, but he's also cynical and downright rude to colleagues and patients alike. He's also ridiculously unethical in his approach. In one episode, he gets a junior colleague to break into a patient's apartment to solve the mystery of their condition. In another, he totally breaches patient confidentiality just to prove a point. Of course, this is where the show parts with reality, but I've found it a really useful springboard for my students to discuss ethics, the processes that should've taken place and how to improve bedside manner.

2
When I see the mass of printouts in their hand, my heart just sinks. I just know they'll have been searching the Internet for every possible diagnosis or quack cure you can think of! It's like that joke: a man goes to his doctor and tells him he's suffering from a long list of illnesses. 'The trouble with you,' says the doctor, 'is that you're a hypochondriac.' 'Oh no,' says the man, 'don't tell me I've got that as well.' Seriously, though, these people are often timewasters and to my mind they're also kind of undermining my professionalism – twenty years of study dismissed in favour of Google! My main aim is to get them out of the surgery as quickly as possible.

3
There's a cliché that doctors make the worst patients because we don't take the advice we would give to others. That's definitely true. I read a survey that found 80% of Norwegian doctors had reported into work with illnesses that they would've issued a sick note to others for. Underlying this is a bigger problem of how we see our role. Our purpose is not to suffer but to see symptoms, diagnose disease, treat it and cure it.
As a result, we sometimes feel lost if we come across a disease or condition that we don't immediately recognise or know how to treat. We're good at dealing with definites, not the unknown. The truth is, when we're faced with uncertainty, many of us don't deal with it very well and that can lead to communication breakdowns.
As a sufferer of a major chronic condition myself, I've been on the receiving end of this. It can start from the first encounter, where the doctor starts the examination without even introducing themselves; to a wrong diagnosis or poor treatment because they won't admit to not knowing what the problem is; to secrecy and silence when there's a relapse and the news is bad. Being a patient actually taught me the most valuable lesson: see the person first, not the condition.

4

I started my studies back home in Sierra Leone, but I had to stop because of the Ebola outbreak. I volunteered to work with the response teams going from house to house informing people of the dangers and uncovering suspect cases. It made me realise the importance of communication and education in health. I had wanted to be a surgeon, but now I'd like to get into community health. I later won a scholarship to come and study here in France and I should qualify next year.

5

I've worked and carried out research in a number of countries and perhaps the biggest thing I've learnt is how you need to be aware of not just the disease but also the person and culture it occurs in. I remember seeing a guy who suffered from a rare hormonal condition called Addison's Disease. What happens is that two small organs – the adrenal glands – don't produce sufficient amounts of the hormone cortisol, which in turn leads to increased pigmentation in the skin. Essentially, their skin turns black. That perhaps wouldn't be so much of a problem these days, but this was 40 years ago in South Africa when the country imposed strict racial segregation. Imagine what that patient must've gone through?

Teacher development: encouraging students to interact and share understanding while reading and listening

Outcomes aims to encourage students to interact and share information when listening and reading. The task isn't about getting the answers right. It's about working collaboratively to support each other in getting a good understanding. It is about students showing what they can get with a little help from friends. Encourage students to work together as much as possible during these tasks, gradually building up understanding and working with different people in the class.

5   Organise the class into pairs to discuss the questions. Go round the room and check students are doing the task and help with ideas and vocabulary if necessary.
• In feedback, ask different pairs to tell the class what they discussed. Once you have fed back on content, look at good pieces of language that students used, and pieces of language students didn't quite use correctly during the activity.

Possible answers
Work with students' ideas. Here are some possibilities:
The Internet is good because: it has a lot of information; it allows students to find out about their symptoms and to improve their general knowledge; there are blogs and online forums where students can share symptoms and ideas; you can contact medical advice on the web

The Internet is bad because: the ill-informed advice can worry people; people self-diagnose instead of seeking proper advice; rumours can spread on the web which may cause health alarms
Ways of avoiding communication problems: improve your 'bedside manner' by taking time to get to know patients personally; explain things in detail; smile and be polite; be available if patients want to contact them
Apartheid was a system of enforced racial segregation which held sway in South Africa until 1990. The man with Addison's Disease may have found himself suffering from racial discrimination – on public transport, in bars and restaurants, and at work.

Culture notes

The photo shows the main characters from the popular American medical drama *House*, starring Hugh Laurie. Other popular US medical dramas of recent years include *ER* and *Grey's Anatomy*.

Optional extra activity   Ask students to look at the photo on the page and say what it shows, and how it makes them feel. This could work as a lead-in or follow-up to this section.

UNDERSTANDING VOCABULARY
Nouns based on phrasal verbs

Aim
to introduce and practise nouns based on phrasal verbs

6   Read through the information in the box as a class.
• Ask students to tell you any nouns based on phrasal verbs that they can think of from their previous learning experience (for example, *outcome, breakdown, breakup, setback*). Ask students to work individually to complete the sentences. Start them off by eliciting the first answer.
• Let students compare answers in pairs. In feedback, model the pronunciation of words that are difficult to say.

Answers

1 shake-up	5 crackdown
2 upbringing	6 breakthroughs
3 workout	7 run-up
4 outbreak	8 dropout

Background language notes for teachers

Note that while the nouns are based on phrasal verbs, it doesn't mean that the verb can be used like the noun. So, you can say *a police crackdown* or *the police cracked down on unrest*, but *the run-up to an election* can't be expressed as *the politicians ran up to the election*. There are no reliable rules about when to use a hyphen when forming nouns from phrasal verbs. So, *shake-up, run-up*, but *breakup*. When the preposition or adverb goes first, it is usually shown as one word: *upbringing*, for example.

7 Organise the class into pairs to discuss the statements in Exercise 6. Tell students to take a minute first to think about which statements they want to talk about, and to prepare ideas. In feedback, elicit some ideas, and comment on the students' pronunciation and use of nouns based on phrasal verbs.

8 Ask students to read through and discuss the nouns. Encourage them to use both the context and their understanding of the two parts of the nouns to work out meaning. At the end, you could ask students to use dictionaries to check, or you could provide definitions and examples yourself.

Answers
1 a **cover-up** is an attempt to stop people from discovering the truth about something, especially a crime or serious mistake
   it could refer to a terrible crime, financial scandal, or accident in a nuclear power station, etc.
2 a **write-off** is a vehicle so badly damaged it can't be repaired
   it is a car / vehicle of some kind
3 a **break-in** is an act of entering a building illegally – using force – in order to steal things
   they refers to the burglars
4 a **bypass** is a road that goes around a town or city so traffic doesn't have to go through the centre
   They = local council / government
5 a **turnover** is the value of goods / services a company sells at a particular time
   They = a big company
6 a **walkout** is a form of protest when workers leave a building and stop working
   They refers to teachers, factory workers, nurses, doctors – workers of some kind
7 a **falling-out** is an occasion when you have a big disagreement with someone and stop talking afterwards
   We = me and a friend / colleague / family member
8 a **mix-up** is a mistake or problem that happens because of confusion or a misunderstanding
   They refers to doctors or hospital staff
   it refers to a test result

9 The aim here is to personalise the nouns by getting students to share any stories or experiences. You could start students off by providing your own personal example.

Optional extra activity Ask students to write four or five personalised sentences using the nouns in Exercises 6 and 8. You could make this interactive by asking them to write three true sentences and one untrue sentence using the nouns. They then read their sentences out in groups. Other students must guess which sentence is untrue.

GRAMMAR Modal auxiliaries

Aim
to check students' understanding of how to use modal auxiliaries to add meaning

10 Read through the information in the box as a class.
• Organise students into pairs to discuss the sentences. Do the first as an example in open class. Monitor and notice how well students understand the rules.
• In feedback, elicit the students' answers. They can check their answers using the Grammar reference on page 176.

Answers
1a *I just know they'll have been searching the Internet.* (= I'm sure that before they come to see me, they've already done this)
 b *I just know they can't have searched the Internet.* (= I'm sure they haven't done this)
2a *Norwegian doctors had reported into work with illnesses that they would've issued a sick note to others for.* (= if other people had come to them, then definitely they would've given them sick notes – it's a certain guess about an imaginary past)
 b *Norwegian doctors had reported into work with illnesses they could issue a sick note to others for.* (= it's possible for them to issue sick notes for this)
3a *Imagine what that patient must've gone through.* (= think about all the terrible things I'm 99% sure they have already endured)
 b *Imagine what that patient might be going through.* (= think about what the patient is possibly suffering at the moment)
4a *If we come across a disease we don't immediately recognise, we can feel lost.* (= it's possible for us to feel lost)
 b *If we come across a disease we don't immediately recognise, we will often feel a bit lost.* (= this is a certain result)
5a *They give poor treatment because they won't admit to not knowing what the problem is.* (= they're refusing to admit they don't know what the problem is)
 b *They give poor treatment because they mustn't admit to not knowing what the problem is.* (= they're not allowed to admit that they don't know what the problem is)
6a *Nowadays, most TV dramas will have more flawed characters.* (= I'm certain they have; this is what I'm sure is generally true)
 b *Nowadays, most TV dramas should have more flawed characters.* (= they don't yet, but it'd be a good idea if they did; I want them to; it's desirable)
7a *We use it as a springboard for a discussion on the processes that should've taken place.* (= processes I wanted to take place, but didn't)
 b *We use it as a springboard for a discussion on the processes that may take place.* (= maybe take place at some future point)

8a *I later won a scholarship to study here in France and I should qualify next year.* (= I think / hope I will qualify)

b *I later won a scholarship to study here in France and I shall qualify next year.* (= definite / very certain prediction)

G Students complete Exercise 1 in the Grammar reference on page 177.

Answers to Exercise 1, Grammar reference
1 must be, should go, could be
2 should've talked, might've seen
3 may have been murdered, won't know, can't stop
4 shouldn't have been playing, could've been killed, Shall (I) take, can play
5 can't be, must have, could (probably) tell
6 won't say, should tell, could get

Background language notes for teachers

Note the form of modal auxiliaries:
Present or future: modal auxiliary verb + infinitive without *to*
Past: modal auxiliary verb + *have* + past participle / *been + ing*

11 Elicit possible answers to the first situation from the class to get students started. Ask students to work in pairs to discuss further possibilities. Monitor and prompt, and help with ideas and vocabulary. In feedback, elicit ideas, and refer back to rules if students have any problems.

Possible answers
2
He must be homeless.
He might be ill. He could be having some kind of attack or seizure.
They shouldn't have let him on the bus.
Someone should've offered him a seat.
3
There must be a bug going round.
We should have taken on more staff.
4
He should have more tests.
He can't have a serious problem.
He must be OK.
I should check out his diet.
5
She can't have recognised me.
She must be ignoring me.
I must have done something wrong.
She should have spoken to me.

12 Organise the class into new pairs. Give students five minutes to choose and prepare situations.

13 When students are ready, ask them to roleplay their conversations. Tell fast finishers to switch roles and re-enact their roleplays.
• In feedback, ask different groups to briefly tell the class what the outcome of their roleplay was.
• Once you have fed back on content, look at good language that students used, and language students didn't quite use correctly during the activity.

Optional extra activity Bring in an interesting photo about which students can speculate or predict. For example, this could be a photo of a busy scene at an airport, or one of a crowd at a football match. Show the picture and ask students to produce sentences using *will, might, should*, etc.

G For further practice, see Exercise 2 in the Grammar reference on page 177.

Answers to Exercise 2, Grammar reference
1 That must've been painful.
2 He should've stopped smoking earlier.
3 It can't be hard to do.
4 Given their resources, they couldn't have done any more to help.
5 It can't have been cheap.
6 He shouldn't have been taking those pills.
7 You may / might / could need three or four operations.
8 He must've been lying!
9 She might've / may have / could've picked up the cold from my son.
10 She should make a complete recovery after the operation.

VIDEO 5: THE CAT WHO ATE NEEDLES
Student's Book page 94

Aim
to watch a video about the drama of an animal operation; to improve students' ability to follow and understand fast speech in a video extract; to practise fast speech and to improve pronunciation, stress and intonation

1 Lead in to the topic by asking students to look at the photo and say what they can see. Organise the class into pairs to discuss the questions. In feedback, elicit students' ideas and write up interesting ideas or pieces of language on the board. Encourage students to justify their opinions.

Possible answers
Benefits of pets: companionship, fun to be with, rewarding to take care of animals, good and educational for your kids, dogs are a good excuse for a walk, can be useful for security
Downsides: cost of food and vet bills, difficult to go away because you have to find someone to feed and look after them, can be smelly, have to take dog for a walk in bad weather
Rewards of being a vet: good money, get to look after and save animals, can be exciting if it involves exotic animals

Culture notes

The photo shows an elderly man with three pet barn owls on the handlebars of his mobility scooter in Middlesbrough, England.

2 ☐◀ 23 Give students time to read through the task. Students watch and note their answers. Let them compare in pairs before discussing as a class.

Answers
1 A needle got stuck in the back of a cat's mouth and then when the cat closed its mouth, it bit into the needle. The needle has gone through the roof of the cat's mouth and penetrated the back of the cat's eye. The needle is unsterilised. The thread has been swallowed and could get stuck in the intestines.
2 The cat was playing by licking a piece of thread. The thread got stuck on the combs on the cat's tongue and it ended up swallowing it. There was a needle attached to the thread. The needle got stuck in the back of the throat and the cat bit into it.
3 Dr Yessenow immediately put Maxine under anaesthesia to take X-rays and get a better look at the needle.
4 The needle is unsterilised and could cause infection. The thread could cause complications. The worst-case scenario would be that the needle penetrates a major blood vessel and causes a major bleed, or that fluid leaks out of the eye itself and it completely collapses.

3 Organise the class into pairs to compare and discuss answers.

4 ☐◀ 23 Give students time to read through the sentences first. Ask students to watch the video, and to note True or False. Let students compare answers in pairs. In feedback, ask students to justify their answers.

Answers
1 F (only a few inches long)
2 T (we realised that the intestinal problem was not a major concern anymore – that our entire focus then was on the eye problem)
3 T (clamped an instrument to that little portion of the needle that was sticking out)
4 T (took less than a minute)
5 T (I think I slept about maybe three or four hours those first couple of nights. I would go through any lengths to save Maxine)
6 F (back to her old self / back to normal)
7 F (I would go through any lengths to save Maxine / It was worth every minute)
8 T (there were so many things that could have gone wrong. Overall, this cat was very, very lucky)

5 ☐◀ 23 Give students time to check the words first. You could check this by asking them to look in a dictionary, or by explaining the words yourself. Let students work in pairs to order the sentences. Then play the whole video. In feedback, ask students to justify their answers.

Answers
f The combs point backwards.
e Doctor Yessenow immediately puts Maxine under anaesthesia.
h I almost wanted to take her place.
d Doctor Yessenow was very helpful, but also very frank.
c It felt like forever – just that not knowing what was going to happen.
a She needs around-the-clock care over the next few days.
b Catherine's dedication pays off.
g In two weeks' time, Maxine is back to her old self.

Background language notes for teachers

around-the-clock care = being looked after 24 hours every day
pays off = is successful
frank = direct and honest
put under anaesthesia = make unconscious with drugs in order to do an operation
combs = here, small points in rows on the tongue
back to her old self = the same as she was before
take her place = be there in place of her

6 This exercise offers students the chance to relate the topic of the video to their own experiences, ideas and opinions.

• Ask students to discuss the questions in groups of four or five. Monitor and help with ideas and vocabulary.
• When most students have finished, stop the class and give some feedback, either by rephrasing some of the things students tried to say for the whole class or by asking students to correct or fill in gaps in sentences you've written on the board, based on what you heard students saying.

Understanding fast speech

7 ▶ 24 Play the recording. Students listen and write what they hear. Let them compare in pairs. Tell them not to worry if they haven't caught all the words yet.

8 ▶ 25 Students listen again to a slower version to check and improve what they have written. Let them compare answers in pairs.

9 Students check what they wrote in File 10 on page 189 of the Student's Book. Encourage them to practise saying the extract.

Video script ▶ 23

Dr Yessenow: Cats have a tongue with combs on it and the combs point backwards. Cats love to play with strings or the thread in this particular case. The thread gets caught in those combs. If a cat has something on its tongue they go they, they try to get it off, but they can't because it's stuck to the back of the tongue so it ends up swallowing the string. In this particular case, the string was attached to a needle and the needle got stuck in the back of the mouth and then when the cat closed its mouth, it bit into the needle. That's unusual, I had never seen anything like this before.
Narrator: Dr Yessenow immediately puts Maxine under anaesthesia to take X-rays and get a better look at the needle.
Dr Yessenow: This cat had to be in pain. We stopped everything that we were doing here in the hospital. This became our priority.
Narrator: The X-rays revealed the needle is nearly two inches long, and Maxine bit down on it so hard it's gone through the roof of her mouth and penetrated the back of her eye.
Dr Yessenow: I mean we were amazed when we saw this – quite shocking, actually.
Catherine: It was unbelievable when I first saw those X-rays – you could actually see the needle, it almost made it to the top of her head. I just felt bad for Maxine. I almost wanted to take her place.
Narrator: An unsterile needle now exposes Maxine to a laundry list of health problems.
Dr Yessenow: The worst-case scenario would have been that this needle was penetrating a major blood vessel and we would have had a major bleed or that the eye itself, all of its fluid would have leaked out and completely collapsed.
Narrator: And once Maxine is under anaesthesia, Dr Yessenow makes another alarming discovery. The cat has eaten more than just a needle.

Dr Yessenow: There was a thread attached to this needle. I became very concerned about this because if that thread gets stuck in the intestinal track, it becomes a very serious problem and it could be extremely life threatening.
Narrator: Faced with two major issues, the vet sends Catherine off to the waiting room as he considers his options for surgery.
Catherine: Dr Yessenow was very helpful but also very frank. He really wasn't sure what was going to happen. I was afraid the worst-case scenario would be that my Maxine wouldn't make it out of surgery alive.
Dr Yessenow: All the ... of the time involved in this case was the thinking, organising, planning, being prepared and knowing what we were doing.
Catherine: It felt like forever – just that not knowing what was going to happen.
Narrator: After intensive pre-planning, Dr Yessenow preps for surgery and starts the procedure.
Dr Yessenow: I was able to grab a hold of the thread with an instrument and the thread just came out – it was basically only a few inches long. Once that was discovered, we realised that the intestinal problem was not a major concern anymore – that our entire focus then was on the eye problem. We propped the mouth open, clamped an instrument to that little portion of the needle that was sticking out and very, very slowly and carefully pulled the needle through the roof of the mouth and pulled it out. The funny part about all this is that the actual procedure itself took less than a minute.
Narrator: After the successful surgery, Dr Yessenow prescribes four different medicines for Maxine. She needs around-the-clock care over the next few days if there's any hope in saving her eye.
Dr Yessenow: I told Catherine that she was going to have to dedicate the next few days of her existence treating this cat's eye.
Catherine: I had to give her medication every two hours for about 72 hours. I think I slept about maybe three or four hours those first couple of nights. I would go through any lengths to save Maxine.
Narrator: Catherine's dedication pays off. In two weeks' time Maxine is back to her old self.
Catherine: I believe it was very much worth it. Maxine is well now and she's happy, and if that's what it takes to get her to be back to normal, it was worth every minute.
Dr Yessenow: I'm very happy with the way that this worked out because there were so many things that could have gone wrong. Overall, this cat was very, very lucky.

REVIEW 5
Student's Book page 95

Aim
to consolidate vocabulary and grammar from
Units 9 and 10

Answers
Exercise 1
1 turnover / profit
2 breakthrough / discovery
3 could
4 been
5 will
6 would / could
7 have
8 must

Exercise 2
1 should have been paying more
2 They must be struggling
3 won't admit to not
4 have been improving over / getting better over
5 wouldn't be talking to
6 are constantly missing

Exercise 3
1 boring
2 have been looking
3 a fiercely
4 will
5 a walkout
6 can

Exercise 4
clench – body (teeth / fist)
click – body (fingers) work (the mouse / icon)
come up with – work (solution / ideas / proposal)
flutter – body (eyelashes)
implement – work (proposal / policy / strategy)
input – work (data / ideas)
oversee – work (project / staff)
place – work (an order)
schedule – work (meeting)
shrug – body (shoulders)
stretch – body (legs / arms)
wipe – body (hands / forehead)

Exercise 5
1 e   6 c
2 h   7 d
3 a   8 f
4 b   9 g
5 j   10 i

Exercise 6
1 compassionate   5 extensive
2 leadership   6 absenteeism
3 casualisation   7 contractual
4 redundancy   8 mortality

Exercise 7
1 network
2 entertaining
3 attract
4 perk
5 places
6 excruciating
7 rushed
8 insert
9 removed
10 anaesthetic
11 tribunal
12 compensation

11 PLAY

SPEAKING

Aim

to set the scene and introduce the theme with a photo; to get students talking about sports they watch and do

1 Start by telling the class that in this unit they're going to be talking about sports and issues around gaming; students will use irony, link ideas within and across sentences, and use playful language.
• Ask students to look at the photo on pages 96–97. Ask: *What can you see?* Elicit a brief description of the photo, and introduce any key words students might need.
• Organise the class into pairs to discuss the questions. Go round the room and check students are doing the task and help with ideas and vocabulary if necessary.
• In feedback, ask different pairs to tell the class what they discussed.
• Once you have fed back on content, look at good language that students used, and language students didn't quite use correctly during the activity. Show students better ways of saying what they were trying to say. You could write some useful new phrases on the board with gaps and ask the whole class to complete the sentences.

Possible answers
In the photo, some fans are watching the action at a football match, while others seem to have got upset and are abusing the referee's assistant.
Fans go wild when their team scores a goal, boo when a decision goes against the team and chant the name of players they like or who are doing well in the match. Fans get upset when a decision goes against their team, their team makes a mistake, or the opposition score. Fans might abuse the referee if they feel every decision made against their team is wrong, and they abuse opposition players who are really bad, really good, or are just unpopular for some reason.
Spectators might hold their head in their hands when a player misses a chance, or when the opposition threaten the goal or score. When the action is very exciting or very tense spectators may be on the edge of their seat.

Culture notes

The photo actually shows a football crowd at a Premier League football match in England. The fans are supporting Aston Villa, a club based in Birmingham. Mellberg ('There's only one Mellberg') was a Swedish international who played for the club which is why some fans are wearing Viking helmets.

2 Ask students to find a new partner. Ask them to prepare ideas individually first. Go round the room and help with ideas and vocabulary if necessary. When students are ready, ask them to take turns to talk. You could model the activity first, expressing one or two of your choices with reasons, and reminding students that we use the infinitive without *to* after *I'd rather* (*I'd rather watch sport than play sport because ...*).
• Once you have fed back on content, look at good language that students used, and language students didn't quite use correctly during the activity.

Optional extra activity Extend the pairwork in Exercise 2 into a mingle. Students go round and ask each other about their sporting preferences.

Teacher development: modelling activities

Even at the Advanced level, it is a good idea to model activities before students begin. Here are some reasons why:
1 It avoids a long-winded instruction – students are immediately clear on what to do.
2 It provides a good example of what you want students to try to say. They have a benchmark to try to achieve.
3 It motivates students to get talking.
4 It allows you to show language you want students to use (here, for example, it is a chance to remind students of how to use *I'd rather*).

Communicative outcomes
In this two-page spread, students will talk about sports and learn to recognise and use irony.

VOCABULARY Sports and events

Aim
to introduce and practise phrases used when describing sports and events

1 Explain to the students that they are going to learn some vocabulary connected to sports and events. Organise the class into small groups of three or four to answer the questions. Elicit the answer to the first one as an example. In feedback, use examples to check the meaning of any words students are not sure of.

> **Answers**
> 1 The second round will be the second series of games in a competition. If you're knocked out, you lose and are then out of the competition. The team / person that beat you goes through to the next round. If you scrape through, you go through to the next round, but after a very difficult, hard-fought game / match that you only just managed to win.
> 2 They hope the decision will be overturned. They disagree with the decision that has been made and want it to be changed. The opposing player hopes the decision will be upheld.
> 3 They might have to do a blood test or urine test before or after a game or a race. If they're caught doping (taking banned substances), they'll probably get a lengthy ban, or in some cases be banned for life.
> 4 They get beaten very badly and lose by a large margin. The crowd may well boo and abuse their team or demand the manager gets sacked, or they may feel embarrassed or go silent.
> 5 If you're sin-binned, you have to leave the place of play for a short period of time because you've committed a foul that's bad, but not bad enough for you to get sent off. In football, if you're sent off, the referee gives you a red card – which can be after a second yellow card or can be a straight red for serious fouls or misconduct. Being sent off is worse than being sin-binned. Sin-binning happens in ice hockey, roller derby, rugby league, and rugby union.
> 6 If you're suspended, you have to miss one or more games because you were sent off in a previous game. If you're substituted, you're taken off during a game and replaced by someone else. This may be because you're not playing well, or it may be tactical – it may suit the game better to bring a different kind of player on. If you're dropped, you're left out of the team for one or more games because you've not been performing well or have upset the manager in some way.

> 7 Because you're tired and are running out of energy. It could also be because you're losing psychological motivation.
> 8 You have a great chance to win something, but fail to. Often it's because you crack under pressure or lose a crucial game.
> 9 They pay / bribe someone to ensure they get the result they want. Maybe they bribe the officials to encourage them to make unfair decisions; or else they bribe players to encourage them to play badly, make crucial mistakes, etc. They usually do it because they have large bets riding on the results.
> 10 In a close game, the two sides or players are very evenly matched and one wins by a very narrow margin. In a one-sided game, one player or team is much better and thrashes the other. A dirty game has lots of fouls in it, and maybe lots of yellow cards, red cards, and players getting sin-binned.
> 11 If you get cramp while playing / running / swimming, you get sudden severe pains in tired muscles. The muscles become very tight. The day after exercise, your muscles may feel stiff when you move.
> 12 Because they're doing it for charity and you want to give them money if they complete it because the money goes to the charity. Perhaps because they are someone you know, and you want to encourage them.

2 In their groups, ask students to take turns trying to use the new language in personalised examples. You could start them off by focusing on the examples, eliciting one or two possible answers from students, and giving them preparation time to think of things to say. Monitor and notice how well students use the new vocabulary. In feedback, point out any errors students make with use and pronunciation.

Optional extra activity Ask students to say which sports each set of phrases in Exercise 1 are most likely to go with. For example, 1 could be a team sport like football or rugby, but also tennis, 2 is most likely tennis, 3 could be athletics or cycling, 4 could be tennis or a team sport like football or rugby, 5 could be rugby or ice hockey but not football (no sin bin in football), 6 any team sports, 7 could be a cycling race or a long-distance race or in a football, rugby, tennis, etc. match, 8 could be golf or tennis where there is pressure on the individual, 9 could be football, cricket or boxing, 10 is a team sport, 11 could be athletics or a team game, 12 is a long-distance event.

LISTENING

Aim
to listen for general understanding and to hear and complete extracts from sentences used in a listening text

3 🎧 **34** Give students a moment to read through the sentences. Check any words students aren't sure of.
• Play the recording. Students listen and note answers. Let students compare answers before discussing in feedback.

Answers

a Conversation 2 (And I got cramp.)
b Conversation 3 (Arsenal were lucky to draw. Honestly, it could've been about five–nil after the first 20 minutes.)
c Conversation 3 (We'll thrash them in the home game! // I don't know. Two of your defenders are suspended, and you have a couple of other people injured. And Arsenal will be the underdogs, so they won't have any pressure on them.)
d Conversation 2 (I was fading so badly by the end.)
e Conversation 1 (Oh, right. Very close! (said ironically) // No, honestly, it was ... kind of!)
f Conversation 1 (The coaching sessions are paying off then. // No, they definitely are. Let's just say there's still room for improvement.)
g Conversation 3 (they made some substitutions and brought on Wallace, who made a huge difference)
h Conversation 1 (she's not exactly Steffi Graf, but you know ...)
i Conversation 2 (Didn't you sponsor me?)

🔊 34

Conversation 1

A: How was the tennis?
B: Good.
A: Who won?
B: Mena, but it was pretty close.
A: Really?
B: Don't sound so surprised.
A: No, sorry. I just thought you said she was really good.
B: She is. I mean, she's not exactly Steffi Graf, but you know ...
A: Steffi who?
B: She was ... Oh dear. Am I showing my age?
A: Don't worry. I won't tell. So what was the score?
B: 6–4, 6–1, I think.
A: Oh, right. Very close!
B: No, honestly, it was ... kind of! We actually had some pretty long rallies. I even had a couple of shots down the line.
A: Look at you!
B: Seriously, I was very proud. Shame my serving was utterly rubbish towards the end.
A: The coaching sessions are paying off, then.
B: No, they definitely are! Let's just say there's still room for improvement. And Mena's just a bit fitter and stronger than me.
A: Well, that's because you're so ancient and she's so young.
B: Ah, yes, well, there is that! Good job I don't look it.
A: Well, that's true.

Conversation 2

C: Hiya. How's it going?
D: Yeah, alright. Is there enough water in the kettle for me too?
C: Yeah, should be.
D: So, how are you? I haven't seen you for a while? Have you been away?

C: I was back in Spain.
D: Oh, cool. Was that seeing family?
C: Mmm, kind of, but actually the main reason I went was for this big swim. Didn't you sponsor me?
D: Did I? Remind me again.
C: It was a 6K swim from the coast to this island.
D: Oh yeah, yeah, yeah! Sorry – a memory like a sieve. So ... how did it go?
C: Well, I just about made it.
D: Sounds bad.
C: Mmm, it was tough! And I got cramp.
D: You're joking! I've had that playing football and I was just clutching my leg in agony.
C: Yeah, it was horrible.
D: But how does that work when you're in the water?
C: There were some support boats that brought me water and I just kind of floated on my back.
D: Still.
C: Yeah, horrible, but I managed to get over it.
D: Well done.
C: I shouldn't have set off so fast because we got diverted because – how do you say – a swarm of jellyfish?
D: You are kidding!
C: No, no. We maybe did an extra kilometre.
D: Wow!
C: It was about 30 degrees too! I was fading so badly by the end.
D: Hey, I wouldn't have even managed to get off the beach.
C: Ha!
D: So, how much do I owe you?
C: £20.
D: Twenty! That's a bit much? You only did 7K in 30 degree heat round swarms of jellyfish.
C: Ha ha! You forget the swim back.
D: What? You ...?
C: No!

Conversation 3

E: Did you catch the game last night? I had to work.
F: Yeah. It was incredible. For a neutral, anyway. I'm not sure how you'd have felt.
E: 2–2 away. It sounds crazy.
F: Hey, Arsenal were lucky to draw. Honestly, it could've been about five-nil after the first 20 minutes. The Arsenal keeper made some great saves and Manu managed to kick the ball over the bar from about a metre out. Honestly, my granny could've scored it.
E: Ah, Manu ... he's so overrated. There's no way he's worth 60 million, or however much he cost us. He's rubbish.
F: You're right. He is totally useless ... which is why he scored two fantastic goals after that!
E: OK, OK. He is good, just not that good!
F: No, I do know what you mean, and actually for his first goal the Arsenal keeper messed up badly.
E: Right. So how did they manage to get back in the game then?
F: Well, they made some substitutions and brought on Wallace, who made a huge difference.
E: Really?

F: Yeah, really. He scored a great goal, which got the whole team going. Then he won them a very dubious penalty and got a Bayern defender sent off.

E: It wasn't a penalty, then.

F: Well, let's put it this way. If he touched him at all, it certainly wasn't enough to send him crashing to the ground like he'd been shot. Anyway, it was an amazing game. Ridiculously open, even after Bayern went down to ten men.

E: Yeah. We'll thrash them in the home game!

F: Probably. But two of your defenders are suspended and you have a couple of other people injured. And Arsenal will be the underdogs, so they won't have any pressure on them. You never know – you could still get knocked out.

E: By Arsenal? Not a chance.

Culture notes

Steffi Graf was a German tennis player. She won 22 Grand Slam singles titles between 1988 and 1999.
Note the tennis terms in Conversation 1: *serve, rally, shots down the line.*
I have a memory like a sieve = an expression meaning 'I am very forgetful' (water goes through a sieve very easily)
a neutral = here, somebody who supports neither team at a match
2–2 away = the speaker is saying that Arsenal were playing away from home (playing in Germany) and drew the match 2–2
Arsenal is an English premier league football club, based in London, and Bayern (Munich) is a German Bundesliga club.
underdogs = the weaker team that is not expected to win
Note the football terms in Conversation 2: *draw, save, (goal)keeper, over the bar* (the beam across the top of the goal), *substitutions, penalty.*

4 🔊 **34** Organise the class into pairs to discuss and complete the sentences. Students should be able to remember some of the missing words based on their first listening and from the context of the sentences.
• Play the recording again. Students listen and complete answers. Let students compare answers before discussing in feedback.

> **Answers**
> 1 my, was utterly rubbish towards the
> 2 just say, still room for
> 3 and I was just, my, in agony
> 4 have even, to get off the
> 5 way he's worth, or however
> 6 scored a great, which got the whole

5 Ask students to prepare ideas individually first. Go round the room and help with ideas and vocabulary if necessary. When students are ready, ask them to discuss the questions in pairs.
• Once you have fed back on content, look at good language that students used, and language students didn't quite use correctly during the activity.

Optional extra activity Ask students in pairs to choose a sport and find and present five words or phrases that are particular to that sport. For example, they could choose football (*free kick, penalty, striker, centre half, get a yellow card*), rugby (*score a try, a conversion, make a pass, a scrum, a lineout*), or tennis (*court, double fault, 40-love, backhand volley, serve*).

DEVELOPING CONVERSATIONS
Irony and humour

Aim
to introduce and practise ways of expressing irony and humour in conversations

6 Read through the information in the box as a class.
• Give students time to find and read through the underlined expressions in audio script 34 on page 207. Ask them to discuss the questions with a partner and decide what they express. In feedback, elicit, confirm and correct answers.

> **Answers**
> Conversation 1
> *Oh dear. Am I showing my age?*
> Not ironic. It's true that when she mentioned Steffi Graf, she's showing her age.
> *Oh, right. Very close!*
> Ironic. In reality, 6–4, 6–1 isn't close at all.
> *The coaching sessions are paying off, then.*
> Ironic. She means she doesn't think they're worth the money or time spent on them.
> *Well, that's because you're so ancient and she's so young.*
> Ironic. Mena may be younger but this is deliberately exaggerated.
>
> Conversation 2
> *Sorry – a memory like a sieve.*
> Not ironic. He really does have a bad memory and forgot about the sponsorship.
> *I've had that playing football and I was just clutching my leg in agony.*
> Not ironic. It really happened.
> *... but I managed to get over it.*
> Not ironic. It's true.
> *That's a bit much! You only did 7K in 30-degree heat round swarms of jellyfish.*
> Ironic. The real meaning is the speaker thinks doing 7K in 30-degree heat is very impressive.
>
> Conversation 3
> *Manu managed to kick the ball over the bar from about a metre out.*
> Ironic. The meaning is it was very hard to miss.
> *He is totally useless ...*
> Ironic. The player then scored an amazing goal.
> *... the Arsenal keeper messed up badly.*
> Not ironic. It's true.
> *... who made a huge difference.*
> Not ironic. It's true. He scored a great goal.

7 Ask students to work individually to do the matching task. Elicit the first one to get them started. Go round the room and help if necessary. Let students compare answers in pairs before discussing as a class.
• Once you have fed back on answers, ask students to practise the exchanges. Go round and correct any poor pronunciation or any other errors.

> **Answers**
> 1 c
> 2 d
> 3 a
> 4 e
> 5 b

Background language notes for teachers

Notice that the way the phrases in Exercise 7 are said is important in expressing irony and humour. Note the extra-strong stress to emphasise the irony (as underlined below):
You could say that!
It wasn't bad. I didn't exactly go wild, though.
Well, it's not exactly Shakespeare.

8 Ask students to complete the sentences. Go round the room and help with ideas and vocabulary if necessary.

9 Organise the class into groups and let them discuss their ideas.
• Once you have fed back on content, look at good language that students used, and language students didn't quite use correctly during the activity.

> **Possible answers**
> There are no fixed answers here. Work with your students' ideas. However, here are some possible ideas:
> I once managed to ... lock myself out of my house / lose my passport when I was on holiday / forget where I was staying and had to wander round for hours trying to find the place!
> I'm not exactly ... the best speaker of English there has ever been / the greatest musician in the world / George Clooney!

CONVERSATION PRACTICE

Aim
to practise language from the lesson in a free, communicative, personalised speaking activity

10 Organise the class into pairs and ask them to decide which task to choose. Give students four or five minutes to read role cards (pages 191 and 192) or prepare things to say. When students are ready, ask them to do the task. Listen for errors, new language or interesting stories to use in feedback. Ask students to change partners two or three times if you want.
• In feedback, look at good language that students used, and language students didn't quite use correctly during

the activity. Show students better ways of saying what they were trying to say. You could write some useful new phrases on the board with gaps and ask the whole class to complete the sentences.

 26 Refer students to the video and activities on the DVD-ROM.

Teacher development: using the video

The video and activities on the DVD-ROM can be used in various ways:
1 as an alternative to the conversation practice
2 instead of the listening activity in some units, particularly with weaker groups. Students can first practise reading out the dialogues and work on some of the key phrases / structures in a controlled way before having a go themselves.
3 at the end of the unit as a revision exercise

GAME THEORY
Student's Book pages 100–101

Communicative outcomes
In this two-page spread, students read about and talk about games and gaming.

VOCABULARY Talking about gaming

Aim
to introduce words to talk about gaming

1   Ask students to work in small groups to come up with a list of games. In feedback, write up kinds of games they mention on the board.

> **Possible answers**
> arcade games, console games, online games, shooter games, strategy games, roleplaying games, sports games, fighting games, simulation games

2   Give students a moment to read through the words, and elicit the first answer to get them started. Ask students to work individually then compare their answers in pairs. In feedback, elicit answers.

> **Answers**
> 1 provides
> 2 collaborate
> 3 modify
> 4 foster
> 5 are exposed
> 6 stimulate
> 7 defy
> 8 letting

3   Ask students to underline any new phrases. Let them compare in pairs. In feedback, elicit answers and check understanding.

> **Possible answers**
> There are no fixed answers, but expect students to underline some of the following:
> 1 Gaming provides an escape from the stresses and strains of everyday life.
> 2 You often have to work together and collaborate with others to achieve success.
> 3 The fact you can <u>modify your environment</u> to <u>suit your own taste</u> makes things very creative.
> 4 Gaming can actually <u>help foster family relationships</u> if everyone plays together.
> 5 You <u>are exposed to a huge amount of English</u> in most games, so they're a great way of practising.
> 6 A lot of the new multi-player online role-playing games really stimulate the imagination.
> 7 The graphics on some modern games are so incredible they <u>defy description</u>.
> 8 First-person shooter games are a great way of letting off steam.

Background language notes for teachers

collaborate = work together
foster relationships = improve or build relationships

defy description = beyond description – so good (or bad) that it is impossible to describe
let off steam = release feelings of anger or frustration (here in a way that doesn't hurt other people)

4   Students discuss the opinions in pairs. Go round the room and check students are doing the task and help with ideas.
• In feedback, ask different pairs to tell the class what they discussed. Once you have fed back on content, look at good language that students used, and language students didn't quite use correctly. Show students better ways of saying what they were trying to say.

> **Possible answers**
> Benefits: improves reactions, good for your brain, makes you quick-thinking, can make money from gaming, helps you get a job in the gaming industry, helps you understand how modern technology works, making friends with other gamers
> Downsides: can be boring and repetitive, anti-social, makes you tired, bad for your eyes, can cause repetitive strain syndrome, some games encourage violence and aggression, addictive, can end up playing games instead of doing other things in life

READING

Aim
to practise reading for general understanding and for the main argument

5   Start by asking students to look at the headline to the blog post, and ask them what they can predict about the text.
• Ask students to read the blog post and answer the questions. Let students compare answers in pairs before discussing as a class. Ask students in feedback to justify their answers.

> **Answers**
> 1
> online chess and snooker (named as examples of common online games people play)
> first-person shooters (sometimes the teacher gets engrossed in them – especially after a bad staff meeting)
> roleplaying games (half the male students seem addicted to them)
> 2
> Benefits:
> help you let off steam / serve as a stress release
> can help linguistic and social skills develop
> help build / cement friendships
> Downsides:
> addictive – result in students sitting up half the night and coming in to class exhausted
> students doing less homework
> students being less verbal
> don't broaden world knowledge in any way

3
The blogger is not totally anti-gaming as he / she admits to enjoying gaming and says we all can see the appeal. However, he / she seems very concerned by how much time kids spend gaming – and the effect this has on them. The blogger would like to see games used in much more moderation.

6 Organise the class into pairs to discuss the opinions. Tell them to look back at the text if necessary to find support for their views. Elicit ideas in feedback, and ask students to justify answers.

Answers
We suggest the following answers. If students are adamant they're right, however, accept their ideas as possibilities if well argued:
1 Yes = after particularly traumatic staff meetings, I've even been known to get disturbingly engrossed in first-person shooters! (*unwind* = relax)
2 Yes = surely only the most evangelical would claim that gaming comes with no strings attached. (You could also argue that the answer is no. He / She doesn't state this opinion, rather he / she sets it out as a challenge and expresses his / her opinion with 'surely only the most evangelical would claim ...' – so not quite the same thing. We don't actually know from this what he / she thinks.)
3 No = the blog says girls read more, spend less time gaming, and do better at school, but that's not the same as saying they mature earlier.
4 Yes = I've heard the arguments in support of collaborative gaming. I've read research claiming linguistic and social skills develop on account of the hours spent online – and that's all fine so long as it's done in moderation.
5 Yes = It's the effect it seems to be having on the lives of half my students that worries me most – and frankly, I mean the male half! ... Many of the lads I teach are addicts, pure and simple. The roleplay games they're into are a chronic suck on their time: whether or not they start out with the intention of studying, before too long their evenings are lost to the virtual realm. Time flies by and they game till they drop where they sit – and subsequently drag themselves into class in the morning half-asleep at best.
(You could also argue that the answer is no. He / She only says that it is the main reason in his / her class, not in the wider world. He / She does not make such a big claim, he / she's just really talking about personal experience.)
6 Yes = whether or not they start out with the intention of studying, before too long their evenings are lost to the virtual realm. Time flies by and they game till they drop
7 No = because the (potential) benefits are mentioned. Also, the blog is talking about computer games, not computers per se.

8 No = these are issues that senior management are aware of. The best solution they've come up with so far, though? Gamification of the syllabus! I despair sometimes, I really do.

Opinion 5 is probably closest to the main argument of the blog.

Background language notes for teachers

disturbingly engrossed = spending too much time on something in a way that is worrying
the most evangelical = here, the people who believe or support something to an extreme
with no strings attached = without problems or any negative outcomes
a chronic suck on their time = a humorous way to say a big waste of time

7 Ask students to read the comments individually. As a class discuss whether the comments agree or disagree with the article. Give students time to write their own comment.

8 Organise the class into groups of four or five to discuss the comments. Monitor closely and note interesting and useful language, as well as errors. Use the feedback to point out good examples, correct errors, and to provide examples of how students can express their ideas better.

Optional extra activity Ask students to write their comments on a piece of paper and to sign them. Then pin the comments in groups of four or five comments in different parts of the rooms (on the notice board, a wall, a table, the board, etc.). Organise the class into groups of four or five. Tell them to find a set of comments, discuss them, then move round the room and discuss another set of comments.

GRAMMAR Linking words and phrases

Aim
to check students' understanding of how to use linking words and phrases in descriptions of games

9 Read through the information in the box as a class.
• Organise the class into pairs to match linkers to functions.
• Monitor and notice how well students understand the rules of form. In feedback, elicit the students' answers.

Answers
1 contrast: That notwithstanding, Whilst
2 condition: so long as, Otherwise
3 time / order: Meanwhile, subsequently
4 purpose / result: so as to, consequently
5 addition: not to mention, Moreover
6 cause: down to, on account of

Background language notes for teachers

Work with what students come up with in Exercise 9 and don't add extras here yourself, but below is a list of other possible linkers that could fit each function, which aren't in the text:

Contrast – *in spite of, despite, although, even though, but, however, whereas, nevertheless, all the same*

Condition – *if, in case, assuming (that), on condition (that), provided (that), providing (that), unless, in the event (that)*

The time / order things happen – *and subsequently, then, after that, afterwards, at the same time, during, until, for once, when, as soon as, the minute, the second*

Purpose / result – *in order to, as such, so, thus, as a result, therefore*

Addition – *as well as, on top of that, furthermore, in addition, additionally, and, and also*

Cause – *a result of, thanks to, as a result of, due to, because of, owing to*

10   Ask students to work individually to do the task. Do the first as an example in open class. Encourage students to have a guess, or use their knowledge, first, to get answers. Let students compare in pairs.

• In feedback, elicit the students' answers. They can check their answers using the Grammar reference on page 177.

Answers

All the same could replace *That notwithstanding*
as such could replace *consequently*
despite the fact that could replace *whilst*
On top of that could replace *Moreover*
a result of could replace *down to*
as well as could replace *not to mention*
If we don't could replace *Otherwise*
provided could replace *so long as*
as a result of could replace *on account of*
In the meantime could replace *Meanwhile*
in order to could replace *so as to*
then could replace *subsequently*

 Students complete Exercise 1 in the Grammar reference on page 178.

Answers to Exercise 1, Grammar reference
1 Otherwise
2 so as not to / in order to not
3 Nonetheless, That notwithstanding
4 so / thus, On top of that / Additionally
5 unless
6 the second / as soon as
7 on account of / as a result of
8 thanks to / due to
9 Whereas / Whilst
10 as well as / not to mention
11 Even though / Although, so long as / providing

---

11   Ask students to work individually to complete the descriptions before comparing ideas with a partner. In feedback, go through the answers and refer back to the rules and the Grammar reference if necessary.

Answers

1 whether	6 In spite of
2 although	7 Even though
3 as such	8 Whereas
4 down to	9 owing to
5 as well as	10 Similarly

---

12   Organise the class into small groups of four or five. Ask students in each group to work individually and choose a game and prepare their ideas. Allow about five minutes of preparation time first, and monitor to help students with ideas and vocabulary.

• As students speak in their groups, go round and monitor, and note down any interesting language you hear.

• Once you have fed back on content, look at good language that students used, and language students didn't quite use correctly. Show students better ways of saying what they were trying to say. You could write some useful new phrases on the board with gaps and ask the whole class to complete the sentences.

 For further practice, see Exercise 2 in the Grammar reference on page 178.

Answers to Exercise 2, Grammar reference
1 so that he can / so that he is able to
2 in case you missed
3 I, on the other hand,
4 despite the fact (that) I
5 and on top of that
6 on account of product adaptation

Optional extra activity Ask students to write up their description of a game for homework.

Web research activity
• Ask students to choose a game to research and write about.
• Ask students to present their game in the next class.

WORD PLAY
Student's Book pages 102–103

Communicative outcomes
In this two-page spread, students will listen to a podcast about wordplay and word games; they will practise alliteration and play word games.

LISTENING

Aim
to practise listening for general and specific information

1 Organise the class into pairs to discuss the questions. Monitor and note their interest and knowledge. In feedback, point out any errors or good use of language you noticed.

Optional extra activity Ask students to describe any other famous games involving words that they play in their country.

Culture notes

Scrabble is being played in the photo. It is a word game in which two to four players score points by placing tiles, each bearing a single letter, onto a board divided into squares. The tiles must form words which go from left to right in rows or downwards in columns, just like in a crossword. Different letters score different points, e.g. E = 1; J = 8. Players add up their points after each round. The winner is the player with most points when the letters run out.
The skills you need include a large vocabulary, and a good eye for letters – you need to be able to see how any set of seven letters in your hand can be made into words. Top scrabble players memorise long lists of odd, high-scoring words, and play a strategic game which is about blocking the board to stop their opponents scoring.
Scrabble was invented in 1928 by an American architect called Alfred Butts. Today, it is a trademark of the US company *Mattel*. It is available in 29 languages, and as many as 150 million sets have been sold worldwide.

2 ⚫ **35** Give students a moment to read the task.
• Play the recording. Students listen and note answers. Let them compare their answers in pairs before discussing as a class.

Answers
Scrabble is mentioned because a new version has been developed for the endangered Carrier language in Canada. The topic of the podcast is what wordplay and word games can do for language learning.

⚫ 35

C = Christine Wright, A = Antoine Smith, K = Karen Lu
C: Hello, I'm Christine Wright and welcome to *The Wright Word*. Following our recent podcast on dying languages, one listener sent me a link to a

fascinating article about a version of Scrabble developed for the Carrier language in Canada. Now, there are only around 1,000 Carrier speakers left in that region, and this project is part of a campaign to try to encourage the Carrier tribes to maintain their distinct language. As an avid Scrabble and Words With Friends player myself, I was obviously attracted to the idea, but I have been wondering how far this project could work and what word games and, more broadly, wordplay can do for language learners. So, here to discuss this with me today I'm joined by multilingual friends Antoine Smith and Karen Lu, both of whom speak ... I think it's five languages?
A: Yep.
K: Yeah, that's right.
C: So, Antoine, what do you think of the idea of Scrabble for a minority language?

Culture notes

The Carrier language is named after the Dakelh people, a First Nations people of the Central Interior of British Columbia in Canada. Carrier is the usual English name for their language.

3 Organise the class into pairs to discuss the questions.
• As students speak, go round and monitor, and note down any interesting language you hear.
• In feedback, look at good language that students used, and language students didn't quite use correctly.

Possible answers
See answers to Exercise 3 below. However, at this stage, work with students' ideas as they will listen and find answers later.

4 ⚫ **36** Give students a moment to read the task.
• Play the recording. Students listen and note answers. Let them compare their answers in pairs.
• In feedback, elicit answers from around the class, and ask students to justify answers by saying exactly what they heard.

Answers
All of the below could be seen as part of the answers. Decide for yourself how much you want your students to remember and relate, and what you're happy just adding or reminding them of yourself.
1 Antoine Smith: not convinced the project will work or help protect the language because Scrabble isn't about knowing the everyday language, it's about specialised vocabulary and unusual words. One person won a competition in English just by memorising words in a dictionary. Karen Lu: likes the idea of wordplay games but believes that Scrabble maybe isn't the best game to help preserve the language as it's an oral language with an oral tradition. Antoine agrees.

Christine: thinks even if the words aren't useful in themselves, there may be a lot of interesting chat involved in playing the game.

2 Other games mentioned are: crosswords, puns, Taboo, tongue twisters, rhymes, Words With Friends

3 The speakers don't exactly always comment on whether things are good for language learners, but you can extrapolate out and see what they basically think. Ideas below.

Crosswords – probably good but be aware they work differently depending on the alphabet. In Chinese, for example, one character is what in English we might think of as a word, therefore what they have on crosswords are phrases or idioms that share certain words / characters.

Puns – very important in Chinese, as in the story about the same character existing for dates and peanuts as well as for the phrase 'May you soon give birth to a boy'.

Taboo – good as you have to use other words to explain / paraphrase the word you're trying to elicit.

Tongue twisters – all that's mentioned here is that they're fun, can have a competitive element, but not really things you'll ever say in conversation.

Rhymes and alliteration – useful because a lot of common expressions feature it – 'here and there', 'everything's ship-shape', etc.

Words With Friends – lots of chat around the game, some users have even had relationships as a result of using the app!

🎧 36

C = Christine Wright, A = Antoine Smith, K = Karen Lu

A: Well, it's interesting, but I'm not sure how far it'll take the language. I mean, a lot of words you use playing Scrabble in English are pretty random. You know, things like *zho*, which are a hybrid cattle, or *mu*, which is a Greek letter. Not exactly the kind of thing you'd drop into casual conversation! I imagine that a Carrier version of Scrabble would be similar – you'd end up having lots of obscure words just because they get a high score.

C: Yeah, but ...

A: ... and in fact, it's more about maths and strategy. Apparently, one world champion didn't even speak English – he'd just learned the dictionary by heart.

C: But they won't be really playing to win, will they? That's not the point here.

A: What? Not playing to win?

C: Yeah. OK. That's your over-competitiveness! But playing with language is universal, isn't it, Karen?

K: Absolutely, but not all cultures play in the same way. I mean, I'm guessing the Carrier language has an oral tradition ...

A: ... exactly ...

K: ... so maybe Scrabble isn't the best game for this language.

A: You took the words out of my mouth.

K: I mean, in Chinese we don't do crosswords because the language is based on characters.

C: Of course! Yeah.

K: Well, there are some kinds of crosswords but with idioms and sayings ...

C: ... because each character in Chinese is like a word?

K: Yeah, exactly, and the two sayings will share the character where they cross. And sometimes one character has two meanings.

C: Yeah, yeah. Actually, I heard that puns are a big thing in Chinese.

K: Oh yeah, definitely. Like when someone gets married, we sometimes give the couple dates and peanuts because the characters for the words 'dates' and 'peanuts' are pretty much the same as the saying 'May you soon give birth to a boy.'

C: Not a girl.

K: No, I know. It is a bit sexist, but that's the tradition.

C: OK. Well, let's not get into that now! Are there any other word games which might be good for practising language?

K: We have another one with idioms. So, I give a saying and then you have to say another one starting with the last word or sound in my one.

A: Doesn't sound so easy.

K: No, maybe not. We also play something like Taboo – you know that, right?

C: Yeah. Where you explain a word – say, 'library' – for others to guess, without using words like 'book' or 'borrow'.

K: Exactly. That's good. We also do tongue twisters.

A: Oh yeah, I like them. I learnt one in Spanish: El perro de San Roca non tiene rabo porque ... oh man, it's slipped my mind now ... er ...

C: And what does it mean?

A: Oh, the dog of San Roca doesn't have a tail because ... I think it was a mouse stole it.

C: Ha ha. Not the kind of thing you'd drop into casual conversation.

A: Er, no, that's true.

C: Mind you, we did a podcast recently on how you get a lot of this kind of alliteration or rhyming just in our normal choice of words, you know, like 'everything's ship-shape' or 'here and there' – maybe because it makes it more memorable.

A: Although apparently it hasn't helped me!

C: Well, there's always an exception that proves the rule.

A: Ha ha. Whatever! It wasn't just about learning. Doing that tongue twister was fun – like a competition with my classmates – and then it spun off into a general discussion on what we found difficult in Spanish.

C: Well, that's the point I was trying to make before with Scrabble. The words themselves might not be so useful, but it's all the chat that goes on around the game.

A: Yeah, no, you're right. I actually heard that some people on Words With Friends have got married through the app's chat feature.

C: Well, I wouldn't go that far, but I think it does prove my point, which is always a good place to call it a day!

K: Absolutely.

A: Who's competitive now!

C: I'd never deny it. Anyway, thanks to you both and thanks to everyone who's listened.

5 🔊 **36** Give students a moment to read through the sentences and decide on any answers they can remember based on the first listening.
• Play the recording again. Let students compare their answers in pairs. In feedback, elicit answers and ask students to justify.

Answers

1 The word *zho* means 'hybrid cattle', and is an example of the kind of obscure word people often use in Scrabble.
2 The fact it's basically an oral language is mentioned because it explains why Scrabble – with its emphasis on obscure words from the written language – isn't the best game for practising / preserving it.
3 Chinese crosswords aren't based on words, like Western ones, but on phrases / idioms that share words. Scrabble wouldn't work as it's based on words and the way letters intersect across them. It may, of course, be theoretically possible to do a version using idioms / phrases with intersecting characters, but Chinese has so many characters, it wouldn't work.
4 In China, when someone gets married, the couple are sometimes given dates and peanuts because the characters for dates and peanuts are pretty much the same as the saying 'May you soon give birth to a boy'.
5 The saying 'May you soon give birth to a boy'.
6 Alliteration – the use of the same letter / sound at the start of words in a phrase or sentence – is shown in 'everything's ship-shape'. Tongue twisters often feature alliteration.
7 Because some people playing the Words With Friends app got to know each other so well through the chat feature of the app that they ended up getting married.
8 Because she wants to finish on a high and ending by her 'winning'.

---

6 Organise the class into groups of four or five to discuss the questions.
• As students speak, go round and monitor, and note down any interesting pieces of language you hear.
• Once you have fed back on content, look at good language that students used, and language students didn't quite use correctly. Show students better ways of saying what they were trying to say. You could write some useful new phrases on the board with gaps and ask the whole class to complete the sentences.

Possible answers

Languages may become extinct because: more people learning major languages because it helps them get a job, travel, get opportunities; many minority languages have low status in society and students need to speak another, need mainstream language to get educated; people who speak the language are dying out
Language can be sexist in terms of using words which are gender specific (*spokesman*, *air hostess*), in using *he* to mean all people, etc.

Optional extra activity Write the following letters on the board: V B E E N M R O. Ask students in pairs to write down as many genuine English words of four letters or more as they can in four minutes. Tell them that they must also find one word of eight letters. At the end, find out which pair got the longest list. Answers: *veer, move, mover, been, beer, born, bore, even, ever, never, rove, over, oven, omen, norm, reborn, morn, NOVEMBER*

UNDERSTANDING VOCABULARY
Alliteration

Aim
to introduce and practise tongue twisters and idioms that use alliteration

7 🔊 **37** Read through the information in the box as a class. Ask students if they can think of any examples of alliteration from their previous learning. Give students a moment to read the tongue twisters.
• Play the recording. Students listen and notice how the speakers say the tongue twisters.
• Organise the class into pairs to practise the phrases. Go round and help with pronunciation.

🔊 **37**
1 Three free throws.
2 A really weird rear wheel.
3 She sells seashells on the seashore.
4 Peter Piper picked a pickled pepper.
5 How can a clam cram in a clean cream can?
6 How much ground would a groundhog hog if a groundhog could hog ground?

Background language notes for teachers: pronunciation

When monitoring students' pronunciation, as in Exercise 7 above, it is handy to have a few ideas up your sleeve to show students how to pronounce particular sounds.
Three free throws = model the tongue going past and touching the top teeth when making the hard 'th' sound, and the teeth biting the bottom lip to show the 'f' sound.
Weird rear wheel = show the tightly rounded mouth for the 'w' sound, and the wider mouth when making 'r'.
Peter Piper = show the plosive 'p' sound by placing a piece of paper in front of your mouth as you say 'p' – note how the paper is blown by the sound.

8 Ask students to complete the sentences individually. Let them compare in pairs.
• In feedback, elicit answers from the class.

Optional extra activity Ask students to find other examples of alliterative phrases in the sentences.

Answers
1 stop the rot
2 love lost
3 bite the bullet
4 doom and gloom
5 on the tip of my tongue
6 peer pressure
7 the lap of luxury
8 reserve the right
9 give as good as she gets
10 jump the gun

The examples of other alliterative phrases in the sentences are:
1 deeply disappointing
2 meeting of minds
3 break the bank
4 far from it
5 –
6 –
7 same old story
8 strictly speaking
9 –
10 simply superb

• In feedback, look at good language that students used, and language students didn't quite use correctly during the activity. Show students better ways of saying what they were trying to say. You could write some useful new phrases on the board with gaps and ask the whole class to complete the sentences.

Optional extra activity Ask fast finishers to choose and play another game, or to write their own list of words to practise.

Background language notes for teachers

stop the rot = stop the sequence of bad things happening (e.g. a run of poor results)
little love lost = they don't get on very well
bite the bullet = do something that is unpleasant
doom and gloom = bad news
on the tip of my tongue = something that you can't quite remember
jump the gun = here, say something before we know all the facts

9 Ask students to work in pairs to try the memory word game.

10 Ask pairs to produce their own true sentences to help them try to remember the phrases. You could change pairs so that students share their sentences with someone new.

SPEAKING

Aim
to play word games

11 Organise the class into new pairs. Tell students to choose a game. Give them time to read their files (pages 190 and 193) and plan how to describe, draw or act out the words depending on which game they chose. Monitor and help with ideas at this stage, and suggest language students might use. When students are ready, ask them to play their games. As students speak, go round and monitor, and note down any interesting language you hear.

12 HISTORY

SPEAKING

Aim
to set the scene and introduce the theme with a photo; to get students talking about a historically significant event

1 Start by telling the class that in this unit they're going to be describing key events in people's lives, giving presentations and discussing important historical events; students will be using similes and presenting and debating arguments and theories.
• Ask students to look at the photo on pages 104–105. Ask: *What can you see?* Elicit a brief description of the photo, and introduce any key words students might need.
• Organise the class into pairs to discuss the questions. Go round the room and check students are doing the task and help with ideas and vocabulary if necessary.
• In feedback, ask different pairs to tell the class what they discussed. Use the opportunity to correct any errors or rephrase what students are trying to say. Look at good language that students used, and language students didn't quite use correctly during the activity. Show students better ways of saying what they were trying to say. You could write some useful new phrases on the board with gaps and ask the whole class to complete the sentences.

> **Answers**
> The photo shows a demonstrator celebrating while sitting on top of the Berlin Wall. The event is the fall of the Berlin Wall on November 9th, 1989.
> Reasons for having an understanding of history: to know about your own country and culture, and its place in the world; to know where we came from and how our predecessors lived; to help understand art, music and literature by understanding the context it was created in; to understand the debt we owe to previous generations who may have fought in wars or other struggles; to learn from the mistakes of history so we don't repeat them; to understand politics or economics which depend on knowing history; to be able to make wiser decisions about what to do next politically or economically

Culture notes

After World War II, and the defeat of Nazi Germany, the city of Berlin in Germany was divided into four sectors. Britain, France and the USA each controlled a sector. The Soviet Union controlled the fourth sector. Once East Germany was established as a separate, communist country from West Germany, the British, French and American sectors of the city were effectively hemmed in by the new communist state. By 1960, the appeal of freedom and a new life was so attractive to many living

in communist East Berlin that millions of people were moving from the Soviet-controlled sector of the city to those controlled by the Western powers. In response, the government of East Germany ordered the construction of a wall to separate East Berlin from West Berlin. Its construction began in August 1961.
Between 1961 and 1989 the wall stood as a Cold War symbol of the stand-off between communism and capitalism. About 150 people died trying to escape over the wall and were shot by East German soldiers. As the Cold War ended across Europe in 1989, and as civil unrest broke out across East Germany, the authorities announced that it was legal for its citizens to cross into the west. On the evening of November 9th 1989, thousands celebrated from both sides of the wall by climbing on it and over it. The Cold War was over. Between 1990 and 1992 much of the wall was demolished. Only a few remnants remain as tourist attractions.

2 Ask students to prepare their role. Set a five-minute limit for students to make short notes in response to each question. Make sure they don't write full sentences. Go round and help with ideas and vocabulary.

3 Mix the pairs so that students are working with someone new. Ask students to take turns to play the role of the man on the wall. Monitor and note errors and interesting uses of language by the students.
• Once you have fed back on content, look at good language that students used, and language students didn't quite use correctly during the activity.

Optional extra activity Bring in or show on your class alternative photos of an individual / people at a great moment in history and give students a choice of events to role play. Other possibilities include iconic photos of people celebrating the end of World War II, Americans planting their flag at Iwo Jima, a lone protestor in front of a tank in Tiananmen Square, Beijing.

Teacher development: using a photo to initiate a roleplay

Think about using photos to initiate discussions, conversations or roleplays. As well as the idea above (asking students to imagine they are a person in a photo and to describe their experience), you could also try some of the following in other lessons:
1 Find a photo of different types of people at a scene in which an event has taken place – a classic example is the scene of an accident. Students play the people in the photo and interview each other to find out what happened.

2 Find a photo of people showing strong emotions – crying, shouting, running, etc. Ask students to discuss why and to play the person who must say what has happened.

3 Find a photo of an event or scene and ask students to imagine they are there. Students must say where they are, what they can see, how they feel.

4 Explore photos or clips from the Internet. They are a great resource for stimulating your students' imaginations.

Communicative outcomes

In this two-page spread, students will practise describing personal histories and key events in people's lives.

VOCABULARY Personal histories

Aim

to introduce and practise phrases used to describe personal histories

1   Organise the class into pairs to discuss the situations. Check the words in bold. Do the first situation as an example to get students started.

• Monitor and note how well students understand the vocabulary. In feedback, elicit ideas, and check any words that students are still unsure of. You will need to provide examples and situations to show meaning.

Possible answers

There are no definitive fixed answers on the positive and negative effects. Let students argue their ideas and accept or reject according to how well they argue. Here are some ideas to help explain, though:

1 If you have a sheltered upbringing, you're protected from outside influences and the big bad world. Plus side: a nice, safe childhood away from harm and hurt. Downside: may end up being a bit naive and vulnerable as not very streetwise.

2 If you're from a deprived background, you grew up without many of the things people associate with a comfortable life. Downside: may not have had many chances in life; may be embittered and damaged. Plus side: streetwise, may well be tough and driven.

3 If you had to flee your country, you left it quickly because of danger. A military coup is when the army takes control of the country. Downside: maybe lost everything, had to apply for asylum elsewhere, maybe experienced discrimination. Plus side: tough and driven, may have a network of others from the country around the world – the diaspora community.

4 Radical politics are politics geared towards big social change of some kind. Plus side: may well still be engaged and interested, or may have put it all behind him and now be very mellow and content. Downside: may have been arrested or beaten-up, may be bitter and disillusioned now.

5 *Evacuated* means 'helped to leave a city or building or other place because it wasn't safe'. Plus side: missed bombing and destruction, survived the war. Downside: maybe never get to go back, may have been separated from family, may have been a refugee.

---

6 People who saw active service served in the army, air force or navy during the war and fought. Plus side: survived, maybe got rewarded for this in some way, maybe has close relationships with ex-soldiers, maybe learned discipline, etc. Downside: may have seen or done some awful things, may be suffering post-traumatic stress disorder or have psychological damage.

7 *To do something from scratch* means 'starting from nothing'. Plus side: must be very determined, will have control over own destiny more, must have developed many skills. Downside: less job security, may have to work longer hours.

8 A broken home is where the parents divorce or separate and the children then grow up with only one parent. Downside: psychological damage, anger and bitterness, insecurity, need for therapy, lack of certain role models. Plus side: very close to at least one parent, may be more driven.

9 A close-knit community is where everyone knows everyone else and they all do things together. Plus side: everyone watches out for you, may well help you. Downside: hostile to strangers, nosy, no privacy.

10 *A privileged background* means 'coming from a very wealthy family'. Plus side: probably had good education, has lots of connections, may well be ambitious and perform well socially. Downside: may lack drive or ambition or focus, not streetwise or tough. Maybe a bit naive.

11 *Winning a scholarship* means 'being awarded an amount of money by an organisation to go and study somewhere'. Plus side: get to study somewhere maybe you wouldn't otherwise be able to, get a better education and qualification, more opportunities, broaden social circle, etc. Downside: may feel out of place or conscious of lack of money.

12 If you're orphaned, both your parents die and you become an orphan. Downside: grow up in care or with foster families, traumatised, may end up separated from brothers or sisters, etc. Plus side: may be more driven.

2 Organise the class into pairs to describe people. As students speak in pairs, monitor closely and note interesting and useful language, as well as errors. Use the feedback to point out good examples, correct errors, and to provide examples of how students can express their ideas better.

Culture notes

The phrase 'evacuated during the war' has particular resonance for British people. During World War II, London was heavily bombed. Between 1939 and 1941, as many as 3.5 million people, mostly children, were evacuated and relocated to host families in the countryside to escape the bombing.

LISTENING

Aim
to practise predicting the content of a listening text and listening for key information; to recognise chunks of language in a listening text

3 Ask students to read the task and the words in the box carefully. Check any words students aren't sure of before asking them to discuss in pairs how the words and phrases are connected to the father's life. Give them a time limit of three to four minutes. Don't feedback on this stage.

Background language notes for teachers

Key words to check:
first generation = the first generation of people from a family to live in a country (i.e. the generation that left one country to settle in another country)
drop out = here, it is likely to mean to drop out of college or school (i.e. stop studying and leave before the end of the course)
textiles = cloth – cotton, etc.
the States = the United States of America
a peasant = a person who works on the land, especially in pre-industrial times

4 ● 38 Play the recording. Students listen and check predictions. Let them compare answers and discuss how the words related to the story in pairs. In feedback, elicit answers.

> **Answers**
> He's from a first-generation Chinese immigrant family.
> He grew up in total poverty.
> His dad passed away when he was thirteen so he had to drop out of school and start working to help support the rest of the family.
> He started off selling ice creams on the streets.
> He then moved on to selling textiles door-to-door.
> He moved to the capital when he was about 21.
> He started a company selling outboard motors.
> He's been able to send all his kids to the States to study.
> He still has rough edges / working class roots and still eats like a peasant.

> ● 38
> A: So ... how did it go with Kim's parents, George?
> B: Oh, it was surprisingly good, actually. The whole visit passed off far better than I'd dared to hope it would.
> A: Yeah? Even with her father?
> B: Yeah. It turns out that his bark is much worse than his bite. We had a long talk over dinner on Saturday and got on really, really well. He's a pretty amazing guy, actually.
> A: Yeah? In what way?

B: Well, he's just had an incredible life. I mean, he's from a first-generation Chinese immigrant family, and he grew up in this very strict, very close-knit community, not really speaking Indonesian or any of the local languages in Borneo, where he was living, and basically just living in total poverty.

A: Wow! You'd never know any of this from just meeting Kim, would you? I mean, not a clue!

B: No, I know, but it sounds like a properly deprived kind of background, you know. And then to make matters worse, when he was thirteen, his dad passed away and as the oldest son he found himself having to support the family.

A: Seriously? Is it a big family?

B: Yeah, enormous. Twelve brothers and sisters! So he had to drop out of school and start working.

A: That's very young to be working. What was he doing?

B: He started off selling ice creams on the streets of Pontianak and then moved on to selling textiles door-to-door, and by the time he was about seventeen he was going off all round the island selling and making deals.

A: That's amazing. I was still living at home stressing about my end-of-school exams at that age.

B: Yeah, exactly. Then when he was about 21, he decided that if he really wanted to get ahead, he'd have to move to the capital, and so he set off to make his fortune. He got there, somehow managed to start up his own company selling outboard motors for boats and then just slowly built things up until he got to where he is today, where he can afford to have all his kids educated in the States and go off on holiday whenever he feels like it.

A: So he really is a proper self-made man, then.

B: Yeah, completely. I mean, he created his whole empire from scratch, you know. But what's great about him is that he's still quite rough around the edges. Like, for instance, he still eats like a peasant and belches after dinner and stuff, which – me being me – I kind of found quite endearing.

A: And what did he make of you and the idea of his daughter dating an artist, then?

B: Well, he's still coming to terms with that, obviously, trying to get his head round it all, but his eyes lit up when I told him how much I got for that portrait I sold last year. Basically, I think he just wants to see that she'll be provided for.

A: Despite the fact she's earning twice as much as you are already!

B: Yeah, well. I didn't dwell on that fact too much.

5 🌀 38 Let students read through the sentences first, and try to complete as many as they can based on their first listening. Tell them to guess the missing words, if they can't remember them from the listening, by using their knowledge of phrasal verbs.

• Play the recording again. Let students compare answers in pairs. In feedback, go through the answers and write up the phrasal verbs on the board.

Answers
1 passed off (= took place, happened)
2 turns out (= used to say something develops in a particular way or has a particular result)
3 passed away (= a 'gentle' euphemism for *died*)
4 started off, moved on to
5 get ahead, set off
6 start up, built (things) up
7 lit up (= became bright with pleasure or anticipation or excitement)
8 dwell on (= spend time thinking about or talking about something)

Background language notes for teachers: phrasal verbs

Phrasal verbs can be transitive (i.e. they take an object) or intransitive (i.e. they don't take an object). They can also be separable or non-separable. Ask your students to look at their completed sentences in Exercise 5 and to categorise the phrasal verbs:
Transitive: *set up, built (things) up, dwell on*
Intransitive: *passed off, turns out, passed away, started out, move on (to), get ahead, set off, lit up*
Separable: *set up, built (things) up*
Non-separable: *dwell on*, all the intransitive phrasal verbs

6 Organise the class into pairs to discuss the questions. Go round the room and check students are doing the task and help with ideas and vocabulary if necessary.
• In feedback, ask different pairs to tell the class what they discussed. Correct any errors or rephrase what students are trying to say.

Possible answers
Pros: lots of brothers and sisters makes you competitive, resourceful, sociable; you have lots of support from siblings through life
Cons: lack of attention, having to compete for everything, perhaps feeling deprived
You might be held back because you don't speak the language, understand the culture or ways of doing things, have family or connections to help you, or because you might be a victim of racism or some other form of discrimination.
It might benefit you because you have drive and ambition, think differently from people in your new country which makes you stand out, have a skill which most people in your new country don't have, have connections from your old culture to help you.
A self-made person is someone who has made their fortune through their own hard work and endeavour, and not from inherited wealth or social or family connections.
If someone is 'quite rough round the edges', they are not polite or well-mannered in a conventional way. Here, it is used to describe someone who has come from a poor, rural background and has retained aspects of that (eating rudely, perhaps being very direct or crude, for example). George perhaps likes this fact because he admires how his father-in-law

has worked hard to get where he is, likes his simple directness, likes the fact that he isn't falsely trying to be someone new, and is proud of or unconcerned about his background.

Teacher development: follow-up questions in pairs or groups

Discussing a set of personalised questions as follow-up to a listening or reading is a feature of *Outcomes Advanced*. Think about how to manage this activity. Here are some suggestions:

1 Think about whether this activity works best in pairs or in groups, and organise the class accordingly. Do your students prefer to work with the same partner or to get to talk to new partners?

2 Think about having a 'chair' to organise the discussion. It is their job (if students work in groups) to ask the questions and make sure everybody gets a chance to speak. Another student in the group could be 'secretary'. It is their job to remember or note what others say, and to report what they discussed to the class in feedback.

3 Let students prepare for this activity by reading the questions individually first, and taking a minute to note things to say, and to ask you for any vocabulary you need.

4 Tell students not to slavishly discuss every question but to choose two or three that interest them and to discuss these.

Optional extra activity Ask students in pairs to think of two other questions to discuss based on the listening, and to write them down. Ask pairs to swap questions with another pair and to then discuss the new questions they have been given.

UNDERSTANDING VOCABULARY
Similes

Aim
to introduce and practise similes

7 Read through the information in the box as a class. Ask students to give you examples of similes from their own language learning experience.

• Before students do Exercise 7, you could write a handful of incomplete similes on the board and ask students to guess how to finish them. For example:
Jo smokes like ...
She went as white ...
That joke is as old ...
I've got a memory like ...
That explanation is as clear ...
Elicit students' ideas. In feedback, after Exercise 7, find out if students guessed the similes correctly.

• Alternatively, ask students to match the sentence halves to make similes. Elicit the first to get them started. Organise the class into pairs to compare answers.

Background language notes for teachers

Simile is pronounced /ˈsɪmɪlɪ/.
Grammatically, *like* is a preposition followed by a noun, and *as ... as ...* are adverbs describing an adjective. They both mean 'in a similar / comparable way to'.
Note that while the phrase *as ... as ...* often is the same as *very* + adjective (*He's as old as the hills* = He's very old), it can sometimes actually mean the opposite (*That's as clear as mud* = That isn't clear at all). The phrase *as clear as day* means 'very clear'. Note that this is checked in Exercise 8 below.
You may wish to point out that *as ... as ...* is not stressed (the main stress is on the adjective), so *as* is reduced to /əz/ in continuous speech. Briefly drill two or three of the similes to check this.

8 Organise the class into pairs to discuss the meaning of the similes by answering the check questions.

Possible answers
1 You feel like a fish out of water when you feel strange and uncomfortable, especially in a group setting. You feel like you're the different / unusual one. The opposite is *feel at home / feel comfortable / feel OK*.

2 You might avoid someone like the plague because you don't like them, or they're a bore or a bully. It might be done by not going to places where you might bump into them.

3 If you're chalk and cheese, it means you are very different or opposite in character. It doesn't necessarily mean you don't get on – you may do, but, if you do, it's notable as such different people often don't. The opposite is something like: they are very similar, have a lot in common, are very alike, or are 'like two peas in a pod'.

4 Athletes who are hard as nails are tough and durable, so examples would be rugby players, long-distance athletes, boxers, or people who have overcome tough physical challenges. Gangsters, bouncers and hard men can be described in this way, but also business people, negotiators, etc.

5 Someone might go as white as a sheet when very shocked or surprised. It could be when you've seen or heard something very unexpected or weird and surprising.

6 If something is as clear as mud, it's not clear at all. It's not possible to understand it. The opposite is very clear, easy to understand, or 'as clear as day'.

9 In the same pairs, ask students to compare the expressions in Exercise 7 with their own language. Monitor, help and prompt students, and in feedback elicit ideas and answers. If you have a monolingual class, discuss how L1 differs from English when forming similes. If you have a multilingual class, use it as an opportunity to share interesting differences between languages.

10   Ask students to work individually first to prepare their own similes. Set a four- or five-minute time limit and be available to help with any vocabulary.

11   Organise the class into groups of four or five to share ideas. In feedback, elicit the funniest or most creative ideas. You could use the possible answers below to show students what answers native English speakers might have produced.

> **Possible answers**
> Students' own ideas. Here are some similes native speakers might come up with:
> 1 ... like a dog, a horse, a Trojan
> 2 ... like slaves, animals, adults
> 3 ... like the United Nations, Prime Minister's question time
> 4 ... as Larry, a lark, the day is long
> 5 ... as nails, old boots, they come
> 6 ... as lovely / beautiful / clear as a child's, an angel's, a songbird's /... a million dollars, like an angel, a movie star

CONVERSATION PRACTICE

Aim
to practise language from the lesson in a free, communicative, personalised speaking activity

12   Ask students to choose and prepare their tasks individually. Monitor and help with ideas and vocabulary.

13   Once students feel confident, organise them into groups of four or five. It doesn't matter if they have prepared different tasks. Ask students to ask each other questions to find out about their lives or the lives of people they know. Listen for errors, new language or interesting conversations to use in feedback.
• In feedback, look at good language that students used, and language students didn't quite use correctly during the activity. Show students better ways of saying what they were trying to say. You could write some useful new phrases on the board with gaps and ask the whole class to complete the sentences.

▶ 27 **Refer students to the video and activities on the DVD-ROM.**

Teacher development: using the video

The video and activities on the DVD-ROM can be used in various ways:
1 as an alternative to the conversation practice
2 instead of the listening activity in some units, particularly with weaker groups. Students can first practise reading out the dialogues and work on some of the key phrases / structures in a controlled way before having a go themselves.
3 at the end of the unit as a revision exercise

> **PRESENTING HISTORY**
> **Student's Book pages 108–109**

Communicative outcomes
In this two-page spread, students listen to a presentation about an aspect of history; they make their own presentation on important historical events.

LISTENING

Aim
to practise listening to a presentation and noticing how it is structured and organised

1   Organise the class into groups of four or five to discuss the questions and do the tasks. Go round the room and check students are doing the task and help with ideas and vocabulary if necessary.
• In feedback, elicit which five tips each group chose and agree on a class list. However, there is no need to provide any definitive answers here as students will have an opportunity to reflect on the tips the speaker follows after listening to the presentation in Exercise 2. Use the feedback to point out good examples, correct errors, and to provide examples of how students can express their ideas better.

Optional extra activity   Before students listen to the presentation, ask students to look at the photos on the spread. Ask: *What can you see? What period of history is this? What do the pictures say about society at that time? What do you think the presentation will be about?* Elicit ideas from the class.

2   ◐ 39 Give students a moment to read the task.
• Play the recording. Students listen and note answers. Let students compare their answers in pairs before discussing as a class.

> **Answers**
> 1 The presentation is about the impact of the Second World War and, in particular, the impact of the war on society and especially on women. It is also about welfare / state intervention.
> 2 2, 4, 5, 6, 7
> (2) She introduces herself to the audience (*As you know, I'm er Courtney and I'm doing History and Politics*).
> (4) She explains the structure of the talk (*Obviously, I've only got a very short time today, so what I'm going to do is focus on two main areas: // I'll conclude with ... // If you have any questions from the presentation, I'll be happy to answer them at the end*).
> (5) She limits her talk to some extent (*this is my presentation on the impact of the Second World War both in Europe and the wider world*); students may argue that this isn't a very narrow area.
> (6) She makes her opinion clear – that the war had huge consequences that continue to this day.

(7) She asks the audience a question, but only in a rhetorical way that doesn't require an answer (*... maybe you think 'So what? Old people, old times. It's nothing to do with me and today's world.'*). Note that, although it is not covered in this introduction, point (11) is covered in the full presentation – she does add a kind of final conclusive point before she finishes.

♫ 39

Hi. Thanks for coming. As you know, I'm, er, Courtney and I'm doing History and Politics. So this is my presentation on the impact of the Second World War both in Europe and the wider world.

So, yeah, I guess many of you may have seen commemorations of the First and Second World Wars in recent years and maybe you think, 'So what? Old people, old times. It's nothing to do with me and today's world.' But what I want to suggest is that nothing could be further from the truth. The consequences have been massive – whether you look at geography, politics, culture or society. I mean, huge numbers of countries we know today gained independence thanks in part to the fact that the old colonial powers were so crippled by debts they incurred during the war that they could no longer maintain their colonies. The UN, NATO and a number of other international institutions were all established then and are still powerful today. In addition, our views on human rights date back to this event, as does society's embrace of science and technology. Even the modernist architecture that dominates many cities today can be traced back to those years. Obviously, I've only got a very short time today, so what I'm going to do is focus on two main areas: the impact of the war on society and particularly on women, and then I'll tackle welfare and state intervention. I'll conclude with a few comments on how this all contrasts with responses to financial catastrophes more recently. If you have any questions from the presentation, I'll be happy to answer them at the end.

3 Ask students to work in pairs to make a list. Start them off by eliciting one or two examples from the class. Monitor and prompt with ideas and vocabulary. You could elicit two or three ideas at the end, just to see what students thought of. However, the aim here is to prepare a prediction task for the listening, so there is no need to feedback on answers in any great detail.

Optional extra activity If you feel students need some support in this task and in preparing a suitable list for their prediction task, you could write a list of headings on the board before they start the task in Exercise 3: *Women and society, Welfare, State intervention*. Ask students to think of three ideas under each heading. In feedback, elicit students' ideas and write them in brief form under each heading. This will then support you in feedback to Exercise 4 as you will have a list of topics to tick or not.

4 ♫ 40 Play the recording. Ask students to listen and make notes next to 'impacts' they had in their lists, noting whether they were mentioned. Let students compare answers with their partners.
• Feedback on students' answers briefly and find out what students predicted correctly.

♫ 40

So, first of all, society. I think life would be quite different for women now but for the war. For example, women in countries such as France, Italy and Japan achieved the right to vote following the war. In France, for example, many women had been central to the resistance movement that had fought against the German occupation and it was simply untenable to continue their exclusion from politics. Everywhere women had entered the workforce in large numbers – often for the first time – to support the war effort while the men were fighting. Alongside this was an increase in independence for women, a greater mixing of women and men from different backgrounds and there was also more widespread sexual freedom during the war years. So, even though the 1950s were very conservative for a while, I would argue that the war sowed the first seeds of women's liberation that flowered in the 60s and 70s and that has brought us to where we are today.

Which brings me to welfare. One of the other social shifts caused by the war was the number of women who were widowed, the thousands of children who were orphaned and the millions of men who were left disabled after serving in the army. In many European countries, welfare systems simply hadn't existed before the war or were fragmented, so there was a real need to establish more comprehensive and joined-up systems. We somewhat take for granted the existence of state-run social support for those from broken homes or the unemployed, the disabled, and sick, but it may never have developed to what we now have but for the war.

Yeah, um, state intervention also extended to the huge process of rebuilding and re-establishing businesses and kick-starting the economy. I think it's difficult for us now to get our heads round the sheer scale of the devastation that took place. Keith Lowe's book, *Savage Continent*, gives a very vivid account of this. But anyway, in many countries, to enable the recovery to take place, lots of companies and banks, even whole industries, were nationalised and they were supported through the Marshall Plan, where the US provided a huge amount of money to do it. Part of the deal for this support was that the US demanded Europe work more closely together, and that eventually led to the formation of what was then called the EEC and went on to become the European Union.

What I think is interesting about this response is it's kind of almost the opposite of what's happened in response to the financial devastation many countries experienced at the start of this century. Certainly in the UK, but maybe elsewhere as well, there's a lot of evidence to suggest that cuts to public spending and changes to work regulations have affected women adversely. Where the rebuilding of economies was once funded on the back of debt, there now seems to be a deep fear of borrowing. This has been coupled with an effort to reduce state intervention and welfare spending and increasingly serious threats to break up the EU. So I guess that begs the question of whether we are doing the right thing and perhaps whether we could learn lessons from our history. Um ... and that's it. Thank you. Er ... any questions?

5 🔊 **40** Ask students to work in pairs to order and discuss the extracts.
• Play the recording again for students to check their ideas.
• In feedback, ask students to justify their answers by telling you what they heard on the recording. You will have to decide how much of the explanations you expect students to come up with, and how much information you would like to give in feedback.

Answers
1b: She claims life would be very different today if it hadn't been for the war. One example she gives is that after the war in some countries, women won the right to vote. In France women had been a key part of the resistance, so it would've been unacceptable for them to be excluded from politics.
2h: This is another example of how the war changed women's status and attitudes. The war saw more mixing of the sexes and more sexual freedom. This fed into the sexual revolution in later years.
3d: This is cited as one reason for why the welfare systems were created.
4a: This is another example of the impact the war had. State-run social support started as a result of it and today we are so used to having it that we don't think about not having it.
5f: We can't imagine the massive devastation that led to huge state intervention.
6g: Another example of the impact of the war and how the state intervened more after the war.
7c: She makes the point that the way we've responded to the recent financial crisis is almost the opposite to the response after the war. Recent austerity measures have hit women more than men.
8e: It's another example of how we've responded differently to the recent financial crisis. After the war there was a lot of borrowing, the EU was formed and women were given more rights. Now there's less state intervention and welfare spending, and the EU is under threat of break up.

---

6 Organise the class into groups of four or five to discuss the questions. Go round the room and check students are doing the task and help with ideas and vocabulary if necessary.
• In feedback, ask different pairs to tell the class what they discussed. Use the feedback to point out good examples, correct errors, and to provide examples of how students can express their ideas better.

Background language notes for teachers

Note the following high-level vocabulary in the listening that you may wish to check:
untenable = an untenable position or argument is one that is impossible to defend (i.e. one that is clearly wrong)
sowed the seeds of = started; was a root or initial cause of something
fragmented = broke into pieces; here, broke down completely so that it did not function
kick-start the economy = (from kick-start a motorbike) – it means 'restart the economy with a sudden act' (e.g. a massive investment)
It's difficult to get our heads round (something) = it's difficult to understand (something), often because it is so enormous or challenging
a vivid account = a very clear account

Culture notes

• Between 1940 and 1944, much of France was occupied by German forces.
• Keith Lowe is a British writer and historian, whose works have been translated into more than a dozen languages. Published in 2013, *Savage Continent* is a history of the chaos and lawlessness that gripped Europe in the aftermath of the Second World War.
• Officially called the European Recovery Program (ERP), the Marshall Plan was an American initiative to aid Western Europe, in which the United States gave $13 billion (approximately $130 billion in today's money) in economic support to help rebuild Western European economies after the end of World War II. It was named after George Marshall, who was United States Army Chief of Staff during the war, and Secretary of State from 1947 to 1949.
• The EEC (European Economic Community) was created by the Treaty of Rome in 1957. It aimed to bring about economic integration between its member states. Its named changed to the EC (European Community) in 1993, and to the EU (European Union) in 2009.

Optional extra activity Ask students to look at audio script 40 on page 209. Tell them to find and underline key phrases used in a presentation.

DEVELOPING CONVERSATIONS
Contextualised questions

Aim
to introduce and practise contextualised questions

7 Read through the information in the box as a class. Ask students to work individually to underline useable phrases in the questions. Elicit the first to get them started. Let students compare their answers in pairs before discussing as a class. Check the meaning of *elaborate* (= give more detailed information) and *cited* (= quoted or referred to).

Answers
1 <u>At one point you said something about</u> the effect of inflation on the decline of the Roman Empire. <u>Could you elaborate on that a bit?</u>
2 <u>I didn't quite understand the point you were making about</u> the role of Christianity in the fall of the Romans. <u>Could you go over that again?</u>
3 <u>You mentioned</u> the rise in divorce after the war. <u>Do you have any specific statistics on that?</u>
4 <u>In your introduction, you gave a quote</u> from Churchill. <u>Could you tell me what the source for that is?</u>
5 <u>You seem to be arguing that</u> the reforms failed. <u>Don't you think that that's a bit of an overstatement?</u>
6 <u>I think you cited a study by</u> Brooks and Hart. <u>Do you have the full reference for that?</u>
7 <u>You referred to something called</u> the Doppler Effect. <u>Could you just explain exactly what that is?</u>
8 <u>I think you claimed that</u> doing grammar is a waste of time. <u>What evidence do you have for that?</u>

8 Ask students to work individually to prepare questions. Tell students to refer back to their answers in Exercises 4 and 5 to remind them of what Courtney said, or tell them to look at audio script 40 on page 209. Monitor and help if necessary.

9 🔊 **41** Play the recording. Students listen and note answers. Let them compare their answers in pairs. In feedback, summarise what questions were asked and discuss as a class whether the questions were answered well or not.

🔊 **41**

C = Courtney, S1, 2, 3, 4 = students

S1: You seem to be suggesting women's liberation wouldn't have happened without the war. Don't you think it was already happening before then?

C: Er, yes, um, that's an interesting point. Yeah, I mean, that is kind of true to some extent. I mean, obviously in some countries, women already had the vote, but, but I think, you know, the points I made are still very valid. I guess, you know, it was more a catalyst. Maybe it would've happened anyway, but it was the spark. It kind of made sure these things happened for sure.

S2: You referred to something called the Marshall Plan. Could you just explain exactly what that is?

C: Um, yes. It was basically just a big fund to support European reconstruction. It's named after the US secretary of State at the time, George Marshall ... I think. I'm not absolutely sure.

S3: You mentioned the scale of the devastation. Do you have any specific statistics on that?

C: Um, yeah. I think across Europe something like 20% of all property was either destroyed or damaged, but that was a lot higher in some cities. I mean, in Warsaw it was I think over 90%. I don't know if you've been there, but like the centre looks medieval. It was totally reconstructed after the war, though. It's amazing. And in, like, other countries, I mean, Japan it was really high too. But, but yeah, I think Lowe's book has more details if you want.

S3: OK, thanks. Do you have the reference for that?

C: Oh, right. No. Yeah, I should've ... yeah, I can get that for you. I don't have it on my notes here, but you can find it on the Internet. It's Lowe, L-O-W-E and it's called *Savage Continent*. I think he's got another one coming out soon about the impact of the Second World War.

S4: You said something about cuts affecting women. Could you elaborate on that a little?

C: Oh, er, yeah. Thanks for asking. Yeah, there's quite a bit of evidence about that, but I'm afraid I've run out of time now. If you catch me after the other presentations, I can tell you more about it then though. OK. Thanks.

10 Organise the class into pairs to ask and answer the questions they prepared in Exercise 8. Monitor and note errors, as well as interesting uses of language.
• In feedback, look at good language that students used, and language students didn't quite use correctly.

VOCABULARY Historical events

Aim
to introduce and practise phrases used to describe historical events

11 Ask students to work individually to complete the sentences. Do the first as an example. Ask students to compare answers in pairs and to make sure they understand any new words by explaining them to each other with reference to the context, and / or by using a dictionary to check the words. Monitor and note which words are particular problems and concentrate on explaining them in class feedback.

Answers
1 introduction, saw
2 success, strengthened
3 election, marked
4 reforms, sowed
5 break-up, entered
6 massacre, restrict
7 declaration, fled
8 overthrow, established
9 revelations, undermined
10 victory, pointed

Teacher development: learning vocabulary in chunks

A feature of *Outcomes Advanced* is to teach vocabulary, not as isolated words, but in useable chunks. In Exercise 11, students have to place words in the context of a sentence. Not only does this get students to think about and guess meaning, but it also provides them with a chunk of language they can then use to express themselves in speaking activities to follow, and in their future language use. Here are two follow-up ideas:
1 Ask students what they notice about collocations in the chunks of language in the sentences in Exercise 11. Tell them to look for fixed expressions

(e.g. *sow the seeds of*), less fixed but common verb + noun collocations (e.g. *undermine people's faith*), and dependent prepositions (e.g. *the success of*).

2 Ask students to choose four or five phrases and rewrite them, using other verbs or nouns. Ask them to share their sentences in pairs or small groups and to discuss whether they are accurate.

12 Organise the class into pairs to discuss the questions. Give students two minutes' preparation time first, and encourage them to use some of the phrases in Exercise 11. When students are ready, ask them to talk with their partner. Monitor and notice any errors or examples of good language use to focus on in feedback.

Optional extra activity Ask students in pairs to write two sentences about two different important historical events this century. Tell them to try not to give away what the events are. Other students must guess the events.

SPEAKING

Aim
to practise a presentation about history

13 Ask students to work in groups of four to choose a task. This will depend on whether your students are from the same country or not. Ask students to spend five minutes preparing their ideas individually.
• When students are ready, ask them to take turns to present their ideas. Monitor closely and note interesting and useful language, as well as errors. Use the feedback to point out good examples, correct errors, and to provide examples of how students can express their ideas better.

Optional extra activity You could make this a more demanding 'presentation' activity by telling students to include three phrases used by Courtney to structure her presentation when they present their ideas to their group. Alternatively, once students have decided on the five most important events in their groups, you could ask them to prepare and present the five ideas to the class, using some of the phrases Courtney uses.

Web research activity
• Ask students to research a historical event that is important to them and prepare to present it to the class in the next lesson.

Communicative outcomes
In this two-page spread, students will discuss arguments and theories about historical events; they will practise using dramatic inversion and discuss historical figures.

SPEAKING

Aim
to introduce the theme of the reading; to get students to talk about a picture

1 Organise the class into groups of four to discuss the questions. Monitor and note errors and interesting uses of language. In feedback, elicit a few ideas.
• Once you have fed back on content, look at good language that students used, and language students didn't quite use correctly.

Possible answers
Work with your students' ideas.
Hopefully, students should say it is from Europe in the Middle Ages. People are walking, leaving a town, going somewhere, being arrested and taken away, dancing. They seem to be peasants – poorer people. Some musicians are playing bagpipes. Some people seem exhausted or faint and are being supported.

Culture notes

The picture is a coloured engraving of an original painting by renowned Flemish painter Pieter Brueghel the Younger (1564 – 1638). It is a depiction of dancing mania on the pilgrimage of epileptics to the church at Molenbeek in what is now Belgium. The town was known for its miraculous well of Saint Gertrude, which attracted thousands of pilgrims. Today, it is a suburb of Brussels.

READING

Aim
to practise reading for general and detailed understanding; to work out the meaning of words in context

2 Ask students to read the task and the questions. Check any key words (*tackle the problem* = deal with or solve the problem). Ask students to read the article. Let them compare answers in pairs.
• In feedback, elicit answers from the class. Ask students to justify their answers with reference to the text.

Answers
1 There was an outbreak of dancing mania in Strasbourg in the summer of 1518.
2 The medical experts said the outbreak was because of 'hot blood'.

3 Usually hot blood would have been treated by the withdrawal of blood to restore the 'correct balance'. This time, though, it was decided that those afflicted needed to keep dancing until they recovered. They were sent to special places to dance until it was out of their system.
4 It was brought to an end after all the dancers started being taken to a special healing shrine.
5 (1) It is the best documented instance of dancing mania. (2) It was the last major outbreak of its kind. (Students could also argue that it is historically significant because there is still a debate about what caused the outbreak.)

3 Ask students to discuss the meaning of the words in the article in pairs, and to work together to complete the phrases. Let students compare answers with their partner before checking in feedback.

Answers
1 outbreak
2 shrine
3 phenomenon
4 withdrawal
5 consumed by
6 epidemic
7 ruled out
8 assigned to

Background language notes for teachers

trigger the outbreak = cause the start of something; examples of things that have an outbreak: outbreak of war, unrest, disease
a holy shrine = a shrine is a place of religious significance – they are found in many of the world's religions and range from the burial place of a saint or a box of relics from a religious person to a natural site such as a large rock
a phenomenon = an unusual or amazing happening
withdrawal = the withdrawal of an army means they are moved back, away from a fight; the withdrawal of support means you stop giving support; the withdrawal of funding means the supply of money is stopped
consumed by = literally eaten up by, so if you are consumed by grief you are so destroyed by feelings of sadness that you can't function normally
epidemic = a disease that is spread by contagious infection
rule out = decide firmly not to do something
assigned to = put in (a particular group)

4 Ask students to work in the same pairs to discuss what theories they can think of. In feedback, ask different pairs to tell the class what they discussed. There are no fixed answers, so work with whatever ideas the students have. Ask further questions about any interesting or unusual theories they may have.

5 🔊 42 Ask students to read the questions.
• Play the recording. Students listen and note answers. Let them compare answers in pairs before discussing as a class.

Answers
1 The dancers had eaten poisoned wheat, which can cause hallucinations and aches and pains.
2 They were cult members of some kind, and pushing their bodies to extremes in pursuit of ecstasy.
3 It was a kind of mass hysteria brought about by a long period of disease and famine.
The most likely explanation is the last one. This would explain the trance-like states and loss of self-control. Hysterical communal states often happen during extreme situations.
Poisoned wheat is unlikely as it's never been known to cause behaviour like that described.
The cult theory is unlikely as they weren't ecstatic: they seemed unhappy and troubled.

🔊 42
While numerous theories for the cause of the dancing mania have been proposed, it still remains unclear whether it was an actual illness or whether it was more a result of some kind of social process. Some assert that the Strasbourg situation was a result of dancers having eaten poisoned wheat, which is known to result in hallucinations and physical aches and pains. Never has it caused the strange behaviour most associated with dancing disease, though.
Others have put forward the theory that the dancers were members of some kind of cult, pushing their bodies to extremes in pursuit of religious ecstasy. However, contemporary reports highlighted the fact that dancers were unhappy and begged onlookers to help them stop.
The most plausible explanation is that as the whole area was severely affected by disease and famine, these factors played a significant role in the explosion of some kind of mass hysteria. This would also explain the trance-like states and loss of self-control that dancers claim to have experienced.

VOCABULARY Discussing arguments and theories

Aim
to introduce and practise phrases used when discussing arguments and theories

6 Organise the class into pairs to discuss the words in italics. You could elicit the first answer to get students started. In feedback, check the difference in meaning between the pairs of words.

Answers
1
put forward / proposed have the same meaning in this context
established that = proved something was true
claimed that = argued something was true (but didn't necessarily prove it)

2
argue / contend have the same meaning in this context
significant = a large role
minor = a small role
3
asserted = stated firmly it was true (but didn't show / prove it)
demonstrated = showed clearly that it was true
stemmed from = was caused by
gave rise to = led to, resulted in
4
allegedly / supposedly have the same meaning in this context
cast doubt on / questioned have the same meaning in this context
5
highlighting / emphasising have the same meaning in this context
challenged = questioned the truth of
accepted = believed the truth of

READING

Aim

to read and make notes on a text; to do a jigsaw reading activity in which students ask and answer questions about their texts

7 Organise the class into new pairs. Ask each pair to decide who is A and who is B. Tell them to find their information pages (pages 194 and 193), then give them time to read their files. Ask them to make notes on the main facts. Tell them to do this as bullet points and tell them not to write complete sentences.
• Note that these are quite long texts. You may wish to prepare students carefully for this task, allowing them plenty of time to prepare (see teacher's notes below).

Answers
Students' own notes. There is no need to go over answers. However, here are some notes to help prompt students as they prepare or speak.
JFK text
Main facts: JFK – US President in Jan 1961; Space Race, Berlin Wall, US-USSR tensions, Cuban missile crisis; health problems and extra-marital affairs; assassinated 22 Nov 1963 – open-topped car – Dallas, Texas; Lee Harvey Oswald arrested – US Marine – had defected to USSR; Oswald shot by Jack Ruby; Ruby died 1967; inquiry – both killers acted alone; later inquiries challenged findings – suggested 2 gunmen
Things attracting debate: 1) Soviets / KGB did it – Krushchev ordered it; 2) Mafia did it; 3) Cubans did it – logical; 4) Lyndon Johnson did it – ambition – CIA helped
Stonehenge text
Main facts: 150 upright stones in Wiltshire – 9 metres high and over 20 tons – smaller stones from 150 miles away in Wales; erected over 100s of years; 30 million man hours
Things attracting debate: Who? Aubrey claimed Druids; 1950s – carbon dating – 1,000 years before

Celts – three tribes built it; How? Stones rolled on tree trunks or stones – ice glaciers – aliens – magic; What for? Astronomers – calendar to track sun and moon – built on site for sun worship – bones found so ancient burial ground for high-ranking people

8 When students are ready, ask them to share the information in their articles. You may need to give them some preparation time in order to plan what to say using phrases from Exercise 6. Monitor closely and note interesting and useful language, as well as errors. Use the feedback to point out good examples, correct errors, and to provide examples of how students can express their ideas better.

Teacher development: organising a jigsaw reading

If you feel the texts may be demanding, either because of their length and complexity, or because of the cultural and historical awareness your students may require, you could break this activity down into more stages:
1 Start with a lead-in stage. Write *JFK* and *Stonehenge* on the board and brainstorm what students know about each topic. If your students know little or nothing, you could ask them to look at the two photos that go with the texts and ask them to predict from those, or you could write some key words from the texts on the board and ask students to say what they might refer to.
2 Divide the class into pairs. Half the pairs work together to read about JFK. Half read about Stonehenge. Students then compare and make notes with a partner who has read the same text. When ready, ask the pairs to work together to use the vocabulary in Exercise 6 to prepare their interpretations.
3 When students are fully prepared, mix the pairs so that students are working with someone who read the other text. Students then tell their partner about their article and discuss the interpretations.

Culture notes

• Archaeologists believe Stonehenge was constructed between 3000 BC and 2000 BC. It is a Neolithic monument, predating the arrival of the Celts in England in about 600 BC. It's located in the county of Wiltshire in south-west England. It is a UNESCO World Heritage Site. It is owned by the Crown – effectively this means that the state owns it on behalf of everybody in the country – and managed by English Heritage, a charity that protects historical monuments.
• The Cuban Missile Crisis occurred between October 16th and 28th 1963. There was a tense stand-off between the US and the USSR. The Soviet Premier Nikita Krushchev agreed to place nuclear missiles on the island of Cuba, which was under the control of the communist leader Fidel Castro, in order to deter the United States from invading Cuba. Eventually, the two sides came to an agreement to dismantle missiles on both sides. It was the closest the Americans and Russians came to direct conflict during the Cold War.
USSR = Union of Soviet Socialist Republics, or Soviet Union

KGB = the main security agency for the Soviet Union from 1954 until its break-up in 1991
CIA = Central Intelligence Agency, the main US security agency
Lyndon Johnson was vice-president under Kennedy, so, under the US constitution, he succeeded to President after JFK's assassination.

GRAMMAR Dramatic inversion

Aim
to introduce and practise dramatic inversion

9 Read through the information in the box as a class.
• Organise students into pairs to complete the sentences. Do the first as an example in open class. Monitor and notice how well students understand the uses.
• In feedback, elicit the students' answers. They can check their answers using the Grammar reference on page 179.

Answers
1a The epidemic only came to a halt after dancers started being taken to a special healing shrine.
 b It has never caused the strange behaviour most associated with dancing disease.
 c The theory wasn't disproved until the 1950s.
 d He became the youngest man ever to hold office and he is also the only Roman Catholic to have ever sat in the White House.
 e As soon as news of the killing started spreading around the world, the local police announced the arrest of Lee Harvey Oswald.
2 The auxiliary (if there is one) goes before the subject and the verb.
3 If there is no auxiliary, we add *do / does* for sentences in the present simple and *did* for sentences in the past simple.
4 We use negative adverbials. The negative is removed from the auxiliary verb and is put instead onto a negative adverb.
5
 1 <u>Only</u> after dancers started being taken to a special healing shrine did the epidemic finally come to a halt.
 2 <u>Never</u> has it caused the strange behaviour most associated with dancing disease.
 3 <u>Not until</u> the 1950s was the theory disproved.
 4 <u>Not only</u> did he become the youngest man to hold office, but he is also the only Roman Catholic to have ever sat in the White House.
 5 <u>No sooner</u> had news of the killing started spreading around the world than the local police announced the arrest of Lee Harvey Oswald.

 G **Students complete Exercises 1 and 2 in the Grammar reference on page 179.**

Answers to Exercise 1, Grammar reference
1 Not only   4 Not until
2 at no time   5 Nowhere else, Only
3 Never before

Answers to Exercise 2, Grammar reference
1 Never before had we witnessed an international relief operation on such a scale.
2 Not until 1996 did the first women's team come into existence.
3 At no time did anyone / anybody try to prevent the tragedy.
4 Only once in our recent history have we had an honest leader.
5 Nowhere else in the world can business and pleasure be combined quite so well.
6 It was made very clear that under no circumstances were the soldiers to surrender or take their own lives.
7 Only after America rebelled against the high import taxes imposed on tea in 1773 did coffee become more popular.
8 Not only was he a poet, but he was also a military leader.
9 No sooner had the government taken office than they put up taxes.
10 Only when it became obvious that the scandal could no longer be contained did he admit his involvement in it.

Background language notes for teachers: reporting speech

Negative adverbial phrases are 'fronted' (placed at the start of a sentence) and the auxiliary goes before subject and verb (e.g. *It has never been ...* becomes *Never has it been ...*). Note that, when spoken, the adverbials at the front of the sentence need to be strongly stressed. Essentially, the problem with getting the hang of these structures is one of learning the complex form. It is worth taking time at written accuracy stages (the Grammar reference exercises and Exercise 10) to make sure students notice and use the forms accurately.

10 Ask students to complete the sentences. Elicit possible answers to the first one to get students started. Tell them to discuss their answers in pairs. Monitor and notice how well students manipulate the forms.
• In feedback, elicit the students' answers. If they make errors, refer them back to the rules in the Grammar reference.

Possible answers
Work with students' ideas. Here are three ideas (on a military theme) you could use as examples if students are slow to get going:
Only when the army reached the river did they realise that the enemy had a lot more soldiers.
No sooner had the battle begun than the leader was killed.
Not only had they won the battle, but the road to the capital lay open.

Optional extra activity Ask students in pairs or groups to write five sentences about a historical event they are familiar with, using dramatic inversion. Ask them to present their sentences to the class as a mini history lecture.

 For further grammar practice, see Exercise 3 in the Grammar reference on page 179.

Answers to Exercise 3, Grammar reference

1 Never before **had** so few people ~~did~~ **done** so much for so many.
2 Not only **did she campaign** ~~she campaigned~~ against injustice of all kinds, but she was also the first female minister.
3 Only when a society refuses to acknowledge its past failings ~~it starts~~ **does it start** to lose its moral authority.
4 No sooner ~~the truce had~~ **had the truce** been called than peace talks began in earnest.
5 Only after tighter checks were introduced **was** corruption finally ~~was~~ tackled.
6 A law was passed saying that on no account **would** foreigners ~~would~~ be allowed into the city centre.
7 Had the missiles reached their intended target, the result would **have been** ~~be~~ disastrous.
8 ~~Such~~ **So** severe was the damage after the attack that the whole area needed to be rebuilt.
9 So sure of victory ~~he was~~ **was he** that he spent the afternoon sleeping in his tent.
10 If ~~were~~ the management **were** to agree to our terms, the strike would end tomorrow.

SPEAKING

Aim
to discuss historical figures and use lexis and structures from the lesson

11 Ask students to work in groups of four. Tell them to spend two minutes writing their own brief notes about each of the historical figures first. Tell them to focus on those they know most about.
• When students are ready, ask them to take turns to share and discuss their knowledge and ideas. Monitor closely and note errors or examples of good language use to feedback on at the end.

Optional extra activity To encourage students to use language from the lesson, write five to ten phrases on the board and tell the class they must use each of them in their discussion at some stage. Possible phrases: *What triggered the outbreak of ... was ..., One theory put forward is that ..., I accept the view that ..., Not only did ... but ..., Only when ... did ...*

Web research activity
• If you have access to the Internet in the classroom, you could ask each individual in a group to research two different people from the list. That way, you create experts in each group for the discussion task.

Culture notes

• Karl Marx (1818 – 1883) was a German philosopher, economist, sociologist, journalist and revolutionary socialist. He spent much of his life in London. Marx's work in economics is the basis for much of the current understanding of labour and its relation to capital, and subsequent economic thought. He published numerous books, notably *The Communist Manifesto* (1848) and *Das Kapital* (1867). He is the founder of Marxism and influenced the 1917 Revolution in Russia and the spread of Communism.
• Charles Darwin (1809 – 1882) was an English naturalist and geologist, who developed evolutionary theory (all species of life have descended over time from common ancestors, through a process he called natural selection). He published *On the Origin of Species* in 1859.
• Albert Einstein (1879 – 1955) was a German-born theoretical physicist who developed the general theory of relativity, a pillar of modern physics. He is best known in popular culture for his mass–energy equivalence formula $E = mc^2$.
• Isaac Newton (1642 – 1726) was an English physicist and mathematician. He was one of the most influential scientists of all time and a key figure in the scientific revolution. His book *Mathematical Principles of Natural Philosophy* (1687) laid the foundations for classical mechanics. He influenced optics, the development of calculus, and, most famously, discovered the law of gravity.
• Galileo Galilei (1564 – 1642), was an Italian astronomer, physicist, engineer, philosopher, and mathematician, whose contributions to observational astronomy include the telescopic confirmation of the phases of Venus, the discovery of the four largest satellites of Jupiter (named the Galilean moons in his honour), and the observation and analysis of sunspots. He established that the sun was at the centre of the solar system.
• Leonardo da Vinci (1452 – 1519) was an Italian Renaissance Man, whose interests were wide-ranging. He is famous for his art (the *Mona Lisa*, *The Last Supper*) and his designs and drawings (he mapped the human body and produced designs for the parachute, helicopter and tank).
• Archimedes (c. 287 BC – c. 212 BC) was an Ancient Greek mathematician, physicist, engineer, inventor, and astronomer. Considered the greatest mathematician of antiquity and one of the greatest of all time, he developed theorems to work out the area of a circle, the surface area and volume of a sphere, and the area under a parabola. He also derived an accurate approximation of pi, and founded hydrostatics and statics, including an explanation of the principle of the lever.
• Sigmund Freud (1856 – 1939) was an Austrian neurologist and the father of psychoanalysis, a clinical method for treating psychopathology through dialogue between a patient and a psychoanalyst.
• Nicolaus Copernicus (1473 – 1543) was born in what was then the Kingdom of Poland. He formulated a model of the universe that placed the sun rather than the Earth at the centre.

VIDEO 6: THE SWORD EXCALIBUR
Student's Book page 112

Aim
to find out about investigations into the myth of King Arthur; to improve students' ability to follow and understand fast speech in a video extract; to practise fast speech and to improve pronunciation, stress and intonation

1 Lead in to the topic by asking students to look at the picture and say what they can see. Organise the class into pairs or small groups to discuss the questions. In a brief feedback session, elicit students' ideas and write up interesting ideas or language on the board. Encourage students to justify their opinions and argue their cases.

Culture notes

• King Arthur is a legendary British leader who, according to medieval histories and romances, led the defence of Britain against Saxon invaders in the late fifth and early sixth centuries AD. In the medieval romances, he leads a group of brave and courtly knights who meet with him sitting around a Round Table like in the picture.
• The story of the sword in the stone is told on the video.
• Mordred (Sir Mordred) is one of the knights of the Round Table, and in some versions the illegitimate son of King Arthur. He is a traitor who fights Arthur resulting in the death of both men.
• Camelot is the castle where Arthur and his knights live.
• The Holy Grail (a cup or dish) is supposed to contain Christ's blood and Arthur's knights set off on expeditions to find it and this was the quest for the Holy Grail.
• Galahad (Sir Galahad) is renowned for his bravery and sets off to find the Holy Grail, a task he accomplishes.
• Guinevere is the wife of Arthur and lover of Sir Lancelot.
• The Lady of the Lake is the ruler of Avalon and in the legend gives Arthur his sword, which rises from the waters of the lake.
• Merlin is the magician who educates and protects Arthur.
• Lancelot (Sir Lancelot du Lac) is the greatest of the Knights of the Round Table, and Arthur's champion until he falls in love with Guinevere and causes the war that brings Arthur's reign to an end.

2 ▢◄28 As students watch the video, they should note the answers. Let students compare answers in pairs before discussing as a class.

Answers
The story told is of the young Arthur being the only person who could pull the sword Excalibur from a stone. One explanation is that the myth is based on the old way of making swords, where they were pulled from a stone mould.

3 ▢◄28 Organise the class into pairs to discuss the phrases. You could have a brief class feedback session and find out what students think. Play the video again so

that students can check ideas and make further notes. Let them compare their answers with their partners before discussing as a class.

Answers
1 All the other soldiers and warlords **tried in vain** to pull the sword out of the stone.
2 Then young Arthur **stepped forward** to try.
3 He was able to remove the sword from the stone because he was **the rightful and true king**.
4 The metalworker they met still uses **the practices of the Ancients** to make his swords.
5 The historian hopes that ancient sword-making techniques may **cast some light on** this Arthurian legend.
6 Swords were **a very expensive piece of technology** back in Arthur's day.
7 **Tin** and **copper** were heated to form molten **bronze**.
8 This is then **poured into a mould** which forms the stone.
9 Metallurgy is **a pretty magical process**.
10 It's a process by which you **transform raw material** into something amazing and magical like the sword.

4 This exercise offers students the chance to relate the topic of the video to their own experiences, ideas and opinions.
• Give students a minute to read the questions and to ask about anything they're not sure of.
• Ask students to discuss the questions in pairs. Monitor students' discussions and help with ideas if necessary.
• When most students have finished, stop the class and give some feedback, either by rephrasing some of the things students tried to say for the whole class or by asking students to correct or fill in gaps in sentences you've written on the board, based on what you heard students saying.

Understanding fast speech

5 ▢◄29 Play the recording. Students listen and write what they hear. Let them compare in pairs. Tell them not to worry if they haven't caught all the words yet.

6 ▢◄30 Students listen again to a slower version to check and improve what they have written. Let them compare answers in pairs.

7 Students check what they wrote in File 10 on page 189. Encourage them to practise saying the extract.

Video script ▢◄28
Narrator: The story describes a gleaming sword thrust into a huge stone and only the rightful King of Britain could pull it out. The fiercest warlords and the strongest soldiers tried in vain to free the blade, but then young Arthur stepped forward.
Mary-Ann Ochota: It was easy because Arthur is the rightful and true King of the Britons.

Narrator: Mary-Ann Ochota meets with a metalworker who uses the practices of the Ancients. She's investigating the origins of the sword in the stone story.

Mary-Ann Ochota: What I want to do is go and find out more about ancient sword-making techniques because I think that might cast some light on this element of Arthur's legend.

Neil Burridge: I suppose the sword we're gonna cast would look something like this when it's finished.

Mary-Ann Ochota: That is beautiful. Is this the kind of sword for a warrior king?

Neil Burridge: Definitely. They are swords belonging to the aristocracy. They're a very expensive piece of technology.

Narrator: A charcoal furnace heats a crucible containing tin and copper to form molten bronze. The bronze is poured into a single stone mould that forms the sword.

Neil Burridge: Right, what we're gonna do now is draw the sword out of the stone mould.

Mary-Ann Ochota: Or draw the sword out of the stone, even.

Neil Burridge: Yes, definitely.

Mary-Ann Ochota: That's absolutely incredible. From that you can see where the myth from the sword in the stone comes from.

Neil Burridge: Yes.

Mary-Ann Ochota: Metallurgy is a pretty magical process. You take this raw material and with skilled hands you can transform it into a glittering weapon. That might be – and I have to give it some weight – that might be the origin of the story of the sword in the stone.

REVIEW 6
Student's Book page 113

Aim
to consolidate vocabulary and grammar from Units 11 and 12

Answers
Exercise 1
1 speaking
2 had
3 so
4 that
5 pressure
6 like
7 hand
8 other
9 Despite
10 until

Exercise 2
1 else in the world are
2 the film deeply disappointing
3 as white as a sheet
4 under no circumstances were we
5 so as to
6 not all doom and gloom

Exercise 3
1 like chalk and cheese
2 had the new currency been introduced
3 as old as the hills
4 your convictions
5 had the region experienced
6 on account of

Exercise 4
assert – theory
He asserts it is true but offers no evidence.
claim – theory
He claims modern behaviour is down to evolution.
uphold – sport
The referee's decision was upheld after looking at video evidence.
drop – sport
She was dropped from the team.
emphasise – theory
The theory emphasises the importance of Thatcher in late twentieth-century history.
establish – theory
Einstein established the theory of relativity.
fade – sport
He faded badly towards the end of the race and finished last.
put forward – theory
He put forward the idea that revolution was inevitable.
scrape through – sport
They scraped through to the second round on penalties.
highlight – theory
Marx highlights the role of the working class in history.
sponsor – sport
The team is sponsored by Emirates airline.
contend – theory
I would contend that we need to cancel debt to get a recovery.

Exercise 5

1 h
2 f
3 j
4 i
5 g
6 b
7 a
8 e
9 c
10 d

Exercise 6

1 description
2 declaration
3 instability
4 liberation
5 substituted
6 revelations, corruption

Exercise 7

1 background
2 emphasised
3 orphaned
4 exposed
5 rise
6 allegedly
7 collaborated (colluded / co-operated)
8 soul-searching
9 radical
10 massacre
11 fled
12 scholarship

13 NEWS AND THE MEDIA

SPEAKING

Aim

to set the scene and introduce the theme with a photo; to get students talking about a significant news story and their attitude to news stories

1 Start by telling the class that in this unit they're going to be commenting on news stories and discussing celebrity and the media; they will be using rhetorical questions and reporting what people said.
• Ask students to look at the photo on pages 114–115. Ask: *What can you see?* Elicit a brief description of the photo, and introduce any key words students might need.
• Organise the class into pairs to discuss the questions. Go round the room and check students are doing the task and help with ideas and vocabulary if necessary.
• In feedback, ask different pairs to tell the class what they discussed. Once you have fed back on content, look at good language that students used, and language students didn't quite use correctly. Show students better ways of saying what they were trying to say. You could write some useful new phrases on the board with gaps and ask the whole class to complete the sentences.

Answers

The photo shows the 2010 Copiapó mining accident, known around the world as the Chilean mining accident. On August 5th, 2010 there was a significant cave-in at the San José copper-gold mine in the Atacama Desert in northern Chile. 33 men were trapped 700 metres underground, but they survived for an amazing 69 days before their rescue. Rescuers were able to speak to them during their ordeal and send food and drink to them. Eventually, they drilled a hole and winched the men to safety. A TV audience of more than one billion viewers around the world watched the rescue live.

Optional extra activity Ask students to tell the class about a 'rescue' story from their own country.

IN THE HEADLINES
Student's Book pages 116–117

Communicative outcomes

In this two-page spread, students will practise talking about news headlines and news and using rhetorical questions.

Preparation You could bring in English language tabloid newspapers or a selection of headlines from tabloids.

VOCABULARY Newspaper headlines

Aim

to introduce language used in newspaper headlines

1 Read through the information in the box as a class. Try to elicit other typical impactful words headlines use. For example: *hit, fail, fall, beat, crash.*
• Ask students to match the words in the box to the phrases in italics which define their meaning. Elicit the answer to the first one as an example. Let students compare answers in pairs. In feedback, go through the answers and use definitions and further examples to show meaning.

Answers

1 toll	7 leak
2 hails	8 ups
3 bars	9 clash
4 cleared	10 rule out
5 seize	11 pulls out of
6 brink of	12 vows

Background language notes for teachers

Newspaper headlines follow the following conventions:
• they use the present tense to report news when the subject comes first: *Killers break out of jail*
• they use the past participle to report news when the object comes first: *20 injured in blast*
• they use the infinitive to refer to a future event: *Government to raise taxes*
• they omit unnecessary words such as auxiliaries and articles: *Dolphins dying out; Man killed in train wreck.*

2 Organise the class into pairs to discuss the headlines. In feedback, elicit ideas and ask students to explain and justify their ideas.

Answers

Answers to b in particular will vary. Some suggestions are given below:

2 a the (US / French / Brazilian, etc.) president has given a speech praising progress made in resolving a dispute

  b where the speech was given; who the dispute is between; what the breakthrough entails; what else needs to be done to reach an agreement and long-term peace; possible threats to the process

3 a a (football) club has banned some fans (from attending matches) to try and reduce hooliganism

  b what fans had done (fighting / vandalism / rival fans); how long they're banned: how will they be banned; policing

4 a a person called Sanders who was standing trial for bribery has been proved innocent and released

  b who Sanders is; who he was accused of bribing (or receiving bribes from); what evidence showed he was innocent; what Sanders will do next

5 a police have raided a house and found £10 million worth of drugs

  b where the house was; who it was owned by; any arrests made; how it fits in with current policing and government policy; war on drugs

6 a Boca (football / basketball, etc.) team have won a game which means they are very likely to win the league they are competing in

  b who they beat (maybe rival team); the score; who scored; how many more points or wins they need to win the title; who are their rivals; comments from the manager (maybe refusing to count their chickens!)

7 a the government or big business has a plan to cut jobs

  b who exactly is cutting jobs and why; what sector the jobs are in; how many; response (denial maybe) from the 'cutters'; response of other political parties if government is cutting the jobs; response from the unions or workers (shock / concern / defiance); plan for industrial action

8 a a businessperson / company called Kirov has bought a lot more shares in a company called Mac Industries because they want to take it over

  b who Kirov is; what Mac does; how big Kirov's stake is (before and now); why they want to take over Mac; what their plans are; current financial state of Mac; share price

9 a there was a union rally where people came together to listen to speeches and at some point there was some trouble between the people in the crowd and police

  b what the rally was for; who held it and where; what caused the disturbance; how the police responded; any arrests or injuries; response from police and demonstrators or union (blaming each other?)

10 a a group / union representing teachers has said they are not going to go on strike as a way of fighting against their pay being cut

  b why the teachers' pay is being cut and by how much; why they have decided not to strike; what their employers or the government have said

11 a a sportsperson called Kohl has been in the news because of an affair or because of some incident involving sex, and has decided not to participate in the Open as a result to avoid being in the spotlight (both golf and tennis have Open championships so it's probably one of these sports)

  b what the sex scandal was; why he or she pulled out; what the event organisers say

12 a a person called Hector (politician / sport star / business person) is promising to continue in their position having said something that has offended people

  b who Hector is; what he or she said; response of the people who were offended by outburst

3 Organise the class into groups of four or five. Ask students to discuss the questions. The aim here is to check meaning by asking students to provide personalised examples. In feedback, elicit any interesting stories or experiences from different groups.

Optional extra activity Ask groups to look at the headlines in the photo on page 116. Ask them to choose one and to think of the story behind the headline.

LISTENING

Aim
to listen for general and specific understanding; to listen for specific chunks of language in a text

4 🎧 43 Give students a moment to read through the situation and questions.

• Play the recording. Students listen and note answers. Let students compare answers in pairs before discussing in feedback.

Answers

Conversation 1
1 Story 4: Sanders cleared of bribery charges (got off / has been lining his own pocket)
2 Agree
Conversation 2
1 Story 7: Leak reveals plan to slash jobs
2 Agree
Conversation 3
1 Story 11: Kohl pulls out of Open over sex scandal (having affair / playing tennis)
2 Agree
Conversation 4
1 Story 12: Hector vows to continue despite outburst
2 Disagree
Conversation 5
1 Story 3: Club bars fans in crackdown on hooliganism
2 Agree

🎧 43
Conversation 1
A: Have you seen the news today?
B: Yeah. Did you see that MP got off?
A: Well, what did you expect? It's one rule for us and another for them, isn't it?
B: It makes me sick. It was so obvious he's been lining his own pocket. I don't know how he's got away with it.
A: Apparently, the case was dismissed on some kind of technicality.
B: Typical. As you say, if it'd been someone lower down, they'd have been convicted.

Conversation 2
C: What do you think of this story about the government's proposals for public sector cuts?
D: I'll believe it when it happens.
C: You don't think it will?
D: No. I mean, look at it from their point of view. Why would they? What do they have to gain? There's an election coming up in just over a year. It'd be a disaster for them.
C: That's true. Maybe the opposition is just stirring up trouble.
D: More likely. I don't think they've said the source of the story, have they?

Conversation 3
E: I can't believe they're still going on about this guy and his affair. They're making such a fuss about nothing.
F: I don't think she'd see it like that!
E: No, I know. It's obviously a big deal for her, but I don't see how having it all over the papers will help. What's it got to do with us? And what's it got to do with playing tennis?
F: Nothing. It's all to do with money and sponsorship, isn't it?
E: Exactly. As if anyone cares. It's such nonsense.

Conversation 4
G: Did you see that thing about the Secretary of State and what he said?
H: Yeah. I can't believe he's refusing to resign!
G: I don't know. Put yourself in his shoes. Can you imagine the pressure politicians are under when there's so much news coverage? It amazes me they don't make more slips.
H: I know, but it's not the first time and I think it undermines our standing in the world. What are other countries going to think?
G: Oh, it's just a storm in a teacup. It'll blow over quickly enough.
H: You think so?

Conversation 5
I: Did you see that business with the Hampton supporters?
J: Yeah, it was a disgrace. They're just animals. They should do something about them.
I: Didn't you hear? They have! A whole load of them have had their season tickets confiscated.

J: Well, it's about time, though why on earth aren't they being prosecuted? The amount of damage they caused! Not to mention the intimidation.
I: I know. They're thugs. They should be locked up.

5 🎧 43 Let students read through the sentences first, and try to complete them based on their first listening.
• Play the recording again. Let students compare their answers in pairs before discussing as a class.

Answers
1 a 's been lining
  b was dismissed
2 a coming up
  b is, stirring up
3 a 're making
  b cares
4 a Put yourself
  b 'll blow over
5 a aren't, being prosecuted
  b should be locked up

DEVELOPING CONVERSATIONS
Rhetorical questions and common opinions

Aim
to introduce and practise rhetorical questions and common opinions

6 Read through the information in the box as a class.
• Organise the class into pairs. Ask students to look at audio script 43 on page 210 to find, underline and discuss the rhetorical questions. Elicit the first one to get students started. Let them compare answers in pairs. Elicit answers in feedback.

Answers
The following are the rhetorical questions and opinions:
Conversation 1
Well, what did you expect? It's one rule for us and another for them, isn't it?
= I didn't expect him to be found guilty.
Conversation 2
(example used in Student's Book)
Conversation 3
What's it got to do with us? And what's it got to do with playing tennis?
= Having an affair has nothing to do with us or playing tennis.
Conversation 4
Can you imagine the pressure politicians are under when there's so much news coverage?
= I think politicians are under huge pressure which is why I have sympathy if they make a slip.
What are other countries going to think?
= I think they will think badly of us.
Conversation 5
... why on earth aren't they being prosecuted?
= I think they should be prosecuted.

7 It is a good idea to elicit situations for the first one from the class to get students started. Organise the class into groups of four to discuss in which situations they might express the other opinions. Leave students to work out meanings in their groups, but monitor closely and note interesting and useful language, as well as errors.
• Use the feedback to point out good examples, correct errors, and to provide examples of how students can express their ideas better. Make sure you check meaning.

> **Possible answers**
> 1 When a wealthy / powerful person is not punished or is punished lightly for a crime.
> 2 When talking about a particularly horrible crime.
> 3 When talking about politicians and corruption.
> 4 When a young person has insulted an old person or done something crass like taking a selfie at a war memorial.
> 5 When talking about the chances of a sports team in a competition.
> 6 When powerful countries threaten to invade another or impose sanctions.
> 7 When there has been another example of something bad and nothing has been done.
> 8 When someone behaves a certain way and subsequently receives particular treatment as a result of the way they have behaved (for example, if you are violent, people are likely to be violent to you in return).

Optional extra activity Ask students if they can think of any other common expressions they have come across in their learning.

CONVERSATION PRACTICE

Aim
to practise language from the lesson in a free, communicative, personalised speaking activity

8 Ask students to prepare notes on news stories individually. Monitor and help with ideas and vocabulary.

9 Once students feel confident, organise the class into pairs to practise. Let pairs have a go at telling their stories more than once – practice makes perfect. Mix pairs so that they can retell their stories with a new partner. Listen for errors or examples of good uses of language to use in feedback.
• In feedback, look at good language that students used, and language students didn't quite use correctly during the activity. Show students better ways of saying what they were trying to say. You could write some useful new phrases on the board with gaps and ask the whole class to complete the sentences.

Optional extra activity Bring in some recent English language tabloid newspapers. Let students read and then tell stories from the newspapers. Alternatively, cut out some headlines from recent stories which will remind and prompt students to tell the story behind the headline.

31 Refer students to the video and activities on the DVD-ROM.

Teacher development: using the video

The video and activities on the DVD-ROM can be used in various ways:
1 as an alternative to the conversation practice
2 instead of the listening activity in some units, particularly with weaker groups. Students can first practise reading out the dialogues and work on some of the key phrases / structures in a controlled way before having a go themselves.
3 at the end of the unit as a revision exercise

Communicative outcomes
In this two-page spread, students read about and discuss the paparazzi; they use and discuss common sayings.

SPEAKING

Aim
to introduce the theme of the reading text and get students talking about celebrity news and the paparazzi

1 Organise the class into groups of four or five to discuss the questions. Monitor as students speak, and notice what sort of magazines and celebrities they bring up. After four or five minutes, ask students to share ideas with the class. In feedback, look at good language that students used, and language students didn't quite use correctly.

> **Possible answers**
> Well-known international celebrity magazines:
> *Hello, OK*
> Ways of gathering celebrity news: reporting official announcements by celebrities (e.g. on their websites or when promoting a film); reporting what celebrities say in interviews or on TV shows; calling agents, publicists, family and friends and celebrities themselves; paying for information from the general public (e.g. photos taken of a celebrity in a nightclub by a club-goer, information from waiters or doormen of clubs or restaurants); getting 'exclusives' from exes or from disaffected people who once worked for or with a celebrity; following a celebrity or waiting for them outside their house or at places they go to (e.g. paparazzi photographers); following the tweets of a celebrity; stalking celebrities or going through their bins, or otherwise invading their privacy

Optional extra activity Before organising the group work activity in Exercise 1, write the names of magazines, newspapers, programmes or websites that focus on celebrity news on the board. Then write the names of two or three celebrities that are currently in the news. Ask students to say what connects the things on the board, what they know about them, and how interested they are in celebrity news stories.

READING

Aim
to practise reading and responding to a text; to read intensively to work out where missing extracts go in a text

2 Ask students to read the statements first, and to say what they can predict about the article from the statements and from the title. Then ask students to read the article and decide which statements they agree with.

3 Ask students to compare their answers in pairs. As you monitor, note any areas of disagreement or things they didn't understand to use as a basis for some feedback. In feedback, elicit answers and ask students to justify their answers by referring to particular parts of the text.

> **Possible answers**
> 1 Students may (or may not) share the sympathy (and respect) of the writer with the fact that 'paps' work long hours, often for not much money.
> 2 The students may (or may not) find the story of 'paps' and teens hanging around together amusing: they are moaning about different things, waiting for a boy band star who isn't even there to come out of a restaurant. The downbeat 'optimism' of the final paragraph is funny, too.
> 3 Students may possibly find Miguel's defence and justification of his profession, and his analogy to hunting, annoying; the writer's sympathy may annoy them, as might her complaint about hard work and her writing style.
> 4 Most would probably agree with this. However, Miguel's assertion that 'respect' between hunter and hunted is important may be questionable.
> 5 Students might argue that she is on the side of the 'paps', sharing their experiences, and coming round to their views and quoting their justifications; she doesn't present or empathise with an alternative view.
> 6 Students' own views

Culture notes

Paparazzi /pæpəˈrætsi/ are independent photographers who take photos of celebrities while they are going about their everyday routines. The word derives from the name of a character in Federico Fellini's classic film *La Dolce Vita* (1960), which is about celebrity life in Rome. Paparazzo is the name of the character of the news photographer who travels around the city on a moped, taking photos of the famous.
'Paps' = an abbreviation of *paparazzi*
A-list celebrity = a celebrity who is on the 'A-list' – i.e. somebody who is really famous – this accolade is reserved for leading actors in Hollywood or the biggest sports stars or most well-known royals
Jen = probably Jennifer Aniston, who became famous in the comedy *Friends*, and has starred in many romcoms
The Village = Greenwich Village is a neighbourhood on the west side of Lower Manhattan, New York, famous for its creative and bohemian inhabitants
Tribeca = a trendy part of lower Manhattan, famous for the Film Festival staged there
Leo = probably Leonardo di Caprio
Up&Down = a New York nightclub

4 Ask students to work individually or in pairs to decide where the extracts go. If you ask students to work individually first, let them take time to discuss answers in pairs. You could elicit the first answer to get students started. In feedback, provide answers, and work with students to explain what clues helped students make their choices.

Answers

1 A day ago I would've looked at the figure on the page jumping out of a cab on a damp street and pitied her for the life she has to lead – the intrusions, the hassle, the lack of privacy.
2 'She's wearing the same outfit as always. She knows we won't be able to sell on the photos.' He shows me an almost identical shot from a week before.
3 We spend the next three hours hanging around, the paps gossiping and moaning about the business – the dream shot, rumours of affairs, agencies squeezing prices – and the teenage fans discussing ...
4 The best we get is a minor soap star, who Miguel spots en route eating a hotdog on a street corner. He seems happy enough to be recognised (though I didn't know him!) and poses for us.
5 Still, Miguel sees it as steadier than the photojournalism he used to do. He also supplements his income teaching at an art college.
6 You can spend time preparing a hide and sit for hours up a tree waiting for a deer to appear and then, when it does, you screw up the shot and it's gone – you've literally blown your chance.
7 There's a phone call. Apparently, Leo is at Up&Down. The chase is on again.

Teacher development: missing phrases in a text

It is challenging to work out where missing extracts go in a text. If you feel your students need more support to do this task, try some of the following:

1 Do the first as an example. Ask students to say why it goes in that place, and elicit a list of things to look for when trying to work out where an extract goes.
2 Write the list of 'clues to look for' on the board. A list could be: lexical clues (similar or synonymous words in the extract to those in the text); reference clues (words like *he* and *this* which refer back or forward to words in the text); grammatical clues (the same tense in the extract as in the text, for example); other contextual clues (using conjunction words like *however*, for example).
3 Do some prediction. Ask students to look at an extract and say what it is talking about or referring to. This will help students to be able to predict its location in a text.

5 Ask students to work in pairs to discuss the meaning of the words and phrases. Do the first as an example. In feedback, ask students to define the words or give example sentences using the words.

Answers

landing our own big fish – this is a play on words in part because they are outside a fish restaurant called Catch. *Big fish* here means 'someone important'. When you land a fish you catch it. You can also land a big prize.

revulsion – feel disgusted or revolted (rather than *I feel admiration / respect*; revulsion here is the opposite of admiration / respect)
on the go – working / travelling non stop (*sixteen hours* and *very tired* + link with *go*)
dead on my feet – absolutely exhausted (link with *dead* and being *on the go*)
scuttle – move quickly like a crab (scuttle *down the street* helps to guess general meaning)
slipped out – leave quietly / secretly (as above: the pattern of *slipped out of a side entrance* will help. If students know *slip* as in *slip on a banana skin* maybe it will also help)
en route – on the way (students will know *route* and / or recognise French). Note the pronunciation in English: /ɒn 'ruːt/.
click bait – eye-catching headlines which tempt you to click on them to find out more – this generates advertising revenue (example of a headline given in the text)
remains upbeat – stays positive / happy (the context of the story – despite the slow day they are still positive)
screw up the shot – make a mess of the shot (*it's gone* shows they didn't catch it / but other times you *hit the target*)

6 Organise the class into groups of four or five to discuss the rights or wrongs of restricting the paparazzi. Give students time to organise their ideas and arguments individually first. Go round the room and check students are prepared for the task and help with ideas and vocabulary if necessary. When students are ready, ask them to discuss as a group. Monitor and listen for errors or good examples of language use to feedback on at the end.

Possible answers

For: invasion of privacy; can hurt people emotionally; can drive celebrities to despair, even suicide; everybody has a right to privacy; unfair on celebrities to have such intrusion; unfair on the families and friends of celebrities; can lead to fights, accidents
Against: freedom of the press; celebrities want publicity when it suits them, so why should they have privacy when it doesn't suit them?; it's part of the business – without the public's need for gossip, there would be no celebrities; they have fame and wealth, so why should they have privacy?; if our privacy laws were really strict, the press wouldn't be able to report on and expose the bad things people do

Optional extra activity You could turn Exercise 6 into an extended class debate. Write on the board: *The paparazzi should be prohibited from publishing personal stories about the lives of celebrities*. Ask students to decide whether they support or oppose the motion. Try to get a 50 / 50 split in your class (and, if you don't, gently persuade students into one camp or another until you have a more or less equal split). Groups have five minutes to prepare five arguments in favour of their view. Each group takes turns to present an argument in formal debate (ask different speakers for each point). At the end, the class votes on the motion.

Understanding vocabulary
Common sayings

Aim
to check students' understanding of how to recognise and use common sayings

7 Read through the information in the box as a class.
• Organise students into pairs to match sentence halves to make sayings. Go round the room and check students are doing the task and help with vocabulary if necessary. In feedback, elicit the students' answers.

Answers
1 c When the going gets tough, the tough get going
2 f People in glass houses shouldn't throw stones.
3 k When in Rome, do as the Romans do.
4 h If you can't beat them, join them.
5 g It takes all sorts to make a world.
6 b The early bird catches the worm.
7 e Never look a gift horse in the mouth.
8 j If it ain't broke, don't fix it.
9 l Too many cooks spoil the broth.
10 d Every cloud has a silver lining.
11 a The grass is always greener on the other side.
12 i Don't count your chickens before they hatch.

Background language notes for teachers

1 Strong people can be relied on to act when a situation is difficult.
2 You shouldn't criticise if you are guilty of the same faults.
3 Behave like the people of the country you are in.
4 Instead of resisting or criticising what people are doing, do the same.
5 Let's recognise that people are different, and not be critical.
6 The first person to do something is successful.
7 Don't refuse something good that is being offered.
8 If something is working, don't change it or try to improve it unnecessarily.
9 If too many people participate in a task, the task will not be done very well.
10 Even in bad times, there is something positive that may happen.
11 We always think that things are better in another place, but that isn't always the case.
12 Don't make plans that depend on something good happening before you know it's actually happened.

8 Elicit the first possible saying from the class to get students started. Then ask students to work in pairs to discuss which saying to use and why. There is no need to feedback here as students will hear answers in the recording.

9 🔊 44 Play the recording. Students listen and check their answers. Note that in the recording many of the answers are actually in shortened form.

• In feedback, discuss which answers were the same, and ask students to say why they came up with identical or different answers. Note that there may be other possibilities to those in the audio script. If answers are different, encourage students to explain their choice and any additional things they would say before judging whether to accept their answer or not.

Answers
1 Takes all sorts
2 let's not count our chickens
3 when in Rome
4 glass houses and all that
5 too many cooks
6 if it ain't broke

🔊 **44**
1 A: Apparently, he loves being a paparazzo.
   B: Really? <u>Takes all sorts</u>, I suppose.
   A: I know. I can't think of anything worse.
2 A: Maybe we could get a bigger place after you get the new job.
   B: Hey, <u>let's not count our chickens</u>. I haven't even had the interview yet.
   A: I know, but I have confidence in you!
3 A: What? We have to eat with our hands?
   B: Hey – <u>when in Rome</u>.
   A: I'd rather not, though. Do you know the word for 'spoon'?
4 A: Honestly, he gets away with murder. He didn't lift a finger to help.
   B: Yeah well – <u>glass houses and all that</u>. We didn't exactly do a lot either.
   A: We did! Well, more than him anyway.
5 A: Honestly, the organisation of the whole event was terrible.
   B: I know. I think it was a case of <u>too many cooks</u>.
   A: Probably. There did seem to be quite a lot of contradictory information flying around.
6 A: I wish they hadn't interfered. We were doing fine without them.
   B: Absolutely. I mean, if <u>it ain't broke</u> ...
   A: Exactly.

10 Organise the class into new pairs. Ask them to choose four other sayings from Exercise 7 and prepare dialogues. Tell them to make them shorter, two-line dialogues. Go round and help with ideas and vocabulary. In feedback, elicit a dialogue from each pair, and ask the class to say how well the common saying was used in each dialogue.

Possible answers
One possible example for each of the remaining sayings:
A: I can't believe you carried on running with that blister on your foot.
B: Hey well, you know what they say – when the going gets tough.

A: Even Dad was up dancing by the end and he hates
   dancing.
B: Well, if you can't beat them.

A: Are you really going to get up at five to go down
   to the market?
B: Hey, the early bird catches the worm.

A: Can't be a genuine Rolex.
B: Almost certainly not but never look a gift horse – it
   seems to work OK.

A: I got quite a good redundancy payment in the end.
B: Oh well, every cloud.

A: I keep thinking maybe I'd be better off working for
   a bigger company.
B: Yeah maybe, but the grass is always greener, isn't
   it? There'll be frustration there too.

Optional extra activity When students have prepared
their dialogues, ask them to practise them in their
pairs and try to memorise them, instead of just reading
them out.

Web research activity
• Ask students to choose a celebrity they are interested
in, and to find out five interesting pieces of news about
the celebrity which they didn't know before.
• In the next lesson, ask students to present their
celebrity news, and to say where and how they
discovered it. Tell them not to go through bins!

Communicative outcomes
In this two-page spread, students will listen to a news
bulletin and discuss news stories; they will practise
using patterns after reporting verbs.

SPEAKING

Aim
to introduce the theme of the listening text and get
students talking about the news

1   Organise the class into groups of four or five
to discuss the questions. Monitor closely and note
interesting and useful language, as well as errors. After
four or five minutes, ask students to share ideas with
the class. Use the feedback to point out good examples,
correct errors, and to provide examples of how students
can express their ideas better.

2   Organise the class into pairs. Ask students to check
they know the meaning of the words and phrases in
bold. Ask students to discuss the opinions. In feedback,
elicit definitions and examples to explain the words, and
elicit students' opinions.

Background language notes for teachers

feeling helpless = feeling that you can't do anything to
change or influence the world
In the hands of media barons = under the control of
individuals who own the big newspapers and news
outlets (e.g. Rupert Murdoch)
keep up with the news = know what's happening in the
latest news
foreign affairs = news about what is happening away
from your country
suppress = stop, censor, prevent from being published
rolling 24-hour news = news that is on all the time, and
keeps changing as new news stories come in
totally hooked on it = can't stop watching or following it
speculation = here, making guesses about things
hard facts = providing facts that are indisputable and
obviously true

Optional extra activity Ask students in pairs to write
their own sentence that shows their view of the news.
Ask pairs to share their view with the class.

LISTENING

Aim
to practise listening for general and detailed
understanding

3   ◐ **45** Play the recording. Ask students to listen and
take notes.

Answers

1 Politician (Finance Minister) has retired (or been sacked – countered rumours she'd been forced out)
2 Two people died in a riot in Manova
3 Interest rates are going to rise
4 Footballer (Jermaine Johnson) is not playing in match (World Cup qualifier)
5 Celebrity couple have won a court (libel) case
6 A (sniffer) dog has won a medal

🔊 **45**

A = announcer,   N = Natalie Davis,   C = Carol Dixon

A: And now on SBC, the six o'clock news with Natalie Davis.
N: Good evening and welcome. The headlines this evening: Finance Minister Carol Dixon has today announced her retirement, and has swiftly moved to counter rumours she's being forced out of her post.
C: At this stage, I'm not willing to comment further other than to say this has been my decision and mine alone, and the reasons for it are personal, not political.
N: And also tonight: two people have died as rioting continues in Manova; interest rates are set to rise; Jermaine Johnson is out of the final World Cup qualifier; the celebrity couple Simon Crouch and Jennifer Ponting have won their libel case against the News Enquirer, and there's a medal for a very special sniffer dog.

Culture notes

In case students ask, none of the characters in the news bulletin are real, and nor is Manova.

4 Ask students to compare answers in pairs. Students match the nouns or noun phrases to the stories they took notes on in Exercise 3. You may need to check some phrases (*sham marriage* = a false marriage, e.g. when two people get married so that one of them can gain citizenship; *tear gas* = a gas used by police to disperse crowds). Monitor and prompt, and find out what students think at this stage.
• In feedback, ask students to share their thoughts with the class, and ask them to justify their ideas.

5 🔊 **46** Give students time to read the task carefully.
• Play the recording. Ask students to listen and answer the questions. Let students compare their answers in pairs.
• In feedback, ask students to retell stories and say how the words are connected.

Answers

1 health grounds, a private matter – the minister is apparently resigning on health grounds and doesn't want to say more because it is a private matter

2 petrol bomb, tear gas – there's been rioting over government reforms – police say two men apparently died when a petrol bomb hit a car which exploded; demonstrators say the two men were crushed when the crowd fled from police tear gas by running down narrow side streets. Government rejected demands to change course.
3 the base rate, inflation – the base rate is set to rise to 4% in order to control inflation (and it may rise higher – refused to rule out); it's feared increase may trigger an economic slowdown, but food and fuel costs still rising
4 thigh strain, on good form – goalkeeper and captain can't play because of a thigh strain, but the manager is confident the replacement will be fine as he's on good form
5 sham marriage, an appeal – the celebrity couple were accused by a paper of being in a sham marriage and they took the paper to court where they won the case (awarded $560,000 damages which they are donating to charity). The newspaper is thinking of appealing against the decision.
6 bomb disposal, bravery – a sniffer dog (Bodge) received a medal for bravery for his work in a bomb disposal unit – helped to find 200 bombs and mines which were deactivated

🔊 **46**

N = Natalie Davis,   C = Carol Dixon,   P = Paul King,
M = Malaika Hussain,   F = François Houllier,
A = Anita Karaji,   L = lawyer,   H = Hassan Cleaver

N: Finance Minister Carol Dixon has confirmed rumours that she is to retire on health grounds. She categorically denied that her retirement was connected to recent criticism of the government's decision to build two new nuclear power stations, although she acknowledged there had been division on the issue.
C: There was a dispute over nuclear energy. I've never hidden that and I've never denied being a long-term opponent, but I lost that argument. And on broad policy I remain totally behind this government.
N: However, she refused to comment further on the health reasons for her departure, stating only that it was a private matter. Elsewhere, rioting over government reforms has continued in Manova, with two men being killed. Crowds throwing missiles confronted armed police in the main square and conducted running battles in the surrounding streets throughout the day. Paul King reports.
P: There are conflicting reports about the deaths. A police spokesman assured reporters that the men died when a car exploded after being set alight by a petrol bomb thrown by rioters. Meanwhile, demonstrators claim the victims were crushed when police fired tear gas to disperse the crowd in the square, forcing people down narrow side streets.

As the news of the deaths spread, protesters rampaged through the surrounding area. The rioting lasted most of the day until an uneasy calm fell upon the city this evening. Addressing the country on television, the President blamed the rioting on subversive groups trying to destabilise the country and rejected demands for the government to change tack. He urged what he termed the silent majority to make their voices heard. However, there are no signs that that call will be heeded. Paul King, Manova.

N: Interest rates look set to rise by half a point, taking the base rate to a ten-year high of 4%. The National Bank refused to rule out further increases this year as it bids to control inflation. Malaika Hussain reports.

M: Thanks Natalie. Yes, today's announcement had been widely expected after recent warnings by the head of the National Bank that caution was needed in the battle against inflation. Now, of course, there will surely be concerns that the rise could trigger an economic slowdown, but it seems those fears are outweighed by real concern about rising food and fuel costs and, as you said, it wouldn't be a surprise if there were further hikes later on in the year.

N: And now sport, and the national football team have been dealt a further blow in the run-up to their crucial World Cup qualifying match against Russia. Goalkeeper and team captain Jermaine Johnson has been ruled out with a thigh strain. The team have struggled and must win if they are to go through to the finals next year. Manager François Houllier expressed confidence in Johnson's replacement, Paul Harrison.

F: Obviously it is not ideal, but, er, Paul is a great keeper and has been on good form, so I am not so worried.

N: The Hollywood couple Simon Crouch and Jennifer Ponting have won their libel action against the paper News Enquirer, following allegations that theirs was a sham marriage. Anita Karaji reports.

A: During the compelling three-day hearing, the court heard claim and counterclaim about the state of Crouch and Ponting's marriage, which, yes, the Enquirer had accused them of entering into purely for their mutual benefit. In the end, though, the judge found in their favour, awarding $560,000 damages. In a statement read by their lawyer, the couple thanked supporters and promised to donate the money to charity.

L: Simon and Jen would like to thank all those fans who never doubted the outcome of this case. They would also like to make clear that all the proceeds from this decision will be given to good causes because this case was never about personal gain, only personal truth.

A: News Enquirer said it disagreed with the decision and was considering an appeal.

N: And finally tonight: a sniffer dog has received a medal for bravery for his work in a bomb disposal unit. Bodge has worked in several war zones over the last six years and has helped find over 200 bombs and mines to be deactivated. His handler, Corporal Hassan Cleaver, said it was a proud day and praised the work of the whole unit.

H: It's just fantastic. He deserves it, as do lots of the dogs we work with. What they do is unbelievably important. They're fantastic.

N: And that's the news from SBC. Good evening.

6 🔊46 Organise the class into groups of four. Let students read through the statements first, and discuss whether they are definitely true, definitely false or still unclear based on their first listening.

• Play the recording again and ask students to listen and check answers. Let students compare their answers in groups before discussing as a class. Tell them to look at audio script 46 on page 210 to confirm their answers before going through answers as a class.

Answers

1 True: *... I've never denied being a long-term opponent, but I lost that argument.*
2 Still unclear: *she refused to comment further on the health reasons for her departure.*
3 Still unclear: *There are conflicting reports about the deaths.*
4 Still unclear: *the President claims the silent majority should speak up*
5 True: *... as you said, it wouldn't be a great surprise if there were further hikes later on in the year.*
6 Still unclear: not mentioned how he got the injury
7 False: *The team have struggled and must win if they are to go through to the finals next year.*
8 True: *... promised to donate the money to charity. / They would also like to make clear that all the proceeds from this decision will be given to good causes, because this case was never about personal gain, only about personal truth.*
9 Still unclear: not mentioned
10 False: he works for the Army (work in a bomb disposal unit, worked in several war zones, his handler, Corporal Hassan Cleaver)

---

7 Ask students to work in the same groups to discuss the stories. Monitor closely and note interesting and useful language, as well as errors.

• Once you have fed back on content, look at good language that students used, and language students didn't quite use correctly. Show students better ways of saying what they were trying to say. You could write some useful new phrases on the board with gaps and ask the whole class to complete the sentences.

GRAMMAR Patterns after reporting verbs

Aim
to check students' understanding of how to recognise patterns used after reporting verbs

8 Read through the information in the box as a class.
• Organise students into pairs to make sentences from the prompts. Do the first as an example in open class. Tell them that their sentences need not be identical to those on the recording. Monitor and help students apply the patterns by reminding them to look at the rules in the box.

• In feedback, elicit the students' answers. They can check their answers using the Grammar reference on page 180.

Possible answers
1 She acknowledged there had been division on the issue.
2 She denied being a long-term opponent.
3 She refused to comment on the health reasons for her departure.
4 Police assured reporters that the men died when a car exploded.
5 The president rejected demands for the government to change tack.
6 The president urged the silent majority to make their voices heard.
7 The newspaper accused them of entering into the marriage purely for their mutual benefit.

 Students complete Exercise 1 in the Grammar reference on page 180.

Answers to Exercise 1, Grammar reference
1 cited (*state that something is ...*)
2 urged (*reiterate that everyone who could, should ...*)
3 refused (*rejected the idea of cooperating*)
4 blamed (*criticise for*)
5 announced (*notify someone*)
6 instructed (*demand someone do*)
7 pleaded (*beg for*)
8 boasting (*praise someone for*)
9 considered (*threaten to do something*)
10 warned (*criticise someone for doing something*)

9 Ask students to work individually to decide which options are correct before comparing with a partner. Let them work together to correct the patterns. Do the first as an example to show how students will need to add / change words to make sentences correct.
• Feedback briefly on students' answers. Refer them to the patterns in the box.

Answers
1 I heard on the news that he'd *admitted / denied / ~~been accused~~* stealing over £1,000,000.
   ... been accused **of** stealing ...
2 In the end, she *convinced / ~~suggested~~ / persuaded* us all to go to the show.
   ... suggested **we all go** to the show.
3 When I saw her, she was *~~telling~~ / grumbling / insisting* that she can't handle the weather here.
   ... telling **me** that ...
4 My aunt *urged / ~~recommended~~ / advised* me to go and get it looked at by a specialist.
   ... recommended **that I** go ...
5 He's *~~confirmed~~ / ~~discussed~~ / vowed* never to marry again.
   ... confirmed **that he's** never **going** to marry again
   ... discussed never **marrying** again ...

10 Organise the class into groups of four or five. Give students time to read the questions. Make it clear that they should try to use the patterns accurately when

discussing their examples. You could provide one or two examples that are true for you to get students started. Monitor and notice errors and examples of good language use which you could focus on in feedback.
• In feedback, ask different groups to tell the class which examples they came up with.
• Once you have fed back on content, look at good language that students used, and language students didn't quite use correctly. Show students better ways of saying what they were trying to say. You could write some useful new phrases on the board with gaps and ask the whole class to complete the sentences.

 For further practice, see Exercises 2 and 3 in the Grammar reference on page 180.

Answers to Exercise 2, Grammar reference
1 anger at the tax
2 to me that she had
3 he would have it done / it would be done
4 urged us to visit him
5 voiced / expressed concern that the situation
6 threatened to get / have me sacked
7 acknowledged that the plan was

Answers to Exercise 3, Grammar reference
1 assurance that
2 criticism about
3 invitation to
4 announcement that they are getting married
5 confession to
6 recommendations for
7 refusal to
8 encouragement to students who want to

Optional extra activity Ask students in pairs to write a list of things they have said in the last week. Tell them to include: a boast, a complaint, a promise, a threat, a criticism, an announcement and a confession. Give an example or two: *I'll give you extra homework; There'll be a test on Monday*. Once students have produced a list, ask them to exchange it with another pair. Each pair must then report the sentences on the list using appropriate verb patterns.

14 BUSINESS AND ECONOMICS

SPEAKING

Aim
to set the scene and introduce the theme with a photo; to get students talking about buying things at auction and investing money in things

1 Start by telling the class that in this unit they're going to be discussing running a company, businesses, crime, banks and economics; students will network and make small talk, use loanwords, and take part in meetings.
• Ask students to look at the photo on pages 122–123. Ask: *What can you see?* Elicit a brief description of the photo, and introduce any key words students might need.
• Organise the class into pairs to discuss the questions. Go round the room and check students are doing the task and help with ideas and vocabulary if necessary.
• In feedback, ask different pairs to tell the class what they discussed.
• Once you have fed back on content, look at good language that students used, and language students didn't quite use correctly.

> **Possible answers**
> The photo shows an auction at Sotheby's. There are a number of paintings on show. People in the audience are making bids.

Culture notes

Sotheby's was established as an auction house in London in 1744. It is now a multinational corporation, and its headquarters are in New York. It has divisions in New York, London, Hong Kong and Moscow. It specialises in fine art but also has subsidiaries selling houses, cars and wine among other expensive items.
In the photo, people are bidding to buy a Chagall painting at Sotheby's fine art auction, New York.

2 Organise the class into groups of four. Start by checking any key words in the list of potential investments (*a start-up* = investing money to support somebody else in being able to quickly start a company or project). Then ask students to discuss which investments they would make. Go round the room and check students are doing the task and help with ideas and vocabulary if necessary.
• Once you have fed back on content, look at good language that students used, and language students didn't quite use correctly during the activity.

> **Possible answers**
> Students' own ideas
> Other good investments might be in stocks and shares, diamonds, a local company you know about, your own business.

Optional extra activity Ask students to rank the potential investments on a scale from 'safe' to 'risky'. In feedback, ask them to explain their ranking.

Teacher development: creating a task

The emphasis in lead-in speaking tasks in *Outcomes Advanced* is on getting students to personalise the material by expressing their own ideas and experiences. However, there are other ways of getting students to use and consider the words, and these involve creating a task. Here are some possibilities:
1 categorising: ask students to organise ideas into different categories (in Exercise 2, students could categorise the potential investments into 'safe' or 'risky' or 'possible' or 'unlikely')
2 ordering or ranking: ask students to order or rank different categories (in Exercise 2, students could rank the potential investments from 'safest' to 'riskiest')
3 matching: ask students to match ideas (in Exercise 2, students could match potential investments with a similar degree of risk).

BUSINESS MATTERS
Student's Book pages 124–125

Communicative outcomes
In this two-page spread, students will practise describing a business and making small talk.

SPEAKING

Aim
to introduce the theme of the listening text and get students talking about running a business

1 Start by giving students a few minutes to read through all the questions and tell them to ask questions about the vocabulary if they need to (see below).
• Organise the class into groups of four or five to discuss the questions. Monitor closely and note any interesting personal views or experiences you could draw on in feedback. After a few minutes, ask students to share ideas with the class. Use the feedback to point out good examples, correct errors, and to provide examples of how students can express their ideas better.

Possible answers
Good things about running a business include being your own boss, being able to make your own plans and fulfil your own dreams, the chance to become rich if you are successful, the sense of achievement. Bad things include the pressure and stress, the risk of losing a lot of money or going bankrupt if you fail, the long hours.

Background language notes for teachers

raising start-up funds = trying to get people to invest in a company (start-up) that's only just beginning to operate, especially a high-tech company
building team morale = making or improving the confidence and enthusiasm of a group of workers
networking = interacting with others to build contacts who may be useful to you in your work
book-keeping = keeping an accurate record of the accounts of a business
managing cash flow = checking and controlling the movement of money into and out of a business as goods are bought and sold

VOCABULARY How's business?

Aim
to introduce and practise language used to describe how business is going

2 Ask students to work in pairs to discuss the words. In feedback, elicit answers and ask students to say how the words differ. Use definitions and examples to help show the difference. Model and drill some of the words for pronunciation.

Answers
1 different: an upturn in sales = sales increase // a decline in sales = sales go down
2 same meaning in context: you have lots of people who know, like and buy your product
3 same meaning in context: you've received a lot of orders
4 same meaning in context: relocating and moving
    different: rent = only the money you pay to use the office or factory space // overheads = rent as well as wages, gas, electricity, water, etc.
5 different: lay off = make redundant // employ = give jobs to
6 same meaning in context: start to sell shares to the public for the first time
7 same meaning in context: pick up and get better = improve
    different: end up going under = go bankrupt and thus have to close // have to make serious cutbacks = survive as a company, but only after cutting costs dramatically
8 same meaning in context
9 different: diversify the range = branch out and start selling a wider range of products and services // consolidate = stick with what you have, focus on core strengths and protect and develop what's already there
10 different: take staff on = employ people // make staff redundant = make them unemployed
11 same meaning in context
12 different: terminating = you already have a contract but have decided to end it // pitch for a contract = try to win the contract

---

Background language notes for teachers: pronunciation

Note the stress: <u>up</u>turn, <u>in</u>undated, relo<u>ca</u>ting, di<u>ver</u>sify, con<u>so</u>lidate, re<u>dun</u>dant, <u>ter</u>minating.

3 Students work in the same pairs. Encourage them to use their knowledge and imagination to think of situations. Monitor and note some of the more interesting ideas students have.
• In feedback, elicit answers from the class. Look at good language that students used, and language students didn't quite use correctly.

Possible answers
There are no definite fixed answers, and it is best to work with what students come up with. However, in case they get stuck, here are some probable responses:
1 *upturn in sales* – better advertising and marketing, economy is picking up, product is becoming better known
    decline in sales – product is becoming outdated, cheaper rival products have appeared
2 *solid client base / loyal customers* – years of work building this up, good product, excellent after-sales service, good reps

---

3 *inundated / flooded* – the result of advertising, celebrity endorsement, being picked up on by the media, etc.

4 *relocating / moving* – usually a cost-cutting measure, but could be to be nearer manufacturing centre, nearer transportation links or where the main business is

5 *lay off* – need to cut costs, business could be in financial trouble or could want to increase profits by cutting costs
employ – business is booming, expanding, demand is up so need more people

6 *floating / launching* – need investment and this is one way to get it whilst retaining basic control of the firm

7 *pick up / get better soon* – things need to improve through better advertising or improving product, business is in financial trouble, losing money, need to make major savings; maybe there's a recession or products are outdated
end up going under – going out of business because sales aren't improving
have to make serious cutbacks – have to make people redundant, reduce quality of goods, reduce salaries

8 *hanging in / surviving* – company has maybe cut back a bit, cut down on lavish spending, salary cuts, diversifying range of products and services or sending business overseas where salaries and costs are less

9 *diversify* – because core products are no longer as profitable as they once were
consolidate – no money to really expand or add new products so what there is now is good enough but needs updating to make it more saleable, build on what there is

10 *take staff on* – business is doing really well, company is expanding, demand is up, more people needed
make staff redundant – company is in financial trouble so need to cut costs so fewer people needed

11 *downturn / drop in sales* – product is perhaps becoming outdated, cheaper rival products have appeared

12 *terminating* – maybe had a row with the Russian partner; feel treated unfairly, don't trust them anymore; contract is impossible to fulfill; they've breached the contract, etc.
pitching – you want to win the contract as it'd be lucrative for you; need the contract in order to expand

Optional extra activity Write the name of a well-known company on the board – preferably one that has been in the news in the students' country. Ask the class to describe the company's recent fortunes using words from Exercise 2.

LISTENING

Aim
to practise listening for general understanding and to hear chunks of language in a text

4 🔊 **47** Introduce the situation, and ask students to briefly read the questions.
• Play the recording. Students listen and note answers. Let students compare answers in pairs. In feedback, elicit answers.

Answers
Conversation 1
1 to check whether the delivery sent out on Monday has arrived yet
2 Business is OK. They're hanging in. Sales have actually picked up a bit this quarter. They've taken on a couple of new people.
3 second speaker's child, her husband / partner, her holiday in Crete

Conversation 2
1 to sort out a time for a meeting during the trade fair next week
2 Not too bad. Planned relocation will save money as overheads will be cheaper, but some staff are threatening to leave the company if it goes ahead.
3 the draw for the European Championships

🔊 **47**
Conversation 1
K = Katherine, S = Susie
K: Hello, InTech Corporation. Katherine speaking. How can I help you?
S: Oh, hello there, Katherine. It's me, Susie.
K: Oh, hi. How're you?
S: Not too bad, thanks. Listen, I'm just calling to check whether the delivery we sent out on Monday has reached you yet.
K: It has, yeah. It came in this morning, I believe.
S: Oh, that's good. I was just panicking over nothing, then.
K: Well, better safe than sorry, isn't it?
S: Exactly. Anyway, how're you? How're things your end?
K: Oh, you know. We're hanging in there. Sales have actually picked up a bit this quarter, so that's good, and we've actually taken on a couple of new people, so can't complain, you know. How's life with you? How's the little one?
S: Oh, she's good. She's just coming up to one now and she's crawling around everywhere and babbling away to herself all the time.
K: Ah!
S: Yeah. I'll send you pictures if you want.
K: That'd be lovely, yeah. And how's Mark?
S: He's OK. He's been away a lot with work recently, actually, which has been a bit of a pain, but hopefully that'll ease off a bit soon.
K: Mmm, yeah ... that can't be easy. Hey, how was your holiday? Didn't you go away somewhere recently?

S: Yeah, that's right, we did. Two weeks in Crete. Oh, it was lovely. Over far too quickly, of course, but much needed.

K: Oh, that's good though.

S: Yeah.

Conversation 2
M = Matt, D = Dietmar

M: Hello. CNC.

D: Hi, is that Matt?

M: Yeah, Dietmar. Hi. I was just thinking of you, actually. I saw the draw for the European Championships.

D: Oh yeah. I'm sorry, but England have to lose to someone.

M: Don't count your chickens yet! Let's wait and see.

D: I admire your optimism.

M: Well, you have to look on the bright side, don't you? Especially in our line of work.

D: Tell me about it! How're things, anyway?

M: Oh, not too bad, all things considered.

D: And what's happening with the relocation?

M: Well, it's still on the cards, apparently. We've told them it's a bad idea, but they just won't listen!

D: Well, just think of all the savings you'll make on your overheads.

M: And on wages if half the staff who're threatening to leave actually do!

D: A lot of that's just talk, I'd imagine. They'll soon come round.

M: I hope you're right. Anyway, what can I do for you today?

D: Well, I was just wondering if we could maybe sort out a time for a meeting during the trade fair next week. It'd be good to talk through Mexico with you.

M: Yeah, of course. Is Thursday any use to you?

D: Yeah, maybe. What time?

M: Um ... well, I could squeeze you in in the morning, if you want. Say 10? 10.15?

D: Yeah, 10.15 should be fine. I'll pencil it in.

M: Great. See you then, then.

5 ✿ 47 Organise the class into pairs. Ask students to try to remember what chunks of language included the words / phrases based on their first listening. You could elicit the first answer to get students started.

• Once students have tried to remember all of them, play the recording again. Students listen and note the missing words. In feedback, elicit answers, and point out the weakly stressed words students may have missed. You could refer students to audio script 47 on page 211 to check their answers.

Answers
1 I was just panicking over nothing
2 Sales have actually picked up a bit this quarter
3 we've actually taken on a couple of new people
4 she's crawling around everywhere (and babbling away to herself all the time)
5 (He's been away a lot with work recently), which has been a bit of a pain, (but hopefully that'll ease off a bit soon).

6 I saw the draw for the European Championships
7 Don't count your chickens yet!
8 just think of all the savings you'll make on your overheads
9 And on wages if half the staff who're threatening to leave actually do!
10 Is Thursday any use to you?

Background language notes for teachers

this quarter = this three month period of business
babbling away = talking nonsense (like babies do)
Is Thursday any use to you? = Is Thursday a day when you are free (for a meeting)?

DEVELOPING CONVERSATIONS
Small talk

Aim
to introduce and practise small talk in business contexts

6 Read through the information in the box as a class. Organise the class into pairs to discuss the questions. In feedback, elicit answers and ideas.

Culture notes

In the UK, small talk may involve asking about health, family and the trip someone made to get there; it may involve talking about the weather, the economy, a favourite team, programmes on TV, plans for the weekend.

7 Ask students to work in pairs to decide on the questions. Let them read each answer carefully first and to take time to think what the question might be before comparing ideas with their partner. Elicit an example to get the pairs started. In feedback, elicit answers and make sure students have come up with appropriate questions.

Possible answers
1 How's business? / How're things going?
2 How did you end up in this job? / How did you get this job?
3 How are things over there? / How's the economy (doing) there?
4 How are the kids? / How are your kids?
5 Lovely weather, isn't it? / Isn't it amazing weather?
6 How's your week been? / Good week? / Have you had a good week?
7 How's your team doing? / Is your team having a good season?
8 What are you doing / up to tonight?
9 How was your holiday? / So what was your holiday like?
10 How was your journey / the flight?

8 Ask pairs to practise small talk by asking the questions they prepared and improvising their own responses. Monitor, prompt, and note good or incorrect examples of language use. In feedback, point out some good examples of small talk, and correct any significant errors.

CONVERSATION PRACTICE

Aim
to practise language from the lesson in a free, communicative, personalised speaking activity

9 Organise the class into pairs. Ask each pair to decide which reason to choose and also to decide who is A and who is B. Give students a short amount of preparation time to think of what to say. Monitor and help, if necessary, encouraging students to make small talk.

10 When students are ready, ask them to act out their roleplays. Monitor each pair and note their language use, noting down any errors, which you could focus on at the end.

11 Ask students to choose another reason and roleplay again this time with Student B as the caller. You could change pairs if you wish to increase the amount of practice. Practice makes perfect.
- In feedback, look at good language that students used, and language students didn't quite use correctly during the activity. Show students better ways of saying what they were trying to say. You could write some useful new phrases on the board with gaps and ask the whole class to complete the sentences.

▶️ **32** Refer students to the video and activities on the DVD-ROM.

Teacher development: using the video

The video and activities on the DVD-ROM can be used in various ways:
1 as an alternative to the conversation practice
2 instead of the listening activity in some units, particularly with weaker groups. Students can first practise reading out the dialogues and work on some of the key phrases / structures in a controlled way before having a go themselves.
3 at the end of the unit as a revision exercise

BANKING ON CHANGE
Student's Book pages 126–127

Communicative outcomes
In this two-page spread, students read and discuss a text about malpractice in banking; they practise using relative clauses and loanwords from other languages.

READING

Aim
to give students practice in reading for general and specific information

1 Organise the class into small groups to brainstorm and then rank banking crimes. In feedback, elicit crimes and write them on the board.

Answers
There are no fixed answers. Work with whatever students come up with. You may want to give one example to get the ball rolling.
For example: hacking into someone's bank account and stealing money, making counterfeit money, banks illegally fixing certain rates to guarantee more profits

2 Ask students to look at the headline on page 127. Ask what the blog post might be about. Then ask students to read the blog post and discuss what the headline refers to in pairs. Discuss as a class in feedback.

Answers
Work with your students' answers. However, here are four possible ways of interpreting the headline, plus a summarising statement:
a four Icelandic bankers have been prosecuted (for fraud)
b the writer thinks this is good because it's one of the first times people who've committed crimes inside banks have been prosecuted – rather than just the banks as institutions getting fined – so it's putting the people first before the institutions
c this may make some people inside banks think twice and take more individual responsibility for their actions
d finally – and students may not get this – it means banks may now become more people-friendly and people-centred and better with customers too

In short, putting people first in terms of the legal process may help banks get better at putting customers first, rather than simply seeking profit.

3 Ask students to discuss the questions with a partner. Tell them to work together to look back at the post to confirm or correct answers. In feedback, ask students to justify their answers.

Answers

1 No. It was because they knew about the poor financial state of the bank and to try and cover this up and calm shareholders, they illegally lent money to someone who bought a share in the firm. This was intended to boost confidence, but they had actually lent the buyer the cash illegally. This is what they were arrested for: fraud, in essence.

2 Not explicitly stated, but presumably because they hired excellent lawyers, evidence was hard to access, the bank itself may not have been cooperative, there were bankruptcy procedures to go through first, etc.

3 That it's easy to see – you don't have to be good at maths to see that the money the UK government has given the banks to bail them out is much more than the money the banks have paid in fines.

4 A period of austerity is a time when the government dramatically reduces public spending and makes lots of cuts to the public sector. The writer clearly doesn't agree with it as the writer is angry about the amount spent bailing out banks – and points to Iceland to suggest another way of sorting out this problem is possible.

5 Banks were part of local communities and so were more likely to protect investments, support local firms, and avert risks as people working in the banks may even have known the people whose money they held.

6 Optimistic. The writer sees the Icelandic situation as offering an alternative model of hope, believes we can change things for the better and believes banks can return to a more people-centred way of working.

Teacher development: inferring from a text

In the Comment section of newspapers, or on blog posts in which experts comment, the writer's opinions are strongly-felt, but not always stated in simple black-and-white terms. Instead, it can be often inferred. Inferring how the writer feels can be a demanding task. It involves reading between the lines, or recognising irony, humour, overstatement or understatement, and is therefore trickier than merely comprehending meaning. Here are some things to guide students to watch out for:

1 the writer's interjections. Point out the phrase 'It's happened again' in paragraph 1, 'Well said indeed' in paragraph 3, and 'You do the maths' in paragraph 4. These show the writer's strength of feeling, and encourage the reader to agree.

2 the use of capitals (£1.2 TRILLION) and italics (*people, same community*) to emphasise or show strength of feeling

3 words that carry the weight of someone's opinion or bias: *finally, of course*

4 the use of rhetorical questions: *Is it so crazy to imagine we could go back to that situation?*

Culture notes

the noughties = the years between 2000 and 2010
£1.2 trillion to bail the banks out = a bank rescue package

(initially of £500 billion) was announced by the British government on 8th October 2008 as a response to the ongoing global financial crisis. Effectively, they bought shares to take the banks into a form of public ownership. High Street banks such as Lloyds TSB and Royal Bank of Scotland were financially rescued (bailed out) in this way.
the Icelandic situation = the Icelandic financial crisis was a major economic and political event in Iceland in which all three of the country's major privately owned commercial banks defaulted in late 2008. It led to economic depression in the country.

4 Ask students to read the comments individually and to prepare their own comment.

5 Organise the class into small groups to discuss the comments on the post and the ones each student has prepared. In feedback, open up anything interesting for class discussion.

GRAMMAR Relative clauses

Aim
to check students' understanding of how to use defining and non-defining relative clauses

6 Read through the information in the box as a class.
• Organise students into pairs to discuss the underlined relative clauses. Do the first as an example in open class. Monitor and notice how well students understand the relative clauses.
• In feedback, elicit the students' answers. They can check their answers using the Grammar reference on page 181.

Answers
1 Defining the noun: 1, 2, 3, 6, 9, 10, 11
  Adding extra non-essential information: 4, 5, 7, 8, 12
2
  1 some kind of organism
  2 some kind of organism
  3 people
  4 jail sentences
  5 the sale of a 5% stake in the bank
  6 the people
  7 a period of recession and austerity
  8 the Icelandic situation
  9 more important reason
  10 a time
  11 the bank
  12 local people
3
  1 *that* – to refer to the organism as a thing, which is the subject of this clause here
  2 *whose* – to refer to purpose 'belonging to' the organism: its purpose / the organism's purpose
  3 no relative pronoun – see 4 at end
  4 *of which* – to refer back to two of the jail sentences, which are the subjects of the relative clause here
  5 *whereby* – to show the process by which something happened, to explain the reason for a previously mentioned action
  6 *who* – to refer back to the people, who are the subject of this clause

7 *during which time* – to refer back to the period of recession and austerity and to introduce what happened within that time

8 *where* – to refer to the situation and to introduce what happened in this situation

9 *why* – it links with the 'reason' and introduces which reason is being talked about here

10 *when* – refers back to 'a time' and introduces what happened in this time

11 no relative pronoun – see 4 at end

12 *some of whom* – refers back to the people, the subjects of this clause

4 no need for a relative pronoun in 3 and 11 because we often don't use a relative pronoun / adverb in defining relative clauses when the noun they relate to is the object of the clause

 Students complete Exercises 1 and 2 in the Grammar reference on pages 181–182.

Answers to Exercise 1, Grammar reference

1 a correct

1 b correct

2 a correct

2 b incorrect – need to add a preposition: The company **in** which he invested all his savings went bust.

3 a incorrect – should be *whose* not *who's*

3 b correct

4 a correct

4 b incorrect – can't use *that* to introduce a non-defining relative clause, should be *who* here instead

5 a correct

5 b incorrect – need another comma added in to enclose the non-defining clause: Taxpayers, many of whom have debts themselves**,** are paying for the banks' losses.

Answers to Exercise 2, Grammar reference

1 We have to identify areas in which improvements can be made.

2 My boss, whose office is next to mine, heard everything.

3 In January, we borrowed €10,000, most of which has already been spent.

4 For the starting point of our study we chose 2004, the year in which our president submitted his first budget.

5 I wanted to explore the extent to which large corporations influence the economic health of nations.

6 We have over 9,000 employees, the vast majority of whom are based in China.

7 We've reached a crucial point, beyond which we cannot cut costs any further without having to lay people off.

8 The S and L bank, which was bailed out by the government and whose executives were imprisoned for fraud, has finally returned to profit.

Background language notes for teachers: relative clauses

Students have lots of problems applying form rules when manipulating relative pronouns and relative clauses. It is worth taking time to look at the rules in the grammar, and to thinking carefully about which of the four accuracy practice exercises in the Grammar reference to do. There is no need to set all of them. Make sure the exercises practise areas of difficulty for your students. Problems students at this level face:

1 When to leave out the pronoun and when to prefer *that* to *which* (*The plane he boarded; the plane that / which was leaving* and *The last plane, which was about to depart* ...).

2 How to use prepositions with *which* or *whom* (*one of the co-founders about whom ...; the top of which was broken ... ; some of whom* ...). Here students have to recognise what is being referred to by the pronoun, whether it is an object or subject, and what preposition is dependent.

7 Ask students to prepare their own personalised sentences first. You could elicit two or three examples from the class to get them started. Monitor and help with ideas and vocabulary.

• When students are ready, ask them to compare their sentences with a partner. Elicit some answers in feedback, and comment on errors or examples of good language use.

Answers

There are no fixed answers needed here. Work with what students come up with. Here is a sample answer to provide as an example:

1 In our country, we are currently in a situation ... *we have never faced before / which could lead to serious unrest / in which thousands face a life of unemployment*

Note that the phrases provided can be followed by a preposition and a relative pronoun, so make sure students are aware of the following:

1 a situation in which

2 cases in which

3 the point at which

4 no reason for / why

5 the way in which

6 the extent to which

 For further practice, see Exercises 3 and 4 in the Grammar reference on page 182.

Answers to Exercise 3, Grammar reference

1 f Our founder was Mr Johnson, after whom the company is named.

2 e We're lucky enough to have an incredible team, without whom we would never have survived this difficult year.

3 c After much research, we've come up with a prototype with which we're all very satisfied.

4 a We're conducting research into the Kazakh market, about which we currently know very little.

5 b I'd like to say thanks in particular to my boss, from whom I've learned a huge amount.

6 d Naturally, we are all influenced by the things with which we surround ourselves.

Answers to Exercise 4, Grammar reference

1 Our founder was Mr Johnson, who the company is named after.

2 We're lucky enough to have an incredible team, which we would never have survived this difficult year without.

3 After much research, we've come up with a prototype which we're all very satisfied with.

4 We're conducting research into the Kazakh market, which we currently know very little about.

5 I'd like to say thanks in particular to my boss, who I've learned a huge amount from.

6 Naturally, we are all influenced by the things (which / that) we surround ourselves with.

Web research activity

• Write the following chunks on the board: *the point at which, no reason why, the way in which, the extent to which.*

• Ask students to type the chunks in a search engine and see which full sentences are provided.

• Ask students to note a few interesting sentences to share with the class.

UNDERSTANDING VOCABULARY

Loanwords

Aim

to introduce and practise loanwords from other languages

8 ✎48 Read through the information in the box with the class. Elicit any loanwords students can recall from their previous learning.

• Play the recording. Students listen and notice the pronunciation of the words. Ask students to work in pairs to discuss their meaning. Let students practise saying the words (with an English accent!).

Answers

plus ça change (French) = the more things change, the more they stay the same; a way of saying, in a resigned way, that nothing changes no matter what you do

prima donna (Italian) = literally the first woman, so used to describe the lead female dancer or singer in an opera; often used to describe someone (male or female) who is egotistical and demanding

fait accompli (French) = a situation or choice which has already been made (so you can't change it – you have to accept it)

a faux pas (French) = literally, a false step; an embarrassing mistake

déjà vu (French) = literally, already seen; when you feel you have been somewhere or done something before

zeitgeist (German) = spirit of the age; used to describe something that captures that spirit

en route (French) = on the way (to)

guerrilla (Spanish) = revolutionary fighter; a positive word to describe freedom fighters or revolutionaries

chef (French) = cook; used to suggest a cook with status (i.e. in a good restaurant or hotel); people sometimes say 'compliments to the chef' to be polite when complimenting the person who has cooked, whether they are professional or not

plaza (Spanish) = big square in a town

angst (German) = feeling of worry about how to behave and what will happen

macho (Spanish) = stereotypically masculine; often used negatively in English to describe overly-aggressive or 'showy' behaviour

au fait (French) = knowledgeable about

fiasco (Italian) = a disaster; used to describe a situation that has become chaotic

kitsch (German) = popular but bad taste

trek (Afrikaans*) = long walk or hike through difficult terrain

*Afrikaans is a derivation of Dutch and is spoken in South Africa.

✎48

plus ça change	chef
prima donna	plaza
fait accompli	angst
faux pas	macho
déjà vu	au fait
zeitgeist	fiasco
en route	kitsch
guerrilla	trek

Background language notes for teachers: pronunciation

The best advice for students here is to try to say the words with their best English pronunciation. It is worth noting that English people do attempt a French pronunciation (sometimes) but rarely attempt one with other languages. So, *café* may be /ˈkæfeɪ;/ or /ˈkæfɪ/ depending on the speaker, and the English *en route* /ɒn ˈruːt/ is like the French /ɑ̃ rut/ but without a rolled 'r'. Spanish speakers may be surprised that in English /l/ is pronounced in *guerrilla* and /z/ in *plaza*.

9 Ask students to work in pairs to replace the words in italics with loanwords. Feedback briefly on the answers before asking students to answer the questions. You could reorganise the class into small groups to discuss the questions. In feedback, ask students to share any interesting comments, and feedback on any errors made.

Answers
1 zeitgeist
2 plazas
3 guerrillas
4 fait accompli
5 macho
6 angst
7 a faux pas
8 kitsch
9 deja vu

Optional extra activity Other loanwords used in English include: *aubergine, bungalow, schadenfreude, cul-de-sac, berserk, pyjamas, raccoon, laissez-faire*. Write them on the board. Ask students to make guesses about what the words mean, and which languages they came from, before looking them up.

Web research activity
• Ask students to research words from their L1 that are in use in English, and words from English that are in use in their L1.
• In the next class, ask students to compare their results in groups.
• In feedback, make a list of the ten most common words.

ANY OTHER BUSINESS
Student's Book pages 128–129

Communicative outcomes
In this two-page spread, students will practise language used in business situations, in particular when taking minutes or when taking part in a business meeting.

VOCABULARY Business situations

Aim
to introduce and practise language used in business situations

1 Ask students to work in pairs to brainstorm words associated with each topic. In feedback, elicit ideas and write up any interesting words and phrases students come up with.

Possible answers
Work with students' ideas. Here are some possibilities (but note that these are expanded on largely in Exercise 2):
business taxes: too high / too low, avoid / evade
cutting costs: losing jobs, profit and loss
an industrial dispute: unions, strike, a breakdown of relations
a new product: launch, sales and marketing, innovation
sales: competitive, marketing, losing, increasing
a takeover: losing jobs, hostile, redundancies

2 Ask students in their pairs to match the groups of phrases to the topics in Exercise 1. Encourage students to explain words to each other and check meaning in a dictionary if necessary. Monitor and notice what students say and prompt and help if necessary. Elicit answers in feedback.

Answers
1 a new product
   You *launch a prototype* of a new product to get feedback on it from possible users / reviewers, to see if it works OK, etc.
   If you can identify *a gap in the market*, it might mean there's a space / an opportunity to sell your new product into. You usually first identify the gap, then start designing and making the product.
   You *conduct focus groups* to identify gaps in the market, see how people feel about existing products, get feedback on prototypes.
   You may get *positive feedback* on existing products, prototypes or new products from focus groups or users.
2 an industrial dispute
   There are *ongoing negotiations* between unions and management to try and avert a strike or to come to an agreement on pay increases or hours. A union or workers make *pay demands* when they want more money.

If both sides can *reach an acceptable compromise*, the industrial action will be averted or end if already started.

Both sides probably need to *have a plan B* in case their main plan of action doesn't work.

Unions may *threaten to call a strike* if their demands aren't met

3 a takeover

A small company may be happy to be taken over if they feel the big company *is a good fit* for them.

If the offer is large enough, the board will *recommend it to shareholders*, who may well then decide to sell.

If an offer is rejected, the prospective buyers may *up the offer* (come back with an increased offer).

A hostile bid is when a company tries to buy a company which doesn't want to be bought and which will fight the attempted takeover.

If shareholders *raise their stake* in a company, it means they buy more shares. This may mean they are closer to overall control / ownership and put pressure on other shareholders to sell the whole firm to them.

4 cutting costs

A company will *undertake restructuring* to reorganise the way it is run to make it more efficient and profitable.

A company will *scale back* output / production, advertising or recruitment to cut costs.

A company will *outsource* work to get it done more cheaply somewhere else.

To cut costs a company may *lay people off* (make them redundant).

A company will *negotiate new deals with suppliers* to get better prices and cut costs.

5 sales

Companies hope their staff will *exceed targets* by selling more than they were asked to do.

When a new company or product appears they *start from a low base* – they don't expect to sell many to begin with, and so make it easy to, say, increase by 100% over a number of years.

A company or sales person always hopes to *seal a major deal* and sell a lot of products at a good profit.

Perhaps having sealed a major deal, company sales or profit might *increase fourfold* – sell four times more than previously achieved.

A company's products might *be dropped by a client* because they are no longer popular.

6 business taxes

Big firms may *lobby* the government not to increase business taxes – they may well *win concessions* from the government, who reduce increases they were planning to make.

Businesses will claim that more taxes will hit profits, which will *affect their bottom line*, and make them less profitable and *less competitive*.

If business taxes are increased, this money could be used to *fund* more *government programmes*.

3 Organise the class into groups of four or five. Ask students to discuss the questions. Monitor closely and note interesting and useful language, as well as errors. Use the feedback to point out good examples, correct errors, and to provide examples of how students can express their ideas better.

Teacher development: collocation

A good way of getting students to build their vocabulary is to get them to brainstorm or research (using dictionaries) as many words and phrases that go with one word or set of words as they can.

Lots of words collocate with *sales*, for example. Write the word in the middle of the board and ask students to give you verbs and nouns that go with the word. Here are some possible answers:

Verbs: *lose, increase, reduce*
Nouns: *sales force, sales tax, sales pitch, sales rep, sales figures*

LISTENING

Aim
to listen for general understanding and to practise taking minutes

4 Organise the class into pairs. Ask students to discuss the questions. Monitor and notice what students say and elicit interesting ideas or experiences students have. In feedback, ask different pairs to tell the class what they discussed. Use the opportunity to correct any errors or rephrase what students are trying to say.

Answers
1 *agenda* = a list of things to be discussed at a meeting
2 *the chair* = the person in charge of running the meeting
3 *sales* = the department responsible for selling what's in stock; *marketing* = this department liaises with customers, promotes the product in the market, helps the organisation see how it needs to modify its product offerings, pricing and communication so that it meets the needs of the distribution channel or end customers
4 *minute-taker* = takes minutes, which are the official written records made during the meeting
5 *AOB* = any other business. At the end of a business meeting, there is an opportunity for anyone present to bring up anything important that needs to be discussed or a decision made that wasn't on the agenda.

5 🕭 **49** Give students time to read the situation and the questions.
• Play the recording. Students listen and match the speakers to their roles. Let students compare their answers in pairs before discussing as a class. Encourage students to justify their answers.

Answers
2 f
3 b
4 e
5 a
6 d

🔊 49

Katrin: I've also been approached by the unions, but perhaps that can wait till AOB at the end of the meeting.

Peter: OK, so let's move on to the next item on the agenda.

Henry: OK. Well, I've handed out the spreadsheet of current figures and, as you can see, we're set to make a substantial loss this year.

Rachel: We've exceeded our sales targets in Eastern Europe.

Alex: So, this is a prototype of what we're calling the 'Shoe Saver'.

Marta: We'd be looking for it to retail at between €100 and €120.

6 🔊 50 Read through the information as a class. Focus students on the task and make sure students are ready with pen and paper to take minutes.
• Play the recording. Students listen and take notes.

🔊 50

K = Katrin, P = Peter, H = Henry, R = Rachel, A = Alex, M = Marta

K: I've also been approached by the unions but perhaps that can wait till AOB at the end of the meeting.
P: OK. Thanks Katrin. I've got that noted. We'll come back to that later on, then. OK, so let's move on to the next item on the agenda. We've already touched on the background to this, but perhaps, Henry, if you could just restate the situation?
H: OK. Well, I've handed out the spreadsheet of current figures and, as you can see, we're set to make a substantial loss this year. Obviously, it's been a volatile year for everyone in the industry, but we can't simply blame economic problems. We've also underperformed.
R: Well, not entirely! We've exceeded our sales targets in Eastern Europe.
H: Yes, that offers some hope, Rachel, but that was starting from quite a low base. I know there are high hopes for this new product, but I really feel the way forward is to cut back on costs.
K: Cutting costs? I would've thought we were at the limit, to be honest. People are already overstretched.
H: It doesn't have to mean more work. We could renegotiate deals with suppliers and then scale back operations.

K: You mean layoffs?
H: Well, some redundancies, maybe, but hopefully they'd be voluntary.
K: Really? I ...
P: OK. Katrin, I think we're getting ahead of ourselves here. Henry, why don't you put together some costed proposals for cutbacks to present at the meeting next week? Then we can see what the possible implications might be. Is that OK with everyone? Now, moving on to our next item. Marta, I believe you and Alex have something exciting to show us.
M: We certainly do. And, as Henry suggested, we do have high hopes for it. If we can tap into the right market for this, it may even help to ease some of the financial problems that have just been highlighted. I'll let Alex talk you through things. Alex.
A: Yeah, thanks Marta. So this is a prototype of what we're calling the 'Shoe Saver'. As you can see, it's basically a compact box. This is a basic design, but we're planning others. Essentially, you pop your shoes inside and give it a blast to remove all the smells. I've brought along a pair of my son's trainers to demonstrate.
R: Oh, they smell dreadful!
A: Yeah. They've been left damp in a bag to show you just how effective the box is. So, I put them in ... and switch it on. It takes a minute. Yes, Rachel?
R: How does it work? I mean, what's the science here?
A: Yeah, right. So what it does is it uses tiny particles of silver, which have antibacterial properties once ionised, and they essentially kill the microbes that cause the odours.
R: Right. OK. I'm not sure what 'ionised' means but isn't the silver expensive?
A: Yeah, but we're talking tiny amounts. ... OK ... There. Done. Have a sniff.
R: Wow! That's amazing.
P: Yeah, great.
K: Very impressive.
H: Very. So what margins are we looking at with this?
A: Well, unit costs are between €35 and €45.
M: And we'd be looking for it to retail at between €100 and €120.
R: Which would certainly improve our bottom line.
H: Why such uncertainty about production costs? That's quite a big range you've given.
A: Well, we're looking at a deal to outsource production, which could bring significant savings. The higher figure would be if we used our own factories and that's also very much erring on the side of caution.
H: Sure. And what kind of sales projections do you have? Rachel?
R: We've estimated something in the region of 10,000 units in the first year, followed by 30,000 in year two, 100,000 in year three and a quarter of a million by year four.
K: Gosh.
M: I know that sounds ambitious, but we're all really excited about this product. Henry, you don't look convinced.

H: Yeah, I don't want to be the bad guy, but have you really thought this through? You know, there's already a range of products that can solve this problem. Will people really want to pay €120 euros for this?

M: No, it's a fair question. I think the first point is that this is far more effective than the sprays and insoles currently on the market. We estimate it could extend a shoe's life by up to 50%, so it'd pay for itself. Secondly, our initial market is not actually homes but health clubs and gyms. Longer term, growth would come from high-end consumers and we've already had some positive feedback from focus groups.

P: I think Katrin wants to come in.

M: Sure.

K: Er, yes, erm. What about patents? Is this original technology?

A: I'll take this one, if I may.

M: Sure.

A: Well, the technology's been around for a while, so that's not something we control, but we have patented a couple of the manufacturing processes that we think will give us an edge over any competitors.

M: Plus, of course, we'll have a head start in establishing the brand.

7 Organise the class into groups of four or five to compare their minutes and the questions. As students speak, go round and monitor, and note how accurate their minutes are. You may decide to play the recording again if students have problems.

• In feedback, elicit three key things they should include in their minutes about the financial loss, and three key things to include about the new product.

Possible answers

There are no fixed answers to this, nor is there an expected way of students taking minutes. However, here is a short possible set of minutes:

Item 1
Henry stated that the company is set to make a substantial loss this year.
Reasons: volatile year for everyone in the industry; also the company underperformed
Rachel pointed out that sales in Eastern Europe exceeded targets.
Henry feels the way forward is to cut back on costs by renegotiating deals with suppliers and scaling back operations, with only voluntary redundancies.
Peter asked Henry to put together some costed proposals for cutbacks to present at the meeting next week.

Item 2
Alex presented a prototype of the Shoe Saver – a compact box that removes all shoe smells. It uses tiny particles of silver to kill the microbes that cause odours.
Alex stated that unit costs are between €35 and €45.
Marta looks to retail at between €100 and €120.

Alex hopes to outsource production to bring significant savings.
Rachel estimated sales in the region of 10,000 units in the first year, followed by 30,000 in year two, 100,000 in year three and a quarter of a million by year four.
Henry questioned whether people want to pay €120 euros for the Shoe Saver.
Marta argued that the Shoe Saver is far more effective than sprays and insoles currently on the market. It could extend a shoe's life by up to 50%, so it'd pay for itself.
Marta pointed out that the initial market is not actually homes but health clubs and gyms. Longer term, growth would come from high-end consumers and already had some positive feedback from focus groups.
Alex said that they had patented a couple of the manufacturing processes involved to give the company an edge over any competitors.

8 Ask students to discuss and improve the sentences in their groups. Monitor closely.

9 Ask students to look at audio script 50 on page 212 and check their answers. In feedback, elicit answers and use the board to show correct answers if necessary.

Answers
1 Not quite accurate – he does say it's been a volatile year for everyone in the industry *but* that they can't blame that and have to accept they've underperformed
2 Not accurate – she points out they've exceeded sales targets, so have done very well there
3 Accurate – she says, 'I would've thought we were at the limit, to be honest. People are already overstretched.'
4 Not accurate – he said there would be some but that hopefully they'd be voluntary, not compulsory
5 Accurate – amazing / very impressive and general sounds of agreement
6 Not accurate – Marta expects them to retail at between €100 and €120 – not €130
7 Accurate – 'we're looking at a deal to outsource production, which could bring significant savings.'
8 Accurate – 'a quarter of a million by year four'
9 Accurate – '... have you really thought this through? You know, there's already a range of products that can solve this problem. Will people really want to pay €120 for this?'
10 Not quite accurate – she did estimate shoes will last 50% longer but main market isn't rich homes, but health clubs and gyms – and it's not initial sales that were very good, but feedback from focus groups – only a prototype
11 Accurate – 'What about patents? Is this original technology?'
12 Accurate – '... that's not something we control, but we have patented a couple of the manufacturing processes that we think will give us an edge over any competitors.'
Marta says, 'we'll have a head start in establishing the brand.'

Optional extra activity Show the following sentences on the board and ask students to write them in their language:

That's also very much erring on the side of caution.
Well, you have to look on the bright side, don't you?
Fortunately, my boss saw the funny side of the situation.
On the plus side, sales in Eastern Europe were up.
Their stuff is a bit on the expensive side.

Remove the English sentences from the board, and ask students to translate their sentences back into English. Then show the originals again for them to compare.

SPEAKING

Aim

to practise language from the lesson in a free, communicative, personalised speaking activity

10 Organise the class into groups of four (or five if you have an odd number – have two heads of marketing in any group with five in it). Ask each group to decide on their roles. Tell them to find their information pages (pages 189, 191 and 192), then give them time to read their files, and to think of what to say. Monitor and help with ideas and vocabulary.

11 When students are ready, ask them to sit in a circle or around a table in order to mimic a business meeting. Tell the chair to start the meeting, and to decide when to move on to each item of the agenda. Set a time limit which will depend on how much time you want to devote to this class (anything between ten and twenty minutes). As they discuss the items on the agenda, monitor and note down any interesting pieces of language you hear.
• In feedback, look at good language that students used, and language students didn't quite use correctly during the activity. Show students better ways of saying what they were trying to say. You could write some useful new phrases on the board with gaps and ask the whole class to complete the sentences.

VIDEO 7: COUNTERFEIT STRATEGY
Student's Book page 130

Aim

to consider how we can combat counterfeiters; to improve students' ability to follow and understand fast speech in a video extract; to practise fast speech and to improve pronunciation, stress and intonation

1 Lead in to the topic by asking students to look at the photo and say what they can see. Make sure you check *counterfeit goods* (see Culture notes below). Organise the class into small groups to discuss the questions. In feedback, elicit students' ideas and write up interesting ideas or pieces of language on the board. Encourage students to justify their opinions.

> **Possible answers**
> People buy counterfeit goods because they are cheap, because they want to have designer brands but can't afford them, and sometimes to protest against big businesses that charge a lot for their products. Banknotes have a serial number, a watermark, a line through them, a complex design and colouring, and use a very particular type of paper.

Culture notes

counterfeit goods = products that have been produced illegally, including pirate DVDs and CDs (which have been copied without permission) and fake designer products such as sunglasses, watches or T-shirts which have been manufactured without permission from the company that owns the rights; other common counterfeit goods are cigarettes and sports-related clothing

2 [▶ 33] Give students time to read through the task. Students watch and note their answers. Let them compare in pairs before discussing as a class.

> **Answers**
> 1 The notes are printed on special paper – a cotton and linen combination. Red and blue security fibres are woven into the paper.
> A fluorescent thread printed with microscopic text is also woven in.
> They use optical variable ink, which changes colour in different lights.
> 2 They bleach lower denomination notes and reprint them with higher values. They use drugstore glitter to mimic the way optical variable ink changes colour in different lights.

3 Organise the class into pairs to discuss how the words are connected to the topic. Give students time to read through and look up / ask about any words they're not sure of before they start discussing them.
• In feedback, elicit ideas from the whole class. Ask students to explain why they think what they think. There are no fixed answers to how students predict these words will be used so accept all ideas within the realms of the possible.

Background language notes for teachers

You may need to briefly gloss the following vocabulary:
If you buy *in bulk*, you buy in large quantities to save money.
victim = the person the bad thing (usually a crime) happens to
If you *offload* something, you get rid of something you don't want by giving or selling it to someone else.
If you get something *at a discount*, you get a special price; you get it cheaper than usual.
If you *avoid detection*, you manage not to be noticed.
in a matter of seconds = in a surprisingly short time; in only a few seconds
genuine bills = real official notes, not counterfeit ones
solution = here, *solution* means 'a liquid with another substance dissolved in it'
revamp = to improve the way that something operates or looks by making major changes to it
large volumes = large amounts

4 ▭ 33 Give students time to read through the task. Students watch and note their answers. Let them compare in pairs before discussing as a class.

> **Possible answers**
> Expect something like this, if not these exact words. You could listen to their answers and if necessary say the words yourself.
> The counterfeiter approaches a *victim* saying he needs to *offload* a large sum of what he claims is genuine currency – *at a discount*.
> The counterfeiter claims the money has been dyed black to *avoid detection* by the police.
> The *victim* is shown how the bills can be cleaned *in a matter of seconds* and they'll use *a genuine bill* that has been dyed black for this trick.
> The *victim* is often given *a special solution* when they pay for the (counterfeit) currency to clean the notes but often it's little more than water and vitamins.
> US currency is given a *revamp* every seven to ten years to stop counterfeiters.
> *Large volumes* of counterfeit currency have been coming out of Colombia. It's usually very high quality.

5 This exercise offers students the chance to relate the topic of the video to their own experiences, ideas and opinions.
• Give students time to choose and prepare a topic. Organise the students into groups and give them seven or eight minutes to discuss them. Monitor and help with ideas and vocabulary.
• When most students have finished, stop the class and give some feedback, either by rephrasing some of the things students tried to say for the whole class or by asking students to correct or fill in gaps in sentences you've written on the board, based on what you heard students saying.

Understanding fast speech

6 ▭ 34 Play the recording. Students listen and write. Let them compare with a partner. Tell them not to worry if they haven't caught all the words yet.

7 ▭ 35 Play the recording again. Students listen and write. Let them compare with a partner. This time, if students have problems, you could play a second time.

8 Students check what they have written by looking at File 10 on page 189. Tell students to work on their own for a few minutes to practise saying the extract. They could then practise saying it to a partner.

> **Video script** ▭ 33
> **Narrator:** The security features of US currency are constantly re-designed. At Secret Service headquarters in Washington DC, agents see a never-ending array of clever techniques that counterfeiters use to keep up. One of the most difficult features for a counterfeiter to copy is also the most basic – the paper it's printed on.
> **Kelley Harris:** Genuine US currency is a cotton and linen combination that actually has a very distinct feel, and there are red and blue security fibres that are mixed in with the currency paper as it's being made.
> **Narrator:** Woven into the paper is another tough detail to reproduce: a fluorescent thread printed with microscopic text.
> **Kelley Harris:** On a genuine bill, security thread should fluoresce a particular colour. Typically on the counterfeits, their security threads do not fluoresce at all.
> **Narrator:** To avoid having to reproduce real currency paper, some counterfeiters use a simple but clever technique. They bleach lower denomination notes and reprint them at higher values. With a little bleach and some ink, a five-dollar note can suddenly become a hundred.
> Even if a counterfeiter gets the paper right and has a detailed printing plate, a final challenge is hidden in the ink itself. The US Treasury uses a proprietary pigment called 'optical variable ink', which changes colour in different light. Counterfeiters often mimic this effect using the most basic materials, like drugstore glitter.
> Good counterfeit notes can be passed one at a time – they only need to be good enough to fool the victim. But even bad notes are sometimes passed in bulk through a distribution scheme known as 'the black money scam'. The counterfeiter approaches a victim saying he needs to offload a large sum of what he claims is genuine currency – at a discount as low as twenty cents on the dollar. He says the money has been dyed black to avoid detection by police.
> **Special Agent "x":** The victim is shown as an example how the bills can be completely cleaned in a matter of seconds and that'll be done with a genuine bill that was dyed black, cleaned in front of them and given to them as an example.

Victim's free to go spend it, they'll feel comfortable, they'll gather as much money as they can afford to come back and buy what they think is more genuine currency dyed in black.

Narrator: When the victim pays for the currency, they're given a special solution to clean the notes – often a simple combination of water and vitamins – only to discover the cash is all counterfeit. It's the price to pay for doing business in the criminal world. US currency is revamped every seven to ten years and the Bureau of Engraving and Printing consults with the Secret Service to make sure the new notes are as difficult as possible to counterfeit. With each new design many of the first and best counterfeits come from Colombia.

Kelley Harris: Counterfeits coming out of Colombia have ... we have seen those for, for a long time. The Colombian counterfeiters are counterfeiting in very large volumes using more sophisticated printing presses and that alone gives it a much better quality than often what we see on digital counterfeits that come off of inkjet printers. They are definitely above average quality counterfeiters.

Aim
to consolidate vocabulary and grammar from Units 13 and 14

Answers
Exercise 1
1 during
2 when
3 *fait*
4 whom
5 told / urged / advised / warned
6 *accompli*
7 where
8 threaten
9 admit
10 lining

Exercise 2
1 forgive him for forgetting
2 The grass is always greener
3 don't count your chickens
4 the point where
5 blame myself for not noticing
6 by which means they had

Exercise 3
1 of
2 most of which
3 *en*
4 applying
5 on going
6 for whom

Exercise 4
1 f
2 a
3 g
4 i
5 j
6 e
7 d
8 c
9 h
10 b

Exercise 5
1 from
2 with
3 of
4 in
5 over
6 in, on

Exercise 6
1 fourfold
2 diversify
3 shareholders
4 concessions
5 projections
6 relocate

Exercise 7
1 upturn
2 take on
3 weather
4 scale back
5 laying, off
6 pick up
7 hanging in
8 gone under
9 solid
10 cash flow
11 consolidate
12 pitching

15 TRENDS

SPEAKING

Aim
to set the scene and introduce the theme with a photo; to get students talking about fashion, music and social trends

1 Start by telling the class that in this unit they're going to be discussing trends, describing clothes and hairstyles, giving opinions on style, discussing the fashion industry, and defining themselves in different ways; they will learn how to repair misunderstandings and use some snowclones.
• Ask students to look at the photo on pages 132–133. Ask: *What can you see?* Elicit a brief description of the photo, and introduce any key words students might need.
• Organise the class into pairs to discuss the questions. Go round the room and check students are doing the task and help with ideas and vocabulary if necessary.

> **Possible answers**
> The photo looks like it comes from an advertisement or magazine supplement of the 1950s or 1960s. However, as it is poking fun at the times, it could be a more modern photograph, designed to make a statement about women's roles at that time. From the fashions, styles and the appearance of the models, it could be European or American.
> The photo shows mod cons of the 1960s, and 'modern living' with functional furniture, and modern appliances.
> It may be trying to sell the vacuum cleaner – with this vacuum cleaner, it's easy to clean the house. It may be making a statement about how women have to be 'superwomen' – looking great, and doing all the household chores. Or it may be amusingly mocking the conventions of the period – women were expected to do everything about the house while the rest of the family took her role for granted. The photo, probably in jest, reflects an era when men went to work and women were housewives, when families were nuclear (mum, dad and children), and when families were aspirational in a growing, thriving, optimistic capitalist society – everybody wanted all the new modern conveniences.

2 Organise the class into groups of four or five to work together to think of ideas. In feedback, ask different groups to briefly tell the class what they discussed.
• Once you have fed back on content, look at good pieces of language that students used, and pieces of language students didn't quite use correctly.

> **Answers**
> 1920s: women's fashion entered the modern era, they started wearing short skirts or trousers, loose dresses with no waistline / beads or long necklaces; men's fashion became less formal, shorter jackets, wider trousers (Oxford bags) and sweaters; known as 'The Jazz Age' – jazz music became widely popular, the Charleston was a very popular dance; post-war boom, trade union movement and Labour party – socialist politics (post-revolution in Russia) on the rise, plus increasing rights for women
> 1940s: plain clothes, 'sensible' shoes because of the war and rationing; in the early 40s the most popular music style was swing, later crooning singers like Frank Sinatra as well as big bands were popular; during the war more women were working because men were fighting – see Unit 12; in UK the Labour government in 1945 led to the NHS and Welfare State
> 1960s: skinny sharp suits and short hair (early 60s), long hair and hippy look (late 60s), women's fashion = mini skirts, high boots, bell-bottom jeans; more acceptable for women to wear trousers; rise of pop music – Beatles, Rolling Stones; Women's liberation movement, free love, some breaking down of traditional families
> 1980s: power dressing – shoulder pads and big hair, New Romantic fashion, lots of accessories, men wearing make-up; electronic music, hard rock, hip-hop, New Romantics and pop; conservative politics, privatisation, increasing role of business, undermining of unions, beginning of globalisation
> 1990s: the grunge look, the 'Rachel' haircut (from the character in *Friends*), increase in tattoos and piercings, longer hair for men; teen pop and dance-pop were popular = Spice Girls, Backstreet Boys, alternative rock = Nirvana, grunge = Foo Fighters, rock = Oasis and Blur; Tamagotchi (the electronic pet from Japan), home computers and mobile phones become popular, the fall of Communism, release of Nelson Mandela
> 2000s: mix of many previous fashions – revivals of 1950s, 1960s and 1980s, loose hanging jeans, baseball caps, general informality, hair = bobs and beehives for women, spiky hair for men; hip-hop, teen pop, rock music; wars, anti-war movements, fear of terrorism, growth of the Internet and social media like Facebook and Twitter, increased globalisation, global financial crisis

Optional extra activity Ask students to say how they would expect a photo from a magazine supplement today to differ from the photo on the spread.

IN STYLE
Student's Book pages 134–135

Communicative outcomes
In this two-page spread, students will talk about clothes, style and fashion; they will practise ways of backtracking and correcting in conversations.

VOCABULARY Style and fashion

Aim
to introduce and practise words and phrases used to talk about style and fashion

1 Lead in briefly by asking students to look at the photos. Ask: *What words do you know to describe the fashions and hairstyles? What adjectives would you use to describe them?* Take brief feedback from the class and write any interesting words or phrases on the board. Only choose words or phrases you think students will find most useful to copy and learn on the board. You could leave them on the board so students can re-use them when doing speaking activities later in the lesson.
• Ask students to discuss the questions in pairs. Elicit ideas from the class.

2 Organise the class into pairs to match words to descriptions. In feedback, elicit answers and ask pairs to justify their choice of odd one out.

Answers
1 c seam = sewn joint of the clothes
2 i skinny = describes a very thin person or sometimes jeans, dress or top
3 f zipped = has a zip instead of buttons
4 e spotted = a pattern with spots; you can have a spot (of oil or food) on your shirt
5 g laces = string to tie your shoes
6 d a strap = part of a bag, watch, dress, etc. that you hold or keeps it fixed in place
7 a a wig = false hair used when someone is bald or dressing up – it replaces or covers hair and could be of various styles
8 h flares = usually jeans with wide bottoms
9 b sturdy = usually shoes – big, strong, difficult to break and usually comfortable for walking in

Background language notes for teachers

tartan and *paisley* = patterns; tartan = Scottish; paisley = of Persian or Indian origins but name comes from town in Scotland (Paisley) where paisley designs were produced
lapel = the part on each side of a coat or jacket immediately below the collar that is folded back on either side of the front
bangle = a loose-fitting metal bracelet
a bob = a short haircut for women in which the hair is cut straight around the head at about jaw-level, often with a fringe at the front
a ponytail = long hair tied at the back

3 Ask students in pairs to say which of the words from Exercise 2 they can see in the photos on pages 134 and 135. In feedback, elicit answers. You will need to decide how much detail you want here. You could ask students to find four words per photo.

Possible answers
from left to right
Photo 1: wool (jacket / cardigan), zip, trendy, sleeve, laces
Photo 2: polyester (catsuit), trendy, collar, a bangle, bushy, a wig, wedges, summery, loud, knee-length
Photo 3: silk (dress), smart, formal, flowery; collar, sleeve, loud
Photo 4: denim, smart, formal, collar, pocket, lapel, sleeve, a belt
Photo 5: denim, silk, scruffy, trendy, stained, frayed, split, ripped, sleeve, loud, revealing
Photo 6: silk, flowery, sleeve, summery

4 Ask students in pairs to discuss the questions. Monitor and prompt, and see how well students know and use the new vocabulary. Use the feedback to check or revise words students weren't sure of.

Optional extra activity Bring in random photos from a fashion magazine. Ask students in pairs or small groups to choose a photo and prepare a description of the fashion, styles and haircuts in the photo. Collect the photos and pin them on the board. Ask each pair or group to describe their photo. The rest of the class say which one it is.

LISTENING

Aim
to practise listening for gist and discovering the meaning of expressions in a text

5 🔊 51 Let students read through the task and the sentences first.
• Play the recording. Students listen and match each conversation to one of the sentences. Let students compare their answers in pairs before discussing as a class. In feedback, ask students to justify their answers by telling you what they heard on the recording.

Answers
Conversation 1
d (*you were a bit of a rock god* = past tense, *did you spray those on, even in those days*)
Conversation 2
a (*dress split down the seam, it ended up being a bit more revealing than I wanted it to be!*)
Conversation 3
e (*smarten up a bit, clients ... expect something a bit more conventional*)
Conversation 4
g (*look at her outfit, not a trend I like.* The general way of talking is not what you would say directly to a person – her legs look as if they'd snap in two.)

Conversation 5

c (*not interested in my dress sense, I'll be in a lab all day if I get it, don't want you tripping over when you walk in the room*)

Conversation 6

b (*I just fancied a change, you can have it in a ponytail … I was a bit sick of it*)

🎧 51

Conversation 1

A: Oh my word, you were a bit of a rock god.

B: That's kind.

A: I had no idea. Look at those skinny jeans! <u>Good grief</u>! Did you spray those on?

B: Yeah, it was a bit of a struggle getting them on even in those days.

A: And all that bushy hair!

B: Hmm …

A: Where did it all go wrong?

B: Well, I like to think I've made up for the loss in other areas.

Conversation 2

C: So, how was it?

D: Well, I thought it was going to be a very formal do so I even borrowed an outfit from a friend and these ridiculous high-heels. And then when I got there I'd obviously got my wires crossed somewhere because no-one else seemed to be that dressed up and I <u>stuck out like a sore thumb</u>.

C: Oh well. Still, I'm sure you looked gorgeous.

D: Yeah well, not after my dress split down the seam when I was dancing.

C: Oh no!

D: Yeah, it ended up being a bit more revealing than I wanted it to be!

Conversation 3

E: Jason, could I have a word?

F: Sure.

E: Do you mind taking the shades off?

F: Oh right, yeah, sure. Have I done something wrong?

E: No, no, not at all – we <u>see you as a great asset</u>. In fact, we'd like you to take on a bit more responsibility.

F: Cool.

E: It's just that … well … you might want to smarten up a bit.

F: Do you think I look scruffy?

E: No, that's not what I meant to say. I know the ripped jeans and paisley shirts are your thing, but what I'm trying to say is if you're interacting with clients a bit more … well, they expect something a bit more conventional.

F: Right, OK. No, that's fine. Sure.

E: Good. You might want to <u>go a bit more easy on</u> the gel too.

Conversation 4

G: Oh, my gosh, Fi! Look at her outfit.

H: You don't like it?

G: A flowery dress with a checked shirt? And the ribbon in her hair? And then those army boots!

H: Hey, it wouldn't work for me, but I think <u>she pulls it off</u>. It's quite a funky look. I might lose the ribbon, but those kind of clashing patterns <u>are really in</u> at the moment.

G: Well, it's not a trend I like. And the boots?

H: Well, they kind of show off her legs in a funny way.

G: I think they make them look like sticks. They look as if they'd snap them in two. She'd be better off in some heels or wedges.

Conversation 5

I: Are you going in that?

J: You don't think it's suitable?

I: No, it's not that. But you've got a stain on the lapel.

J: What, that? You can hardly see it.

I: Let me see if I can rub it off.

J: <u>Don't fuss</u>. It'll be fine. Anyway, they're not interested in my dress sense. I'll be in a lab all day if I get it.

I: Well, at least tie up your laces properly – don't want you tripping over when you walk in the room!

Conversation 6

K: Gosh! That's a bit radical, isn't it?

L: You don't like it?

K: No, no, you look fantastic. It just took me aback when I first saw you. So what brought this on?

L: Oh, I just fancied a change and I've taken up running again and, well, I mean, you can have it in a ponytail or tie it up but … I don't know … I was a bit sick of it.

K: No, I know what you mean. <u>I wish I could get away with having it</u> like that – it'd be so much easier.

L: You don't think you could?

K: No – my face is too round. I'd look like a lollipop!

L: That's a bit of an exaggeration! You could have it in a bob. That'd work.

K: Hmm, I'm not convinced.

6 Organise the class into pairs. Ask students to find the underlined words in audio script 51 on page 212 and discuss the expressions. In feedback, elicit answers from students and check any words students are unsure of.

Answers

Good grief = an expression of surprise

stuck out like a sore thumb = look obviously and uncomfortably different to the others

see you as a great asset = we think you are good for the company

go a bit more easy on = use less

she pulls it off = she makes it work / is successful

are really in = are very fashionable

Don't fuss = don't worry and interfere

I wish I could get away with having it (like that) = I wish I could make it work without looking stupid

7 Organise the class into small groups to discuss the questions. Monitor closely and note interesting and useful language, as well as errors. Use the feedback to point out good examples, correct errors, and to provide examples of how students can express their ideas better.

Optional extra activity Organise the class into groups of four. Tell them that they are all going clubbing on Saturday night. Tell each group to decide together what each member of the group should wear to the night out.

DEVELOPING CONVERSATIONS
Backtracking and correcting

Aim
to introduce and practise ways of backtracking and correcting

8 Read through the information in the box as a class. Ask students to complete the sentences individually and then compare their answers in pairs. Go round the room and check students are doing the task and help with ideas and vocabulary if necessary.
• In feedback, elicit and check answers.

> **Possible answers**
> Answers will vary, but here are some examples:
> 1 it's not the kind of thing I'd wear.
> 2 I really like the way it is now.
> 3 that I think the event is going to be quite formal so you might want to wear something else.
> 4 that we don't always agree on certain things.
> 5 it would be a shame to lose his talents here.
> 6 it's a great course, if you want to become a teacher, but you have to be absolutely sure that's what you want to be.

9 Ask students in their pairs to practise their conversations in Exercise 8. Practice makes perfect, so encourage the students to repeat dialogues and to spend lots of time getting their dialogues right.
• In feedback, correct any errors of form and pronunciation.

10 Organise the class into new pairs. Give students three or four minutes to prepare their phrases to express misunderstandings. You could elicit one or two examples to get them started. When students are ready, they take turns to read out a misunderstanding to a partner. The partner must backtrack and correct, improvising phrases from the lesson. You could model this with a strong student.

Optional extra activity Turn Exercise 10 into a mingle. Students walk round the class expressing misunderstandings to different classmates. The classmates backtrack and correct.

CONVERSATION PRACTICE

Aim
to practise language from the lesson in a free, communicative, personalised speaking activity

11 Organise the class into pairs and ask students to decide on a task. If they choose task b, they should also choose which roles to take. Tell them to find their information page (page 196). Give students four or five

minutes to prepare, and to think of what to say. When students are ready, ask them to do the task. Listen for errors, new language or interesting opinions to use in feedback. Ask students to change partners two or three times if you want.
• In feedback, look at good language that students used, and language students didn't quite use correctly during the activity. Show students better ways of saying what they were trying to say. You could write some useful new phrases on the board with gaps and ask the whole class to complete the sentences.

 36 Refer students to the video and activities on the DVD-ROM.

Teacher development: using the video

The video and activities on the DVD-ROM can be used in various ways:
1 as an alternative to the conversation practice
2 instead of the listening activity in some units, particularly with weaker groups. Students can first practise reading out the dialogues and work on some of the key phrases / structures in a controlled way before having a go themselves.
3 at the end of the unit as a revision exercise

Communicative outcomes

In this two-page spread, students talk about why trends rise, peak and fall; they recognise and use snowclones; they look at how prepositions work with nouns, verbs and adjectives.

SPEAKING

Aim

to introduce the topic of the reading text; to get students talking about trends

1   Start by asking students to look at the photo. Ask: *What can you see in the photo? How would you describe the man's appearance?* Elicit students' ideas and write any interesting descriptive words or phrases on the board.
• Organise the class into pairs. Ask students to discuss the questions. Monitor the students and note errors and good uses of language. At the end, elicit ideas, opinions and experiences. Then feed back on errors with the class.

> **Possible answers**
> The man has short hair at the side, long on top with a flick, tattoos and a long beard (all very popular trends among young men in 2015).
> Trends may begin because: a celebrity wears a certain style, a film or TV show popularises something, something trends on Twitter or another social network, a major sporting occasion such as the World Cup starts trends, sometimes they start as a joke or a serious world event may affect how people feel about life and the world and cause a trend. Explanations for the rise, peak and fall are provided in the text.

READING

Aim

to read for general and specific understanding

2   Give students a minute to read through the four pieces of information they must find out from the text. Ask them to predict what the article might be about from the information and the photo and elicit ideas.
• Ask students to read the article and discuss answers with a partner. In feedback, elicit answers from different pairs.

> **Answers**
> 1 Roots in 2008 global financial crisis – men (having lost power of wealth / control) chose to emphasise their masculinity with extra hair. Then spread through celebrity endorsement.
> 2 Fish who happen to be born with different colouring are able to avoid predators, and their unusual looks can make them more attractive. Bearded men can also appear more attractive because they look different.

> 3 People follow the trend that beards are attractive and in doing so it becomes common / not rare, so the non-bearded man becomes more attractive because they are in the minority.
> 4 They follow a similar pattern in building up slowly, but then reaching a tipping point where they explode.

3   Let students read through the sentences first, and decide whether they are true or false based on their first reading. Then ask them to try to find answers they aren't sure about in the text. Let students compare their answers with a partner.
• Elicit answers from the class in feedback. Ask students to explain and justify their answers.

> **Answers**
> 1 F (*little could he have known … his choice of phrase was set to become a trend …*)
> 2 F (*'peak plastic surgery'* is mentioned by social commentators, not the writer)
> 3 T (Brooks claims there's a deeper underlying cause: *evolution.* This infers that if something has happened as part of evolution then it's not new.)
> 4 F (*in a bid to explain this, he speculates* – it can be interpreted that the paper hasn't proved anything, it's a hypothesis)
> 5 T (*This will make it less likely to fall prey to predators … This, in turn, makes it a more attractive partner.*)
> 6 T (*As the fashion spread, however, it lost its edge and female preferences started shifted again.*)
> 7 T
> 8 F (*… I'm not alone in wanting to see the back of grumpy cats …*)

Culture notes

The semi-fixed phrases explored in this section have a variety of cultural sources. For example, *Keep calm and …* started life as a slogan on a WWII poster (it was originally *Keep calm and carry on*) but has recently been revived as an amusing 'typically English' expression which can be found on T-shirts and mugs in souvenir shops across the UK.

4   Ask students to work individually to find the nouns or noun phrases that go with verbs in the article. Do the first as an example in open class to get students started. Let students compare answers in pairs before discussing as a class.
• In feedback, explore the meaning of the phrases, and ask how common the collocation between verb and noun is, in the opinion of the students.

> **Answers**
> **pinpoint** *a very specific tipping point in our culture*
> *the question 'Have we reached peak X?' started to* **trend**
> **emphasise** *another aspect of masculinity*
> *celebrities* **pick up** *the fashion*
> *women* **rate** *bearded men as more attractive*

the paper **speculates**
enjoy an advantage
the fashion **loses** its edge
trendsetters **champion** ideas / concepts / products
postcards **urge** people

5 Organise the class into groups of four or five to discuss the questions. In feedback, ask different groups to briefly tell the class what they discussed.
• Once you have fed back on content, look at good language that students used, and language students didn't quite use correctly. Show students better ways of saying what they were trying to say. You could write some useful new phrases on the board with gaps and ask the whole class to complete the sentences.

Optional extra activity Write 'In' and 'Not In' on the board. Then write up or just read out a list of things that may or may not be in right now. Ask the class to discuss and decide whether the things you list are in or not, and why. A possible list (but make your own): *short hair for women, long hair for men and boys, long skirts, tight jeans, beanies, baseball caps, neck chains for boys, the colour blue, hip hop, board games, Twitter.*

UNDERSTANDING VOCABULARY
Snowclones

Aim
to introduce and practise snowclones

6 Read through the information in the box as a class.
• Ask students to work in groups of three or four to discuss the meaning of the phrases and then adapt them. Have an extended feedback session, discussing and deciding on which adaptations really work.

Possible answers
1 It was the mother of all burgers. = It was the biggest and best / worst.
   It's the mother of all cocktails.
   It was the mother of all headaches.
2 If you look up the word 'cute' in the dictionary, you'll find a picture of my son! = to describe someone or something as being the very essence of the word
   Look up the word 'idiot' in a dictionary and you'll find a picture of Joe!
3 It's politics, but not as we know it. = used to comment on what's seen as a new innovation
   It's a phone, but not as we know it.
4 It's a fine line between love and hate. = to say something can easily change from one thing to another even if apparently opposite
   It's a fine line between pleasure and pain.
   It's a fine line between clever and stupid.
5 Life's too short for boring shoes. = to say something is a waste of time or should be avoided
   Life's too short to get into arguments.
   Life's too short to sit through another 'Mission Impossible' film.

6 Orange is the new black. = it means 'the latest trend / thing, etc. that shares traits with an older trend / thing'
   Gardening is the new rock and roll.
   Staying in is the new going out.
7 The neighbours from hell! = to say that they are the worst example of a thing you could imagine
   It was the holiday from hell.
   He's the boss from hell.
8 Trouble is my middle name. = to say you have a very strong trait or characteristic
   Charm is her middle name.
   Fun is his middle name.
9 What is this Internet of which you speak? = to pretend that you don't know something everyone knows – especially when it is given as part of a suggestion
   What is this microwave oven of which you speak?
   Who is this Obama of which you speak?
10 You can take the boy out of the city, but you can't take the city out of the boy. = to explain that someone retains a characteristic of a particular place
   You can take the boy out of Texas, but you can't take Texas out of the boy.
   You can take the girl out of Spain, but you can't take Spain out of the girl.

Culture notes

A 1980s song called *Star Trekkin'* featured the line: *It's life, Jim, but not as we know it* (spoken by Mr Spock). The song was inspired by the science fiction TV series *Star Trek*. *It's a fine line between stupid and clever* was first used in the 1980s spoof rock documentary *Spinal Tap*.
It has been claimed that Iraqi president Saddam Hussein's 1991 speech promising 'the mother of all wars' gave rise to the snowclone 'the mother of all ...'.

Teacher development: snowclones and memes

In 2004, (when the term was introduced), linguist Geoffrey Pullum described *snowclones* as 'instantly recognizable, time-worn, quoted or misquoted phrases or sentences that can be used in ... different variants'. Often they start out as quotes or misquotes from movies, TV shows or songs.
The word *meme* originated with Richard Dawkins' 1976 book *The Selfish Gene*. It can be defined as an idea, behaviour, or style that spreads from person to person within a culture. Like genes, a cultural idea or trend can be passed on through, and can influence, generations. The study of memetics investigates this cultural phenomenon.

Optional extra activity Try out the search engine activity suggested in the information box if your class have access to the Internet. Ask different pairs to choose and research a snowclone and report findings to the class.

GRAMMAR Prepositions

Aim

to check students' understanding of how we use prepositions with adjectives, nouns, short phrases, and when a verb follows a preposition

7 Read through the information in the box as a class.
• Organise students into pairs to match the words and phrases in the article to the patterns. Do the first as an example in open class. Monitor and notice how well students understand the rules.
• In feedback, elicit the students' answers. They can check their answers using the Grammar reference on pages 182 and 183.

> **Answers**
> 1 opt for
> 2 alone in
> 3 choice of
> 4 in turn
> 5 with some young men responding

 Students complete Exercise 1 in the Grammar reference on page 183.

> **Answers to Exercise 1, Grammar reference**
> 1 the game on purpose to
> 2 to his arrival
> 3 reducing costs we have enabled
> 4 in the long term
> 5 accounts for almost / nearly / just under
> 6 were selected / chosen at random
> 7 There was stiff resistance to
> 8 succeeded in bringing
> 9 on a daily basis
> 10 with regard to the overall design

Background language notes for teachers: prepositions

For the most part, using dependent prepositions correctly is down to simply memorising which preposition goes with which adjective or noun. If your students have a language that can easily be compared to English, you could explore whether L1 is the same or different. This will shed light on which phrases need to be learnt and memorised.
You might wish to compare examples of the preposition + *ing* form with full phrases with the same meaning. For example:
On finishing college, she ...
When / After / Once she had finished college, she ...

8 Ask students to work individually to choose the correct options and then compare their answers in pairs. Do the first as an example in open class to get them started.
• In feedback, elicit answers from the class.

> **Answers**
> 1 Are there any contemporary fashions you really object ~~with~~ / to / ~~for~~? Why?
> 2 Had you heard about / ~~from~~ / of hipsters before this lesson?
> 3 Do you know anyone who'd benefit ~~of~~ / from / ~~by~~ a style makeover?
> 4 Can you think of anything that you're pretty much alone ~~for~~ / in / ~~on~~ liking?
> 5 Have you ever bought any clothes or accessories you were very disappointed with / ~~by~~ / ~~in~~?
> 6 Do you have a preference ~~to~~ / for / ~~of~~ any particular brands? If so, why?
> 7 Do you think things are better or worse where you live, compared to / ~~from~~ / with five years ago?
> 8 Do you know anyone who shows real dedication ~~for~~ / to / in keeping up with trends?

Background language notes for teachers

hear about = be informed of, gain knowledge of (*Did you hear about Simon? He got the job.*)
hear of = become aware of someone or something's existence (*I'd never heard of Taylor Swift before my granddaughter started talking about her.*)

9 Organise the class into groups. Ask students to discuss the questions. Monitor closely and note interesting and useful language, as well as errors.
• Once you have fed back on content, look at good language that students used, and language students didn't quite use correctly. Show students better ways of saying what they were trying to say. You could write some useful new phrases on the board with gaps and ask the whole class to complete the sentences.

Optional extra activity Ask fast finishers to write other interesting discussion questions using prepositions that are dependent on a noun, verb or adjective. Tell them to discuss their own questions in their groups.

 For further practice, see Exercises 2 and 3 in the Grammar reference on page 183.

> **Answers to Exercise 2, Grammar reference**
> 1 A number of factors have contributed **to** the trend towards small families.
> 2 The news that girls are **at** more risk of online negative experiences comes as no surprise.
> 3 We'd simply never thought it'd be necessary to take out insurance **against / for** natural disasters.
> 4 Reactions **to** the new trend have been very mixed so far, it must be said.
> 5 The magazine prides itself **on** being cutting edge.
> 6 She just seems to be famous **for** being famous.
> 7 The arrival of the miniskirt in the early 1960s symbolised a rejection **of** conservative values.
> 8 **On** gaining power, Napoleon introduced new dress codes in court.

Answers to Exercise 3, Grammar reference
1 CORRECT
2 Hats were essential clothing ~~during~~ **for** centuries, but during the 20th century they fell out of fashion.
3 They have grown ~~in~~ **into** one of the biggest companies in the country.
4 It's a translation ~~of~~ **from** Arabic.
5 We sometimes have to work ~~until~~ **up to** / **for** seven hours without a break.
6 CORRECT
7 I somehow managed to crash ~~to~~ **into** the car in front of me.
8 We were very close. She was ~~as~~ **like** a mother to me.
9 CORRECT
10 CORRECT

Communicative outcomes
In this two-page spread, students will discuss the fashion industry and issues such as objectification and self-esteem.

SPEAKING

Aim
to introduce the topic of the listening text; to get students talking about the fashion industry

1 Start by asking students to look at the photo. Ask: *What can you see in the photo? How would you describe the appearance of the two people?* Elicit students' ideas and write any interesting descriptive words or phrases on the board.
• Organise the class into groups to discuss the questions. Go round the room and check students are doing the task and help with ideas and vocabulary if necessary.
• In feedback, elicit ideas, opinions and experiences.

Possible answers
Popular fashion magazines in the UK: *Elle, Harper's Bazaar, Red, Glamour, Vogue, Grazia, Porter, GQ, Marie Claire*
Some big fashion stars (top models): Kate Moss, Gisele Bundchen, Cara Delevingne, Kendall Jenner

LISTENING

Aim
to listen for general and specific detail; to listen to see how words and phrases are connected to the topic

2 ⚫52 Ask students to read the questions, and ask what they can predict about the listening from the questions (it's going to be about Dove's advertising campaign).
• Play the recording. Students listen and note answers. Let students compare answers in pairs before discussing as a class.

Possible answers
1 four
2 how the media impacts on our mental states
3 She's a size 26 model – largest with a mainstream agency – and a 'body-positive activist' who has a campaign to broaden our idea of beauty.
4 Dove sells toiletries. Its advertising campaign is called Campaign for Real Beauty, and it started ten years ago.
5 Both aim to broaden the definition / images of beauty in the fashion industry and to see beauty as a personal choice.

⏴ 52

A = announcer, S = Sheila Tinkelman, M = Margot van der Stegen

A: And next on Radio Talk we have Mixed Media with Sheila Tinkelman.

S: Hello! Role models, Twitter storms and sweet soul music – today we'll be looking at how the media can impact on our mental states. Are footballers really role models and to whom? Or is it an excuse by the media to justify click bait? Jon Ronson's book on the very real and devastating impact of committing a faux pas in the virtual world, and the researcher discovering the power of music in calming Alzheimer's patients.

But first, images of beauty and the fashion industry. The model Tess Holliday has attracted a certain amount of press attention with her growing Instagram following and social media campaigns against what she calls 'beauty standards'. Holliday is a size 26 and supposedly the largest woman to be signed by a mainstream modelling agency. She styles herself as a body-positive activist and has been held up as a force for change in the fashion industry. But haven't we been here before? It's over ten years now since the toiletries brand, Dove, launched its Campaign for Real Beauty, with its first iconic adverts of women of various shapes and sizes, and since then a number of its commercials have gone viral. A recent video featured large public buildings round the world where a pair of entrances had been labelled either 'Beautiful' or 'Average'. Women were secretly filmed hesitating as they chose which door to go through and some were then interviewed about their choice. Holliday's social media campaign may be somewhat more grassroots and in-your-face than Dove's, but both essentially aim to broaden the images of beauty beyond those presented by the fashion industry and to see beauty as a personal choice. The question is whether campaigns like these are needed at all. And if they are, do they make any real difference? So, here to discuss these and other issues with me is the academic, Margot van der Stegen. Margot, thank you for joining us.

M: My pleasure.

Culture notes

Tess Holliday was named by *Vogue Italia* as one of the top six plus-size models in the world in 2013. In 2015, Milk Model Management announced that they had signed her, making her the largest plus-size model to be signed to a mainstream modelling agency.

Dove is a personal care brand owned by Unilever originating in the United Kingdom. It produces body lotions, hair care products and hand creams.

Margot van der Stegen is fictitious.

3   Organise the class into pairs. Ask students to discuss the questions. Go round the room and check students are doing the task and help with ideas and vocabulary if necessary.

• In feedback, elicit ideas, opinions and experiences.

Possible answers
A 'body-positive activist' promotes the idea that everybody should feel positive about their body shape and not feel they should be trying to achieve an ideal shape.
The message of the Campaign for Real Beauty (according to Dove) is to celebrate the natural physical variation embodied by all women and inspire them to have the confidence to be comfortable with themselves. Cynics would say it is a way of marketing their own products, and linking their company with the 'body-positive' movement.

4   Ask students to predict how the words and phrases link to the topic with their partner. Monitor closely and note what students are saying. You could have a brief feedback session to find out what students predict. There is no need to comment on or correct any predictions at this stage but check the meaning of any terms students are not sure of (see Background language notes below).

Background language notes for teachers

objectification = if you objectify someone, you treat them as an object to study or admire (like a vase or ornament)
shield = protect (you might draw a shield to show the meaning)
manipulative = if you manipulate someone, you make them do something or believe what you say; it is a negative word as it implies being dishonest
eating disorder = a mental health problem around eating (e.g. anorexia, bulimia)
role model = a person you admire and perhaps imitate because they represent something good or ideal
selfies = photos you take of yourself
skin lightening = a procedure that makes your skin lighter in pigmentation

5   **⏴ 53** Play the recording. Students listen and check their ideas. They can take notes if they wish. Let students compare ideas with their partner and discuss how the words are connected to the information on the recording.
• In feedback, decide what to accept from students as the exact wording varies. Note there is a second more detailed listening to follow that will help students, as well as a vocabulary focus where they could listen a third time.

Answers
objectification: women are objectified in fashion photos / art; they sometimes engage in self-objectification by criticising themselves
selfies: a Dove advert asked teenagers to take selfies and analyse them, and the speaker suggests this is making people address their beauty in objectifying ways!
eating disorder: it's suggested that eating disorders are connected to this self-objectification
manipulative: the speaker finds the Dove adverts manipulative (because they are selling 'beauty products'); Tess Holliday's campaign is less manipulative, but they are both selling beauty

a maths test: in an experiment, women who had previously had to try on a swimsuit did worse in the test than those who'd had to try on a sweater – the implication is that wearing a swimsuit created more self-objectification and anxiety which distracted them from doing the test well

shield: parents need to protect children from the fashion industry

skin-lightening: Dove's parent company sells skin lightening products – it shows how they are encouraging people to conform to an idealised look

role model: parents are better role models than fashion if they don't objectify women or self-objectify

---

♺ 53

S = Sheila Tinkelman, M = Margot van der Stegen

S: So Margot, your research is in the area of self-objectification, which I think would argue that the kinds of fashion images we are bombarded with these days have a consistent impact on women's mental states.

M: Absolutely. Basically with all of these images, women are essentially objects of the male gaze. The argument is that for women this objectification has become internalised and part of their way of being. In other words, we look at ourselves as outsiders and monitor our appearance – generally in critical ways and in comparison to the dominant idealised look.

S: Beautiful, white, young, tall and skinny.

M: Exactly. Of course, this process has existed for centuries, particularly through Western art, but we now live in an age of unprecedented visual saturation, which affects all corners of the world and all classes of society.

S: And it's affecting our mental health and giving rise to eating disorders such as anorexia?

M: Well, yes. I mean, that's a bit of an oversimplification – there's obviously a number of factors involved in eating disorders. But what experimental studies have shown is how simply flicking through fashion magazines can trigger self-criticism. There's also one seminal study that found women who were asked to try on a swimsuit suffered more anxiety than those who tried on a sweater. What's more, the researchers found the higher levels of anxiety had a knock-on effect in that the women who had tried on the swimsuit got lower marks in a maths test they were given afterwards! None of these things were true of men in the study. So it seems reasonable to believe that self-objectification may at least contribute to mental health issues for women.

S: Certainly that also chimes with Dove's research that found that while over 70% of girls between the ages of ten and seventeen felt pressure to be beautiful, only 4% of women worldwide would describe themselves as such.

M: Yes, that pressure is very real and, both as a mother and a researcher, it's certainly something I worry about.

S: So, do you think campaigns such as Dove's or Tess Holliday's make a difference?

M: Well, I think there's certainly a contradiction at the heart of Dove's campaign in that it's essentially a brand selling shampoo and body wash, and I don't see that as having much to do with self-esteem. Indeed, in some parts of the world, its parent company sells cosmetics such as skin-lightening products that don't exactly support the idea that we are all equally beautiful.

S: Sure, but you don't think women should be encouraged to 'spend less time analysing the things they don't like and more time appreciating what they do' – as one of the participants in a Dove ads puts it.

M: Of course that's a good message for anyone but actually I'd say most of their adverts are forcing women to define themselves in terms of looks. I mean, why not choose between doors marked 'Average' and 'Intelligent' instead, or, I don't know, 'Caring' and 'Selfish'? And then a previous advert actually encouraged teenagers to take selfies and analyse them! OK, Dove would say it's done in a positive way, but it's pure self-objectification. And do they know how many women photoshop their selfies?

S: Well, perhaps as the actress Cameron Diaz once said, we all actually want to be objectified. Maybe we just need to change the terms. Isn't that what Tess Holliday is saying too?

M: Yeah, I mean personally, I find her campaign less emotionally manipulative in that it doesn't play upon women's existing insecurities and simply says I am beautiful, you are too. But ultimately, yes, she's a model and it's about beauty.

S: So, not fully empowering?

M: No. I mean, within the fashion industry it is good to have people like her, but for me, real change has to come from the home. I think generally parents should shield their kids from the whole fashion industry. They should strengthen their children's self-esteem by basing it on being a good person rather than appearance. Fathers can be role models by not objectifying women. Mothers can be role models in not openly self-objectifying – difficult though that might be.

S: Well, that brings us rather neatly to our next item on role models and footballers, so I'll stop you there. Margot van der Stegen, thank you.

M: Thank you for inviting me.

---

6 ♺ 53 Start students off by eliciting whether the first point is made or agreed with by Margot. Ask students to discuss the rest with their partner based on their first listening.

• Play the recording again to let students check their answers in pairs before discussing as a class.

• In feedback, ask students to justify their answers by telling you what they heard on the recording.

Answers
1 Makes
2 Margot doesn't make this point. She says that the *process has existed for centuries*. It's not a new phenomenon.
3 Agrees
4 Margot doesn't say whether the research was valid or not
5 Agrees
6 Makes
7 Not stated
8 Makes

7 Ask students to complete the sentences individually first. Do the first as an example. Let students check answers in pairs before working together to find answers in audio script 53 on page 213.
• In feedback, write up the missing words on the board.

Answers
1 unprecedented visual saturation
2 simply flicking through
3 a knock-on effect
4 also chimes with
5 at the heart
6 in terms of
7 women's existing insecurities
8 rather neatly to

Background language notes for teachers

unprecedented visual saturation = a huge number of visual images in numbers never seen before
simply flicking through = looking through a magazine, turning over the pages quickly without reading any articles
a knock-on effect = an effect that happens as a result of something that happened earlier
chimes with = is similar to
at the heart of (the campaign) = central to (the campaign)
in terms of = in relation to a particular aspect of, with respect to
women's existing insecurities = the fears and concerns women already have
bring (us) rather neatly to = connects the previous point to the next one in a good way

8 Ask students to discuss the questions in groups of four or five. Monitor closely and note interesting and useful language, as well as errors.
• Once you have fed back on content, look at good language that students used, and language students didn't quite use correctly. Show students better ways of saying what they were trying to say. You could write some useful new phrases on the board with gaps and ask the whole class to complete the sentences.

DEVELOPING CONVERSATIONS
Defining yourself

Aim
to introduce and practise ways of defining yourself

9 Read through the information in the box as a class.
• Ask students to use the pattern to write sentences. Monitor closely and prompt students to correct any errors.

Possible answers
As a father, I want girls like my daughter to have equal opportunities to boys.
As a teacher, I think doing hours of homework is unnecessary.
As a daughter, I worry about what will happen when my parents get old.
As a good citizen, I always try to vote.
As someone who often plays football in parks, I find it annoying when dog owners don't clean up after their dogs.
As a conservative, I believe government should reduce its influence on daily life.

10 Organise the class into pairs to compare and discuss their sentences. In feedback, elicit some of the more interesting definitions students produced.

Optional extra activity Ask fast finishers to work on definitions for you!

UNDERSTANDING VOCABULARY
Verb forms and word families

Aim
to introduce and practice verb forms and word families

11 Read through the information in the box as a class.
• Ask students to complete the sentences. Let students compare answers in pairs.
• In feedback, elicit the students' answers.

Answers
1 idealised
2 fattening
3 justification
4 heightened
5 overgeneralisation
6 whiteners / whitening
7 widening
8 commercialisation
9 demystified
10 disheartening (*heartening* is also possible depending on your point of view!)

Optional extra activity Show the following sentences on the board and ask students to write them in their language:
There's no guarantee that what replaces them will be any more to our own liking.

*There is simply no justification for girls under sixteen being
used to model adult clothes.*
*It is no great surprise that the fashion industry refuses to
accept responsibility.*
There is no real demand for larger models.
I'm no expert, but it can't just be coincidental, can it?
The impact images have is obviously no small matter.
Remove the English sentences from the board, and ask
students to translate their sentences back into English.
Then show the originals again for them to compare.

12   Organise the class into pairs to choose sentences
and discuss the topics.
• Go round the room and and note down any interesting
pieces of language you hear.
• Once you have fed back on content, look at good
language that students used, and language students
didn't quite use correctly. Show students better ways
of saying what they were trying to say. You could write
some useful new phrases on the board with gaps and
ask the whole class to complete the sentences.

Optional extra activity   Choose one of the topics to
debate as a whole class activity.

Web research activity
• Ask students to find an advertisement for a product
that uses a model / models.
• Ask them to present the advertisement to the
class, saying what it's promoting, and whether it is
successful or not.
• Ask students to say whether the model is being
objectified and presented positively or not.

16 DANGER AND RISK

SPEAKING

Aim
to set the scene and introduce the theme with a
photo; to get students talking about risk taking

1   Start by telling the class that in this unit they're going
to be learning how to describe accidents and injuries, talk
about law and regulations, compensation culture, and
discuss Internet use; students will practise interjecting
and thinking critically about texts.
•   Ask students to look at the photo on pages 140–141.
Ask: *What can you see?* Elicit a brief description of the
photo, and introduce any key words students might need.
•   Ask students to read the sentences and choose the one
which describes their feelings about the photo.

2   Organise the class into groups of four or five to
compare their answers to Exercise 1 and discuss the
questions. Go round the room and check students are
doing the task and help with ideas and vocabulary if
necessary.
•   In feedback, ask different pairs to tell the class what
they discussed.
•   Once you have fed back on content, look at good
language that students used, and language students
didn't quite use correctly during the activity. Show
students better ways of saying what they were trying
to say. You could write some useful new phrases on the
board with gaps and ask the whole class to complete
the sentences.

Possible answers
Reasons for taking risks: fame, money, the adrenaline
rush, the desire to be different, showing off to friends
Consequences: death or serious injury, heartbreak
for their family, worry and concern for friends and
family, arrest by the police, incredibly high life
insurance premiums
Everyday risks: driving a car, crossing the road,
playing sports

Background language notes for teachers

out of your mind = crazy
get the appeal = understand the appeal or attraction of
something
give it a go = try to do it
totally up for (something) = very enthusiastic about
wanting to try something or do something
the adrenaline rush = the feeling of pleasure you get
from being in dangerous, exciting situations

Culture notes

The photo actually shows urban climber Yaroslav Segeda
taking a selfie on top of one of the highest buildings in
his home city, Kiev, in Ukraine.

ACCIDENT-PRONE
Student's Book pages 142–143

Communicative outcomes
In this two-page spread, students will practise describing accidents and injuries; students will notice how interjections are used in conversations.

VOCABULARY Accidents and injuries

Aim
to introduce and practise ways of describing accidents and injuries

1 Ask students to work in pairs to replace the words with synonyms. Elicit the answer to the first one as an example. In feedback, go through the answers and use definitions and examples to show meaning.

Answers

1 ripped	7 sliced
2 came to	8 cut
3 pouring	9 burnt
4 panicked	10 fainted
5 banged	11 break
6 heavily	12 terrible pain

Background language notes for teachers

Note that some phrases are colloquial: *freaked out, came to*. Some are very dramatic, and therefore used in stories to make the story more dramatic and gory: *tore* and *ripped* are both stronger than *pulled*; *whacked* is stronger than *hit*; *snap* is more dramatic than *break*; *gash* is more dramatic than *cut*.
Pronunciation: highlight the /ɔː/ sound in *tore*, *pouring* and *scalded*; the stress in *consciousness* and *profusely*.

2 Organise the class into pairs to test each other. As you monitor, watch out for pronunciation difficulties and correct them. In feedback, find out which words students had problems remembering. Swap roles if you have fast finishers.

Teacher development: student vocabulary testing

A good way of getting students to show understanding is by getting them to test each other. This can be either collaborative or competitive. It is student-centred, can be fun, and encourages students to take responsibility for both their own learning and that of others in their class. Here are some ideas:
1 After introducing a set of words, ask students to test each other (as in Exercise 2 above). This could take the form of one student providing synonyms, definitions or antonyms from which the other must say or guess the word. It could also involve students preparing and producing sentences in which they say *X* instead of the word they are testing. The other student must guess which word *X* is.

2 Organise the class into groups to prepare a vocabulary test. Students prepare definitions or examples to show the meaning of words. When groups are ready, they test other groups by reading out their definitions or examples, and the other groups guess the word. Award points for good definitions or examples as well as correct answers.
3 Set the preparation of a vocabulary test as a homework activity. For example, at the end of a unit, tell each student to find five words or phrases from the unit that they have learned. Tell them to prepare 'clues' or explanations for the words or phrases as part of their homework. In the next lesson, students present their clues to the class (or in groups if your class is large). The class or group has to guess which words or phrases they are describing.

Optional extra activity Ask students in pairs to mime the words or phrases. Their partners must guess.

SPEAKING

Aim
to practise using vocabulary to describe accidents and injuries in an extended speaking activity

3 Ask students to prepare individually first for one or two minutes. Tell them to choose which places or situations they have most to say about and to think about what to say. When students are ready, organise them into pairs to discuss the accidents. Go round the room and check students are doing the task and help with ideas and vocabulary if necessary.
• In feedback, ask different pairs to tell the class what they discussed. Once you have fed back on content, look at good language that students used, and language students didn't quite use correctly during the activity.

Possible answers
a beach: drowning, cut feet on rocks and bits of glass in the sand
a campsite: hit by collapsing tent, hit finger with hammer
cooking dinner: burnt on cooker, cut finger when chopping
cycling: injuries from falling off bike or being knocked off by a car or lorry, serious head injuries if not wearing helmet
doing DIY: cut finger or hand with tools, falling off a ladder
driving: a crash or collision, head or neck injuries
a football pitch: break a leg or twist or sprain an ankle from a badly-timed tackle or turn
gardening: cut finger from pruning the roses, falling off a ladder
an ice rink: falling on the ice and breaking an arm or leg, cut by ice skate
jogging: hit by car, slipping and falling
a nightclub: slip and hurt ankle from exuberant dancing
a mountain: breaks, sprains and cuts from slipping on mountain path

Optional extra activity Make use of the photo on the page. Ask students: *Where are the boys? What are they doing? What is about to happen? How will both boys react?* You could exploit this photo before or after Exercise 3, or as a lead-in to the whole spread.

LISTENING

Aim
to listen for general and specific understanding; to work out the meaning of words and phrases in context

4 🔊 **54** Give students a moment to read through the situation and questions.
• Play the recording. Students listen and note answers. Let students compare their answers in pairs before discussing in feedback.

Answers
Conversation 1
1 Brian's brother – his front teeth and his wrist
2 A wall collapsed when he was trying to climb it and he landed face first, knocking his teeth out (and snapped his wrist).
3 His false teeth fell out at dinner and he put them back in in front of them.

Conversation 2
1 Doug – his forehead (and chin)
2 He hit his head on a shelf. He got blown over and fell and hit his chin on the road.
3 The woman notices and asks about a scar.

🔊 **54**
Conversation 1
A = Anita, B = Brian
A: Well Brian, I have to say, I certainly wasn't expecting your brother to do that!
B: What? The business with the teeth?
A: Yeah. I mean ... yuck! Seriously. In the middle of the meal as well. That really freaked me out.
B: I guess it was a bit odd. I'm sort of used to it now, though.
A: It was gross. I mean, couldn't he have kept it hidden and just sneaked off to the loo - instead of bashing it back in right in front of us? Incredible! Honestly! Just ... wow!
B: Ha ha. I'd take it as a compliment. It means he's comfortable in your presence now!
A: Lucky me!
B: Have I ever told you how that happened?
A: No, but I'm not sure I want to know, to be honest.
B: Oh, it's not that bad. It was back when we were kids. We'd just moved to this place out in the country and we were exploring, you know, having a wander around, and there was this big old wall at the end of the garden. We were trying to haul ourselves up it, but then when he got near the top, the whole thing collapsed and he came crashing down and landed face first, knocking those two front teeth out.

A: Fff! Ouch! Nasty.
B: Yeah, there was blood everywhere, you know, pouring down his face ...
A: Oh, stop it! You're just saying it to make me feel worse now.
B: And to top the whole thing off, he didn't even really notice because he somehow snapped his wrist in the fall as well.
A: Aww, poor guy.
B: Yeah, he was in agony.
A: I guess perhaps I should cut him some slack, then.

Conversation 2
C = Chloe, D = Doug
C: How did you get that scar, if you don't mind me asking?
D: Which one? The one on my chin?
C: No, I meant the one on your forehead. It's pretty nasty.
D: Oh, that. Yeah, well, I was smart enough to somehow walk straight into a head-height shelf when I was eighteen. I was working at this summer camp in the States and I'd been out to a party with some friends one night, stumbled home and whacked myself when I got back to my cabin. I decided that, while it hurt a bit, it'd probably be OK and that what I really needed was my bed. I woke up in the morning to find there was blood everywhere – all over the bed, the floor – and most shockingly, when I looked in the mirror, I realised my face was covered in dried blood, which I really hadn't been expecting! The doctor said he could've stitched it if I'd seen him right away, but that it was unstitchable the following day! Just my luck.
C: Oh, that's awful.
D: Yeah, well, it's my own stupid fault, really.
C: And ... um ... I'm scared to ask now, really, but what about that other one?
D: You won't believe me when I tell you. Honestly.
C: Um ... OK. Is it gruesome?
D: Not really. Just odd. I don't know if you remember but a couple of years ago, there were all these reports of people getting blown off their feet by high winds and even someone getting killed by being blown head first into a door.
C: No! That must just have completely passed me by somehow.
D: Yeah? Well, it was pretty crazy. What happened with me was that one night I just got totally blown down the drive at the side of my house – completely out of control! I somehow managed to go head first between two parked cars, whacking my head on both of them and landing on my chin in the middle of the road.
C: Aww, ouch!
D: Yeah, and when I came to, I found my chin completely split open ... and my wisdom teeth weren't too happy either!
C: Woah! You're fairly accident-prone, really, aren't you?
D: I've got another one, actually, if you want to hear about it ...

Background language notes for teachers

You could point out the words used to mean 'really horrible' in the context of describing injuries: *nasty, gruesome, gross*.

cut him some slack = stop criticising him or giving him a hard time

wisdom teeth = the large back teeth that don't usually appear until your teens

5 🔊 **54** Let students read through the sentences first, and decide whether they are true or false based on their first listening. Check *stitches* (= thread used to join skin together after it has been cut in an accident). You might also pre-teach one or two difficult words needed to answer the questions: *haul yourself up* = pull yourself up; *cut (somebody) some slack* = not be too demanding or critical; *it passed me by* = I didn't notice it.

• Play the recording again. Let students compare their answers in pairs before discussing as a class. In feedback, ask students to justify their answers by telling you what they heard on the recording.

Answers

1 F (*I guess it was a bit odd. I'm sort of used to it now, though.*)

2 F (*Ha ha. I'd take it as a compliment. It means he's comfortable in your presence now! A: Lucky me!* (Note that Anita is being sarcastic.)

3 T (*We were trying to haul ourselves up it*) (Note that *haul* means 'pull up using your arms and with great difficulty'.)

4 T (*He didn't even really notice because he somehow snapped his wrist in the fall as well.*)

5 T (*I guess perhaps I should cut him some slack then.*)

6 T (*I was working at this summer camp in the States*)

7 T (*while it hurt a bit, it'd probably be OK and that what I really needed was my bed*)

8 F (*he could've stitched it if I'd seen him right away, but that it was unstitchable the following day!*)

9 F (*it's my own stupid fault, really*)

10 F (*That must just have completely passed me by somehow.*)

---

6 Ask students to discuss the words and phrases in pairs. Go round the room and check students are doing the task and help if necessary.

• In feedback, ask different pairs to tell the class what they think the words mean. Ask them to say how the context helped to show meaning. You could ask students to check any words they aren't sure of in a dictionary at the end of the activity.

Answers

1 *business* here means 'strange or controversial thing that happened'

2 *freaked me out* here means 'made me feel really unsettled / uncomfortable'

---

3 *sneaked off* here means 'to go quietly so people don't notice'; *the loo* is an informal word for the toilet; *bashing* here means 'hitting it so that it is in place'

4 *to top the whole thing off* is used here to introduce the last of several bad events

5 *smart* is used ironically here – normally it means 'clever', but here it means 'stupid'

6 *stumbled* here means 'walked unsteadily'

7 *just my luck* is used ironically to mean 'I always have bad luck'

8 *weren't too happy* is used to mean his teeth were painful too

---

7 Ask students to discuss the questions in groups of four or five. Monitor closely and note interesting and useful language, as well as errors.

• In feedback, ask different pairs to tell the class what they discussed. Once you have fed back on content, look at good language that students used, and language students didn't quite use correctly during the activity.

Possible answers

Work with your students' answers.

The first sounds really painful because it involves loss of teeth and a broken wrist. The second and third involve blows to the head, which could be more serious.

The first and second are perhaps most avoidable. The first and second involve blame on the part of the person who got injured. In the first, he shouldn't have been climbing over a wall. In the second, he had been to a party and wasn't concentrating. Responses could include giving first aid, calling an ambulance, fainting with shock at the sight of blood, and panicking.

DEVELOPING CONVERSATIONS

Interjections

Aim

to introduce ways of using interjections to express emotions or show you want people to do something

8 🔊 **55** Read through the information in the box as a class. Ask students if they can think of any interjections they know in English.

• Play the recording. Ask students to listen and note down the interjections. Let them compare answers in pairs. In feedback, elicit answers and write them up on the board.

🔊 **55 and answers**

1 Wow!	7 Ahem!
2 Fff! Ouch!	8 Mmm
3 Yuck!	9 Umm
4 Gosh!	10 Oi!
5 Phew!	11 Sshhh!
6 Mmm!	12 Oops!

Background language notes for teachers

It is worth noting that when saying these words it is important to mime or act out the feeling behind them. So, *wow!* needs to be said with wide-eyed enthusiasm otherwise it suggests disinterest or cynicism. You could drill the words with appropriate facial expressions to get students practising this. The words are onomatopoeic for the most part – they sound like what they mean.

9 Organise the class into pairs to discuss the meaning of the interjections. Elicit the meaning of the first to get students started. In feedback, elicit a few predictions but don't reveal the answers as this activity creates a prediction task for the listening to follow.

10 🔊 56 Play the recording. Ask students to check predictions. Let them compare their answers in pairs. In feedback, elicit answers.

Answers
1 Wow! = surprise / show you're impressed
2 Fff! Ouch! = sympathy for pain suffered
3 Yuk! = disgust
4 Gosh! = surprise
5 Phew! = relief
6 Mmm! = you like the taste
7 Ahem! = trying to get attention or expressing annoyance where you might be ignored
8 Mmm = uncertainty or a non-committal noise (neither yes or no) – in this case because you weren't listening
9 Umm = hesitation
10 Oi! = you've seen someone doing something wrong
11 Sshhh! = asking people to be quiet
12 Oops! = old fashioned / polite way to say you made a mistake or dropped something, etc.

🔊 **56**
1 A: She speaks six different languages.
   B: Wow! That's impressive.
2 A: I was running and I heard something in my knee just snap!
   B: Fff! Ouch! Painful!
3 A: His false teeth fell out onto the floor and he just picked them up and put them straight back into his mouth again.
   B: Yuk! That's disgusting!
4 A: I've still got a scar. Look.
   B: Gosh! That's awfully big!
5 A: The doctor I went to for a second opinion said I'd been given the wrong diagnosis and it wasn't as serious as they'd thought.
   B: Phew! That's a relief, then.
6 A: Mmm! This is delicious! What's yours like?
   B: Yeah, not bad.
7 A: Ahem!
   B: What? ... Oh, sorry.

8 A: And then she said, like, you know, that she thought it was a bit too big, you know, not really the right fit, but I wasn't sure so ... are you listening to me?
   B: Mmm. Yeah. Course.
9 A: So how come you decided to do that, then?
   B: Umm. That's a good question, actually. I'd have to think about that.
10 A: Oi! What do you think you're doing?
   B: Quick! Run!
11 Sshhh! The baby's sleeping.
12 A: And then I realised I'd copied my boss in on the email by mistake!
   B: Oops! That wasn't very clever.

11 Ask students to discuss the questions with their partner. Go round the room and check students are doing the task and help with ideas and vocabulary if necessary. In feedback, ask different groups to tell the class what they discussed.

Possible answers
Reasons for using interjections: to show interest, to respond naturally, to keep conversations going, to be natural by using English interjections rather than ones you would use in your language
Reasons against: don't need them, could sound unnatural when using them

---

Optional extra activity Ask students in pairs to prepare and act out three short conversations, each containing a different interjection. Ask some pairs to act out their conversations for the class.

CONVERSATION PRACTICE

Aim
to practise language from the lesson in a free, communicative, personalised speaking activity

12 This is an opportunity to bring together the different threads of the lesson, and for students to practise describing accidents.
• Ask students to choose a task and prepare notes. Monitor and help with ideas and vocabulary.

13 Once students are ready, organise them into groups of four or five to share their stories. Listen for errors, new language or interesting conversations to use in feedback.
• In feedback, look at good language that students used, and language students didn't quite use correctly during the activity. Show students better ways of saying what they were trying to say. You could write some useful new phrases on the board with gaps and ask the whole class to complete the sentences.

🎥 **37 Refer students to the video and activities on the DVD-ROM.**

Teacher development: using the video

The video and activities on the DVD-ROM can be used in various ways:

1 as an alternative to the conversation practice
2 instead of the listening activity in some units, particularly with weaker groups. Students can first practise reading out the dialogues and work on some of the key phrases / structures in a controlled way before having a go themselves.
3 at the end of the unit as a revision exercise

Communicative outcomes
In this two-page spread, students read and discuss compensation cases.

SPEAKING

Aim
to introduce the topic of the reading text; to get students talking about risk or risk aversion

1 Start by explaining *risk aversion* (= ways of avoiding risks). Organise the class into groups of four or five to discuss the questions. Go round the room and check students are doing the task and help with ideas and vocabulary if necessary.
• In feedback, ask different groups to tell the class what they discussed. Once you have fed back on content, look at good language that students used, and language students didn't quite use correctly.

Possible answers
from top to bottom
Photo 1: this illustrates the risk of terrorists taking explosives in cans or tubes on to a plane – fluids and pastes are currently prohibited from flights
Photo 2: this illustrates the need to wear visible clothing in the street. These school kids have been given hi-vis jackets, presumably so that they won't be hit by motorists, or perhaps so that the teachers can make sure they don't lose any kids.
Photo 3: this illustrates the risk involved in putting up scaffolding in a high rise building
Photo 4: this is a joke. It is making fun of the fact that signs are often put up to warn us of unimportant things or unlikely risks – here, the sign is warning us about itself.

READING

Aim
to practise reading for general understanding; to prepare students for the extended reading

2 Ask students to read the situation and the task. Set a two-minute time limit for them to read and note answers.

3 Ask students to work in pairs to compare answers. In feedback, ask pairs to share their ideas with the class.

Answers
1 photo 4 – it is a possible example of overcautiousness and worry about compensation claims while not dealing with more important issues (though students may have other ideas which they will need to justify)
2 Answers will vary depending on students' attitudes

3 Answers will vary depending on students'
   countries and attitudes
4 *negligent* = irresponsible
   damages = compensation / payment
   dismissed on the grounds = rejected for the reason ...

Optional extra activity Note that students will soon
read about this case. However, you could open it out at
this stage into a debate. Ask students to discuss the case
and court decision in open class, and encourage them to
share their diverse opinions.

VOCABULARY Laws and regulations

Aim
to introduce and practise words to describe laws and
regulations

4 Ask students to match the words to the definitions.
Elicit the answer to the first one as an example. Let
students compare their answers in pairs. In feedback,
elicit answers.

Answers
1 an appeal   6 non-compliance
2 negligence   7 damages
3 liability   8 grounds
4 legislation   9 precedent
5 a lawsuit

Background language notes for teachers:
pronunciation

Point out the strong stress in these words: *appeal,
negligence, liability, legislation, non-compliance, damages,
precedent*.

5 Ask students to complete the sentences. Let students
compare their answers in pairs. In feedback, elicit
answers from different pairs.

Answers
1 was held   6 admitted
2 was awarded   7 set
3 sued   8 repealed
4 was overturned   9 was dismissed
5 filed

Background language notes for teachers

Point out common collocations, and ask students if they
can think of other common collocations. For example: *be
(liable), be held (liable), find yourself (liable);
award (someone damages), award (an amount) in
damages, pay damages, receive damages;
overturn, dismiss, uphold on appeal*, etc.

Teacher development: the importance
of collocation

Recognising the patterns of words, the way particular
words collocate with others and the way they habitually
go together, is important in language learning and
attaining fluency. While these sequences of words
are instantly recognisable to native speakers, they are
difficult for second language learners to acquire and
use properly. That's why it is essential to make sure your
students notice patterns and sequences, categorise
them, expand on them, and notice how fixed they are.
Pay particular attention to unusual collocations which
students will never guess, and which do not translate
from L1 (e.g. *hold someone liable*).

Optional extra activity Ask students to use dictionaries
to research other collocations and sequences for the
words in the sentences in Exercise 5.

6 Ask students to work in pairs to come up with
examples. You may want to set a limit (say: *give me
five examples in total*), depending on your students'
knowledge and experience. Don't expect students to
have ideas to incorporate all the language. Monitor and
help with ideas and vocabulary. In feedback, elicit any
interesting stories or experiences from the class.

Possible answers
Some possible examples related to the UK and
US below:
1 BP was held liable for the accident on its oil rig in
   the Mexican gulf and forced to pay damages.
2 & 6 In a case of medical negligence at a Rhode
   Island hospital, they operated on the wrong side
   of someone's brain.
3 A Conservative MP, Jonathan Aitken, once sued
   a newspaper for libel over a claim he had been
   involved in corruption, but he lost the case and
   ended up in prison.
4 A man who was jailed for killing Jill Dando, a TV
   presenter in the UK, eventually had his conviction
   overturned on appeal.
5 A number of cancer sufferers / smokers filed (and
   won) a class-action lawsuit against a number of
   cigarette companies.
7 The ruling of the European Human Rights court
   set a precedent for the example in item 7.
8 In the UK there is opposition to some security
   legislation and people want to see it repealed.
9 Many cases are dismissed for this reason.

Optional extra activity 1 Ask students to word build
from the words in Exercises 4 and 5. For example,
students could make this list: *liable, liability, precedent,
precedence, legislate, legislative, libel, libellous, convict,
conviction, compensate, compensation, oppose,
opposition, dismiss, dismissal*.

Optional extra activity 2 Ask students to play a word
game with the words from the lesson. In pairs, students
take turns to say a word. Their partner must create a
sentence using that word.

READING

Aim
to practise reading for general and specific
understanding; students read and respond to
information and opinions in texts

7 Remind students of the news report by asking them
to look at the headline. Ask: *What do you remember of
the story? From the headline, what do you expect the
point of view of the editorial to be?* Ask students to read
the situation and the task. Let students compare their
answers in pairs before discussing as a class.

> **Answers**
> 1 They think it was stupid and a waste of time.
> 2 – not taking responsibility for own actions
>   – wasted court time
>   – people see risk and danger everywhere (health
>   and safety culture)
>   – extra costs for business (such as increased
>   insurance premiums)
>   – extra red tape for business
>   – inconvenience when travelling
>   – 'smothering children' (i.e. not giving them
>   sufficient freedom)
> 3 It wants fewer of these cases brought to court
>   and some health and safety regulations to be
>   repealed.
> 4 It's a more 'popular' / tabloid-type paper given the
>   exaggerated language (list of shame / wrapped
>   in red tape), but it takes the subject seriously.
>   Generally it could be characterised as right-wing –
>   with arguments to reduce the burden of the state
>   and a focus on individual freedom and business.

8 Ask students to read the list and prepare their
own opinions. Go round the room and check students
are doing the task and help with ideas and vocabulary
if necessary.

9 Organise the class into pairs to share their opinions.
• In feedback, ask different pairs to tell the class what
they discussed. Use the opportunity to correct any errors
or rephrase what students are trying to say. You could
extend this into a class debate (see below).

Optional extra activity Choose one of the items on the
list of shame which some of your students put a tick
next to while others put a cross next to. Ask students
to form groups or pairs made up of students who have
the same opinion about whether the item is mad or
not. Give students time to prepare short arguments
to support their point of view. Then ask each group to
present their points to the class. At the end, find out
whether anybody changed their mind depending on the
arguments put forward by each side.

SPEAKING

Aim
to practise language from the lesson in a free,
communicative, personalised speaking activity

10 Students will read three or four short texts, each
of which provide information that sheds a different light
on the issues raised in the text, notably the true story
behind the Liebeck case. They will then have the same
questions to discuss as their partner.
• Organise the class into pairs. Ask each pair to decide
who is A and who is B. Tell them to find their information
pages (pages 188 and 195), then give them time to read
their files and prepare. Monitor and help with ideas and
vocabulary.
• Ask students to tell each other what they read in their
texts. Then ask them to discuss the questions. Monitor
and note errors and good uses of language.
• In feedback, look at good language that students used,
and language students didn't quite use correctly. Show
students better ways of saying what they were trying
to say. You could write some useful new phrases on the
board with gaps and ask the whole class to complete the
sentences.

> **Answers**
> Answers will vary. The additional information is
> aimed at showing some alternative views, but
> students may legitimately argue that it is irrelevant
> or unreliable / biased or reinforces how they feel as
> well as undermining their initial assumptions.

Optional extra activity As the texts require some
understanding before students can report and discuss
them, you might consider breaking this activity down
into further stages.
• Start by organising the class into A pairs and B pairs.
• Ask the A pairs to work together to read and prepare,
and the B pairs to do the same. Take time to monitor,
explain words, and make sure students are fully prepared.
• Then mix the pairs so that the As are with the Bs so
they can summarise and discuss their texts and the
questions.

Communicative outcomes
In this two-page spread, students will talk about Internet dangers; students will roleplay a phone-in about future risks and fears.

SPEAKING

Aim
to set the scene and introduce the theme of the listening; to get students talking about digital technology

1 You could start with an open-class activity, books closed, by writing *digital* on the board, and asking students to think of as many words as they can that collocate with *digital*.
• Organise the class into groups to discuss the terms. Go round the room and check students are doing the task and help with ideas and vocabulary if necessary.
• In feedback, ask different pairs to tell the class what they discussed. Once you have fed back on content, look at good language that students used, and language students didn't quite use correctly during the activity.

Possible answers
digital detox: taking a break from using any digital product, especially in the case of excessive use
the digital divide: inequality being created between those who understand and have access to Internet and those who don't
digital disruption: how companies using digital technologies are disrupting and taking over from traditional providers, e.g. the Uber taxi app is taking over from licensed cabs in many cities worldwide
the digital economy: money made through online trading
digital footprint: all the details you leave of yourself online and in your mobile phone usage
digital hermits: people who adopt a digital-free lifestyle
digital literacy: ability to use software and hardware and understand aspects of digital content
digital natives: young people who have grown up with and have a natural understanding of digital products and social media

Optional extra activity Ask students to look up *digital* in dictionaries or online and find out how many collocations they can find.

UNDERSTANDING VOCABULARY

Synonyms

Aim
to check students' understanding and use of synonyms, and how they collocate differently

2 Read through the information in the box as a class. Ask students to work individually to choose the correct option. Let students compare answers in pairs before discussing as a class.

Answers

1 peril	6 menace
2 threat	7 risk
3 hazard	8 danger
4 menace	9 risk
5 threat	10 danger

Background language notes for teachers

grave danger = very serious
fraught with danger = full of danger (also *fraught with concern, difficulties, ambiguities*)

3 Ask students to work individually to underline the whole phrase. Let students compare answers in pairs before discussing as a class.

Answers
1 ignore ... at your peril
2 under threat from
3 poses a real health hazard
4 combat the menace of
5 poses a great threat to
6 (some kind of) menace to society
7 run the risk of
8 is fraught with danger
9 putting yourself at risk
10 is in serious danger of

4 Ask students to discuss the statements in pairs. This activity aims to personalise the new language and collocations, and get students to use them. You could choose one of the sentences to discuss in more detail as a class.

LISTENING

Aim
to practise listening and note-taking; to listen for specific information

5 ✪ 57 Give students a moment to read the situation and task.
• Play the recording. Ask students to listen and take notes.

6 Let students compare answers in pairs before discussing in feedback.

Answers
Internet addiction
created a generation of idiots
plagiarism
young people 'over-sharing'
dangers of online profile causing problems for you in the future
spammers / fraudsters

🎧 57

**M = Michael (presenter), J = Joyce,
O = Oliver, N = Nigel**

M: Now I'm guessing that many of you – like me – may have raised an eyebrow this week when you heard that kids as young as eight are receiving treatment for Internet addiction. And this is a problem that's surely set to get worse, of course, given that it's just been announced that over 40% of the world's population – a whopping three billion people – is now online. Three billion! Can you believe it? And that's why today we're turning our attention yet again to the World Wide Web – and asking whether the Internet is becoming more of a curse than a blessing. As ever, if the show's to work, we need you to call up and tell us what's on your mind. And I think we have our first caller on line one. It's Joyce in Crawley. Joyce, hello.

J: Oh hello, Michael. Thank you. Yes, erm, well, I've been a university lecturer for some 40 years now and I'm on the verge of retiring. I'm due to stop work in the summer and I must say I'm awfully glad about it.

M: Why's that, then, Joyce?

J: Well, to be frank, I think the Internet has created a generation of idiots and I honestly don't think things are likely to get any better in the foreseeable future.

M: Well, that's a fairly bleak appraisal. What is it about the Web that particularly concerns you, Joyce?

J: Well, the main thing is simply the ease of access it provides. I'm obviously not opposed to people being able to access useful information, but most students nowadays have lost the ability to construct their own essays or think their own way through a question. They simply cut and paste and hand things in, which appals me.

M: So, plagiarism, in short?

J: Exactly. But you try telling them that!

M: Well, luckily, I don't have to, Joyce, and on the plus side, you won't have to either for that much longer. Next up, I think it's Oliver phoning in from Barnstable. Are you there, Oliver?

O: Yes, Michael. Can you hear me?

M: Loud and clear, Oliver. What's on your mind?

O: Well, what worries me, Michael, is the fact there's no delete button on the Web.

M: OK. You're going to have to expand on that a bit, Oliver. I'm not quite sure I know what you mean.

O: Well, look. People like me, what you might call digital natives, right. We've grown up with the Internet and sharing online is a normal part of how we live. Most young people don't think twice about what they share when – and I just think that's bound to cause problems in the long run.

M: You think there's some over-sharing going on then, Oliver?

O: I do, yeah, and I think people are pretty naïve too. You know, they'll post up crazy photos from parties and fire off comments in the heat of the moment and just assume that they can delete it all later.

M: Well, there are firms that can tidy up your online profile these days, aren't there?

O: Yeah, sure, to a degree ... but you can never really know if someone's copied what you've posted, can you? And things can easily come back to haunt you later on.

M: And you're saying the chances of people avoiding all this are pretty slim?

O: To put it mildly, yes. People need to wake up – and wise up, really.

M: Sound advice, I'd say. Next up is Nigel, in Manchester. Hello.

N: Hello there, Michael. Nice to be with you. Long-time listener here. What I wanted to say was it's time we got tough and cracked down more on the Web.

M: And how do you propose we do that, then?

N: Well, if it were up to me, I'd arrest anyone caught looking at banned websites. I mean, they must know who these people are, mustn't they, the government?

M: That's a huge online policing presence you're suggesting there, Nigel, and in all likelihood, most offenders are actually pretty harmless when it comes down to it.

N: Yeah, OK, but maybe we should make an example out of one or two people, then, you know. Hit them with the toughest sentences we can. Like all the spammers and online fraudsters, and so on. Do that and the odds are you'll put others off.

M: Or do that and there's a distinct possibility you'll end up involved in a legal dispute about appropriate punishments, I would've thought, to be honest.

7 🎧 **57** Play the recording again. Ask students to listen and note answers. Organise students into pairs to discuss and check answers. In feedback, elicit brief answers.

Answers
1 kids addicted at eight years old, 40% of world population online
2 Students have lost their ability to construct an essay and just cut and paste, basically engaging in plagiarism.
3 He is one himself. They are people who have grown up with the Internet.
4 His main concern is with young people 'over-sharing' and the danger of online profiles causing problems for young people in the future.
5 He'd arrest anyone caught looking at banned websites.
6 It would require a huge online policing presence, and most offenders are probably pretty harmless.
7 He'd make an example of one or two people to put others off.
8 The possibility of ending up involved in a legal dispute about appropriate punishments.

8 Organise the class into groups of four or five to discuss the questions.
• As students speak, go round and monitor, and note down any interesting pieces of language you hear.
• At the end, look at good language that students used, and language students didn't quite use correctly during

the activity. Show students better ways of saying what they were trying to say. You could write some useful new phrases on the board with gaps and ask the whole class to complete the sentences.

GRAMMAR Talking about the future

Aim
to check students' understanding of how to use various verb and noun structures to talk about the future

9 Read through the information in the box as a class.
• Ask students to complete the sentences individually. Monitor and notice how well students understand how to use these patterns.

10 🔊 58 Organise students into pairs to compare their ideas in Exercise 9.
• Play the recording so that students can listen and check their answers.
• In feedback, elicit the students' answers and discuss any problems. They can check their ideas and answers using the Grammar reference on page 184.

> **Answers**
> 1 's, set to get   6 verge
> 2 's to work   7 chances
> 3 'm due to stop   8 likelihood
> 4 are likely to get   9 odds
> 5 bound to cause   10 possibility

> 🔊 58
> 1 This is a problem that's surely set to get worse.
> 2 If the show's to work, we need you to call up and tell us what's on your mind.
> 3 I'm due to stop work in the summer.
> 4 I honestly don't think things are likely to get any better in the foreseeable future.
> 5 I just think that's bound to cause problems in the long run.
> 6 I'm on the verge of retiring.
> 7 And you're saying the chances of people avoiding all this are pretty slim?
> 8 In all likelihood, most offenders are actually pretty harmless.
> 9 Hit them with the toughest sentences we can. Do that and the odds are you'll put others off.
> 10 Do that and there's a distinct possibility you'll end up involved in a legal dispute.

 Students complete Exercise 1 in the Grammar reference on page 184.

> **Answers to Exercise 1, Grammar reference**
> 1 distinct / ~~probable~~ (It is probable that you'll experience ...)
> 2 about to be / on the verge of being
> 3 due to / ~~just about to~~ (just about to = more immediate and not usually with time phrase)
> 4 slim / slight (both mean small)

5 probable / likely
6 ~~chances~~ / likelihood (chances doesn't fit the phrase – collocation = in all likelihood)
7 set to announce / on the brink of announcing (though first is far more common)
8 high / ~~likely~~ (there are some examples on Google, but very unusual compared to high / low odds)
9 bound to / ~~set to~~ (set to suggests readiness so it doesn't work here when it is out of your control like this)
10 is to / ~~will~~ (will isn't usually used in the If clause of a conditional sentence. Use present forms with future meaning.)

11 Do the first as an example in open class. Then ask students to work individually to rewrite the sentences before comparing with a partner.

> **Answers**
> 1 The situation is bound to deteriorate.
> 2 It's (very) likely that our jobs will be at risk.
> 3 They're on the verge of finalising the deal.
> 4 Gamble online and in all likelihood you will lose.
> 5 The work is due to be finished by May.
> 6 Inflation is set to rise above 10% next month.

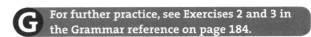 **For further practice, see Exercises 2 and 3 in the Grammar reference on page 184.**

> **Answers to Exercise 2, Grammar reference**
> 1 of   5 for
> 2 in   6 of
> 3 for   7 In
> 4 on
>
> **Answers to Exercise 3, Grammar reference**
> 1 is to be overseen by
> 2 is sure to damage
> 3 on the brink of finding
> 4 are about to be
> 5 success is bound to
> 6 are highly likely to rise

SPEAKING

Aim
to provide communicative speaking practice in a personalised activity

12 Organise the class into groups of four or five and ask them to choose a topic for discussion.
• Ask each group to select a host. Tell the host (Student A) to find their information page (page 197), then give them time to read the file, and to think of what to say. Ask the other students to prepare points.
• Give students four or five minutes to prepare ideas. Monitor and help with vocabulary and encourage students to make brief notes to help them when they talk.

13 When students are ready, ask them to roleplay the phone-in programme. Monitor and notice errors and examples of good language use which you could focus on in feedback.
• In feedback, ask different groups to tell the class what they discussed.
• Once you have fed back on content, look at good language that students used, and language students didn't quite use correctly during the activity. Show students better ways of saying what they were trying to say. You could write some useful new phrases on the board with gaps and ask the whole class to complete the sentences.

Web research activity
• The Internet is full of lists. Ask students to find a list connected with dangers or risks. For example, they could research the top ten dangers in the home, the top ten most dangerous cities or the top ten holiday health risks.
• In the next lesson, ask students to present their lists and say which dangers they agree or disagree with and why.

Aim
to find out about the long-necked women of Myanmar; to improve students' ability to follow and understand fast speech in a video extract; to practise fast speech and to improve pronunciation, stress and intonation

1 Lead in to the topic by asking students to look at the photo and say what they can see. Organise the class into pairs or small groups to discuss the questions. Elicit students' ideas and write up interesting ideas or language on the board. Encourage students to justify their opinions and argue their cases.

Answers
Although it may not be immediately obvious to your students, the photo shows a row of public payphones in front of a large poster. It may well be at an airport or railway or bus station.
Work with what students say, but the most likely explanation is that the photo was taken somewhere in south-east Asia (Thailand or Burma), and the purpose is to advertise the country or region.

Culture notes

The 'long neck women' are Kayan people, originally from Burma (or Myanmar as it is also called). However, some hill tribes also live in northern Thailand, having fled there in the 1980s and 1990s after coming into conflict with Burma's military regime. There has been criticism of the Thai villages as they are exploited by people selling tours to go and look at the long-necked villagers. Tribes of long neck people are actually quite rare among the Kayan. The majority became Roman Catholic in the nineteenth century.

2 [38] Give students time to read through the questions. As students watch the first part of the video, they should note answers. Let them compare their notes in pairs before discussing as a class.

Answers
1 tattoos, implants, piercings, hair colouring, skin colouring
2 the remote Thai-Burmese border
3 The brass rings they wear around the necks are valuable. They need armed guards to protect from bandits who might try to steal the rings.

3 Organise the class into pairs to prepare questions. As they discuss, monitor and note down the six most common questions. If some pairs had problems preparing questions you could have a brief feedback session in which the class share their questions. That way all the students will be prepared for the next task.

4 ⏵38 Play the second part of the video and ask students to note answers to any of their questions. Let them compare answers in pairs before discussing as a class.

5 Organise the class into pairs. Ask students to look at the words and numbers first to see what they remember based on their first viewing. As students watch the second part of the video again, they should add to and correct their ideas. Let them compare answers in pairs before discussing as a class.

Answers
1 Mar Nang is the matriarch of the hill tribe – the female leader of the community.
2 Mar Nang's coil is long enough to form 25 concentric rings – it's over twelve inches high.
3 To outsiders, the rings may appear to be shackles of slavery or suffering.
4 The heavy coils are made from solid brass rods.
5 Neck pieces can weigh as much as a standard car tyre.
6 They start off by adding just a few rings, then as each extra coil is added, they start pushing the clavicle (the bone from your shoulder to the bottom of your neck) down – and then the ribs are squeezed and flattened.
7 Folklore says a women's neck will break if coils are removed and it's unsupported. (Mar Nang has proved this is not true many times.)
8 Today a nineteen-year-old comes to Mar Nang complaining about her sixteen rings. Mar Nang will take all the rings off and refit them.

6 This exercise offers students the chance to relate the topic of the video to their own experiences, ideas, opinions and general knowledge.
• Give students time to read the questions. Put them into groups to discuss them.
• Monitor and help with ideas, facts and vocabulary.
• When most students have finished, stop the class and give some feedback, either by sharing some ideas you heard with the whole class or by asking students to correct or fill in gaps in sentences you've written on the board, based on what you heard students saying.

Understanding fast speech

7 ⏵39 Play the recording. Students listen and write what they hear. Let them compare in pairs.

8 ⏵40 Students listen again to a slower version to check and improve what they have written. Let them compare answers in pairs.

9 Students check what they wrote in File 10 on page 189 of the Student's Book. Encourage them to practise saying the extract.

Video script ⏵38

Narrator: Tattoos, implants, piercings, hair colour, skin colour. As a species, we're either trying to stand out or to fit in. The changes we make to our bodies don't just define ourselves – they define the very culture we live in. So what interpretation of beauty would lead these women to extend their necks beyond recognition?
On the remote Thai-Burmese border local women seek thatch grasses for their village. Their world is as beautiful as it is dangerous – a haven to smugglers and outlaws. An armed guard watches for bandits – ready to protect them – because even though they're poor, these women carry one item of great value: their brass neck rings.

Mar Nang: I started to wear the rings when I was five years old.

Narrator: 51-year-old Mar Nang is the matriarch of a hill tribe known as the Kayan. To the outside world they are the 'Long Necks' – wearers of shining rings of brass that disfigure and deform the bodies of those who wear them.

Mar Nang: Feeling pain and feeling some discomfort is part of living.

Narrator: Mar Nang is one of the longest of the Long Necks. Her coil is long enough to form 25 concentric rings over twelve inches high.

Mar Nang: I had all these rings when I was sixteen years old, I didn't want to put on any more.

Narrator: Kayan women have worn these bonds of brass for centuries. To outsiders, they might appear shackles of slavery or suffering. The heavy brass coils are fashioned from solid brass rods. Neck pieces can weigh up to 22 pounds, the same as a standard car tyre. Mar Nang has felt the weight of hers for 46 years, and even though she and the Kayan women are known as 'Long Necks', their coils do not actually extend the spine.
An initial coil of about five rings weighing nearly four and a half pounds presses down on the shoulders. As each new coil is added the extra weight compresses the body, pushing the clavical down, squeezing and flattening the ribs until the shoulders fall away, giving the appearance of an elongated neck.
Folklore says a woman's neck, long supported, can break if the collar is removed. Village matriarch Mar Nang has challenged that legend many times removing and repairing the neck pieces of longneck women. Today nineteen-year-old Mar Bling has come to Mar Nang complaining of discomfort with her heavy sixteen-ring brass coil. Mar Nang will readjust and refit it for her.

Mar Bling: At first it's painful, but it's worth the initial pain because it's beautiful.

Narrator: Mar Bling has adapted to years of washing, sleeping and eating wearing her metal collar.

Mar Bling: Sleeping and washing is difficult, but you get used to it.

Narrator: She hasn't seen her own neck in over five years and wonders what she will find.

Mar Bling: I haven't seen my neck for a long time. Today is a big occasion and I'm very excited.

REVIEW 8
Student's Book page 149

Aim
to consolidate vocabulary and grammar from
Units 15 and 16

Answers
1

1 likelihood / probability	6 capable
2 chances / odds	7 slim
3 peril	8 to
4 threat	9 in
5 for	10 of

2

1 congratulate you on passing
2 unaware of the existence of
3 is fraught with danger
4 on the verge of becoming
5 a fine line between genius
6 in the medium / long term

3

1 in thinking	4 due
2 it's likely	5 risk
3 to	6 of which

4
top half: bangles (on your wrist), bushy (hair), lapel
(on jacket), wig (on head), shades (sunglasses), sleeve
(of shirt / jacket)
bottom half: flares (jeans), flats (shoes), sturdy (shoes),
trainers (shoes), wedges (shoes), sandals (shoes)

5

1 h	3 g	5 a	7 c
2 f	4 b	6 d	8 e

6

1 in
2 in
3 over
4 off
5 out

7

1 insufficient
2 non-compliance
3 liability
4 consciousness
5 negligence, compensation

8

1 scruffy	7 knock, out
2 frayed	8 came to
3 fancy	9 gash
4 highlighted	10 pouring
5 knee-length	11 top
6 heels	12 ripped

AN INTRODUCTION TO WRITING IN *OUTCOMES*

In this section we will look at two broad reasons for writing in a foreign language: to practise and play, and for the real world. We explain what we mean by them and how they may differ in teaching, tasks and feedback.

Practice and play The first reason for writing in a foreign language is simply to practise new language, experiment and learn more English. Writing may have significant benefits for students learning English. In contrast to speaking, students have time to plan what they want to say; they can look words up in a dictionary, they can check and rewrite grammar and they may be more able to notice how English works. That might then give benefits in terms of their overall competence in English. Writing for the purpose of practice and play does not depend on any particular genre or standard organisation in writing; it could be short sentences, paragraphs, dialogues, etc.; it could be about anything the student wants or it could be on a theme the teacher chooses; it could be random connections of sentences – true or imagined. Some grammar and vocabulary tasks in the Student's Book are of this nature, with students having to complete sentences using their own ideas. Below are some more tasks. The ideas focus on revising language, but it doesn't have to be so. Here are some ideas your students could try:

- Write a diary about your day, trying to include new words or structures that you've learnt.
- Write five to ten lines of English every day about anything you like.
- Write every day / week about a story you saw or read about in the news.
- Write a poem or story using a new word you've learnt.
- Write a conversation based on one you had with someone during the class.
- Write an imagined conversation with someone you know based on a topic you've studied.
- Write an imagined conversation that takes place in a particular place.

As these kinds of writing tasks are unconnected to any particular genre, they require no 'teaching' or preparation, and can be set at any time. In terms of feedback, you may want to simply write a personal response to what the student wrote such as, *This really made me laugh* or *That's interesting*. Alternatively, you could engage in a dialogue with the student by asking them genuine questions, which they answer in writing. You may want to correct aspects of the key structure or words that they practised, or use common errors from different students as a way to re-teach language in class. However, we feel correction should be kept to a minimum with these kinds of texts. The aim is not assessment – it is to encourage students, to engage with them and get them to play with language.

For the real world The second broad reason for writing is that students need to write a specific kind of text for an assessment or for a 'real life' task such as sending an email. These texts are generic in some way. They often have specific vocabulary (including large chunks or expressions) or grammar connected with them. They also have rules about the way they are presented, how they are paragraphed and ordered and other aspects of discourse. The problem for foreign learners of English is that these rules of discourse might be different in their languages. Unlike speaking, where listeners might accept errors because they can see other things to help interpret the message, with writing a reader may misunderstand a message or even be offended when the rules or conventions of a genre are broken. For this reason, students need careful preparation for writing such texts, and feedback should be more thorough.

The writing units in the Student's Book aim to provide this careful preparation. They are based on genres commonly tested in international exams such as PET, Cambridge First and IELTS, or on functional writing tasks we may perform at work or when studying in an English-speaking context.

WHAT'S IN *OUTCOMES* WRITING UNITS?

Each double-page spread teaches a different style of writing. You can follow them in any order or do them after every two units in the main Student's Book. The units contain:

Speaking The units aim to be interactive. Speaking activities provide a warmer, relate to the topic, discuss the text types or may be part of planning for writing.

Writing The writing sections present model texts. While there may be some basic comprehension questions around these, the main focus is noticing useful language for the genre and how the texts are organised.

Key words This section focuses on words / expressions which link sentences and clauses and give texts coherence. They follow a similar pattern to grammar exercises, with a short explanation or guided questions and a controlled practice.

Vocabulary and grammar There are often short grammar or vocabulary sections if there is a close relation to the text type. Note there's *no* link to the Grammar reference.

Practice This is a task for students to write a similar kind of text to the one they looked at in **Writing** and try to incorporate some of the other language they have learnt in the unit. This section can be set as homework or be done in class. Doing the practice in class can be interactive, particularly if using a 'process writing' approach.

Process writing

Process writing approaches focus on the fact that good writers often go through several stages to produce a good piece of writing. They may:

- brainstorm ideas
- write a plan
- write a draft
- discuss their draft with someone
- write a second draft
- put it through a spell-checker
- have corrections made by someone
- write the final draft.

Obviously, we don't always go through these stages when we write, but in the case of our students, having different stages and allowing for more than one draft gives more opportunity for teaching and learning. In fact, brainstorming and planning stages are often included in **Practice** or at some other stage of the lesson. However, there is no reason why any of the stages above shouldn't be done in pairs in class. Another way you might want to incorporate a process approach is to give the **Practice** task for homework *before* they do the actual writing lesson. They then rewrite their work in light of what they learn.

Marking and feedback

There are a number of options available to teachers to mark and give feedback on students' writing.

Using symbols You can mark essays using symbols above the inappropriate word or grammar. Here are some examples:

- t = wrong tense
- wf = wrong word form (e.g. noun not adjective)
- col = wrong collocation (e.g. the noun is the right meaning but doesn't go with the verb)
- voc = you have the wrong word (it makes no sense here)
- prep = you need a different preposition
- pl = plural is wrong or should be plural
- sp = wrong spelling
- wo = the word order is wrong
- art = the article is wrong or absent

The idea of doing this is to make students notice their errors and try to find answers. You could do this as pairwork in class. It may help them to become more aware of their common errors and edit their own work more carefully. The difficulty is that mistakes don't fit neatly into categories and students may still get the language wrong. You should mark the text again.

Re-formulation You may simply want to cross out and rewrite things that are 'wrong' in the text. This may have the advantage of teaching students the correct language (though note they may still be unclear *why* it was wrong). It may also be time-consuming for you and demoralising for students if they see lots of crossing out.

In this case – and indeed with all cases of teacher feedback – you need to strike a balance. At Advanced, you will expect a high degree of accuracy. Students should also be able to deal with a variety of text types, employing informal and formal registers. Students should also be able to structure their writing and use language appropriate to their readers.

Content and structure When you mark the texts you could ignore 'grammar' and individual vocabulary mistakes and focus only on whether the writing answers the question and is organised well. You simply write comments on the writing or at the end. This is often quicker for you, the teacher.

Marking this way trains students to appreciate the importance of these aspects of writing over basic 'accuracy'. Readers in fact will often ignore mistakes if the overall structure of the text is clear and the content is relevant, logical and / or interesting.

However, students will want to know if their writing is correct unless you clearly warn them beforehand that you'll only deal with content and structure.

Peer correction Students can also give feedback. Get them to read each other's writing and evaluate the texts and / or suggest changes. To do this they really need a 'mark scheme', this could be a list of statements they tick or adapt such as:

- *I enjoyed this.*
- *I wanted to know more about …*
- *I didn't understand the bit about …*
- *You used some words / grammar I didn't know how to use.*

Another way is to give them marking criteria from an established source such as the Cambridge First exam. Check they're not too difficult for your students.

The advantage of peer correction is that it's interactive and based on genuine readers' responses. It's also easy on the teacher! However, it is not so good for dealing with language, apart from general statements, as students may not trust each other's judgement – often with good reason! However, it is a useful stage and may save you time by reducing mistakes or inconsistencies before you come to mark the texts.

WRITING AND PORTFOLIOS

Whichever way you choose to correct the students' texts, we suggest you get students to rewrite them. This would guarantee that the students focus on their errors and produce an improved text which they could then keep in a portfolio. Portfolios of work are recommended by the Common European Framework of Reference (CEFR) and can provide evidence of students' progress and level.

WRITING LESSONS 1–8 ANSWER KEY

1 DESCRIBING VISUAL DETAIL
Student's Book pages 150–151

2
1 by population (not by area)
2 rural to urban (not the other way round)
3 chart is 2012–2030 not 2014–2030
4 not true that the global urban population is expected to rise 25%
5 population of Dhaka predicted to rise by 60% (not 90%)
6 majority (not minority) of cities are on the coast or major rivers

4
1 the vast majority
2 almost a fifth
3 more than halved, fourfold
4 four out of five, slightly higher
5 a tiny percentage
6 a significant minority

5
1 By 2025, the population is projected to rise to 15 million.
2 In the next 20 years, the rural population is predicted to fall.
3 African cities are expected to grow rapidly over the next few years.
4 China is forecast to become the world's largest economy in the next ten years.

7
1 The government donates 0.6% of GDP as aid, the bulk of which goes to countries in Africa.
2 There were 2,650 fatalities from car accidents last year, the vast majority of which were caused by driver error.
3 The city has around 200,000 inhabitants, of whom 25,000 are students.
4 There was a significant fall in crime in the last decade, a large part of which was put down to rising living standards.
5 The survey interviewed 950 people altogether, most of whom were 18–25 years old.

2 BUILDING AN ARGUMENT
Student's Book pages 152–153

6
1 Indeed
2 as such
3 such
4 While
5 Furthermore
6 however
7 Firstly
8 Secondly
9 In short
10 otherwise

8
1 After much questioning, he was eventually forced to admit that there was indeed something wrong.
2 There are those in society who do not pay sufficient attention to their own health. Indeed, many actively abuse it.
3 Following repeated accusations, it was later proven that the test results had indeed been falsified.
4 The final results of the experiment were very strange indeed.
5 Putting such a theory into practice would be hard. Indeed, you might say almost impossible.
6 Cultural identities in any society vary so widely as to make the extraction of common features very difficult indeed.

3 REVIEWS
Student's Book pages 154–155

2
1 Based + set
2 rhyme + collection
3 album + encores
4 sets + choreography
5 abstract + sculptures
6 production + plot
7 technique + partner
8 prose + multi-layered
9 orchestration + role
10 symphony + finale

3
1 see films at the cinema
2 read poetry
3 go to small gigs
4 see musicals
5 go to exhibitions
6 see plays at the theatre
7 go to the ballet
8 read novels
9 go to the opera
10 go to big concerts

6
1 b   2 d   3 f   4 e   5 a   6 c

4 DESCRIBING PROCESSES
Student's Book pages 156–157

3
1 parabolic troughs
2 heat exchanger
3 generator

4 turbine
5 cooling tower
6 supplementary gas-powered heaters

4

1 whereby
2 thus
3 meanwhile
4 As
5 which

7

1 Plastic is removed from the rubbish manually.
2 The pipes are insulated with foam to minimise heat loss.
3 The final product is screened for impurities.
4 The tea leaves are categorised into different grades according to size and quality.
5 Nothing is discarded during the process, to maximise efficiency.
6 Potential jury members are selected at random from the electoral roll.
7 The parts are assembled in a central plant.
8 The final manuscript is proofread for spelling mistakes and other errors.
9 The oranges are boxed and loaded onto lorries.
10 The turbines are powered by forcing water through them.
11 Microbes are used to break down the oil into droplets.
12 They only take payment after the order is shipped from the warehouse.

9

1 whereby
2 thereby
3 whereby, thereby
4 whereby

5 COVERING LETTERS
Student's Book pages 158–159

4

1 am writing
2 as
3 would
4 having spent
5 worked
6 which
7 put
8 all
9 should
10 hearing

6

1 arranged
2 promoting
3 advised
4 achieved
5 conducted
6 dealt with
7 implementing
8 diagnosed
9 devised
10 budgeted
11 negotiated
12 represented

8

1 Please do not hesitate to contact me should you require further information.
2 References are available on request, should you require them.
3 Should any vacancies become available, please contact me at the earliest opportunity.

4 After 60 days you can retake the test should you wish to do so.
5 Please phone to make an appointment should you wish to discuss this matter further.

9

1 Feel free to get in touch if you want more information.
2 I've got references if you need them.
3 Get in touch with me as soon as possible if any jobs come up.
4 You can do the test again after a couple of months if you want to.
5 Phone and make an appointment if you want to talk any more about this.

6 MAGAZINE ARTICLES
Student's Book pages 160–161

3

1 photo 3

4

2 Paragraphs end at *Museum* and *maintenance*.
   paragraph 1 – introduces inventor and invention
   paragraph 2 – describes how he came to invent the cat's eye
   paragraph 3 – talks about applications of cat's eye and compares it with other inventions
3 a I believe Percy Shaw is a great inventor and his cat's eye should be displayed in the Design Museum.
   b ... but how many of these were really invented by one man?
   c It made its inventor millions of pounds, yet few know his name.
   d Their inventors 'stood on the shoulders of giants' ...
   e ... telephones, cars, computers, etc. ...
   f *yet few know his name* – sentence 2, *Surely, therefore, Percy Shaw* ... – last sentence, *Besides, few inventions can* ... – last sentence but one

5

1 There was enormous interest in the new device, yet sales were sluggish.
2 It was cheap to produce. Besides, it was beautiful to look at. / Besides being cheap to produce, it was beautiful to look at.
3 Surely this is the greatest achievement of the 21st century so far.
4 Some may argue that many others were working on the problem, but surely his was the biggest and most decisive contribution.
5 The train was fast and comfortable, and besides, it was the cheapest option.
6 He made millions from his invention, yet he died in poverty.

6

1 little
2 Little, much
3 A few, little
4 little, many, few
5 much, many, few

7 APPLYING FOR FUNDING
Student's Book pages 162–163

3
1 give + realise
2 allow + benefit
3 raise + feed back
4 devote + forge
5 facilitate + carry out
6 communicate + attracts

7
1 enrol on
2 trust
3 enhancing
4 stay abreast
5 optimise
6 do not hesitate to

8
1 c   2 e   3 b   4 a   5 d

8 GIVING INFORMATION
Student's Book pages 164–165

4
1 Housing   5 entering
2 Founded   6 Walking
3 Situated   7 featuring
4 Following

5
1 Entering the museum, we ...
2 Walking round the museum, I ...
3 Removed from Greece at the start of the 19th century, the Elgin Marbles ...
4 Being redecorated, the galleries ...
5 Not having long before closing time, we ...
6 Being a regular visitor to the city, I'm ...
7 Being about ten miles outside of town, the museum ...
8 A new law was introduced about ten years ago, resulting in all entrance fees being scrapped.
9 Visiting the museum during the morning, you will find it much less crowded.
10 The guide, pretending not to hear her questions, carried on with the tour.

6
1 d   2 c   3 g   4 b   5 f   6 a   7 e

GRAMMAR REFERENCE ANSWER KEY

1 CITIES
Student's Book pages 166–167

Perfect forms

Exercise 1
1 a haven't called
  b don't call
2 a was done up
  b has been done up
3 a had been struck
  b was struck
4 a will have changed
  b will change
5 a consult
  b have consulted
6 a was / were here (*was* is more common)
  b had been
7 a Having spent
  b Spending
8 a underwent
  b had undergone

Exercise 2
1 will have left by
2 had never seen anything
3 having been there recently
4 had been initiated
5 people had not been evacuated
6 to have improved

2 RELATIONSHIPS
Student's Book pages 167–168

Would

Exercise 1
1 would completely agree with you
2 would not say he was / would say he was not
3 would not accept any of
4 would not get involved
5 he would not bitch about people
6 I would kick him out
7 would not imagine I would get / buy // would imagine I will not buy / get
8 I would expect it to

Exercise 2
1 correct
2 I often got into trouble at school just because I ~~would have~~ **had** really long hair.
3 correct
4 My parents wish we ~~would live~~ **lived** a bit closer to them.

5 I wouldn't be here if I ~~wouldn't have~~ **hadn't** had the surgery.
6 correct
7 Seriously, I wish my brother **would** shut up sometimes.
8 correct
9 It doesn't surprise me. I knew ~~he'll~~ **he'd** say that! He's so predictable!
10 correct

3 CULTURE AND IDENTITY
Student's Book pages 168–169

Cleft sentences

Exercise 1
1 it, that
2 was, way, that / which
3 did, suggest, what, is
4 thing, me, that
5 reason, he, happened, was

Exercise 2
1 frustrates + lack
2 upsets + seeing
3 disturbs + stance
4 drives + way
5 concerns + number
6 worrying + level
7 angered + the fact
8 amazes + amount

Exercise 3
1 surprised me was how cosmopolitan the city is
2 disturbs me is how nationalistic he can be
3 concerns me is the growing wealth gap
4 I find scary / scares me is the alarming rate that the whole society is ageing (or how fast society is ageing)
5 makes me angry / angers me is the way people assume I must love football just because I'm Brazilian

4 POLITICS
Student's Book pages 169– 171

Conditionals 1

Exercise 1
1 don't
2 bound / sure / likely / going
3 would
4 should (or could)
5 never (or not), would
6 puts
7 knew, don't

8 be, was / were
9 'd, didn't (or 'll, don't)
10 couldn't / wouldn't, had (or don't, 's)
11 does, will (or did, would)
12 would, did

Exercise 2

1 Unless they win / have / get popular support
2 provided they do not spend / provided it does not cost
3 whether you like it or
4 Supposing an accident happens / happened (or *Supposing there was / were an accident*)
5 as / so long as the economy
6 or things / the situation will get
7 Assuming (the) opinion polls are

Conditionals 2

Exercise 1

1 could've / would've won, had changed
2 would've voted, didn't like
3 might / would be, hadn't been mixed up
4 wouldn't be, hadn't made
5 hadn't given, might not / wouldn't be
6 needed, would be / was, had, would go

Exercise 2

1 a, b, d   2 a, d, e   3 a, c, e   4 a, c, e

5 GOING OUT, STAYING IN
Student's Book pages 171–172

Noun phrases

Exercise 1

1 Joel Riley gives a talk.
2 Solitary retreat is explored in this book.
3 The parents are seeking damages.

Exercise 2
Suggested answer
John Moffit, the 37-year-old award-winning character actor from Canada, playing in his first leading role, stars in the three-hour action-packed road movie *The Dying* based on the book by Tom Daley.

Exercise 3

1 Visit the awe-inspiring cathedral designed by the architect Antonio Gaudi.
2 I read a fascinating article in the paper by the novelist Anne Tyler.
3 The exhibitions held in the centre are accompanied by workshops suitable for all ages.
4 There is a wealth of exhibits on show, dating back thousands of years.

Exercise 4

1 The six-week course provides guidelines for quick and effective weight loss.
2 The supply of arms to other countries is a controversial matter / a matter of controversy.
3 There's a lot of opposition to the creation of a new car tax.

4 The building / erection / construction of the monument celebrated the centenary / 100th / 100-year anniversary of Jonson's birth/ of the birth of Jonson.

6 CONFLICT AND RESOLUTION
Student's Book page 172

Wish and *if only*

Exercise 1

1 had, didn't, would've / might've
2 was / could, could, 'll
3 had, would've, wasn't / weren't, would
4 weren't, 'll, could've
5 hadn't, wouldn't, wouldn't

Exercise 2

1 only I had not spoken / hadn't spoken
2 wish I could have gone
3 wish you were not so
4 would not fight so / as
5 we did not have to
6 If only you had told me / 'd told me

7 SCIENCE AND RESEARCH
Student's Book page 173

Passives

Exercise 1

1 has been achieved
2 was given an injection
3 is believed to be
4 had one of my wisdom teeth taken
5 be supported by
6 being / getting employed by
7 is thought to be caused by a mineral
8 to be funded by

Exercise 2

1 is being carried out
2 affected, have been vaccinated
3 undertaking, be produced
4 have been caused, being exposed
5 being extracted / having been extracted, was tested
6 set back, is hoped, prevent

8 NATURE AND NURTURE
Student's Book page 174

Auxiliaries

Exercise 1

1 am, are	6 did, Wouldn't
2 won't (*wouldn't* also possible)	7 wasn't / weren't, can't
3 does, does, doesn't	8 haven't, will
4 wouldn't	9 did, am
5 won't	

Exercise 2
1 He **does** live up to
2 I **did** like the country
3 My son **does** really enjoy
4 species **does** participate
5 Tigers **did** use to be
6 He **does** talk over you

Exercise 3
1 I did
2 It doesn't
3 We will
4 It does
5 It is

9 WORK
Student's Book pages 175–176

Continuous forms

Exercise 1
1 have drawn up, have been drawing up / am drawing up
2 were losing / had been losing, lost
3 will be dealing with / is dealing with, will deal with
4 were having / had been having, had had
5 are processed, is being processed
6 wouldn't be sitting, wouldn't sit
7 was being interviewed, was interviewed
8 show, be showing

Exercise 2
1 correct
2 He must've been doing at least 80km/h when he crashed.
3 The company took over a chain of shops last year so they own over 1,000 stores now.
4 We can't meet in the office at the moment because it's being done up.
5 We're actually supposed to be taking on some new people soon, but I don't know when.
6 Apparently, he's been seeing the boss's daughter for the last year, but the boss still doesn't know.
7 correct
8 correct
9 I'll be sorting out those files later, so if you finish early, come and give me a hand.
10 I don't know why he's being such a pain, he's not normally like that.

10 HEALTH AND ILLNESS
Student's Book pages 176–177

Modal auxiliaries

Exercise 1
1 must be, should go, could be
2 should've talked, might've seen
3 may have been murdered, won't know, can't stop
4 shouldn't have been playing, could've been, Shall (I) take, can play
5 can't be, must have, could (probably) tell
6 won't say, should tell, could get

Exercise 2
1 That must've been painful.
2 He should've stopped smoking earlier.
3 It can't be hard to do.
4 Given their resources, they couldn't have done any more to help.
5 It can't have been cheap.
6 He shouldn't have been taking those pills.
7 You may / might / could need three or four operations.
8 He must've been lying!
9 She might've / may have / could've picked up the cold from my son.
10 She should make a complete recovery after the operation.

11 PLAY
Student's Book pages 177–178

Linking words and phrases

Exercise 1
1 Otherwise
2 so as not to / in order to
3 Nonetheless, That notwithstanding
4 so / thus, On top of that / Additionally
5 unless
6 the second / as soon as
7 on account of / as a result of
8 thanks to / due to
9 Whereas / Whilst
10 as well as / not to mention
11 Even though / Although, so long as / providing

Exercise 2
1 so that he can / so that he is able to
2 in case you missed
3 I, on the other hand,
4 despite the fact (that) I
5 and on top of that
6 on account of product adaptation

12 HISTORY
Student's Book page 179

Dramatic inversion

Exercise 1
1 Not only
2 at no time
3 Never before
4 Not until
5 Nowhere else, Only

Exercise 2
1 Never before had we witnessed an international relief operation on such a scale.
2 Not until 1996 did the first women's team come into existence.
3 At no time did anyone / anybody try to prevent the tragedy.

4 Only once in our recent history have we had an honest leader.
5 Nowhere else in the world can business and pleasure be combined quite so well.
6 It was made very clear that under no circumstances were the soldiers to surrender or take their own lives.
7 Only after America rebelled against the high import taxes imposed on tea in 1773 did coffee become more popular.
8 Not only was he a poet, but he was also a military leader.
9 No sooner had the government taken office than they put up taxes.
10 Only when it became obvious that the scandal could no longer be contained did he admit his involvement in it.

Exercise 3

1 Never before **had** so few people ~~did~~ **done** so much for so many.
2 Not only **did she campaign** ~~she campaigned~~ against injustice of all kinds, but she was also the first female minister.
3 Only when a society refuses to acknowledge its past failings ~~it starts~~ **does it start** to lose its moral authority.
4 No sooner ~~the truce had~~ **had the truce** been called than peace talks began in earnest.
5 Only after tighter checks were introduced **was** corruption finally ~~was~~ tackled.
6 A law was passed saying that on no account **would** foreigners ~~would~~ be allowed into the city centre.
7 Had the missiles reached their intended target, the result would **have been** ~~be~~ disastrous.
8 ~~Such~~ **So** severe was the damage after the attack that the whole area needed to be rebuilt.
9 So sure of victory ~~he was~~ **was he** that he spent the afternoon sleeping in his tent.
10 If ~~were~~ the management **were** to agree to our terms, the strike would end tomorrow.

13 NEWS AND THE MEDIA
Student's Book pages 180–181

Patterns after reporting verbs

Exercise 1

1 cited (*state that something is ...*)
2 urged (*reiterate that everyone who could, should ...*)
3 refused (*rejected the idea of cooperating*)
4 blamed (*criticise for*)
5 announced (*notify someone*)
6 instructed (*demand someone do*)
7 pleaded (*beg for*)
8 boasting (*praise someone for*)
9 considered (*threaten to do something*)
10 warned (*criticise someone for doing something*)

Exercise 2

1 anger at the tax
2 to me that she had
3 he would have it done / it would be done
4 urged us to visit him
5 voiced / expressed concern that the situation
6 threatened to get / have me sacked
7 acknowledged that the plan was

Exercise 3

1 assurance that
2 criticism about
3 invitation to
4 announcement that they are getting married
5 confession to
6 recommendations for
7 refusal to
8 encouragement to students who want to

14 BUSINESS AND ECONOMICS
Student's Book pages 181–182

Relative clauses

Exercise 1

1 a correct
  b correct
2 a correct
  b incorrect – need to add a preposition: The company **in** which he invested all his savings went bust.
3 a incorrect – should be *whose* not *who's*
  b correct
4 a correct
  b incorrect – can't use *that* to introduce a non-defining relative clause, should be *who* here instead
5 a correct
  b incorrect – need another comma added in to enclose the non-defining clause: Taxpayers, many of whom have debts themselves**,** are paying for the banks' losses.

Exercise 2

1 We have to identify areas in which improvements can be made.
2 My boss, whose office is next to mine, heard everything.
3 In January, we borrowed €10,000, most of which has already been spent.
4 For the starting point of our study we chose 2004, the year in which our president submitted his first budget.
5 I wanted to explore the extent to which large corporations influence the economic health of nations.
6 We have over 9,000 employees, the vast majority of whom are based in China.
7 We've reached a crucial point, beyond which we cannot cut costs any further without having to lay people off.
8 The S and L bank, which was bailed out by the government and whose executives were imprisoned for fraud, has finally returned to profit.

Exercise 3

1 f Our founder was Mr Johnson, after whom the company is named.
2 e We're lucky enough to have an incredible team, without which we would never have survived this difficult year.
3 c After much research, we've come up with a prototype with which we're all very satisfied.
4 a We're conducting research into the Kazakh market, about which we currently know very little.
5 b I'd like to say thanks in particular to my boss, from whom I've learned a huge amount.
6 d Naturally, we are all influenced by the things with which we surround ourselves.

Exercise 4

1 Our founder was Mr Johnson, who the company is named after.
2 We're lucky enough to have an incredible team, which we would never have survived this difficult year without.
3 After much research, we've come up with a prototype which we're all very satisfied with.
4 We're conducting research into the Kazakh market, which we currently know very little about.
5 I'd like to say thanks in particular to my boss, who I've learned a huge amount from.
6 Naturally, we are all influenced by the things (which / that) we surround ourselves with.

15 TRENDS
Student's Book pages 182–183

Prepositions

Exercise 1

1 the game on purpose to
2 to his arrival
3 reducing costs we have enabled
4 in the long term
5 accounts for almost / nearly / just under
6 were selected / chosen at random
7 There was stiff resistance to
8 succeeded in bringing
9 on a daily basis
10 with regard to the overall design

Exercise 2

1 A number of factors have contributed **to** the trend towards small families.
2 The news that girls are **at** more risk of online negative experiences comes as no surprise.
3 We'd simply never thought it'd be necessary to take out insurance **against / for** natural disasters.
4 Reactions **to** the new trend have been very mixed so far, it must be said.
5 The magazine prides itself **on** being cutting edge.
6 She just seems to be famous **for** being famous.
7 The arrival of the miniskirt in the early 1960s symbolised a rejection **of** conservative values.
8 **On** gaining power, Napoleon introduced new dress codes in court.

Exercise 3

1 CORRECT
2 Hats were essential clothing ~~during~~ **for** centuries, but during the 20th century they fell out of fashion.
3 They have grown ~~in~~ **into** one of the biggest companies in the country.
4 It's a translation ~~of~~ **from** Arabic.
5 We sometimes have to work ~~until~~ **up to / for** seven hours without a break.
6 CORRECT
7 I somehow managed to crash ~~to~~ **into** the car in front of me.
8 We were very close. She was ~~as~~ **like** a mother to me.
9 CORRECT
10 CORRECT

16 DANGER AND RISK
Student's Book page 184

Talking about the future

Exercise 1

1 distinct / ~~probable~~ (It is probable that you'll experience …)
2 about to be / on the verge of being
3 due to / ~~just about to~~ (just about to = more immediate and not usually with time phrase)
4 slim / slight (both mean small)
5 probable / likely
6 ~~chances~~ / likelihood (chances doesn't fit the phrase – collocation = in all likelihood)
7 set to announce / on the brink of announcing (though first is far more common)
8 high / ~~likely~~ (there are some examples on google, but very unusual compared to high / low odds)
9 bound to / ~~set to~~ (set to suggests readiness so it doesn't work here when it is out of your control like this)
10 is to / ~~will~~ (will isn't usually used in the If clause of a conditional sentence. Use present forms with future meaning.)

Exercise 2

1 of
2 in
3 for
4 on
5 for
6 of
7 In

Exercise 3

1 is to be overseen by
2 is sure to damage
3 on the brink of finding
4 are about to be
5 success is bound to
6 are highly likely to rise

TESTS

GRAMMAR

1 Complete the sentences with the correct perfect forms of the verbs in brackets.

1 By the time the explorers reached the Pole, they _____ (cover) over a thousand kilometres on foot.
2 In recent years, council employees _____ (give) two separate pay rises.
3 _____ (design) the new national stadium, Ferguson then went on to design many other sports arenas.
4 By the end of the next quarter, the Treasury _____ (recover) over 30 million euros in unpaid taxes.
5 The city's commitment to art and culture in recent years _____ (recognise) across the world.
6 The building doesn't meet current standards, and that's why inspectors _____ (declare) it unsafe.
7 Jack became a successful businessman despite _____ (leave) school twenty years previously with few qualifications.
8 Although he _____ (not visit) the monument, he knew all about its history from books.
9 Before long, mankind _____ (work) out a way of building a space colony on Mars. I hope I'm still around to see it!
10 If we _____ (know) there was an exhibition on, we would have come to the gallery with you.

/ 10

2 Complete the text with the correct perfect forms of the verbs in brackets.

The old city of Montevideo

   Montevideo, the capital city of Uruguay, lies on the north-eastern bank of the Rio de la Plata. It was founded by the Spanish in 1724. Although fortifications ¹_____ (build) in the region by the Portuguese 40 years earlier, they offered no resistance to the arrival of a rival Spanish expedition. ²_____ (take) control of the region, the new settlers soon began establishing a city. By the end of the eighteenth century, Montevideo ³_____ (grow) in size to become the main naval base of the Spanish Empire in the South Atlantic. A huge wall was built around the city, which is believed by many historians to have saved the city from a catastrophic attack. The Portuguese probably would have tried to capture the city if it ⁴_____ (not be) so well-defended.
   Today, the old city of Montevideo is just one of many barrios, or districts, of a much larger city. Millions of dollars ⁵_____ (spend) in recent years on renovating the old buildings. ⁶_____ (become) a run-down area during the late twentieth century, the old city was in need of a make-over. By the end of this decade, construction companies ⁷_____ (complete) a transformation of the historical centre. They ⁸_____ (create) an attractive district full of pedestrianised streets, theatres and restaurants. Montevideo ⁹_____ (know) for its culture and beauty ever since its earliest days. It's no wonder that, since the beginning of the twentieth-century, Montevideo ¹⁰_____ (rate) as having the highest quality of life of any city in Latin America.

/ 10

VOCABULARY

3 Choose the correct word to complete the sentences.

1 The pollution from cars in the city centre is so bad that people are _____ on the fumes.
   a choking   b dropping   c crawling
2 The economy is so strong that new companies are _____ all over the country.
   a showing off   b springing up   c coming out
3 In the evening, there's an exciting _____ about the place because the bars and restaurants are popular with students.
   a trace   b buzz   c choke
4 Vandals have been fined _____ for damaging the city hall.
   a hardly   b smoothly   c heavily
5 The crime _____ in the city is awful. Thousands are mugged each year.
   a show   b amount   c rate
6 The pollution was so bad that a layer of _____ hung over the centre, and everybody had to wear masks.
   a slum   b smog   c consumption

/ 6

4 Rewrite the sentences replacing the words in italics with a phrase of emphasis or exaggeration formed using the word in brackets.

1 From this vantage point, you can see *a very long way*. (miles)

   _____

2 There were *a large number of* people waiting outside the stadium. (loads)

   _____

3 Living in such a crowded city *is comparable to* being in a sardine can. (like)

   _____

4 I've had this old T-shirt *a very long time*. (ever)

   _____

5 The outside toilet is *very dirty*. (absolutely)

   _____

6 It was *very crowded* in the nightclub. (completely)

   _____

/ 6

5 Complete the sentences using the verbs in the box in the correct form. There are two verbs you don't need.

undergo	initiate	pour	demolish	flourish
soar		impose	be neglected	

1 The local council have decided _____ the old cinema in the city centre to make way for a car park. How dare they destroy such a historic building!
2 The government intends _____ sanctions on any regime which does not accept the UN resolution.
3 During the last recession, unemployment figures _____ from 8% to 28% in some parts of the country.
4 This part of the city _____ by the authorities for decades. The lack of investment has resulted in poor housing and rising crime.
5 Last year, the city centre _____ a complete transformation. A new shopping centre was built as well as a cinema complex.
6 New businesses _____ in this positive economic atmosphere. They are all making profits.

/ 6

6 Complete the sentences with one verb from the box in the correct form which can be used in both pairs of sentences. There are two words you don't need.

calm	emerge	raise	compel	spark	grip	drug

1 a The government have _____ fears of an imminent attack by terrorists.
  b He wasn't sure, so he _____ his doubts at the meeting.
2 a This region is _____ by recession. Thousands are unemployed.
  b The nation was _____ by the soap opera. Everybody watched to find out what would happen.
3 a I felt _____ to respond to the reviewer's criticism. Why should they be allowed to be so rude?
  b Although he didn't want to speak against his friend, Jones was _____ to appear as a witness in the trial.
4 a The minister's comments _____ criticism from those he had accused of being lazy.
  b When the government banned the film, it _____ a wave of protests from people opposed to censorship.
5 a I drink herbal tea to _____ my nerves. It helps me relax.
  b Harrison tried to _____ the angry crowd by telling them that the government would listen to their demands, and take action to improve the situation.

/ 5

7 Complete the binomials in each sentence with one word.

1 Frankly, I'm sick and _____ of having to make excuses for your bad behaviour.
2 I go swimming every now and _____, but not often, I'm afraid.
3 There was a complete breakdown of law and _____ in the town.
4 We should think of how we can help ordinary working families first and _____.
5 Although there are lots of theatres, the quality of shows is a bit hit and _____. Read the reviews before you book.
6 You should think long and _____ before you take the job.
7 We went to the mountains for a bit of peace and _____.

/ 7   / 50

UNIT 2 TEST

GRAMMAR

1 Rewrite the sentences replacing the words in italics with *would* or *wouldn't* whenever possible. If not possible, write *NP*. Do not change the meaning of each sentence.

1 Jack *refused to help us* tidy up.
Jack _____ tidy up.
2 Sarah *used to live* on a canal boat.
Sarah _____ on a canal boat.
3 I really wish we *had prepared better* for the race.
I really wish we _____ for the race.
4 I thought the film *was never going to end*. It was so boring!
I thought the film _____. It was so boring.
5 Some colleagues *used to commute* long distances before the office relocated.
Some colleagues _____ long distances before the office relocated.
6 I *advise you not to listen to* a word he says.
I _____ a word he says.
7 My car *failed to start* this morning. That's why I was late.
My car _____ this morning. That's why I was late.
8 There's a big football match on, and it's about to start. *Is it OK if I switched the TV on?*
There's a big football match on, and it's about to start. _____ if I switch the TV on?
9 I'm glad you've decided to shave off your moustache. *You'll look* much better without it.
I'm glad you've decided to shave off your moustache. _____ much better without it.
10 I wish you *didn't insist on smoking* all the time.
I wish you _____ all the time.

/ 10

2 Complete the text with the correct form of the verbs in brackets. Use *would* whenever possible.
David Bowie
Many ¹_____ (describe) David Bowie as the most iconic pop star of the 1970s. Despite growing up in London, he ²_____ (be) a fan of American musicians like Bob Dylan in his early career. He ³_____ (aspire) to be a folk musician, and his early songs ⁴_____ (influence) by this genre. In the 1960s, he realised that he ⁵_____ (have to) change his real name, which was David Jones, to something different. This was because the vocalist of the pop group The Monkees ⁶_____ (name) Davy Jones. He chose Bowie – after the famous knife. Few ⁷_____ (imagine), back in 1969, when he ⁸_____ (have) his first hit with Space Oddity, that he ⁹_____ (go) on to influence not just the music industry, but the world of art and fashion. More than that, he changed the lives of millions by challenging concepts of gender politics and identity. It is fair to say that, without Bowie, who died in 2016, the late twentieth century ¹⁰_____ (be) a much duller time.

/ 10

VOCABULARY

3 Choose the correct word to complete the sentences.
1 Personally, I find Simon terribly _____. I mean, he clearly thinks he's cleverer and more talented than anyone else.
a charming   b arrogant   c cynical
2 Susie is a real _____. I've never met anyone so lazy!
a bitchy   b slacker   c laid-back
3 I'm more than _____ to help you with the assignment. Just give me a call and we'll talk it over.
a willing   b wilful   c willed
4 I suppose I admire Henry's strong _____. It's just frustrating that his views are so different from mine.
a stubborn   b arrogance   c principles
5 Dan is a real _____! He's always telling annoying jokes and playing tricks on everybody.
a snob   b pain   c cynic

/ 5

4 Complete the sentences with one word.
1 Take no _____ of Ben. He's just being silly and wants attention. It's better to ignore him.
2 I think Jill has already _____ her mind up. She's going to study astrophysics, and there's no way you'll change her mind.
3 Amy is very ambitious. She'll do anything to _____ ahead at work.
4 You're being too serious. Come on. Lighten _____ and enjoy the party.
5 I know you're angry, but I think you should _____ down and apologise to Tom. Both of you can't be right.
6 It's important to _____ up for principles you believe in. That's why I have joined the campaign.
7 Changing the way you do things is a good way of _____ things fresh in a relationship.
8 Adele's new album may well _____ to be the best of her career so far.
9 Despite falling 30 metres down the mountainside, Clark lived to _____ the tale.
10 These days, far too many marriages end _____ divorce.

/ 10

5 Rewrite the sentences replacing the words in italics with a phrasal verb formed from the verb in brackets. Add any other words necessary. Do not change the meaning of each sentence.
1 Thomas *seems to be* the sort of guy you can rely on. (come)
Thomas _____ the sort of guy you can rely on.
2 Stephen and Paul have *had a really good relationship* ever since they were kids. (get)
Stephen and Paul have _____ ever since they were kids.
3 If you need any help in *arranging* your financial affairs, just ask me. I'm an accountant. (sort)
If you need any help in _____ your financial affairs, just ask me. I'm an accountant.

4 We *had to go through* a thorough investigation by the border police before they let us enter the country. (subject)

We were _____ a thorough investigation by the border police before they let us enter the country

5 The council are planning to *introduce* new guidelines. (bring)

The council are planning to _____ new guidelines.

6 The block of flats at the end of our street has been *demolished*. (knock)

The block of flats at the end of our street has been

_____.

7 After he was released from jail, Jonathan was able to give up crime and *return to* the straight and narrow. (get)

After he was released from jail, Jonathan was able to give up crime and _____ the straight and narrow.

8 In the end, *the most important thing is* money. (come)
In the end, it _____ money.

    / 8

6 Complete the sentences with a relationship phrase using the words in the box.

shock   ourselves   patch   eye   weight
nerves   terms

1 My sister Samantha really annoys me! She constantly gets _____.

2 We don't like strangers around here. We prefer to keep

_____.

3 Unfortunately, my boss and I rarely agree. In fact, there are hardly any issues that we see _____ on.

4 Frankly, Jack is lazy and doesn't work hard enough. He should be fired because he isn't pulling _____.

5 My wife and I are arguing a lot at the moment. Our relationship is going through _____.

6 The news of her death surprised us all. It really came

_____.

7 Arnold and Graham are so angry they refuse to say a word to each other. For days now, they haven't been

_____.

    / 7   / 50

UNIT 3   TEST

GRAMMAR

1 Complete the sentences with the words in the box.

```
main   way   why   how   did   thing   upset
find   what   place
```

1 The _____ I get really angry about is having to pay so much tax.
2 The reason _____ we left early was because we were worried about the traffic.
3 _____ was unacceptable was not what Jo said, but the way she said it.
4 All I _____ was ask if she needed anything, and she just started shouting at me.
5 The _____ I was born is still a very quiet village not far from the sea.
6 What I _____ strange about Karen's behaviour is the way she looks right past you all the time.
7 The _____ thing I wanted to say was that I thought the meeting was useful despite all our arguments.
8 What _____ me most was Emily's refusal to even say hello.
9 _____ she manages to run that place all on her own I'll never know. It's a remarkable achievement.
10 What I love most is the _____ everybody gets together and helps each other at this time of year.

/ 10

2 Rewrite the second sentence in each pair so that it has a similar meaning to the first.

1 Kids today only want to play with their mobile phones.
All _____
2 I find John's arrogance really annoying.
What I _____
3 I'd really love to go to New Zealand one day.
The place _____
4 We go to the south of France each year because my wife's parents live there.
The main reason _____
5 I find the extreme violence in his films upsetting.
It _____

/ 10

VOCABULARY

3 Choose the correct word to complete the sentences.

1 Traditions _____ a significant role in our society.
a show   b play   c make
2 It is rude to _____ the mickey out of people wearing historical costumes, even if they do look funny.
a keep   b take   c set
3 We don't mind what people do around here. Everybody's free to express themselves. It's a case of live and _____.
a let live   b stay alive   c show life
4 In traditional societies young people are expected to _____ to the demands of their families and culture.
a revolve   b interfere   c conform

5 There is much greater _____ mobility these days. We can all choose what to study, where to work, and who to marry.
a social   b sociable   c society
6 The way people relate _____ each other is important
a at   b to   c for

/ 6

4 Match the sentence starters to the sentence endings.

1 Despite being afraid of heights, Stuart climbed   a the cloth.
2 Adam and Grant managed to lay   b the dishwasher.
3 After wiping up the mess, Emma used all her strength to wring out   c the carpet.
4 The hardest thing about sewing is having to thread   d the ladder.
5 When you've finished, don't forget to flush   e the needle.
6 It's my job to load   f the toilet.

/ 6

5 Complete the sentences with the verbs in the box in the correct form. There are three words you don't need.

```
mend   spill   flood   spread   run   cover   stick   in
```

1 Place the pudding in a large bowl and _____ it with a clean cloth until it cools down.
2 If you _____ any of the liquid on carpets or rugs, don't worry as it washes out easily.
3 When we opened the washing machine, water poured out and _____ the kitchen.
4 Sylvia used to _____ her own skirts when they were torn. The family didn't have money for new clothes.
5 _____ a little glue on the back of each strip of paper and put them in the correct spaces in the album.

/ 5

6 Circle the odd word out.

1 pin   needle   pan
2 wire   screw   cable
3 sweep   wipe   stain
4 drill   mop   brush
5 rinse   soak   rip

/ 5

7 Complete the sentences with an expression using the word *thing*.

1 Don't worry. I don't mind missing the play. In fact, it's no _____ at all. I can always get tickets to go another time.
2 I'd love to go to California, but I have neither money nor free time. Chance would _____.
3 We're so sorry we broke the plates, but the party got out of hand. You know how it is. One _____ another.
4 I always go for a jog first _____ morning. It's great to be outside so early.
5 Riding my motorbike on country lanes is great fun. It's the sort of _____ to be alive.
6 Talking with your mouth full is rude where I come from. It's just not the _____ in polite society.
7 Right now, I'm so busy at work that taking a holiday is the _____ mind.
8 What with one _____, I just haven't had any time to look at the essay you sent me. Sorry.

/ 8   / 50

UNIT 4   TEST

GRAMMAR

1 Choose the correct word to introduce the condition.

1 *As long as / Even if* the weather doesn't get any better in the next few days, we'll still play the match.
2 I'd drive home now *whether / if* I could.
3 *If / Unless* I get a significant pay rise, I won't stay with this company much longer.
4 *Supposing / Providing* you could live anywhere in the world, where would you choose?
5 I'm going to close the shop later, *if / whether* you like it or not.
6 I'll put up the money for the project *supposing / assuming* you are prepared to put in the hard work to make it profitable.
7 *Otherwise / Provided* the cheque is enclosed, we will process your claim immediately.
8 You'd better write back *or / if* I'll want to know why.

`/ 8`

2 Complete the sentences with the correct form of the verb in brackets.

1 Why didn't you phone? If I _____ (know) you were coming over, I _____ (cook) something special.
2 Just think. If Paul _____ (not send) me that love poem all those years ago, I _____ (not be) married to him now.
3 Thanks for helping. What on earth _____ (I / do) if you _____ (not be) there for me every day?
4 I _____ (not stand) in this election right now if it _____ (not be) for the support of my wife for all these years.
5 I _____ (send) Danny a Valentine's Card if you _____ (remind) me to. Why didn't you tell me that yesterday was February 14th?
6 I can't see this weather affecting tomorrow's match, but, supposing the match _____ (postpone), how _____ (the club / refund) all the spectators?
7 To be honest, I feel quite fresh despite the long hike. I guess we _____ (feel) a lot more tired if Fred _____ (not pick) us up at Devil's Pike. That meant we didn't have to walk the last three kilometres in the dark.
8 The world _____ (be) so different today if those people _____ (not give) their lives to the cause of freedom.
9 We won, of course, so this question is merely hypothetical, but, if the election _____ (lost), _____ (the party leader / resign)?
10 I _____ (fail) in my bid for president if I _____ (not nominate) by all of you back in January. Thank you.
11 Unless you _____ (stop) telling lies all the time, people _____ (not take) you seriously. You really need to rethink your behaviour.
12 Supposing you _____ (give) a million dollars, _____ (you / spend) it wisely?

`/ 12`

VOCABULARY

3 Complete the sentences with the correct form of a verb in the box which has an opposite meaning to the word in italics.

| reduce | bankrupt | lead | undermine | discourage |
| boost | trigger | benefit | | |

1 Although there has been an *increase* in gun crime, figures show that overall crime figures _____.
2 Despite offering his *support* during last year's election campaign, the millionaire businessman's comments actually _____ our efforts – they had a negative rather than a positive effect.
3 The coach's speech *inspired* some of the team but _____ those who felt they weren't part of her plans.
4 Although they may _____ those in work to a small extent, the reforms will most certainly *harm* the prospects of those out of work,
5 After years of *decline*, the rising price of textiles will _____ the economy of the town by about 20%.
6 The leader's intention was to *draw back* from the precipice of war, but his actions _____ to an even greater conflict.
7 While Jim's company *made a profit*, his brother's company _____ by rising prices, meaning that he didn't have enough money to pay his creditors.
8 The aim of the legislation was to *block* the import of arms, but, in the end, it _____ an even greater influx.

`/ 8`

4 Circle the odd verb out.

1 grab	clutch	chuckle	grasp
2 whisper	mutter	mumble	giggle
3 hop	gasp	step	skip
4 cheer	stroll	scream	shout
5 chuckle	stagger	stroll	creep
6 peer	stare	yell	glare

`/ 6`

5 Choose the correct verb to complete the sentences.

1 Professor Talbot *peered / glared* through the microscope once more. He was amazed by what he saw.
2 Two of the students were *chuckling / mumbling* at the back of the class. Clearly, they found something funny.
3 Once we reached the top of the mountain, we *gazed / glared* in wonder at the waterfall crashing down into the valley below.
4 Although we *muttered / yelled* at the top of our voices, Susie didn't hear us. She was too far away.
5 Late for work, Ian *raced / crept* out of the house at top speed and headed for the bus stop.
6 We have an hour before the train leaves. Let's *stroll / stagger* around the city centre. It's quite historical.
7 Could you just *grab / clutch* my bag for me? It's on the top shelf.
8 Be careful when you *step / skip* off the bus. There's a big gap between the floor of the bus and the pavement.

`/ 8`

6 Choose the correct word to complete the sentences.

1 The role of the leader of the main _____
party is to challenge and criticise the actions of the
government.
a opposition   b representative   c satirical

2 Sadly, political _____ among young people is
in decline. Fewer and fewer people are actively taking
part in political activities.
a identity   b engagement   c emergence

3 Although once seen as a _____ of fun in his
own party, Watson rose to be leader. Nobody laughed
at him then.
a person   b figure   c protest

4 The prime minister has announced _____.
People won't be voting for any political party. They'll
be voting on whether to stay in the European Union or
not.
a an election   b a petition   c a referendum

5 Alleged vote-_____ was not proved, so the
result stood and the People's Party formed the new
government.
a striking   b rigging   c lining

6 It was a _____ victory! The party won 80% of
seats in the new parliament and celebrated wildly!
a landslide   b hollow   c consensus

7 I didn't _____ my vote in the last election. I wish
I had voted for somebody.
a throw   b cast   c set

8 In a recent opinion _____, the government's
position was shown to be very unpopular.
a poll   b lobby   c petition

| / 8 | | / 50 |

UNIT 5 TEST

GRAMMAR

1 Rewrite each sentence with the words and phrases in the box. They each go with the underlined nouns.

> deserted   beyond the rocks   small

1 We came across a <u>beach</u>.

_____

> stalking a mouse   elderly   of a cat

2 My <u>mother</u> bought a <u>painting</u>.

_____

> of primitive art   held in a barn   inspiring

3 We went to an <u>exhibition</u>.

_____

> living in India   cooked with lots of spices   curried

4 <u>People</u> eat <u>food</u>.

_____

> cut from river banks   traditional   thatched with reeds

5 <u>Roofs</u> are made.

_____

/ 10

2 Complete the texts with the words and phrases in each box in each space.
The Tower of London

> central
> known as the Tower of London
> of the River Thames
> historic
> on the north bank

Her Majesty's Royal Palace and Fortress,
¹_____, is a ²_____ castle located
³_____ ⁴_____ in ⁵_____ London.

> ruling
> by William the Conqueror
> much resented
> in 1078
> which gives the entire castle its name

It was founded ⁶_____, the king of England,
⁷_____. The White Tower, ⁸_____, was
a ⁹_____ symbol of oppression, inflicted upon
London by the ¹⁰_____ elite.

/ 10

VOCABULARY

3 Complete the sentences with the correct words.

1 The film was really dull and lasted over four hours. I was bored out of my _____.
2 The play was OK, but not half as good as all the critics had claimed. It didn't live up to all the _____.
3 Clara was so upset when the heroine died near the end of the film that she burst into _____, and couldn't stop crying.
4 The comedian was so funny that we were all on the floor in _____. We couldn't stop laughing.
5 I have never felt so embarrassed in public. I didn't want to be there. I wanted the ground to open up and _____ me.
6 Henry was so young when he died. At his funeral, his friends and family were inconsolable. They were in _____ of tears.
7 Her outrageous behaviour at the party caused a bit of a _____. Everybody there was shocked.
8 Graham is so _____ of himself that he thinks everything he says is really interesting, and, believe me, it isn't!

/ 8

4 Complete the sentences with words in the box.

> bored   mortified   awkward
> overwhelmed   yawning

1 At the farewell party, Kingsley was _____ by all the kind words his colleagues said. He was both proud and moved.
2 The speaker went on and on and we all felt horribly _____.
3 I was _____ when I realised that I had reversed my car into my boss' car in the car park.
4 I bumped into my ex-boyfriend at a party last week. We both felt quite _____. We didn't know what to say to each other.
5 We were so tired that we couldn't stop _____. We just wanted to go to bed.

/ 5

5 Match the words to make expressions.

1 a herd of   a labour
2 signs of   b flowers
3 floods of   c sheep
4 a supply of   d bees
5 a bunch of   e tears
6 a swarm of   f life

/ 6

6 Complete the sentences with the words in the box. Add any other words necessary. Do not use more than five words. There are two words you don't need.

> manner   tip   amount   performance
> content   pleasure   creation   rear

1 I think that was probably _____ *Hamlet* I have ever seen in a London theatre in my entire life!
2 The answer is _____ tongue, but I just can't remember the artist's name.

3 Following _____ the United Nations in 1945, there was at last an international organisation intent on the maintenance of peace.
4 All _____ events will take place at this year's festival ranging from song and dance to live theatre.
5 We had _____ Dan's company last weekend. He really is a funny and charming guest.
6 A large _____ rubbish has been dumped in the street near our house. I'd like to know who put it there.

/ 6

7 Choose the correct word to complete the sentences.
1 The novel's main _____ is a young man who has lost his job and his direction in life.
   a star   b representative   c protagonist
2 The story is told in the _____ person by the narrator.
   a first   b major   c main
3 The novel _____ important themes of identity and personal crisis.
   a treats   b revolves   c deals with
4 The film is _____ on a novel of the same name, and more or less follows the plot of the novel.
   a set   b based   c rooted
5 The novel is, by _____, both funny and moving.
   a goes   b moves   c turns

/ 5   / 50

UNIT 6 TEST

GRAMMAR

1 Complete the sentences with the correct form of the verbs in brackets. Use *would* or *could* whenever possible.

1 My regrets? Well, I wish I _____ (listen) to my friends when they told me not to go out with Roger.
2 I wish you _____ (switch) that radio off. Why do we have to listen to football commentaries all afternoon?
3 I wish Paul _____ (stop) going on about his trip to Brazil. It's all he ever talks about.
4 I wish I _____ (dance) a bit. I always find it embarrassing whenever I have to dance.
5 Most of the students wish they _____ (be) somewhere else right now.
6 If only I _____ (buy) that dress. I want it more than anything, but it's much too expensive for me.
7 I wish I _____ (complain) about the terrible service, but my wife told me not to bother. Frankly, I regret not doing so.
8 If only it _____ (not be) so late. I'd love to stay longer.
9 We wish we _____ (meet) Joe while he was staying in London.
10 If only I _____ (have) my guitar with me. I'd love to play you a tune.

/ 10

2 Complete the dialogue with an auxiliary verb or modal auxiliary verb.

A: Why didn't you invite Jim to the party?
B: I wish I ¹_____. It ²_____ have been better all round. How was I supposed to know that he's your sister's new fiancée?
A: Yes. Sorry. I meant to tell you that. I wish I ³_____ keep forgetting things. Perhaps you should call and explain things to my sister.
B: I wish I ⁴_____. But she's not answering calls – at least, calls from me. They go straight to voicemail. If only she ⁵_____ pick up the phone.
A: Perhaps I should phone.
B: Well, yes. I wish you ⁶_____. She is your sister after all. She always listens to you.
A: I wish she ⁷_____. If only that ⁸_____ true. In reality, she treats me like a fool.
B: You're joking!
A: I wish I ⁹_____.
B: Well, anyway, I'd appreciate it if you would phone her. We need to explain the situation before her opinion of both of us gets any worse.
A: OK. I will. I just wish you ¹⁰_____ invited poor Jim in the first place!

/ 10

VOCABULARY

3 Complete the sentences with a phrase using the words in brackets.

1 Calm down and don't shout. There really is no need _____ (raise).
2 You're not listening to my opinion. Try to see it _____ (point).
3 I am really sorry I said that. That came _____ (wrong).
4 We've been talking about the same thing for ages. We're just going _____ (circles).
5 Don't worry about what has already happened. There's no point _____ (spilt).
6 The situation isn't as bad as you think. It really isn't _____ (world).
7 I know you're still angry with me after I shouted yesterday, but it's time we _____ (air).
8 We don't seem to understand each other very well. I think we've got _____ (wires).
9 I didn't mean that at all. You're _____ (words).

/ 9

4 Complete the sentences with the words in the box.

annual   lasting   former   diverse   notable

1 Both current soldiers, and _____ soldiers who have left the army, are being treated for stress-related illnesses.
2 Although not particularly well-thought-of, the festival is a well-attended _____ event in the countryside. This year, just three bands are playing there.
3 One of the most _____ campaigners of recent years has been arrested by the police.
4 A _____ range of people, from all parts of society, came to the meeting.
5 The treaty has brought decades of _____ peace to the region.

/ 5

5 Match the verbs 1–6 to the words a–f.

1 plant   a a coup
2 stage   b a ceasefire
3 lose   c a bomb
4 declare   d the enemy
5 defeat   e on trial
6 put   f ground

/ 6

6 Complete the sentences with the missing words connected with war.

1 The supermarkets are in the middle of a price _____. They're all cutting the prices of key foods.
2 During the election we were _____ with emails and leaflets urging us to vote for various candidates. It was really annoying.
3 The body's _____ against viruses can be reduced by a poor diet.
4 The judge said that the press coverage added up to a serious _____ of the actress' privacy.
5 In a real _____ of wills, both players refused to give in. The match lasted hours.
6 The right to privacy of ordinary citizens is under _____ from government agencies who want to access our personal data.
7 Thanks to a very successful marketing _____, we have raised the profile of the new product.
8 Rather than competing against each other, we should join _____ and work together to achieve more.
9 All the big _____ in the energy industry are working together to prevent smaller companies from being competitive in the market.
10 A huge _____ of volunteers have turned up to help clean up the festival site.

/ 10   / 50

UNIT 7 TEST

GRAMMAR

1 Complete the sentences with the correct passive forms of the verbs in brackets.

1 While we _____ (show) around the castle, one of the people in our tour group slipped and fell off the battlements. It was awful.
2 The trees near the centre _____ (cut) down today to make space for the new cinema complex.
3 Both of these gadgets _____ (can / use) to slice hard-boiled eggs, but this one is much cheaper.
4 Some of these vases _____ (think) to be over a thousand years old. They're probably worth millions!
5 Andy _____ (must / give) that pullover at Christmas. I haven't seen him wear it before.
6 Last term, Simon and I _____ (ask) to sing at the concert by the head teacher.
7 I remember _____ (not allow) to stay up late to watch the final of the World Cup when I was ten. I was really upset that I couldn't watch it.
8 Many _____ (know) to have died in the disaster, but the authorities are not releasing names yet.
9 I've heard that Harrison _____ (may / present) with a medal for his bravery.
10 Don't worry about _____ (not / give) a ticket. You'll get one as soon as you board the boat.

/ 10

2 Choose the correct form to complete the sentences.

1 One athlete, *choosing / chosen / having chosen* at random, will be asked to light the torch.
2 What happened next shouldn't ever *be allowed / being allowed / to be allowed* to happen again. It was and is a disgrace.
3 As a kid, I *got told off / told off / had told off* on a daily basis. Mind you, I was really naughty most of the time.
4 The disease *thought / was thought / has thought* to be caused by poor-quality drinking water.
5 My grandmother *was the tumour removed / got removed the tumour / had the tumour removed* last February, and she's been fine since.
6 That cut needs *see / to see / seeing* to. It looks serious to me.
7 Did you know that you can *play / be played / playing* that game online?
8 It *has argued / has been argued / has arguing* that the penal system is not fit for purpose.
9 A boat *made / was made / has made* out of paper has sailed across the Mediterranean.
10 Steve *had fixed his bike / had his bike fixed / had been fixed his bike* last week at the local bike shop.

/ 10

VOCABULARY

3 Circle the word(s) which do not collocate in each sentence.

1 Scientists *undertook / carried out / extracted* the survey to find out about public conceptions of their work.
2 Scientists made a major *breakthrough / condition / step forward* in the fight against cancer.
3 Researchers *stuck / devised / invented* a way to measure the amount of gas produced.
4 Biochemists *reproduced / inserted / duplicated* the results of the earlier experiment under stricter conditions.
5 The *underlying / due / root* cause of the problems remains to be discovered.
6 The patients all had a rare genetic *condition / disorder / reproduction* which may prove fatal in the long term.

/ 6

4 Complete the text with the correct form of the verbs in the box.

pave	stand	come	resonate	prompt
address	unfold	reflect		

2001: A Space Odyssey

The novel *2001: A Space Odyssey*, which was written by Arthur C Clarke, and the film based on the book, directed by Stanley Kubrick, both ¹_____ important issues facing humanity. They explore the dangers associated with the nuclear age, and warn against the destructive power associated with technological innovation in the military arena. At the time of the film's release, these fears ²_____ with many in the audience who also feared the rapid development of technology.

Although it ³_____ out in 1969, the film has ⁴_____ the test of time. One reason for this is that it so clearly ⁵_____ the fears and anxieties felt at that time. Another reason is that it ⁶_____ each of us to speculate about our role in the universe. As the story ⁷_____, we gradually realise that the computer Hal has a mind of its own. This ⁸_____ the way for a tense showdown between man and machine that results in a mind-bending trek through space and time.

/ 8

5 Complete the sentences with the correct form of the words in the box.

remake	impress	cynic	exploit	stupid	imply
colony	technology				

1 Susie made a very _____ speech during her first conference. I was surprised by how good it was.
2 I can't believe the _____ of the council in placing the school crossing so near the dangerous corner.
3 There have been so many _____ advances in the world of science during the last decade that it's hard to keep up.

4 Some people were very _____ about Don's plans at first. They thought they wouldn't work and made sarcastic comments.
5 I preferred the _____ to the original film, actually.
6 During _____ times, European settlers paid little attention to the rights of native peoples in the region.
7 Asking us to work extra hours without pay amounts to _____. We're going on strike!
8 It will take a long time before we are fully aware of the _____ of the government's decision. It may change our way of dealing with childcare.

☐ / 8

6 Choose the correct word to complete the sentences.
1 There is no causal _____ between the new road signs and the rise in the number of accidents.
   a join   b link   c connection
2 A number of _____ need to be taken into consideration before we can reach an accurate interpretation of the data.
   a variables   b varieties   c various
3 I think these figures are statistical _____. We can disregard them.
   a disabilities   b enemies   c anomalies
4 You shouldn't _____ the figures to suit your own preconceptions.
   a revolve   b turn   c twist
5 Henning Corporation should not be part of the enquiry because the company has a _____ interest in the results being shown to be inaccurate.
   a vested   b tested   c conflicted
6 Contrary to popular _____, the drug has no effect on intelligence.
   a view   b belief   c knowledge
7 Crowther's figures simply don't _____ up to scrutiny.
   a shift   b set   c stand
8 The entire experiment was fundamentally

   _____.
   a error   b flawed   c anomaly

☐ / 8   ☐ / 50

UNIT 8   TEST

GRAMMAR

1 Complete the sentences with the correct form of an auxiliary verb.

1 People like us generally play by the rules, _____ they?
2 Jo's better at lying than most, _____ she?
3 Although some people _____ try their best to support the event, most, I'm afraid, were of no help at all.
4 I'd love to tell him what I think, I really _____.
5 I'm tired, and so _____ Donna. Why don't we just stay in?
6 Although everybody in the village has been invited to next weekend's do, many _____ come, I'm sure of it.
7 So, you want to come with me now, _____ you? I wonder why you've changed you mind. Could it have something to do with the fact that I've offered to pay for the tickets?
8 I'm pleased Jack's got himself a job, but I'm also surprised he _____, to be honest.
9 We bought a season ticket, and, in _____ so, saved at least £50 on travel costs.
10 I don't have a ticket and neither _____ Sam.

/ 10

2 Complete the dialogue with the correct auxiliary verb.

Tom: Barry's not coming over this evening.
Dan: ¹_____ he? I thought he ²_____.
Tom: He has an essay to write, apparently.
Dan: Well, so ³_____ I, but that hasn't stopped me coming, ⁴_____ it?
Tom: Well, no. But last week he said he ⁵_____ be able to come this week.
Dan: He ⁶_____. He said he'd come unless the traffic was bad, and it ⁷_____. The roads are clear.
Tom: OK. Well, I'm not happy about his absence either, ⁸_____ I? But there's no need to get angry.
Dan: Yes, there ⁹_____. He's our best darts player! He plays better than either of us ¹⁰_____. Without him, we're going to lose badly, tonight.

/ 10

VOCABULARY

3 Match the adjectives to the nouns they best collocate with.

1 barren   a water
2 murky   b rainforest
3 sandy   c track
4 lush   d cliff
5 sheer   e grassland
6 dirt   f beach

/ 6

4 Complete the sentences with phrases using the words in brackets. Do not use more than five words.

1 I'm aware that the gossips among you _____ (rumours) me. None of them are true, so please stop.

2 Karen is always supportive if you feel down and need _____ (shoulder) on.
3 The thing about Jack is that he says exactly what he thinks. He doesn't _____ (mince).
4 Look, say what you want to say. Just _____ (point). I haven't got all day.
5 When Shelley is telling one of her longwinded stories, she dominates the conversation. Nobody else can _____ (edgeways).
6 Let me explain what I want to say instead of always _____ (putting) mouth.
7 We're not talking to you. Don't _____ (butt) the conversation!
8 So far you haven't said what you want. Stop _____ (bush) and say what you want.

/ 8

5 Circle one word that does not belong in each group.
1 **Birds**
  a beak   b wings   c feelers   d claws   e tail
2 **Lions**
  a claw   b hoof   c tail   d teeth   e fur
3 **Rabbits**
  a toes   b tail   c fur   d horn   e nostrils
4 **Camels**
  a teeth   b hump   c breast   d scales   e legs
5 **Fish**
  a tail   b scales   c horn   d eyes   e teeth

/ 5

6 Complete the sentences using the correct form of the verbs in the box.

| roam   leap   let   gnaw   draw   breed |

1 Once, huge herds of bison _____ widely across America's Midwest.
2 Many hibernating animals are able to _____ upon fat reserves to help them get through the winter.
3 We used to have a hamster, and one day it escaped and _____ through the electric cable under the living room floor and all the lights went out.
4 Zoos use captive _____ programmes to ensure the survival of some of the world's rarest mammals.
5 When in danger, the creature _____ out a really loud squeal.
6 Tigers hide downwind from prey animals, and don't _____ out and catch them until they are really close.

/ 6

7 Complete the compound adjective in each sentence by adding one word.

1 The award-_____ novel has sold millions of copies.
2 New Stop & Go Shampoo is tailor-_____ for today's busy lifestyles.
3 In the US, they have six-_____ motorways, or freeways as they call them. Can you believe it?
4 It was a last-_____ decision to book the holiday. We just went online and booked a flight for the next day!
5 We have no regular place to meet. Using the social centre is not really a long-_____ solution to the problem, but it will have to do for now.

/ 5   / 50

UNIT 9 TEST

GRAMMAR

1 Complete the sentences with the correct continuous forms of the verbs in brackets.

1 I _____ (think) of living in Ireland at one time. That was before I married Joanne.
2 The roof _____ (repair) when we visited, so we didn't really get to see the palace because of all the scaffolding.
3 I _____ (not ask) you for help if I weren't in such dire need.
4 Welcome on board. The Rocky Mountain train is about to depart. On today's journey, we _____ (travel) through some of the country's most wonderful scenery, so sit back and relax.
5 You must _____ (joke) if you think I'm going to wear that. It's awful.
6 It _____ (get) harder to find a good plumber these days.
7 A number of other guests _____ (join) us before the end of the weekend.
8 Jack's supposed to _____ (do) his homework upstairs, but I bet he isn't.
9 Everything _____ (do) to track down your missing suitcase, sir. Please take a seat and I'll inform as soon as I have any news.
10 I'll pick you up at the airport tomorrow. Look out for me. I _____ (wear) a green pullover.

/ 10

2 Complete the text with the correct form of the verbs in brackets. Use continuous forms whenever possible.
The death of the desk

Architects [1]_____ (start) to rethink the way we work, and a move away from the office desk as the main place of productivity [2]_____ (see) now as an inevitable development in workplace design. Nowadays, large corporations [3]_____ (believe) that making employees sit at desks reduces both creativity and productivity. As a result, over the last few years, they [4]_____ (seek) out architects who can help them redesign the places we work in. The headquarters of the Royal Institute of British Architects in London [5]_____ (be) just one building which [6]_____ (redevelop) in recent times to reflect this new thinking. Influenced by computer technology, it [7]_____ (make) up of interconnected offices, and platforms instead of stairs, and huge open landings where employees can meet. The idea is that, in the future, employees [8]_____ (not sit) at a desk, but [9]_____ (use) the space around them to find inspiration and meet colleagues. It is a fascinating idea. We [10]_____ (might / witness) the start of a brave new world of work.

/ 10

VOCABULARY

3 Choose the correct word to complete the sentences.

1 It's sometimes hard to _____ your deadlines in a busy office like this.
   a meet   b stay   c take
2 We have _____ an ad in the local newspaper to try to recruit new staff.
   a lain   b placed   c stood
3 How can we _____ on budget if your department continues to overspend?
   a stay   b put   c let
4 Just _____ your expense claims to me and I'll process them for you.
   a draw up   b bring off   c pass on
5 We've already _____ a number of successful events.
   a put on   b put up   c put in
6 Could you _____ this issue, Lillian? I'm busy at the moment.
   a come up   b deal with   c get over
7 We're trying to _____ new business by sending out flyers and leaflets.
   a attract   b network   c oversee

/ 7

4 Circle the adjectives that collocate best with the adverbs.

1 financially   a demanding   b rewarding
2 mind-numbingly   a boring   b competitive
3 physically   a demanding   b efficient
4 blissfully   a interesting b happy
5 fiercely   a rewarding   b competitive
6 highly   a efficient   b happy
7 utterly   a interesting b draining

/ 7

5 Complete the sentences with the words in the box. There are two words you don't need.

| perk notice leave dismissal absenteeism casualisation crèche redundancy quit cuts |

1 If there wasn't a _____ at work, I'd have to pay a fortune in childcare.
2 After my mother died, I was given compassionate _____. I didn't work for three months.
3 If you resign, you'll have to give two months' _____. You can't just quit immediately.
4 The tribunal decided that Kim shouldn't have been sacked. It was a case of unfair _____ and she was awarded damages.
5 Perhaps the best _____ of my job is the free store card we are given. I get 50% off anything I buy in the store I work at.
6 Many employees took _____ because the factory owners were offering a generous amount of money to anyone who chose to leave and seek work elsewhere.
7 Swingeing _____ by the government have reduced the social welfare budget.
8 _____ at the factory continues to be a problem. Some employees are calling in sick five or six times a month.

/ 8

6 Circle one word that does not collocate in each list.

1 a week's
   a leave   b retirement   c notice
2 sack
   a an employee   b a manager   c a career
3 quit
   a your job   b your salary   c the firm
4 subsidised
   a days off   b travel   c healthcare
5 launch
   a a scheme   b a crackdown   c a cut
6 raise
   a salaries   b perks   c wages
7 voluntary
   a absenteeism   b redundancy   c retirement
8 secure
   a jobs   b unions   c contracts

⬚ / 8   ⬚ / 50

1 a week's
   a leave   b retirement   c notice
2 sack

UNIT 10   TEST

GRAMMAR

1 Complete the sentences using the correct modal verb from the box and the verb in brackets. Sometimes more than one answer is possible.

should   may   can   must   can't   mustn't

1 The organisers were at fault for letting so many people come into the hall at once. They _____ (plan) the event better to avoid such overcrowding.
2 Simpson was a fabulous doctor and a wonderful human being. We _____ (never / see) the like of her again.
3 These tablets _____ (produce) by Arrow Pharmaceuticals because they are the wrong shape.
4 Styles that were once criticised _____ (get) a new lease of life with changing fashions.
5 By the end of evening, we _____ (finish) wrapping all these presents. At least, I expect that to be the case.
6 There's no point ringing. The dentist _____ (go) home by now. It's almost nine o'clock in the evening.
7 The patient _____ (try) to get out of bed when she slipped and fell, but, frankly, there's no way of knowing for sure. She has died of her injuries.
8 Some mammals _____ (do) things that humans are simply incapable of.
9 I'm disappointed we missed the start of the film. We _____ (get) here earlier.
10 You _____ (tell) Susie what I told you. Please keep it a secret.

/ 10

2 Rewrite the sentences so that they have the same meaning as the first sentence. Use an appropriate modal auxiliary verb in each new sentence.

1 You were supposed to pick us up half an hour ago.
You _____
2 It's impossible to find a cure for this disease.
A cure _____
3 There's a chance that the boy's still wandering around out there.
The boy _____
4 We're all certain Tracey paid for the prescription.
Tracey _____
5 We expect Tom to win all the games he plays.
Tom _____

/ 10

VOCABULARY

3 Complete the sentences with a verb in the correct form.

1 Jo's knee joint _____ up after someone kicked it during the match. She could hardly bend it.
2 Wendy has _____ her arm in three places and had metal rods inserted into it.
3 I had to _____ my tooth out when it became infected.

4 Fortunately, Sue's tumour has _____ into remission. She's feeling much better.
5 The patient was _____ an anaesthetic before the operation.
6 Dan has been _____ with a tropical disease. However, the doctor says that there is a cure.
7 As soon as she reached hospital, the doctors _____ her on a drip.
8 You'll need to _____ a scan to see how badly damaged it is.

/ 8

4 Match the phrases 1–6 to the things they describe a–f.

1 'I doubt that the survey was at all reliable.'   a mortality
2 'The patient has a sore throat, a fever and a headache.'   b downward spiral
3 'You won't believe how much it hurts.'   c symptoms
4 'Let's look at the number of deaths there have been in this region.'   d neural connections
5 'Nerve cells transmit information through electrical and chemical signals.'   e scepticism
6 'Things just seem to go from bad to worse.'   f excruciating pain

/ 6

5 Circle the words that collocate best with the verbs.

1 flutter   a your eyelashes   b your shoulders
2 raise   a your belly   b your eyebrows
3 click   a your fingers   b your forehead
4 shrug   a your elbows   b your shoulders
5 clench   a your fist   b your head
6 stretch   a your eyes   b your legs
7 pat   a your back   b your fingers
8 drop   a your head   b your heart

/ 8

6 Complete the sentences using nouns based on the phrasal verbs in the box.

crack down   get together   bring up   pass by
work out   break through   break out   run up

1 _____ ignored the family of beggars sitting on the side of the road.
2 The government is worried about the latest _____ of cholera in the impoverished south of the country.
3 My old college friends and I have a _____ in a restaurant once a year. It's always great to see them again.
4 I did a _____ at the gym this morning – lots of press-ups and stretching. I'm exhausted now.
5 In the _____ to the last election, there were three debates between leaders of the main parties.
6 A significant _____ by scientists seeking a cure for cancer has been announced. Hopefully, it will lead to improved treatment.
7 A _____ on drug smuggling by border police has been successful. Over a hundred arrests have been made.
8 I had a difficult _____. Both my parents died and I lived with three or four sets of foster parents.

/ 8   / 50

UNIT 11 TEST

GRAMMAR

1 Complete the sentences with the correct words and phrases in the box.

> otherwise   whilst   down to   provided   despite
> consequently   whether   owing to   meanwhile
> moreover

1 _____ the fact that Mike hated board games, his wife insisted on forcing him to play them on holiday.
2 The popularity of these computer games is _____ the novelty of their state-of-the-art graphics.
3 _____ you have the right visa, you will be able to stay in the country for up to six months.
4 We're heading off in 20 minutes _____ you're ready or not.
5 The train will be delayed by 40 minutes _____ the bad weather conditions. We apologise for any inconvenience.
6 Try to buy the game online. _____, we'll have to buy it from a high street shop at a much higher price.
7 Our games industry is underfunded. _____, in other parts of the world, the state is supporting the industry with huge subsidies.
8 The games industry is both prolific and profitable. _____, it is a significant employer, providing excellent training for many young people interested in a career in technology.
9 _____ I'd like to work for a games manufacturer, I think I should go and get a degree at university first.
10 Amy invented a new board game and promoted it successfully on the Internet. _____, it sold in the millions and she became a wealthy woman.

/ 10

2 Complete the text with linking phrases. Each phrase is made up of three words including the word in brackets.

Board Game Review

You'll love the brand new board game *Crisis At Sea*, [1]_____ (so) you are a fan of strategy games. [2]_____ (as) having an interesting narrative, the game also comes with a really well-designed board and playing cards. In the game, each player has to navigate his or her 'ship' through stormy waters [3]_____ (in) reach the safety of their home port. [4]_____ (on) that, they have to complete a series of tasks, including rescuing drowning sailors and attacking hostile pirates.

An enormous number of new titles are currently being developed for general sale, [5]_____ (on) the growing popularity of strategic board games. *Crisis At Sea* is just one of them. Others include *Death In The Mountains*, *Roller Park* and *Crazy Canyon*, [6]_____ (not) *Super Cars* and *Lazy Day*, two games at an early stage of development. Games manufacturer Timothy Pratt told me that his designers were having to work day and night [7]_____ (so) meet the current demand for new games. [8]_____ (in) the fact that board games are selling well, prices remain high [9]_____ (as) the high costs involved in production. Some have criticised the cost, urging customers not to pay such inflated prices. [10]_____ (all) though, there seems to be no end in sight for the boom in the popularity of board games.

/ 10

VOCABULARY

3 Choose the correct word to complete the sentences.

1 The crowd _____ wild when Hughes scored.
   a went   b made   c got
2 Players love it when the crowd starts _____ their name.
   a booing   b chanting   c screaming
3 In ice hockey, players who commit a foul are sent to the _____ .
   a foul-hall   b bad-spot   c sin-bin
4 I think I've got a bit of _____ from running around so long. I need to stretch my legs.
   a cramp   b stiff   c pull
5 An international betting syndicate has been _____ matches for ages.
   a fixing   b mending   c making

/ 5

4 Complete the sentences with the missing words. The first letter is given.

1 We scored the only goal in the last minute of the match and just s_____ through to the second round of the cup.
2 The horse was way out in front for most of the race but f_____ over the last hundred metres and finished second.
3 Griffiths was s_____ off by the referee for punching the goalkeeper in the mouth.
4 We got k_____ out of the cup on penalties. We scored four, but the opposition scored all five of theirs.
5 We b_____ it! We should have won but made mistakes and ended up losing.
6 Pilling was s_____ in the 60th minute of the match because he picked up an injury.
7 In a one-s_____ game, City won 8–0.
8 After being c_____ doping by officials, the sprinter was banned for two years.
9 Barcelona completely outplayed us and we got t_____ 6–0. We were awful.
10 Edwards has played poorly in the last couple of matches and is likely to be d_____ by coach Sam Stone.

/ 10

5 Complete the sentences with the correct form of the verbs in the box. There are two verbs you don't need.

stimulate   defy   foster   provide   collaborate
let   modify

1 The quality of the graphics _____ description. It really is that good.
2 I play games just to relax and _____ off steam at the end of a long, stressful day.
3 Our organisation aims to _____ positive relationships between young people and their families by providing support and understanding.
4 The writing course really _____ our imagination. It helped us become more creative.
5 I have _____ with three other gamers in developing this new shooter game. It really is a joint effort.

/ 5

6 Complete the sentences with an appropriate alliterative word.

1 Don't give up. You need to have the _____ of your convictions.
2 _____ speaking, this cafeteria is only for use by staff members.
3 In these difficult economic times it's hard to make ends _____ .
4 Fortunately, there was a real _____ of minds at the conference and a lot of progress was made.
5 Teenagers feel a lot of _____ pressure to behave in certain ways.
6 Since she won the lottery, Rani has been living in the _____ of luxury.
7 I expect everything to be _____-shape when I get back, so start tidying.
8 I can't think of the word. It's on the _____ of my tongue.
9 Don't worry about Clare. She's not afraid of those boys. She'll give as _____ as she gets.
10 After we lost the match 6–0, it was all doom and _____ in the changing room. Everyone was down.

/ 10   / 50

UNIT 12   TEST

GRAMMAR

1 Complete the second sentence so that it has a similar meaning to the first sentence using the word given.

1 There has never been a war as brutal as this one at any other time in history.
At _____

2 Soldiers have never been expected to fight in such conditions before.
Never _____

3 The rest of the army wouldn't have been able to retreat if those soldiers had not given their lives.
Had _____

4 We didn't know what he had achieved until after the campaign was over.
Only _____

5 The journey was so dangerous that few ever attempted it.
Such _____

☐ / 10

2 Rewrite each sentence in the text so that they have a similar meaning to the first. Use the first words provided.
The Museum of Egyptian Antiquities in Cairo
As soon as we entered the museum, we saw our first statue. The statue was so amazing that we just stared at it. You can't see so many ancient Egyptian artefacts anywhere else in the world. We had no idea how remarkable the collection was until we had seen it for ourselves. The collection was both extensive and well-organised.

1 No _____
2 So _____
3 Nowhere _____
4 Not _____
5 Not only _____

☐ / 10

VOCABULARY

3 Complete the sentences using the verbs in the box in the correct form.

shelter   close   scratch   deprive   orphan   break

1 We live in a very _____-knit community in which everybody knows what everybody else is up to.
2 I built up this business from _____. When I started, I had nothing.
3 I guess I came from a _____ home. My dad walked out when I was six. We weren't short of money though, even after my parents divorced.
4 It's tough living in a _____ area where nobody has a job or much money.
5 My _____ upbringing didn't prepare me for this. As a child, I had everything I needed, and I didn't know how hard life could be.
6 Agnes was _____ at the age of six when her parents died in a car crash.

☐ / 6

4 Complete the common similes with one word.
1 My great-grandfather is as old as the _____.
2 My uncle Frank smokes like a _____.
3 Although brothers, Tim and Simon are like _____ and cheese. They have nothing in common.
4 When I first arrived in New York, I was like a fish out of _____. Everything was so strange.
5 Sally went as white as a _____ when she heard the news.
6 At university, Delia avoided me like the _____. I think she thought I was boring.

☐ / 6

5 Match the sentence halves to make similes.
1 The actions sowed   a the way to a brighter future.
2 The reforms saw   b the seeds of recovery.
3 The party overthrew   c the old regime.
4 The election pointed   d a lengthy period of unrest.
5 The country entered   e inflation rise as a result.

☐ / 5

6 Circle one word that is the most unlikely collocation.
1 an outbreak of
  a troops   b violence   c war   d disease
2 consumed by
  a grief   c desire
  b disappointment   d rage
3 assigned to
  a the case   c the entertainment
  b their groups   d the London branch
4 a shrine to
  a the gods   c primitive art
  b the dead   d the traffic
5 the withdrawal of
  a funding   b light   c support   d troops

☐ / 5

7 Match a word or phrase in the box to the words in italics in each sentence with the same meaning.

gave rise to	casting doubt on	put forward
highlight	stemmed from	demonstrate
contend	accepted	

1 I would *argue* that there is a need to investigate this area of historical study further.
2 Lewis *proposed* a new theory to explain the reasons behind the general's success.
3 It's important to *emphasise* the role of women in these significant social changes.
4 The historian's new book fails to *show* why the war was lost.
5 The TV documentary's enquiries ended up *questioning* the committee's initial findings.
6 The decline in the industry *was caused by* various economic factors.
7 The discovery of gold in California *resulted in* the development of that region.
8 Professor Davis *finally agreed with* the findings of other scholars.

☐ / 8   ☐ / 50

UNIT 13 TEST

GRAMMAR

1 Choose the correct word to complete the sentences.

1 The editor has _____ us to find a really interesting lead story.
   a ordered   b demanded   c insisted
2 Publicists have _____ that the two Hollywood stars are to wed.
   a acknowledged b notified   c assured
3 We _____ getting a qualification before going into journalism.
   a promise   b declare   c recommend
4 She _____ stealing my briefcase.
   a confessed b apologised c denied
5 The politician _____ that he knew nothing of the plot.
   a stated   b refused   c defended
6 May I _____ you that the poll closes at midnight?
   a consider   b remind   c express
7 The president _____ to introduce reforms.
   a refused   b urged   c recommended
8 I _____ leaving now.
   a warn   b suggest   c vow
9 Sam _____ with the judge to let him go.
   a pleaded   b threatened c urged
10 I _____ the riot on the poor state of the economy.
   a criticise   b accuse   c blame

/ 10

2 Complete the text with the correct form of the words in brackets.

The phone hacking scandal

The News of the World used to be Britain's best-selling newspaper. It was famous for its exclusive stories about the private lives of celebrities. In 2011, however, many of its editors and journalists ¹_____ (accuse / use) illegal means to get stories. They had hacked into the phones of famous people, listening in to their private conversations, and using the information they heard to write stories. At first, senior editors at the newspaper ²_____ (declare / they / not know) anything about the phone hacking before the accusations were made, and ³_____ (assure / readers / they / never do) such a thing at any time in the past. However, as the evidence mounted, they ⁴_____ (confess / they / be) involved in the crime, and ⁵_____ (apologise / act) in the way they did. Some journalists ⁶_____ (admit / hack) the telephones of members of the royal family, celebrities with mental health problems, and a teenager who had been murdered. This outraged the public. Many ⁷_____ (criticise / the newspaper / have) no sense of decency. Politicians ⁸_____ (vow / take) action to make privacy laws stricter, and the newspaper's owner had to ⁹_____ (promise / never /accept) such disgraceful behaviour from

journalists again. Realising that the reputation of the 160-year-old newspaper was destroyed, its owner ¹⁰_____ (announce / he / close) the publication. In July 2011, the last copy of the News of the World was printed.

/ 10

VOCABULARY

3 Read the opening of the news stories. Complete the headlines with a verb commonly used in headlines in the correct form.

1 MINISTER _____ EFFORT
   Volunteers clearing pollution from local beaches were highly praised for their hard work by fisheries minister Justine Clark on a …
2 COACH _____ TO CARRY ON
   City coach Slaven Modric promised fans he would not resign despite recent poor results …
3 CUSTOMS _____ RECORD HAUL
   Border police have found and confiscated a record number of guns from smugglers in the last month.
4 JENKINS _____ OF MURDER
   In a sensational judgment, Clive Jenkins was found not guilty at Clerkenwell Court yesterday …
5 TEENS _____ FROM ARCADE
   Following a series of disturbances, under-18s are now prohibited from entering the City Centre arcade.
6 POLICE _____ WITH RIOTERS
   During yesterday's riots, there were numerous fights between police and troublemakers intent on …
7 CINDY CLARK _____ OUT OF POP STARS SHOW
   At the last moment, singing sensation Cindy Clark has told organisers she cannot take part in this year's Pop Stars Show due to ill health.
8 FINANCE MINISTER _____ OUT TAX RISE
   The finance minister has said that there will definitely be no rise in the basic rate of income tax this year.

/ 8

4 Choose the best definition for each sentence.

1 I've been on the go all day long.
   a I've been busy all day.
   b I've been relaxing and doing nothing.
2 I'm dead on my feet.
   a I'm hopeless at dancing.
   b I'm absolutely exhausted.
3 The photographer screwed up the shot.
   a He prepared to take a photo.
   b He didn't take a good photo.
4 She slipped out through a different door.
   a She fell as she was leaving.
   b She left secretly so nobody would see her.
5 We prefer to remain upbeat.
   a We prefer to be positive.
   b We prefer to be at the heart of the action.
6 I felt revulsion at the news.
   a I felt really really disgusted.
   b I felt really really disappointed.

/ 6

5 Complete the common sayings with one word.

1 Too many cooks spoil the _____ .
2 Never look a gift horse in the _____ .
3 The early bird catches the _____ .
4 Every cloud has a silver _____ .
5 People in glass houses shouldn't throw _____ .
6 Don't count your chickens before they _____ .
7 In for a penny, in for a _____ .
8 The grass is always _____ on the other side.

/ 8

6 Circle one word that is the most likely collocation.

1 I _____ up with the news online.
   a keep   b make   c put
2 Power in this country is concentrated in the
   _____ of just a few people.
   a fists   b arms   c hands
3 She took a few weeks off work on _____
   grounds.
   a illness   b health   c hard
4 During the crisis, we watched _____ 24-hour
   news channels to find out what was happening.
   a turning   b rolling   c sliding
5 Murdoch is a media _____ who controls many
   of the world's English language news outlets.
   a baron   b duke   c earl
6 It was a _____ marriage. They had just
   pretended to marry to claim the money.
   a false   b sham   c freak
7 I'm totally _____ on soap operas. I watch them
   all day, every day.
   a hung   b taken   c hooked
8 A newspaper editor demands _____ facts, not
   gossip, before he considers publishing a news story.
   a hard   b tough   c main

/ 8   / 50

UNIT 14   TEST

GRAMMAR

1 Complete each sentence with a relative pronoun or adverb. If no word is necessary, write –.

1 We visited one of the locations _____ the supermarket chain hoped to open a new store.

2 The authorities have introduced a new regulation _____ employers are held responsible for any accidents.

3 Nobody _____ was present at the time remembered seeing Ferguson leave.

4 One of the most compelling reasons _____ the government decided to investigate was the existence of an off shore banking account in the owner's name.

5 Investors, many of _____ had lost their life savings, insisted on the government taking action.

6 The point at _____ regulars need to step in has been reached.

7 The company _____ I worked for allowed us to leave early on Fridays.

8 One of the company directors, _____ Ferrari is parked outside, has just been arrested by the police.

/ 8

2 Rewrite each of the pairs of sentences below as one using a defining or non-defining relative clause.

1 The city appears to be abandoned at this time of night. It is usually crowded with people.
The city _____

2 Selhurst Holdings have made an offer. We cannot accept it.
We cannot _____

3 Three youths were arrested by the police. They had committed serious offences.
The police _____

4 Danny Clark has been elected vice-president. His brother was my friend at school.
Danny Clark _____

5 The stadium was on a high security alert. The cup final was being held there.
The stadium _____

6 The conference came to an end early. It had been an unqualified success.
The conference _____

/ 12

VOCABULARY

3 Complete the second sentence so that it has a similar meaning to the first. Use the correct form of a verb in the box.

| upturn   lay off   pitch for   inundate   diversify |
| pick up   go under   take on   hang in   float |

1 Thousands of workers have lost their jobs as a result of the factory's closure.
Thousands of workers _____ as a result of the factory's closure.

2 Sales have begun to improve in recent weeks.
Sales have begun to _____ in recent weeks.

3 The company is in danger of being out of business unless we become more competitive.
The company is in danger of _____ unless we become more competitive.

4 It's important to stay in business during these tough times.
It's important to _____ during these tough times.

5 Employing new staff is essential now that we're looking to open new branches.
_____ new staff is essential.

6 We ought to try to win new contracts.
We ought to _____ new contracts.

7 We started to sell the company's shares on the stock market in 2014.
We _____ on the stock market in 2014.

8 Sales have improved thanks to the recent positive improvement in the economy.
Sales have improved thanks to the _____ in the economy.

9 Our company is aiming to develop new products and services.
Our company is aiming to _____ .

10 Since we started the online business, we have been flooded with orders.
Since we started the online business, we _____ with orders.

/ 10

4 Match the loan words 1–8 to the sentences a–h that best describe them.

1 plaza   a Some may find the decorations attractive, but I think they're horrible and are in bad taste.

2 kitsch   b It was really embarrassing. We cooked chicken for our guests ... and they were vegans!

3 angst   c The dinner party was a disaster – the food was undercooked and everyone got food poisoning.

4 zeitgeist   d I'm really concerned about why I exist on this planet at all.

5 fiasco   e We found ourselves in a huge square full of cafes and restaurants.

6 trek   f Hannah knew everything there was to know about where to go and what to do in the city.

7 au fait   g Pop music and mini-skirts captured the spirit of those exciting times.

8 faux pas   h Will walked alone across the Kalahari Desert.

/ 8

5 Complete the business news report with one word in each space. The first letter is given.

And here is the business news.

Union representatives are threatening to
[1] c_____ a strike after they failed to
[2] r_____ a compromise over a new pay
[3] d_____ with representatives of the Babar
Steel Corporation. The Corporation refused to
[4] u_____ its offer of a 2% pay rise.

    Car manufacturers in the Midlands have
[5] l_____ a prototype of their new electric car.
Chief executive Clive Wilson explained that there was
a [6] g_____ in the market for affordable electric
cars.

    Retail giant Holdsworth's have announced they
will be [7] s_____ back their operations in Asia
because of the volatile economic climate. Over 50
stores will be closed. [8] 'C_____ costs is our
priority,' a spokesperson said.

    Following months of negotiations, Stanwick
Aerospace has [9] s_____ a major deal with
India to supply jet engines. It seems the company
will now [10] e_____ its target of selling 2,000
engines this year. A new target figure of 4,000
engines has been set.

    In a [11] h_____ bid on the city's stock
exchange this afternoon, chocolate manufacturer
Jupiter Cocoa attempted a [12] t_____ of rival
company Kelly's Cakes. The board of Kelly's Cakes
resisted, however, and the company is still in the
hands of its original shareholders.

| / 12 | | / 50 |

UNIT 15 TEST

GRAMMAR

1 Complete the sentences with the correct preposition.

1 The idea of going away for such a long time doesn't appeal _____ me.
2 This album reminds me _____ the time I was at college.
3 Scientists in the 20th century finally succeeded _____ creating artificial intelligence.
4 One of the advantages _____ being bilingual is a lower risk of developing Alzheimer's disease.
5 There's been a recent decline _____ the number of people suffering from depression.
6 My sister's preference _____ eating a low-carb diet hasn't changed over the years.
7 This toy isn't suitable _____ children under the age of three.
8 I was unaware _____ the fact that I had to switch off the computers before leaving.
9 I am writing to congratulate you _____ winning a place at the University.
10 I don't think you can be capable _____ judging art if you haven't studied its history.

/ 10

2 Complete the second sentence so that it has a similar meaning to the first sentence using the word given. Do not change the word given. You must use between three and five words, including the word given.

1 Nobody could control the situation in the war zone at all. CONTROL
The situation in the war zone was completely _____.
2 Smokers are more likely to get heart disease than non-smokers. RISK
Smokers _____ heart disease than non-smokers.
3 After I finished school, I found a job at a local call centre. ON
_____, I found a job at a local call centre.
4 Many passengers have had to sleep at the airport because all the flights have been delayed. WITH
_____, many passengers have had to sleep at the airport.
5 You must eat chocolate within reasonable limits or you'll put on weight. MODERATION
You must eat chocolate _____ avoid putting on weight.
6 Thomas was slower than the others and couldn't keep up. PACE
Thomas was _____ and couldn't keep up.
7 The restaurant changes the menu every day. BASIS
The menu is changed by the restaurant _____.
8 As the economy gets worse, the company is planning to cut down on salaries. WANE
With the _____, the company is planning to cut down on salaries.

9 A study of Ebola survivors has revealed a group of people who don't get ill after contacting with the virus. IMMUNE
A study of Ebola survivors has revealed a group of people who _____ the virus.
10 Bill loved poetry from early childhood. FOR
Bill _____ poetry from early childhood.

/ 10

VOCABULARY

3 Complete the sentences with the correct words. The first letter is given.

1 My best friend brought me a scarf made of genuine s_____ when she was in Japan.
2 Jack often wears a pair of old s_____ jeans when he does the gardening.
3 I bought this gorgeous f_____ skirt. It has pink roses on a white background.
4 I always wear s_____ clothes to work – a suit, a tie, a well-ironed white shirt.
5 There is a thick l_____ on the inside of my ski jacket which keeps me warm.
6 My new necklace is made up of lots of individual b_____.
7 One of the latest trends is having your hair h_____ to get a sun-kissed look.
8 I decided to take up jogging, but I still haven't bought a good pair of t_____.
9 I must get some s_____ shoes for walking in the hills.
10 When the actor put the w_____ on his head, he finally became the character.

/ 10

4 Choose the correct word to complete each snowclone.

1 We have _____ peak home furnishings.
   a accomplished   b achieved   c reached
2 Keep _____ and carry on.
   a silent   b calm   c relaxed
3 Pride is the _____ of all sins.
   a mother   b aunt   c sister
4 It's life, Jim, but not _____ we know it.
   a that   b as   c how
5 There's a _____ line between genius and insanity.
   a thin   b final   c fine
6 Life's too _____ for a bad coffee.
   a short   b precious   c quick
7 Good is the _____ bad.
   a opposite   b popular   c new
8 The neighbours from _____.
   a above   b hell   c south
9 Danger is my _____ name.
   a first   b middle   c surname
10 You can _____ the girl out of the country, but you can't _____ the country out of the girl.
   a get   b bring   c take

/ 10

5 Complete the sentences using words based on the verbs, adjectives and nouns in the boxes. There is one extra word in each box.

> strong   justify   broad   mystery   authorise
> simple

1 The ad claims this mouthwash is good for you as it is supposed to _____ your gums and teeth if used regularly.
2 I know it's an over-_____ but I think boys like football because they get to run around a lot.
3 One of the most _____ events was the complete disappearance of a submarine. Nobody knows what happened to it.
4 Most users want to protect their webpages from _____ access to their personal information.
5 A homeowner shot a burglar. The court decided that his act was _____ as he was trying to protect his life.

> heart   general   destroy   ideal   commercial   light

6 The increasing _____ of the movie industry means that many movies are just glorified advertisements for top-end products.
7 The _____ of the rainforest is a great ecological disaster which must be stopped now.
8 The life of a celebrity is often _____ by ordinary young people, but in fact it is not as perfect as they imagine.
9 When talking to children about love and relationships you should avoid _____ as everybody experiences such things in their own way.
10 It's _____ to hear that the tests went so well. Perhaps there is hope that a cure will be found.

☐ / 10   ☐ / 50

UNIT 16   TEST

GRAMMAR

1 Choose the correct word or phrase to complete the sentences.

1 The unemployment rate looks _____ to rise in the next couple of months. Lots of people are going to lose their jobs.
  a set   b on the verge   c a possibility
2 There's a _____ chance Jane might get the job.
  a short   b slim   c narrow
3 The president _____ to the press at 3. She has an important announcement to make.
  a is to speak
  b is bound to speak
  c will end up speaking
4 Such a derisory offer is highly _____ to be rejected.
  a set   b bound   c likely
5 The next train _____ leave at 6.45.
  a is likely to b is set to   c is due to
  `/ 5`

2 Complete the sentences with the correct prepositions.

1 We're just _____ to leave. What do you want to ask?
2 The likelihood _____ this happening is small.
3 I'm due _____ a rest. I've been working really hard.
4 The stage is set _____ a significant election victory.
5 We have a good chance _____ winning.
  `/ 5`

VOCABULARY

3 Complete the second sentence so that it has a similar meaning to the first sentence using the word given. Do not change the word given. You must use between two and five words, including the word given.

1 It's highly likely Claire will lose the match. SURE
  Claire _____ the match.
2 I don't think James will win the election. CHANCES
  I think the _____ the election is pretty low.
3 This medication hasn't been tested yet, but it is likely to be safe to use. PROBABILITY
  In _____, this medication is safe to use.
4 He is going to leave the company. BRINK
  He's _____ the company.
5 We will probably have to cut down on extra expenses. IS
  The _____ we will have to cut down on extra expenses.
6 It's possible that the oil prices will continue to fall. ODDS
  _____ the oil prices will continue to fall.
7 It is just possible that he'll become the chairman of the committee. SLIM
  There's _____ becoming the chairman of the committee.
8 I can't talk to you right now as I'm leaving. ABOUT
  I can't talk to you right now as _____.

9 I'm sure this project won't work. CHANCE
  There is _____ this project working.
10 It's highly likely that the number of tourists will drop next year. DISTINCT
  There's _____ that the number of tourists will drop next year.
  `/ 10`

4 Circle the correct words to complete each sentence. If both options are correct, circle both words.

1 I accidentally dropped a pan of really hot soup and *scalded / burnt* my foot quite badly.
2 I can't stand the sight of blood. I *freak out / pass out* and have to leave the room.
3 As a child, I once fell off my bike and *banged / whacked* my head on the road.
4 When I *came to / came about*, I realised I was in hospital.
5 She was in a bad car crash. She was losing a lot of blood – it was *streaming / leaking* down her face.
6 He showed me a large *gash / cut* on his leg, which he said was the result of falling from a tree.
7 As Kim was climbing over the fence, she caught her skirt on a nail and *ripped / tore* it.
8 Ben *sliced / ripped* open his finger while he was peeling potatoes.
9 Low blood pressure or low sugar level can make you lose *consciousness / faint*.
10 The injection was so painful that it made me cry. I was in *agony / terrible* pain.
11 I heard the bone in my arm *cut / snap*. It was a horrible experience.
12 By the time he reached the hospital, he was bleeding *strongly / profusely*.
  `/ 12`

5 Choose the correct word to complete the sentences.

1 The hospital staff was accused of medical _____ after the death of a newborn baby.
  a failure   b negligence   c inattentiveness
2 The wife of a man who was killed by a fallen tree, has finally filed a _____ against the local authorities.
  a law   b case   c lawsuit
3 New _____ is being introduced in the European Parliament to encourage international adoptions.
  a regulation   b reference   c legislation
4 The judge ordered the college to pay _____ to a former student after she'd proved she'd been bullied.
  a fines   b damages   c fees
5 The lawyers hope this court case will set a legal _____ which will help protect the Arctic in the future.
  a precedent   b model   c example
6 The local residents disagree with the judge's decision and are preparing an _____.
  a application b objection   c appeal
7 The employer's _____ doesn't cover any accidents that you have outside the office premises.
  a drawback   b duty   c liability

8 Major instances of _____ towards patients were revealed after a number of inspections in health centres. It was revealed that the staff consistently failed to perform their duties.
   a objection   b non-compliance c negligence

9 This company was _____ liable for its negligent actions which led to the catastrophe.
   a brought   b held   c lifted

10 It is the job of a lawyer to find any _____ on which a case could be dismissed.
   a causes   b grounds   c reasons

[/ 10]

6 Complete the sentences with *danger, peril, threat, hazard, menace* or *risk*.

1 Those warning signs are there for a reason. You ignore them at your _____.

2 The peace and quiet of the village is under _____ from the government's plan to build a new motorway.

3 Leaving uncooked chicken in the kitchen area is a health _____.

4 Local people are getting together to combat the _____ of drug use on the estate.

5 If we stay here, we run the _____ of getting cut off by the tide.

6 Extreme sports are fraught with _____.

7 The arms build-up in the region poses a _____ to all of us.

8 You'll be in serious _____ of being arrested if you don't move.

[/ 8] [/ 50]

REVIEW TEST 1   UNITS 1–6

GRAMMAR

1 Complete the sentences with one word in each space.

1 Frankly, I _____ describe his behaviour as unacceptable. He was so rude! It's not something I _____ expect from someone in his position.

2 The housing crisis _____ not be what it is today if the government _____ taken action sooner.

3 The _____ I _____ most irritating about Jack is his arrogance.

4 I expected more support from Karen but _____ she did when asked to help _____ make a few phone calls.

5 _____ is the banking sector rather than the government _____ is to blame for the problems we face.

6 _____ happened next was so remarkable _____ I'll never forget it.

7 If you _____ calling her day after day, she _____ definitely get annoyed with you.

8 _____ payment is received in the next 24 hours, we _____ have no choice but to take legal proceedings.

9 It is an old, industrial building _____ a tall chimney made _____ brick.

10 I wish I _____ stay longer, but I _____, I'm afraid.

/ 10

2 Complete the text with the correct form of the verbs in brackets.

Discos for older people, anyone?

All my life, I ¹_____ (love) discos, but I'm 46 now, and where in London can you go clubbing if you're getting on? To be honest, I ²_____ (consider) giving up dancing altogether until a friend told me about a regular disco dancing get-together in a community centre in Hither Green, a suburb in the south-east of the city. If only I ³_____ (know) about this place earlier. ⁴_____ (spend) many a night embarrassing myself dancing among kids half my age, I suddenly found I was among disco fans who were the same age as me, and just as keen on the music. I ⁵_____ (dance) all night but for the fact that the place closed at eleven, perhaps because, in truth, despite loving the music, we oldies really couldn't keep up the pace. It was a great night out, though, and I can't wait to go again.

I ⁶_____ (describe) the place as a cross between a village fete and a scene from *Saturday Night Fever*. Half the people there were dressed in spandex and glitter! In fact, I really ⁷_____ (should / wear) something more exciting that first time. I intend to remedy that before I go again. By this time next week, I ⁸_____ (buy) myself some disco dancing gear and a ticket for the next

---

dance night. Assuming they ⁹_____ (not cancel) the event, it'll be another amazing night out. I wish other clubs ¹⁰_____ (put on) great nights out for older people in this way. 46 is the new 21, you know.

/ 10

VOCABULARY

3 Complete each sentence with one word.

1 The crime _____ in the city is already high, and likely to rise.

2 There's not a _____ of litter anywhere in the park. It's all been picked up by volunteers.

3 After the twins had finished making biscuits, the kitchen was _____ a war zone.

4 I enjoy going to the cinema every now and _____.

5 Frankly, Claire is a bit of a _____. She's difficult, demanding and annoying!

6 It's your decision. Have you made up your _____ what to do yet?

7 We have managed to _____ down the shortlist of candidates for the job from twelve to three.

8 Mark doesn't _____ his weight at work. He should work harder.

9 I'm sorry, but, what with one _____ and another, I haven't had time to book the tickets.

10 What is the word? It's on the _____ of my tongue. I just can't remember it.

/ 10

4 Choose the correct word to complete the sentences.

1 Graffiti artists live on the edge. They can _____ fined heavily for damaging public property.
   a have   b get   c make

2 Liz lived in a run-_____ part of the city where there was both poverty and crime.
   a through   b down   c torn

3 I'm sick and _____ of having to commute to work each day.
   a tired   b ill   c bored

4 Have you sorted _____ somewhere to stay yet?
   a up   b out   c upon

5 Mel and Adam aren't on speaking _____. They are really annoyed with each other.
   a terms   b forms   c words

6 In some societies, people have _____ touch with traditional ways.
   a missed   b failed   c lost

7 Have you _____ the floor yet?
   a swept   b spilled   c rinsed

8 It was so funny we were all on the floor in _____.
   a floods   b stitches   c yawns

9 Let's not worry about what happened. There's no point in crying over spilt _____.
   a milk   b beer   c water

10 Hardwick was _____ on trial for murder.
   a set   b stood   c put

/ 10

LISTENING

5 ▶ Listen to the radio interview and choose the best answer.

1 How does the presenter introduce Amy at the start of the interview?

a as somebody who has recently left her post in the New York City planning department

b as a person with a strong record of success in dealing with difficult planning issues

c as somebody who has just been given a new role in the New York City planning department

d as a person with a significant amount of experience in carrying out her job as a planning director

2 What does Amy say about construction projects in New York since she started her current job?

a There have been considerable alterations to the whole city's infrastructure.

b One part of the city has been completely transformed.

c Financial constraints have resulted in only a limited amount of building being done.

d She has had to work to correct errors made by previous architects.

3 How does Amy defend herself when accused of agreeing to two controversial construction projects?

a She denies having any involvement in either of the projects.

b She says the presenter has exaggerated the level of protest involved.

c She admits to the buildings being over-budget but argues they were necessary.

d She argues that the opponents of the project did not fully understand its aim.

4 Which planning issue is most important to Amy?

a the need to ensure that New York's neighbourhoods can cater for all who visit

b the need to help more people move into New York from surrounding areas

c the need for homes that even people on relatively low incomes can buy

d the need to help entrepreneurs with start-up schemes to help them open shops

5 In what way is New York ahead of all other American cities?

a It is a city where fewer people rely on using a car.

b The city has excellent schemes for water collection.

c It has learnt how to store solar power better than others.

d The city has a much better public transport system than other cities.

/ 15

SPEAKING

6 Talk about one of the following topics.

• how you would improve the appearance, infrastructure and facilities of a town or city you know well

• the aspects of culture and identity which help define you as a person

• how you intend to vote in a forthcoming election or referendum and why

/ 15

READING

7a Read the text and choose the best heading.

1 Why do the English never celebrate St George's Day?

2 Why should the English celebrate St George's Day?

3 Why are the English unsure about celebrating St George's Day?

/ 1

7b Read the text and decide where each extract should go. There is one extract you don't need.

1 However, there is no great desire in the most populous and historically most dominant part of Great Britain to do the same.

2 The Mayor of London spearheaded a recent campaign to organise a huge celebration centred on Trafalgar Square in London, for example.

3 The blame for this can hardly be put on St George himself, who is undoubtedly a patron saint to be proud of.

4 That notwithstanding, interest in celebrating such a controversial patron saint was to decline over the following centuries.

5 Later, during the early fifteenth century, the saint's feast became a major celebration in England, on a par with Christmas.

/ 8

7c Read the text again and answer the questions.

In which paragraph (A to D)

1 do we learn nothing of the life of the real St George?

2 does the writer describe a time when English people changed their view of St George's Day?

3 do we hear why other nations differ from the English in their view of saints' days?

/ 6

A

In common with other European countries, England has a patron saint, St George, whose feast day falls on April 23rd each year. As a rule, however, the average English person has very mixed feelings about celebrating the event. ᵃ_____ Celebrated in legend for his ability to kill dragons, St George has been described as the epitome of the warrior saint of medieval legend. The indifference with which the majority of English people treat his feast day has more to do with the history of England, and conflicting notions of what constitutes English identity.

B

On medieval battlefields the name and spirit of St George was invoked by English soldiers, and the saint's banner, a red cross on a white background, was adopted and worn. The cross, a symbol of the martyrdom of the historical figure of St George, who was executed for his faith, was believed to offer protection in battle. b_____ The English Reformation, however, put an end to St George's prominence. Catholicism was overthrown as the established faith of the country and with Protestantism came apathy, or even mistrust, towards saints and saints' days. The feast of St George ceased to be a public holiday, and, by the eighteenth century, when the political union between England and Scotland encouraged people to think of themselves as British rather than English, the saint's hold on the national consciousness was much reduced.

C

Some scholars argue that there are reasons other than the switch to the Protestant faith for the reluctance of ordinary English people to embrace the feast day of their national saint, a man who, during his actual lifetime, lived and died in what is now the Middle East, and never came anywhere near the coast of England. St Andrew's Day in Scotland and St David's Day in Wales are celebrated enthusiastically, as assertions of national identity distinct from that of England. c_____ Indeed, many English people are reluctant to express patriotic sentiments so openly, seeing them as a distasteful expression of national superiority. It is fair to say that the flag of St George has been to some extent appropriated by groups with nationalist, racist or anti-EU agendas, and many ordinary people would consider it to be an exclusive rather than an inclusive emblem.

D

Despite all the history, and the nervousness about fully embracing St George's Day, there have been many attempts in recent years, by both politicians and interested lobby groups, to persuade the English to change their attitude towards the day. d_____ In truth, though, while some do mark the occasion, it continues to pass most people by. No doubt St George himself, a soldier of the Roman Empire who converted to Christianity, but who never, incidentally, killed any dragons, would be neither impressed nor particularly concerned about the English reluctance to make more of his day.

WRITING

8 Write one of the following.
- an email advising a friend who is visiting a city you know well on where to stay, what to do and what places to visit
- an opinion essay about this statement: *People aged 16 to 18 should be allowed to vote in elections.* Discuss.
- a review of a film you have recently seen

/ 15 / 100

LISTENING

5 ▶ Listen to the radio interview and choose the best answer.

1 The presenter says that Sir Anthony Clark
   a has only ever written history books about the USA.
   b has largely specialised in one particular age in American history.
   c is an expert on twentieth-century world history.
   d began writing American history books as a teenager.

2 How did Sir Anthony first become interested in history?
   a It happened as a result of experiences he had in the 1960s.
   b It arose from his love of academic life at college.
   c He says he became a historian by accident.
   d His job as a diplomat led him to an interest in history.

3 In Sir Anthony's opinion, which quality is most important in a historian?
   a Being both very patient and very persistent.
   b Having a good relationship with your reader.
   c Working hard to gain a detailed level of knowledge.
   d Being able to come to clear judgments or explanations.

4 What does Sir Anthony say a historian should most avoid?
   a examining the actions of people from history by today's standards or morals
   b expressing their own personal bias when drawing conclusions
   c using contemporary material instead of going back to original sources
   d being tempted to use history to criticise modern events

5 Which of the following best summarises Sir Anthony's view with regard to the lessons we can learn from history?
   a Knowing about history helps us predict possible outcomes in the future.
   b We may as well take no notice of the lessons from history.
   c We should be cautious about which lessons from history to follow.
   d Knowing about history prevents politicians from leading us into disaster.

/ 15

SPEAKING

6 Talk about one of the following topics.
• describe a place of great natural beauty that you have visited
• describe an occasion when you experienced great highs or lows when watching or participating in sport
• make a presentation about a historical event that was important in your country's history

/ 15

READING

7a Read the text. Match the sub-headings below to three of the paragraphs A–E in the text. There are two paragraphs that do not match with any of the sub-headings.

1 How office workers reversed a trend
2 How a revolution in the way we build led to the open plan office
3 How social change led to a new way of working

/ 3

7b Read the text and decide where each extract should go. There is one extract you don't need.

1 Instead of freeing office workers to discuss and debate, it has exposed them to the annoying habits and unwanted chatter of their co-workers.
2 Of course, there was nothing even remotely liberating for workers about this.
3 During the coming decades, planners will continue to work tirelessly to transform the office environment.
4 Historians have argued that this was a natural reaction to the structured, top-down political systems previously imposed on people in Europe.

/ 6

7c Read the text again and answer the questions with the number of the correct paragraph.

In which paragraph (A to E)
1 does the writer not mention any negative aspect of the office environment described?
2 does the writer compare the office to other environments in which people gather in large groups?
3 does the writer give reasons why the design of an office environment did not achieve what it set out to do?

/ 6

The rise and fall of the open plan office

A _____
Many of us will spend much of our working lives in open-plan offices, wondering, as we sit at our carefully placed desks among the pot plants, irritated by our colleague's droning voice or pen-clicking habit, whether office life in wide spaces really is the best way of passing a career.

B _____
Unsurprisingly, it was the Americans, at the end of the nineteenth century, who first came up with the idea of freeing employees from their individual offices and gathering them together in one great space. Liberated by the opportunity afforded by exciting new construction techniques, which used steel girders to hold up ceilings, thus negating the need to have lots of walls, office planners placed desks in rows, making it easier for workers to pass paper between each other, and easier for bosses to see what was going on. a_____ Far from it. Placed in rows as if at school, and overseen by managers who had their own private offices, they were expected to sit in industrious silence like automatons, the office experience reminiscent of that of the assembly line on the factory floor.

C _____

After the Second World War, a new thinking took hold with regard to open plan office design, notably, at first, in Germany. The idea was that offices should be more organic, and less hierarchical. ᵇ_____ Be that as it may, the new office landscape involved scattering desks in an apparently chaotic fashion, and in such a way that they encouraged workers to meet and talk with each other. Managers found themselves in among secretarial workers, and the most lowly clerk sometimes found him or herself right next to the boss. Much of the elitism and snobbery of old-style offices was lost as the size or location of a desk suddenly had little or nothing to do with the seniority or salary of an employee.

D _____

Idealistic and revolutionary though the new office plan was back in the 1940s and 1950s, it has, in the eyes of many workers, failed to deliver the ideal workplace environment it promised. ᶜ_____ Constantly interrupted, many are driven to distraction, and the environment created can be both stressful and confrontational as employees mark out their territory, or fall out with colleagues who invade their space. It is also incredibly difficult to get the noise levels right in an open plan office, some of which are so noisy it's hard to concentrate, while others are deathly quiet, making it hard to have private meetings as they are so easily overheard.

E _____

Ironically, it is in Germany, as well as in Scandinavia, that the open-plan office has come to be most roundly rejected in recent years. Orchestrated largely by employees themselves, who, having been consulted at last, overwhelmingly rejected what office designers had previously considered good for them, there has been a move back to an environment in which workers have their own personal space. This may be private offices, but it might also be carefully designed 'cellular' spaces in which everybody has access to a window with a view, a door, or a wall to call their own. Nowhere is ever perfect. An office with walls can be lonely and isolating. However, it seems that, by and large, in the office we prefer having a place to call our own to a shared environment.

WRITING

8 Write one of the following.
- a covering letter for a dream job that you would like to apply for
- a magazine article entitled *The Day That Shook The World*
- an essay discussing the pros and cons of having the Olympics in your country

| / 15 | | / 100 |

GRAMMAR

1 Complete the sentences with one word in each space.

1 We were accused _____ breaching the peace and warned _____ to do it again.

2 Blamed by his own staff _____ losing money, Higgins was threatened _____ the sack.

3 There are many ways in _____ we can try to support people _____ relatives were killed in the disaster.

4 The police feared that people would try to break into the building. That is the main reason _____ the place in _____ the murders took place was demolished.

5 In cases _____ there is little or no proof, there is no reason _____ the judge shouldn't order a mistrial.

6 Andy's fondness _____ team sports stems _____ the positive experiences he had doing sport at school.

7 I am grateful _____ all those who have shown belief _____ me during this difficult time.

8 By _____ the most significant reason for such a sharp rise _____ the homeless figures is the removal of the housing subsidy by the government.

9 Although he was _____ trial, and _____ oath, Smethurst was rude and disdainful in court.

10 There's only a very slim _____ of finishing the project tonight. _____ all probability, we'll have to stay and work on it over the weekend.

/ 10

2 Complete the text with the correct form of the verbs in brackets.

Tabloids in the dock

A tabloid photographer who, for months,
¹_____ (deny) any involvement in
²_____ (use) illegal means to get close-up photos of a celebrity and his family, was finally found guilty of an invasion of privacy at Hazeley Crown Court last Tuesday. While ³_____ (answer) questions from the prosecution, the photographer admitted ⁴_____ (take) photographs of film star Will Kerry's patio and swimming pool from a location which was clearly in the middle of land owned by the actor. Consequently, the judge had no choice but to award damages. Besides ⁵_____ (fine) for taking the photos, the photographer ⁶_____ (warn) not ⁷_____ (go) within twenty kilometres of land belonging to the actor. In an interview, Will Kerry blamed the police for ⁸_____ (not take) the threats to his privacy seriously, and said he was not alone in ⁹_____ (want) tighter laws. The tabloid's editor has apologised and vowed ¹⁰_____ (change) the policy at the newspaper with regard to taking photographs of celebrities.

/ 10

VOCABULARY

3 Complete each sentence with one word.

1 The early bird catches the _____. That's why I've set my alarm for six.

2 I've been walking around the shops all morning. I'm absolutely _____ on my feet.

3 We have a very solid client _____. That's why we think our sales will hold during the recession.

4 We may have to _____ on new sales staff. We simply don't have enough people working for us.

5 Workers are threatening to _____ a strike if managers don't meet their pay demands.

6 It's your decision. Have you made up your _____ what to do yet?

7 My jeans are worn _____. I've had them for years and need new ones.

8 Susie whacked her head on the pavement and _____ out. She didn't regain consciousness until she got to hospital.

9 The celebrity took the newspaper to court for printing the story about her and won over $1 million in _____. The money was given to compensate for her ruined reputation.

10 By travelling to the infected zone, you run the _____ of catching the disease.

/ 10

4 Choose the correct word to complete each sentence.

1 New police chief _____ to reduce crime.
   a vows   b hails   c seizes

2 Arun must have _____ out through the back door when we weren't looking. He's not here now.
   a tripped   b dropped   c slipped

3 The company _____ 60 employees, some of whom had worked there for a long time, because the only way to reduce costs was to cut the workforce.
   a picked out   b laid off   c turned down

4 I'm not really _____ with the latest computer technology.
   a au fait   b en route   c faux pas

5 The German car manufacturer is hoping to _____ a contract to sell in China.
   a launch   b reach   c seal

6 In the 1970s, everybody wore jeans with _____.
   a collars   b flares   c lapels

7 She was bleeding _____ from the wound.
   a streamingly   b profusely   c openly

8 I _____ my hand with boiling water.
   a scalded   b ripped   c freaked

9 The court's decision has _____ a precedent which will have to be followed in future.
   a put   b set   c stood

10 The spread of the virus poses a real health _____.
   a peril   b menace   c hazard

/ 10

LISTENING

5 ▶ Listen to the radio interview and choose the best answer.

1 What did Ken Logan achieve during his time as editor of a newspaper called the Chronicle?
 a He tried to design the first online news website.
 b He helped instruct reporters in digital technology.
 c He transformed the design of the newspaper.
 d He introduced a new broadsheet form of the newspaper.

2 What do we find out about Ken's journalistic background?
 a He became editor of the Chronicle immediately after leaving the news bureau in Warsaw.
 b He spent ten years working at the London Media College.
 c He learnt about new technology while employed by Press International.
 d He left Press International to go and work abroad.

3 What does Ken say about his role in starting an online newspaper at the Bugle?
 a The fact that he got to start up a newspaper website was accidental.
 b Nobody had designed a newspaper website before his team did.
 c He wanted a newspaper website with a commitment to good research.
 d He aimed to cover different stories to what you usually find in a paper.

4 What personal challenges did Ken face when setting up the website?
 a The technology was to cause him a lot of problems.
 b There were significant financial difficulties to face.
 c He felt responsible for both the technical and journalistic operations.
 d Getting the right sort of staff was a demanding problem.

5 Nowadays, to what extent are the reporters who work on the website different from those who work on the regular newspaper?
 a There isn't much difference as many reporters work on both.
 b Journalists on the regular newspaper are, by and large, older.
 c Reporters on the website are expected to react more quickly to tight deadlines.
 d There tends to be a lot of competition between the two reporting teams.

/ 15

SPEAKING

6 Talk about one of the following topics.
• trends that are currently 'in' and why they are so popular
• a politician or business person who has influenced you
• a law you would change and why

/ 15

READING

7a Read the text and decide where each extract should go. There is one extract you don't need.

1 What we do, the everyday risks we take, can have a powerful influence on the people around us, perhaps far more than we are willing to admit.

2 The startling disparity between the responses surprised researchers, and led them to seek explanations.

3 No amount of reasoning can lead us to draw any conclusion with regard to risk-taking other than this one.

4 On the contrary, it is one influenced by our emotions and by the behaviour of those around us.

5 In other words, if we see lots of people doing something dangerous, we tend to think it's alright for us to be doing it, too.

/ 8

7b Read the text again and decide if each statement is true (T) or false (F).

In paragraph one
1 The experiment proved that people are more concerned about risk to themselves than others. T / F
2 The writer provides an example of common risk-taking behaviour. T / F
3 The result of the experiment into risk-taking was not expected by those who carried it out. T / F

In paragraph two
4 The writer singles out one particular group of people who may tend to take more risks than others. T / F
5 The writer gives at least one reason why people take risks which couldn't be categorised as 'cognitive bias'. T / F

In paragraph three
6 The writer concludes that the main reason for extreme risk-taking behaviour is peer pressure. T / F
7 The writer concludes with advice on what we can all do to tackle the problem of risk-taking. T / F

/ 7

Risk taking

A recent experiment into risk-taking has thrown up an interesting paradox, which is that we take a different view of risks when we take them than we do if asked to evaluate how dangerous they are for others. In other words, plenty of people are quite happy to bomb down the motorway over the speed limit but would be horrified if their much-loved partner suggested they were about to do the same. In the experiment, one group was asked whether they would engage in certain perilous activities, while another group were asked to decide whether they would recommend them to someone they loved. ᵃ_____ Indeed, on first glance, one might consider the results of the experiment to be counter-intuitive. Aren't we supposed to look after our own safety above that of all others?

The conclusion drawn by researchers was that being sensible and impartial was perfectly feasible for people when asked to put themselves in another's shoes, but a concept that went out of the window when applied to their own actions. The very act of trying to work out how hazardous something might be for another person obliges us to be objective, and this leads us to come to a conclusion which errs on the safe side. By contrast, other factors are at play when we have to make decisions about our own behaviour. For a start, we let our emotions get in the way. Young people, in particular, are prone to doing dangerous things just for the buzz, or just to show they can. We are also influenced by cognitive biases. Psychologists use this term to describe outside influences that affect our reasoning. Perhaps the clearest example of a cognitive bias is the way the actions of others legitimise our actions. b_____ There is, if you like, legitimacy in numbers.

This study has significant implications for those of us keen to discourage people we know from taking part in activities which put them at risk. It shows that our attitude to personal risk isn't a reasoned, evaluated, impartial judgment, as it would be were we to be thinking of others. c_____ In turn, it proves the link between peer pressure and the choices we make, something that all parents are, no doubt, already well aware of. Personal risk-taking will always be higher when hanging out with risk-takers. That notwithstanding, the study shows that it's not necessarily the actions of those closest to us, but the actions of society as a whole, which influence us. d_____ In consequence, if we as a society want to stop people from acting in ways that put themselves in danger, then we should look to ourselves first, and have greater awareness of the consequences our own actions can lead to.

WRITING

8 Write one of the following.
- an email requesting funding for a business project you have
- an opinion essay about this statement: *People who get the news online are better informed than those who watch TV news bulletins.* Discuss.
- a magazine article about a current trend and the reasons behind it

/ 15   / 100

MID-YEAR TEST | UNITS 1–9

GRAMMAR

1 Complete the sentences with the correct form of the verbs in brackets.

1 _____ (win) medals at two Olympics Games, Borzov decided to retire.
2 By the end of the year, the council _____ (demolish) all the old buildings in the city centre. They have plans to build a cinema complex in their place.
3 I knew the expedition _____ (end) in disaster. I said as much before they even set out.
4 Nobody _____ (mind) if you'd just taken a day off. There was no need to turn up with such a bad cold.
5 She _____ (not pass) even if she does loads of revision.
6 Where _____ (you / go) if you'd had the chance?
7 I wish you _____ (stop) criticising me! Whatever I say, it's wrong in your opinion!
8 I wish I _____ (not have to) work next weekend. I could do with a few days off.
9 Brownlee hates _____ (ask) to attend public engagements.
10 Since last summer, a number of similar events _____ (hold) in venues across the country.
11 We ran four marathons in five days, and, in _____ (do) so, raised thousands for charity.
12 Adam is supposed _____ (do) his homework upstairs right now, but I wouldn't be surprised if he's on that computer game again.

[/ 12]

2 Complete the second sentence so that it has a similar meaning to the first sentence.

1 Many believe that this painting is his masterpiece.
This painting _____
2 I remember he wore a large, black hat.
What _____
3 Ensure all your documents are in order or you won't be allowed to enter the country.
As long as _____
4 They won't make a profit without investing in the business.
Unless _____
5 I regret not going on that holiday.
If only _____
6 You can use this gadget to control machines in your house.
This gadget _____

[/ 6]

3 Complete the dialogue with one word in each space. Use auxiliaries and modal auxiliaries in the correct positive or negative forms.

Sam: You're a big fan of Jimi Hendrix, [1]_____ you?
Stan: Yeah. That's right. I idolise him, I really
[2]_____. Over the years, I [3]_____ spent at least £5,000 on records by the great man and on

memorabilia he once owned. In [4]_____ so, I have managed to fill the back room of my flat from floor to ceiling with stuff.
Sam: Well, the place in London where he lived has just [5]_____ opened to the public.
Stan: [6]_____ it?
Sam: Yeah. [7]_____ you bought tickets to go yet? I thought you [8]_____ have.
Stan: Well, I [9]_____ now. Do you have the address of the website? Why didn't you tell me about this earlier?
Sam: I'm sorry. I [10]_____ have, but I just expected you to know already.

[/ 10]

VOCABULARY

4 Complete each sentence with one word.

1 We bought a country cottage because we want a bit of peace and _____.
2 I'm sick and _____ of having to commute to work each day.
3 Joe _____ me as the sort of guy you can trust.
4 Keep an _____ on the kids for me, will you? I'll be back in a minute.
5 We need to buy some washing-up _____ and a sponge.
6 I go for a jog first _____ in the morning. It's a great way of starting the day.
7 Jones was seen as a _____ of fun after he made that embarrassing speech.
8 The film was so sad we were all in _____ of tears by the end.
9 The novel is _____ on a true story.
10 Stop shouting! There's no need to _____ your voice.
11 There is no sign of an end to the fierce price _____ between the two leading supermarkets.
12 The government's refusal to invest yet again represents the thin end of the _____. It looks like they have no intention of supporting the project.
13 This film is _____ -numbingly boring.
14 Alan took compassionate _____ from work after the accident.

[/ 14]

5 Complete the sentences with the correct form of the verbs in the box.

| break spring end set shut |
| put make stand |

1 The town centre is booming right now. New shops and offices _____ all over the place.
2 In the last few months, the local council _____ ambitious plans to transform this district.
3 It took Paul a while to _____ his mind to take the job, but once he'd decided he was glad he had.
4 Kelly always _____ for what she really believes in. She won't compromise.
5 If you're not careful, you'll _____ with no money. Think carefully about what you're spending it on.
6 Sadly, talks _____ between the rebels and the government, and we expect fighting to recommence.

7 Once he starts talking, Ian never _____ . He can talk for hours!

8 We are experienced event organisers who, over the years, _____ important events including international conferences and product launches.

/ 8

LISTENING

6 ▶ Listen to the radio interview and choose the best answer.

1 What does Gaby say about her company?
   a There is nowhere else quite like it.
   b It is a company that is successful and growing.
   c They sell gadgets in major stores and online.
   d All their gadgets are inexpensive and modern.

2 What is the most popular range or category of gadgets on the website?
   a the most economical gadgets are most popular
   b a range of gadgets powered by sunlight
   c gadgets which are good for the environment
   d the most user-friendly gadgets

3 According to Gaby, what is useful about the earphones she is selling?
   a You can continue listening to the TV even when you leave the room.
   b They have high-quality wires or cables so you can hear sound better.
   c They are a low-cost alternative to more traditional headphones.
   d They control the sound level that comes out of the television.

4 In Gaby's opinion, what sort of gadgets do customers most want?
   a gadgets that are practical and serious
   b gadgets that are really weird
   c gadgets that have both style and function
   d gadgets at an economical price

5 What does Gaby say about the flying alarm clock?
   a It's not really very practical.
   b She would love to have one herself.
   c Sales of the clock have not really taken off.
   d It's fun but also serves its purpose.

/ 10

SPEAKING

7 Talk about one of the following topics.
• three important but different relationships that you have with people in your life
• the best way of spending a Saturday night in your town or city
• the scenery and natural landscape of a part of the world you know well

/ 10

READING

8 Read the text and choose the correct answer.

1 What does the writer say about his job?
   a He says that he finds it very difficult to do each day.
   b He suggests it isn't a job everybody would want to do.
   c He expresses some doubts about how best to do the job.
   d He offers no sympathy for those he works with in his job.

2 How does the writer describe young offenders?
   a They have to appear more grown up than their age.
   b They come across as people who are unsure of themselves.
   c They are irresponsible and untrustworthy.
   d They are always very serious.

3 How does the writer compare the juvenile criminals he works with to himself?
   a He says that he too committed crimes but was never caught.
   b He admits to having been punished by the prison system himself.
   c He suggests that, in other circumstances, he may have shared their fate.
   d He feels lucky to have been given support to stay out of trouble.

4 Which of the following is a view expressed by the writer?
   a Many young offenders deserve to be locked in prison for long periods.
   b Society should be more sympathetic to the fact that an offender is young.
   c The victims of crime have a right to expect criminals to face punishment.
   d It is better for society that all serious offenders are off the streets.

5 In the text, it is argued that the prison system is 'counter-productive'. Which of the following is not stated as a reason why this is the case?
   a Many young offenders often feel they have been unfairly imprisoned.
   b Many young offenders are let down by not being taught properly in prison.
   c Many young offenders learn the skills of more experienced criminals in prison.
   d Many young offenders are soon back in prison after they are released.

/ 15

Society and the juvenile criminal

I suspect few would envy my job as a mentor to teenagers locked up in a young offender prison in the south of the country. Each day, as I sit and talk with these troubled youngsters, I am struck by their immaturity and insecurity. While I never find their demands on my time stressful, I am touched by their stories. At the same time, I have to remind myself that they are not wholly innocent, or, necessarily, to be pitied. There is no doubting the seriousness of their offences. These youths have messed up their lives and those of others. They are responsible for acts of senseless violence, for crimes which betray a callous disregard for other people. To my mind, however, it is questionable whether locking up young people like those I encounter on a daily basis is the right thing to do. Is it fair to impose long sentences in tough institutions on people who are still searching for their own identity? Can teenagers be held responsible for their actions in the same way as adults? I always think back to my own teenage years, to the impulses I couldn't control, and to how easily I could have ended up in trouble. Rather than punishing and brutalising young people, shouldn't the state try to understand why they behave as they do, and support and educate them, giving them second and third chances, helping them learn from their mistakes?

There are always two sides to any argument, and, within the prison system itself, there are diverse views on this issue. I had a conversation with a professional within the prison I work in about my concern with regard to the heavy sentencing of these young men, sentences equivalent to those of an adult, and got a curt response. I was told I didn't understand the true nature of these young men and that they were fully responsible for their actions. I was reminded that many of these boys were repeat offenders who had plagued their neighbourhoods for years, and that society could only be protected by sentences which kept them off the streets. I was told to consider the victims and their families. Without the sense of retribution that a long prison sentence brings, it is often hard for the victims of violence to move on.

On the other hand, many who work within the prison system believe that putting young offenders into a harsh regime with hardened criminals is counter-productive. Young offenders toughen up. Rather than reflecting on how to reform their lives, they learn criminal behaviour. One youth I spoke to described how he had learned to fight in prison, how he had learned to hit and hurt people quickly before the prison officers could stop the fight. Instead of tackling the causes of offending, prison lumps young criminals together under one roof, exposing them to violence, poor education provision and long periods of boredom. Moreover, the frequency with which young offenders return to prison shows up the futility of the system. It is an astonishing statistic that around three in four teenagers sentenced to custody will reoffend within a year of release. To my mind, it is about time we change the way we seek to punish rather than rehabilitate young people who fall foul of the law.

WRITING

9 Write one of the following.
- a story based on an urban myth
- an opinion essay about this statement: *The legal age at which someone can drive should be raised to 21.* Discuss.
- a review of a book you have read

/ 15   / 100

END-OF-YEAR TEST 1   UNITS 1–16

GRAMMAR

1 Complete the second sentence so that it has a similar meaning to the first sentence using the words given.

1 The sheer scale of the refugee problem concerns me.
   What _____

2 George hopes to get a scholarship to Harvard University.
   It _____

3 If Sally hadn't slipped, she may well have won the race.
   Had _____

4 I regret breaking up with Debra.
   If only _____

5 In the end, we lost the match.
   We ended up _____

6 Both universities were offering places to applicants from abroad.
   Applicants from abroad _____

7 After she had received her award, Penny began to cry.
   Having _____

8 We posted the news online as soon as we heard it.
   No sooner _____

9 Sylvia's injury didn't affect her performance at all.
   In no way _____

10 Senator Clark said that he had never told a lie.
   Senator Clark denied _____

                                                      ☐ / 10

2 Complete the text with one word in each space.

A robotic age
The world is on the [1]_____ of change, and breakthroughs in the field of robotics look [2]_____ to lead that change. The place [3]_____ we will, in all [4]_____, see the most significant transformation is the workplace. A new idea is to design robots that can perform routine jobs [5]_____ being controlled by a person in a different country. This may seem a strange thing to do at first glance. Why on earth [6]_____ you want the operator to be in a different country? However, imagine [7]_____ a robot cleaner in a big company in Japan, which was [8]_____ controlled by an operator in Thailand or Vietnam. It would create jobs in developing countries, [9]_____ jobs are difficult to find and salaries are low.
   [10]_____ many predict is that it will become possible to rent a robot to do our shopping, visit an elderly relative, or check out a hotel that we're thinking [11]_____ visiting. [12]_____ only would that transform our lives, [13]_____ it would also leave us free time to do what we really want to do. [14]_____ a possibility was unthinkable not so long ago, but now it seems inevitable. Naturally, some may not approve [15]_____ living in a society in [16]_____ we rely [17]_____ robots so much. [18]_____ they to be given a choice, many would prefer to do

things for themselves. The threat of [19]_____ replaced by robots is also a concern for many workers. [20]_____ notwithstanding, it seems clear that a new robotic age will be with us soon.

                                                      ☐ / 20

VOCABULARY

3 Complete each sentence with one word.

1 The journalists were caught up in an _____ conflict between government and rebel forces intent on killing each other.

2 I'm just going to the shops to buy a few bits and _____. Do you want anything?

3 Jim and Moira's marriage is going through a bit of a _____ patch. They aren't talking to each other at the moment.

4 Samantha just _____ into tears when she was told her dog had died.

5 We're just going round in _____ here. Let's stop talking about things and come to a decision.

6 I don't support this line of research. It's a _____ slope leading to unforeseen consequences.

7 If you need a _____ to cry on, give Pam a call. She's very supportive.

8 John is on _____ leave. His father died and he needed time off to get over it.

9 Anderson has been _____ from the team following a string of poor performances.

10 She was shocked. She went as white as a _____.

11 The newspaper was _____ for libel by the actress.

12 Too many cooks spoil the _____.

                                                      ☐ / 12

4 Complete the sentences with the correct phrasal verb form of the verbs in the box.

end	send	go	sort	butt	freak

1 Our region has _____ a lot of changes in recent years. It's a more interesting place as a result.

2 We should try to _____ our differences. Ignoring each other is not the best way to behave.

3 If you go on like this, you'll _____ making yourself ill. Take a rest.

4 Paul's so rude. He's always _____ other people's conversations.

5 The captain was _____ for foul play in the last minute of the match.

6 Ellie _____ when she saw all the blood. She just screamed and screamed.

                                                      ☐ / 6

5 Choose the correct word to complete the sentences.

1 New buildings have been _____ up everywhere. There is a lot of construction going on.
   a springing   b showing   c throwing
2 Marine life is under _____ from pollution and fishing.
   a danger   b peril   c threat
3 Every cloud has a silver _____ .
   a covering   b lining   c lacing
4 She just needs to _____ her fingers and he comes running.
   a click   b clench   c beat
5 We're in danger of failing to _____ the deadline.
   a lose   b meet   c see
6 Both horses and deer have _____ .
   a beaks   b claws   c hooves
7 _____ to the path or you'll get lost.
   a Stray   b Stick   c Stay
8 The rebels began to _____ ground to the government forces.
   a miss   b lose   c fail
9 The novel _____ on the relationship between Gillian and her ex-husband.
   a centres   b bases   c revolves
10 Lewis _____ as an independent in the last election.
   a set   b stood   c lay
11 I don't know why the girls were _____ . It wasn't at all funny.
   a giggling   b mumbling   c muttering
12 She's easy-going and charming, and very good at _____ other people at their ease.
   a showing   b putting   c making

/ 12

LISTENING

6 ▶ Listen to the radio interview and choose the best answer.

1 Why is Amanda Fowler researching the life of one of Britain's best-known businesswomen?
   a for a television documentary about Sarah Henderson's life
   b as part of her research into gender discrimination in business
   c to include aspects of Sarah's career in her book about businesswomen
   d to put together a newspaper article about inspirational business people
2 By the time she died, what had Sarah Henderson achieved?
   a She had founded one of the most successful magazines of the last century.
   b She had promoted ethical trading practices across the world of business.
   c She had founded an organisation to campaign for human rights.
   d She had started the world's most successful cosmetics business.

3 How is Sarah's relationship with her producers described?
   a She ensured her producers were paid appropriately.
   b She insisted on using only the very best materials.
   c She inspired producers to improve their own work practices.
   d She stuck with the same producers year after year.
4 What does Amanda say about fair-trade products in the 1970s?
   a They were quite common then but rarely purchased.
   b Sarah Henderson encouraged people to buy them.
   c There were more fair-trade products than there are now.
   d Most ignored Sarah's call for people to use fair-trade products .
5 How did Sarah Henderson get the law changed?
   a by campaigning for improved women's rights in the workplace
   b by leading a campaign to increase the amount of testing on beauty products
   c by refusing to carry out any tests on the products she was selling
   d by opposing animal testing on cosmetics and getting people to support her

/ 10

SPEAKING

7 Talk about one of the following topics.

- TV programmes, films, books and / or music you remember and reasons why they were culturally important
- an event in recent history that has had an effect on you
- your experience of your first day at work, school or college

/ 10

READING

8a Read the text and decide where each extract should go. There is one extract you don't need.

1 Having spent millions on trying to solve this problem, countries in the developed world have nowhere to go.
2 That said, a failure to police and restrict the use of antibiotics continues to lie at the heart of the problem.
3 For a century, doctors have been able to make use of a near miraculous cure-all which has changed the status of bacterial diseases from that of mass murderers to mild nuisances.
4 Used as a way of protecting a patient when their immune system is compromised by chemotherapy or surgical procedure, millions would die if the drugs were to become ineffective.
5 As enemies go, bacteria have proved to be remarkably combative, and the all-out offensive waged against them by previous generations of medical practitioners has failed.

/ 4

8b Read the text again and answer the questions.

Which paragraph (A–D)

1 describes a current change of approach by doctors?

2 explains why bacteria have been able to resist drugs?

3 mentions more than two current uses of antibiotics?

/ 6

The war against bacteria

A

Imagine a future in which the slightest cut to your finger might well lead to an untreatable bacterial infection and a lingering death. That is the fear of many medical experts currently grappling with the approaching nightmare of a time when antibiotics no longer work. a_____ These days may now be behind us. Already, there are signs of a coming catastrophe. In some parts of the world, there are strains of tuberculosis resistant to all but a couple of drugs, and even hospitals in wealthy countries are rife with hard-to-treat bugs that increasingly threaten the lives of elderly or frail patients.

B

Often described in terms of a war we cannot afford to lose, doctors who were once happy to sanction bombarding their patients' immune systems with drugs like penicillin are now having to rethink what they routinely do. b_____ Instead of wiping out bacteria, the widespread use of antibiotics has enabled them to adapt and come again. This has led to a world in which diagnosing antibiotics as a cure is now restricted in many countries. c_____ Poor sanitation and over-use of antibiotics has helped resistance spread in developing countries, and the fact that anybody can hop on a plane has meant that new bacterial strains are impossible to restrict to one country or region.

C

While our species has failed to discover a new class of antibiotics since the 1980s, bacteria have not let up in their fight to survive by mutating. Capable of doubling in population every 20 minutes, and able to swap bits of their genetic code with other bacteria, their armoury is spectacular, and their fighting capacity seemingly irresistible. We were aware of this from the start. Back in the 1940s, Alexander Fleming, the man who discovered penicillin, warned that using the drug inappropriately could lead to disaster. He feared that practitioners would give inadequate quantities of the drug, thus battling but not defeating the bacteria, and allowing it to quickly mutate and develop resistance. This observation has proved prescient. There is no doubt that our over-diagnosis of the miracle drug has contributed to the survival of our ancient, microscopic enemies.

D

Losing the battle against bacteria is unthinkable. Not only would it mean the return of diseases such as tuberculosis, but it would severely compromise the ability of doctors to treat non-bacterial killers such as cancer or to carry out routine operations. d_____ Steps need to be taken soon, ranging from the internationally proscribed use of drugs in some situations, to greater steps to impose extremely high levels of hygiene so as to prevent bacterial disease in the first place. Some campaign for restricting the supply or raising the price of drugs. Increasingly, such steps seem essential, but potentially ineffectual. The post-biotic age is approaching fast.

WRITING

9 Write one of the following.

- an email inviting a friend from abroad to a cultural event in your country, advising him or her on what to wear, bring, do, eat and / or say
- an opinion essay about this statement: *Zoos are necessary.* Discuss.
- a description of a process with which you are familiar

/ 10   / **100**

negative

END-OF-YEAR TEST 2   UNITS 1–16

GRAMMAR

1 Complete the second sentence so that it has a similar meaning to the first sentence using the words given.

1 I haven't seen the test results so I don't want to offer an opinion.
  Not _____

2 I missed the performance because the traffic was so bad.
  If the traffic _____

3 Harry was upset by the fact that nobody congratulated him.
  What _____

4 Amy's constantly moaning about the weather.
  If only _____

5 Scientists may well interpret the data in a number of different ways.
  The data _____

6 We need to give Joe more time to decide.
  Joe needs _____

7 He was skiing far too fast.
  He shouldn't _____

8 I know you don't want to go, but you have no choice.
  Whether _____

9 Nobody had ever completed a lap in such a fast time before.
  Never before _____

10 I don't think it is right that children should be allowed in.
  I don't approve _____

  / 10

2 Complete the text with one word in each space.

A Productive Way to Punish

[1]_____ lost both his job and his home at the age of 40, New Yorker Carl Hammond took to a life of crime, and, nowadays, barely a day goes by during [2]_____ he doesn't steal something. Indeed, you could say that [3]_____ he does for a living is commit petty theft. [4]_____ lifting goods from the city's department stores on a regular basis, and selling them on the street, may seem [5]_____ a pretty depressing way of life to most, to Carl it makes sense. 'If I [6]_____ better qualified, I'd get a proper job,' he says, 'but I have no prospects, and neither [7]_____ my friends on the street. We haven't been given any choice but to steal, [8]_____ we?' [9]_____ is with sadness in his voice that he says this.

The reason [10]_____ Carl offends and reoffends over and over again is that his shoplifting [11]_____ so petty as to warrant only the shortest of standard sentences – 60 to 90 days at the most. It is no deterrent, and no incentive to change his ways. [12]_____ the fact that he isn't getting any younger, Carl continues to waste his life. [13]_____ is the system that seems to be failing him. Carl [14]_____ probably jump at the chance

of changing his ways [15]_____ he genuinely to be given that opportunity, but instead he is stuck in a cycle of crime, poverty and prison.

Threatened with time in jail, habitual criminals like Carl merely shrug their shoulders. [16]_____ effect, they have ceased to care what is done to them. [17]_____ a different approach can be found, people like him will just spend their lives going in and out of cells. That's why a new project is [18]_____ tried out in the city, which sentences petty criminals to community service instead of prison. The hope is that this new approach will succeed [19]_____ giving Carl and others a greater feeling of self-worth, and will help them change their ways, and, even [20]_____ it fails, it will at least get Carl to do an honest day's work for once.

  / 20

VOCABULARY

3 Complete each sentence with one word.

1 The prime minister's comments sparked a _____ of protests from civil rights activists opposed to his reforms.

2 Think long and _____ about what you want to study before choosing a course.

3 Sam isn't pulling his _____ in the team. He just doesn't work hard enough. We should drop him and pick another player.

4 The play was so dull I was bored out of my _____.

5 There's no point in crying over _____ milk. Let's just move on.

6 The conspirators were put on _____ for planting a bomb in the city centre.

7 Two international athletes were _____ of doping by the athletics federation and banned.

8 We've lost every match this season. We need to improve our performances to stop the _____.

9 Tom built up his business from _____. He had nothing when he started.

10 After standing in the queue for three hours I was _____ on my feet.

11 Poor sales are likely to affect the business' _____ line.

12 The case was thrown out on the _____ of insufficient evidence.

  / 12

4 Complete the sentences with the correct phrasal verb form of the verbs in the box.

lay	come	sound	let	stand	give

1 When you first meet her, Amy _____ as a really nice person. I'd like to get to know her better.

2 Why don't you _____ other people in the company and see what they think.

3 Before he died, Hughes _____ all his money to charities. He was penniless at his death.

4 These figures don't _____ to scrutiny. I think they are unreliable.

5 The small mouse _____ a squeal when I tried to pick it up.
6 Cybertechnics have _____ 20 employees because the company hasn't enough contracts to keep them in work.

/ 6

5 Choose the correct word to complete the sentences.
1 I like smart shirts with long _____.
   a sleeves   b lapels   c flares
2 We may need to _____ staff redundant.
   a give   b take   c make
3 Henry is as hard as _____.
   a nails   b stones   c swords
4 Police have _____ down on drug use in the neighbourhood.
   a broken   b smashed   c cracked
5 I could see Tina _____ at me with anger in her eyes. I didn't know what I'd done wrong.
   a fluttering   b grinning   c glaring
6 Louise never _____ her words. She says things very directly and clearly.
   a turns   b minces   c slices
7 There's a narrow _____ across the top of the mountain range that we'd like to climb to.
   a cove   b ridge   c gorge
8 We employ a large sales _____.
   a army   b force   c regiment
9 The name of the place we went to is on the _____ of my tongue. I wish I could remember it.
   a top   b end   c tip
10 Once everybody has _____ their vote, we will find out who has won.
   a thrown   b pulled   c cast
11 I'm sorry, but that isn't acceptable. It's not the _____ thing in our club.
   a shown   b made   c done
12 I've _____ my trousers at the back. How embarrassing!
   a ripped   b spilled   c flushed

/ 12

LISTENING

6 ▶ Listen to the radio interview and choose the best answer.
1 Which of the following details are mentioned in the description of the crime Bentley and Craig committed?
   a Both Derek Bentley and his friend Christopher Craig came from South London.
   b Derek Bentley shot at a policeman during the course of a burglary.
   c Christopher Craig shot at least two policemen while trying to escape.
   d Bentley was caught by the police after Craig was caught and arrested.
2 During the attempted burglary, someone was heard to shout 'Let him have it!' What does Claudia say about the phrase?
   a She admits the phrase might be interpreted to mean different things.
   b She says Bentley shouted the phrase as Craig jumped from the roof.

c She argues that Bentley meant to tell Craig to give himself up.
d She acknowledges that it's likely nobody actually said the phrase at all.
3 When describing the murder of the policeman, which of the following does Claudia mention?
   a The killer was clearly scared as he ran from the police.
   b The killer was being held down by a policeman as he fired.
   c The killer was holding a weapon he had adapted in some way.
   d The killer clearly didn't intend to kill the policeman at all.
4 How is Derek Bentley described?
   a as a vulnerable young man who wasn't very smart
   b as someone who may have been insane at the time of the murder
   c as a person who knew exactly what he was doing
   d as someone who bore more responsibility for the crime than Craig
5 How does the presenter feel about the trial and execution of Derek Bentley?
   a He considers it a sad but just decision.
   b He appears concerned it was an error.
   c He tries to be neutral in his view.
   d He seems more worried about Craig.

/ 10

SPEAKING

7 Talk about one of the following topics.
- think of a wedding, birthday party or other social occasion you have been to. Describe it to somebody as if they are from a very different culture.
- talk about what you think we can learn from animals
- describe current trends in your country, which ones you have taken part in, and which ones you think will last

/ 10

READING

8a Read the text and decide where each extract should go. There is one extract you don't need.
1 In contrast, local people have consistently refused to work with overseas environmental agencies.
2 Such enlightened thinking would not only save the trees, but would reverse an attitude in the west which has often bordered on the hypocritical.
3 As great tracts of tropical forests are cut down each day, we lose the great trees that once absorbed so much harmful CO_2, and, as we burn and log them, we release even more of the gas.
4 In consequence, it is undoubtedly true that, while the demand remains for timber on the world's markets, trees will come down.
5 Much has already been lost, but so much could still be saved were we to act more resolutely now.

/ 4

8b Read the text again and answer the questions.

In which paragraph (A to D)

1 does the writer explain why local people can't be expected to cease logging without incentives?
2 does the writer give a reason to stop logging other than that of the threat to the world's climate?
3 does the writer say who should take responsibility for changing the situation as it currently is?

/ 6

OPINION: Why we must stop logging

A

Should ten million of us suddenly leap on board planes and fly from Paris to New York, the amount of carbon dioxide released would be shocking, right? Well, believe it or not, the logging industry is responsible for releasing an equivalent amount of carbon dioxide on a daily basis. ᵃ_____
Just about everybody, from the most innocent of children in primary school to the most powerful of world leaders at climate change summits, knows and accepts the error of logging. That notwithstanding, nothing of any import is ever done bar a little lip service, and a shrug of the shoulders.

B

Of course, the daily catastrophe of deforestation threatens to deprive us of so much more, too. While climate change may well be what really focusses the minds of politicians when they ponder how to halt stripping the tropical world of its trees, to many the loss of habitat and species is of comparable concern, not to mention the undiscovered medicines lost to science, or the sheer wonder of nature denied to future generations. ᵇ_____

C

One thing that needs to be acknowledged is that deforestation makes sense financially, not least to the people on the ground, many of whom are impoverished. ᶜ_____ A profit can be made from the wood sold, and, once all the trees have gone, cash crops can be planted in the spaces left. Various peoples have lived for millennia in rainforests by slashing and burning the trees, exhausting the fertile land, then moving on to another part of the forest. Why should they take any notice of environmentalists from wealthy countries whose own lives lack hardship? It is unreasonable to merely demand that poorer countries ignore the financial potential of exploiting this natural resource.

D

The onus then has to be on the wealthier nations of the world to change the dynamics, creating a situation in which protecting rainforests makes more sense financially than tearing them down. ᵈ_____ It is scandalous, for example, that while there are many financial incentives for landowners in Europe to protect natural habitats, there are virtually no incentives for landowners in poorer countries to do the same. It is high time that rich countries used their finances to stop deforestation in its tracks. Imagine a world in which forests were sponsored by major multinationals and prosperous governments, who didn't just ban logging, but invested in jobs for locals as tourist guides, animal welfare officers or even botanists and zoologists.

WRITING

9 Write one of the following.
- a magazine article about a medical discovery that you think is of great importance
- a web page providing information about a place in your country people should visit
- a covering letter for your dream job

/ 10   / 100

UNIT 1

1

1 had covered	6 have declared
2 have been given	7 having left
3 Having designed	8 hadn't visited
4 will have recovered	9 will have worked
5 has been recognised	10 had known

2

1 had been built	6 Having become
2 Having taken	7 will have completed
3 had grown	8 will have created
4 hadn't been	9 has been known
5 have been spent	10 has been rated

3

1 a   2 b   3 b   4 c   5 c   6 b

4

1 From this vantage point, you can see for miles and miles.
2 There were loads and loads of people waiting outside the stadium.
3 Living in such a crowded city is like being in a sardine can.
4 I've had this old T-shirt for ever.
5 The outside toilet is absolutely filthy.
6 It was completely packed in the nightclub.

5

1 to demolish	4 has been neglected
2 to impose	5 underwent
3 soared	6 are flourishing

6

1 a & b raised	4 a & b sparked
2 a & b gripped	5 a & b calm
3 a & b compelled	

7

1 tired	3 order	5 miss	7 quiet
2 then	4 foremost	6 hard	

UNIT 2

1

1 wouldn't help us	6 wouldn't listen to
2 NP	7 wouldn't start
3 NP	8 Would it be OK
4 would never end	9 NP
5 would commute	10 wouldn't smoke

2

1 would describe	6 was named
2 was	7 would have imagined
3 aspired	8 had
4 were influenced	9 would go
5 would have to	10 would have been

3

1 b   2 b   3 a   4 c   5 b

4

1 notice	4 up	7 keeping	10 in
2 made	5 calm	8 prove	
3 get	6 stand	9 tell	

5

1 comes across as	5 bring in
2 got on really well	6 knocked down
3 sorting out	7 get back on
4 subjected to	8 comes down to

6

1 on my nerves	5 a rough patch
2 ourselves to ourselves	6 as a shock
3 eye to eye	7 on speaking terms
4 his weight	

UNIT 3

1

1 thing	4 did	7 main	10 way
2 why	5 place	8 upset	
3 What	6 find	9 How	

2

1 All kids want to do today is play with their mobile phones.
2 What I find really annoying is John's arrogance.
3 The place I'd really love to go to one day is New Zealand.
4 The main reason we go to the south of France is because my wife's parents live there.
5 It is the extreme violence in his films (that) I find upsetting.

3

1 b   2 b   3 a   4 c   5 a   6 b

4

1 d   2 c   3 a   4 e   5 f   6 b

5

1 cover	3 flooded	5 Spread
2 spill	4 mend	

6

1 pan   2 screw   3 stain   4 drill   5 rip

7

1 big thing	5 thing that makes you happy
2 be a fine thing	6 done thing
3 thing led to	7 last thing on my
4 thing in the	8 thing and another

UNIT 4

1

1 Even if	3 Unless	5 whether	7 Provided
2 if	4 Supposing	6 assuming	8 or

2

1 had known, would have cooked
2 hadn't sent, wouldn't be
3 would I do, weren't
4 wouldn't be standing, wasn't
5 would have sent, had reminded
6 was postponed, would the club refund
7 would have felt, hadn't picked
8 would be, hadn't given
9 had been lost, would the party leader have resigned
10 would have failed, hadn't been nominated
11 stop, won't take / aren't going to take
12 were given, would you spend

3

1 have reduced	4 benefit	7 was bankrupted
2 undermined	5 boost	8 triggered
3 discouraged	6 led	

4

1 chuckle	3 gasp	5 chuckle
2 giggle	4 stroll	6 yell

5

1 peered	3 gazed	5 raced	7 grab
2 mumbling	4 yelled	6 stroll	8 step

6

1 a	3 b	5 b	7 b
2 b	4 c	6 a	8 a

UNIT 5

1

1 We came across a small deserted beach beyond the rocks.
2 My elderly mother bought a painting of a cat stalking a mouse.
3 We went to an inspiring exhibition of primitive art held in a barn.
4 People living in India eat curried food cooked with lots of spices.
5 Traditional thatched roofs are made with reeds cut from river banks.

2

1 known as the Tower of London
2 historic
3 on the north bank
4 of the River Thames
5 central
6 by William the Conqueror
7 in 1078
8 which gives the entire castle its name
9 much resented
10 ruling

3

1 mind	3 tears	5 swallow	7 scene
2 hype	4 stitches	6 floods	8 full

4

1 overwhelmed   4 awkward
2 bored   5 yawning
3 mortified

5

1 c	2 f	3 e	4 a	5 b	6 d

6

1 the best performance of   4 manner of
2 on the tip of my   5 the pleasure of
3 the creation of   6 amount of

7

1 c	2 a	3 c	4 b	5 c

UNIT 6

1

1 had listened   6 could buy
2 would switch   7 had complained
3 would stop   8 wasn't / weren't
4 could dance   9 had met
5 were   10 had

2

1 had   6 would
2 would   7 did
3 didn't / wouldn't 8 was / were
4 could   9 was / were
5 would   10 had

3

1 to raise your voice   6 the end of the world
2 from my point of view   7 cleared the air
3 out all wrong   8 our wires crossed
4 round in circles   9 twisting my words
5 in crying over spilt milk

4

1 former   4 diverse
2 annual   5 lasting
3 notable

5

1 c	2 a	3 f	4 b	5 d	6 e

6

1 war   6 fire
2 bombarded   7 campaign
3 defences   8 forces
4 invasion   9 guns
5 battle   10 army

UNIT 7

1

1 were being shown   6 were asked
2 are being cut   7 not being allowed
3 can be used   8 are known
4 are thought   9 may be presented
5 must have been given 10 not being given

2

1 chosen   6 seeing
2 be allowed   7 play
3 got told off   8 has been argued
4 was thought   9 made
5 had the tumour removed 10 had his bike fixed

3

1 extracted   3 stuck   5 due
2 condition   4 inserted   6 reproduction

4

1 address   3 came   5 reflects   7 unfolds
2 resonated 4 stood   6 prompts   8 paves

5

1 impressive   5 remake
2 stupidity   6 colonial
3 technological   7 exploitation
4 cynical   8 implications

6

1 b	3 c	5 a	7 c
2 a	4 c	6 b	8 b

UNIT 8

1

1 don't	4 would	7 do	10 does
2 isn't	5 is	8 has	
3 do	6 won't	9 doing	

2

1 Isn't	4 has	7 isn't	10 do
2 was	5 wouldn't	8 am	
3 do	6 didn't	9 is	

3

1 e	2 a	3 f	4 b	5 d	6 c

4

1 are spreading rumours about   5 get a word in edgeways
2 a shoulder to cry   6 putting words into my
3 mince his words   7 butt into
4 get to the point   8 beating about the bush

5

1 c	2 b	3 d	4 d	5 c

6

1	roamed	3	gnawed	5	lets
2	draw	4	breeding	6	leap

7

1	winning	3	lane	5	term
2	made	4	minute		

UNIT 9

1

1	was thinking	6	is getting
2	was being repaired	7	will be joining
3	wouldn't be asking	8	be doing
4	will be travelling	9	is being done
5	be joking	10	'll be wearing

2

1	are starting	6	has been redeveloped
2	is being seen	7	is made
3	believe	8	won't be sitting
4	have been seeking	9	will be using
5	is	10	might be witnessing

3

1	a	3	a	5	a	7	a
2	b	4	c	6	b		

4

1	b	3	a	5	b	7	b
2	a	4	b	6	a		

5

1	crèche	5	perk
2	leave	6	redundancy
3	notice	7	cuts
4	dismissal	8	Absenteeism

6

1	b	3	b	5	c	7	a
2	c	4	c	6	b	8	b

UNIT 10

1

1	should have planned	6	must have gone
2	may never see	7	may have been trying
3	can't have been	8	can do
4	should / may get	9	should have got
5	should have finished	10	mustn't tell

2

1 should have picked us up half an hour ago.
2 can't be found for this disease.
3 may / might / could still be wandering around out there.
4 must have paid for the prescription.
5 should / ought to win all the games he plays.

3

1	swelled	3	have	5	given	7	put
2	broken	4	gone	6	diagnosed	8	have

4

1	e	2	c	3	f	4	a	5	d	6	b

5

1	a	3	a	5	a	7	a
2	b	4	b	6	b	8	a

6

1	Passersby	5	run-up
2	outbreak	6	breakthrough
3	get-together	7	crackdown
4	workout	8	upbringing

UNIT 11

1

1	Despite	5	owing to	9	Whilst
2	down to	6	Meanwhile	10	Consequently
3	Provided	7	However		
4	whether	8	Moreover		

2

1	so long as	5	on account of	9	as a result of
2	As well as	6	not to mention	10	All the same
3	in order to	7	so as to		
4	On top of	8	In spite of		

3

1	a	2	b	3	c	4	a	5	a

4

1	scraped	5	blew	9	thrashed
2	faded	6	substituted	10	dropped
3	sent	7	sided		
4	knocked	8	caught		

5

1	defies	3	foster	5	collaborated
2	let	4	stimulated		

6

1	courage	5	peer	9	good
2	Strictly	6	lap	10	gloom
3	meet	7	ship		
4	meeting	8	tip		

UNIT 12

1

1 At no time in history has there been a war as brutal as this.
2 Never before have soldiers been expected to fight in such conditions.
3 Had those soldiers not given their lives, the rest of the army wouldn't have been able to retreat.
4 Only after the campaign was over did we know what we had achieved.
5 Such is the danger of the journey that few have ever attempted it.

2

1 No sooner had we entered the museum than we saw our first statue.
2 So amazing was the statue that we just stared at it.
3 Nowhere else in the world can you see so many ancient Egyptian artefacts.
4 Not until we had seen the collection for ourselves did we have any idea how remarkable it was.
5 Not only was the collection extensive, but it was also well-organised.

3

1	close	3	broken	5	sheltered
2	scratch	4	deprived	6	orphaned

4

1	hills	3	chalk	5	sheet
2	chimney	4	water	6	plague

5

1	b	2	e	3	c	4	a	5	d

6

1	a	2	b	3	c	4	d	5	b

7

1 contend	5 casting doubt on
2 put forward	6 stemmed from
3 highlight	7 gave rise to
4 demonstrate	8 accepted

UNIT 13

1

1 a	3 c	5 a	7 a	9 a
2 a	4 c	6 b	8 b	10 c

2

1 were accused of using
2 declared (that) they hadn't known
3 assured readers (that) they had never done
4 confessed that they had been
5 apologised for acting
6 admitted hacking
7 criticised the newspaper for having
8 vowed to take
9 promise never to accept
10 announced (that) he was closing

3

1 hails	3 seize	5 barred	7 pulls
2 vows	4 cleared	6 clash	8 rules

4

1 a	2 b	3 b	4 b	5 a	6 a

5

1 broth	3 worm	5 stones	7 pound
2 mouth	4 lining	6 hatch	8 greener

6

1 a	3 b	5 a	7 c
2 c	4 b	6 b	8 a

UNIT 14

1

1 where	3 who	5 whom	7 that
2 whereby	4 why / -	6 which	8 whose

2

1 The city, which is usually crowded with people, appears to be abandoned at this time of night.
2 We cannot accept the offer which Selhurst Holdings have made.
3 The police arrested three youths who had committed serious offences.
4 Danny Clark, whose brother was my friend at school, has been elected vice-president.
5 The stadium, where the cup final was being held, was on a high security alert.
6 The conference, which had come to an end early, had been an unqualified success.

3

1 have been laid off	6 pitch for
2 pick up	7 floated
3 going under	8 upturn
4 hang in	9 diversify
5 Taking on	10 have been inundated

4

1 e	3 d	5 c	7 f
2 a	4 g	6 h	8 b

5

1 call	4 up	7 scaling	10 exceed
2 reach	5 launched	8 Cutting	11 hostile
3 deal	6 gap	9 sealed	12 takeover

UNIT 15

1

1 to	3 in	5 in	7 for	9 on
2 of	4 of	6 for	8 of	10 of

2

1 out of control
2 are at greater risk of
3 On finishing school
4 With flights having been delayed
5 in moderation to
6 off the pace
7 on a daily basis
8 economy on the wane
9 are immune to
10 had a fondness for

3

1 silk	5 lining	9 sturdy
2 scruffy	6 beads	10 wig
3 flowery	7 highlighted	
4 smart	8 trainers	

4

1 c	3 a	5 a	7 c	9 b
2 b	4 b	6 a	8 b	10 c

5

1 strengthen	6 commercialisation
2 simplification	7 destruction
3 mysterious	8 idealised
4 unauthorised	9 generalisations
5 justifiable	10 heartening

UNIT 16

1

1 a	2 b	3 a	4 c	5 c

2

1 about	2 of	3 for	4 for	5 of

3

1 is sure to lose	6 The odds are (that)
2 chances of James winning	7 a slim chance of him
3 all probability	8 I'm about to leave
4 on the brink of leaving	9 no chance of
5 likelihood is that	10 a distinct possibility

4

1 scalded	7 ripped / tore
2 freak out	8 sliced
3 banged / whacked	9 lose consciousness / faint
4 came to	10 agony / terrible
5 streaming	11 snap
6 gash / cut	12 profusely

5

1 b	3 c	5 a	7 c	9 b
2 c	4 b	6 c	8 b	10 b

6

1 peril	3 hazard	5 risk	7 threat
2 threat	4 menace	6 danger	8 danger

REVIEW TEST 1 UNITS 1–6

1

1 would, would
2 would, had
3 thing, find
4 all, was
5 It, that
6 What, that
7 keep, will
8 Unless, will
9 with, of
10 could, can't

2

1 have loved
2 had considered
3 had known
4 Having spent
5 would have danced
6 would describe
7 should have worn
8 will have bought
9 don't cancel
10 put on / would put on

3

1 rate
2 trace
3 like
4 then
5 pain
6 mind
7 narrow
8 pull
9 thing
10 tip

4

| 1 b | 3 a | 5 a | 7 a | 9 a |
| 2 b | 4 b | 6 c | 8 b | 10 c |

5

| 1 d | 2 c | 3 b | 4 c | 5 a |

7 a

3

7 b

| a 3 | b 5 | c 1 | d 2 |

7 c

| 1 A | 2 B | 3 C |

REVIEW TEST 2 UNITS 7–12

1

1 needs, get
2 Can't, do
3 Isn't, was
4 neither, anyone
5 being, been
6 Despite, same
7 As, said
8 only, but
9 sooner, than
10 Were, would

2

1 has been studied
2 was carried out
3 was needed
4 were arguing
5 were plans approved
6 could have gone
7 had it tested
8 had been undertaken
9 was fluoride added
10 ensuring

3

1 wedge
2 came
3 stand
4 edgeways
5 notice
6 diagnosed
7 mix
8 caught
9 broken
10 put

4

| 1 a | 3 b | 5 c | 7 a | 9 c |
| 2 c | 4 b | 6 c | 8 b | 10 b |

5

| 1 b | 2 a | 3 c | 4 a | 5 a |

7 a

| 1 E | 2 B | 3 C |

7 b

| a 2 | b 4 | c 1 |

7 c

| 1 C | 2 B | 3 D |

REVIEW TEST 3 UNITS 13–16

1

1 of, not
2 for, with
3 which, whose
4 why, which
5 where, why
6 of, from
7 to, in
8 far, in
9 on, under
10 chance, In

2

1 had denied
2 using
3 answering
4 taking
5 being fined
6 was warned
7 to go
8 not taking
9 wanting
10 to change

3

1 worm
2 dead
3 base
4 take
5 call
6 mind
7 out
8 passed
9 compensation
10 risk

4

| 1 a | 3 b | 5 c | 7 b | 9 b |
| 2 c | 4 a | 6 b | 8 a | 10 c |

5

| 1 b | 2 c | 3 c | 4 d | 5 a |

7 a

| a 2 | b 5 | c 4 | d 1 |

7 b

| 1 F | 3 T | 5 T | 7 T |
| 2 T | 4 T | 6 F | |

MID-YEAR TEST UNITS 1–9

1

1 Having won
2 will have demolished
3 would end
4 would have minded
5 won't pass
6 would you have gone
7 would stop
8 didn't have to
9 being asked
10 have been held
11 doing
12 to be doing

2

1 is believed to be his masterpiece.
2 I remember was that he wore a large, black hat.
3 all your documents are in order, you'll be allowed to enter the country.
4 they invest in the business, they won't make a profit.
5 I'd gone on that holiday.
6 can be used to control machines in your house.

3

1 aren't	4 doing	7 Have	10 should
2 do	5 been	8 would	
3 have	6 Has	9 will	

4

1 quiet	5 liquid	9 based	13 mind
2 tired	6 thing	10 raise	14 leave
3 strikes	7 figure	11 war	
4 eye	8 floods	12 wedge	

5

1 are springing up
2 has set out
3 make up
4 stands up
5 end up
6 have broken down
7 shuts up
8 put on

6

| 1 b | 2 c | 3 a | 4 c | 5 d |

8

| 1 b | 2 b | 3 c | 4 b | 5 a |

END-OF-YEAR TEST 1   UNITS 1–16

1
1 What concerns me is the sheer scale of the refugee problem.
2 It is hoped that George will get a scholarship to Harvard University.
3 Had Sally not slipped, she may well have won the race.
4 If only I hadn't broken up with Debra.
5 We ended up losing the match.
6 Applicants from abroad were being offered places at both universities.
7 Having been presented with an award, Penny began to cry.
8 No sooner had we heard the news than we posted it online.
9 In no way did Sylvia's injury affect her performance.
10 Senator Clark denied that he had ever told a lie.

2
1	brink	11	of
2	set	12	Not
3	where	13	but
4	likelihood / probability	14	Such
5	while	15	of
6	would	16	which
7	having	17	on
8	being	18	Were
9	where	19	being
10	What	20	That

3
1	armed	7	shoulder
2	pieces	8	compassionate
3	rough	9	dropped
4	burst	10	sheet
5	circles	11	sued
6	slippery	12	broth

4
1	gone through	4	butting into
2	sort out	5	sent off
3	end up	6	freaked out

5
1 a	3 b	5 b	7 b	9 a	11 a
2 c	4 a	6 c	8 b	10 b	12 b

6
1 c	2 b	3 c	4 b	5 d

8 a
a 3	b 5	c 2	d 4

8 b
1 B	2 C	3 D

END-OF-YEAR TEST 2   UNITS 1–16

1
1 Not having seen the test results, I don't want to offer an opinion.
2 If the traffic hadn't been so bad, I wouldn't have missed the performance.
3 What upset Harry was that nobody congratulated him.
4 If only Amy would stop moaning about the weather.
5 The data might be interpreted in a number of different ways.
6 Joe needs to be given more time to decide.
7 He shouldn't have been skiing so fast.
8 Whether you like it or not, you're going.
9 Never before had anybody completed a lap in such a fast time.
10 I don't approve of children being let in.

2
1	Having	11	is
2	which	12	Despite
3	what	13	It
4	Whilst / Although / While	14	would
5	like	15	were
6	was / were	16	In
7	do	17	Unless
8	have	18	being
9	It	19	in
10	why	20	if

3
1	wave	4	mind	7	convicted	10	dead
2	hard	5	spilt	8	rot	11	bottom
3	weight	6	trial	9	scratch	12	grounds

4
1	comes across	3	gave away	5	let out
2	sound out	4	stand up	6	laid off

5
1 a	3 a	5 c	7 b	9 c	11 c
2 c	4 c	6 b	8 b	10 c	12 a

6
1 c	2 a	3 c	4 a	5 b

8 a
a 3	b 5	c 4	d 2

8 b
1 C	2 B	3 D

TESTS AUDIO SCRIPTS

P = presenter, A = Amy

P: I'm delighted to welcome New York City's Planning Director Amy Hurdle to today's programme to give us an insider's view on the sort of complex planning issues facing major cities around the world. Welcome to the programme, Amy.

A: Hello. It's good to be here.

P: Having spent the best part of a decade in your role as planning director, you must have witnessed wholesale changes to the city over the years.

A: Well, you'd think so, but, to be frank, since the last economic downturn, which coincided with my promotion to this, my current role, building work has been more geared to maintaining the city's fabric than transforming it. I am responsible for advising the Mayor on all matters relating to the development and improvement of the city, but, with budgets limited, we've much less ambitious or grandiose plans than previous generations of architects.

P: It would be fair to say, though, that you're no stranger to controversy, having been involved in giving the green light to two recent construction projects, both of which caused a storm of protest from New York residents?

A: Well, you're referring to the housing projects in north Manhattan, and in Brooklyn. I have to say that I think you're overstating the opposition there, much of which was from environmental groups who have their own agenda. The need for affordable housing, and the high design standards of the construction work you're referring to, more than justified their completion. What I would accept is that any project, no matter what it is, will have its opponents. Parisians really hated the Eiffel Tower when it was first put up, you know.

P: OK. I guess that's always the case. What would you say was the most significant planning issue currently facing the city?

A: I'd say that what we need to maintain, more than anything else, is the economic diversity of the various neighbourhoods of the city. Anyone who's been on vacation to New York will know that every part of the place has its own atmosphere, its own feel, with different shops and restaurants, and a real buzz about the place. It's only by encouraging affordable housing that we can keep that feel. If people have to move out of the city because rents are too high, all this will be lost.

P: So, that's where your focus lies?

A: Absolutely. Historically, New York has always been full of entrepreneurs, keen to set up businesses or open shops, but local businesses need local customers. Our role is to make sure people who've always lived in the city can still live there.

P: What about other cities? What can you learn from them?

A: That's an interesting question. We've been exploring how the cities of Chicago and Berlin have been making the most of their roof space to develop solar energy. That's something we can learn from. The city of Seattle has been really innovative in collecting and using storm water, which saves money and means they have a ready water supply in times of drought. We're behind in that regard although we do have plans to be better. Also, despite being proud of the fact we're less dependent on cars than any other American city, I guess we're behind in such things as having bike lanes or a really well-integrated bus transport system.

P: Lots to improve on then.

A: I guess so. There always is.

P: OK. Well. Thanks for your insight. After the break, I'll be asking …

P = presenter, SA = Sir Anthony Clark

P: Sir Anthony Clark's interest in history, and American history in particular, started in his early teens and has barely wavered since. He has published widely on topics such as the depression of the 1930s and the New Deal that followed it, and he has gained a reputation as one of the world's greatest authorities on US history in the first few decades of the twentieth century. In recent years he has branched out, with some success, to write about other eras and other countries. His new book, however, *America in 1910*, returns to the period with which he is most comfortable and most respected. We're delighted to have Sir Anthony with us in the studio. Welcome to the programme.

SA: Hello. And thank you for mentioning my new book.

P: Well, we'll come to that. It's a great read, I must say. But first I'd like to take you back a little – to the very beginning, in fact. Would you say there was a moment when you decided to become a historian, or was it something that just happened along the way?

SA: Well, I'd say most historians fall into it, as it were, quite by chance. You know, they take history because they can't think of anything else, and get so involved with it, and stuck in books, that they're 30 and unemployable outside of the academic life before they know it. For me, though, it was undoubtedly a calling.

P: A calling?

SA: Oh, yes. My father is to blame. During the 1960s, he worked in the British embassy in Washington, and, being something of a history buff himself, he let me loose on the fabulous library of American history books there, and encouraged me to seek out places of interest in the city. Before long I was hooked. I knew what I wanted to be.

P: What qualities does a good historian need?

SA: I'm tempted to say patience. When researching a book, there is an awful amount of source material you need to get through just to get a thorough working knowledge of the subject. But what's more important is the ability to weigh up the evidence and interpret the facts correctly.

P: I guess that's what the reader requires from a good historian.

SA: Absolutely. And I'm not talking about being biased, or having an agenda. It's about discovering all there is to know, and presenting it in a way that is clear and accurate. One temptation you have as a historian is to see things through a contemporary lens. I think that's an error that is often made. A good historian should not judge a historical figure by today's values, but should show how that figure would have been judged in his or her own time.

P: Some would say we study history in order to learn from the past. Do you hold with that theory?

SA: Well, cynics would say we tend to ignore any lessons. I'm not someone who believes that an understanding of history will stop leaders, or anyone else for that matter, repeating some of the many mistakes that have plunged civilisation into catastrophe over the centuries. But a careful analysis of history can give pointers as to what may or may not happen if you follow a comparable course of action.

P: So, I'm taking that as a yes. Politicians should take note of the lessons of history.

SA: Politicians with an understanding of history tend to be more cautious. That's my opinion.

P: OK. Thank you, Sir Anthony. Now let's talk about your new book.

REVIEW TEST 3 UNITS 13–16

P = presenter, K = Ken

P: Ever since he took on his first editorial role with the Chronicle way back in the nineties, Ken Logan has always had an eye on how technology was likely to transform the newspaper business. He was instrumental back then in training journalists to use computers when writing, editing and designing, and, later, when he became editor of the Bugle, he oversaw one of the first attempts by the press to set up an online news website in parallel with the publication of a paper copy broadsheet. It is fair to say that he foresaw the development of the Internet, and the importance it would have for the industry. I'm happy to welcome Ken Logan on the line from New York. Hello Ken.

K: Hello.

P: Tell us a little about your background, Ken.

K: Well, I graduated from the London Media College 30 years ago now, then spent a decade working for Press International, on what was called the wire service, finding and passing on stories from news bureaus in places as far afield as Stockholm, Zurich and Warsaw. It was a great grounding for my later career as I got to work with what was then cutting-edge technology. It made me realise how important it was. After stints as a deputy editor on various newspapers, I got my first chance to head up a news team with the Chronicle, as you said.

P: You're credited with pioneering online newspapers. How did that come about?

K: Well, by design, not by accident. The main reason I got the job at the Bugle was to head up a team devoted to putting content on the web. We weren't the first, by the way. There were online newspapers before us. But what we did was provide a service which aimed to be as thorough in the way it found and checked stories as a regular newspaper. Before us, online news content was just stuff that people had copied from other sources, and put out there. It wasn't verified in any way. We put out the same quality of news as you'd find in a paper you'd buy in a newsagent's. And that was new.

P: Revolutionary, I'd say. What challenges did you personally face when trying to set up an early online news site?

K: Well, I daresay the technological challenges were immense. The site kept crashing often early on, I remember. But, as editor, these were challenges I left to others. My main concern was one of recruitment. In those days, finding someone good enough to produce copy for a well-established paper like the Bugle, but who could also find their way around digital technology was not easy, I can tell you. I more or less travelled the world looking for the right sort of talent.

P: And was money an issue? I'd guess setting up a news website from scratch involved a lot of finance.

K: It did, you're right. But the newspaper was brilliant in that respect, and happy to invest what it took. I think this reflects the long-standing values of the Bugle, a paper that has always embraced new ideas.

P: How did old-style journalists take to the idea of news online?

K: I guess there was some resistance at that time in press offices other than ours to the idea of moving away from journalists who spent their time out there looking for stories, to journalists who spent their time on computers. At the Bugle though, probably because we got the right people in, that was never an issue. It's true that, early on, the website was put together by a quite separate team of journalists, who were younger than most of those working on the regular newspaper, but that quickly changed, and now there is a real crossover between staff who largely work on the website, and those who devote most of their time to producing stories for the broadsheet.

MID-YEAR TEST UNITS 1–9

P = presenter, G = Gaby

P: Hello and welcome to World of Science, the show that explores amazing new ideas and inventions. Today, I'm talking to Gaby Clarke, who once taught engineering at a leading London university but gave it all up to run her own web-based company called Super Gadgets. Super Gadgets, what's that all about then, Gaby?

G: Well, we're a modern company specialising in selling useful gadgets, ranging from the state-of-the-art and somewhat pricey to the dirt cheap and very cheerful. Our gadgets are not just loads of fun but also just happen to make life easier, too.

P: And on the web?

G: Yes, that's right. We're a web-based business, and, as more and more people are getting into shopping online, we're expanding faster than we can manage. To be honest, we'd be nowhere without the Internet because all our business comes from that source.

P: So, you won't find any of this stuff in your local department store?

G: None of our stuff, no. And our suppliers only sell through us, so no. If you're looking for time-saving, trouble-free gadgets, check us out.

P: OK. So, which gadgets are flying off the webpage right now?

G: The buzz word right now when it comes to gadgets is eco-friendly. Our customers want to do their bit for the planet by not using so much electricity. I guess it saves them money, too. That's why our top sellers are all in this category. We've been selling a lot of wind-up radios. You wind a lever on the back and they work without batteries or mains electricity. They're a bit tricky to get the hang of, to be honest, but, once you do, they're great. Then there is the solar-powered charger. Placed under direct sunlight, it stores energy. Plug in your mobile phone and you're effectively charging it up for free.

P: Mmm. I think I'd like one of those.

G: Well, they're only £19.99.

P: Sounds pricey.

G: Not when you consider that it lasts a life-time.

P: OK. Sold. What else have you got?

G: Marc Wireless earphones, anybody? No wires or cables so you can walk around the house while you're listening to the TV or radio. They're really handy if you're watching TV in your bedroom and want to go to the kitchen to get a drink. You don't have to stop listening.

P: I bet they'd work for anyone keen to cut down the noise level in their house, too. You know, buy them for your teenage kids. They sound great. I'd love to try them out.

G: Well, why don't you? We've found that our customers want gadgets that are elegant in appearance, but also quirky and fun. I guess practicality is essential, too. A couple of our best-selling items sound pretty weird but actually really work well. For instance, one of our biggest sellers is the flying alarm clock. Whenever the alarm goes off, the clock takes off and flies across the room. You can't turn it off until you've found it so it makes you get out of bed. Really practical, you see. To be honest, I wouldn't want to buy something that would deprive me of my beauty sleep, but our customers love it.

P: Not my cup of tea, either, I think. It'd drive me mad. What else are your customers really into?

G: Oh, well my personal favourite would have to be the microwaveable woolly hat. Brand new, so who knows whether our customers will take to it or not, but I'm a fan already, I can tell you. I had one on all weekend because I had a bit of a cold.

P: OK. So how does that work?

G: Well, you put it in the microwave to warm up, then put it on your head. It's great to wear when it's chilly out.

P: Well, I can't say I've heard anything as mad as that before, but, yeah, I can see it working. Thanks for coming on the show, Gaby.

G: It's been a pleasure.

END-OF-YEAR TEST 1 UNITS 1–16

P = presenter, A = Amanda

P: In the studio today, I'm talking to journalist and broadcaster Amanda Fowler who is here to talk about British businesswoman Sarah Henderson. Welcome to the show, Amanda. So, why are you so interested in Sarah Henderson?

A: Well, I guess she's always been someone I've looked up to. The business world has historically been dominated by men, and, with far too few exceptions, it continues to be a place where women are under-represented. That's why it's important to celebrate the achievements of businesswomen who have made their mark.

P: You're researching her life currently. As a broadcaster, the fact that so much of her life was in the public eye must be of help to you.

A: Well, yes, the newspaper cuttings and excerpts from TV programmes featuring her have obviously helped. There's a lot of material to be discovered and explored. I'm working on a book called *Women In Management*, and I intend to place the key parts of Sarah Henderson's life's work at the heart of my book.

P: In a recent article you wrote that Ms Henderson had been truly inspirational throughout her career. Can you elaborate on that?

A: Certainly. At the time of her early death at only 60, she had become one of the most successful businesswomen of her generation. In fact, Millennium magazine described her as the most important woman in business of the twentieth century. She founded Cosmo, which is now a worldwide chain of shops selling cosmetics. From the outset though, Sarah said that she would use her position as a successful entrepreneur to campaign for human rights and ethical trading. And this is what she did. She promoted these ideals in her work and consequently she changed the world of business.

P: How exactly did she do that?

A: By promoting environmental issues, and bringing them to the attention of the general public through her business. She insisted on using sustainable raw materials in her products, and demanded that producers in developing countries were paid a fair wage. She inspired both consumers and businesses to become socially aware and environmentally responsible. It simply hadn't been done before and in that way she was a pioneer and an inspiration to so many people. We're used to seeing eco-friendly and fair-trade products now, but when Sarah was campaigning for these in the 1970s it was unheard of.

P: She also became a notable and committed campaigner against animal testing.

A: Yes. Perhaps this is what she is best known for, or, at least, in the public consciousness, this is what people think of when they recall Sarah Henderson. Her campaign against animal testing on beauty products was instrumental, some would say, in eventually getting the law changed. We take it for granted now, but things would never have changed if ordinary businessmen and women like Sarah hadn't changed the way they did business. She proved that ethical business practices can be a force for good.

P: Well, thank you, Amanda. It has been really interesting. After the break, we'll be looking at …

END-OF-YEAR TEST 2 UNITS 1–16

P = presenter, C = Claudia

P: There have been many cases of miscarriages of justice over the years, but the trial and execution of Derek Bentley in the 1950s is a case which still resonates today. On this week's show, I'm talking to documentary filmmaker Claudia Wright, who has just released a new film which re-investigates many of the issues surrounding the notorious case. Welcome to the show, Claudia.

C: Hello.

P: Let's start by reminding listeners of what happened on that fateful night in 1952.

C: Well, the bare facts seem pretty straightforward when you first hear them. Derek Bentley was a nineteen-year-old petty criminal who lived in South London. On the night of November 2nd 1952, Derek and an accomplice, called Christopher Craig, broke into a warehouse. Somebody spotted them and called the police, who followed the young burglars up on to the roof. One policeman grabbed hold of Bentley, and it was then that he is supposed to have shouted, 'Let him have it, Chris!'

P: Let him have it?

C: Yes. He shouted 'Let him have it', at which point Craig turned round and shot at the policeman, injuring him. Then more policemen arrived and chased Craig across the roof, with Craig shooting at them. Eventually, Craig was cornered, and ran out of ammunition. He leapt from the building and injured himself, but not before one of his shots had struck Sidney Miles, a young policeman, who was killed instantly.

P: So, it was Craig not Bentley who shot someone that night?

C: That's right. Bentley had already been arrested by the time PC Miles was killed. But both teenagers were arrested and charged with murder. Under British law at the time, both were guilty of 'malicious intent' and 'common purpose'. In other words, both of them were equally guilty of the consequences of the crimes they planned together. They were both guilty of intending to commit burglary and violence, so they were both responsible for murdering the policeman.

P: OK. So was it considered an open and shut case at the time?

C: No, not at all. There was a lot for the jury to consider. For a start, both Bentley and Craig denied that Derek had shouted 'Let him have it!' It was police witnesses who insisted he had said the words. And even if he had said them, did he really mean to tell Craig to shoot the policeman?

P: 'Let him have it' could mean almost anything, couldn't it?

C: Well, in the parlance of the criminal underworld at that time, it obviously meant 'shoot'. But, yes, you're right. Theoretically, it could have meant give the gun to the policeman.

P: Absolutely.

C: There was also some doubt as to whether Craig was actually intending to shoot PC Miles. The barrel of Craig's gun had been sawn off, which made it shorter and more powerful, but also wildly inaccurate. It was far from clear that Craig had actually aimed at PC Miles at all. Perhaps he had only intended to scare off the police by firing bullets indiscriminately. Not only that, but Bentley was under arrest when the policeman was shot. The defence argued that he couldn't be responsible for murder if he was in police custody.

P: Well, no, I don't see how he was responsible.

C: Indeed. But what you have to remember is that under the law of the time both teenagers were equally culpable. They both had criminal intent, so it was hard for the defence to show that Bentley was not guilty.

P: But Bentley had learning difficulties, didn't he? Couldn't they prove that he wasn't bright enough to be responsible for his actions?

C: Derek Bentley had a mental age of eleven, and was very impressionable, but, again, under the law of the time that was no defence. A plea of insanity was the only way of avoiding responsibility, but Derek wasn't insane. He was of low intelligence.

P: So, they found him guilty?

C: He was convicted of murder and faced execution. Although his defence team appealed against the judgment, it was unsuccessful, and he was hanged in January 1953.

P: And what about Craig? Was he hanged, too?

C: Christopher Craig was only sixteen at the time of the murder, so he was too young to hang. You had to be over eighteen. He spent ten years in prison, and is still alive today, as far as I know, having been free for over 50 years.

The nurse

You are a nurse working both day and night shifts at a busy city centre hospital. City centre rental costs are now too high for you as a single person on a low salary. From the suburbs, travelling to and from work is difficult because you can't afford a car, night buses are few and irregular, and in daylight hours traffic jams are common on the ring road.

The ex-factory worker

Since the city's major employer closed the doors of its manufacturing plant, you have been out of work. There is no longer any factory work in or near the city, and blue collar workers are largely unemployed. Families in your community are living on the breadline. You left school early and, like many of your former co-workers, have no qualifications.

The teenager

In your run-down suburb of the city, there are high-rise blocks, a few shops, and no other amenities. Teenagers have nowhere to go. As a result, they hang out in gangs, on wasteland, and cause a nuisance. Drug use, vandalism and petty crime are commonplace in the area.

The young person

You live in a smallish town which is quite run down. There are lots of ugly 1970s buildings, poor housing, empty shops and very few green areas. Transport links with the neighbouring city are poor. There's an air of hopelessness – lots of young people are moving away, businesses are closing. Something needs to be done to halt the decline.

The single parent

You live in council-run accommodation on the tenth floor of a high-rise block with three children and an elderly relative. You don't work and live on benefits. The lift breaks down often and there is damp in your apartment, which is bad for your children's health. The council seem uninterested in improving the place you live in, or finding better accommodation for you.

The wheelchair user

You live and work in the busy city centre. On a daily basis, you face challenges. Older buildings in the city have narrow doorways and corridors. Many of the pavements in the city are narrow and uneven. Buses in the city are not adapted for easy access by wheelchair users. There are no city centre bathroom facilities for wheelchair users. Car parks are difficult to manoeuver through.

There is always some madness in love. But there is also always some reason in madness.

(Friedrich Nietzsche, philosopher, 1844–1900)

You can discover more about a person in an hour of play than in a year of conversation.

(Plato, philosopher, c. 425–348 BC)

Shared joy is a double joy; shared sorrow is half a sorrow.

(Swedish Proverb)

Love is never lost. If not reciprocated, it will flow back and soften and purify the heart.

(Washington Irving, 1783–1859)

It is one of the blessings of old friends that you can afford to be stupid with them.

(Ralph Waldo Emerson, poet, 1803–1882)

A friend is someone who knows all about you and still loves you.

(Elbert Hubbard, writer, 1856–1915)

One loyal friend is worth ten thousand relatives.

(Euripides, tragedian, 480–406 BC)

Three things in human life are important: the first is to be kind; the second is to be kind; and the third is to be kind.

(Henry James, writer, 1843–1916)

It is better to have loved and lost than never to have loved at all.

(Alfred Lord Tennyson, poet, 1809–1892)

The way to love anything is to realise that it may be lost.

(Gilbert K. Chesterton, writer, 1874–1936)

If you would be loved, love, and be loveable.

(Benjamin Franklin, author, politician and inventor, 1706–1790)

Anybody can sympathise with the sufferings of a friend, but it requires a very fine nature to sympathise with a friend's success.

(Oscar Wilde, playwright, 1854–1900)

3 THE CULTURE AND IDENTITY QUIZ

1 Where were you born?

2 What's your nationality?

3 What's your first language?

4 Name three characteristics or personality traits that you associate with people in your culture.

5 Which of the three characteristics do people in your culture value the most?

6 Which characteristic or personality trait do you think foreigners most associate with your country?

7 Name two important cultural events that take place in your country.

8 Describe how one of these events reflects the values and / or personality of people in your country.

9 In what way are you typical of somebody from your country and culture?

10 In what way are you untypical?

11 Which national characteristic in yourself would you be most happy to lose?

12 What do people from other countries most misunderstand about your personality?

13 Do you have much experience of living or staying in other countries?

14 What things did you find difficult about the culture of the country? What things did you like?

15 If you could choose a different country to live in for six months, where would you choose and why?

16 Which national characteristic in yourself would help you fit in if living abroad?

17 If you lived abroad, what would you most miss about your country and culture?

18 If you could take one thing with you when moving abroad, what would it be?

As a pair, think of two more questions to ask to find out about a person's culture and two more about a person's identity.

4 POLITICAL DILEMMAS

Dilemma 1

A left-wing politician who has always campaigned for a public health service and state education has a ten-year-old son who is doing badly at his local state school. The private, independent school nearby has a much better reputation for helping students reach their potential. The politician's partner would like to send their son to this school, but the press would be very critical if this happened.
What would you do if you were the politician and why?

Dilemma 2

A politician is campaigning on a left-wing platform against an opponent who is much better-funded, and can afford lots of campaign advertising. Unexpectedly, a wealthy businessman offers to fund the politician's campaign, saying that they agree with most of what they stand for. Although the businessman is asking for no favours right now, it is clear that he may want favours in the future.
What would you do if you were the politician and why?

Dilemma 3

At a press conference during an election campaign, a journalist asks a politician if she has ever committed a petty crime – shoplifting, for instance, or speeding. At the back of her mind, the politician recalls being taken to the police station and reprimanded for stealing some chocolate from a shop when she was fourteen. She is tempted, however, to just say no to the question.
What would you do if you were the politician and why?

Dilemma 4

Two politicians who were in the same club together at university find themselves on opposite sides of a hotly-contested election campaign. One of the politicians remembers an example of seriously bad behaviour by the other politician when they were in the club. He knows it would damage his opponent's campaign if it were revealed to the press.
What would you do if you were the politician and why?

Dilemma 5

A politician is flying high in the polls, but a focus group study carried out by her party shows that her policy to ban the sale of all firearms in her country is extremely unpopular with core voters and could, potentially, cost her party the election. At the same time, it is a policy close to her heart which she has always believed in.
What would you do if you were the politician and why?

Dilemma 6

The leader of a political party has asked politicians in her party to support her view on climate change when they next have to vote on closing the country's coal mines. A member of the cabinet who has always been loyal to the leader before disagrees strongly with that policy and doesn't believe in climate change. The politician knows that the leader will win the vote even if he votes against the closure and he expects that he will lose his job.
What would you do if you were the politician and why?

Dilemma 7

Every year, a politician and his family go on holiday to a hot, sunny country where they have a family villa. Unfortunately, however, the leader of that country has recently been very critical of the politician's country, and has threatened a trade embargo. It is already June, and the politician's family is keen to pack for their holiday.
What would you do if you were the politician and why?

Dilemma 8

An old business partner who helped a politician early on in his career now wants his old friend to support a bill that will be good for his business. He wants his friend, who is now an MP in parliament, to use his influence to get a planning application passed. However, the planning application is for a building on a green field site in an area of natural beauty, and building in such places is generally opposed by the politician's party.
What would you do if you were the politician and why?

5 EVENINGS OUT AND EVENINGS IN

STUDENT A

hours / watch TV / a week	hours / watch TV / yesterday	what / device / use / watch TV	kind of TV series / watch
who / favourite TV characters	what / most time / ever / watch TV	who / talk to / about TV programmes	watch / foreign TV programmes
what / favourite TV channels	watch / live TV / downloads / recorded		

Use the prompts to make questions to ask your partner about their habits and preferences. Think of two more questions and write them in the boxes. Think of follow-up questions.
A: *How many hours a week do you usually spend watching TV?*
 B: *Probably about fifteen.*
A: *Do you watch more TV on some days than others?*

 -

STUDENT B

how many / evenings / go out / a week	what / kind of things / do / go out	ever / watch TV / in public places or with other people	prefer / TV or cinema
how late / stay out / weekday / weekend	what / favourite way / spend / evening out	what new places / like to go	how far / travel / evening out
how much / spend / one evening out	prefer / go out / couple / large group		

Use the prompts to make questions to ask your partner about their habits and preferences. Think of two more questions and write them in the boxes. Think of follow-up questions.
B: *How many evenings a week do you usually go out?*
 A: *Probably about three or four.*
B: *Do you often go out on weekday evenings?*

6 CONFLICTS AND RESOLUTIONS

I was really busy this year doing extra-curricular activities. I played rugby for my university team, and did a lot of drama. I also got a part-time job in a café so I could earn some money to travel in the summer. I left all my revision until the end of the year, and then I got ill and couldn't work for two weeks. Now I've failed my end-of-year exam and I'll have to retake the year.

- -

I've fallen out with my best friend. I said something really stupid to her and she misunderstood and got really angry. That was two weeks ago. I haven't seen her since, and now it feels too late to apologise or explain. I really miss her; we were really close and had a lot in common.

- -

I've spent nearly all my money for the year already, and I still have three months of term left. Now I have no money left to buy food or do anything. I spent quite a lot of money on going out, and I bought lots of clothes, too. My parents work really hard and they've already given me as much help as they can, so I really can't ask them for any more.

- -

I made friends really quickly at the start of the year with a group of students from another course. Now I'm starting to realise that some of them are not very nice; they've been really picking on me and it's making me really unhappy. All the students on my course have already made their own friendship groups and I feel really left out.

- -

I've been here for two terms now and I'm starting to think I chose the wrong course. What I really enjoyed was doing art, painting and drawing and stuff, but I thought Law was a much more sensible thing to do and that I'd earn lots of money. I'm really not enjoying the studying, the course is boring and I'm just not that interested in the subject. I don't like this town very much either.

- -

I have a group project to do with a group of friends from my course, but I've really messed up. I misunderstood my part of the project, so I spent hours doing the wrong thing and now I have to start all over again. But I'm also behind on my other work now, so I don't have much time to spend on it. My friends are quite angry with me and feel that I've let them down.

The shoe umbrella
Walk in the rain while your shoes stay dry!

Expected retail price: from £5 to £10
Materials: plastic, metal
Material and manufacturing costs: £2

Diet water
Get slim by drinking water with the calories taken out!

Expected retail price: from £1 to £2
Materials: plastic bottle, tap water
Material and manufacturing costs: £0.15

The walking sleeping bag
Warm, comfortable, and you can walk around!

Expected retail price: from £50 to £200
Materials: nylon, polyester, possibly down / feather
Material and manufacturing costs: £15 (synthetic) to £25 (natural fibre)

Battery-operated scissors

Expected retail price: from £15 to £20
Materials: plastic, metal
Material and manufacturing costs: £3.50

The baby mop
A onesie for babies which gets them to mop the floor as they crawl!

Expected retail price: around £20
Materials: cotton
Material and manufacturing costs: £5

The pet talker
A digital translator from cat or dog language to English

Expected retail price: from £30 to £35
Materials: plastic casing, silicon chip
Material and manufacturing costs: £2

Electronic pet stroker

Expected retail price: from £10 to £15
Materials: plastic, metal
Material and manufacturing costs: £4

The flask tie
A tie that carries your favourite beverage

Expected retail price: from £15 to £20
Materials: polyester, plastic
Material and manufacturing costs: £2

8 FIND YOUR SOULMATE

1 Read the sentences and circle the appropriate answer.

1 I don't like spending money.
   A very true   B true   C partly true   D not true

2 I'm an early bird rather than a night owl.
   A very true   B true   C partly true   D not true

3 I take responsibilities seriously and always finish work on time.
   A very true   B true   C partly true   D not true

4 People see me as an open, generous person.
   A very true   B true   C partly true   D not true

5 Hiking, trekking and mountain climbing are the best types of sport for me.
   A very true   B true   C partly true   D not true

6 The best holiday for me would involve chilling out on the beach.
   A very true   B true   C partly true   D not true

7 My worst nightmare would be having to give a public speech.
   A very true   B true   C partly true   D not true

8 I'm often quick-tempered, but I calm down quickly.
   A very true   B true   C partly true   D not true

9 I'm good at fixing things and making things.
   A very true   B true   C partly true   D not true

10 Not having enough time for myself is depressing.
    A very true   B true   C partly true   D not true

11 I tend to agree with other people to please them.
    A very true   B true   C partly true   D not true

12 I prefer to email or text people instead of calling.
    A very true   B true   C partly true   D not true

13 I make friends easily but find it hard to keep in touch with them.
    A very true   B true   C partly true   D not true

14 It's important for me to have clear rules and regulations in life.
    A very true   B true   C partly true   D not true

2 Compare your answers with other people in your group or class. Find out what you have in common, and whether you have a soulmate (somebody who has more than ten answers similar to you). What do you think the answers say about your personality?

3 Discuss the following:
Which of the aspects of personality in the questionnaire do you think are determined by your environment or simply by nature?
Which have always been true for you, and which have changed during your lifetime?

HAMLEY'S INTERNATIONAL CONSTRUCTION IS RECRUITING

Choose the job that suits you and apply now!

ENGINEER

Are you enthusiastic and good at getting to grips with technical data? Do you enjoy solving practical problems? Are you passionate about maintaining standards and producing a safe and high-quality product? Can you work to deadlines and work to a budget? Do you have the experience and personality to motivate people and build an effective team?

Apply now.
£35,000 pa with pension scheme

SALES MANAGER

Do you have what it takes to guide, motivate and support your team members? Do you enjoy travelling and working with people from different cultures and backgrounds? Are you good at giving presentations and selling ideas and products?

If you have the necessary skills and experience in these areas, apply now.
£30,000 pa with health insurance

DESIGNER

Do you enjoy creative but meticulous visual work? Are you self-motivated and able to work well on your own and meet deadlines? Are you flexible enough to work to a client's brief while maintaining your own artistic standards? Do you have the interpersonal skills to meet with clients and discuss projects, and the business acumen to agree realistic fees and maintain profit margins?

Apply now.
£25,000 pa – training provided

Recruiters
1 Decide what skills and attributes you are seeking in applicants for the three jobs advertised.
2 Prepare questions to ask applicants to help you identify the perfect candidate.
3 Interview a variety of applicants and decide who to offer each job to.

Applicants
1 Decide which job to apply for.
2 Make a list of the skills and attributes you have which make you suitable for the job.
3 Attend interviews and do your best to make a good impression.

Rehabilitation *help drugs give up*	**Injection** *needle syringe drug*	**Remission** *time illness severe*
Drip (n) *liquid medicine blood*	**Relapse** *ill again better*	**Mortality rate** *death number country*
Life expectancy *length time to live*	**Outbreak (n)** *start disease to die*	**Workout (n)** *exercise physical to train*
Infection *disease medical virus*	**Scratch (n)** *cat nail blood*	**Operation** *cut open body*
Scan (n) *organs pathological information*	**Burn (n)** *skin injury light*	**Anaesthetic (n)** *drug operation pain*
Physiotherapy *massage advice posture*	**Graft** *skin burn transplant*	**Diagnose** *name symptoms problem*
Procedure *anaesthetic treatment operation*	**Stitches** *cut thread needle*	**Joint** *knee part bone*

11 WHAT DOES THAT WORD MEAN?

Group A

hat-trick (n)

1   This is a term used in football when a player scores three goals in a single match. It's also used in other team sports such as hockey and rugby.   ☑

2   _____

3   This term comes from gymnastics. It describes a type of headstand in which the gymnast bends backwards to place her feet on the floor while her head is till touching the floor.

stinger (n)

1   _____

2   This is a type of injury that players get in high-contact sports such as rugby or American football. When a player is hit or kicked, they may briefly feel a sudden burning pain.   ☑

3   This is the name given to the spray that physiotherapists use when they run on to the pitch during a match. It quickly deadens the pain felt by an injured player.

streak (n)

1   If a player is continually doing well in matches we say that he or she is 'on a winning streak'. If a player is continually doing badly in matches then we say that he or she is 'on a losing streak'.   ☑

2   This is a verb and has a similar meaning to 'give up' or 'surrender'. Imagine a team is losing 8-0 in a football match. The players might streak – in other words, they lose heart and give up.

3   _____

crab (n)

1   This is a swimming stroke, like the butterfly or backstroke, but one you won't find in the Olympics. If you crab, or do the crab, it means you swim with your head up and your arms and legs splashing under the water. It's how babies often swim.

2   This is a term from the sport of rowing. In a race, if a rower 'catches a crab' it means they mistime putting their oar in the water. The oar is the long wooden stick rowers use, and it is important to put it in and out of the water at the same time as the other rowers.   ☑

3   _____

ace (n)

1   In tennis, if the server hits the ball so well that his or her opponent can't even touch the ball with their racket, it is an ace.   ☑

2   In basketball, a shot from the halfway line (or further) is called an ace if it goes in the basket.

3   _____

dead ball (n)

1   Quite simply, a ball that has burst and can't be used. The term is used in both football and rugby.

2   _____

3   In football, if a ball goes out of play, behind the goal, it is called a dead ball. The goalkeeper then will collect the ball and take a dead ball kick to restart the match.   ☑

corker (n)

1   _____

2   This is an alternative word to *goalkeeper*. It is often used in hockey to describe the person who stands in the goal.

3   The word *corker* can be used to describe any person and many things that are really amazing. In sport, therefore, it is often used to describe a great goal or a great throw.   ☑

✂ -

Group B

journeyman (n)

1   In team sports, a journeyman is a player of average ability who plays for lots of different teams in his career.   ☑

2   This is a slang term for a long-distance runner or triathlete, especially those who compete in ultra-distance races.

3   _____

deuce (n)

1   _____

2   This is a score in tennis, equivalent to 40-40. It means that both players have won three points in a game.   ☑

3   If a player does a trick to beat an opponent, we say that he has deuced his opponent. It means to beat someone with skill.

cauliflower ear (n)

1 _____

2 A word used to describe the ear of a sports person whose ear has been badly damaged. In rugby, for example, players get 'cauliflower ears' from constantly banging their heads together. ☑

3 This is used in racket sports to describe a shot that went badly wrong. So, if a player hits a ball and it flies backwards into the crowd, it's a cauliflower ear.

spear tackle (n)

1 In fishing, this is equipment used to catch very big fish.

2 In rugby, this is foul play. If a player picks another player up, turns him upside down, and lets go of him, it is a spear tackle. It's very dangerous. ☑

3 _____

set (n)

1 Tennis players play three sets or five sets in a match. A set, therefore, is made up of games. A player might win a set 6–3. ☑

2 In snooker or billiards, when you place the balls in a triangle on the table at the start of the match, we say that the balls are 'in the set'.

3 _____

bullseye (n)

1 In volleyball, if you hit a high ball very hard with your hand and it wins the point without touching an opponent, it is called a bullseye.

2 _____

3 This is the small circle in the middle of a dart board. If you hit it with a dart, it is worth 50 points. ☑

open goal (adj)

1 _____

2 In football, an open goal is when a footballer is right in front of the goal and it is easy to score. If a player misses an open goal, it is a great catastrophe! ☑

3 When a goal is disqualified because of foul play, we say that it is an open goal.

12 HISTORY IN A MINUTE

Speak for one minute on: a historical event that had a positive impact on your family	Speak for one minute on: a historical event you witnessed	Speak for one minute on: a time when you got a sports or other injury
Speak for one minute on: a political figure that changed the world	Speak for one minute on: a time when you met a famous person	Speak for one minute on: a person that played an important role in your life
Speak for one minute on: a historical event you wish hadn't happened	Speak for one minute on: a time when you tried some food for the first time	Speak for one minute on: the first time you travelled on your own
Speak for one minute on: a scientific invention that changed the history of mankind	Speak for one minute on: a time when you got an unusual or exciting present	Speak for one minute on: a place you'd like to return to

13 AMBIGUOUS HEADLINES

1   **MARS BARS PROTEST**

2   **ATTACKS ON REFEREES GETTING UGLY**

3   **MAN EATING FISH MISTAKENLY SOLD IN PET SHOP**

4   **EYE DROPS OFF SHELF FOLLOWING HEALTH PROBE**

5   **STOLEN STATUE FOUND BY TREE**

6   **DEALERS TO HEAR IMPORTANT CAR TALK AT NOON TODAY**

7   **POLICE HELP DOG BITE VICTIM**

8   **FACTORY WORKERS REFUSE TO WORK AFTER DEATH**

9   **RED TAPE HOLDS UP NEW BRIDGE**

10 **CONMAN JAILED IN GUITAR CASE**

11 **STUDENTS MAKE NUTRITIOUS SNACKS**

12 **BANK CHIEF GRILLED BY MPS**

A large company has banned employees from bringing in their own cans of fizzy drinks because there are vending machines selling cans on the premises.

A large accountancy company has banned facial hair on men.

Employees in a publishing company are not permitted to lift parcels or boxes of paper. If the photocopier is empty, they have to call maintenance.

A large distribution warehouse has banned its employees from wearing hats, caps, beanies, etc.

An IT company has ruled that employees should only be permitted to check their personal email accounts twice a day.

All employees at a telesales office have been told to wear a smart business suit at all times.

A restaurant chain has decided that all tips should be shared between waiting staff, kitchen staff and cleaning staff instead of being kept by individual waiters.

Teachers at a large language school are only permitted to make 30 photocopies a day. If they make any more, they have to pay 5p per photocopy.

Employees are not permitted to move any desks, filing cabinets or other office furniture. They have to call and schedule official furniture movers if they want anything changed.

A department store has banned staff from using water bottles. Instead they have installed one water dispenser with small, disposable, cone-shaped cups.

A publishing company is docking employees' pay if they arrive at work after nine in the morning.

A legal firm has banned the display of personal items on desks, notably family photos.

All employees at an insurance call centre are only allowed to be away from their desks for a short time. After eight minutes a flashing light goes off.

Workers at a large distribution warehouse are not allowed to chew gum.

A
Wearing woolly hats in summer
Posting photos of your dinner on social media
Young men with long beards

_____

_____

_____

_____

_____

B
Men with ponytails
Posting sentimental comments about loved ones on Facebook
Wearing 'fake' glasses to look cool

_____

_____

_____

_____

_____

C
Coloured contact lenses
Low-slung trousers showing your underwear
Multiple piercings on the face

_____

_____

_____

_____

_____

16 ARE YOU A RISK TAKER?

MONEY

1   Imagine someone gave you $100 and a coin, and invited you to toss the coin, saying that if it landed on 'heads' they would give you another $100, but if landed on 'tails' you would have to give the money back. You'd toss the coin, right? It's the obvious thing to do.

   A That sounds like me! Go for it!
   B Er ... I'd probably keep the money, unless they agreed to give me $200 if it came down 'heads'.
   C Oh, no, I'd keep the $100.

2   Having inherited money from an aunt, your financial advisor suggests investing the money in a secure account at 2% interest or buying shares in an exciting new technological company where the investment could go under, but will probably pay off handsomely. You buy those shares!

   A Definitely! No risk, no reward, I say.
   B I'd ask to split the risk. I'd put half my money into the shares.
   C I'd rather not take the risk – 2% on a secure account is a sound investment.

STUDIES

3   Your tutor has set an assignment to hand in a month from now. While others may be heading to the library, you're heading home. You always leave assignments to the last minute. It concentrates the mind.

   A That's me. I do things the night before.
   B I'd probably write it up at the last minute, but I'd do my research before.
   C Not me! I'd be the first in the library.

4   The final exams of your course are approaching. Your teacher offers extra, optional sessions for anyone that's concerned about them. However, as you have been doing well on the course, and have no reason to think you'll do badly in the exam, you decide not to do the extra sessions.
   A Absolutely. Why waste my time?
   B I might go to one or two sessions.
   C I'd be the first to sign up.

WORK

5   There is an important meeting at work tomorrow with overseas clients. You will be expected to make a pitch and secure the deal. Naturally, with your charm, charisma and experience, there is no need to prepare. You feel more alert walking into a meeting with just your wits to rely on.

   A If you know your stuff, preparation is a waste of time.
   B I think I'd want a few notes to look at during the meeting.
   C I'd be up all night preparing.

6   You love your job, but a vacancy in another part of the company has come up at a higher level and with a higher salary. Naturally, you're going to apply for it even though it is a job in which you will have to quickly learn new skills, and a job which doesn't necessarily suit your personality.

   A I'd go for it. It's the only way to the top.
   B I'd want to know a bit more about the job first.
   C I'd stay put. I feel happier if I'm confident about my job.

HEALTH

7   You've booked a two-week beach holiday, and your travel company is asking you whether you want to take out holiday insurance. Naturally, you don't take it out. You're only going to sit on a beach. What could possibly go wrong?
   A Absolutely. Waste of money.
   B I'd take some sort of insurance – to cover medical expenses, perhaps.
   C No travel insurance? You must be joking!

8   You are part of a sports team on the verge of heading to a tropical country for a tournament. However, there has been an outbreak of a killer virus in the region. Your government's health service says that it is serious but travel is possible if you take precautions. Although some of your tour group have pulled out, you are still determined to go.

    A I'm sure it'll all be fine!
    B I'd want more guidance and advice before deciding.
    C No way would I go!

SPORT

9   Every week, you go to an aerobics class, which you really enjoy. Then one week, there is a new teacher who asks whether you would like to stick to the previous trainer's routine or try a new one that's a bit more challenging. Naturally, you are keen to try the new routine.

    A It's great to try new things and I like a challenge.
    B I'd try it once then ask to go to the old routine again unless I really like it.
    C I'd ask to stick with the old routine, I wouldn't want to overdo it.

10 During an organised trip around New Zealand, you are given a choice of how to spend the day. The choice is between a boat trip across a lake or an 'adventure' day spent water skiing, bungee jumping and doing a rope walk in the forest. You are the first to sign up for the 'adventure' day!

    A Weeeehaaaaa!
    B I'd like to try water skiing but not the others.
    C See you on the boat. Is there a life vest?

Key
Mostly A: You are a serious risk-taker. Remind me not to ask you for a lift.
Mostly B: You generally play it safe but seem prepared to push the boundaries from time to time.
Mostly C: You play things so safe! I bet you have insurance for your insurance, and wear a mask on the underground.

TEACHERS' NOTES TO COMMUNICATIVE ACTIVITIES

1 URBAN SOLUTIONS

Aim: to practise giving solutions
Activity type: groupwork
Before the lesson: Photocopy one worksheet for every group of six students. Cut up each worksheet into six sections.
Procedure: Organise students into groups of four to six.
• Hand out the six role cards in a pile to each group. Each student takes a card. Tell them to imagine they are the person on the card and to prepare to describe the problem they face in their own words.
• When students are ready, ask the first student to describe their problem to their group. Tell them to summarise and expand on the problems on their cards, using their own words rather than reading from the card. After listening to the problem, the rest of the group must discuss what solutions they would offer.
• When students have finished discussing the first problem, ask the second student to describe the next problem until all the problems have been discussed.
• In feedback, ask groups to summarise the solutions they came up with. Ask individuals to say whether they felt the solutions met their demands.

2 RELATIONSHIPS

Aim: to practise giving opinions
Activity type: groupwork
Before the lesson: Photocopy one worksheet for every group of students. Cut up each worksheet into twelve sections.
Procedure: Organise the class into groups of three or four.
• Hand out the cards around the group, so each student has three or four cards.
• Tell students to read the quotes and decide what they mean. If you prefer, you could give students the option of choosing the two quotes they find most interesting.
• Students should work individually to decide if they agree with the quote or not, justifying their views and backing them up with examples. This might include examples from personal experience, from celebrity lives or from films or literature.
• Students take turns to read out one of their quotes and explain to the rest of the group what they think it means, whether they agree with it or not, and why / why not.
• Students as a group decide whether they think it is a good quote or not. They could give each quote a mark out of ten, then at the end of the discussion choose the best quote.
• Take feedback from the whole class and see if they agree on which is the best quote.

3 THE CULTURE AND IDENTITY QUIZ

Aim: to practise asking and talking about culture and identity
Activity type: pairwork and groupwork
Before the lesson: Photocopy one worksheet for every student.
Procedure: Start by asking students what characteristics define people from their country. If your students are already living abroad in an English-speaking country, you could start by asking what characteristics define people in their host country, or the country they are visiting.
• Organise the class into pairs and give each student a worksheet. Tell students to work in pairs to discuss the questions and prepare their own answers. Tell them to prepare follow-up questions as instructed which they will ask other students. Monitor and help students with vocabulary and ideas.
• Organise the class into groups of four or five. Make sure that you split up pairs so that they are not in the same group. Tell students to interview the other students in their group, and find out everybody else's answers to the questions. Tell them to ask their follow-up questions.
• After they have finished, ask students to find their original partner and to share and discuss their findings.
• Your feedback will depend on whether you have a class of students from the same culture or from a variety of cultures. If they're from the same background, find out and agree on typical aspects of culture and identity that the students shared. If they're from different backgrounds, find out the differences.

4 POLITICAL DILEMMAS

Aim: to describe and discuss moral dilemmas in a political context
Activity type: groupwork
Before the lesson: Photocopy one worksheet for every group of four students.
Procedure: Organise the class into groups of four or five and hand out the list of dilemmas to each group.
• Ask one student to read out the first dilemma. Students take turns to discuss what they would do and why. Once they have fully discussed the dilemma, a different student reads out the second dilemma, and students discuss it. Students continue until they have discussed all eight dilemmas.
• In class feedback, ask different groups to say what they would do and why. You could open this out into a class discussion in which students agree on the 'correct' moral course in each case.
• Alternatively, this could be done on more of a 'for and against' basis, so students are actually encouraged to argue the case rather than all agree on an easy option. Split the dilemmas in two sets and give each set to a group to decide what they would do. They then have to defend their own decisions and attack the decisions of the other side.

5 EVENINGS OUT AND EVENINGS IN

Aim: to discuss preferred ways of spending free time in the evenings
Activity type: pairwork
Before the lesson: Photocopy one worksheet for every pair of students in the class. Cut the worksheets into two along the cutting lines.
Procedure: Organise the class into pairs and hand out an A and B card to each pair.
• Ask students to look at the prompts on their card and think of the questions they would ask. Depending on the class, they can write down the questions or just prepare them in their head.
• They should write two more questions on the same topic (staying in or going out) in the empty boxes.
• They then use the prompts to ask and answer questions about each other's habits and preferences.
• Encourage students to discuss and explain their preferences (e.g. *I like going out at weekends, but not during the week. I feel too tired to study the next day if I've been out late.* or *I really like documentaries, there are some really good nature and history documentaries on channel 4. But I hate soaps, I don't watch any, I think they're really boring.*).
• Put student pairs together to form groups of four. Each student then reports to the rest of the group about their partner's preferences.
• Ask each group to report back to the class. Find out if they feel the same about going out and staying in, or if different members of the group have very different preferences.

6 CONFLICTS AND RESOLUTIONS

Aim: to practise talking about regrets and giving advice
Activity type: groupwork or pairwork
Before the lesson: Photocopy one worksheet for every pair of students or group of students in the class. Cut up each worksheet into six sections.
Procedure: Give each pair or group of students a full set of cut up cards, and put them face down on the table.
• Explain that they will have two minutes to write as many regrets as possible for each situation. They can add their own invented details if they wish, as well as using the information on the card.
• Ask them to turn over the top card and write as many regrets as they can, using *I wish ...* and *if only ...* . Set a timer and stop them after two minutes. They should then turn over the next card and do the same.
• The winner is the pair or group with the most correct sentences.
Extra
• Look at each situation and ask the students to give some advice about what each person should do next to put things right.

7 AMAZING INNOVATIONS

Aim: to make a short presentation about an invention, to persuade or challenge
Activity type: groupwork
Before the lesson: Photocopy one worksheet for every group of three students in the class.
Procedure: Tell the class that every year millions of new inventions are tested and patented worldwide but only a fraction become popular and mass-produced. Discuss the possible reasons for this and what happens to the inventions that do not become popular.
• Organise the class into groups of three, and allocate each group the role of inventors or businesspeople. Give each group of businesspeople a full worksheet, and allocate each group of inventors one or two inventions.
• Tell the inventors that they need to prepare a presentation of their invention(s) to persuade the businesspeople that their product will sell well and be a good investment. They are competing with other investors for a grant of £1,000,000. They should think about:
  • Design and visual appeal
  • Usefulness
  • Manufacturing costs and likely price
  • Target market
  • Eco-friendliness
• Tell the businesspeople that their company has done well this year, and they are looking to invest some of the profit in a new invention which could potentially be commercially successful. They will have to choose the best invention, and award it a grant of £1,000,000. Think about:
• General appeal – how attractive, useful, etc. is the product?
• Is there a credible market? How much are people likely to pay?
• How unique is the product? Does it fulfil a need / a gap in the market?
• How eco-friendly is it? (materials, manufacture)
• Allow some time for inventors to prepare their presentation, and for businesspeople to prepare questions to ask.
• Inventors give their presentation to the class. After each presentation, the businesspeople should ask questions to challenge the inventors to defend their product.
• After all the presentations have been made, each group of businesspeople should choose the best product.

8 FIND YOUR SOULMATE

Aim: to talk about personalities
Activity type: groupwork
Before the lesson: Photocopy one worksheet for every student in the class.
Procedure: Ask students to read through the statements individually and choose the best answer for them. Deal with any unknown vocabulary. Emphasise that there is no right or wrong, good or bad answer; they should answer honestly.
• Organise students into groups of three or four. Ask students to compare their answers to see if they can find somebody similar to them and discuss what their answers say about their personality.
• Ask students to what extent they think their answers are determined by nature or nurture.
• After they have finished, get class feedback and discuss the answers.
• Ask students to think of one new thing they found out about themselves. Compare in groups.
Extra
• Ask students to work in pairs to write a short description of their personality, based on their answers to the questionnaire.

9 WHICH JOB IS FOR ME?

Aim: to prepare and carry out a job interview; revising ways of describing skills and attributes
Activity type: pairwork
Before the lesson: Photocopy one worksheet for every student in the class.
Procedure: Write the three jobs on the board and ask students what skills and attributes people will need to apply for such jobs.
• Organise students into pairs. Hand out the worksheets to each student. Divide the pairs into recruiters and applicants. Tell the recruiters to read the ads then prepare questions to ask. Tell the applicants to choose a job to apply for and prepare what to say. Give them the option of choosing the same job as their partner and preparing together, or choosing different jobs and preparing individually. Give students five minutes and monitor to help.
• When students are ready, ask the applicants to stand up, walk round and sit next to a recruiter. Tell the recruiters they have one minute to interview their applicant. After one minute, say stop, and tell the applicants to stand up and go and find a new recruiter. Again, set a one-minute time limit for the recruiters. After four or five interviews, say stop and ask students to return to their original seats.
• In feedback, ask recruiters to say who they will offer jobs to and why.

10 WHAT'S THE MATTER?

Aim: to revise vocabulary connected to health and illness
Activity type: groupwork
Before the lesson: Photocopy one worksheet for every group of four students in the class. Cut up each worksheet into 21 cards.
Procedure: Organise the class into groups of four students. Give each group a copy of the worksheet cut into individual cards and place them face down.
• Ask students in their groups to shuffle the cards. Tell one student to look at the top card (without letting their partners see) and provide a definition of the word in bold. When giving a definition, students mustn't use any of the three words written in italics on the card. Other students in the groups must guess the word described. The first student to guess the word 'wins' the card and keeps it. The game continues with another student looking at the next card.
• If a student can't give a definition of the word in bold, they can place the card back at the bottom of the pile, and take another card.
• When students have guessed all the words, the game ends. The winner is the student with the most cards.
• With smaller classes, you could put students in pairs instead of groups.

11 WHAT DOES THAT WORD MEAN?

Aim: to practise speculating
Activity type: group game
Before the lesson: Photocopy one worksheet for every two groups of three students in the class. Cut the worksheet in half along the cutting line.
Procedure: Tell students that they are going to play a game called 'Call My Bluff' based on a popular TV quiz show in the 1960s.
• Organise the class into groups of three. Tell half the class they are A groups and the other half they are B groups. Hand out an A worksheet to each A group, and a B worksheet to each B group.
• Ask students to look at the first word and definition on their worksheet. Tell them to work together to use their imagination to prepare one further alternative believable definition of the word provided. For example, students might describe a *hat-trick* as 'a very tall player in basketball'. Point out that students should use the look and sound of the word to help them come up with ideas for definitions. Once students have three definitions for their first word (including the correct one provided), tell them to prepare alternative definitions for the other words on their worksheet. Go round the class and help with ideas and vocabulary.
• When students are ready, pair A groups with B groups round the class. Tell them to take turns to play the game. Each student in the A group reads out one of their three prepared definitions of *hat-trick* in a random order. When they've heard all three definitions, the B group decide together which definition is most likely to be correct. If they guess correctly, they get a point. It is then Group B's turn to provide the three definitions they prepared for their first word.

- At the end of the game, find out which group got most points by guessing most answers correctly.

Extra

- You could play this game with a dictionary. Ask groups to find a few unusual words in a dictionary and prepare three alternative definitions for the words, including the correct one.

12 HISTORY IN A MINUTE

Aim: to practise talking about history and time
Activity type: personalised groupwork
Before the lesson: Photocopy one worksheet for each group of four or five students in the class. Cut up each worksheet into twelve cards.
Procedure: Organise the class into groups of four or five. Hand out the cards in a pile to each group and ask the students to shuffle the cards and place them face down in front of them.

- Tell one student to be the timekeeper. Ask another student to turn over the first card. When the timekeeper says go, that student must start talking about the topic on the card. Explain that they must talk without repetition or hesitation for one minute. In other words, if they repeat any important words or phrases, or if they stop talking for two or three seconds, a team member can say 'challenge'. The team member must then say why they challenged, and if the group agree that it was an accurate challenge, the topic then passes to the next person in the group, or the person who challenges. That encourages students to pay attention, a) to think of what they might say, and b) to get the other person out. The timekeeper notes down how many seconds they spoke for before being challenged.

- For the second round, change the timekeeper and ask a different student to turn over a card and start talking. Play as before. After two or three rounds, students will get the hang of it. The timekeepers keep score of how many minutes each person speaks for. At the end, the winner is the student who spoke without repetition or hesitation for longest.

13 AMBIGUOUS HEADLINES

Aim: to speculate about the meaning of headlines
Activity type: groupwork
Before the lesson: Photocopy one worksheet for every student in class.
Procedure: Write the first headline on the board. Ask: *What's the news story about?* Elicit ideas from students and establish that the headline has two possible meanings – the serious, intended meaning, and a second possible meaning which is funny. In 1, the actual story is about the fact that the Mars chocolate company has barred its employees from taking part in a protest on the company's premises. However, the way the headline is written makes it sound as if the actual chocolate bars themselves (called *Mars bars*) have taken part in a protest.

- Organise students into groups of four. Hand out a worksheet to each student.
- Ask students to read each headline and discuss what they think the actual story was about, and how the headline might be misunderstood.

- Ask them to make small changes and rewrite the headline so that it is no longer ambiguous. Explain that this might mean just adding an extra word or changing one or two words to make the meaning clearer.
- In class feedback, elicit and confirm students' ideas, and have a discussion about what makes each headline ambiguous.

Extra

- Ask students to write a short article for a local newspaper, reporting the story behind one of the headlines.

Answers

A = intended meaning
B = possible misunderstanding

1 A There was a protest against changes to the size of the Mars bar.
   B The Mars bars are protesting.
2 A There have been unpleasant ('ugly') attacks on referees.
   B People have been complaining about referees being ugly.
3 A A man-eating fish has been sold in a pet shop by mistake.
   B A man eating a fish was sold in a pet shop by mistake.
4 A Bottles of eye drops have been removed from sale because of a health scare.
   B An eye dropped off a shelf because of a health scare.
5 A A statue was found by somebody and it was next to a tree.
   B A tree found the statue.
6 A An important talk about cars, for car dealers, is happening at midday today.
   B An important car is going to be actually talking to dealers.
7 A The police are helping a person (victim) who was bitten by a dog.
   B The police are helping the dog to bite somebody.
8 A A person has died at the factory and the workers are refusing to work.
   B The factory workers are refusing to work after they themselves have died.
9 A The building of a new bridge is being delayed because of red tape (red tape = bureaucracy).
   B The red tape is literally holding the new bridge together.
10 A A criminal (conman) has been jailed for his part in a police case about a guitar.
    B The criminal has been jailed inside a guitar case.
11 A Students have been preparing snacks that are nutritious.
    B Students are nutritious snacks (i.e. good to eat!).
12 A The bank chief was asked a lot of difficult questions (grilled) by MPs.
    B The bank chief was put on a grill and cooked by MPs.

14 OFFICE RULES

Aim: to practise giving opinions
Activity type: groupwork
Before the lesson: Photocopy one worksheet for every group of four students in the class. Cut up each worksheet into fourteen cards.
Procedure: Organise the class into groups of four. Hand out the cards in a pile to each group and ask the students to shuffle the cards and place them face down in front of them.

• Tell students to assign themselves a letter, A–D. Student A turns over and reads out the card at the top of the pile. He / She can decide whether to argue for or against the office rule. Student B must argue the other side of the case.

• Students A and B take turns to make arguments in favour of or against the rule until the other pair (C and D) decides that the debate has been won by either A or B. This winner takes the card.

• Student C now turns over the next card and debates it with Student D. Continue round the group, with all students taking turns at taking a card and choosing their side of the argument.

• You could, alternatively, just manage this as a discussion or debate without any competition. Give one uncut photocopy to each group of four and ask them to discuss and debate the pros and cons of each of the office rules on the handout.

15 THE ROOM OF DOOM

Aim: to practise talking about trends
Activity type: pairwork and groupwork
Before the lesson: Photocopy one worksheet for every three pairs of students in the class. Cut each worksheet into three along the cutlines.
Procedure: Ask students: *What's in? What's out? What current trends do you find really annoying?* Elicit ideas.

• Organise the class into pairs. Hand out the worksheets to students in pairs. Each pair should get either an A, B or C worksheet. Ask students to read their three examples of current trends and decide whether they think they are in or not, and whether they find the trend annoying or not. Have a brief feedback, and ask students to give reasons why they think any one of the trends is annoying.

• Write THE ROOM OF DOOM on the board. Explain to students that you want them to work in pairs to think of three or more current trends that they find really annoying. Tell them to write them down on their worksheet. Once they have ideas, tell them to think of reasons why they think their trends should be sent to THE ROOM OF DOOM, never to be seen again. Give students five minutes to think of trends they hate and arguments for sending them to THE ROOM.

• When students are ready, organise the class into groups of three. Split the pairs who prepared together. In threes, students choose one of their trends, introduce it to their partners, and say why it should be sent to THE ROOM OF DOOM. Once all three people in each group has spoken, the group must decide together which annoying trend to send to THE ROOM (they can only send one). Have a brief class feedback, and find out which trends went to THE ROOM and why.

• You could continue the game by reorganising the class into different groups of three, and asking them to describe and condemn a new annoying trend from their list. Continue until lots of trends have been sent to THE ROOM OF DOOM.

16 ARE YOU A RISK TAKER?

Aim: to do a risk assessment quiz and to practise speculating about different situations
Activity type: pairwork and groupwork
Before the lesson: Photocopy one worksheet for every student in the class.
Procedure: Start by asking: *Are you a risk-taker?* Elicit answers from the class and ask for examples of when students feel they tend to take risks in life.

• Organise the class into pairs. Hand out the worksheets. Ask students to work together with their partner but to choose their own personal answer to each question. Monitor and help with any vocabulary problems.

• Once students have completed the questionnaires, pair each pair with another pair and ask them to discuss and justify their answers. Tell them to elaborate on exactly how they would react if faced with each situation.

• In class feedback at the end, find out which students in the class are risk-takers, and which are risk adverse.

WORKBOOK ANSWER KEY

1

1 congested
2 spotless
3 sprawling
4 run down
5 well-run
6 vibrant

2

| 1 e | 3 c | 5 h | 7 d |
| 2 g | 4 a | 6 b | 8 f |

3

c

4

| 1 E | 3 A | 5 A+E | 7 E |
| 2 A+E | 4 – | 6 A | |

5

1 How are you doing? (b)
2 When would be best for you? (a)
3 What's it like? (d)
4 Is there anything good on? (c)

6

nightlife
food
what's on
atmosphere
shopping

7

1 out and about
2 tired
3 miss
4 run down
5 done
6 out

8

1 hit the town
2 be spoilt for choice
3 a (tourist) hot-spot
4 pick (someone) up

Workbook pages 6–7

1

1 The room was really, really cold/freezing.
2 You could see for miles and miles (around).
3 The way people drive is totally insane/crazy. It's rather like being on a race track.
4 I had to leave the restaurant because it was unbearably hot (inside).

2

1 loads and loads
2 literally
3 packed
4 miles and miles
5 totally
6 really, really
7 absolutely
8 spotless

3

1 I swear, the shop was filthy inside!
2 The woman in the baker's was incredibly helpful.
3 Honestly, the stench was unbearable!
4 It was really, really great to see you again!
5 Seriously, he drove like crazy to get here!
6 Getting across town was a nightmare!

5

population increase 5
a method to deal with waste 1
protest against changes 4
the creation of green spaces 2
concerns for the future 6
an idea to improve travel 3

6

| 1 F | 3 F | 5 T | 7 T |
| 2 T | 4 F | 6 F | 8 T |

7

1 with   2 up   3 in   4 over   5 up   6 under

Workbook pages 8–9

1

1 demolished
2 initiating
3 decline
4 neglected
5 soaring
6 undergo
7 flourished
8 poured

2

1 She said she ~~hasn't~~ hadn't been to Buenos Aires before last year.
2 My family ~~has lived~~ lived in Milan until 1994.
4 The town hall was reopened last year, ~~had~~ having been completely rebuilt after the fire.
5 It is believed that the number of university graduates will ~~had doubled~~ double / have doubled by 2020.
6 By the time we got there, the concert ~~finished~~ had finished.
7 Where ~~had~~ have you been? We've been waiting here for hours and hours!

3

1 had been destroyed
2 has been developing
3 has been
4 have recovered
5 had been travelling
6 have encouraged
7 Having been done / Done
8 will have been completed / will be completed

4

| 1 d | 2 c | 3 f | 4 e | 5 a | 6 b |

5

1 on and off
2 sick and tired
3 peace and quiet
4 first and foremost
5 here and there
6 long and hard

6

| 1 quiet | 3 pieces | 5 now |
| 2 long | 4 off | 6 regulations |

Unit 1 Vocabulary builder quiz

1

| 1 hard | 3 now | 5 sick |
| 2 initiated | 4 compelled | 6 out |

2

| 1 career | 3 tip | 5 nerves |
| 2 plans | 4 a service | 6 a crowd |

3

1 muggings	4 entitled	6 thrilled
2 consumption	5 sprawling	7 demolition
3 congestion		

4

| 1 underwent | 3 run-down | 5 upturn |
| 2 downturn | 4 spotlessly | 6 re-housed |

UNIT 2
Workbook pages 10–11

1

1 snob (c)   3 bitchy (b)   5 pain (e)
2 incompetent (d) 4 principled (f)   6 laid-back (a)

2

1 b   2 a   3 a   4 b   5 b

3

Speaker 1: married couple
Speaker 2: brothers
Speaker 3: grandmother and granddaughter

4

a 3   c 1   e 1   g 1
b 2   d 2, 3   f 2

5

1 make   3 the feeling   5 seemed to
2 across   4 get   6 strikes

6

relationships

7

compassionate, forceful, outraged

8

1 to tell   6 were
2 shouldn't be treating   7 would refuse
3 would have called   8 had better end
4 ask   9 get hurt
5 would you rather have   10 Staying

Workbook pages 12–13

1

1 away   5 of   9 up
2 down   6 into   10 down
3 through   7 out
4 on   8 up

2

1 I would have thought you would have been delighted!
2 He will have finished it by tomorrow.
3 She said there would be rain later, but I do not know if there will.
4 She could not have known who would be there.
5 I would not have helped you, even if I could.
6 These are mine, but I do not know whose those are.

4

c

5

1 T   3 F   5 T   7 F
2 F   4 T   6 F   8 T

6

1 point   3 vain   5 faced
2 set   4 rescue   6 action

Workbook pages 14–15

1

1 e   3 j   5 a   7 b   9 i
2 h   4 f   6 c   8 d   10 g

2

a 4   c 1, 7   e 6, 8
b 5   d 9   f 2, 3, 10

3

1 wouldn't pay   4 wouldn't back
2 Would (you) give   5 would lighten
3 wouldn't lift   6 'd have

4

1 He would never mince his words when commenting on their behaviour.
2 I'd say she did that on purpose.
3 Would you mind helping me with this application form?
4 She would get upset over such trivial things!

5 I would have thought that Peter knew all about that!
6 She warned him that she would leave if he didn't stop yelling.
7 I wouldn't have shouted if you hadn't kept interrupting me.
8 I'd go and talk to her if I were you, and try to patch things up. / If I were you, I'd go and talk to her and try to patch things up.

5

1 F   2 T   3 T   4 F   5 F   6 T

6

1 going through a bit of a rough patch
2 be getting on each other's nerves
3 get on
4 a scene
5 ended up
6 been on speaking terms
7 collaborating
8 see eye to eye
9 back down
10 friction
11 confrontation
12 his weight
13 on first name terms
14 makes it so awkward
15 When it comes down to it
16 came as a real shock
17 sparked her interest
18 keeping an eye on him
19 came to his aid
20 put him at his ease

Unit 2 Vocabulary builder quiz

1

1 back   3 out   5 down   7 up
2 down   4 over   6 out

2

1 bitchy   3 snobbish   5 intensity
2 incompetence   4 willing

3

1 subjected   3 determined   5 confided   7 draw
2 narrowed   4 pull   6 slacking

4

1 F   2 F   3 T   4 T   5 F   6 T

UNIT 3
Workbook pages 16–17

1

1 a   2 b   3 c   4 b   5 a   6 c

2

1 touch   3 revolves   5 let
2 superficial   4 outlook   6 male

3

1 c   2 b   3 a

4

1 H   2 C   3 M   4 H   5 M   6 C

5

1 They take place in springtime.
4 People believe they may bring good luck.

6

1 about   4 way   7 overstatement
2 far   5 see   8 sure
3 exaggeration   6 harsh

7

a 1, 4   b 3, 6   c 2, 7   d 5, 8

8

1 down
2 up

10
1 What bothered me was the number of homeless people on the streets.
2 The one thing I found incredible was the lack of crime.
3 The thing that worries me is the amount of money politicians are wasting.
4 What annoys me the most is that no one seems to be listening.
5 One thing that drives me mad is all the red tape.

11
1 What ~~found I~~ I found difficult to cope with were the crowded streets.
2 The thing that amazes me the most ~~are~~ is the strict censorship laws.
5 One thing I hated was ~~that~~ the fact that the officials were so corrupt.
6 The thing that ~~me disturbs~~ disturbs me the most is the fact that everyone seems scared.

Workbook pages 18–19

1
1 needle 4 oven 7 toilet
2 dishwasher 5 cloth 8 pin
3 drill 6 tap

2
1 brush 4 stairs 7 hammer
2 rope 5 pads 8 washing-up liquid
3 screws 6 wires

3
1 C 2 A 3 B

4
1 a 2 g 3 h 4 f 5 c 6 b 7 d

5
1 f 2 e 3 a 4 d 5 b 6 c

Workbook pages 20–21

1
1 f 2 d 3 c 4 a 5 b 6 g 7 e

2
The writer is doing 2, 4, 5 and 6.

3
1 not to be missed 4 go wild
2 light up the skies 5 like there's no tomorrow
3 electric 6 bring a smile to my face

4
1 warm 3 back 5 showered
2 rule 4 food 6 clockwork

5
a like clockwork
b a warm reception
c like the back of my hand
d as a rule
e showered us with
f provided plenty of food for thought

Unit 3 Vocabulary builder quiz

1
1 c 2 f 3 e 4 a 5 d 6 b

2
1 revolves 4 misinterpret 7 stained
2 retain 5 scrubbed
3 stick 6 conform

3
1 hospitality 3 outlook 5 assumption
2 appliances 4 roots 6 normality

4
1 I 2 C 3 C 4 C 5 I 6 I

UNIT 4
Workbook pages 22–23

1
1 compassion 6 bravery
2 charismatic 7 compromise
3 communication 8 honesty
4 flexibility 9 passion
5 self-confident 10 ruthlessness

2
1 charisma 3 hasty 5 downturn
2 ruthlessness 4 charming 6 issue

4
a 3, 5 b 2, 6 c 1, 4

5
1 some slight reservations 4 a good idea in theory
2 completely opposed 5 totally against
3 totally in favour of 6 far outweigh

6
1 of 4 reservations about
2 I stand on 5 in, think it's
3 to 6 the whole

7
1 c 2 a 3 c 4 c 5 a 6 b

8
1 If ~~you'd be~~ you were elected, what would you do about housing?
2 You're going to get the sack if ~~you'll be~~ you're late again!
4 If they asked for a raise tomorrow, he definitely ~~won't~~ wouldn't give it to them.
5 What if you were unemployed, though, what ~~will~~ would you do then?
6 I would consider running for office, if I were you.
7 If the scandal ~~might break~~ broke, he would lose the election.

9
1 triggered 3 compound 5 benefit
2 discourage 4 undermine 6 reduce

10
1 lead 5 compound
2 boost 6 undermine
3 triggered 7 bankrupt
4 devastated

Workbook pages 24–25

1
conservation

2
1 over-exaggerated 5 the economy
2 irreversible 6 hospital
3 idealism 7 heavily populated
4 politician 8 local politics

3
1 d 2 e 3 b 4 f 5 a 6 c

4
1 giggled 3 crept 5 gazed
2 raced 4 chattered

5
1 muttering 3 gazed 5 grabbed
2 staggered 4 giggled 6 strolled

6
women

7

1 56% = percentage of Rwandan parliamentary seats held by women
2 1/3 = share of cabinet positions held by women in Rwandan government
3 800,000 = the approximate number of Rwandans killed in the genocide of 1994
4 70% = percentage of females in the population immediately after the genocide
5 30% = approximate percentage of women in parliamentary seats in South Africa and Mozambique

8

1 e   2 h   3 b   4 a   5 g   6 d   7 c

9

1 genocide	3 abolition	5 detractors
2 archaic	4 facilitating	6 hamper

Workbook pages 26–27

1

positive way

2

1 presents	4 forward	7 However
2 overall	5 grows	8 sum
3 following	6 drop	

3

1 small   4 longer / more unhappy
2 more ruthless   5 so / such
3 the most difficult

5

1 reached	3 landslide	5 rigged	7 prominent
2 cover up	4 outspoken	6 conducted	8 strike

6

1 If it hadn't been for their support, we would never have won.
2 If she hadn't been in a meeting, she'd have seen you.
3 If I didn't have to finish this report, I'd stop and talk.
4 If we'd been in power, this would never have happened.
5 If she had campaigned longer, she might / would be in office now.

Unit 4 Vocabulary builder quiz

1

1 carry on a	4 an emerging	7 an alleged
2 cover up an	5 establish an	8 a narrow
3 set up a	6 a broad	

2

1 allegations	4 representation	7 satirical
2 outweigh	5 opposition	
3 satirical	6 stance	

3

1 F   2 T   3 F   4 T   5 T

4

1 for   3 at   5 to
2 about   4 for

UNIT 5
Workbook pages 28–29

1

1 c   2 e   3 a   4 b   5 f   6 d

2

1 live up to the hype   4 burst into tears
2 caused a scene   5 was in bits
3 was mortified   6 feel / am feeling a bit rough

3

d **** outstanding

4

1 winning	4 successful	7 stunning
2 cracking	5 fearsome	8 exhilarating
3 powerful	6 admirable	

5

1 wooden	4 irresistible	7 spine-tingling
2 spectacular	5 stilted	
3 disjointed	6 devastating	

7

2 that was awkward
3 have been bursting / ready to burst
4 have been pleasant
5 be feeling rough
6 be serious

8

1 You must be getting quite good at it.
2 It must've been amazing.
3 I bet that was awful.
4 I imagine she was quite relieved.
5 I bet she was mortified.
6 You must be getting pretty tired of it.

Workbook pages 30–31

1

1 bunch	4 swarm	7 floods
2 tip	5 supply	8 creation
3 pleasure	6 sign	

2

1 fraction	4 awkwardness	7 thrill
2 manner	5 record	8 pack
3 front	6 production	

3

c   a proposal

4

1 e   2 a   3 f   4 b   5 d

5

1 The club is conveniently located.
2 Membership is inexpensive.
3 Chess helps develop prediction skills.
4 Playing helps people to relax.
5 Chess improves ability in certain subjects.
6 The club could create money for the council.

6

1 outwit	3 disability	5 unwind
2 innumerable	4 international	6 aforementioned

Workbook pages 32–33

1

1 a   2 c   3 d   4 b   5 e   6 d

2

Suggested answers:
2 Ken Wilson's talk proved very popular, receiving thunderous applause.
3 Macbeth is a gloomy play written by Shakespeare.
4 Look at the actress with the designer dress.
5 The National Theatre Company is producing a number of new plays.
6 The Frankies gave a superb concert, which was watched by millions.

3

Conversation 1 d
Conversation 2 a

4

1 T	3 F	5 F	7 T
2 F	4 T	6 F	8 T

5

1 a   2 c   3 c   4 a   5 b   6 b

6

1 around	3 to	5 in
2 in	4 by	6 on

Unit 5 Vocabulary builder quiz

1

1 tale	3 stitches	5 yawning
2 centres	4 bunch	

2

1 dialogue	3 narrator	6 memoir

3

1 synonymous	3 oppression
2 acceptance	4 creation

4

1 in   2 by   3 into   4 of   5 on   6 At   7 off

5

1 swarm	2 pleasure	3 hype

UNIT 6
Workbook pages 34–35

1

Speaker 1 a   Speaker 2 d   Speaker 3 c

2

Speaker 1 f   Speaker 2 c   Speaker 3 a

3

a Speaker 2	c Speaker 3	e Speaker 1
b Speaker 3	d Speaker 1	f Speaker 2

4

1 f	3 d	5 a	7 b
2 h	4 c	6 e	8 g

5

1 are trying to	3 in discussing	5 take
2 of taking	4 prove	6 are missing

6

1 didn't come out right
2 point in discussing / talking about it now
3 twist my words
4 your point
5 clear the air
6 got our wires crossed

7

1 I wish I ~~know~~ knew the answer to these questions.
4 I wish you ~~can~~ could come to support me when I see the boss later.
5 If only I ~~would be~~ were / was better at remembering facts when I'm arguing with someone.
6 I wish I ~~didn't go~~ hadn't gone to class yesterday.

8

1 you'd / would let
2 I could take
3 we hadn't fought
4 tree hadn't been
5 I hadn't yelled
6 you could find

9

1 phone would work properly
2 would stop being late / wouldn't always be late
3 hadn't agreed to help my brother move house
4 I didn't have to go to work today
5 I could come to your party
6 there weren't so many commercials on TV

10

1 b   2 e   3 f   4 a   5 c   6 d

11

1 /s/ re**c**eive	3 /dʒ/ intelli**g**ent
ceasefire asso**c**iated	rage legitimate
2 /k/ **c**areful	4 /g/ **g**o
nu**c**lear **c**asualty	negotiation agreement

13

1 a   2 b

Workbook pages 36–37

1

1 conflict	5 defeated	9 violations
2 troops	6 negotiating	10 tension
3 invades	7 track down	11 are surrounded
4 breaks out	8 join forces	12 seize control

2

c

3

1 ✗	3 ✓	5 ✓	7 ✗	9 ✓
2 DC	4 DC	6 ✗	8 DC	

4

1 civilians	3 reconciliation	5 compromises
2 casualty rate	4 retribution	6 overcome

Workbook pages 38–39

1

to complain about the service of an online DVD rental club

2

1 recently	3 largely	5 evidently
2 Unfortunately	4 desperately	6 extremely

3

1 a   2 a   3 a   4 a   5 a   6 b

4

Suggested answers:
1 In spite of / Despite promising to call us back, he never did.
2 Due to the wrong instructions we couldn't use the product.
3 As there was a fault in the camera, we couldn't take any photos.
4 Due to the casing being cracked, the game didn't work.
5 In spite of / Despite asking for a red model, I was sent a yellow one.
6 I wish to return this camcorder as the lens is scratched.

6

1 launched	5 combat	9 challenge
2 targets	6 capture	10 aggressive
3 defence	7 bombard	
4 guns	8 invaded	

Unit 6 Vocabulary builder quiz

1

1 continuation	4 complexity	7 fatalities
2 aggressive	5 harassment	
3 notable	6 hostility	

2

1 d   2 e   3 a   4 b   5 f   6 c

3

1 V+N   2 V   3 V+N   4 V+N   5 V+N

4

1 made	5 take
2 rose / escalated	6 staged
3 negotiate	7 withdraw / recall
4 broke	

UNIT 7
Workbook pages 40–41

1
1 created
2 breakthrough
3 negative
4 undertook
5 due to
6 reproduced
7 pave the way

2
1 negative
2 condition
3 down to
4 underlying
5 devised
6 undertake

3
2 How on earth did they manage (to do) that?
3 How on earth do they achieve that?
4 What on earth was it?
5 Why on earth are you going / do you want to do that?
6 But how on earth did they make them? / were they made?
7 How on earth can he / will he be able to afford that?

4
1 <u>Why on earth</u> do you want to do that? (↗)
2 <u>Believe me</u>, you're making a mistake. (↘)
3 <u>On the whole</u>, it went very well. (↗)
4 It was a disaster, <u>to say the least</u>. (↘)
5 <u>What in the world</u> were you thinking of? (↘)
6 <u>Funnily enough</u>, the experiment was unsuccessful. (↘)

6
Suggested answers:
A Introduction
B Course content
C Facilities
D Encouraging participation

7
a 3
b 5
c 8
d 2
e 6
f 1
g 7
h 4

8
1 R
2 A
3 R
4 A
5 R
6 A
7 A
8 R

Workbook pages 42–43

1
1 an outline of the issue
2 media relations
3 online coverage
4 visual media
5 an idea for the future

2
Suggested answers:
1 communication
2 are employed
3 science blogs
4 liveliness
5 pop musician
6 physicist
7 less
8 videos
9 trained
10 studying

3
1 present
2 inspire
3 estimate
4 stimulate
5 release
6 assess

4

	adjective	verb	noun
1	exploratory	explore	exploration
2	manipulative	manipulate	manipulation
3	diverse	✗	diversity
4	implied	imply implicate	implication
5	preventative	prevent	prevention
6	abundant	abound	abundance
7	varied	vary	variable variety
8	probable	✗	probability

5
1 cynical
2 aggressive
3 capabilities
4 variables
5 fatalities
6 manipulative

6
1 non-fatal
2 improbable
3 illogical
4 incapable
5 Unfortunately, irreversible
6 unexplored

Workbook pages 44–45

1
1 e   2 d   3 a   4 f   5 b   6 c

2
1 Contrary
2 up
3 suit
4 interest
5 anomaly
6 link

3
b   an entrepreneur

4
1 b   2 a   3 c   4 b   5 c   6 c

5
1 Statistics are twisted by government agencies to suit their own ends.
2 The animals are checked regularly for signs of deterioration in their health.
3 Acoustics can be tested by virtual ears which were invented by a scientist from Cardiff.
4 It is reported that 30,000 elephants have been killed illegally by rangers.
5 The award was given to the scientists in recognition of their work.
6 It is thought that the language barrier will be bridged by online translation services.

6
1 previously thought
2 doubts have been raised
3 bees resemble
4 findings will be presented
5 flower once belonged

Unit 7 Vocabulary builder quiz

1
1 C   2 I   3 I   4 C   5 C   6 I   7 I

2
1 with
2 in
3 for
4 of
5 up
6 to

3
1 test
2 wreaked
3 slope
4 disorder
5 holes
6 conclusive

4
1 acceleration
2 twisted
3 insertion
4 revelations
5 stimuli
6 undertaking

UNIT 8
Workbook pages 46–47

1
1 crater 3 plain 5 cliff
2 dune 4 gorge 6 glacier

2
1 cliff 3 crater 5 plain
2 dunes 4 gorge 6 glaciers

3
1 c 2 e 3 f 4 b 5 a 6 d

4
c a professional rock climber

5
Monique agrees with 3, 5 and 6.

6
a If I were you, I'd move back a bit, I really ~~wouldn't~~ would.
b Mmm. The scenery can be incredibly varied, ~~they~~ it really can.
c Yes. Amazing. I love the sea, I really love it.
e Incredible. I've never seen wildlife like this so close before, I really ~~have never~~ never have / I really haven't.
f That sounds terrifying, it really ~~is~~ does!

7
1 d 2 e 3 a 4 f 5 c 6 b

8
1 The mountains are awesome, they really are.
2 It is normally safe but sometimes problems do occur.
3 'Did you see James? Was he on the tour?' 'He was, but she wasn't.'
4 The scenery can be stunning, it really can.
5 You're not well, are you?

10
c mountainous

11
1 doesn't 5 doing 9 have
2 did 6 would 10 Is
3 Has / Does 7 can't
4 do 8 do

Workbook pages 48–49

1
1 butting 5 bush
2 into your mouth 6 cry
3 minces 7 edgeways
4 struggle 8 point

2
1 shoulder to cry on
2 get to the point
3 put words into my mouth
4 me get a word in edgeways
5 mince your words
6 stop beating about the bush
7 it a struggle to express
8 butting in (to our conversation)?

3
a concerned
g fascinated

4
1 e 2 a 3 b 4 h 5 g 6 d 7 c

5
a confounded c alluring e vulnerable
b poaching d make way f misnomer

Workbook pages 50–51

1
1 claws 3 fur 5 feelers
2 scales 4 horns 6 humps

2
1 leaps – shark 4 sense – spider
2 withstand – penguin 5 tunnels – mole
3 blends – chameleon 6 gnawing – beaver

3
1 d 3 f 5 g 7 e 9 a
2 h 4 i 6 b 8 j 10 c

4
1 tailor-made suit 5 life-threatening disease
2 self-help guide 6 child-friendly environment
3 award-winning charity 7 long-term unemployment
4 water-resistant watch 8 five-mile run

5
dolphin-spotting boat trip, excursion to the seal colony

6
1 Wander 4 Sign up 7 Beware, make
2 Gaze 5 Don't forget
3 Take 6 Avoid

7
1 d 2 f 3 a 4 b 5 c 6 e

Unit 8 Vocabulary builder quiz

1
1 narrow 3 lush 5 barren
2 murky 4 sweeping

2
1 I hate the way he butts in when we're talking.
2 The beaver gnawed through the wooden fence.
3 Authorities are cracking down on illegal poaching.
4 Stop beating about the bush and just say it!
5 The insect can blend in with its surroundings.
6 He saw the snake and let out a scream!
7 The blowfish will puff up when it is alarmed.
8 Researchers draw on their knowledge of the species' nocturnal habits to locate it.

3
1 scrambled 4 popularise 7 Predators, prey
2 mince 5 vital
3 dismissed 6 defy

4
1 superstitious 3 intuitively 5 ancestral
2 resistant 4 extensively

UNIT 9
Workbook pages 52–53

1
1 CEO 4 Admin 7 R&D
2 rep 5 HR
3 PA 6 IT

2
1 liaise 4 input 7 process
2 oversee 5 come up with 8 schedule
3 troubleshoot 6 draw up

3
Suggested answers:
1 HR / PA 4 Admin 7 HR
2 R&D 5 R&D 8 PA
3 IT 6 HR

4
They have b and e in common.

5
1 F 3 F 5 T 7 T
2 T 4 T 6 F 8 F

6
1 harness 3 patented 5 generate
2 days 4 process 6 catchy

7
2 She doesn't have a lot of free time, then.
3 You must be able to speak Swedish, then.
4 She won't be able to finish that report, then.
5 You must have handed in your notice, then.
6 He must be a good person to talk to about this new product, then.

8

2 A number of new colleagues will be ~~join~~ joining us over the next couple of weeks.
3 I ~~work~~ have been working for the same pharmaceutical company for 15 years.
5 We'll have ~~been finishing~~ finished the project by next week.
7 This time next week we're supposed to ~~celebrate~~ be celebrating the book launch, but I'm not sure it'll be ready in time.
8 I've been having a lot of trouble with that photocopier ~~before~~ since it broke down.

9

1	broken	5	contained	9	have felt
2	've been	6	's been	10	was going
3	been looking	7	'd been		
4	'd left	8	was		

Workbook pages 54–55

1

1 Advertising is fiercely competitive and can be quite stressful.
2 I'm not remotely interested in working with children because I have no patience with them!
3 Caring for people with Alzheimer's can be emotionally draining, so I try to remain detached.
4 Factory workers should take reasonably frequent breaks to stay alert.
5 Accountancy was financially rewarding, but I hated it.
6 I'm blissfully content with my present job and have no plans to retire.
7 Working as a receptionist is technically straightforward, although problems occasionally arise.
8 I'm utterly exhausted by the work and really need a break.

2

1 F	2 A	3 C	4 C	5 A	6 F

4

1 d   2 a   3 b

5

They'd generally agree with 2, 3 and 6.

6

1	makes mistakes	4	make amends	7	learning, improve
2	Think, tell	5	Avoid		
3	blame	6	trust		

7

1 T   2 T   3 F   4 T   5 T

Workbook pages 56–57

1

1	industrial	4	subsidised	7	early
2	voluntary	5	compassionate	8	state
3	unfair	6	minimum		

2

1	early retirement	4	minimum wage
2	industrial tribunal	5	voluntary redundancy
3	state pension	6	compassionate leave

3

1	perks	4	childcare	7	absenteeism
2	subsidised	5	opposition	8	grateful
3	crèche	6	crackdown		

4

Suggested answer: a, b, d and f

5

a, b, d and f

6

1	demonstrated	3	awarded	5	realise
2	developed	4	impressed	6	relish

Unit 9 Vocabulary builder quiz

1

1 d   2 a   3 c   4 e   5 b

2

1	tribunal	3	liaise	5	enthusiastically
2	condemn	4	inherently	6	screw

3

1	inevitability	5	dismissal
2	blissfully	6	redundancy
3	fiercely	7	technical
4	mind-numbingly		

4

1	set	3	Pull
2	troubleshoot	4	mind-numbingly

5

1 back   2 perk   3 screw

UNIT 10
Workbook pages 58–59

1

1 f	3 g	5 a	7 h
2 c	4 d	6 e	8 b

2

1	undergo	3	insert	5	scan	7	stitches
2	fast	4	swelled	6	take part	8	broke

3

1 It may take a few years ~~so~~ until they find a cure.
2 When Martin was in a coma, I knew he could ~~hear somehow me~~ hear me somehow / somehow hear me.
3 He made a kind of bandage or ~~somehow~~ something.
4 I knew I needed to do some sort of exercise but I wasn't sure what type.
6 He somehow managed to mix up the children's medical records.

4

1	kind of / somehow	5	somehow
2	or so	6	kind of
3	something	7	or so
4	some kind of		

5

Juri cut his head badly and had to go to hospital.

6

1	introducing the story; setting the scene	Have I ever told you about the time …? It all started when … It was (back) in … when …
2	moving from one event to the next; re-establishing the situation	But the … part of … was yet to come … In the middle of all this, … So there we were, … While all this was going on, …
3	concluding the story; giving the outcome of an event	After all that, … I ended up … One thing it's taught me is …

7

1 It was at this point that I ~~did notice~~ noticed my foot was bleeding quite badly.
2 It ~~was~~ wasn't until we had been walking for a couple of hours that we remembered our flashlights.
3 It was only when Lois reached the village that ~~felt she~~ she felt a sense of relief that the trip was over.
4 Not until midnight ~~we could~~ could we find our way back. / It was not until midnight that we could find our way back.
5 Only after standing up did I realise how much I ~~have~~ had hurt myself.

Workbook pages 60–61

1
1 mind / drift
2 clench / fist
3 flutter / eyelashes
4 raise / eyebrows
5 shrug / shoulders
6 stretch / legs

2
1 pat
2 shrug
3 spit
4 hug
5 sniff
6 wipe

3
1 ~~stretched~~ fluttered
2 ~~glared~~ blinked
3 ~~raised~~ clutched
4 ~~support~~ stretch
5 ~~fluttered~~ crouched
6 ~~blinked~~ raised
7 ~~crouch~~ support
8 ~~clutched~~ glared

4
She has cyberchondria.

5
1 b   2 c   3 a   4 c   5 b   6 a

6
1 turned out
2 headed off to
3 clear up
4 come up with
5 taken up

Workbook pages 62–63

1
a to discuss ways in which hospital services could be improved

2
1 I   3 B   5 I   7 B
2 B   4 I   6 B   8 I

3
1 A   3 A   5 A   7 D
2 D   4 D   6 D   8 D

4
1 c   3 e   5 f   7 d
2 g   4 b   6 a

5
1 breakthrough
2 upbringing
3 dropouts
4 runup
5 outbreak
6 shakeup
7 workout

6
1 b   3 c   5 e   7 f
2 a   4 d   6 h   8 g

7
1 must be feeling
2 can't possibly have seen
3 shouldn't have been driving
4 could have had a vaccination if
5 might / may / could have been the hamburger that gave me
6 should have told / ought to have told your parents about not

8
2 I don't know why he felt unwell.
3 You shouldn't have ignored your injury.
4 I think it was some kind of natural medicine.
5 The doctor asked me to get dressed again.
6 He could have picked up the disease on holiday.
7 I was put on a waiting list for my heart operation.

Unit 10 Vocabulary builder quiz

1
1 swollen
2 dietary
3 eradication
4 anaesthetised
5 underpinned
6 extensive

2
1 write-off
2 walkout
3 falling-out
4 bypass
5 break-in
6 shake-up

3
2, 5 & 6 describe a form of treatment.

4
1 mortality
2 cure
3 aftercare
4 disease
5 your fingers
6 remission
7 head

UNIT 11
Workbook pages 64–65

1
1 sponsoring
2 sending
3 fading
4 challenging
5 substituting
6 doping
7 thrashing
8 blowing

2
1 out
2 underdog
3 overturned
4 fading
5 scrape
6 close
7 suspended
8 fixed

3
1 a current sportsperson
2 a doctor
3 a referee
4 a fitness instructor
5 a retired sportsperson

4
a 3   b 1   c 2   d 5   f 4

5
1 a   2 b   3 b   4 a   5 a   6 b

6
1 b   2 a   3 b   4 a+b   5 b   6 a

7
1 f   2 d   3 b   4 a   5 e   6 c

8
1 engrossed
2 confronted
3 grasped
4 informed
5 attached

9
1 ~~with~~ **in** moderation
2 universal ~~fact~~ **truth**
3 ~~true~~ **pure** and simple
4 ~~cooperative~~ **collaborative** games
5 Multi-~~tasking~~ **player**

Workbook pages 66–67

1
1 even though
2 otherwise
3 Although / Even though
4 whether
5 in order to / so as to
6 Provided / So long as

2
1 c   3 a   5 d   7 i   9 g
2 b   4 e   6 f   8 h

3
1 Johnson's taking some rest so he can recover from his injury.
2 You won't improve unless you train more.
3 Marc was disqualified, even though he protested.
4 You must have cheated, otherwise you wouldn't have won.
5 I'm unable to give up my job in order to train professionally.

4
a a concerned parent

5
1 F   3 F   5 F   7 F
2 T   4 DS   6 T   8 F

6
1 of   3 between   5 of   7 to
2 in   4 to   6 with   8 in

Workbook pages 68–69

1
a

2
1 The question is
2 in two respects
3 In other words
4 Moreover
5 On the other hand
6 In summary

3
1 belief
2 ability / abilities
3 participation
4 comparison
5 determination
6 Resentment
7 development
8 freedom

4

1 b	3 a	5 a	7 b
2 a	4 a	6 b	8 b

6

1 marriage	4 bred	7 disappointed
2 lost	5 nothing	
3 family	6 kith	

7

Love's Lesson Learned, Rob and Rose, far from

8

Accept all answers. Suggested answer:
'Rose and I are head over heels,
And despite what you may think
Our love will stand the test of time,
We'll battle through thick and thin
Inseparable.'

9

bluff / tough, coach / show, court / pawn, down / ground, cushion / football, hurdle / world

Unit 11 Vocabulary builder quiz

1

1 chanted	3 substitutes
2 chants	4 substitute

2

1 bite	3 let	5 dragged	7 nodded
2 flies	4 fosters	6 jump	8 stop

3

1 moderation	3 abusive	5 traumatic
2 suspension	4 simulation	6 attentive

4

1 I	2 C	3 I	4 C	5 I	6 C	7 C

UNIT 12
Workbook pages 70–71

1

1 flee, coup	4 orphaned
2 radical	5 saw active service
3 deprived	6 broken home

2

1 deprived	4 scholarship	7 fled
2 sheltered	5 privileged	8 scratch
3 knit	6 evacuated	

3

b historical biographer

4

1 fascinating	5 timeline
2 scandalous	6 diaries
3 the general public	7 reserved
4 organisation	8 detective

5

1 like a fish ~~in a sieve~~ out of water
2 as hard as ~~a dodo~~ nails
3 as old as the ~~plague~~ hills
4 smokes like ~~mud~~ a chimney
5 as clear as ~~a chimney~~ mud
6 like chalk and ~~nails~~ cheese
7 avoid ... like ~~mud~~ the plague
8 a memory like a ~~sheet~~ sieve

6

Your profile should include b and e.

7

Paragraph 1: b, e
Paragraph 2: a, f
Paragraph 3: c, d

8

Suggested answers:
a The recession brought a time of great hardship.
b She was arrested on suspicion of theft.
c For many years, we were consumed by guilt.
d She struggled to make sense of it all.
e Her book is a very moving account of the events.
f It pays tribute to the bravery of / shown by some of the people.

Workbook pages 72–73

1

a

2

1 F	3 T	5 F	7 F
2 T	4 T	6 T	8 F

3

1 Cleopatra
2 Sir Francis Drake
3 Alexander the Great
4 Alexander the Great
5 Marie Antoinette
6 Alexander the Great, Sir Francis Drake

4

1 manipulate	4 maligned
2 portrayed	5 contended
3 condemn	

5

2 You cited ...	5 You made the point that ...
3 You suggested that ...	6 You referred to ...
4 be arguing that ...	7 You claimed that ...

6

1 d	2 a	3 b	4 f	5 g	6 e	7 c

Workbook pages 74–75

1

1 e	3 i	5 j	7 f	9 d
2 g	4 a	6 c	8 b	10 h

3

1 ●○○	uprising editor industry scholarship
2 ○●○	employer portrayal reflection
3 ○○●	employee engineer refugee
4 ○●○○	reliable assassinate validity
5 ○○○●	evacuee Vietnamese

5

1 establishing	5 challenged
2 put	6 claimed
3 played	7 gave
4 stemmed	8 cast

6

1 Sirimavo R. D. Bandaranaike
2 Marie Curie
3 Virginia Apgar
4 Anna Akhmatova
5 Corazon Aquino
6 Fanny Blankers-Koen
7 Gabrielle Chanel
8 Shirley Chisholm

7

1 At no time	4 Nowhere else
2 No sooner	5 Not until
3 Not only	6 Only after

8

1 Never before had I seen such a huge crowd of people gathered in one place.
2 Only when the police fired tear gas at them did the crowd disperse.
3 Not only did the tsunami kill eleven villagers, but it also destroyed nearly all of the fishing boats in the area.
4 Two people signed the Declaration of Independence on 4 July, but not until five years later was the last signature added.
5 No sooner had war been declared between Britain and Zanzibar in 1896 than the latter surrendered.
6 Despite being afraid, at no time during the earthquake did the little boy cry.

Unit 12 Vocabulary builder quiz

1

1 evacuation	3 intervention	5 overstatement
2 declaration	4 nationalised	6 crippling

2

1 cheese	3 sieve	5 mud
2 sheet	4 plague	6 chimney

3

1 to	3 out	5 on	7 over
2 up	4 from	6 on	8 round

4

1 massacred	3 challenged	5 upbringing
2 privileged	4 nails	

UNIT 13
Workbook pages 76–77

1

1 a	3 d	5 c	7 g
2 h	4 f	6 e	8 b

2

Suggested answers:

2 Cole to pull out of Arsenal contract / Cole pulls out of Arsenal contract
3 Chancellor rules out tax increase / Tax increase ruled out by Chancellor
4 President Carver to slash / slashes arms spending / Arms spending slashed by President Carver
5 Drugs seized in warehouse raid / Police seize drugs in warehouse raid
6 Landlords vow to bar hooligans from city centre pubs / Hooligans will be barred from pubs, vow landlords

3

1 g	2 e	3 a	4 f	5 c	6 b

4

B Appeal of the station
C Types of programme
D Community

5

1 attract	3 broad	5 generate	7 an asset
2 encourage	4 appeal	6 allow	8 improve

6

1 A review supplement would make the paper appeal to a wider readership.
2 Clear headings would make the web page more accessible to users.
3 Colourful images would make the page more attractive to a broad readership. / Colourful images would attract a broader readership to the page.
4 A careers supplement would encourage more advertisers / more businesses to advertise.

Workbook pages 78–79

1

1 Don't count your chickens before they hatch.
2 The grass is always greener on the other side.
3 Every cloud has a silver lining.
4 It takes all sorts to make a world.
5 too many cooks spoil(ing) the broth.
6 the early bird catches the worm.
7 when in Rome, do as the Romans do.
8 When the going gets tough, the tough get going.

2

A 3	B 5	C 1	D 2

3

1 c	2 d	3 a	4 c	5 d	6 d

4

1 circulation	3 took	5 isolated
2 discerning	4 narrow	6 detriment

Workbook pages 80–81

1

1 d	2 b	3 a

2

1 A	2 M	3 R	4 A	5 M	6 A	7 R

3

2 natural	4 risen	6 advertising
3 society	5 legislature	7 statute

5

	reporting verb pattern	verbs
1	verb + (*that*) clause	acknowledge, claim, confirm
2	verb + object + (*that*) clause	assure, confirm, express, reject
3	verb + *to*-infinitive	refuse, vow
4	verb + object + *to*-infinitive	urge
5	verb + noun phrase	acknowledge, deny, reject
6	verb (+ object) + preposition	blame, praise

6

1 expressed	3 assured	5 claimed
2 acknowledged	4 praising	6 confirmed

7

1 The Prime Minister vowed to cut taxes in the next six months.
2 The speaker urged the crowd to sign the petition and make the outcry too loud to be ignored.
3 Gerard rejected the committee's offer.
4 The physicist acknowledged that s/he had been misguided in his / her calculations.
5 The company spokesperson denied that the company / they had tried to play down the importance of the problem.
6 Marie blames the nanny state for children's loss of contact with nature.
7 The minister confirmed that Parliament is / was going to pass the new education bill this / that year.
8 The MP refused to discuss the issue with the press until the next day.

Unit 13 Vocabulary builder quiz

1
1 pulls 2 hails 3 clash 4 slash 5 raid

2
1 denied 2 tipped 3 join 4 thrown 5 slash

3
1 profits 2 cover up 3 praise 4 rise

4
1 of 2 to 3 on 4 of 5 in 6 to 7 for

5
2 ✓ 4 ✓

UNIT 14
Workbook pages 82–83

1
1 flooded 4 relocating 7 downturn
2 taken on 5 making 8 client base
3 picked up 6 hanging in 9 overheads

2
1 c 2 e 3 g 4 b 5 f 6 a 7 d

3
1 d 2 c 3 a

4
1 c 2 a 3 e 4 d 5 f 6 b

5
1 action plan 4 work-life balance
2 job satisfaction 5 time management
3 rest break 6 to-do list

6
1 a checking 3 a to leave 5 a to eat
  b to have   b reading   b getting
2 a putting 4 a to inform
  b to do   b spending

8
c a business advisor

9
1 ✗ 2 ✓ 3 ✗ 4 ✗ 5 ✓ 6 ✓ 7 ✗

10
1 employees 3 competitors 5 discounts
2 capital 4 catalogue 6 repeat

Workbook pages 84–85

1
1 c 3 c 5 a 7 a
2 a 4 b 6 c 8 b

2
1 FSO 3 MS 5 MS 7 FSO
2 MS 4 FSO 6 FSO

4
A Jason

5
1 B 3 A 5 A 7 C 9 D
2 C, D 4 B 6 D 8 C

6
1 spin 3 buzz word 5 agenda 7 undercut
2 grey area 4 Plan A 6 do-gooder 8 give it a go

Workbook pages 86–87

1
2 which 8 (that / which)
3 (which) 9 to whom / to who
4 (where) 10 (that)
5 when / that 11 (that)
6 in which / that 12 whose / for whom / for who
7 which 13 what

2
2 (d), whose policy of employing experienced staff was very successful.
3 (a), when / whereupon a number of changes to company policy were made.
4 (f), none of which were of good quality / which were all of poor quality / , all of which were of poor quality.
5 (c) that / which described how profits had plummeted.
6 (b) by which time / point it was too late to win back their solid customer base / when it was already too late to win back a solid customer base.

3
1 gap 3 deal 5 line
2 stakes 4 meeting 6 concessions

4
1 exceeded 4 recommend 7 conduct
2 seal 5 undertake 8 demands
3 bid 6 ongoing

5
1 competitive 4 drop 7 threat
2 lobby 5 outsource 8 make
3 scale 6 upped

Unit 14 Vocabulary builder quiz

1
Sentences 1, 2, 4 and 6 relate to money.

2
1 served time 4 sealed the deal
2 weathering the storm 5 bottom line
3 won (mining) concessions

3
1 flotation 3 diversifying 5 termination
2 relocating 4 ongoing 6 upturn

4
1 in 3 on 5 through 7 with
2 to 4 out 6 under 8 to

UNIT 15
Workbook pages 88–89

1
1 scruffy 3 revealing 5 beads 7 collar
2 high heels 4 split 6 linen 8 a ponytail

2
1 e 2 c 3 a 4 f 5 d 6 b

3
1 silk, knee-length 4 checked, spotted
2 conventional, formal 5 bob, shades
3 worn out, trainers 6 lining, ripped

4
Speaker 1: g fashion designer
Speaker 2: f male model
Speaker 3: d consumer
Speaker 4: c manufacturer of beauty products
Speaker 5: a online shopping consultant

5
1 India, Speaker 3
2 Japan, Speaker 1

6
a 4 c 1 e 2 g 3
b 3 d 2 f 4 h 5

7
1 skimpy 3 eye-catching 5 bland
2 flamboyant 4 feminine

8
1 then 3 wrong 5 Are you saying
2 lose 4 clash 6 on

9

a 4   b 3   c 1   d 6   e 2   f 5

10

1 c   2 a   3 d   4 e   5 f   6 b

11

1 A: You didn't like him, then?
   B: But I <u>did</u>, actually.
2 A: So, you liked the show?
   B: No, I said I <u>dis</u>liked the show.
3 A: You must have overslept!
   B: No, <u>you're</u> <u>early</u>!
4 A: So it's true. You were laughing at me!
   B: No, I <u>wasn't</u> laughing. That's <u>not</u> true!
5 A: It's your turn to do the shopping.
   B: No, it's <u>not</u> my turn. I did it <u>yesterday</u>.
6 A: You must have seen her!
   B: No, I <u>can't</u> have seen her. I <u>wasn't</u> <u>there</u>!

Workbook pages 90–91

1

b

2

1 g   2 h   3 d   4 b   5 e   6 a   7 c

3

1 speaks volumes
2 dragged around
3 do the leg work
4 ripped off
5 go about
6 build a rapport with

4

1 in
2 to
3 At
4 in
5 from
6 with
7 from
8 by
9 into

5

1 not as we know it
2 the flatmate from hell
3 my middle name
4 It was the mother of all
5 of whom you speak?
6 the word 'mutt' in the dictionary
7 the new 'speak'
8 life's too short

Workbook pages 92–93

1

verb	noun	adjective
simplify	simplification	simple / simplified
(de)mystify	mystery	mysterious / mystifying / mystified
commercialise	commercialisation	commercial / commercialised
lighten	lightening	lightening / lightened
authorise	authority	(un)authorised
justify	justification	(un)justified / (un)justifiable
idealise	ideal / idealisation	ideal
widen	width	wide / widening

2

1 unjustified
2 mystified
3 Self-objectification
4 over-simplification
5 lightening
6 disheartened

3

Yes

5

1 tricky
2 How's it going?
3 stuff like that
4 pay was pretty good
5 Let me know
6 full-on
7 beyond my reach
8 About

Unit 15 Vocabulary builder quiz

1

1 stuck out like a sore thumb
2 opted for
3 pulled it off
4 is set to
5 take new fashion items on board
6 on the wane

2

1 incidence
2 traits
3 masculinity
4 pinpoint
5 profound
6 endorsements
7 disorientated

3

1 seam
2 laces
3 flares
4 shades
5 zip
6 bushy

4

1 (set) to (top)
2 (take) on (board)
3 (opted) to
4 (on) the (wane)
5 (shield their children) from
6 (hair) in (a ponytail)

UNIT 16
Workbook pages 94–95

1

Speaker 1: d member of a rescue team
Speaker 2: b writer
Speaker 3: c office worker

2

1 a   2 b   3 b   4 a   5 a   6 b

3

1 They've come with the <u>right</u> gear.
2 Wait. I'll <u>just</u> catch my breath.
3 'The <u>next</u> step could have been fatal.' 'Quite.'
4 We're leaving on the first of March.
5 He was sent home to get over a leg wound.
6 I remember <u>quite</u> clearly. I left it there.

5

1 b   2 a   3 c   4 c   5 c

6

1 Whoa! / Oh! / Yuck!
2 Oops!
3 Wow! / Gosh!
4 Oi! / Whoa!
5 Sshhh! / Umm …

7

1 tearing
2 came to
3 banging
4 consciousness
5 burn
6 deeply
7 sliced
8 whacked

8

1 dismissed, grounds
2 awarded, damages
3 conviction, overturned
4 sued, libel
5 set, precedent
6 opposed, legislation

Workbook pages 96–97

1

c

2

1 C
2 A
3 B
4 A
5 D
6 B
7 A
8 D
9 C
10 B
11 C

3

1 churn
2 draw
3 conjure
4 head
5 rush
6 word

4

1 threat
2 peril
3 hazards
4 menace
5 risk
6 danger
7 threat
8 risk

5

1 menace   2 hazard   3 threat   4 danger

Workbook pages 98–99

1
1 it: the government
2 this: the intention to get tough on crime
3 these: adolescent road accidents, drink- and drug-driving, illegal drag racing
4 What: the facts about the dangers of driving
5 so: taking driving courses to keep skills current

2
| a But still | c Indeed | e As well as this |
| b therefore | d As for | f in order to |

3
| a Nevertheless | c In fact | e On top of this |
| b consequently | d With respect to | f so as to |

4
1 As well as this / On top of this
2 Indeed / In fact
3 in order to / so as to
4 As for / With respect to
5 But still / Nevertheless
6 therefore / consequently

6
| 1 for | 3 In | 5 to |
| 2 bound | 4 possibility | 6 chances |

7
1 The President is set to meet the Prime Minister in December.
2 Your contract is due for renewal next month.
3 Logan is bound to have an accident.
4 The odds are that we'll reach the summit within a couple of days.
5 The researchers believe that they are on the verge of finding a cure.
6 I think there's a slim chance that Nathan's plan will work.
7 In all likelihood, Prash won't survive the operation.
8 The search party has just announced that they are on the point of quitting.

Unit 16 Vocabulary builder quiz

1
| 1 to | 3 with | 5 to |
| 2 off | 4 off | 6 against |

2
1 d   2 e   3 g   4 c   5 b   6 a   7 f

3
| 1 verge | 3 peril | 5 absurd |
| 2 confiscated | 4 scalded | |

4
1 plagiarism	4 appraisal	7 liability
2 unprecedented	5 disruption	
3 Menacing	6 negligence	

CD 1: Units 1–8
Unit 1
Track 1
Track 2
Track 3
Unit 2
Track 4
Track 5
Track 6
Unit 3
Track 7
Track 8
Track 9
Track 10
Unit 4
Track 11
Track 12
Track 13
Unit 5
Track 14
Track 15
Track 16
Unit 6
Track 17
Track 18
Track 19
Unit 7
Track 20
Track 21
Track 22
Track 23
Unit 8
Track 24
Track 25

CD 2: Units 8–14
Unit 8
Track 26
Track 27
Unit 9
Track 28
Track 29
Track 30
Track 31
Unit 10
Track 32
Track 33
Unit 11
Track 34
Track 35
Track 36
Track 37
Unit 12
Track 38
Track 39
Track 40
Track 41
Track 42
Unit 13
Track 43
Track 44
Track 45
Track 46
Unit 14
Track 47
Track 48
Track 49
Track 50

CD 3: Units 15–16 + Class tests	
Unit 15	
Track 51	
Track 52	
Track 53	
Unit 16	
Track 54	
Track 55	
Track 56	
Track 57	
Track 58	
Class tests	
Track 59	Review test 1
Track 60	Review test 2
Track 61	Review test 3
Track 62	Mid-year test
Track 63	End-of-year test 1
Track 64	End-of-year test 2